CASE
PROBLEMS IN
INTERNATIONAL
FINANCE

McGraw-Hill Series in Finance

CONSULTING EDITOR

Charles A. D'Ambrosio, *University of Washington*

CASE PROBLEMS IN INTERNATIONAL FINANCE

W. Carl Kester
Timothy A. Luehrman

Graduate School of Business Administration
Harvard University

McGRAW-HILL, INC.

New York St. Louis San Francisco Auckland Bogotá Caracas
Lisbon London Madrid Mexico Milan Montreal
New Delhi Paris San Juan Singapore Sydney Tokyo Toronto

This book was set in Times Roman by The Clarinda Company.
The editors were Kenneth A. MacLeod, Peitr Bohen, and Bernadette Boylan;
the production supervisor was Denise L. Puryear.
The cover was designed by Leon Bolognese.
R. R. Donnelley & Sons Company was printer and binder.

CASE PROBLEMS IN INTERNATIONAL FINANCE

Case material of the Harvard Graduate School of Business Administration is made possible by the cooperation of business firms and other organizations which may wish to remain anonymous by having names, quantities, and other identifying details disguised while maintaining basic relationships. Cases are prepared as the basis for class discussion rather than to illustrate either effective or ineffective handling of an administrative situation.

1 2 3 4 5 6 7 8 9 0   DOH   DOH   9 0 9 8 7 6 5 4 3 2*

ISBN 0-07-034263-6

Library of Congress Cataloging-in-Publication Data

Case problems in international finance / [edited by] W. Carl Kester,
    Timothy A. Luehrman.
        p.   cm. — (McGraw-Hill series in finance)
    Includes index.
    ISBN 0-07-034263-6
    1. International finance—Case studies.   I. Kester, W. Carl.
II. Luehrman, Timothy A.   III. Series.
HG3881.C324   1993
658.15′99—dc20   92-27871

ABOUT
THE AUTHORS

W. CARL KESTER is Professor of Business Administration at Harvard Business School where he teaches international finance in Harvard's MBA and Executive Education Programs. He became a member of the faculty at Harvard in 1981.

Professor Kester is the author or coauthor of more than thirty-five case studies and fifteen published articles on various finance topics. His articles have appeared in the *California Management Review*, *The Continental Journal of Applied Corporate Finance*, *Financial Management*, the *Harvard Business Review*, *Japan and the World Economy*, and the *Sloan Management Review*, among others. His research into Japanese mergers and acquisitions was supported by the 1987 O'Melveny & Myers Centennial Grant, and culminated in his recently published book, *Japanese Takeovers: The Global Contest for Corporate Control*. He is also co-editor of the tenth edition of *Case Problems in Finance*.

An economics graduate of Amherst College, Professor Kester also holds advanced degrees from Harvard Business School (MBA, 1977) and the London School of Economics and Political Science (M.Sc., 1974). He received his Ph.D. in Business-Economics in 1981 from Harvard University's Graduate School of Arts and Sciences.

TIMOTHY A. LUEHRMAN is Associate Professor of Business Administration at Harvard Business School where he teaches corporate finance in Harvard's MBA and Executive Education Programs. He became a member of the faculty at Harvard in 1986.

Professor Luehrman's research has focused on companies' operating exposure to real exchange rate changes, and international differences in the cost of capital. He is the author of more than twenty case studies and a dozen published articles. His articles have appeared in the *Harvard Business Review; Japan and the World Economy;* the *Journal of International Business Studies*, for which he serves as Associate Editor; and the *Sloan Management Review*, among others.

Professor Luehrman is a graduate of Amherst College where he studied economics and English literature. He received his MBA from Harvard Business School and his Ph.D. from Harvard University's Graduate School of Arts and Sciences in 1983 and 1986, respectively.

To Our Teachers and Students

CONTENTS

INTRODUCTION

Once considered the specialty of financial officers working at large multinational corporations, international finance today has become everyone's business. The ability to source funds quickly in different currencies and markets; the evolution of truly global product markets in industries such as automobiles, semiconductors, and pharmaceuticals, among many others; and the increasing availability and attractiveness of cross-border investment opportunities have thrust managers of all stripes and from all types of companies into the international financial area. Monitoring exchange rates and foreign capital costs has become as much a part of the general financial manager's routine as monitoring domestic interest rates and stock prices has always been. Indeed, even companies that source all their factors of production and sell all their output at home must now keep a watchful eye on shifting exchange rates and off-shore interest rates if they face substantial foreign competition in their home markets.

The cases selected for inclusion in this volume reflect the current breadth and sophistication of skills employed by today's corporate financial managers. They are drawn from Harvard Business School's MBA course *International Managerial Finance*. Reflecting their use in that course, the cases are designed to stimulate critical thinking, active discussion, and the development of sound business judgment predicated on fundamental principles of financial economics. Accompanying the cases are technical notes designed to provide background and some fundamental skills for analyzing associated cases. They are not a substitute, however, for more comprehensive treatments provided in textbooks and other outside readings.

Although some cases have been disguised to protect confidential information, all but a handful describe actual administrative situations requiring analysis and a decision. As such, they replicate the multifaceted character of the problems faced by modern financial managers. The corporate finance slant of the cases is obvious enough, but this should not obscure the need to consider corporate strategy, organizational constraints, and many other exigencies in the course of recommending specific actions.

While the development of analytic skills and managerial judgment are the primary goals of these cases, the conveyance of general institutional knowledge about international finance is an important secondary one. Many of the cases and notes contain sections providing background about local markets, local financing techniques, local managerial practices, historical events preceding contemporary problems (e.g., the Latin American debt crisis), and so forth. Collectively, the administrative situations described in these cases span fifteen different countries, twenty-five different industries, and thirty-seven different companies ranging in size from $20 million to $16 billion.

As a group, this collection of cases develops several themes about international finance. First is the fundamental point that finance is an important determinant of corporate performance. By recognizing attractive international financing and investment opportunities, analyzing them correctly, and executing transactions prudently, corporate financial officers can add considerable value to the companies they manage.

Unbridled pursuit of any and all attractive deals available in today's complex markets will seldom be desirable, however. Financial execution must be governed by internally consistent financial policies, which are themselves part of a coherent financial strategy designed to support a corporate strategy. Thus, the interdependence of corporate and financial strategy, and the need to coordinate the two, constitutes a second major theme of these cases.

A third theme is that exchange rate changes matter, though often in ways that are subtle and indirect. Not all exchange rate shifts that critically influence a company's competitive position and value will show up in its financial accounts using generally accepted accounting principles. Likewise, not all of those that are reflected in financial reports affect value. The questions of which exchange rate exposures matter most and how they should be managed are addressed here within the traditional finance paradigm of value maximization.

Finally, through the analysis of international mergers, acquisitions, and corporate restructurings, fundamental differences in national systems of corporate governance are brought to light. As markets integrate and the volume of cross-border investment increases, these differences are being drawn in sharper relief. It is too common a mistake, however, to ascribe such differences solely to cultural factors. Thus, a final theme of these cases is that one must go beyond cultural norms and carefully analyze the economic purposes served by different governance institutions found in different parts of the world. What at first appears to be a peculiar idiosyncrasy driven by cultural norms is often seen, upon closer inspection, to serve rational economic purposes. The sharp contrasts among German, Japanese, and Anglo-American systems of corporate governance, for example, and the relative success of corporations domiciled in those three countries, raise provocative questions about the most effective means of governing organizations competing in today's international markets.

A considerable debt of thanks is owed to the many people and organizations around the world who have contributed to the development of this collection of cases. Clearly, these cases could not have been written without the cooperation and generous sacrifices of time made by scores of managers interviewed at those companies providing the decision-making settings. Sheer numbers and the need to respect condfidentiality prohibits naming them all; but they know who they are and it is our sincere hope that they will realize the full extent of our gratitude and derive some satisfaction from having had an impact on the pedagogy of international financial management.

As we assembled the cases into a book, many helpful suggestions were provided to us by a number of scholarly reviewers. These include Esther Ancel, University of Wisconsin-Milwaukee; James N. Bodurtha, Jr., University of Michigan; Kirt C. Butler, Michigan State University; John M. Geppert, University of Nebraska-Lincoln; Luc A. Soenen, Cal Poly San Luis Obispo; and Anant K. Sundaram, Amos Tuck School of Business of Dartmouth College. Their thoughtful comments provided a rich resource for us to draw upon throughout the development of the manuscript.

We also thank the hundreds of executive and MBA students who analyzed and discussed these cases in classes at Harvard Business School. Their many insights and comments helped us "season" the cases appearing here. We are also most grateful for editorial support provided by Jane Manilych, and the production and proofreading of the manuscript by Dale Abramson, Brenda L. Fucillo, and the Word Processing Center of Harvard Business School.

Finally, special thanks and recognition go to Professors Dwight B. Crane; Steven R. Fenster; William E. Fruhan, Jr.; Samuel L. Hayes, III; Scott P. Mason; Thomas R. Piper; Henry B. Reiling; and G. Peter Wilson, each of whom graciously extended permission to include cases or notes developed by them in this collection. Glyn Ferguson Aepple; William B. Allen, Jr.; Rajiv A. Ghatalia; Robert W. Lightfoot; Richard P. Melnick; Julia Morley; William T. Schiano; and James J. Student are also warmly thanked for their invaluable assistance in the preparation of our cases and notes during the last several years. We are grateful for generous financial support provided by Harvard Business School's Division of Research in the course of developing these cases, and to Harvard Business School's Publishing Division for its cooperation in granting permission to include them in this volume.

W. Carl Kester
Timothy A. Luehrman

CASE
PROBLEMS IN
INTERNATIONAL
FINANCE

PART ONE

FOREIGN EXCHANGE MARKETS AND EXCHANGE-RATE DETERMINATION

MANAGING THE U.S. DOLLAR IN THE 1980s

Starting in 1980, the value of the U.S. dollar increased steadily against other currencies and reached record levels by early 1985. An index of the trade-weighted nominal value of the U.S. dollar rose from 100 in 1980 to nearly 170 by late 1984 (see **Exhibit 1**). The same general pattern could be observed in the bilateral exchange rates of the dollar with the four currencies of the other major industrial countries, France, Germany, the United Kingdom, and Japan (see **Exhibit 2**).

The strong dollar, coupled with the booming U.S. economy, fueled growth in sales and profitability for many industrial companies around the world. For 4 years, export sales to the United States increased with widening margins. The effect of the strong dollar on U.S. companies, however, was quite different. It made U.S. exports less competitive in foreign markets, allowed less expensive foreign-made goods to flood U.S. markets, and cost an estimated three million U.S. jobs. The adverse effects were so pronounced that the U.S. Congress gave serious consideration to various trade protection measures proposed by business and labor leaders. Complicating the public debate on this issue was the fact that a wide variety of theories had emerged to explain the dollar's strength.

THE 1985 DOLLAR DEBATE

The debate on causes of the dollar's rising value, although far from resolved, focused primarily on the impact of relative inflation rates and interest rates on the dollar.

This case was prepared by Professor W. Carl Kester and Research Associate Richard P. Melnick. Copyright © 1991 by the President and Fellows of Harvard College. Harvard Business School case 292-001.

Closely linked to these determinants were discussions concerning the balance of trade, the federal government's deficit, monetary growth, real economic growth, and international capital flows.

Briefly, the United States ran an increasingly negative trade balance, current account, and federal government budget deficit beginning in 1980. The U.S. gross national product, however, grew at a slow but healthy rate in 1983 and 1984. Inflation slowed after reaching a peak of 13 percent in 1980, and interest rates generally declined after peaking in 1980 and 1981. **Exhibit 3** provides statistics on several key economic variables for the United States, France, Germany, Japan, and the United Kingdom.

Traditionally, nations with continuing balance-of-trade, current-account, and budget deficits experienced depreciations in the international value of their currencies. It seemed a paradox, therefore, that the United States enjoyed a strong dollar while suffering from expanding deficits of these very same types.

Some economists explained the paradox by noting that in the 1980s a happy side effect of the U.S. trade deficit was a substantial capital surplus. Although the federal budget deficit stimulated aggregate demand in the United States, thus increasing demand for imports, it was also the primary stimulant behind the capital inflows needed to finance the trade deficit.

Martin Feldstein, former chairman of the Council of Economic Advisors, and his wife, Kathleen, an economist, also blamed the budget deficit for the strong dollar. However, they viewed the trade deficit primarily as a consequence of that strength:

> The current huge trade deficit is not due to any fundamental weakness of American industry or to increases in unfair trade practices of other nations . . . the real trade problem [is] the overvalued dollar.
>
> The major and fundamental change that has occurred during the Reagan years is, of course, the unprecedented increase in the federal budget deficit. The government borrowing to finance this deficit has absorbed more than half of all net savings generated in the United States and has kept real interest rates much higher than abroad. These high interest rates attract investment from abroad and push up demand for the dollar.[1]

Allan Meltzer, a professor of political economy and public policy at Carnegie-Mellon University, had a very different view of the role budget deficits played in the dollar's strength:

> The effect of large budget deficits is to weaken currencies, not strengthen them. A country with continually large budget deficits eventually will have to pay the bill by raising taxes or printing money and creating more inflation. Both taxes and inflation chase away foreign investors, so either course is poison for the value of the country's currency. The exchange markets recognize this immediately, and the dollar weakens. The dollar is strong despite the budget deficit, not because of it.[2]

It was Professor Meltzer's opinion that the dollar was strong because of growth in the U.S. economy, particularly in the area of investment spending. This growth, he

---

[1]Martin and Kathleen Feldstein, "Time to Raise Taxes," *Boston Globe,* October 1, 1985, p. 42.
[2]Allan H. Meltzer, "How to Cut the Trade Deficit," *Fortune,* November 25, 1985, p. 177.

believed, was stimulated by the lowering of effective tax rates on capital spending and the lowering of inflation, which raised the real value of depreciation write-offs.

Analysts at Morgan Guaranty Trust Company emphasized yet another view on this issue. They believed that "While the large federal deficit may have contributed to a strong dollar in the past, insofar as it has increased real interest rates, continued failure to come to grips with the deficit is likely to erode confidence in the dollar."[3]

So-called "monetarist" economists tended to discount the importance of budget deficits and focused instead on monetary policy to find an explanation for the dollar's strength. They attributed this strong dollar to the U.S. Federal Reserve's low-inflation monetary policy adopted in the early 1980s. Indeed, some monetarists argued that the dollar would stay high so long as the Fed held monetary growth within reasonable bounds, no matter what happened to the budget deficit.[4] As *The Wall Street Journal* claimed, "With a given set of outside influences, the value of the dollar in marks depends on how many dollars are created by the Fed and how many marks are created by the Bundesbank, period."[5]

The Group of Five (G-5) Agreement

In the midst of this confusion, the Reagan administration initiated a meeting of the finance ministers and central bankers from five major industrial countries (the "Group of Five," or "G-5"): France, Germany, Japan, the United Kingdom, and the United States. The participants met at the Plaza Hotel in New York and announced a three-point program on September 22, 1985, consisting of the following elements:

• A new U.S. commitment to join other nations in lowering the U.S. dollar's value. Although an explicit plan of intervention was only hinted at, it was clear that such a commitment would require coordinated bank sales of dollars in foreign exchange markets in return for British pounds, German marks, Japanese yen, and French francs.

• Tax cuts and other measures to spur growth in Europe and Japan, and to increase the value of the foreign currencies against the dollar.

• Continued Reagan administration efforts to reduce U.S. budget deficits and resist protectionist pressures in Congress.

As a rationale for the program, it was stated in the communiqué that "recent shifts in fundamental economic conditions . . . together with policy commitments for the future . . . [had] not been reflected fully in the exchange markets." Nevertheless, it was clear that any attempt to engineer a devaluation of the dollar through market intervention would face serious risks and skepticism.

One such risk was that if this program were too successful it might result in a free-fall of the dollar. This could rekindle inflation and raise interest rates. At the other end of the spectrum was the risk that the dollar would not depreciate much at all. This was

---

[3]Morgan Guaranty Trust Company, *World Financial Markets,* August 1985, p. 2.

[4]"The 'Cambridge Mafia' and the Friedmanites Debate the Dollar," *Business Week,* September 9, 1985, pp. 22–23.

[5]"Only Schizoid Intervention," *The Wall Street Journal,* September 23, 1985, p. 30.

especially likely if the markets interpreted the program as being merely lip service, or if the Group of Five did not fulfill their commitments to improve investment and growth prospects in their own countries.

The general skepticism with which the G-5 announcement met was summarized by Ronald Holzer, a vice president and chief foreign-exchange dealer of Harris Trust & Savings Bank, Chicago, who stated:

> The past has shown us that whenever the finance ministers from the Big Five get together there's a lot of rhetoric and little action. Any time there's talk of intervention and outside forces in the market, it creates volatility and uncertainty. But in the long term it doesn't have any lasting impact.[6]

THE 1987 DOLLAR DEBATE

Following the G-5 agreement in September 1985, the dollar depreciated rapidly (see **Exhibits 1** and **2**). By February 20, 1986, the dollar had dropped 30 percent against the deutsche mark and the yen, exceeding most expectations and prompting Federal Reserve Chairman Paul Volcker to say the dollar had fallen enough. In an October 1986 meeting, Treasury Secretary James Baker and Japanese Finance Minister Kiichi Miyazawa agreed that the dollar should not fall much below ¥155. However, the Reagan administration, under pressure to decrease the trade deficit, leaked word in January 1987 that it wanted the dollar to fall further. As the dollar continued to drop, public officials and economists debated what, if anything, could or should be done about the dollar, interest rates, and the trade deficit.

The Administration's Strategy

Nearly everyone in Washington had an opinion about the trade deficit and the dollar's fall. One argument held that the dollar's January 1987 plunge centered around the Reagan administration's effort to avoid protectionist legislation in Congress in the spring. Secretary Baker had masterminded a comprehensive exchange-rate, interest rate, and global growth strategy because "We feel that we are engaged in a life-or-death struggle to preserve the world economy."[7] His strategy appeared to center on using the weak dollar as leverage to encourage Germany and Japan to stimulate their economies with tax and interest rate cuts. These actions, it was hoped, would support the dollar by creating demand for American exports and making it relatively attractive to invest in the United States. However, Secretary Baker denied that the administration had "talked the dollar down" in January, and noted, "There's a limit to what you can do. The fact of the matter is, the market will determine what the appropriate level for the dollar is."[8]

---

[6]"Central Banks' Intervention to Influence Currency Prices Is a Game of Skill and Timing Played amid Uncertainty," *The Wall Street Journal*, September 23, 1985, p. 26.
[7]*The New York Times*, February 1, 1987, Business section, p. 1.
[8]*The Wall Street Journal*, January 27, 1987, p. 3.

Paul Volcker expressed deep concerns about a continued dollar devaluation. He feared that too much downward pressure on the dollar could send it into a free-fall like the decline of 1976 to 1980. "The danger of movements from the present level is that you get a more complete pass-through, I think, into import prices,"[9] he told the Congressional Joint Economic Committee. This outcome might yield increased domestic inflation, capital flight, higher interest rates, and eventually a recession. Chairman Volcker added a further problem: "Declining currencies do not provide for extra flexibility in the conduct of monetary policy."[10] Instead of driving the dollar down, he recommended that the administration attack the more fundamental cause of the trade deficit. Specifically, he thought the United States must decrease its federal budget deficit while increasing private investment in new equipment and technology.

Was the Dollar Correctly Valued?

Arguing that the dollar was in fact still *overvalued,* Martin Feldstein wrote, "The only thing that can achieve a sustained reduction of the U.S. trade deficit is a continued substantial decline of the dollar. And that decline is coming."[11] Professor Feldstein added that small differences between U.S. interest rates and Japanese and German interest rates could not prevent the fall of the dollar because investors realized that the dollar's current level was unsustainable.

Ronald I. McKinnon, professor of economics at Stanford University, in contrast, felt the dollar was highly *undervalued.* He explained:

> At 200 yen and 2.3 marks by the end of 1985, the dollar was more or less correctly aligned with the currencies of our Japanese and European trading partners in two closely related aspects. First, there was approximate purchasing power parity. . . . Second, rates of price inflation (as measured by changes in their respective wholesale-price indexes in three areas) were virtually the same, and close to zero.[12]

Professor McKinnon said the reason the dollar was undervalued was that the United States followed the "false academic doctrine" that says a devaluation of a currency can by itself reduce that country's trade deficit. Since real interest rates were still too high, he believed, the U.S. government should reduce its budget deficit instead of pressuring other governments to expand their economies. Once the trade deficit was no longer a problem, Professor McKinnon wrote, the G-7 (the G-5 plus Canada and Italy) should meet to realign exchange rates at purchasing power parity and to coordinate their monetary and fiscal policies.

Martin Feldstein believed that intervention in the markets, as Professor McKinnon proposed, was futile. He wrote:

[9]*The Wall Street Journal,* February 3, 1987, p. 2.
[10]*The Wall Street Journal,* January 23, 1987, p. 3.
[11]*The Wall Street Journal,* November 25, 1986, p. 28.
[12]*The Wall Street Journal,* February 2, 1987, p. 22.

The decline of the dollar began in March 1985, six months before the Plaza G-5 meeting. Moreover, the dollar's value (relative to a weighted average of other industrial currencies) declined as fast between March and September of 1985 as it has since the meeting. The evidence indicates that the dollar's decline has been caused by private investors responding to economic fundamentals rather than government pronouncements or exchange-market interventions.[13]

The Continuing Trade Deficit

Surrounding the debate about the weak dollar were those who tried to explain why the trade situation had not improved despite the dollar's decline (see **Exhibit 3**). Deborah Allen Olivier, president of the Claremont Economic Institute, said, "The dollar's two year plunge is benefitting American industry very little and very unevenly."[14] A lot of the problem arose because the currencies of several major trading partners such as Canada, Brazil, and South Korea had either been stable or had even fallen against the dollar (see **Exhibit 4**).

Ms. Olivier emphasized the importance of using a broad trade-weighted measure of the dollar when gauging its value. While the Federal Reserve Board said the dollar had depreciated 39 percent against our 10 major trading partners since early 1985, the Federal Reserve Bank of Dallas said the dollar had decreased only 5 percent relative to the 131 countries with which the United States traded. Ms. Olivier argued that there were "very few U.S. industries . . . more competitive today than they were 2 years ago." Furthermore, there was "tremendous variation in the amount by which various goods are influenced by currency changes."[15]

Others offered different reasons to explain why our trade deficits with Germany and Japan had not decreased. Deputy Secretary of the Treasury Richard Darman accused America's big corporations of being "bloated, risk-averse, inefficient and unimaginative."[16] The Japanese, it was said, were defending their U.S. market shares by holding dollar prices constant despite the yen's appreciation. Burk Kalweit, senior economist for the National Association of Machine Tool Builders, noted: "The Germans aren't selling on price; they're selling on engineering and features."[17]

A more basic question was asked by Vermont Royster, editor emeritus of *The Wall Street Journal,* who wrote, "One of the things that's always puzzled me is how those who manage our economic affairs think they know what is the 'right' price for a dollar in terms of francs, pounds, yen or whatever. And if they do, why do they keep changing their minds?"[18]

Part of the problem, as the *Financial Times* pointed out, was that "There is no scientific way of calculating a 'correct' value for the dollar."[19] Aside from pegging

[13]*The Wall Street Journal,* November 25, 1986, p. 28.
[14]*The Wall Street Journal,* January 30, 1987, p. 22.
[15]Ibid.
[16]*The Wall Street Journal,* January 7, 1987, p. 1.
[17]Ibid., p. 18.
[18]*The Wall Street Journal,* January 27, 1987, p. 34.
[19]*Financial Times,* January 23, 1987, p. 16.

currencies to gold, which would be too confining, Mr. Royster was not sure how to stabilize exchange rates.

Nevertheless, many people had strong feelings about the dollar. The French finance minister, Edouard Balladur, called the slide of the dollar "excessive, unjustified and harmful to the world economy."[20] Karl Otto Poehl, president of West Germany's central bank, said, "It's very important that we try to stabilize the current exchange-rate pattern. . . . We are approaching a risky point in the exchange markets. . . . [Further devaluation of the dollar] could cause a crisis of confidence in the dollar, and then the whole thing could get out of control."[21] Meanwhile, Rimmer de Vries, chief international economist at Morgan Guaranty Trust Company, said, "The dollar has to decline further, and the earlier the better. It is the only way we can hope for a quick turnaround."[22]

The Paris Accord

Clearly, in early 1987, there was very little consensus among experts about whether or not the dollar was correctly priced on foreign exchange markets, and whether or not anything should, or even could, be done about it. Beryl Sprinkel, chairman of the President's Council of Economic Advisers, admitted, "Many of us prefer to have more stable exchange rates than we've had of late." But he added, "We have no objective about what the dollar price should be."[23]

This position was ultimately reflected in the Paris Accord that was reached among six major industrial nations (the G-5 plus Canada) on February 22, 1987. The finance ministers of the six nations agreed that they were ready to intervene in the currency markets, if necessary, to stabilize exchange rates at "about their current levels."[24] Italy also was party to the meeting, but the Italian minister walked out before the communiqué was signed because he felt the G-5 countries had worked out the major details among themselves the day before. The communiqué released by the six remaining countries said that exchange rates were then "within ranges broadly consistent with underlying economic fundamentals."[25] Yet the ministers reiterated that they had not established target or reference zones for the currencies. The basis of the communiqué rested on the pledges by the United States, Germany, and Japan to resolve the trade deficit problem without further devaluing the dollar. Germany would increase the size of its 1988 tax cuts, Japan would propose new measures to stimulate its economy, and the Reagan administration would work to decrease the U.S. federal budget deficit. Mr. Baker allowed for the possibility of talking the dollar down further if other nations did not fulfill their promises.

[20]*The Wall Street Journal*, January 15, 1987, p. 3.
[21]*The Wall Street Journal*, January 26, 1987, p. 25.
[22]*The Wall Street Journal*, January 20, 1987, p. 14.
[23]*The Wall Street Journal*, January 22, 1987, p. 24.
[24]*The Wall Street Journal*, February 22, 1987, p. 3.
[25]Ibid.

DISCORD AND PUZZLEMENT

Reactions to the Paris meeting varied. Its mere announcement on February 19 caused the Tokyo stock market to rally to a record level in hope that the Bank of Japan would cut its discount rate to 2.5 percent. The dollar increased sharply but then fell back when Paul Volcker spoke against target zones. After the meeting, Edouard Balladur expressed delight with the results and said, "We are not at the end of the road. . . . But we are on the right track."[26] Kiichi Miyazawa, the Japanese finance minister, said, "I also am very, very happy with the results of the meeting."[27] However, the pledges of cooperation were unconvincing to the Italian representative, who had walked out, and the Canadian minister, who was not much happier. One senior official remarked, "Will the markets be more impressed by the threat of intervention or the size of the imbalance this year in the absence of any new policy moves? That is the real question."[28]

Despite the Paris Accord, Vermont Royster's earlier words might prove prophetic: "[the] powers-that-be, no matter what they say, are going to keep tinkering with our dollar on the foreign exchange markets while they search for the dollar's 'right' price. . . . But what I don't understand is how they're going to know when they've found that 'right' price. To me it's a puzzlement."[29]

[26]*Financial Times,* February 22, 1987, p. 1.
[27]*The New York Times,* February 22, 1987, p. D10.
[28]Ibid.
[29]*The Wall Street Journal,* January 27, 1987, p. 34.

EXHIBIT 1   **NOMINAL AND REAL EXCHANGE RATES AND EXPECTED REAL INTEREST DIFFERENTIAL**

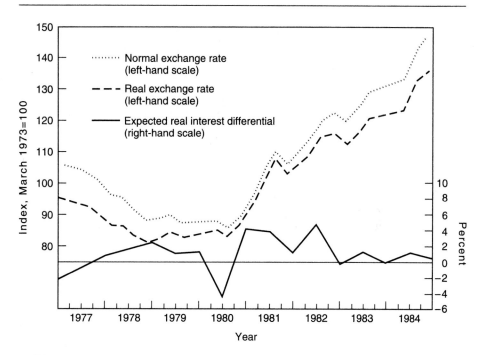

.... Normal exchange rate
(left-hand scale)

– – – Real exchange rate
(left-hand scale)

——— Expected real interest differential
(right-hand scale)

[1]Multilateral trade-weighted dollar.
[2]Nominal exchange rate adjusted by relative consumer prices.
[3]U.S. interest rate (3-month) minus trade-weighted average interest rate (also 3-month) for six industrial countries adjusted by corresponding OECD inflation forecasts.

EXHIBIT 1
(continued)

MULTILATERAL TRADE-WEIGHTED VALUE OF THE U.S. DOLLAR (1980 = 100)

Year	Nominal	Real
1975	112.7	110.7
1976	120.8	114.7
1977	118.2	109.8
1978	105.7	99.3
1979	100.8	98.1
1980	100.0	100.0
1981	117.7	118.9
1982	133.4	131.7
1983	143.4	138.3
1984	158.1	151.8

Quarter	Nominal	Real
1983		
I	136.6	132.2
II	140.7	136.0
III	147.3	142.1
IV	149.0	143.2
1984		
I	150.6	144.3
II	151.9	145.4
III	162.1	156.0
IV	168.4	161.2
1985		
I	179.1	170.0
II	170.6	161.6
III	159.3	151.5
IV	146.7	139.5
1986		
I	136.7	129.8
II	130.7	123.2
III	123.9	117.8
IV	122.4	116.4

Sources: Board of Governors of the Federal Reserve System and Organization for Economic Cooperation and Development (OECD).

EXHIBIT 2   NOMINAL BILATERAL EXCHANGE RATES FOR THE U.S. DOLLAR (CENTS PER UNIT OF FOREIGN CURRENCY)

Year, month, or quarter	French franc	German mark	Japanese yen	U.K. pound
1975	23.354	40.729	0.33705	222.16
1976	20.942	39.737	0.33741	180.48
1977	20.344	43.079	0.37342	174.49
1978	22.218	49.867	0.47981	191.84
1979	23.504	54.561	0.45834	212.24
1980	23.694	55.089	0.44311	232.58
1981	18.489	44.362	0.45432	202.43
1982	15.293	41.236	0.40284	174.80
1983	13.183	39.235	0.42128	151.59
1984	11.474	35.230	0.42139	133.56
1983				
I	14.517	41.513	0.42436	153.28
II	13.403	40.256	0.42109	155.21
III	12.561	37.828	0.41252	150.95
IV	12.251	37.344	0.42714	146.91
1984				
I	12.060	37.052	0.43326	143.50
II	12.004	36.891	0.43539	139.58
III	11.160	34.251	0.41055	129.65
IV	10.673	32.726	0.40635	121.50
1985:01	10.305	31.540	0.39342	112.71
1985:02	9.908	30.280	0.38391	109.31
1985:03	9.923	30.320	0.38772	112.53
1985:04	10.590	32.314	0.39708	123.77
1985:05	10.545	32.162	0.39725	124.83
1985:06	10.705	32.641	0.40186	128.08
1985:07	11.298	34.384	0.41470	138.07
1985:08	11.720	35.795	0.42112	138.40
1985:09	11.547	35.235	0.42278	136.42
1985:10	12.401	37.813	0.46581	142.15
1985:11	12.643	38.530	0.49003	143.96
1985:12	13.013	39.806	0.49312	144.47
1986:01	13.365	41.010	0.50028	142.44
1986:02	13.971	42.887	0.54098	142.97
1986:03	14.293	43.952	0.55963	146.74
1986:04	13.877	43.991	0.57113	149.85
1986:05	14.091	44.889	0.59869	152.11
1986:06	14.043	44.769	0.59687	150.85
1986:07	14.425	46.475	0.63048	150.71
1986:08	14.878	48.494	0.64859	148.61
1986:09	14.962	48.984	0.64629	146.98
1986:10	15.237	49.865	0.63910	142.64
1986:11	15.104	49.400	0.61406	142.38
1986:12	15.315	50.302	0.61709	143.93
1987:01	16.127	53.775	0.64587	150.54

EXHIBIT 3 KEY ECONOMIC STATISTICS OF THE FIVE MAJOR INDUSTRIAL COUNTRIES*

	Nominal interest rates,† % per annum	Premium/(discount) on 3-month forward exchange rate,‡ % per annum	Growth rates, % per annum				Federal government deficit, billions of local currency	Balance of payments, $ millions			
			Real GNP	Money	CPI	WPI		Trade balance	Current account	Net capital flow	Overall balance
France											
1980	12.99	5.85	1.1	8.0	13.8	8.8	(1.0)	(13,419)	(4,208)	(8,480)	6,060
1981	15.66	n.a.	0.3	12.3	13.4	11.0	(85.6)	(9,970)	(4,809)	(8,887)	(4,766)
1982	15.56	(3.51)	1.6	14.8	11.8	11.1	(110.6)	(15,785)	(12,082)	1,239	(3,606)
1983	13.61	(2.37)	0.5	11.2	9.6	11.1	(150.5)	(8,754)	(4,904)	9,396	4,166
1984	12.41	(2.00)	1.8	7.3	7.4	13.3	(145.1)	(4,089)	(14)	5,204	2,786
Germany											
1980	8.50	8.17	1.8	2.4	5.4	7.6	(26.91)	8,970	(16,003)	1,930	(15,650)
1981	10.38	3.16	(0.1)	0.9	6.3	7.8	(35.86)	16,570	(5,419)	6,830	1,560
1982	8.95	3.28	(1.0)	3.2	5.3	5.9	(30.86)	25,280	3,135	50	2,920
1983	7.89	3.94	1.3	10.3	3.3	1.5	(31.04)	22,270	4,170	(6,020)	(1,230)
1984	7.78	2.92	2.5	3.4	2.4	2.9	(28.48)	22,340	6,074	(10,780)	(1,130)
Japan											
1980	9.22	7.00	4.9	0.8	8.0	17.8	(14.524)	2,130	(10,750)	18,880	5,030
1981	8.66	6.46	4.0	3.7	4.9	1.4	(13.013)	19,960	4,770	(1,560)	3,640
1982	8.06	1.87	3.2	7.1	2.6	1.8	(13.811)	18,080	6,850	(16,200)	(4,700)
1983	7.42	3.70	3.0	3.0	1.8	(2.2)	(13.844)	31,460	20,800	(21,320)	1,550
1984	6.81	1.85	5.8	2.9	2.3	(0.3)	(13.263)	44,260	35,000	(36,540)	2,120
United Kingdom											
1980	13.79	3.34	(2.6)	4.4	18.0	14.0	(10.81)	3,715	8,690	(7,631)	(1,443)
1981	14.74	(1.51)	(1.3)	10.2	11.9	9.6	(10.40)	7,756	15,070	(15,060)	(825)
1982	12.88	(0.99)	2.3	8.2	8.6	7.7	(7.86)	3,423	8,435	2,228	5,673
1983	10.81	(0.72)	2.5	14.2	4.6	5.4	(14.49)	(1,813)	4,862	(7,659)	(1,247)
1984	10.69	(1.21)	2.0	14.6	5.0	6.2	(10.19)	(5,677)	733	(13,469)	(10,719)
United States											
1980	11.39	n.r.	(0.3)	6.4	13.5	14.1	(68.72)	(25,500)	1,860	(34,830)	(7,890)
1981	13.72	n.r.	2.5	7.1	10.4	9.1	(72.62)	(27,980)	6,620	(25,750)	(1,250)
1982	12.92	n.r.	(2.1)	6.6	6.2	2.0	(130.72)	(36,470)	(9,230)	(21,490)	2,030
1983	11.34	n.r.	3.7	11.2	3.2	1.3	(190.41)	(62,020)	(40,860)	25,190	(4,050)
1984	12.48	n.r.	6.8	6.9	4.3	2.4	(184.46)	(108,270)	(101,600)	77,030	150

*n.a. = not available; n.r. = not reported.
†Government bond yields (average yields to maturity).
‡Based on end-of-year quotations for each currency against the U.S. dollar.
Source: IMF *International Financial Statistics,* 1985.

	Nominal interest rates,[†] % per annum	Premium/discount (−) on 3-month forward exchange rate,[‡] % per annum	Growth rates, % per annum		Balance of payments, $ millions			
			CPI	WPI	Trade balance	Current account	Net capital flow	Overall balance
France								
1985: I	12.27	(1.81)	5.6	6.7	(2,190)	(1,712)	71	595
II	11.83	(3.16)	7.4	3.5	(501)	965	1,519	1,281
III	11.97	(2.80)	3.9	(5.3)	(1,107)	37	80	(184)
IV	11.33	(2.00)	2.5	(8.9)	(734)	1,617	2,167	689
1986: I	9.19	(4.84)	0.5	n.a.	(1,215)	(416)	(519)	80
II	8.65	(0.53)	2.8	n.a.	(1,010)	1,021	(1,438)	6,706
III	8.51	(2.08)	2.5	n.a.	(553)	n.a.	n.a.	n.a.
IV	9.89	(5.78)	2.7	n.a.	n.a.	n.a.	n.a.	n.a.
Germany								
1985: I	7.44	2.63	4.4	4.1	5,070	1,540	(950)	(3,950)
II	7.02	2.28	2.3	1.7	6,070	3,001	(160)	1,730
III	6.55	3.60	(1.0)	0.0	6,970	1,990	(620)	1,870
IV	6.57	6.72	1.3	(0.7)	10,550	7,210	(470)	1,240
1986: I	6.21	2.88	0.0	(3.9)	11,480	6,870	9,070	840
II	6.17	2.34	(1.0)	(5.8)	12,840	8,230	250	(3,880)
III	6.26	1.51	(2.0)	(4.0)	14,850	8,010	4,720	2,100
IV	6.25	1.36	(1.3)	(5.7)	n.a.	n.a.	n.a.	n.a.
Japan								
1985: I	6.97	2.76	0.7	1.6	8,930	6,810	(10,350)	150
II	6.53	1.56	3.6	(2.7)	14,190	13,270	(17,040)	950
III	6.36	1.80	0.7	(4.3)	15,080	13,090	(17,810)	(410)
IV	6.10	4.73	1.4	(8.9)	17,790	16,000	(18,060)	(550)
1986: I	4.80	2.16	0.3	(9.1)	14,560	12,670	(19,890)	1,180
II	4.83	2.28	1.0	(15.8)	23,910	23,100	(28,990)	5,720
III	4.65	1.24	(2.1)	(10.6)	26,590	24,210	(37,760)	7,300
IV	4.66	1.83	0.0	(6.2)	n.a.	n.a.	n.a.	n.a.
United Kingdom								
1985: I	10.34	3.86	5.1	6.7	(2,012)	(765)	(5,914)	1,567
II	10.45	4.56	4.4	8.1	(519)	1,342	(2,175)	(2,595)
III	10.15	3.25	1.1	2.3	(670)	2,095	(4,847)	(1,700)
IV	10.35	3.64	2.0	3.5	916	2,669	(4,206)	(419)
1986: I	8.75	3.79	2.8	5.8	(2,578)	229	(3,946)	894
II	9.32	2.96	5.4	6.6	n.a.	n.a.	n.a.	n.a.
III	10.31	4.60	0.3	1.7	n.a.	n.a.	n.a.	n.a.
IV	10.17	4.52	5.3	3.0	n.a.	n.a.	n.a.	n.a.

*n.a. = not available; n.r. = not reported; values in parentheses.
†Government bond yields (average yields to maturity).
‡Based on end-of-year quotations for each currency against the U.S. dollar.
Source: IMF, International Financial Statistics, 1985.
Exhibit 3 continued on p. 16.

EXHIBIT 3 (*continued*)   KEY ECONOMIC STATISTICS OF THE FIVE MAJOR INDUSTRIAL COUNTRIES*

	Nominal interest rates,[†] % per annum	Premium/discount (−) on 3-month forward exchange rate,[‡] % per annum	Growth rates, % per annum		Balance of payments, $ millions			
			CPI	WPI	Trade balance	Current account	Net capital flow	Overall balance
United States								
1985: I	11.92	n.r.	2.5	(0.7)	(23,460)	(23,550)	13,450	10,850
II	10.62	n.r.	5.1	0.3	(30,350)	(30,380)	14,620	(7,530)
III	10.67	n.r.	2.8	(2.8)	(33,650)	(32,340)	17,840	(2,420)
IV	9.49	n.r.	3.7	2.5	(36,980)	(31,480)	25,090	4,720
1986: I	7.50	n.r.	0.9	(5.8)	(34,560)	(31,040)	6,750	(2,050)
II	7.79	n.r.	(0.9)	(7.5)	(35,930)	(35,500)	20,240	(14,060)
III	7.95	n.r.	3.1	(1.8)	(39,620)	(40,210)	14,920	(15,170)
IV	7.79	n.r.	2.1	1.5	n.a.	n.a.	n.a.	n.a.

EXHIBIT 4 THE LARGEST U.S. BILATERAL TRADE DEFICITS

Country	Deficit, $ 1986 Nine months*	Deficit, $ 1985 Nine months*	Change in U.S. dollar vs. foreign currency, % (9/85–12/86)†	Products exported to U.S.
Japan	43,871	34,659	−34.0	Automobiles and parts, steel, electronics
Canada	18,803	16,474	+0.3	Automobiles and parts, lumber, machinery
West Germany	11,415	8,367	−32.0	Automobiles and parts, chemicals, machinery
Taiwan	10,716	9,085	−12.0	Apparel, electronics, telecommunications gear
South Korea	4,788	2,926	−3.0	Textiles, electronics, automobiles, steel
Italy	4,549	3,711	−29.0	Apparel, footwear, machinery
Hong Kong	4,303	4,150	−0.2	Apparel, electronics, telecommunications gear
Mexico	4,013	4,326	+135.0	Automobiles and parts, oil, machinery
Britain	3,534	2,540	−7.0	Oil, vehicles, chemicals, machinery
Brazil	2,516	3,622	−109.0	Iron, steel, coffee, oil
Switzerland	2,485	1,026	−31.0	Chemicals, machinery, pharmaceuticals
France	2,455	2,656	−25.0	Automobiles and parts, steel, machinery, wine
Indonesia	1,981	2,898	+47.0	Oil, rubber, coffee
Sweden	1,886	1,751	−19.0	Automobiles, steel, machinery
Venezuela	1,659	2,025	0.0	Oil, metals
Nigeria	1,591	1,568	×	Oil
Algeria	1,042	1,473	×	Oil
Singapore	1,017	635	−0.9	Apparel, electronics, telecommunications gear
South Africa	891	631	−17.0	Metals, chemicals
Denmark	712	671	−28.0	Furniture, meat
Ecuador	639	886	+34.0	Wood, oil, textiles
India	633	602	+8.0	Fibers, apparel, oil, misc. manufactured items
Malaysia	512	513	+4.0	Rubber, apparel, electrical machinery
Philippines	493	590	+11.0	Apparel, electrical products, wood
Angola	438	629	×	Oil

*In millions.
†Note: × = No quotes available—insufficiently traded.
Source: The Wall Street Journal, January 7, 1987.

THE FOREIGN EXCHANGE MARKET: BACKGROUND NOTE AND PROBLEM SET

International finance plays a large though often hidden role in all of our lives. Whether we are driving to work in a Japanese car, wearing clothes tailored in Hong Kong, or having a German beer before dinner, we are using products originally purchased with currencies traded through the foreign exchange market. An understanding of this market is essential to firms that operate globally because they are exposed to foreign-currency fluctuations. Moreover, the market has grown substantially in recent years because of floating exchange rates, deregulation, and the advancement of communications technology. Though it is difficult to measure the size of the foreign exchange market, in 1985 the Group of Thirty research organization estimated the *daily* foreign exchange turnover at $150 billion. By 1986, however, a survey of the central banks from the United States, the United Kingdom, and Japan reported that daily turnover in the top three centers alone was $188 billion. Continued reform will make the foreign exchange market an increasingly innovative and exciting arena in which to participate.

MARKET PARTICIPANTS

The foreign exchange market involves participants buying and selling currencies all over the world. Elaborate communications systems, including telephones, telexes, computers, and news wires, link individuals worldwide. Trading takes place throughout most of each day, starting in Tokyo; moving west to Singapore and Hong

This case was prepared by Research Associate Richard P. Melnick and Professor W. Carl Kester. Copyright © 1987 by the President and Fellows of Harvard College. Harvard Business School case 287-033.

Kong; continuing to Zurich, Frankfurt, and London; and then ending in New York, Chicago, and San Francisco.

Participants in the market include individuals, corporations, commercial banks, and central banks. Each has different motives for transacting. Commercial banks with large foreign exchange sales and trading departments act as dealers when they buy and sell foreign exchange for clients. Their clients, usually corporations, need to transfer purchasing power to and from other countries in order to buy foreign goods and services and to invest in foreign assets. Commercial banks profit from the spread between buying currencies low at a "bid" price and selling them at a higher "ask" or "offer" price. Individual speculators profit when there is a change in general price levels and they have predicted the change better than the market. Individuals, including tourists, importers, and exporters, use the foreign exchange market to conduct trade or investment transactions.

Central banks have two official reasons for participating in the foreign exchange market: (1) to monitor the market and (2) to intervene for purposes of policy implementation. A central bank might intervene, for example, to smooth out extreme currency fluctuations or to meet obligations under formal agreements such as the European Monetary System (EMS).[1] A striking example of the central banks' ability to influence the market was the Group of Five's effort to depreciate the dollar in September 1985. Through the sale of billions of dollars, the dollar depreciated 35 percent in 10 months. Intervention on this scale was unprecedented.

Profiting on their currency reserves has increasingly become an additional motive for some central banks to enter the foreign exchange market. The Soviet Union, acting through its Vneshtungbank trade bank, reportedly has been so profitable in its foreign exchange dealings that many suspect information leaks from the U.S. Commerce Department and the German Bundesbank.[2]

Central banks can act discreetly or conspicuously, and they often exploit the market power derived from their mere threat of action. The Bank of England is reported to be the most professional bank and has cleverly used the market to discourage speculation against sterling. The German Bundesbank is considered sophisticated, but with a somewhat tarnished reputation as it has been thought to give domestic banks advantageous information. By telling their national banks outright what to do, the Bank of Japan acts aggressively without trading directly. Traders generally like to avoid the U.S. Federal Reserve Bank, whose intervention is often thought to be clumsy and inept.[3]

---

[1]The European Monetary System is an organization composed of all the European Economic Community members. It was founded in 1979 to stabilize exchange rates among the European countries. Their currency basket, called the European Currency Unit (ECU), is composed of a predetermined quantity of each currency, where the components reflect each member's relative size. Each nation's currency may not deviate from the ECU by more than 2.25 percent (the British pound does not follow the ECU restrictions), but the ECU itself floats against the rest of the world.

[2]Henry Sender, "Games Central Banks Play with Currencies," *Institutional Investor,* November 1985, pp. 100–110.

[3]Ibid., p. 108.

A 1986 survey of central banks in the United States, the United Kingdom, and Japan shows that London, New York, and Tokyo, with $90 billion, $50 billion, and $48 billion, respectively, in estimated *daily* turnover are the leading foreign exchange centers. London is the world's largest foreign exchange center because it has several advantages: history, geography, and a healthy regulatory environment. Expertise and tradition go back to the days when the pound was the most widely traded currency. More important, however, is the fact that London can trade with Tokyo and Hong Kong in the morning and New York in the afternoon, as well as Frankfurt and Zurich continually. Trading has increased substantially since 1979, when foreign exchange regulation decreased in Britain and banks were permitted to trade directly rather than through brokers.

Tokyo's foreign exchange market has grown dramatically from an estimated daily turnover of only $8 billion in 1985. Under pressure from the United States, the Japanese have also decreased market regulation and have thereby surpassed Hong Kong and Singapore in average daily turnover.

New York's foreign exchange system grew during much of the early 1980s, but suffered under the weak dollar of 1986 and the increased power of European central banks. Nonetheless, the greatest volume occurs in the European afternoon when New York is open. Because of the deep market, this is the safest time to execute large transactions.

THE SPOT MARKET

The *spot* exchange rate allows for the buying and selling of foreign exchange with settlement in 2 business days, known as the *value date*. According to the aforementioned central bank survey, spot transactions accounted for 73 percent of all business in London and 63 percent in New York. Spot rates are quoted in terms of both currencies in *The Wall Street Journal,* one just being the reciprocal of the other. On September 2, 1986, for example, the spot rate for Swiss francs (SF) against U.S. dollars was SF = $0.60994, and the cost of the U.S. dollar was therefore 1/0.60994 or 1.6395 Swiss francs.

Quotes are said to be direct or indirect. A *direct* quote is the price of a foreign currency unit in terms of the home currency. According to the previous example, the direct quote for Swiss francs in the United States was $0.60994. An *indirect* quote is the price of a unit of home currency measured in the foreign currency. Thus, the indirect quote for Swiss francs in the United States was SF1.6395.

With this system, a quote's definition depends on the country of reference. To clarify this ambiguity, New York bankers established the *European terms* convention, which uses the U.S. dollar as the common denominator. Thus, traders in the United States, Switzerland, or any other country would all quote Swiss francs as SF1.6395/$. The exceptions to this rule are British sterling and the currencies of several former British Commonwealth countries including Australia and New Zealand. The exceptions exist because the British pound (£) was formerly not a decimal currency and it was easier to quote sterling in terms of other currencies. Today, these currencies are still quoted around the world in "American terms," which is the number of dollars per unit of their currencies.

Cross Rates and Triangular Arbitrage

If a Swiss bank wants German marks, it could get a rate of Swiss francs per deutsche mark from a German bank. From the perspective of dealers in a dollar-based market, this quote would be a *cross rate*. These rates can be given with either currency serving as the denominator and they are most common among the Western European currencies. These cross rates are typically used by central banks of countries in the EMS trying to determine when they need to intervene.

Cross rates should equal the rates resulting from conversion to and from U.S. dollars (except for small differences attributable to transaction costs). Before using a cross rate, it is useful to see if transacting through dollars as an intermediate currency yields a different rate. For instance, if a dealer offers a dollar for 6.6625 French francs (FF) or 2.0320 deutsche marks (DM), then the cross offer rate should be 3.2788 French francs per deutsche mark. With bids of FF6.6575 and DM2.0310 per dollar, the corresponding cross bid rate would be 3.2779. If the cross bid rate were actually 3.3000 French francs per deutsche mark, traders could engage in *triangular arbitrage* to devalue the cross rate and push the system into equilibrium. Traders would take the following three steps: (1) Sell DM1,000,000 (the "over-priced" currency) for French francs at a cross rate of 3.300 French francs per deutsche mark and receive FF3,300,000; (2) sell French franc holdings against dollars at a spot offer rate of FF6.6625 per dollar and receive $495,310; and (3) sell U.S. dollar holdings against deutsche marks at a spot rate of 2.0310 deutsche marks per dollar and receive DM1,005,975. The potential for this profit of DM5975 would erode quickly as deutsche marks are sold against French francs at the overvalued cross rate.

Newspapers usually give only the bid rates or estimates at the midpoint of dealer spreads under European terms (except for sterling), while actual dealers give buying and selling quotations. "Offer" or "ask" rates under European terms will be higher than bid rates since dealers will want to sell dollars at a higher price than that at which they buy dollars. The difference between the two rates is usually quite small. For example, Citicorp could buy French francs (sell dollars) at FF6.6675 per U.S. dollar and sell francs (buy dollars) at FF6.6625 per U.S. dollar. The spread is FF0.0050 or 50 points, where a "point" refers to the quote's last digit.[4] Though the bank's spread might be as small as 0.0005 of the transaction value, this is how banks profit in the foreign exchange market. With a more typical 10-point spread, bank revenues on $1 billion of transactions could be $1 million. The spread travelers experience can be 10 times as high because executing their many small

---

[4]A "point" or "pip" can refer to two, four, six or any number of decimal places. If the Japanese yen were quoted in American terms with an ask of $0.001235 and a bid of $0.001230, this would still be considered a 5-"point" spread.

transactions requires higher inventory carrying costs and virtually the same amount of paperwork as that of large transactions.

THE FORWARD MARKET

When business deals require individuals and corporations to pay or receive foreign currency in the future, they often prefer to transfer the risk that currency values will change. The *forward market* allows corporations to establish the exchange rate between the two currencies for settlement at a fixed future date. This is known as *hedging* or *covering* foreign currency exposure. The *forward rate* is fixed at the time the contract is made, but payment and delivery are not made until the value date. Forward contracts are often negotiated against dollars, though European traders also exchange domestic European currencies against each other. The most frequent forward contracts are for 1, 2, 3, 6, or 12 months. Banks actively trade in these markets both for their customers and for themselves. "Odd-dated" forward contracts (i.e., maturities other than the most common ones) are possible, but they are more expensive because of the thinner market. Long-dated forwards and special quotes can be arranged for up to 10 years with major currencies.

The ratio at which two currencies will be exchanged on a future date is the *outright* forward rate. These rates are usually printed in newspapers and are used by banks when dealing with their clients. Foreign exchange traders like to abbreviate, however, and quote forward premiums or discounts in terms of points.[5] A *dollar premium* implies that forward dollars are at a premium over spot, and the French, for example, need more French francs to buy dollars forward than to buy dollars spot. Similarly, a *dollar discount* means one needs fewer units of foreign currency to buy dollars forward than to buy dollars spot.

In order to tell if a currency is at a premium or a discount, compare the size of the forward bid points with the forward ask points for a given maturity. If the forward bid points are higher than the forward ask points, the U.S. dollar is at a forward discount. For example, if the 3-month forward points for deutsche marks are 38/35, then the forward bid points of DM0.0038 are greater than the forward ask points of DM0.0035 and the forward market is at a dollar discount. Similarly, if the 3-month forward points on French francs are 50/55, the bid is smaller than the ask, and the dollar is at a forward premium.

To calculate the outright forward rate, one needs to know if the U.S. dollar is at a premium or a discount. Looking at the forward bid-offer points, if forward bid points are greater than the offer points, the currency is at a U.S. dollar discount and the trader should *subtract* the forward bid-offer points from the quoted spot rates. If the forward

---

[5]Dealers often do not use the decimal point for forward bid-offer points. Whether talking on the phone or placing quotes on a screen, traders give the complete first bid of the spot quote (e.g., FF6.6575). All that is given for the ask, however, are the digits that differ from the bid (i.e., 75). A slash (/), communicated orally by the word "to," separates the bid and ask quotes. Thus a spot quotation for the French franc might appear on a screen as 6.6575/625, implying an offer rate of 6.6625, and the corresponding 3-month forward rate would be represented as 263/296. One adds these points to the *last* three digits of the spot rate to get the outright forward quote.

bid points are less than the forward offer points, the currency is at a dollar premium and the trader should *add* the forward points to the respective spot points.

Forward quotes can also be presented as a percent-per-annum (% p.a.) deviation from the spot rate. By convention, the formula for calculating forward premiums and discounts as percentages using European terms, with n equal to the number of months in the contract, is:

$$\text{Forward premium or discount } (\% \text{ p.a.}) = \frac{\text{spot rate } - \text{ forward rate}}{\text{forward rate}} \times \frac{12}{n} \times 100$$

Using spot and 3-month forward quotes for deutsche marks of 2.2605 and 2.2406, respectively, we would have:

$$\frac{2.2605 - 2.2406}{2.2406} \times \frac{12}{3} \times 100 = 3.55\%$$

When using American terms, the formula changes as follows:

$$\text{Forward premium or discount } (\% \text{ p.a.}) = \frac{\text{forward rate } - \text{ spot}}{\text{spot}} \times \frac{12}{n} \times 100$$

Thus, in the above example we would have

$$\frac{0.4463 - 0.4424}{0.4424} \times \frac{12}{3} \times 100 = 3.53\%$$

This differs from the percentage using European terms only by a rounding error.

Covered Interest Arbitrage

Many factors explain the changing values of foreign currencies relative to the U.S. dollar. Spot rates can be quite volatile, influenced by news, rumors, speculation, supply and demand imbalances, and central bank intervention. Over the long run, spot rates are affected by relative interest rates and inflation rates, trade imbalances, and purchases or sales of foreign assets.

Perhaps the dominant factor influencing the forward rate of a currency relative to its spot rate is the difference between nominal interest rates on foreign currency–denominated investments and comparable U.S. dollar investments. Investors will compare interest rates around the world in pursuit of the best possible return for a given level of risk. Large banks and corporations seeking short-term use of cash will generally look at Eurodeposit rates since such deposits are quite accessible, secure, and competitively priced because of the less-regulated nature of the Eurodeposit market.

However, the highest nominal Eurodeposit rate does not necessarily imply the highest expected yield in home currency terms. If the currency in which the deposit is made depreciates against the home currency, then the actual yield on the deposit in home currency terms will be less than the quoted nominal yield. For example, a 1-year Eurofranc deposit may offer a yield of 11⅝ percent compared to a 1-year Eurodollar deposit offering 7⅞ percent. But if the franc depreciates by 3.36 percent or more, the interest rate difference favoring the franc will have been completely offset from a U.S. dollar perspective. The depositor could hedge this risk by selling francs (purchasing dollars) forward at the prevailing market exchange rate, thus locking in the future rate at which the principal plus interest can be converted to dollars. In principle, assuming an efficiently operating foreign exchange market, the prevailing 1-year forward contract rate for French francs will reflect the market's collective judgment about what the spot rate will be 1 year later. In other words, the current forward rate should be an unbiased predictor of the future spot rate, a condition known as *forward parity*.

Because money can flow quickly and in large volume from one Eurocurrency deposit to another, and because forward rates may be thought of as unbiased predictors of future spot rates, Eurodepositors aggressively seeking the highest *effective* return (including expected exchange-rate movements) should drive Eurodeposit rates, spot exchange rates, and forward exchange rates into an interdependent relationship in which expected yields are identical across currencies. This condition is known as *interest rate parity*. It can be expressed notationally by the following equation:

$$F = S\frac{(1+R_F)}{(1+R_\$)}$$

where F = the forward exchange rate expressed as units of foreign currency per dollar (European terms)

S = the spot exchange rate expressed as units of foreign currency per dollar

$R_\$$ and R_F = the Eurodollar deposit rate and the other Eurocurrency deposit rate, respectively

If this condition is violated, a *covered interest arbitrage* opportunity will present itself (for this reason, the above equation is also frequently referred to as the "covered interest arbitrage" condition). For example, consider the terms presented in **Table 1**.

The French franc is selling at a forward discount against the dollar. Using the midpoints of the quotes, the discount is 1.88 percent on an annualized basis. This is

TABLE 1	Exchange Rate and Interest Rate Quotes	Spot	3-Month forward
	French franc	7.7150/200	300/425
	3-month Eurofranc rates	11⅝–11¾%	
	3-month Eurodollar rates	7⅞–8%	

smaller in absolute terms than is theoretically justified on the basis of differences in interest rates:

$$3.68\% = \{[(1 + 11.6875/400)/(1 + 7.9375/400)] - 1\} \times 4 \times 100$$

Consequently, an arbitrageur could profit risklessly by taking the following steps:

1. Borrow 1,000,000 Eurodollars for 3 months at 8 percent.

2. Purchase FF7,715,000 at the spot bid rate.

3. Invest the francs for 3 months at the Eurofranc deposit rate of 11⅝ percent.

4. Simultaneously sell francs (buy dollars) forward at the forward offer rate of 7.7625. The amount of the forward sale should equal the total amount of franc proceeds at the deposit's maturity, or FF7,939,217 [FF7,715,000 × (1 + 0.11625/4)].

In 3 months, the arbitrageur would receive the Eurofranc deposit with interest, execute the forward contract, and obtain $1,022,765 (FF7,939,217/7.7625). This could be used to repay the Eurodollar loan with interest amounting to $1,020,000 [$1,000,000 × (1 + .08/4)], leaving a gain of $2765. Assuming total transaction, brokerage, and cable cost of 0.25 percent, or $250 on the $1,000,000 deal, a net profit remains of $2515. Note that this was obtained risklessly and without any equity directly committed by the arbitrageur. As many people try to exploit this opportunity in volume, interest rates and exchange rates will adjust until parity is restored and riskless profit opportunities are eliminated.

INTERBANK TRADING

The vast bulk of foreign exchange transactions takes place in the *interbank market*, where banks and foreign exchange brokers determine exchange rates. Dealers try to develop a sense for where the market is going and then buy or sell currency either for their clients or for their own portfolios. After dealer A decides what he wants to buy or sell, he calls foreign exchange dealers at other banks and "asks for the market." He wants to know whether the dealers' rates are competitive and does not say whether he intends to buy or sell. Foreign exchange dealer B (being called now) must use her intuition to determine what caller A wants to do before offering a quote. Many techniques are used in an effort to get the best rate. For example, if the first caller wants to buy deutsche marks, he might first ask for the market in pounds to confuse the dealer and only later ask for deutsche marks.

Aside from figuring out what the caller wants to do, dealer B must also devise a strategy that meets her goals. If dealer B wants to *sell* deutsche marks (buy dollars), she might present a bid of DM2.5235 per dollar, 2 points higher than other banks', which are at 2.5233. The dealer must also quote an offer, and this should not be better than the market since she does not want to own deutsche marks. Convention holds that the caller can choose either rate and any amount within 1 minute after the quotes. After the minute, dealer B can change her quotes. When a difference in the fourth decimal place can represent thousands of dollars on a big transaction, good judgment and fast thinking are vital.

The parties exchange confirmation papers after a deal has been arranged over the phone. Settlement occurs on the value date as the currencies are exchanged through the banks' clearing accounts. Client rates are generally determined in the retail bank draft market, while the interbank rate is determined in the wholesale market. The largest corporate clients get rates similar to those offered to other banks.

Sometimes banks cannot make markets among themselves. When a private deal cannot be arranged, foreign exchange brokers are used as intermediaries. Banks call brokers and tell them how much foreign currency they want to buy or sell and at what rate they will do the transaction. The broker then takes many requests to buy or sell and tries to find banks with complementary goals. If two banks' exchange-rate terms can be matched, a trade is made. The banks only learn of each other's identities after a contract is settled. Following the contract's consummation, the broker receives a fee from each bank. Banks always prefer to make their own market since the broker's fee makes the same transaction more expensive.

OTHER FOREIGN EXCHANGE INSTRUMENTS

As indicated, the foreign exchange market allows individuals and corporations to transact in the spot market for immediate delivery and in the forward market for settlements in the future. Other foreign exchange vehicles and markets are also appearing. Although they accounted for less than 1 percent of total foreign exchange transaction volume in 1986, their importance is likely to grow.

While forward rates are quoted by commercial banks, *foreign-currency futures* are homogeneous contracts traded in physical marketplaces such as the International Monetary Market (IMM) in Chicago. Buyers and sellers of foreign-currency futures deal through the exchanges rather than directly. Advantages of these contracts are that they are relatively small and, because of their homogeneity, are highly liquid. However, homogeneity also implies inflexibility, and there are high costs on large futures transactions.

Though complicated, expensive, and relatively illiquid, *foreign-currency options* are becoming an attractive transaction alternative. Options allow a company to hedge against foreign exchange losses, but they also provide opportunities for bold speculation in the market. Unlike futures contracts, options represent the right, but not the obligation, to buy or sell a specific amount of currency at a fixed price on or before some future date. Since the option holder can always avoid exercising the option if it is uneconomical to do so, options make possible large upside gains while limiting downside losses. Costing an average of 5 percent to 6 percent of the underlying contract amount, options are expensive compared to the spreads on interbank forward contracts. Though options are not for everyone, more companies are using them to make a profit and hedge risk in times of volatile exchange-rate fluctuations.

A common tool used to hedge foreign-currency risk is a *foreign currency-swap*. A foreign-currency swap allows one party to swap principal and interest in one currency for principal and interest in another. Usually the participants borrow different currencies, exchange the receipts, and then service each other's debt. This arrangement eliminates exchange risk for the transaction and makes future currency fluctuations irrelevant. Sometimes a domestic company is able to borrow funds at a cheaper rate than a foreign company could. Swaps provide cost savings when two companies with complementary needs and desires get together. The World Bank is a frequent participant in these swaps and arranged the first important swap with IBM in 1981. Interest rate swaps, developed in 1982, allow a company with a fixed-rate asset or liability to convert the security into a floating-rate obligation or vice versa. Since then, foreign-currency and interest rate swaps have typically been used together. Further details concerning swaps are provided in the *Note on Foreign Currency Swaps*.

EXCHANGE-RATE PROBLEMS

The mechanics of exchange-rate arithmetic, though fundamentally simple, can be confusing for those not using it on a regular basis. The questions below are designed to provide practice in the more common manipulations. They are of low to moderate difficulty with the easiest problems occurring first. **Exhibits 1** through **3**, along with the general background information provided in this case, are sufficient to solve the problems.

1. Are the dealer quotes shown in **Exhibit 1** direct or indirect? If DM1,000,000 were sold spot, how many dollars would be received? When would settlement normally take place?

2. Examine the cross spot rates shown in **Exhibit 2**. Are there any triangular arbitrage opportunities among these currencies (assume deviations from theoretical cross rates of 5 points or less are attributable to transaction costs)? How much profit could be made on a $5 million transaction?

3. What would be the $/SDR (SDR = U.S. dollars per unit of currency) bid if the SDR appreciates 15 percent against the dollar? What would be the *SDR/$* offer rate if the SDR appreciates 15 percent?

4. Which currencies are at a dollar discount and which are at a dollar premium? What are the outright forward rates for the pound? For the French franc? Using the midpoints of bid-ask spreads, what are the forward premia or discounts on an annualized percentage basis for both these currencies?

5. A private speculator expects the yen to depreciate 7 percent against the dollar over the next 3 months. How can the speculator try to profit on these expectations through (a) spot market transactions only, and (b) forward market transactions only (assume no margin requirements or restrictions on transactions in credit markets)? What will be the expected dollar profit on a $1 million position in each case? What other considerations should factor into the speculator's choice between the spot and forward markets for purposes of profiting on future movements of the yen?

6. A U.S. corporate treasurer will receive a £2 million payment in 30 days from a British customer. The treasurer has no strong opinion about the direction or magnitude of changes in the sterling spot rate, but would like to eliminate the uncertainty surrounding such movements. Within the context of the rates shown in **Exhibits 1** and **3**, what options are available to the treasurer for hedging the foreign exchange risk associated with the sterling payment? What is the expected cost (expressed as an annualized percentage) of each alternative? Which alternative should the treasurer pursue? How would your answers to the above questions change if the treasurer believed very strongly that sterling would trade at $1.45?

7. Compare the 1-year forward premium or discount on the French franc to the 1-year Eurodollar and Eurofranc interest rates shown in **Exhibit 2**. How can this situation be arbitraged?

8. Examine the spot rate and the 6-month forward rate for the British pound. Suppose a speculator anticipates that the pound's spot rate and the 6-month Eurodollar deposit rates will be unchanged from their present levels in 6 months' time. However, at that future date, the 6-month Eurosterling deposit rates will have changed to 10.0000 percent to 10.0625 percent per annum. What should be the new 6-month forward rate for the pound if covered interest arbitrage opportunities are to be avoided half a year from now? How can the speculator profit from the expected change in the interest rate difference while remaining in a "square" position (i.e., offsetting foreign exchange purchase contracts with sales contracts) at all times? What will be the expected dollar profit per pound? How will this expected profit change if the spot rate 6 months later does not remain constant but changes to 1.5500/10? To 1.4500/10? What circumstances might cause the speculator to realize a loss rather than a gain?

EXHIBIT 1   SPOT AND FORWARD EXCHANGE RATES

Currency	Spot	1 Month	3 Months	6 Months	12 Months
Sterling*	1.4890/00	55/52	160/156	302/289	560/523
Deutsche mark	2.0310/20	22/18	64/54	128/105	277/228
French franc	6.6575/625	73/86	263/296	505/590	1194/1351
Yen	154.20/30	8/6	33/27	75/62	164/137
SDR*†	1.2141/43	5/3	12/8	18/11	24/12

*U.S. dollars per unit of currency.
†Special Drawing Right.

EXHIBIT 2   CROSS SPOT EXCHANGE RATES*

	DM	FF	Yen
DM	——	0.3050/51	1.3169/71
FF	3.2779/88	——	4.3365/84
Yen	75.9232/350	23.1595/618	——

*Quotes should be interpreted as units of the currency represented in the left-hand column per unit of currency shown in the top row. Quotes for the DM/yen and FF/yen are expressed in units per *100 yen.*

EXHIBIT 3   EUROCURRENCY INTEREST RATES

Currency	1 Month	3 Months	6 Months	12 Months
U.S. dollar	5.6875–5.8125	5.5000–5.6250	5.5000–5.6250	5.6250–5.7500
Sterling	10.0625–10.1875	9.8750–9.9375	9.6875–9.7500	9.6250–9.7500
Deutsche mark	4.4375–4.5625	4.3125–4.4375	4.3125–4.4375	4.3125–4.4375
French franc	7.1250–7.2500	7.1875–7.3125	7.1875–7.3125	7.2500–7.3750
Yen	5.1250–5.1875	4.7500–4.8125	4.6250–4.6875	4.6250–4.6875
SDR*	5.9375–6.0625	5.8125–5.9375	5.7500–5.8750	5.8125–5.9375

*Special Drawing Right.

THE BANK FOR INTERNATIONAL DEVELOPMENT

Near the end of October 1985, Maria Mendez, assistant treasurer for the Bank for International Development (BID), was analyzing historical data on borrowing costs in yen and dollars. A proposed new issue of dollar-denominated debt had renewed an internal debate about the bank's financing policies. The debate centered on policies for selecting currencies in which to raise funds for the bank's lending activities. The treasurer's practice of issuing in different currencies, depending on market conditions, had been criticized lately, both internally and by a few of the bank's directors. To help prepare a response to this criticism, the treasurer asked Ms. Mendez to analyze borrowing costs in different currencies.

BACKGROUND

The BID was a supranational financial institution with the mission of promoting worldwide economic development. It was organized and owned by many governments around the world that subscribed and paid into its capital base. As such, BID had no natural "home" currency and, in fact, reported its operating results and financial condition in several currencies. Most of the bank's funds were raised by substantial borrowings on the open market. The bank made loans for many types of projects, especially infrastructure projects designed to promote economic growth in the borrowing nation. All of its loans carried a sovereign guarantee. The bank had steadfastly resisted pressure to make loans for purely political purposes and

This case was prepared by Professors W. Carl Kester and Timothy A. Luehrman. Copyright © 1989 by the President and Fellows of Harvard College. Harvard Business School case 289-034.

consistently refused to consider rescheduling any of its debt. To date, no borrower had ever defaulted on one of its loans.

The bank was careful to maintain its own status as a high-quality credit, as evidenced by its AAA rating. Further reflecting its conservatism, the bank hedged its positions in all currencies; all borrowing in a given currency was matched by loans and low-risk investments (e.g., government bonds) in that same currency. Because of its strict credit guidelines, conservative financial policies, and the support of member governments, BID was able to borrow in capital markets around the world at rates only slightly above the U.S. government's.

CONTROVERSY ABOUT CURRENCIES AND BORROWING COSTS

The primary objective of BID's treasurer was quite clear: to minimize the bank's effective borrowing costs. Because exchange risk was effectively transferred to borrowers, minimizing borrowing costs was not a controversial objective, and the treasurer focused intently on the bank's cost of debt. At first, the only funds available at low cost in large volume were U.S. dollars. However, as surpluses developed in Japan, Germany, and OPEC nations, nondollar borrowings began to expand. **Exhibit 1** provides a breakdown of BID's debt by currency and maturity as of September 1985.

As the menu of currency choices expanded, BID's treasurer increasingly sought to borrow in whatever currencies appeared to offer the best terms at any given time. His opinions about the future course of interest rates and exchange rates had resulted in noticeable shifts in the composition of new issues by the bank. For example, the bank had borrowed heavily in dollars during the period 1975–1978, in 1980, and again in 1982–1983, while turning to other currencies in the remaining intervals of the decade.

This on-again, off-again policy with respect to the dollar had prompted two types of criticisms. First, some critics thought it ill-advised to borrow U.S. dollars when interest rates were significantly lower in other currencies such as Japanese yen, deutsche marks, and Swiss francs. They argued that BID should take advantage of its ability to tap capital markets around the world to select the market offering the lowest interest rate at a given time. However, the treasurer thought it likely that the dollar would depreciate sufficiently over the life of the borrowings to more than offset the higher dollar interest rate.

It was this response that rankled a second group of critics. They argued that if market interest rates reflected expected changes in currency values, then there was no point in trying to "time" the market. The treasurer's switching from one currency to another was sheer speculation that could not be expected to pay off in the long run. This group of critics argued that currency choices should be guided by internal targets for different currencies, rather than by market timing considerations.

THE SITUATION IN OCTOBER 1985

In October 1985, the treasurer was considering a $500 million issue of 7-year Eurodollar floating-rate notes. The issue would float with 3-month US$ LIBOR (the London interbank offered rate), which had fallen by more than 100 basis points since the beginning of 1985. By the end of October, BID could expect to pay 7.95 percent initially on such a dollar issue. However, the rate on a comparable issue of Euroyen notes would be still lower, at 7.75 percent. The bank had successfully issued Euroyen notes since 1983, and some of the bank's officers argued for a similar issue at the present time, despite the fact that yen (¥) rates had risen more than 100 basis points since the beginning of the year. Inflation had been fairly low in both countries. Japan experienced consumer price inflation of 1.9 percent during 1984; U.S. consumer prices inflated at 3.0 percent in 1984. In the first three quarters of 1985, Japanese inflation was running somewhat lower, at an annual rate of 1.5 percent. U.S. inflation was also lower, at an annual rate of 2.8 percent. The spot exchange rate was ¥211.50/$ and the 3-month forward rate was ¥211.61/$.

COMPARING CAPITAL COSTS

It was in these circumstances that Maria Mendez was asked to address the question of whether real capital costs had been lower in some currencies than others during the previous decade. Of particular interest was the question of whether there appeared to have been timing opportunities such as the treasurer had recently tried to exploit. While all concerned realized that her study was being done with hindsight, everyone felt that the debate within the bank would benefit from some data.

Before examining all the major currencies in which the bank transacted, Ms. Mendez decided first to undertake a pilot study of the yen and the dollar. Accordingly, a research analyst had assembled a data base consisting of monthly observations of 90-day interest rates and inflation rates in the United States and Japan, and end-of-month spot exchange rates and 90-day forward rates between the yen and the dollar.[1] The data covered the period from January 1976 to the present. They were arrayed in columns on an electronic spreadsheet as shown in the sample in **Exhibit 2** (the complete spreadsheet is contained in a file on the diskette accompanying this case). For convenience, interest rates and inflation rates, which are normally quoted on an annual basis, were converted to actual 90-day rates on a continuously compounded basis.[2] The observations were arrayed so that the consumer price inflation (CPI) actually experienced during a given 90-day period lined up with the nominal return promised to the holder of a Eurodeposit at the *beginning* of the same 90 days.

The data were ready for analysis. Before examining them, Ms. Mendez resolved to give careful thought to the question of what she should expect to find. She wondered under what circumstances she should expect the bank to prefer to borrow in one currency rather than another. Moreover, if a particular currency did appear to be cheaper at a given time, could the opportunity have been exploited without hindsight?

---

[1]Ninety-day Eurodeposit rates were chosen for the pilot study because of the ready availability of data in both currencies, and because of the close relationship between BID's borrowing costs and short-term Euromarket rates.

[2]Rates expressed on a continuously compounded basis are easily manipulated for the purposes of such a study. For example, the real (inflation-adjusted) return on a 90-day Eurodollar deposit is found by simply subtracting the continuously compounded inflation rate from the continuously compounded interest rate.

If so, how? Finally, how long might such an opportunity persist? The results of the analysis would affect not only the choice of currency for the bank's next issue, but also the larger debate about the bank's borrowing strategy.

EXHIBIT 1   **BANK BORROWINGS BY CURRENCY, SEPTEMBER 1985**

	%
Belgian francs	0.31
British pounds sterling	0.33
Canadian dollars	0.24
Deutsche marks	29.67
French francs	0.14
Italian lire	0.20
Japanese yen	13.94
Kuwaiti dinars	0.98
Netherland guilders	1.48
Saudi Arabian riyals	0.55
Swedish kronor	0.14
Swiss francs	18.51
U.S. dollars	33.11
Venezuelan bolivares	0.40
	100.00

MATURITY STRUCTURE OF BORROWINGS, SEPTEMBER 1985

Years to maturity	%
1	9.14
2	10.62
3	10.10
4	10.26
5	12.64
10	30.52
15	11.82
20	4.90
	100.00

EXHIBIT 2   SELECTED HISTORICAL INTEREST RATES, INFLATION RATES, AND EXCHANGE RATES[a]

Date (end of month)	90-day Euroyen rate	90-day Eurodollar rate	Qtrly. Japan CPI infl.	Qtrly. U.S. CPI infl.	Fwrd. ex. 90-day, ¥/$	Spot ex. rate, ¥/$	Fwrd. ex. qtrly. prem./disct.
Jan. 76	0.0123	0.0128	0.0334	0.0103	303.80	303.70	0.0003
Feb. 76	0.0129	0.0135	0.0307	0.0132	302.30	302.25	0.0002
Mar. 76	0.0150	0.0134	0.0293	0.0146	302.80	299.70	0.0103
Apr. 76	0.0123	0.0131	0.0101	0.0160	299.43	299.40	0.0001
May 76	0.0168	0.0157	−0.0013	0.0159	300.60	299.95	0.0022
Jun. 76	0.0147	0.0146	0.0236	0.0144	298.33	297.40	0.0031
Jul. 76	0.0152	0.0137	0.0247	0.0129	294.00	293.40	0.0020
Aug. 76	0.0144	0.0135	0.0335	0.0100	289.45	288.75	0.0024
Sep. 76	0.0159	0.0140	0.0158	0.0100	288.15	287.45	0.0024
Oct. 76	0.0147	0.0129	0.0193	0.0113	294.93	293.70	0.0042
Nov. 76	0.0162	0.0125	0.0253	0.0197	296.95	295.75	0.0040
Dec. 76	0.0160	0.0122	0.0215	0.0224	293.60	292.80	0.0027
Jan. 77	0.0144	0.0128	0.0283	0.0250	288.80	289.30	−0.0017
Feb. 77	0.0137	0.0125	0.0316	0.0193	284.20	282.70	0.0053
Mar. 77	0.0156	0.0126	0.0199	0.0206	278.55	277.50	0.0038
Apr. 77	0.0131	0.0128	0.0012	0.0163	277.85	277.70	0.0005
May 77	0.0137	0.0147	−0.0081	0.0149	277.21	277.30	−0.0003
Jun. 77	0.0143	0.0140	0.0161	0.0121	266.77	267.70	−0.0035
Jul. 77	0.0146	0.0152	0.0230	0.0108	266.20	266.00	0.0008
Aug. 77	0.0123	0.0152	0.0115	0.0107	266.85	267.30	−0.0017
Sep. 77	0.0098	0.0166	−0.0092	0.0107	263.35	265.45	−0.0079
Oct. 77	0.0098	0.0174	−0.0103	0.0146	248.60	250.60	−0.0080
Nov. 77	0.0020	0.0166	0.0057	0.0159	242.34	245.70	−0.0138
Dec. 77	0.0045	0.0174	0.0171	0.0197	236.93	240.00	−0.0129
Jan. 78	0.0072	0.0175	0.0238	0.0222	239.30	241.40	−0.0087
Feb. 78	0.0062	0.0174	0.0248	0.0259	235.95	238.70	−0.0116
Mar. 78	0.0030	0.0181	0.0101	0.0282	220.30	222.40	−0.0095
Apr. 78	0.0052	0.0184	0.0045	0.0267	220.55	222.90	−0.0106
May 78	0.0066	0.0192	0.0000	0.0227	220.25	223.40	−0.0142
Jun. 78	0.0072	0.0208	0.0178	0.0213	201.65	204.70	−0.0150
Jul. 78	0.0039	0.0204	0.0144	0.0211	187.75	190.70	−0.0156
Aug. 78	0.0062	0.0212	0.0033	0.0210	187.15	190.20	−0.0162
Sep. 78	0.0069	0.0226	−0.0111	0.0172	186.00	189.15	−0.0168
Oct. 78	0.0060	0.0269	−0.0110	0.0183	172.40	176.00	−0.0207
Nov. 78	0.0008	0.0273	−0.0044	0.0253	192.75	197.50	−0.0243
Dec. 78	0.0015	0.0276	0.0055	0.0300	189.80	194.60	−0.0250

[a]*Note:* These data are continued in the worksheet on the diskette accompanying this case.

NOTE ON FUNDAMENTAL PARITY CONDITIONS

For the modern corporate treasurer, an appreciation of the forces underlying exchange-rate movements is important because of the impact such changes can have on the firm's various exchange-rate exposures. This note discusses a simple framework for analyzing expected exchange-rate movements. The framework is founded upon assumptions of rational economic behavior and the ability to transact freely at no cost in the markets for goods and credit as well as the market for foreign exchange. A handful of fundamental parity and market equilibrium conditions describes the connections among these international markets.

The empirical evidence supporting each individual parity condition is mixed. But collectively, they constitute a useful model for ordering one's thinking about the economic forces governing exchange-rate movements. Their usefulness to the financial officer is less as accurate descriptors of international financial markets and more as a unified framework for focusing executive attention on relevant issues and prompting managers to address the right questions as far as exchange-rate movements are concerned.

PURCHASING POWER PARITY

Perhaps one of the earliest and most widely discussed parity conditions is *purchasing power parity* (PPP). In its "relative" form, PPP states that one currency's rate of exchange for another can be expected to change over time at a rate equal to the relative

This note was prepared by Research Associate Richard P. Melnick and Professor W. Carl Kester. Copyright © 1988 by the President and Fellows of Harvard College. Harvard Business School note 288-016.

expected inflation rates in the two countries. The condition can be expressed notationally as[1,2]:

$$(1+\dot{s}) = \frac{(1+\dot{p}_F)}{(1+\dot{p}_D)} \tag{1}$$

where $\dot{s}$ = the expected rate of change in the spot exchange rate (foreign currency per unit of domestic currency) over some relevant time interval, expressed as a decimal fraction (e.g., 0.05 for a 5 percent rate of change)

$\dot{p}_F$ = the expected rate of foreign price inflation over the same time interval, expressed as a decimal fraction

$\dot{p}_D$ = the expected rate of domestic price inflation over the same time interval, also expressed as a decimal fraction

An understanding of PPP begins with the "law of one price" (LOOP), which states that goods priced in different currencies should have the same price when one currency is translated into the other using the spot exchange rate prevailing at the time of the transaction. This can be expressed as $P_F = S \cdot P_D$, where P_F is the price of a commodity in foreign currency, P_D is the price in domestic currency, and S is the spot exchange rate expressed as units of foreign currency per unit of domestic currency.

Economist Gustave Cassel discussed the LOOP when he tried to explain the new parity relationships among major currencies established after World War I. He believed that the LOOP would be enforced by commodity arbitrageurs who would buy and sell across borders to exploit differences in commodity prices not justified by transportation or other transaction costs. Their actions, it was argued, would alter commodity prices and/or the spot exchange rate until a single, worldwide price was obtained.

Even without overt arbitrage, the law of one price was thought to prevail over the long run due to the supply-and-demand forces of international trade. If, for example, the price of coal were higher in France than in Germany or the United Kingdom by an amount not justified by freight costs, then nobody in Europe would buy French coal. Eventually, coal prices in France would have to fall, or those in Germany or the United Kingdom would have to rise, until a single commodity price emerged.

If the scope of economic activity is enlarged from trade in one commodity to that of all goods produced and consumed in two economies, then one obtains an "absolute" version of PPP, which states that national *price levels* are equated by the

---

[1]It is assumed here and throughout the rest of this note that exchange rates are expressed in units of foreign currency per unit of domestic currency. For exchange rates where this is not the convention (e.g., British sterling viewed from a non–British perspective), the parity equations should be modified appropriately by inverting ratios on the side of the equation opposite the exchange rates.

[2]A common alternative expression for PPP is: $\dot{s} = \dot{p}_F - \dot{p}_D$. This is a correct expression whenever rates of change are expressed on a continuously compounding basis [continuously compounding rates of change can be calculated by taking the natural log of one plus the discrete-time rate of change, e.g., $\ln(1.10) = 0.095$]. Both relative PPP formulations will give approximately equivalent results when the relevant rates of inflation are very close to each other. However, when rates of inflation in the two economies are widely divergent, merely taking the simple difference of discrete-time changes rather than the ratio as shown in Eq. (1) can lead to large errors.

spot exchange rate: $p_F = S \cdot p_D$, where p_D is the domestic price level, and p_F is the foreign price level. By converting price levels into inflation rates, one obtains the relative version of PPP shown in Eq. (1).

INTEREST RATE PARITY

The *interest rate parity* (IRP) condition stipulates that the forward premium or discount for one currency relative to another should be equal to the ratio of nominal interest rates on securities of equal risk denominated in the two currencies in question. Notationally, the relationship can be expressed as[3]:

$$\frac{F}{S} = \frac{(1 + R_F)}{(1 + R_D)} \qquad \text{or alternatively} \qquad F = S\frac{(1 + R_F)}{(1 + R_D)} \qquad (2)$$

where F = the forward exchange rate for a given time interval
S = the current spot exchange rate
R_F = the nominal interest rate on a security with a maturity equal to that of the forward exchange rate and denominated in a foreign currency, expressed as a decimal fraction
R_D = the nominal interest rate on a security of equivalent maturity and denominated in the domestic currency, also expressed as a decimal fraction

If this condition does not hold, then it will be possible to engage in covered interest arbitrage: a series of transactions that will provide a riskless profit. For example, if the yield on 1-year deutsche mark government bonds is 4 percent and the yield on 1-year U.S. Treasury notes is 8 percent, the deutsche mark should be trading at a 1-year forward premium to the dollar of $3.7\% = [(1.04/1.08) - 1] \times 100$. Suppose the deutsche mark/dollar spot exchange rate was 1.8000. IRP would imply a 1-year forward rate of $1.8(1.04/1.08) = 1.7333$. If, instead, the deutsche mark were trading in the 1-year forward market at 1.75, a riskless profit could be earned by buying what was cheap and selling what was dear, all the time remaining in a "square" position (i.e., being neither long nor short of deutsche marks or dollars). The arbitrage would work as follows:

1. Borrow deutsche marks today for 1 year at 4 percent.

2. Convert the borrowed deutsche marks to dollars in the spot market at an exchange rate of DM1.8/$.

3. Invest the dollars for 1 year at 8 percent.

---

[3]If interest rates are expressed on a continuously compounding basis, IRP can be approximated as $\frac{(F - S)}{S} = R_F - R_D$. This says that the forward premium or discount on a currency should equal the difference between interest rates.

4. Buy deutsche marks forward 1 year at DM1.75/$.

If an arbitrageur borrowed, say, DM10 million in step 1, received $5,555,556 upon immediate conversion in the spot market, and received $6,000,000 after investing the dollars for one year at 8%, his or her future profit would be $57,143, regardless of what happened to the deutsche mark/dollar exchange rate during the intervening year. This can be determined by calculating the dollar size of the forward contract the arbitrageur would have to execute in order to repay the borrowed deutsche mark principal plus interest 1 year later: DM10,400,000/1.75 = $5,942,857. The difference between this sized forward contract and the $6 million proceeds from the dollar investment yields the riskless profit of $57,143. Note that the arbitrageur could achieve this without any equity commitment of his or her own. As many arbitrageurs acted to exploit this opportunity, exchange rates and interest rates would be modified through the forces of supply and demand until they conformed to the IRP condition shown above.

FORWARD PARITY

A third parity condition is that forward exchange rates are *unbiased* predictors of futures spot rates. This is known as *forward parity* (FP). Notationally, it is expressed as:

$$F = E(S) \tag{3}$$

where E implies the expected future value of the variable within the parentheses.

Note that this condition does *not* say that the forward rate is a perfectly *accurate* predictor of the actual future spot rate. In fact, as will be shown later, forward rates are not accurate predictors. FP merely states that, on average, the forward exchange rate neither systematically over- nor underestimates the future spot rate. Put differently, deviations of the forward rate from the actual future spot rate average about zero when observed over a long enough span of time. An implication of this condition is that an investor cannot hope to profit systematically by speculating on differences between the forward rate and the subsequent spot rate prevailing at the time a forward contract matures.

DOMESTIC FISHER EFFECT

The *domestic Fisher effect* (DFE), named after the economist Irving Fisher, is a general equilibrium condition rather than a market arbitrage condition like the above relationships. It states that the nominal interest rate in every country will be equal to the real rate of interest compounded by expected future inflation[4]:

---

[4]Again, if interest rates and inflation rates are expressed on a continuously compounding basis, Eq. (4) can be expressed in the somewhat more familiar form $R = r + \dot{p}$.

$$(1 + R) = (1 + r)(1 + \dot{p}) \tag{4}$$

where R = the nominal rate of interest
r = the real rate of interest
$\dot{p}$ = the expected rate of inflation

The relationship is premised on the assumption that rational investors have in mind a *real* rate of return that they expect to earn when investing money. Consequently, they will demand higher returns in inflationary environments to compensate themselves for the expected erosion of purchasing power. Thus, if investors sought a real return of 3 percent during a year in which inflation was expected to be 5 percent, an 8.15% = $\{[(1.03)(1.05) - 1] \times 100\}$ nominal yield would be necessary to offset the effects of inflation.

INTERNATIONAL FISHER EFFECT

An important corollary of the DFE is the *international Fisher effect* (IFE), or "Fisher-open" condition. This condition can be thought of as a combination of the interest rate parity and forward parity conditions. It states that the expected rate of change in the spot exchange rate should equal the ratio of nominal interest rates in the two countries:

$$\frac{E(S)}{S} = \frac{(1 + R_F)}{(1 + R_D)} \quad \text{or alternatively} \quad E(S) = S\,\frac{(1 + R_F)}{(1 + R_D)} \tag{5}$$

Thus, returning to the deutsche mark/dollar example used in the discussion of IRP, one would expect the deutsche mark to appreciate against the U.S. dollar over the next year by 3.7 percent. In effect, IFE says that equilibrium can be maintained in global capital markets only if German investors in U.S. dollar securities are compensated for the expected decline of the dollar against the deutsche mark by means of higher nominal dollar interest rates (alternatively, it can be said that U.S. investors in deutsche mark securities must be compensated for lower German interest rates by means of an appreciating deutsche mark).

If the international Fisher effect, the domestic Fisher effect, and relative PPP are combined, yet another important corollary emerges, which is that *real interest rates should be equal everywhere*. Because nominal exchange-rate changes can be expected to offset price inflation differentials between countries, expected profit opportunities would emerge if this were not true.

EMPIRICAL EVIDENCE AND MANAGERIAL IMPLICATIONS

The major parity and market equilibrium conditions discussed so far are summarized in **Exhibit 1** (definitions of variables are the same as those used in this note's main text). If all these conditions held precisely at every point in time, and assuming freely and efficiently operating capital markets, there would be little reason for company treasurers to concern themselves with exchange rates and foreign exchange exposures. Simultaneous satisfaction of all the parity conditions would ensure that no one could profit systematically from foreign exchange transactions (over and above returns just adequate to compensate for risk), that various methods of covering foreign exchange exposure would have equal expected costs (e.g., forward contracting and money market hedges), and that covering oneself would have expected losses or gains equal to that which would result from conducting all future transactions at the then prevailing spot prices. In other words, a corporate policy of proactively covering all transaction exposures would be expected to produce the same gains or losses, on average, over the long run as a passive policy of simply executing all transactions at future spot rates. Furthermore, there would appear to be no net advantage to financing in different currencies or markets. Perfect parity would assure that the *real* cost of capital measured in one's home currency would be equivalent no matter what the source and currency of the capital raised.

Unfortunately, though not surprisingly, the bulk of empirical evidence does not support the strict hypothesis of perfectly efficient markets and perfect parity at all points in time. One of the earliest studied and least well supported conditions is that of purchasing power parity.[5] Many empirical tests involving major currencies and covering different time spans fail to support relative purchasing power parity in the short run. There is evidence that PPP holds over the long run, however, and even those studies that reject relative PPP do find a strong proportional relationship between inflation rates in two economies and the rate of change in the exchange rate between their two currencies.

Despite the generally negative findings, PPP may hold better than the data suggest. One of the central problems in testing PPP is the measurement of inflation. Ideally, for purposes of testing PPP, one should measure inflation across economies using identical "baskets" of goods. One immediately encounters the problem of which basket to use: internationally traded goods only or a broad basket of consumer goods and services. The latter, as measured by a consumer price index, would seem to be the measure of inflation most relevant to most investors seeking to maximize their welfare. But consumer baskets can differ widely from one nation to the next and generally include costs of nontraded items, such as housing, that cannot be arbitraged in international markets. Even if the inflation index problem can be solved, there is the further problem of gauging *expected* inflation, upon which PPP depends. Market expectations cannot be observed directly. Therefore, proxies must be constructed using observed historical rates of inflation. This approximation can impart error to the tests, thus undermining the strength of the statistical results rejecting PPP.

---

[5]See, for example, M. Adler and B. Lehman, "Deviations from PPP in the Long Run," *Journal of Finance* 38, no. 5 (December 1983): 1471–1487; R. Dornbush, "Expectation and Exchange Rate Dynamics," *Journal of Political Economy* 84 (December 1976): 1161–1176; S. P. Magee, "Contracting and Spurious Deviations from Purchasing Power Parity," in *The Economics of Exchange Rates,* eds. J. A. Frenkel and H. G. Johnson (Reading, MA: Addison-Wesley, 1978); L. H. Officer, "The Purchasing-Power-Parity Theory of Exchange Rates: A Review Article," *IMF Staff Papers* 23 (March 1976): 1–60; and R. J. Rogalski and M. S. Vinso, "Price Level Variations as Predictors of Flexible Exchange Rates," *Journal of International Business Studies* 8 (Summer 1977): 71–81.

Evidence on the empirical validity of forward parity is also somewhat mixed. Early tests of forward parity support the hypothesis that forward rates are unbiased predictors of future spot rates. Forward rates are seldom accurate predictors, but some studies have concluded that deviations of future spot rates from levels predicted by forward rates are merely random variations around a mean of zero.[6]

Other studies claim to have detected a "forward bias" that is suggestive of positive risk premia in forward exchange rates.[7] In other words they claim that forward rates have differed systematically from subsequent future spot rates at the end of the contract date. These premia are thought to exist due to market imperfections (e.g., expectations of the imposition of exchange or credit controls) or systematic risk. The latter could arise whenever exchange-rate movements are correlated with returns on other assets. Since risks of this nature cannot be diversified away, a risk premium would be required to induce investors to bear them. These arguments are challenged on the grounds that foreign exchange risk is, in fact, primarily diversifiable. Presently, the upper hand, empirically speaking, appears to lie with those rejecting forward parity.

Roughly the same can be said for the domestic Fisher effect. Paradoxically, there is common acceptance of Fisher's logic concerning the presence of an inflation premium in nominal interest rates, but there is little empirical evidence that DFE holds in its strictest form. Some empirical support is provided by tests involving very-short-term government securities, but little support is provided when longer maturities are examined.[8] It appears that nominal interest rates do not necessarily change to offset precisely changes in expected inflation. Empirical tests of the Fisher effect suffer from the same drawback as those for PPP, however, which is that expected inflation cannot be observed directly. Hence, testing generally takes place using an "ex post" real interest rate, which is the nominal interest rate for a given period of time less realized inflation over the same time period. This has led some researchers to conclude that tests of the Fisher hypothesis to date have been inconclusive.

Interest rate parity is the one condition that has received widespread empirical support, though even this is limited to major currencies and requires recognition of transactions costs. An illustration of this sort of result is provided by **Exhibit 2**, which shows the pattern of potential covered interest arbitrage opportunities between the yen and the dollar from January 1976 to November 1985. Panel A of **Exhibit 2** plots forward premia and discounts on the yen against the national differences in interest rates; note the close conformity. Panel B, however, magnifies the difference between

[6]See J. A. Frenkel, "A Monetary Approach to the Balance of Payments: Doctrinal Aspects and Empirical Evidence," *Scandinavian Journal of Economics* 78, no. 2 (May 1976): 200–224; I. Giddy, "An Integrated Theory of Foreign Exchange Equilibrium," *Journal of Financial and Quantitative Analysis* 11, no. 5 (December 1976): 883–892; S. W. Kohlhagen, "The Forward Rate as an Unbiased Predictor of the Future Spot Rate," *Columbia Journal of World Business* 14, no. 4 (Winter 1979): 77–85; and S. P. Magee, "The Empirical Evidence of the Monetary Approach of the Balance of Payments and Exchange Rates," *American Economic Review: Proceedings* 66, no. 2 (May 1976): 163–170.

[7]See D. L. Kaserman, "The Forward Exchange Rate: Its Determination and Behavior as a Predictor of the Future Spot Rate," *Proceedings of the American Statistical Association* (1973): 417–442; and R. W. Roll and B. H. Solnik, "A Pure Foreign Exchange Asset Pricing Model," *Journal of International Economics* 7 (1977): 161–179.

[8]D. K. Eiteman, A. I. Stonehill, and M. H. Moffett, *Multinational Business Finance*, 6th ed. (Reading, MA: Addison-Wesley, 1992), p. 155.

these two plots. Spikes above and below the zero baseline in panel B represent deviations of the yen-dollar interest rate differential from the yen's forward dollar premium or discount.

At first glance, numerous riskless profit opportunities would appear to exist, suggesting a breakdown of IRP between the yen and the dollar. However, one must recognize that, in practice, an arbitrageur must execute four transactions to exploit a covered interest arbitrage opportunity. Specifically, the arbitrageur must borrow at the offer rate in one currency, convert to another currency on one side of the spot dealer's spread, lend in that currency at the bid rate, and then cover forward on the other side of the forward dealer's spread. Thus, there are two spreads to be spanned as well as the possibility of other transactions costs such as brokerage fees, transmission costs, transaction taxes, etc. These costs, which evidence indicates to be about 25 basis points during this time period, is represented by a band above and below the zero baseline.[9] (The band is drawn as two fixed, horizontal lines for convenience only. In fact, transactions costs could, and probably did, vary over time, with the band widening during volatile periods in the exchange market and narrowing during relatively calm periods.) Truly profitable covered interest arbitrage opportunities are really presented only in those instances where the spikes extend above or below the band. While a number of such opportunities appear to remain, they are fewer in number and less dramatic in size. Indeed, the remaining opportunities could be more apparent than real, resulting from flawed data observations rather than true market opportunities.

This sort of result is typical for most of the world's major currencies: Few truly profitable CIA opportunities are found to exist after transaction costs are considered, and most of those will be fairly short-lived. Indeed, only professionals that watch the market closely are likely to be in a position to exploit such opportunities when they arise, and they will do so in large volume. This very action on their part serves to eliminate the arbitrage opportunity fairly quickly. The same is not likely to be true for less actively traded currencies or currencies in which credit is severely restricted. In these cases, arbitrageurs may not be able to construct their hedges properly due to an inability to borrow, lend, or cover forward in size.

MANAGERIAL IMPLICATIONS

The inconclusive evidence regarding the parity conditions is no great surprise. Despite the increased efficiency and integration of global and capital and foreign exchange markets, there are still sufficient imperfections in those markets to make it unlikely that perfect parity will hold at all points in time. As a consequence, one conclusion that can be drawn is that financing in foreign currencies or engaging in hedging activities need not be a sterile exercise generating no expected gain or loss for shareholders. Genuine opportunities to create or destroy value for the corporation may present themselves from time to time. It may be possible to borrow at low real interest rates in some countries, or set up particularly low-cost hedges.

---

[9]See W. C. Kester and T. Luehrman, ''Real Interest Rates and the Cost of Capital: A Comparison of the United States and Japan,'' *Japan and the World Economy,* 1, no. 3 (1989): 1–23.

Given the highly uneven track record of the parity conditions as accurate descriptions of market behavior, their real value to managers lies in their role as a conceptual framework for recognizing potentially genuine profit- or loss-making opportunities. They offer, in other words, a useful starting point for analyses involving foreign exchange movements. Predictions of future exchange rates derived from one or more of the parity conditions (e.g., PPP, FP, or IRP), for example, may not be especially accurate, but, on average, they are likely to perform no worse than those arising from more complex economic models.

Ultimately, the parity conditions are most useful as a means of organizing and disciplining one's thinking about exchange-rate determination. Even if markets do not operate perfectly efficiently, one should maintain a healthy skepticism of "free lunches." When presented with a scheme for making money in foreign exchange markets, or for covering an exposure at exceptionally low cost, a grasp of the fundamental parity conditions can help one pinpoint the inefficiency being exploited and formulate the relevant questions to pose to those sponsoring the idea. In this way, one can be more certain that a viable economic rationale, not merely a quick sales pitch, underlies the scheme's promised returns.

EXHIBIT 1   SUMMARY OF MAJOR PARITY AND MARKET EQUILIBRIUM CONDITIONS

1. Law of one price (LOOP)

$$P_F = S \cdot P_D$$

2. Purchasing power parity (PPP):
   a. Absolute

$$p_F = S \cdot p_D$$

   b. Relative

$$(1 + \dot{s}) = \frac{(1 + \dot{p}_F)}{(1 + \dot{p}_D)}$$

3. Interest rate parity (IRP)

$$\frac{F}{S} = \frac{(1 + R_F)}{(1 + R_D)}$$

4. Forward parity (FP)

$$F = E(S)$$

5. Domestic Fisher effect (DFE)

$$(1 + R) = (1 + r)(1 + \dot{p})$$

6. International Fisher effect (IFE)

$$\frac{E(S)}{S} = \frac{(1 + R_F)}{(1 + R_D)}$$

EXHIBIT 2 POTENTIAL COVERED INTEREST ARBITRAGE OPPORTUNITIES BETWEEN THE YEN AND THE DOLLAR, 1976–1985

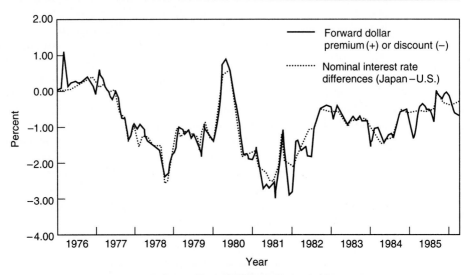

A. Comparison of FX forward premia/discounts
to interest rate difference

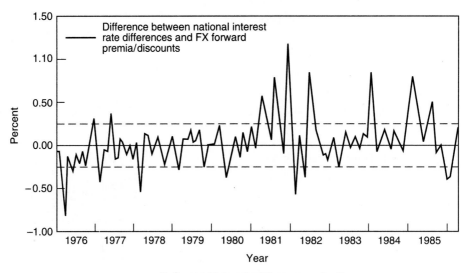

B. Covered interest arbitrage opportunities

Note: Graphs are constructed using monthly observations of 90-day Eurodollar and Euroyen yields and 3-month forward rates for the yen. All data were obtained from the IMF's *International Financial Statistics* computer tapes.

PART TWO

TWO

CAPITAL BUDGETING, INVESTMENT, AND CROSS-BORDER VALUATION

NOTE ON CROSS-BORDER VALUATION

Cross-border investment has assumed a prominent place among the key decisions facing today's corporate managers. In addition to a general relaxation of capital controls by many nations, this has been stimulated by developments such as European economic integration, the opening of Eastern European markets, Latin American debt-equity swap programs, and a global wave of privatizations, to name but several.

As one major form of investment, cross-border acquisitions have been particularly prevalent since 1980. American corporations, for example, increased their acquisitions of foreign targets by 160 percent between 1980 and 1990. Acquisitions of American targets by foreign companies rose about 50 percent during the same period. Some transactions, such as Matsushita Electric's $6.9 billion acquisition of MCA, Inc., in 1991, have been unprecedentedly large. The majority, however, have been well under $100 million in size, suggesting that these transactions are not just the domain of giant multinationals. Evaluating cross-border deals now lies within the purview of executives from a wide array of corporations around the world.

The objective of this note is to review basic methods of valuing cross-border investments and the main issues affecting such valuations. It is intended to be a source of guidance, not a comprehensive review of the topic. The basic principles underlying discounted cash flow techniques for domestic valuations are covered in major finance textbooks.[1]

[1]See, for example, Richard A. Brealey and Stewart C. Myers, *Principles of Corporate Finance,* 4th ed. (New York: McGraw-Hill), pp. 4–283.

This note was prepared by Professor W. Carl Kester and Research Associate Julia Morley. Copyright © 1992 by the President and Fellows of Harvard College. Harvard Business School note 292-084.

In this note, three cross-border valuation techniques are applied to the following simple valuation problem: An American company, US Inc., is considering an expansion of its British subsidiary, UK plc. The cost of the expansion is £50 million, which must be expended in the very near future. In addition, US Inc. will have to fund additional working capital of £6 million at the time of the expansion.

In conformity with its practice at home, US Inc. evaluates capital expenditure proposals by discounting free cash flows at an appropriate weighted average cost of capital (WACC). When applied to cross-border investments, this basic valuation methodology is fundamentally the same as when used to value domestic projects, although there are a number of important issues specific to cross-border valuations that must be resolved. These include:

• The choice of currency, foreign (local) or domestic (home), in which to execute the analysis

• Whether or not to discount foreign cash flows at the time they are earned or only as they are remitted home to the parent

• Whether to use foreign or domestic tax rates

• The proper calculation of the cost of capital used to discount the cash flows

• The appropriate treatment of special risks unique to cross-investments such as foreign exchange risk, political risk, and so forth

These points are addressed below by working through the UK plc valuation example using various methods of valuation.

VALUING FREE CASH FLOWS WITH A WEIGHTED AVERAGE COST OF CAPITAL

The most commonly practiced valuation technique is the discounting of expected free cash flows (FCF) by a weighted average cost of capital. Free cash flow is the cash made available by the project or business and available (in principle) for distribution to the suppliers of capital as a return on their investment. It may be defined as after-tax earnings *before* deductible financing charges such as interest expense, lease rentals, and so forth; plus all deductible noncash charges (e.g., depreciation, deductible amortization, deferred taxes, etc.); and less new cash outlays for required capital expenditures and investment in net working capital.

The rate at which expected free cash flows should be discounted is the *opportunity cost* of investing capital in the assets in question. It would be ideal if the opportunity cost of capital could be observed directly, but this is seldom the case for most capital expenditures by industrial corporations. However, required rates of return can usually be determined for debt and inferred (using observable capital market prices) for equity capital used to fund an investment. By "weighting" the market-determined cost of debt and the cost of equity with the respective proportional claims of each on the value of the investment and adding the two components together, the opportunity cost of capital for the business in question may be inferred. Further, by employing the after-tax rather than pre-tax cost of debt in the weighted average, the tax advantage of using debt to finance the investment will automatically be captured in the discounted-cash-flow analysis. That is, the present value of cash flows discounted at a rate that incorporates the after-tax cost of debt will have included in it the present value of future tax shields created by using debt.

Combining these elements yields the familiar formula for the weighted-average cost of capital:

$$\text{WACC} = \frac{D}{V}k_D (1 - t_c) + \frac{E}{V}k_E$$

where D/V = the proportion of value (V) claimed by debt (D)
E/V = the proportion of value (V) claimed by equity (E)
(note that $D + E = V$)
k_D = the required rate of return on debt capital
k_E = the required rate of return on equity capital
t_c = the marginal corporate tax rate

One of the first decisions that must be made when executing valuations of cross-border investments is the choice of which of two or more currencies to use in the forecasting of free cash flows, and which of these same currencies to use in measuring the WACC. If parity relationships exist among exchange rates, interest rates, and inflation rates, the choice of currency in which to do the analysis will be a matter of indifference as far as the resulting estimate of value is concerned. One must simply be careful to discount foreign-currency cash flows at the appropriate foreign-currency discount rate, and home-currency cash flows at the appropriate home-currency discount rate. Under these circumstances, either approach will yield identical outcomes upon converting the present value in one currency to that of the other using the prevailing spot exchange rate.

Nevertheless, preferences may arise for using one method instead of another from time to time. For example, if it is thought that a project's value might be especially sensitive to future exchange-rate changes, it will be helpful to forecast foreign-currency cash flows and then explicitly convert them to home-currency cash flows using a specific set of forecasted exchange rates. Setting up the analysis this way enables one to engage easily in sensitivity analysis of the exchange-rate assumptions by substituting alternative exchange-rate forecasts. Similarly, if large real exchange-rate changes are anticipated, or management is simply interested in gauging the impact of large real-rate changes on the value of a project, it is also advisable to forecast explicitly the anticipated path of future exchange rates and then use these forecasts to convert foreign-currency cash flows. In still other situations, a manager may have available only very poor information about the likely direction and rate of change of an exchange rate, but a reasonable estimate of what a project's foreign-currency cost of capital might be. Under these conditions, discounting foreign-currency cash flows with a foreign-currency cost of capital may be more appropriate. Given the varying suitability of each method under different circumstances, both will be demonstrated here in the analysis of UK plc's expansion project.

Method A: Discounting Foreign-Currency Cash Flows

As required by US Inc.'s capital budgeting procedures, the controller of UK plc. has provided headquarters with a set of expected future cash flows denominated in pounds sterling (see **Exhibit 1**). The starting point in the construction of total free cash flow is a forecast of earnings before interest and taxes (EBIT), which is itself derived from forecasts of sales and expenses. Some of the general assumptions underlying these forecasts and other pertinent data about prevailing economic conditions are provided in **Table 1**.

TABLE 1   SUMMARY OF KEY ASSUMPTIONS PERTAINING TO THE VALUATION OF UK PLC'S EXPANSION PROJECT

	$	£
General economic assumptions		
Price inflation	3.0%	7.0%
Yield on government bonds	6.0	10.1
Corporate tax rate	34.0	35.0
Equity market risk premium	8.6*	na
Spot exchange rate ($/£)	$1.7000 bid–$1.7010 ask	
Project-specific assumptions		
Cost of debt	9.4%	13.6%
Debt-to-capital ratio	0.40	
Systematic risk		
Asset beta	.76	
Equity beta	.90	

*From Roger G. Ibbotson and Rex A. Sinquefield, *Stocks, Bonds, Bills, and Inflation: Historical Returns (1926–1989)* (Charlottesville, VA: The Research Foundation of the Institute of Chartered Financial Analysts), p. 86.

Taxes   One of the major complexities with which managers must deal in cross-border valuations is the existence of multiple tax regimes. Different countries have different corporate tax rates and different requirements regarding the timing of tax payments. The United States, for example, taxes *worldwide* corporate income at a 34 percent marginal rate and requires payment of taxes on a quarterly basis.[2] The United Kingdom taxes corporations at the slightly higher rate of 35 percent, but permits them to pay taxes as long as 9 months after the end of their accounting period. Many other countries offer tax exemptions and special "tax holidays" to foreign investors to encourage investment inside their borders. A wide selection of marginal corporate tax rates for different countries is listed in the **appendix** to this note.

[2]Generally, income from abroad is treated as part of worldwide income when it is *earned* in the case of a foreign division, and when it is *remitted* as dividends in the case of foreign subsidiaries. Some exceptions to these general rules exist.

The appropriate treatment of foreign taxes in cross-border valuations depends crucially upon the nature of any existing tax treaties between the two countries involved. The two most commonly encountered tax situations and their treatment in cross-border valuations are as follows:

• Many countries use a "tax credit" system: Foreign taxes of virtually all types paid abroad may be claimed as a credit against taxes paid on foreign-source income in the home country. Foreign tax credit limitations generally result in the higher of the two marginal corporate tax rates being paid. Thus, unless specific tax provisions dictate otherwise, the *higher* corporate tax rate should be used in computing after-tax free cash flows for a cross-border project.

• A "tax exemption" system (e.g., as used in the Netherlands) *exempts* foreign-source income from taxation at home if taxes were paid to the foreign country. In this case, the foreign country's marginal corporate tax rate should be used in calculating after-tax free cash flows.

If a tax holiday is provided in the host country, the foreign investor may or may not benefit. Whether or not it does benefit depends upon the existence of a "tax-sparing credit" in the investor's domestic tax system. If it does have such a credit, it will benefit fully from the host country's tax holiday, and a tax rate of zero should be used in the valuation analysis for as long as the holiday is in effect. If it does not have such credit, as is the case in the United States, for example, then a tax liability will be incurred at the investor's domestic corporate tax rate on foreign-source income.

These general descriptions are very much simplified and expert tax advice from an international corporate tax specialist is often required to determine the correct rate to use in a cross-border valuation. In the case of US Inc.'s investment in UK plc, the higher marginal rate of 35 percent should be used. Also, because of the 9-month gap between the incurring of a tax liability and the payment of taxes in the United Kingdom, the cash payment of taxes in **Exhibit 1** is assumed to occur with a one-period lag.

Earned versus Remitted Cash Flows   Cash flows that are earned on an investment in a foreign country may or may not be converted into home currency and remitted directly back to the foreign parent. This may be for any of several reasons. The investing parent may wish to reinvest local funds in the foreign currency in question, it may wish to divert those funds to other offshore investments, or it may be blocked from doing so by local regulations that restrict the free convertibility of the local currency. These possibilities raise the question of whether one should use earned or remitted cash flows in valuing cross-border investments.

In most situations, particularly those involving cross-border investments among major industrialized nations, earned cash flows should be used whether or not they are remitted immediately to the parent. This recommendation is based upon the same principle used in domestic valuation techniques: Even if a company does not actually pay out all its free cash flow as dividends, the cash generated by the company is the amount *available* for distribution to shareholders, and over which the shareholders have an ownership claim. Amounts not paid out as dividends will add to the value of equity's claim, dollar for dollar, as long as the company earns a return on retained earnings equal to the cost of equity.

The same logic applies in the case of UK plc's project. Provided that it can earn the local cost of capital on cash earned in the United Kingdom but not remitted to US Inc., earned cash flows should be used to value the project. Using remitted cash flows would be preferable only if earnings retained by the foreign subsidiary were not expected to earn the local cost of capital, or if it were believed that there was a high risk of expropriation.

Terminal Value   The terminal value of a project often represents a significant proportion of its total present value and must always be included. The appropriate method of computing a project's terminal value depends largely on how and when a project is likely to end, and on the length of the forecasting time horizon. Going concerns with an indefinite life are often best handled by assuming that the last period's free cash flow will be received as a perpetuity or as a long-lived annuity, possibly growing at some reasonable constant rate in either case.

The simple net book value of the investment at the forecasting horizon is also commonly used as an estimate of terminal value. Book value is often used for finite-lived projects under the assumption that all assets can be liquidated and liabilities discharged at their respective book values. If reliable estimates of liquidating values can be determined, however, these will generally be superior to simple book values.

For UK plc, the terminal value in **Exhibit 1** has been represented as a no-growth perpetuity of the final year's EBIT, reduced by taxes assessed at the full marginal rate of 35 percent. Capital expenditures beyond year 5 are assumed to equal depreciation charges, and no further incremental investment in working capital will be necessary. The actual terminal value amount of £78.0 million is computed with the formula EBIT $\times (1 - .35)$/WACC. Because this quantity is considered to be value provided by the project at the end of the fifth period, it must itself be discounted to the present using the project's WACC.

Many cross-border investments are of a strategic nature with the characteristic that much of their total cash inflow will be realized late in the project's development. To the extent this is true, a cross-border project's terminal value will likely constitute a large proportion of its total net present value. Consequently, it is advisable to forecast cash flows for cross-border investments as far into the future as seems reliable (5 to 10 years, if possible), and to engage in sensitivity analysis with respect to the terminal value. It is useful to display the terminal value separately in a set of cash flow forecasts, and to experiment with different formulas or growth assumptions to gauge the robustness of the project's acceptability.

The Discount Rate   In conformity with the principle stated above that *foreign-currency* cash flows must be discounted at an appropriate *foreign-currency* discount rate, UK plc's sterling cash flows must be discounted at a sterling discount rate. However, a sterling WACC need not be constructed directly in sterling. In fact, as a practical matter, it will often be more convenient to compute WACCs in one's home currency—dollars, in this case—and then convert it to a foreign-currency discount rate.

The rate at which a project's expected cash flows should be discounted is ultimately nothing more nor less than the opportunity cost of investing capital in the assets in question. This implies that the correct discount rate depends upon the set of investment opportunities facing a company's investors. Determining what that set looks like is becoming an increasingly challenging task as more and more companies sell equity abroad, thereby becoming owned by shareholders with very diverse patterns of consumption and facing diverse investment opportunities.

Nevertheless, it is often expedient if not, indeed, actually more accurate for many companies to assume that they are owned by investors indigenous to the countries in which they are headquartered. Although not perfectly homogeneous, such investors may be presumed to consume roughly similar baskets of goods and services, and to face roughly similar investment opportunity sets. Thus, it is generally reasonable for these companies first to determine discount rates for foreign-currency cash flows in terms of home-currency rates of return on debt and equity, and then convert to the foreign-currency discount rate using a relationship such as interest rate parity.

In fact, depending upon the countries and currencies involved, it may be *necessary* to determine a home-currency WACC first. In some cases, lack of reliable capital market data for local sources of corporate funds may defeat any attempt to compute a foreign-currency WACC directly. Some countries, for example, may lack markets for riskless domestic securities, or may not have a sufficiently long history of equity market returns to permit accurate measurement of local equity-market risk premiums. These deficiencies make the use of the capital asset pricing model (CAPM) to estimate the local-currency cost of equity capital problematic if not actually impossible.

In the case of US Inc., it shall be assumed that the company is owned by American investors who believe themselves to face a predominantly domestic American investment opportunity set. Thus, the riskiness of a foreign investment and the required rate of return on those assets are effectively determined by reference to U.S. capital market investment opportunities. Using the standard WACC formula and the data provided in **Table 1**, the project's WACC is as follows:

$$10.7\% = .4\ (9.4\%)\ (1 - .35) + .6\ (13.7\%)$$

As in any WACC computation, the **weights** applied to the costs of debt and equity represent the long-term target capital structure of the project and *not* necessarily the parent company's own consolidated capital structure or the proportions of debt or equity used in the initial financing of the project. The use of WACC as a discount rate also implicitly assumes that the ratio of *market values* of debt and equity claims on the project's total value remains more or less constant over the life of the project. If it is known in advance that this will not be the case, it will be necessary either to recompute the WACC for each period, taking into account the project's changing capital structure,[3] or to employ an entirely different methodology (for example, "valuation in parts," which is discussed below).

---

[3]This will generally require not only changing the debt and equity weights in the WACC formula, but also recalculating the levered cost of equity, and possibly also the cost of debt, from period to period.

The pretax **cost of debt** is best measured by the cost of borrowing in the currency in question, 9.4 percent in this case. The relevant **tax rate** to apply to this cost is that marginal rate which is binding upon the company, whether domestic or foreign. As indicated in the discussion of taxes above, this is normally the higher of the two tax rates. For UK plc's expansion project, the after-tax dollar cost of debt is, therefore, the following:

$$9.4\% \times (1 - .35) = 6.1\%$$

The levered **cost of equity** for the project may be determined by employing the capital asset pricing model, using the following formula:

$$k_e^l = R_F + \beta^l(\overline{R}_M - R_F)$$

where k_e^l = the levered cost of equity
R_F = the prevailing risk-free rate of return
β^l = the project's levered beta
$(\overline{R}_M - R_F)$ = the difference between the expected return on the market, $\overline{R}_M$, and the risk-free rate of return, hereinafter called the *equity market risk premium*

Using values obtained from **Table 1**, the project's dollar cost of equity is 13.7% = 6.0% + 0.9(8.6%).

The dollar WACC of UK plc's expansion project can be converted to a sterling WACC by using the *interest rate parity* condition (expected inflation rates could also be used in the application of *purchasing power parity*). Interest rate parity stipulates that the expected rate of change in the spot exchange rate equals the ratio of the prevailing interest rates in the two currencies.[4] In the case of the dollar-sterling exchange rate, the interest rate parity condition is expressed as:

$$(1 + \Delta S) = \frac{(1 + R_\$)}{(1 + R_\pounds)}$$

where ΔS is the expected fractional change in the spot exchange rate during the forecasting period, and $R_\$$ and $R_\pounds$ are the nominal yields during the same period on comparable-risk dollar- and sterling-denominated debt, respectively. If parity holds, it follows that the appropriate sterling WACC to use for discounting purposes is the dollar WACC adjusted for expected exchange-rate changes. Thus,

$$(1 + R_\pounds) = \frac{(1 + R_\$)}{(1 + \Delta S)}$$

[4]Similarly, the purchasing power parity condition stipulates that the expected rate of change in the spot exchange rate equals the ratio in expected rates of inflation in the two currencies. Note that if real interest rates are equal in the two currencies, interest rate parity and purchasing power parity will yield identical expected rates of change in the spot exchange rate.

Using yields on government bonds obtained from **Table 1** (or, if applying purchasing power parity, the expected inflation rates), the factor for determining the expected annual change in the dollar-sterling exchange rate can be computed as: $(1.06/1.101) = 0.9628$. The sterling WACC is, therefore, 15.0% ($1.107/0.9628 = 1.150$).

Segmented versus Integrated Capital Markets   To the extent that the underlying premise of US Inc.'s investors being Americans facing a largely domestic U.S. investment opportunity set is incorrect, both the estimated dollar and sterling discount rates will be inaccurate and biased. If, instead, US Inc.'s investors are presumed to be internationally diversified in their asset ownership or even just to view their potential investment opportunity set as being global in scope, then returns on a *global market portfolio* would offer a more appropriate benchmark for gauging the project's risk and required rate of return. Some of what may appear to be nondiversifiable systematic risk in the U.S. domestic market may prove to be diversifiable *country* risk within the context of a global market portfolio. Thus, a cross-border investment's **beta** is likely to differ according to which market portfolio is used in its computation. Due to the diversifiable nature of many country risks, it will generally be lower when computed using a global market portfolio.

Even if one assumes investors are diversifying internationally, however, relying on U.S. equity-market data to implement CAPM may still be a reasonable expedient. It should be noted that the U.S. equity market by itself accounts for a large fraction (roughly a third) of the total worldwide market value of equity. Consequently, the correlation between U.S. equity-market returns and those on a global portfolio is positive and relatively high (see **Table 2**). Furthermore, the global integration of major equity markets, although less than perfect, is by now sufficiently good to ensure that substantial national differences in the price of risk do not persist for long without stimulating international capital flows and price changes that eventually eliminate the differences.

TABLE 2   CORRELATION COEFFICIENTS FOR RETURNS ON THE U.S. AND SELECTED OTHER EQUITY MARKETS*

	Japan	Germany	France	United Kingdom	World
United States	.283	.347	.428	.499	.842

*Coefficients are computed using monthly returns in U.S. dollars between 1969 and 1990.
Source: Daniel E. Waters, *The Growing Popularity of International Investing* (unpublished independent research report) (Cambridge, MA: Harvard Business School, 1991).

Adjusting for Special Risks   When calculated as shown above, discount rates for cross-border projects reflect the time value of money, the nondiversifiable risk surrounding the expected cash flows, and the tax advantages associated with the use of debt to fund the project. How should foreign exchange risk, expropriation risk, inflation risk, and other country-level risks be factored into the analysis?

Managers often believe that risks such as these must be reflected in the discount rate by adding an additional risk premium to the project's estimated cost of capital. Whether or not such a procedure is valid depends upon the assumptions one is willing to make about the risks in question. Specifically, if the risks of concern are *nondiversifiable* risks that are *not* adequately captured in the cross-border project's beta, then adding a premium to the discount rate is in order. However, if the risks are largely diversifiable, or if they are adequately captured in the project's beta, then it would be inappropriate to penalize the project by adding an additional risk premium to the discount rate.

As a practical matter, even if the project's beta does not reflect all nondiversifiable risks, adjusting the discount rate by adding a premium can often introduce errors into the analysis that may do more to distort than clarify the true value of the project. The chief problem in this regard is determining the correct size of the premium to be added. Too frequently managers arbitrarily add an all-purpose adjustment factor (e.g., 5 percent) without careful regard for the true nature and extent of the risks involved. If the impact of special cross-border risks on the discount rate cannot be measured fairly accurately, it is generally advisable to search for a means of reflecting them in cash flow forecasts rather than the discount rate. The virtue of doing so is that hidden assumptions about the special risks can be made explicit and different assumptions can be tested in sensitivity analysis.

Consider **foreign exchange risk**. Very little (probably much less than half in most cases) of exchange-rate volatility will prove to be systematic risk that should be reflected in the discount rate. Nevertheless, managers may wish to adjust a project's estimated value to reflect exchange-rate risk. Rather than boost the discount rate by a significant amount, an alternative approach for doing so would be to convert foreign-currency cash flows at an appropriate forward exchange rate quoted by a dealer of forward currencies. These cash flows may then be discounted at a home-currency discount rate (see method B below). Whether or not expected foreign-currency cash flows are truly hedged at these forward rates, the dealer quotes effectively proxy for the price of "insurance" against exchange-rate risk that one could, in principle, purchase in the forward market. By effectively "charging" this insurance premium to future periods' cash flows, exchange-rate risk can be captured in the cash flows rather than the discount rate.

Similar adjustments to cash flows are often possible for other risks as well. Insurance against certain types of **expropriation risk** and the risk of **currency inconvertibility**, for example, can be purchased from agencies such as the Overseas Private Investment Corporation (OPIC) in the United States; the internationally well known insurance company Lloyd's of London; or various other national export-import banks. The premiums for this insurance can be deducted from future cash flows as a means of avoiding ad hoc adjustments to discount rates.

A further virtue of this approach is that the timing of exposure to, say, expropriation risk may be reflected more accurately. It may be the case, for example, that the risk of expropriation of a large new mine will be greatest soon after the mine has met performance tests, all necessary financing is in place, and well before substantial depletion has taken place. Increasing the discount rate to reflect expropriation risk implicitly assumes that the risk of expropriation remains constant over time. Adjusting expected cash flows by charging them with premiums for expropriation risk insurance in only those years in which the risk seems substantial may better reflect the political and economic realities impinging upon the project.

Yet another technique for handling expropriation and other forms of political risk is to engage in scenario analysis. By assessing the probabilities of expropriation in each future period at various levels of compensation, an expected cost of expropriation can be estimated for each year and used to adjust expected future cash flows from the project. Although the assumed probabilities and levels of compensation may themselves be highly subjective estimates, they at least have the virtue of being explicit assumptions about the actual timing, likelihood, and value impact of expropriation. These can then be debated and refined by those responsible for making the investment decision.

Inflation risk is most problematic when attempting to value investments in hyperinflationary environments. Hyperinflation is generally characterized by highly volatile rates of inflation from one period to the next, as well as very high rates. Because it is difficult to ascertain long-term expected inflation in hyperinflation economies, it can be extremely difficult to determine an appropriate discount rate. Under these circumstances, the best course of action is to execute the analysis in *real,* not nominal, terms. That is, expected cash flows should be forecasted using real rather than inflated monetary values, and they should be discounted using a real rather than nominal cost of capital. Although such an analysis can, in principle, be executed in any currency, it is often most expedient to do so in a stable currency, such as dollars, for which reliable real rates of return can be estimated.

These special risks will be ignored in the case of US Inc.'s expansion of UK plc. It is assumed that country risks are low in this case and that any relevant, nondiversifiable foreign exchange risk is being adequately reflected in the project's beta.

Completing the Analysis   Using the sterling WACC of 15.0 percent to discount the project's *earned* after-tax sterling free cash flows, a net present value of £15.8 million may be computed (see **Exhibit 2**). Its value in dollars can be determined by multiplying this present value by the spot exchange rate. In this instance, the correct rate to use is the spot bid rate of $1.70 per pound, which yields a dollar net present value of $26.9 million.

Method B: Discounting Foreign-Currency Cash Flows Converted to Home Currency

The second method for valuing foreign-currency free cash flows involves the conversion of foreign-currency amounts into home currency, and then discounting the converted cash flows at the home-currency discount rate. This approach can be particularly useful if a foreign investment's home-currency value is likely to be particularly sensitive to exchange rates and managers wish to engage in sensitivity analysis with respect to exchange-rate changes, or if future rates of exchange are, for some reason, easier to determine than is a foreign-currency WACC.

Forecasting Exchange Rates   The value of UK plc's expansion project obtained by using method B is also shown in **Exhibit 2**. *Interest rate parity* has been used to forecast the exchange rates used to convert expected foreign-currency cash flows. Relying once again on government bond yields obtained from **Table 1**, the factor for determining the annual change in the dollar-sterling exchange rate is $(1.06/1.101) = 0.9628$. Thus, at the end of year 1 the spot exchange rate is expected to be ($1.70/£) $\times (0.9628) = \$1.6367/£$. In year 2, it is expected to decline to ($1.70/£) $\times (0.9628)^2 = 1.5757$, and so on until it reaches \$1.4062/£ at the end of year 5.

Other methods are also available for forecasting future exchange rates. For example, the use of the expected inflation rates in **Table 1** in the application of the purchasing power parity condition yields $0.9626 = (1.03/1.07)$ as the annual factor by which the spot exchange rate can be expected to change. Note that this is virtually identical to the factor obtained using interest rate parity. This result obtains because the *real* risk-free interest rate is identical in both countries at about 2.9 percent [$(1.06/1.03) - 1 = 0.029$, in the case of the dollar, and $(1.101/1.07) - 1 = 0.029$, in the case of the pound].

Quoted interbank forward exchange rates may also be used to convert foreign-currency cash flows under the presumption that such rates are unbiased estimates of future spot exchange rates. This is the condition described as *forward parity*. A common problem with using forward rates, however, is that reliable quotes for many currencies are seldom available for more than a couple of years into the future. Furthermore, forward dealer quotes may not be unbiased as assumed by the parity condition; very wide spreads on long-dated forward contracts may incorporate risk premiums. As noted above, forward rates may be useful to the extent one deliberately wishes to ''charge'' foreign currency cash flows an insurance ''premium'' to reflect foreign-exchange risk in the analysis, but we cannot be sure that they are always providing unbiased estimates of future spot exchange rates.

Finally, of course, any independent set of exchange rates can be used to model a particular path of movements of special interest to management. For example, the impact of a real depreciation of the pound against the dollar could be modeled in the example used here by assuming the dollar-sterling exchange rate declines by a factor less than 0.9626, which would mean that the pound is expected to depreciate at a rate faster than that justified by inflation differences alone. Alternatively, an isolated exchange-rate shock in one year, followed by parity movements in subsequent years, could also be modeled.

Discounting to the Present   Once expected foreign-currency cash flows have been converted to home currency, it is then a relatively straightforward matter to discount these flows to the present using an appropriate *home-currency WACC*. As previously determined in the discussion of method A, the home-currency WACC for

UK plc's expansion project is 10.7 percent. The net present value of the project's free cash flow converted to dollars is estimated at $26.8 million (see **Exhibit 2**).

Note that, except for a rounding error, the two values obtained using method A and method B are the same. This is because the only difference between the two methods is the means by which the expected rate of change in the exchange rate is captured in the analysis. In method B, the expected rate of change was captured directly in exchange rates forecasted for conversion purposes. In method A, it was captured in the estimated cost of capital used for discounting purposes. If a constant discount rate were used but the expected rate of change in the spot exchange were not constant (because, for example, a real exchange rate shock was expected to occur during the forecasting period), the two methods would not yield identical results.

VALUATION IN PARTS

Discounting total free cash flows with a WACC is the most commonly used valuation technique. However, it can be problematic in many situations, particularly when dealing with cross-border investments. The standard application of WACC is not reliable, for example, when the capital structure of a project or foreign acquisition is expected to change over time; if host governments make available subsidized sources of local financing as an incentive to invest; or if a foreign investment entails the incurrence of any of a host of other special financial benefits or costs such as sale-and-leaseback arrangements, tax benefits associated with reserve accounting, and so forth.

When the complexity of an investment becomes great enough, it will generally be more reliable to deconstruct its cash flows into discrete elements, value each separately, and then invoke the principle of value additivity to reconstruct the components into a single estimate of value. To distinguish it from other conventional methods, this technique is often called "valuation in parts," or "adjusted present value."[5] Valuation in parts can be represented as follows:

$$\text{Total value} = \text{present value of total free cash flows} \\ + \text{present value of financial costs and benefits}$$

The first component, the present value of free cash flows, measures the investment's intrinsic worth *without regard for how the investment is financed*. In effect, it is the investment's free cash flows (the same cash flows as would be used when discounting by WACC) discounted by an appropriate opportunity cost of capital that reflects the time value of money and the riskiness of the cash flows.

The second component, the present value of financial costs and benefits, might itself be deconstructed into two or more elements such as the present value of tax shields and the value of financial subsidies. In the case of UK plc's expansion project, the only financial side benefit of the investment is the tax shield associated with the use of debt to finance the assets in question.

[5]See Brealey and Myers, op. cit., pp. 457–480.

Base Net Present Value

Valuation in parts begins in much the same fashion as valuation using WACC: Total free cash flows must first be forecasted. For UK plc's expansion project, the same sterling cash flows shown in **Exhibit 1** may be used in this technique.

The chief departure from the WACC technique is the construction of the discount rate used to value the free cash flows. To separate the base net present value (NPV) of the investment's operating cash flows from the value created by financing choices, the base net present value must be estimated independently of any associated financing decisions. Doing so first requires the estimation of an "asset" (i.e., unlevered) beta for the project's returns. For the project in question, an asset beta of .76 is provided in **Table 1.**[6] It is less than the levered-equity beta of .90 because it does not reflect the additional systematic risk of equity cash flows brought about by the need to make low-risk debt-service payments to creditors.

Using the standard CAPM formula and the asset beta of .76, the appropriate dollar discount rate for deriving the base value of the project is:

$$6\% + .76(8.6\%) = 12.5\%$$

Once again, interest rate parity may be used to convert this dollar rate to a sterling rate, as follows:

$$1.125(1.101/1.06) = 1.1685$$

Discounting the sterling cash flows by 16.85 percent yields a base net present value of £7.4 million (see **Exhibit 3**).

Note that the terminal value is lower than that shown in **Exhibit 2** because of the higher discount rate used in the perpetuity calculation. Indeed, the entire base net present value is lower than that obtained when using WACC because of the higher discount rate, which is a direct reflection of the omitted value attributable to debt financing at this stage of the analysis. In fact, the estimated base net present value of the project reveals that more than half of its total net present value is ultimately attributable to the present value of tax shields created by debt financing.

Present Value of Tax Shields

Discounting free cash flows with WACC, which incorporates an *after-tax* cost of debt, implicitly incorporates the present value of tax shields associated with debt

---

[6]Asset betas are seldom directly observable and are not widely reported. Occasionally, they can be determined from debt-free "pure-plays" in a particular line of business. Alternatively, they may be estimated from levered equity betas using the formula $\beta^u = \beta^l/[1 + (1 - \tau)D/E]$, where β^u and β^l are the unlevered and levered betas, respectively, and τ is a parameter that reflects the net tax savings to investors (after both personal and corporate taxes are taken into account) of a dollar of interest payments. However, because this formula assumes that corporate debt is riskless (i.e., has a beta of zero), and because the value of τ is generally not known outside the United States (even within the United States, experts are divided in their opinion of τ's value; most place it between 0 and .3), the application of this formula in cross-border valuations is often problematic.

financing directly in the computed present value. Valuation in parts requires the explicit discounting of tax shields as a distinctly separate component of value. The first step in this process is the estimation of the future tax shields themselves, period by period.

Normally, estimating tax shields is a straightforward, if somewhat tedious, task. One need only know the cost of debt, its repayment schedule, and the target capital structure for the project. In the case of UK plc's expansion project, debt will cost 13.6 percent (in pounds sterling) and the company will finance 40 percent of the project's cost with debt.

The simplest possible analysis using these assumptions is that the company borrows 40 percent of the £56 million initial outlay (£22.4 million) locally, and then maintains that level of debt indefinitely. This treatment would mean that the company would receive a tax shield of £1.066 million [(0.35) × (0.136) × (£22.4 million)] annually in perpetuity. The present value of this perpetuity is £7.8 million = £1.066/0.136. The cost of debt is used as the discount rate under the assumption that the tax shields are realized with approximately the same degree of risk as that associated with the debt itself.

Yet another possibility would be that the company borrows £22.4 million initially, and then repays it as a term loan over a specified period of time without replacing the debt. Under this assumption, the interest expense and associated tax shield would have to be computed for each year throughout the repayment period and discounted to the present. Clearly, this will produce a smaller present value of tax shields than the above perpetuity calculation. This reflects the suboptimal capital structure (i.e., no debt) for the project beyond the initial loan.

Highly levered transactions often require a combination of both approaches for the computation of the present value of tax shields. These deals generally start with very high levels of debt, which are then paid down rapidly until a long-term target capital structure is reached and maintained in a steady state. To handle this pattern, one should compute tax shields period by period while the debt is being repaid and the capital structure is changing, and then assume that subsequent tax shields are received as a perpetuity once the target level of debt has been reached.

Although it is not a highly levered transaction, UK plc's project also requires a combination of techniques for the estimation of the present value of tax shields. Strictly speaking, to be compatible with the capital-structure assumption implicitly made in the WACC valuation, which is that debt constitutes a fixed proportion of the project's *value* at all points in time, the level of debt used in the expansion project will be both greater than £22.4 million (because the project is worth more than the £56 million outlay from the very start) and changing in amount (because the project's value changes over time until it is assumed to reach a steady state after year 5).

To compute the tax shields for the expansion project, one must first compute the present value of the project at the start of each forecast period, determine the amount of debt accommodated by that value using the 40 percent target proportion, and then compute the annual interest expense using the prevailing sterling interest rate of 13.6 percent. The annual interest expense is then multiplied by the marginal corporate tax rate to obtain the forecasted tax shields. These calculations are shown in **Exhibit 3**.

Note the timing of the tax shield cash flows shown in **Exhibit 3**. Because UK plc is not required to pay taxes until 9 months after the close of its accounting period, the cash realization of the tax shield does not occur until the period *following* the realization of the interest expense itself.

Note also that the tax shields have a terminal value. Once it is assumed that the project's cash flows are received as a level perpetuity, the value of the investment becomes constant at £69.4 million. This means that the amount of debt, the interest expense, and the tax shield also become constant after the end of the forecasting horizon. Therefore, the value of all tax shields realized beyond the first five can be estimated as a level perpetuity using 13.6 percent as the discount rate.

Discounting all the forecasted tax shields to the present yields a present value of £8.3 million. Together with the base net present value of £7.4 million, this valuation methodology assigns a value of £15.7 million to the expansion project.

Most of the small difference between this value and the £15.8 million obtained using WACC is attributable to rounding error. Nevertheless, a slightly lower figure from valuation in parts was predictable because of the timing in the realization of tax shields. The use of WACC implicitly assumes that all tax shields are received simultaneously with the realization of interest expense. Valuation in parts permits the explicit recognition that taxes and, thus, tax shields, are realized with a lag in the United Kingdom. Between the two methods, valuation in parts permits greater accuracy in this case. This advantage can be even larger in situations involving very complex financings, changing capital structures, and off-market interest rates. Indeed, in such situations, the rigidity of assumptions implicitly embodied in the application of WACC can defeat its applicability altogether.

THE VALUE OF GROWTH AND OPERATING OPTIONS

In addition to financial complexities, many cross-border investments frustrate ordinary valuation methods because of intangible benefits such as operating flexibility and valuable new investment opportunities that may accompany an initial investment. Many cross-border acquisitions, for example, are important more because they establish an immediate beachhead in a new country which can later be expanded if conditions warrant. For strategic reasons, these discretionary future expansion opportunities might be considerably more valuable than the initial assets themselves. Locating manufacturing facilities abroad may also be valuable more for the operating flexibility it provides when responding to unexpected real exchange-rate changes (e.g., by permitting the shifting of production or the sourcing of parts from more favorable locations) than for the present value of cash flows expected from the initial investment.

Value attributable to operating flexibility or future investment is generally not easily incorporated into ordinary net present value analysis because it depends upon future business conditions and managerial discretion. That is, growth and operating options will be exercised in some future states of the world and not others. In this regard, they are analogous to contingent claims. Their value is better construed to be that of an *option* to invest in real assets.

By way of analogy to ordinary call options on securities, an operating or growth option's exercise price is the investment required to obtain particular assets. The value of the assets to be acquired (i.e., the underlying "security") is the total present value of their expected cash flows plus the value of any new options expected through ownership and operation of the assets in question. The "time to maturity" is the length of time that final commitment of capital can safely be deferred before the opportunity ceases to exist. This might be many years, months, or, conceivably, just a few days depending upon the nature of the opportunity.

Valuing growth options quantitatively is generally quite challenging. Sometimes, as in the case of natural resource projects in which holders of leases have the right (but not the obligation) to explore for minerals or hydrocarbons in a given area during a limited length of time, the analogy between options on real assets and options on securities may be quite close, and reliable data to implement standard option pricing model (e.g., the Black-Scholes option pricing formula) may be widely available. In other instances, the unique features of growth and operating options requires substantial modification of standard formulas and sophisticated numerical estimation techniques to estimate value.

A thorough discussion of options pricing techniques is beyond the scope of this note.[7] Suffice it to say at this point that, within the context of the valuation-in-parts paradigm, the total value of many cross-border investments can usefully be deconstructed as follows:

Total value = base NPV + present value of tax shields
                        + present value of financial costs and benefits
                        + present value of growth and operating options

Whereas the first three components have forecastable cash flows that can be discounted using well-known techniques, the last component is a discretionary investment (or operating) opportunity, the value of which is best thought of as an option on real assets. As is the case with call options on securities, the growth-option component of value will *increase* in value, all other factors being held constant, as

- The value of the underlying assets increases

- The required capital outlay (i.e., the exercise price) decreases

- Interest rates increase

- The volatility of the underlying assets' value increases

- The length of deferability (i.e., the time to maturity) increases

Notice that two of these variables, the interest rate and volatility (risk), have an effect on the value of growth options that is the opposite of their effect on the present

[7]For further reading and additional references on the application of option pricing theory to corporate finance, see Brealey and Myers, op. cit., pp. 511–534, and W. Carl Kester, "An Options Approach to Corporate Finance," in *Handbook of Corporate Finance,* 6th ed., ed. E. Altman (New York: John Wiley & Sons, 1986), pp. 5.1–5.35.

value of cash flows. Thus, cross-border investments that create many new growth options are likely to be less severely penalized by high discount rates than projects of similar risk that do not create new growth options. Similarly, they will be comparatively more attractive if the growth options represent investment opportunities in volatile business environments. The rapidly changing economic and political environment in Eastern Europe, for example, may make many capital investments in that region attractive primarily for the value of the new growth options they create rather than the cash flows expected from the initial investment. Indeed, many new Eastern European investments may have a negative net present value of free cash flows, but still have positive total value once the value of growth options is taken into account.

SUMMARY

The same fundamental principles of valuation that underlie conventional domestic capital budgeting are also applicable when evaluating cross-border investments. What changes is the application of standard valuation techniques.

At a minimum, cross-border valuation requires that expected changes in exchange rates be incorporated into the analysis. This can be achieved by explicitly forecasting exchange rates, converting foreign-currency cash flows, and then discounting at an appropriate home-country discount rate (method B), or by appropriately incorporating the expected rate of change in exchange rates in the discount rate when discounting foreign-currency cash flows (method A). If parity exists among exchange rates, interest rates, and inflation rates, either method will yield the same present value. A brief summary of the steps in each method is presented in **Exhibit 4**.

In addition to exchange-rate changes, other concerns peculiar to cross-border investments may also have to be addressed. These include problems such as choosing which cash flows, earned or remitted, to discount; adjusting for foreign-currency risk; adjusting for various types of country risk; and capturing special financial benefits and costs associated with cross-border investments.

No one choice will be correct in any and all circumstances; managers must tailor their choices to suit the characteristics of each situation. As a general rule, however, it is best to avoid trying to incorporate special adjustments into the analysis by arbitrarily boosting the discount rate. The potential errors in doing so could be large, unknown, and compounded in the discounting of long-term cash flows, which are frequently an important source of value for strategic cross-border investments. Whenever possible, it is best to reflect adjustments directly in cash flows. Doing so will generally provoke more thoughtful treatment about the size and timing of the risks in questions, afford greater accuracy in the assessment of the risks' impact on value, and make explicit the assumptions underlying their treatment in the analysis.

The complexity of some cross-border investments, however, may be such that they defy ordinary net present value analysis using total free cash flows and WACC. This is particularly true when investments are accompanied by project-specific financial subsidies (or costs), temporary tax breaks, unusually high levels of debt for a short period of time, and so forth. Under these circumstances, it is helpful to deconstruct the project's value into individual elements, each of which may be more analytically tractable than trying to value all of the project's incremental free cash flows with a single discount rate. Valuation in parts begins by determining a base net present value of operating free cash flows using a discount rate that is not modified by capital structure, cost of debt, or tax factors (i.e., an unlevered cost of equity). To this is added the present value of tax shields and other nonoperating sources of cash associated with the project.

Many cross-border investments may also require an expanded concept of total value: one that reflects the value inherent in the operating flexibility afforded by overseas assets or the discretionary future investment opportunities that are created by the investment under consideration. Such operating and growth options are somewhat analogous to call options securities, and our knowledge of option pricing can be used to understand the key determinants of their value. Numerical evaluation of growth options can be rather challenging, however. Nevertheless, growth options can be important sources of value for strategically important cross-border investments and should not be implicitly assumed to have a value of zero. Indeed, their value in some cases could be so substantial as to justify accepting a cross-border project that has a negative net present value of incremental free cash flows.

In short, conventional valuation techniques commonly used in domestic capital budgeting can be applied to cross-border investments, although their application requires careful consideration of numerous factors unique to operations involving multiple currencies, multiple tax rates, and multiple legal and regulatory jurisdictions. However, discounting free cash flows with a WACC is ultimately a fairly simple technique best used in simple situations. The more complex the financial arrangements surrounding a cross-border investment and the more strategic the purpose of the investment, the more helpful it will be to execute valuation in parts and to adopt an expanded concept of value that recognizes the importance of operating and growth options.

EXHIBIT 1   FORECASTED CASH FLOWS FOR THE EXPANSION OF UK PLC BY US INC. (IN MILLIONS)

	Year						Terminal value
	0	1	2	3	4	5	
Earnings before financing charges and taxes	—	£10.0	£12.5	£15.0	£16.5	£18.0	
Taxes*	—	—	3.5	4.4	5.3	5.8	
Earnings before financing charges, after taxes	—	10.0	9.0	10.6	11.2	12.2	
Depreciation expense[†]	—	5.0	5.0	5.0	5.0	5.0	
Capital expenditures	£(50.0)	(4.0)	(4.4)	(5.0)	(5.3)	(5.7)	
Investment in net working capital	(6.0)	(0.6)	(0.7)	(0.9)	(1.0)	(1.1)	
Total free cash flow	£(56.0)	£10.4	£8.9	£9.7	£9.9	£10.4	£78.0[‡]

*Taxes are incurred locally at the full marginal corporate tax rate of 35 percent, and paid 9 months following the end of the tax year. US Inc. receives a tax credit on income remitted from UK plc up to the full marginal U.S. corporate tax rate of 34 percent.

[†]Initial capital expenditures of £50 million are depreciated on a straight-line basis over 10 years, beginning in the first year.

[‡]Estimated as a level, no-growth perpetuity of £11.7 million that begins in the sixth year of the project.

EXHIBIT 2   CALCULATING THE NET PRESENT VALUE (NPV) OF FOREIGN-CURRENCY CASH FLOWS (IN MILLIONS)

	Year						Terminal value
	0	1	2	3	4	5	

Method A: Discount foreign-currency cash flows to present; convert NPV to the home currency at the spot exchange rate

	0	1	2	3	4	5	Terminal value
Free cash flows	£(56.0)	£10.4	£8.9	£9.7	£9.9	£10.4	£78.0
Discounting factor @ 15%	1.000	0.870	0.756	0.658	0.572	0.497	0.497
Present value	(56.0)	9.0	6.7	6.4	5.7	5.2	38.8
NPV	£15.8						
Spot exchange rate	1.70						
NPV	$26.9						

Method B: Convert foreign-currency cash flows to home currency; discount to present at the home discount rate

	0	1	2	3	4	5	Terminal value
Free cash flows	£(56.0)	£10.4	£8.9	£9.7	£9.9	£10.4	£78.0
Exchange rates*	1.7000	1.6367	1.5757	1.5171	1.4606	1.4062	1.4062
Free cash flows	$(95.2)	$17.0	$14.0	$14.7	$14.5	$14.6	109.7
Discounting factor @ 10.7%	1.000	0.903	0.816	0.737	0.666	0.601	0.601
Present value of cash flows	$(95.2)	$15.4	$11.4	$10.8	$9.7	$8.8	$65.9
NPV	$26.8						

*Forecasted exchange rates are determined using interest rate parity. The factor $(1.06/1.101)^n$, where n equals the number of the year in question, was multiplied by the initial spot exchange rate, $1.70/£, to generate each of the exchange rates used in years 1 through 5, including the terminal value at the end of year 5.

EXHIBIT 3   VALUATION IN PARTS (IN MILLIONS)

	Year						Terminal value
	0	1	2	3	4	5	
Base net present value							
Free cash flows	£(56.0)	£10.4	£8.9	£9.7	£9.9	£10.4	£69.4
Discounting factor @ 16.85%	1.000	0.856	0.732	0.627	0.536	0.459	0.459
Present value of cash flows	(56.0)	8.9	6.5	6.1	5.3	4.8	31.8
Net present value	£7.4						
Present value of tax shields							
Project's total value at the *start* of the period	£63.4	£63.7	£65.6	£66.9	£68.3	£69.4	
Value of debt	25.4	25.5	26.2	26.8	27.3	27.8	
Interest expense @ 13.6%	3.5	3.5	3.6	3.6	3.7	3.8	
Tax shield	0.0	1.2	1.2	1.3	1.3	1.3	9.7
Discounting factor @ 13.6%	0.880	0.775	0.682	0.600	0.529	0.465	0.465
Present value of tax shields	0.0	0.9	0.8	0.8	0.7	0.6	4.5
Total present value of tax shields	£8.3						

Total value

Base net present value	£7.4
Present value of tax shields	8.3
Total sterling value	£15.7
Total dollar value	$26.7

EXHIBIT 4   ALTERNATIVE METHODS OF VALUING CROSS-BORDER INVESTMENTS

Initial analysis

1. Forecast foreign-currency free cash flows
   • Incorporate expected foreign-currency inflation rates (except in hyperinflation environments)
   • Use appropriate effective tax rate
   • Include terminal value

Method A	**Method B**

2. Determine foreign-currency discount rate
  • Use project-specific capital structure
  • Use project-specific beta
	2. Forecast future exchange rates using parity relationships and convert cash flows to home currency

3. Calculate present value in foreign currency	3. Determine home-currency discount rate
	  • Use project-specific capital structure
	  • Use project-specific beta

4. Convert to home currency using the spot exchange rate	4. Calculate present value in home currency

APPENDIX: 1991 MARGINAL CORPORATE TAX RATES FOR SELECTED COUNTRIES

Country	Basic marginal corporate tax rate,[a] %
Argentina	20
Australia	39
Austria	30
Bahamas	None
Bahrain	None
Bermuda	None
Belgium	39
Brazil	30
Canada	38[b]
Cayman Islands	None
Channel Islands	20
Chile	35
China	25–40[c]
Colombia	30
Cyprus	20–25[d]
Czechoslovakia	20–55[e]
Denmark	40
Finland	23
France	34[f]
Greece	46[g]
Germany	50[h]
Hong Kong	16.5
Hungary	40[i]
India	40
Indonesia	35
Ireland	40[j]
Italy	36[k]
Japan	40[l]
Kenya	40
Korea	34
Liechtenstein	7.5–15
Luxembourg	20–33
Kuwait	5–55
Malaysia	35
Mexico	35
Netherlands	35–40
New Zealand	33
Nigeria	40
Norway	27.8[m]
Oman	5–50
Pakistan	30–50
Panama	20–50
Philippines	35
Portugal	36[n]

APPENDIX: 1991 MARGINAL CORPORATE TAX
RATES FOR SELECTED COUNTRIES (*continued*)

Country	Basic marginal corporate tax rate, %
Puerto Rico	28–42
Saudi Arabia	25–45
Singapore	31
South Africa	50°
Soviet Union	35^p
Spain	35
Sweden	30
Switzerland	3.63–9.8^q
Taiwan	15–25^r
Thailand	35^s
Turkey	46
United Kingdom	35
United States	34
Venezuela	15–50

[a]A progressive corporate tax system is represented in this table by a range of tax rates.

[b]This rate is reduced to 34.5 percent for domestic manufacturing and processing companies.

[c]This range relates to foreign enterprises operating in China.

[d]An additional tax of 10 percent is levied before the deduction of losses brought forward and certain tax incentives.

[e]For joint ventures where there is more than 30 percent foreign participation, the 55 percent rate is reduced to 40 percent. Banking and financial institutions have all their profits taxed at 55 percent.

[f]The rate is 42 percent on profits distributed to stockholders.

[g]The rate for manufacturing, mining, and quarrying corporations is 40 percent (35 percent if they are quoted on the Athens Stock Exchange). Corporations that do not fall into the above categories, but are listed on the Athens Stock Exchange, are taxed at the rate of 40 percent.

[h]The rate is 36 percent on profits distributed to stockholders.

[i]The rate for a foreign manufacturing corporation is 16 percent for the first 5 years, and 24 percent for the following 5 years. If the corporation is involved in a "priority" industry, these rates are reduced to 0 percent and 16 percent, respectively.

[j]A rate of 10 percent applies to certain manufacturing activities.

[k]A company that distributes more than 64 percent of its taxable income to its stockholders bears an additional tax of 56.25 percent on the excess.

[l]The rate is 35 percent on income set aside for distribution to stockholders.

[m]Companies involved in the production or pipeline transport of oil and gas are liable to a tax of 50.8 percent, plus a special oil tax of 30 percent.

[n]This rate is increased in most cases by a municipal surcharge of 10 percent to 36.9 percent.

[o]Other rules apply for companies involved in the mining of gold, diamonds, oil, and natural gas.

[p]Joint enterprises and foreign entities are subject to tax at 30 percent (the former is also subject to taxes of 80–90 percent of profits exceeding predetermined levels).

[q]Additional surcharges typically raise rates to an average of 25–35 percent.

[r]These rates are based on formulae.

[s]The rate is 30 percent if the company is registered on the domestic securities exchange.

MSDI—ALCALA DE HENARES, SPAIN

On June 24, 1987, John Verniero, financial analyst at Merck & Co., Inc., was reviewing an investment proposal from Merck Sharp and Dohme International (MSDI). The proposal called for the purchase and installation of new automatic inspection equipment for the filling of glass ampules with liquid pharmaceutical products. The equipment was to be installed in a facility operated by MSDI in Alcala de Henares, a suburb of Madrid, Spain. The new machinery was manufactured by Brevetti Cea, S.p.A., an Italian firm, and was expected to result in significant savings of labor and materials. Fully installed, the machinery would cost 61.525 million pesetas (Pts), or nearly $500,000. For investments of this size, Merck required a discounted cash flow analysis and approval from corporate headquarters in Rahway, New Jersey.

MERCK & CO., INC.

Merck is a large multinational producer of pharmaceuticals for human and animal health care. Sales for 1987 were projected to be about $5 billion. For the year ended December 31, 1986, the company reported earnings of $676 million on sales of $4,129 million. **Exhibit 1** presents selected consolidated financial data for Merck.

The company's extensive international operations are conducted primarily through subsidiaries grouped within its MSDI division. These include manufacturing facilities, research laboratories, and experimental farms in twenty countries, and sales and

This case was prepared by Research Associate James J. Student and Professor Timothy A. Luehrman. Certain facts and data have been disguised. Copyright © 1989 by the President and Fellows of Harvard College. Harvard Business School case 289-029.

marketing subsidiaries in many more. In 1986, subsidiaries outside the United States recorded about half of Merck's sales and slightly less than 40 percent of pre-tax income.

OPERATIONS AT ALCALA DE HENARES

The manufacturing facility at Alcala de Henares began operating in 1969 and was located near a research laboratory and an experimental farm, also owned by Merck. The factory produced, among other things, ampules of liquid Lidocaine, a local anesthetic used as a diluent for certain antibiotic powders. Manufacturing inputs were sourced locally and the finished product was sold primarily to Spanish customers. Lidocaine was one of Merck's older products and sales of the drug in Spain were expected to decline gradually over the next decade.

One of the primary production processes at Alcala de Henares consisted of washing, filling, inspecting, and sealing the ampules of Lidocaine. Ampules are small glass containers, about 0.25 to 0.50 inches in diameter, with conical tops. These were purchased from local suppliers and subjected to vigorous washing and sterilization by automated machinery. Washing and sterilization had to conform to stringent quality control guidelines and a number of ampules were inevitably chipped or broken in this process.

Once washed, the ampules were filled by automated machinery with liquid Lidocaine. The filled ampules then proceeded to an inspection station. This was essentially a viewing box that illuminated and magnified the ampules. Particles larger than 50 microns, primarily fragments of glass from the washing process, were then visible and workers pulled the contaminated ampules off the line.[1] Ampules that passed inspection then had their conical tops flame-sealed and were ready for packaging and shipping.

In the spring of 1987, the inspection station at Alcala de Henares was running at 200 percent of planned capacity. An added shift of ten workers was needed to sustain this level of production. Each required 2 to 3 months of training to become proficient with the semiautomatic inspection equipment. MSDI's investment proposal called for replacing this semiautomatic inspection process with photoelectric sensing machinery that would measure electronically the number and size of particles in the ampules. The high-speed equipment manufactured by Brevetti Cea had a rated capacity of nearly six million ampules per year, or about 25 percent more volume than MSDI anticipated in 1988. Inspection criteria and rejection thresholds were easily adjusted by the user and the machinery did not require specially trained operators.

Cost Savings from the Proposed New Equipment

The new equipment could process MSDI's projected volume using four employees rather than ten, resulting in savings of both direct labor and training costs. Under very favorable circumstances, only three workers would be required. It would also eliminate human performance variability, which currently caused many good ampules to be

---

[1] One micron equals one-millionth of 1 meter.

rejected. Tests of the new equipment indicated that the rejection rate would drop from 11 percent of all ampules tested to about 3 percent. Thus MSDI expected savings in materials as well. **Exhibit 2** compares projected operating data for the existing semiautomatic inspection process and the proposed automatic photoelectric process. The projections in **Exhibit 2** assume a constant inflation rate in Spain of 8.0 percent over the life of the project.

The new equipment would have a useful life of 10 years and would be depreciated under the straight-line method for both tax and financial reporting purposes. The equipment being replaced had a book value and tax basis of Pts 1605 thousand, and 3 years of straight-line depreciation remaining. Its market value was thought to be about Pts 950 thousand. After considering Merck's consolidated tax position, Verniero determined that his analysis would use the local tax rate of 35 percent.

The issue that remained unresolved was whether the discounted cash flow analysis should be performed in dollars or pesetas, or indeed, whether it mattered which currency was used. Certainly borrowing costs in the two currencies were different: U.S. banks' prime rate for dollar loans was 8.50 percent, while the rate in Spain on short-term peseta loans had recently risen to about 18 percent. MSDI could obtain longer-term (peseta) funds at 15 percent. The spot exchange rate on July 27 was Pts127.00/$. One- and three-month forward rates were Pts125.85/$ and Pts123.70/$, respectively.

Many analysts were predicting a real appreciation of the peseta against the dollar over the next 5 years. They pointed to recent improvements in the performance of the Spanish economy as the reason for their bullish view of the peseta. Spain's real economic growth was running higher, and inflation lower, in 1987 than in 1986. Still, economists' 5-year forecasts for the peseta/dollar exchange rate covered a wide range, from a low of Pts80/$ to a high of Pts170/$. Selected financial and macroeconomic data are presented in **Exhibits 3** and **4**.

EXHIBIT 1   MERCK & CO., INC.: SELECTED CONSOLIDATED FINANCIAL DATA* (MILLIONS, EXCEPT AS NOTED)

Year ending December 31

	1986	1985	1984	1983	1982	1981	1980	1979	1978	1977
Sales	$4128.9	$3547.5	$3559.7	$3246.1	$3063.0	$2929.5	$2734.0	$2384.6	$1981.4	$1724.4
Net income	675.7	539.9	493.0	450.9	415.1	398.3	415.4	381.8	307.5	277.5
Total assets	5105.2	4902.2	4590.6	4214.7	3655.4	3317.2	2907.7	2649.1	2278.1	1993.4
Long-term debt	167.5	170.8	179.1	385.5	337.3	241.0	211.4	213.7	211.4	213.8
Equity	2541.2	2607.7	2518.6	2409.9	2180.2	1978.2	1841.6	1645.0	1436.3	1260.2
Earnings per share, $	4.85	3.79	3.36	3.05	2.81	2.68	2.77	2.53	2.03	1.84
Dividend per share, $	1.90	1.60	1.50	1.40	1.40	1.30	1.15	.95	.85	.75
Return on sales	16.4%	15.2%	13.8%	13.9%	13.6%	13.6%	15.2%	16.0%	15.5%	16.1%
Return on beginning equity	25.9%	21.4%	20.5%	20.7%	21.0%	21.6%	25.3%	26.6%	24.4%	25.2%
Capital expenditures	$210.6	$237.6	$274.4	$272.8	$295.1	$322.8	$256.5	$170.1	$155.9	$177.2
Depreciation	167.2	163.6	151.6	135.2	121.1	105.0	91.3	80.6	74.3	65.8
Research and development expenditures	479.8	426.3	393.1	356.0	320.2	274.2	233.9	188.1	161.4	144.9

*As reported in the Merck & Co., Inc., 1987 Annual Report.

EXHIBIT 2 COMPARISON OF PROJECTED OPERATING DATA FOR DIFFERENT INSPECTION PROCESSES (THOUSANDS, EXCEPT AS NOTED)

	Years ending December 31									
	1988	1989	1990	1991	1992	1993	1994	1995	1996	1997
Projected ampule volume (×1000)	4590	4258	4166	4020	3854	3702	3566	3443	3335	3240
Projected operating costs, semiautomatic equipment,* Pts										
Materials	14,872	14,900	15,744	16,407	16,988	17,624	18,334	19,118	20,000	20,985
Direct labor	29,376	29,431	31,099	32,410	33,557	34,812	36,216	37,764	39,506	41,451
Overhead†	44,248	44,331	46,843	48,817	50,546	52,436	54,551	56,883	59,506	62,436
Total	88,496	88,662	93,686	97,634	101,091	104,872	109,101	113,765	119,012	124,872
Projected operating costs, new photoelectric equipment,* Pts										
Materials	13,678	13,704	14,480	15,091	15,625	16,210	16,863	17,584	18,395	19,301
Direct labor	11,750	11,773	12,440	12,964	13,423	13,925	14,487	15,106	15,803	16,581
Overhead†	44,248	44,331	46,843	48,817	50,546	52,436	54,551	56,883	59,506	62,436
Total	69,676	69,808	73,763	76,872	79,594	82,571	85,901	89,573	93,704	98,318

*Projections reflect 8 percent annual inflation in per-ampule costs.
†Does not include depreciation.

EXHIBIT 3   SELECTED SPANISH FINANCIAL AND MACROECONOMIC DATA

Date		Average daily interbank rate, Pts%	6- to 12-month deposit rate, Pts%	Short-term commercial lending rate, Pts%	Consumer price inflation, Pts%	Real growth in gross domestic product, %
1980		18.6	13.1	16.9	10.2	1.5
1981		18.7	11.4	15.3	11.5	0.2
1982		20.3	12.3	15.0	14.7	1.2
1983		16.4	12.3	15.0	12.2	1.8
1984	I	14.8	12.5	20.0		
	II	11.9	12.6	17.2		
	III	12.5	12.4	15.0		
	IV	12.2	11.7	14.0	11.3	1.9
1985	I	12.1	11.1	13.7		
	II	14.0	10.7	14.0		
	III	11.1	10.5	14.3		
	IV	9.9	9.9	12.0	8.8	2.2
1986	I	11.3	9.4	11.6		
	II	12.0	9.2	12.4		
	III	11.6	8.9	12.5		
	IV	11.8	8.7	12.3	8.8	3.3
1987	I	14.4	8.6	13.1		
	II	18.1	8.8	17.9		

EXHIBIT 4   SELECTED U.S. FINANCIAL AND MACROECONOMIC DATA

Date		Average yield on 3-month T-bills, $%	Average yield on 10-year T-bonds, $%	Average yield on 6-month commercial paper, $%	Prime commercial lending rate, $%	Consumer price inflation, $%	Real growth in gross domestic product, %
1980		11.5	11.46	12.29	15.27	13.5	−0.2
1981		14.03	13.91	14.76	18.87	10.4	1.9
1982		10.69	13.00	11.89	14.86	6.1	−2.5
1983		8.63	11.10	8.89	10.79	3.2	3.6
1984	I	9.13	11.94	9.45	11.25		
	II	9.84	13.20	10.77	12.75		
	III	10.34	12.87	11.15	12.75		
	IV	8.97	11.74	9.26	11.00	4.3	6.8
1985	I	8.18	11.58	8.69	10.50		
	II	7.52	10.81	7.91	9.75		
	III	7.10	10.34	7.72	9.50		
	IV	7.15	8.76	7.70	9.50	3.6	3.0
1986	I	6.89	8.56	7.41	9.25		
	II	6.13	7.60	6.54	8.50		
	III	5.53	7.31	5.89	7.50		
	IV	5.34	7.26	5.73	7.50	1.9	2.9
1987	I	5.53	7.19	5.95	7.50		
	II	5.73	8.34	6.85	8.50		

OCEAN DRILLING, INC.

On November 16, 1981, the board of directors of Ocean Drilling, Inc., was confronted with a choice between bids by two foreign shipyards on two semisubmersible drilling rigs.[1] The company had planned to purchase the rigs from a U.S. shipyard with financing facilitated by the Maritime Administration's loan guarantee program. To its dismay, President Reagan's determination to cut government programs resulted in a sharp reduction of the Maritime Administration's loan guarantee activities. With $2.7 billion of requests for loan guarantees and only $900 million to allocate for fiscal year 1982, the agency seemed likely to scuttle all drilling loan bids and to concentrate on encouraging ship construction.

Management was forced to choose between two alternative bids: one by a Japanese shipyard for $90 million; a second by a French shipyard for $96 million. Both proposals involved possible exchange risks associated with changes in the value of these currencies. This risk was an important consideration since 75 percent to 80 percent of the cost of the rigs would be financed in the country—and therefore the currency—where the shipyard was located.

The members of the board acknowledged that they were not experts in the foreign exchange market. Indeed, they wondered if such a person existed. Responsibility was assigned to Geoffrey Moore, the assistant treasurer, to analyze in detail the foreign exchange risks involved in the Japanese and French proposals. A summary description of the two proposals is contained in **Exhibit 1**.

---

[1]Semisubmersible rigs are anchored and float in a half-submerged position for greater stability in rough sea environments.

This case was prepared by Professor Thomas R. Piper. Copyright © 1981 by the President and Fellows of Harvard College. Harvard Business School case 282-050.

THE OFFSHORE DRILLING INDUSTRY

The offshore drilling industry had experienced rapid growth since 1973, fueled by the fifteenfold increase in oil prices (see **Table 1**). Revenues rose 25 percent annually as more expensive rigs were added to the fleet, and daily rates were increased. By 1981, every available mobile rig in the world was under contract, often for as long as 2 years, at daily rates that had doubled in less than 3 years to $75,000 a day for the large semisubmersibles.

Ocean Drilling's management was intent on establishing itself among the leaders in the industry. Capital outlays were scheduled at more than $250 million per year through 1985—a substantial undertaking for a company with an estimated net worth at yearend 1981 of only $194 million, a bond rating of BB, and erratic earnings. **Exhibit 2** summarizes Ocean Drilling's past financial performance.

The financial community was not comfortable with the aggressive spending plans. Its concern was reflected in the 20 percent yield on Ocean Drilling's most recent public debt offering. Some industry observers feared that a glut might develop when the 200 rigs on order worldwide came onstream. Rumor had it that one of the industry leaders was holding back on fleet expansion, expecting to pick up rigs from other operators at fire-sale prices.

Ocean Drilling's management was confident, however, that any downturn would be brief. The president commented:

> Right now it is hard to say if the industry is overbuilding because the real impact of thirty-dollar oil is not fully understood. Using historical experience to build future scenarios may not be a valid approach anymore. People cite the so-called cycle theory which says the industry will move into an overbuilt situation every five to six years. However, in the last seven years the price of oil has increased almost fifteenfold. The rig population during this time increased twofold. There is obviously room for a lot of expansion and we plan to capitalize fully on the opportunity.

The large spending program would be financed by a combination of sharply higher earnings and continued heavy use of debt. Shipyard financing at rates of 9 percent to 10 percent (versus the 20 percent yield on the company's most recent public debt issue) would keep total interest expense in line with earnings. (See **Exhibit 3** for projected income statements and capitalizations.)

TABLE 1   GROWTH OF OFFSHORE DRILLING INDUSTRY, 1970–1980

	1970	1980
Number of rigs	194	471
Revenues per day	$1,560,000	$15,000,000
Revenues per rig per day	$8,041	$31,847

FORECASTING EXCHANGE RATES

The magnitude of the proposed shipyard financings required careful analysis of possible changes in exchange rates. Mr. Moore asked his assistants to compile economic data for Japan, France, and the United States. (See **Exhibits 4** through **7**.) He also reviewed information culled from recent reports on each country, as summarized in **Exhibit 8**.

HEDGING POLICIES

Mr. Moore was considering two methods to protect Ocean Drilling against the risks involved in borrowing in a foreign currency. One possibility was to sell U.S. dollars for French francs or Japanese yen in the forward market (see **Table 2**). Moore thought that it would be very difficult to buy a single forward contract to cover the life of the loan from either shipyard. Nervousness over Mitterrand's Socialist policies in France made it unlikely that a contract beyond 2 years could be found at a reasonable price. In contrast, it would be possible to negotiate a 5-year forward contract in yen.

The other possibility was to borrow in the United States at 20 percent, convert the proceeds into French francs or Japanese yen, and invest them in France or Japan at the prevailing rates (**Table 2**). While this seemed fairly straightforward in dealing with the risks, it was also expensive. Moore suspected that management would be unwilling to invest in anything other than a Japanese or French government security. A borrowing/investing hedge would involve a substantial spread due to the difference in creditworthiness.

In view of the disadvantages of each of the hedging alternatives, Moore wondered if the best move was to leave the exchange risk uncovered.

TABLE 2   MARKET RATES, NOVEMBER 16, 1981

Exchange rates*	Spot	6-Month	12-Month	2-Year	5-Year
FF/$	5.570–5.580	5.6775(−4.0)	5.7800(−3.8)	6.0300(−4.0)	Not available
¥/$	227.15–227.30	219.95(+6.3)	212.40(+6.5)	197.25(+6.8)	184.15(+4.1%)

Interbank deposit rates	6-Month	12-Month	5-Year
Eurodollars	13.44%	13.75%	15.50%
Euro French francs	17.50	18.00	19.00
Euroyen	7.62	7.55	8.25

*The figures in parentheses are the annualized percentage rate of change and are based on the bid rate.

EXHIBIT 1   SUMMARY OF SHIPYARD PROPOSALS

	French shipyard	Japanese shipyard
Total bid price of rigs	FF535 million	¥20,444 million
Exchange rate on November 16	5.570 (FF/$)	227.15 (¥/$)
U.S. dollar bid equivalent	$96 million	$90 million
Amount of shipyard financing	75%	80%
Currency	Franc	Yen
Maturity	8 years	10 years
Payment schedule	Equal annual payments	Equal annual payments
Interest rate	10½%	8¾%
Required down payment by Ocean Drilling	$24 million	$18 million

EXHIBIT 2   SUMMARY OF FINANCIAL PERFORMANCE (IN MILLIONS)

	1974	1975	1976	1977	1978	1979	1980
Total revenues	$47	$81	$86	$99	$122	$136	$173
Earnings before interest and taxes	13	11	15	10	21	32	59
Interest	3	4	9	11	11	14	17
Profit before taxes	10	7	6	(1)	10	18	42
Taxes	4	2	1	0	4	3	6
Net income	$6	$5	$5	$(1)	$6	$15	$36
Cash flow from operations	$13	$14	$16	$11	$19	$33	$58
Capital expenditures	$28	$23	$28	$32	$41	$71	$156
Times interest earned	4.3	2.8	1.7	0.9	1.9	2.3	3.5
Return on average equity	13%	10%	9%	—	10%	21%	32%
Per share							
Earnings	$0.37	$0.32	$0.31	($0.06)	$0.36	$0.92	$2.02
Dividends	0.03	0.03	0.03	0.00	0.00	0.00	0.00
Book value	3.10	3.39	3.66	3.60	3.96	4.88	7.80
Market–High	3¼	3⅞	3½	3	4⅛	9¼	43
Low	1⅞	2	1⅝	1½	1¾	2⅞	10

EXHIBIT 2
(continued)

BALANCE SHEET AT DECEMBER 31, 1980 (IN MILLIONS)

Assets		Liabilities and equity	
Cash	$ 8	Accounts payable	$ 13
Accounts receivable	32	Accrued liabilities	15
Inventories	10	Accrued taxes	3
Prepaid expenses	5	Current portion long-term debt	13
Total	55	Total	44
Construction funds in escrow	17	Deferred income taxes	8
Gross plant and equipment	386	Other long-term liabilities	6
(–)Accumulated depreciation	87	Long-term senior debt	124
Net plant and equipment	299	Convertible subordinated debt	50
		Shareholders' equity	139
Total assets	$371	Total	$371

Note: Under the terms of a borrowing agreement, the current ratio must be at least equal to 1.2 and the ratio of senior debt to the sum of subordinated debt plus shareholders' equity may not exceed 1.25.

EXHIBIT 3

PROJECTIONS, 1981–1985 (IN MILLIONS)

	1981	1982	1983	1984	1985
Revenues	$262	$407	$561	$888	$1309
Earnings before interest and taxes	117	180	220	330	500
Interest	30	43	60	80	100
Profit before tax	87	137	160	250	400
Tax	22	32	48	90	172
Net income	$65	$105	$112	$160	$228
Earnings per share	$3.65	$5.90	$6.29	$8.99	$12.81
Number of shares			17.8 million		
Long-term debt	$240	$364	$440	$640	$840
Convertible subordinated debt	50	50	50	50	50
Shareholders' equity	194	299	411	571	799
Total	$484	$713	$901	$1261	$1689

EXHIBIT 4   FRANCE: BALANCE OF PAYMENTS (BILLIONS OF U.S. DOLLARS)

	1975	1976	1977	1978	1979	1980
Trade balance	1.1	−4.6	−2.7	0.7	−2.0	−12.0
Merchandise: exports	50.0	53.9	61.2	74.6	94.3	107.5
Merchandise: imports	−48.9	−58.5	−63.9	−73.9	−96.3	−119.5
Net other goods, services, and income	1.6	1.2	2.5	6.3	7.1	8.3
Private unrequited transfers	−1.5	−1.4	−1.4	−1.8	−2.3	−2.5
Official unrequited transfers	−1.1	−1.0	−1.4	−1.5	−1.7	−1.7
Net capital flows other than reserves	−0.6	0.7	0.1	−3.6	−1.6	8.1
Net errors and omissions	4.1	2.1	3.5	2.8	2.3	5.7
Counterpart items	—	—	0.1	0.1	2.2	5.0
Other	0.5	0.2	−0.6	0.3	0.1	0.5
Total change in reserves	4.1	−2.8	0.1	3.3	4.1	11.4
			Index (1975 = 100)			
Volume of exports	100	109	116	123	136	139
Volume of imports	100	121	122	128	143	152
Unit value of exports	100	109	120	126	138	153
Unit value of imports	100	111	123	125	137	163

EXHIBIT 5   JAPAN: BALANCE OF PAYMENTS (BILLIONS OF U.S. DOLLARS)

	1975	1976	1977	1978	1979	1980
Trade balance	4.90	9.80	17.20	25.30	1.70	2.10
Merchandise: exports	54.6	65.9	79.2	95.3	101.1	126.7
Merchandise: imports	−49.7	−56.1	−62.0	−70.0	−99.4	−124.6
Net other goods, services, and income	−5.3	−5.7	−5.85	−7.04	−9.39	−11.3
Private unrequited transfers	−0.1	−0.14	−0.07	−0.26	−0.25	−0.25
Official unrequited transfers	−0.3	−0.22	−0.33	−0.41	−0.85	−1.26
Net capital flows other than reserves	0.59	−0.09	−5.07	−7.77	−6.77	18.85
Net errors and omissions	−0.48	0.15	0.67	0.15	2.38	−3.12
Counterpart items	−0.09	−0.01	0.13	0.20	0.26	0.09
Total change in reserves	−0.78	3.79	6.68	10.17	−12.87	5.11
			Index (1975 = 100)			
Volume of exports	100	122	133	134	133	155
Volume of imports	100	108	111	119	132	124
Unit value of exports	100	99	98	92	102	114
Unit value of imports	100	103	100	82	107	150

EXHIBIT 6   UNITED STATES: BALANCE OF PAYMENTS (BILLIONS OF U.S. DOLLARS)

	1975	1976	1977	1978	1979	1980
Trade balance	9.1	−9.2	−30.9	−33.7	−27.3	−25.3
Merchandise: exports	107.1	114.8	120.8	142.1	184.5	224.0
Merchandise: imports	−98.0	−124.0	−151.7	−175.8	−211.8	−249.3
Net other goods, services, and income	14.1	18.9	21.7	24.8	35.0	36.5
Private unrequited transfers	−0.9	−0.9	−0.9	−0.8	−0.9	−1.1
Official unrequited transfers	−4.0	−4.4	−4.2	−4.7	−5.2	−6.5
Net capital flows other than reserves	−28.6	−25.3	−20.3	−28.9	−9.2	−41.2
Net errors and omissions	5.7	10.4	−0.6	11.7	21.2	29.8
Counterpart items	−0.5	0.0	0.2	−0.4	−2.8	0.6
Other	5.5	13.1	35.4	31.1	−13.6	14.9
Total change in reserves	0.4	2.6	0.4	−0.9	−2.8	7.7
			Index (1975 = 100)			
Volume of exports	100	104	104	115	126	138
Volume of imports	100	122	135	148	150	138
Unit value of exports	100	103	107	115	134	148
Unit value of imports	100	103	112	121	142	181

EXHIBIT 7 COMPARATIVE DATA

	1975	1976	1977	1978				1979				1980				1981		
				1	2	3	4	1	2	3	4	1	2	3	4	1	2	Aug.
Industrial production*																		
France	100	108	110	110	112	111	113	114	116	117	117	118	116	116	113	108	108	na
Japan	100	111	116	120	122	124	126	129	132	134	138	144	144	140	142	145	146	144
United States	100	111	117	120	123	126	128	129	129	129	129	129	123	121	127	129	130	130
Employment*																		
France	100	99	98	97	96	97	97	96	96	96	95	95	95	96	na	na	na	na
Japan	100	98	97	96	95	95	94	94	94	94	94	94	95	95	95	95	96	96
United States	100	103	107	110	112	113	115	116	117	117	118	118	118	117	118	119	119	119
Earnings per employee in manufacturing																		
France	100	117	133	145	149	155	159	166	173	177	184	191	200	207	214	222	229	na
Japan	100	113	123	128	131	133	135	135	139	141	143	144	148	150	152	152	159	158
United States	100	108	118	124	126	129	133	135	137	140	143	145	148	152	157	161	165	166
Money supply*																		
France	100	108	120	121	124	131	133	139	143	146	149	150	153	158	158	162	169	na
Japan	100	113	122	123	128	132	138	139	141	146	142	142	142	140	139	142	149	149
United States	100	106	115	118	120	122	124	124	126	129	131	133	134	137	136	131	na	na
Consumer prices																		
France	100	110	120	126	129	133	135	138	142	147	151	157	162	167	171	177	184	190
Japan	100	109	118	120	123	124	124	124	127	128	130	133	137	139	140	142	144	143
United States	100	106	113	117	120	123	125	128	133	137	141	147	152	155	159	163	168	171
Industrial prices																		
France	100	107	113	115	117	119	123	128	133	136	139	143	145	145	150	153	162	165
Japan	100	105	107	106	105	104	103	105	109	114	119	127	133	134	133	132	134	135
United States	100	105	111	115	119	121	124	128	133	137	142	148	151	156	159	164	168	169
Rates per U.S. dollar																		
French franc	4.49	4.97	4.71	4.58	4.50	4.33	4.18	4.30	4.29	4.10	4.02	4.08	4.09	4.20	4.52	4.96	5.72	5.82
Yen	305	293	240	222	205	189	195	209	217	223	240	250	218	212	203	211	226	228

EXHIBIT 7 COMPARATIVE DATA (continued)

	1975	1976	1977	1978	1979	1980	1981-I	1981-II	Nov. 1981
Short-term interest rates, %									
France	7.7	8.8	9.1	8.0	9.7	12.2	12.5	16.6	17.9
Japan	10.5	7.0	5.6	4.4	6.0	10.7	8.0	7.1	7.2
United States	6.2	5.3	5.7	8.5	11.2	13.1	15.5	16.9	17.3
Long-term interest rates, %									
France	11.0	11.0	11.6	11.3	11.2	14.3	15.0	15.4	17.9
Japan	9.7	8.8	7.2	6.1	7.8	8.5	8.3	8.1	10.9
United States	8.9	8.2	8.0	8.8	9.6	12.3	13.9	14.6	16.1

*Seasonally adjusted.
Source: *International Financial Statistics* (Washington D.C.: International Monetary Fund, November 1981).

EXHIBIT 8   SUMMARIES OF VARIOUS REPORTS

FRANCE*

President François Mitterrand is moving faster than his critics had feared in imposing far-reaching controls on France's economy. In doing so, his Socialist government may be headed for serious troubles starting in 1983, following a spurt of inflationary growth that is expected in the year ahead as a result of the government's expansionary spending and job-creating policies.

In an attempt to roll inflation back to 10 percent from its current annual rate of 14 percent and halt the erosion of the French franc, Finance Minister Jacques Delors on October 5 clamped a price freeze on basic products. He also took a long step toward imposing an "incomes policy" by announcing that he would confer with labor unions on moderating pay demands.

Withdrawal from the EMS? The moves are seen as part of a growing "radicalization" of the French economy by the government of Mitterrand, which is putting its main emphasis on creating jobs through growth rather than fighting inflation at a time when most other industrial countries are reining in their economies in order to curb spiraling prices. The resulting weakness of the franc, which fell from 22 cents at the beginning of the year to 18 cents on October 2, forced Mitterrand to devalue the franc within the European Monetary System (EMS). Initially, the franc strengthened again, but German bankers predict that further devaluations, possibly culminating in French withdrawal from the EMS, will be an almost inevitable consequence of Mitterrand's "dash for growth."

The centerpiece of Mitterrand's strategy is his first budget, unveiled on September 30, which envisages a $17 billion deficit for 1982, at least 50 percent higher than the 1981 deficit. Delors now says he will try to trim some outlays, but the Keynesian budget is complemented by measures last summer to give consumer spending a quick boost with a 10 percent increase in the minimum wage and big increases in social welfare.

The result next year, most forecasters agree, will be a spurt of real growth that should come close to the government's target of 3.3 percent after near-zero growth in 1981. For the sluggish economies of France's European trading partners, Mitterrand's pump priming may provide a welcome stimulus. But for France itself, economist Ulrich Schroder of Germany's Westdeutsche Landesbank warns, the program is "Socialist short-term policy designed to achieve quick, visible results" without considering the adverse consequences 2 or 3 years down the road. Adds Philippe Scheuer, economist for Data Resources International in Brussels: "The favorable effects of the [French government's] policy will be felt in 1982, and it is only after that they face problems. 1983 is the dangerous year. . . ."

*Based on "France, A Risky Speedup in Mitterrand's Timetable," *Business Week*, October 19, 1981, pp. 58–59.

EXHIBIT 8   (continued)

Numerous obstacles. Not all Europeans are so pessimistic. "I firmly believe the only way to encourage new investment is through growth, not restraint," says Ken E. Mathysen-Gerst, president of Geneva-based Capital International. "Inflation is a consequence, but it can be managed." Nevertheless, he warns, "the French transition is going to be Europe's most difficult question of the next two years."

Numerous obstacles may derail Mitterrand's strategy. One is the disparity between Mitterrand's expansionary internal policy and the sluggishness of the world economy. The risk is that imports will flood into France while exports languish, thus worsening a balance-of-payments deficit on current account that is running at a $7.9 billion annual rate. French attempts to slow the fall of the franc by strict exchange controls and a two-tier structure of interest rates are creating problems for the rest of Europe. There is also a basic contradiction between Mitterrand's vow to "reconquer the internal market" for French industries—a policy dubbed by Italian newspapers as "pink protectionism"—and the need to support open international markets for high-technology industries into which the government plans to pour resources. Equally contradictory are the goals of promoting an innovative and dynamic small- and medium-sized business sector while levying higher taxes on both income and capital.

The umbrella over such goals is a two-stage Socialist strategy for growth, starting with a 2-year push to create jobs and expand consumption. The second stage, following the extensive nationalizations, is a French version of supply-side economics that starts from very different premises than those of its U.S. counterpart. It is based on the judgment that the private sector has failed because, as stated in the preamble to the nationalization bill, "from 1974 through 1980, investment by public-sector enterprises rose 91% in volume, while private investment fell 5%." In this situation, says a top French official, government-controlled enterprises must "run against the tide" and develop long-term strategies that will produce spinoff benefits for private business.

JAPAN[†]

Early in 1981 the year continued to benefit in the exchanges from the rapid adjustment of Japan's economy to the second oil shock. Restrictive monetary and fiscal policies have successfully curtailed domestic demand, limited the buildup of inflationary expectations, and, together with moderate wage settlements, contained the impact of oil price increases on domestic costs. At the same time, changes in production processes under way since the mid-1970s have made industry less dependent on imported raw materials, particularly oil. These developments, together with the impact of the 1979–1980 depreciation of the yen, have led to a marked improvement in the current account, which has swung from a deep deficit to virtual balance. They also

[†]Based on "Treasury and Federal Reserve Foreign Exchange Operations," *Federal Reserve Bank of New York, Quarterly Review* 6, no. 3 (Autumn 1981): 52–54.

EXHIBIT 8 (continued)

---

have impressed international investors sufficiently to attract massive inflows of funds, particularly from OPEC investors eager to increase the share of yen-denominated assets in their portfolios.

Meanwhile, domestic demand has stalled, and with the improvement in Japan's external position, the authorities have begun to relax the tight stance of policy after mid-1980. Yet, by early 1981, consumption and residential construction continued to falter, and business fixed investment, previously the only domestic source of strength, was also decelerating rapidly. The growth of the monetary aggregates has slowed, and yen money market rates have softened. Inflationary pressures have eased, partly reflecting the dampening impact on import prices of the yen's appreciation, so that wholesale price inflation dropped from a year-on-year rate of 24 percent in the spring of 1980 to about 5 percent in early 1981. A major factor was the moderate 7 percent wage increases agreed to by the unions in 1980.

On March 17, the government introduced a fiscal package which accelerated budgeted public-works expenditures and provided low-cost financing to promote housing construction, to aid small companies, and to boost exports of industrial plants. But the authorities were also concerned that the large interest differentials adverse to the yen might trigger volatile capital outflows.

Pressures against the yen intensified considerably during July as the long-awaited decline in U.S. interest rates failed to materialize. With little prospect that large interest differentials adverse to the yen would narrow and that the currency would soon rebound against the dollar, a broad range of participants accelerated their sales of yen in an effort to limit losses. At the same time, foreign corporations stepped up short-term yen borrowings to meet financing needs in other currencies, while commercial leads and lags also shifted against the yen. As the flow of funds gathered force, the decline of the yen began to outpace the fall of the European currencies against the rapidly strengthening dollar. On July 31, the yen closed at ¥240, down 17 percent against the dollar since January.

UNITED STATES[‡]

The economy is entering a critical test period. After 6 months of essentially lateral movement, the big question now is whether cumulative deterioration will set in, tipping the nation into a new recession. Crucial, too, at this juncture is the direction that monetary and budget policies will take in a settling of nervous and unsettled financial markets.

Increased speculation that the economy is in a slump may be premature. There is no certainty that the small slippage in gross national product will continue in light of the lift that will be provided by the tax cuts and the growth in defense spending. The cause

---

[‡]Based on "Economy Watch," *The Morgan Guaranty Survey* (October 1981): 1–5.

EXHIBIT 8   (continued)

of the current softness is essentially Federal Reserve restraint. With that restraint now lessening, there is a good prospect that recessionary tendencies will not cumulate.

Fiscal policy, meanwhile, faces its own critical test. Scarcely 2 months after historic victories in cutting the budget, President Reagan came back with a second slice. The ultimate response in Congress seems unclear.

Since mid-July the demand for credit in the United States has been stubbornly strong in the face of high interest rates. The market seems impressed by Chairman Volcker's reaffirmation of the Federal Reserve's commitment to restrain monetary expansion. In addition, the market is increasingly concerned about the impact of the U.S. government's budget deficits and near-term financing requirements on U.S. financial markets. In this environment, interest rates remain high, and the dollar remains strong. Inflation continues at a 10 percent annual rate.

SIMMONS JAPAN LIMITED

In the waning hours of 1986, Mr. William W. Flanz, senior managing director and chief operating officer of Prudential Asia Investments Limited, left a New Year's Eve party in Hong Kong to take an urgent phone call from the United States. For the last 4 months, he had been engaged in intense and difficult negotiations with the Wesray Capital Corporation to purchase Simmons Japan Limited (SJL) from Wesray in a leveraged buyout involving Prudential Asia and Simmons Japan's management. With other potential buyers of SJL waiting in the wings, a sense of urgency had also pervaded the negotiations. Contributing to the sense of urgency was the opinion of a counsel that an agreement in principle had to be reached before the end of the year if advisory fees connected with the deal were to be deductible for tax purposes in 1986.

A preliminary structure for the deal had been worked out within Prudential Asia, but the final price and several other issues related to present and future equity positions in the company had yet to be resolved. Now, with this phone conversation, Mr. Flanz would seek to bring the negotiations to a point where the various parties concerned would exchange signed faxed copies of a letter of intent that would contain substantially all the terms of a purchase and sale agreement. If the buyout could be completed along the lines proposed by Prudential Asia, it would be the first deal of its kind in Japan and a prominent feather in Prudential Asia's cap.

This case was prepared by Research Associate Richard P. Melnick and Professor W. Carl Kester. Copyright © 1988 by the President and Fellows of Harvard College. Harvard Business School case 289-001.

COMPANY BACKGROUND

Simmons Japan was incorporated in Japan in 1964 as a joint venture between Simmons USA (Simmons) and Tokyo Bed. The joint venture was dissolved in 1966, and Simmons Japan became a wholly owned subsidiary of Simmons International, which was 100 percent owned by the Simmons Company. Recent financial statements for SJL are presented in **Exhibits 1** and **2**.

The parent company was based in Atlanta and manufactured beds, mattresses, and box springs. In October 1978 Gulf and Western Industries, Inc. (G&W), acquired 69 percent of the financially ailing Simmons Company for $93.1 million (G&W already owned 31 percent of Simmons's shares). G&W operated in three principal business areas: (1) financial services, (2) consumer and industrial products, and (3) entertainment and communications. Despite Simmons's poor performance and G&W's promise to restore it to financial health, Simmons's incumbent management was retained in its Atlanta headquarters.

In June 1985, G&W sold its Consumer and Industrial Products Groups to Wickes Co. for approximately $1 billion. As part of the group, the Simmons Company was wholly acquired by Wickes. Wickes's activities included lumber and building materials, general and apparel retailing, and food and drug operations. Wickes had filed for reorganization under Chapter 11 of the Bankruptcy Code in 1982 and emerged in early 1985 by completing the largest nonrailroad reorganization in U.S. business history. Though this acquisition stretched the newly reorganized Wickes's resources in the short term, it created the potential for a manufacturing and retailing empire with sales of $6 billion. Upon acquisition by Wickes, Simmons was legally reorganized to make the company more tax efficient.

Wickes then sold most of Simmons (including the Japanese subsidiary) to the Wesray Capital Corporation and members of Simmons's management for $120 million in October 1986. Wesray was a closely held, private investment firm based in Morristown, New Jersey, owned in part by former Treasury Secretary William E. Simon. One reason for the sale was Wickes's interest in focusing on building materials and home improvement stores. At the time of the transaction, Simmons had annual sales of approximately $350 million.

Simmons Japan Limited's Products

SJL produced a variety of pocket coil and open coil mattresses as well as box springs, all under the Simmons brand name. The premier product was the Beautyrest mattress, which combined strong brand image and the Simmons name to produce a high level of customer recognition. Other leading SJL products were the Dr. Hard and the My Health lines, both of which provided firm mattresses. SJL also sold accessories, headboards, and sheets that were manufactured by outside suppliers and sold as Simmons products. **Exhibit 3** shows a breakdown of sales by product line.

Production of SJL beds took place at one manufacturing facility in Zama City, 40 kilometers west of Tokyo. The factory was built in 1964 with 3700 square meters. An additional 3000 square meters were put into place in 1972. The plant was in good condition and was expected to accommodate the anticipated growth over the next 5 years. Manufacturing capacity was 300 pieces per day; SJL's warehouse could store 5000 pieces. The company consistently strived to improve manufacturing and assembly equipment to increase quality and decrease costs.

Markets and Competition

While 70 percent of the Japanese population still slept on traditional futons (a rectangular cushion rolled onto the floor for sleeping at night and put out of sight during the day), 30 percent were sleeping on spring mattresses in 1986. The Japanese spring bed market had grown 4 percent to 5 percent annually in the mid-1980s. France Bed (the only publicly listed Japanese manufacturer) dominated this market with a 40 percent to 45 percent share. Additional data on market shares within Japan are shown in **Exhibit 4**.

Though SJL controlled only 4 percent of the total market, the company dominated the premium-quality segment, with a 70 percent market share. Simmons's American image and the Beautyrest brand name helped SJL to maintain its foothold. By concentrating on high-quality Western styles, SJL targeted its products toward more affluent Japanese consumers seeking to upgrade their mattresses. A recent government decree that required new houses to include more space per person helped SJL because more Japanese would have room to accommodate Western-style bedding. Twenty percent of SJL's sales came from exports to Singapore and Hong Kong; the company's remaining sales were concentrated in Japan.

Distribution

Japanese retail stores were very demanding and often required suppliers to support the cost of floor space, to deal on a consignment basis, and sometimes to deliver merchandise C.O.D. to the purchaser. SJL had well-established relationships with two major and three smaller distributors. The distributors picked up the products at the factory, stored them at their warehouses, and delivered them to local stores. This system allowed SJL to avoid direct contact with retailers, to keep inventories at minimal levels, and to manage accounts receivable more easily. Consequently, distributors played an important role in marketing SJL products. The company had a sales office in Tokyo to enable quick access to major distributors.

Management

Among the eighty-four employees of SJL were five upper-level managers. Tormod Isetorp, president, 51 years old, was born and educated in Norway. He emigrated to the United States in 1960, worked for the International Division of the First National Bank of Boston, and then moved to the Bank of America. Later he worked for First Savings and Loan Association in San Francisco. In 1970 SJL asked him to take charge of the company. Despite initial difficulties during the early 1970s, Mr. Isetorp learned to speak Japanese, brought product design and production in-house, and assembled a harmonious Japanese management team.

Kazuo Kobaya, vice president, was 57, was married, and had two children. He worked for Chiyoda Textile Company, Pepsi-Cola Bottling Company, in which he rose to Vice President in 1970, and Ray-O-Vac Corporation as general sales manager. Joining SJL in 1981, he oversaw day-to-day operations and assisted Mr. Isetorp.

Kazuhiro Horie, production manager, worked for Mitsubishi Petro Chemical in accounting and then labor management. In 1969 he joined Daito Metal Industrial Company as a general manager assigned to improving labor/union relations. Since coming to SJL in 1980, he had improved quality, productivity, and labor relations. He was married, had three children, and was 52 years old.

Masanori Miura, comptroller/administration manager, worked as an accountant for Helena Rubenstein and later Baskin Robbins. At SJL, he started as a comptroller and designed an accounting system that conformed to the procedures of the parent company. As the administration manager, he promoted a harmonious relationship between management and staff. He was 46 and married with two children.

Masaharu Ichikawa, age 45, was domestic sales manager. He worked previously in the textile department of Sibel Hegner and Company in Yokohama and for the Continental Purchasing Company in Tokyo. He joined SJL in 1981 as sales manager and was responsible for SJL's relationships with its five distributors. Mr. Ichikawa was married and had two children.

PRUDENTIAL ASIA

Prudential Asia Investments Limited (PruAsia) was founded in 1986. It resulted from a combination of investment capital contributed by the Prudential Insurance Company of America and a business plan developed by four partners seeking to start an investment company that would also provide financial advisory services in Asia. Its services were directed primarily toward closely held family companies in the region. It sought to build a broadly diversified direct investment portfolio in the Asia-Pacific region. The initial investment focus was upon Korea, Japan, Taiwan, Hong Kong, Singapore, and Thailand.

PruAsia was led by the four founding principals, who collectively brought to the company more than 50 years of experience as financial and investment professionals in Asia. Dr. Victor K. Fung was the chairman and chief executive officer of PruAsia. He was a fourth-generation Hong Kong Chinese who lectured for a period at the Harvard Business School and then ran the family business, Li & Fung, before founding PruAsia. Douglas Fergusson, senior managing director, was born in India of Scottish parents and raised in Hong Kong, where he spent most of his professional career. He previously worked for Schroders Asia doing corporate and project finance. Michael Kwee, senior managing director and an Indonesian-born Chinese, was formerly director and senior vice president of America's International Assurance. Finally, William W. Flanz, senior managing director and chief operating officer, worked with many of the region's corporate leaders during the 19 years he was with the Chase

Manhattan Bank, ultimately as Chase's Asia-Pacific area director and senior vice president.

THE PROPOSED TRANSACTION

With the sale of Simmons to Wesray, Tom Isetorp seized the opportunity to attempt a purchase of SJL. Since Wesray had itself purchased Simmons with a considerable amount of debt financing, it seemed likely that it would be interested in selling some parts of Simmons as a means of reducing the debt burden. For his part, Tom Isetorp observed, "Our company has been very profitable for 13 consecutive years, and we wanted to expand our business even further on a long-range basis. However, the ownership of our parent company was changed three times during the past three years. We could not work out our own business strategy because of this merry-go-round ownership of the parent company. . . . We, therefore, wanted to become independent, but had no funds to do so. Then came Prudential Asia to help us."[1]

Wesray's need for cash, Simmons's dominant U.S. focus, and SJL's desire to control better its own destiny created the impetus for a management buyout. The problem was how to structure and finance the deal. Following preliminary discussions the following terms began to emerge within PruAsia as a serious leveraged buyout proposal for the other principals to consider:

1. SJL management would subscribe to $1 million of common stock in the newly purchased company, which would give it a 14 percent equity interest.

2. Senior debt totaling $12 million would be arranged by PruAsia prior to closing.[2]

3. PruAsia would also subscribe to $6 million of common stock (representing an 86 percent equity interest) and would finance the rest of the purchase price by underwriting a sufficient amount of subordinated debt prior to closing. Subsequent to closing, it was expected that 60 percent of the subordinated debt and 50 percent of PruAsia's equity interest would be sold to third-party investors.

The target capital structure for SJL following the closing and the specific terms of the debt are shown in **Exhibit 5**. The total capitalization assumes a $29 million purchase price (Wesray's asking price). Although specific third-party investors in the subordinated debt and equity had not been identified, it was hoped that a number of onshore and offshore institutions and wealthy individuals would find the investment attractive. Annual interest payments and the amortization schedules of the new debt are shown in **Exhibit 6**.

RISK AND EXPECTED RETURN

Mr. Flanz of PruAsia was interested in pursuing the deal along the proposed terms, provided, of course, he could be convinced that PruAsia's target pre-tax *dollar* return

---

[1]*Nikkan Gendai,* August 9, 1987.

[2]All debt, including subordinated debt, would be denominated in yen. In December of 1986, the yen-dollar exchange rate reached 160, down from a high of 260 in early 1985.

on capital of 20 percent to 25 percent for this sort of investment was realistically achievable. To aid in that assessment, management of SJL had presented PruAsia with a 5-year plan shown in **Exhibit 7**. This was considered a base case, founded on the assumption that SJL would maintain its current level of business activities with no major expansions. An optimistic scenario would see sales grow at 15 percent annually with 20 percent operating margins. A pessimistic scenario would probably entail 10 percent sales growth and 15 percent margins.

Not reflected in these forecasts were several changes in SJL's operations contemplated by Mr. Isetorp. In particular, Mr. Isetorp hoped to develop markets outside of Japan, Hong Kong, and Singapore and to set up a manufacturing base in Taiwan or Hong Kong. As a way of decreasing distributors' margins (estimated at ¥80 million annually), SJL also considered establishing an offshore distribution company to handle foreign sales. Finally, SJL had considered purchasing 51 percent ownership in a small but rapidly growing furniture company, or possibly setting up a joint venture with a major overseas furniture manufacturer to import and distribute wooden furniture in Japan. It was believed that these changes could diversify and improve SJL's revenue streams while lowering production and distribution costs.

Also not reflected explicitly in the forecasts were a number of risks. One major vulnerability was the concentration of SJL's domestic sales within Japan through a few major distributors. Two distributors alone controlled 93 percent of SJL's Japanese sales. Another vulnerability was that SJL's high-quality product meant it had relatively high production costs. Should a more efficient Japanese manufacturer or a low-cost, high-quality overseas supplier enter the market, SJL's market position could be threatened. Finally, as always, export sales were exposed to the effects of exchange-rate fluctuations. A strengthening yen in 1985 and 1986 had contributed to an 18 percent drop in export sales during the first 10 months of 1986. Exchange rates and interest rates prevailing at the end of 1986 are shown in **Exhibit 8**.

REACHING AGREEMENT

Although a preliminary framework for the financing of the deal had begun to take shape within PruAsia, several key points had yet to be resolved before the deal could be closed. Primary among these was the price to be paid for SJL. Wesray's asking price was $29 million. However, a consultant had advised PruAsia that $22 million was a more accurate appraisal. Most Japanese manufacturers of household furnishings traded in Tokyo at price/earnings multiples of forty to fifty times earnings. France Bed itself had a multiple of forty times earnings. American household furnishings producers sold in New York at multiples in the ten to fifteen range.[3]

Another point of negotiation was a possible continuing equity interest for Simmons USA. Wesray's first proposal to the investor group included the granting to Simmons

---

[3]Estimates of beta—a measure of systematic, nondiversifiable risk relative to a market portfolio of stocks—were not known for Japanese household furnishings producers. However, betas for comparable American producers (measured relative to the Standard & Poor's 500 Stock Index) ranged between .85 and .90 on an *unlevered* basis.

USA of a 5-year option to purchase up to 20 percent of the common equity of SJL on a pro rata basis from each of the original shareholders at an exercise price equal to the price paid by those shareholders for common stock upon execution of the buyout. It also proposed that Simmons USA nominate a director to SJL's board. By the end of December, Mr. Flanz had negotiated the size of the option to 10 percent of SJL's equity and had insisted on SJL's independence. The topic was still open to discussion, however.

Yet another area of concern for Mr. Flanz was the subordinated debt. Given the conservative lending practices of Japanese financial institutions, which generally loaned funds on a strictly senior and fully secured basis, placing the subordinated debt could prove to be problematic. What could be done in the event Japanese financial institutions balked at making an unsecured, subordinated loan?

THE ELEVENTH HOUR

Dressed in black-tie evening wear and surrounded by New Year's Eve celebrants, Mr. Flanz was now being called upon to address these issues. Given the long and difficult road that had brought the negotiating parties to this juncture, he was eager not to let the midnight deadline pass without reaching a final agreement. Were this to happen, the sense of urgency would be lost and negotiations might drag on until PruAsia was outmaneuvered or outbid by another buyer.

If agreement could be reached and the leveraged buyout completed, it would be the first transaction of its kind in Japan—a path-breaking deal that would garner PruAsia considerable exposure in its Asian market. For precisely this same reason, the deal also contained considerable risk for PruAsia: A poorly priced and executed deal would prove to be an embarrassment for the fledgling investment management company. With these thoughts in mind, Mr. Flanz left the party to take his call from Wesray.

EXHIBIT 1   INCOME STATEMENTS (IN MILLIONS)

	12 Months ended December 31*		12 Months ended June 30			
	1986	1985	1985	1984	1983	1982
Net sales	¥3006	¥2958	¥2803	¥2479	¥2347	¥2018
Cost of goods sold	(2026)	(1927)	(1828)	(1712)	(1621)	(1419)
Gross profit	980	1031	975	768	726	599
Total SG&A[†]	(466)	(474)	(455)	(357)	(318)	(277)
Other income/(expenses)	0	0	0	(2)	(2)	(1)
Operating income	514	557	520	409	406	321
Other interest income/(expense)	25	75	84	56	46	33
Other income/(expense)	(5)	(16)	(14)	(5)	(2)	19
Pre-tax income	534	616	590	460	450	374
Income tax	(397)	(266)	(353)	(264)	(259)	(212)
Net income	¥137	¥350	¥237	¥196	¥191	¥162
Margin (percentage of net sales)						
Gross profit	32.6%	34.9%	34.8%	31.0%	30.9%	29.7%
Operating income	17.1	18.8	18.6	16.5	17.3	15.9
Pre-tax income	17.8	20.8	21.0	18.5	19.2	18.5
Net income	4.6	11.8	8.5	7.9	8.1	8.0

*Fiscal yearend changed from June 30 to December 31 in 1985. If an agreement in principle to sell SJL could be reached before January 1, 1987, acquisition expenses of ¥161 million could be deducted from 1986 operating income for tax purposes. Depreciation charges for 1986 were approximately ¥21 million (casewriter's estimates).

†SG&A = Selling, general, and administrative expenses.

EXHIBIT 2   BALANCE SHEETS (IN MILLIONS)

	December 31		June 30			
	1986	1985	1985	1984	1983	1982
Assets						
Cash	¥331	¥1151	¥633	¥258	¥71	¥43
Marketable securities	35	0	284	351	702	259
Trade receivables	766	879	794	672	608	545
Inventories	199	164	219	212	193	217
Other current assets	86	94	18	18	23	23
Current assets	1417	2,288	1948	1511	1597	1087
Net property, plant, and equipment	214	221	233	253	251	270
Other assets	147	95	14	14	3	3
Due from parent company	0	0	454	486	208	400
Total assets	¥1778	¥2604	¥2649	¥2264	¥2,059	¥1760
Liabilities and equity						
Trade accounts payable	¥392	¥378	¥340	¥307	¥261	¥232
Accrued expenses	56	52	68	47	42	28
Income taxes payable	191	167	245	138	195	120
Current liabilities	639	597	653	492	498	380
Due to parent company	209	0	7	4	0	0
Pension liabilities	186	154	142	125	100	81
Deferred income taxes	0	0	(135)	(101)	(88)	(60)
Total liabilities	1034	752	667	520	510	401
Common stock	319	565	310	310	310	310
Legal reserve	78	59	0	0	0	0
Retained earnings	347	1228	1671	1434	1239	1048
Shareholders' equity	744	1852	1981	1744	1549	1358
Total liabilities and equity	¥1778	¥2604	¥2649	¥2264	¥2059	¥1760

Source: Corporate documents.

EXHIBIT 3   SALES BREAKDOWN BY PRODUCT

Product	% of Sales
1 Beautyrest	35.9
2 Headboards, frames, and night tables	30.7
3 Box springs	14.5
4 Open coils	12.7
5 Bed accessories	6.2
	100.0

Source: Corporate documents.

EXHIBIT 4   JAPANESE BEDDING MARKET SHARES

Company	Market share, %
1 France Bed	40
2 Nihon Bed	10
3 Toyota Bed	8
4 Dream Bed	6
5 Simmons Japan Limited	4
6 Suzuran	4
7 Tokyo	3
8 Annel	2
9 Others	23
	100

Source: Corporate documents.

EXHIBIT 5   TARGET CAPITAL STRUCTURE FOR SIMMONS JAPAN LIMITED
($ THOUSANDS; ¥ MILLIONS)[a]

Institution	Seven-year senior term note,[b] $	Ten-year subordinated term note,[c] $	Senior revolving credit[d]	Common stock	Total
PruAsia	—	$4,000	—	$3,000	$7,000
Investors	—	$6,000	—	$3,000	$9,000
Management	—	—	—	$1,000	$1,000
Financial institutions	$6,000	—	$6,000	—	$12,000
Total					
Dollars	$6,000	$10,000	$6,000	$7,000	$29,000
Yen	¥960	¥1,600	¥960	¥1,120	¥4,640

[a]All debt will actually be denominated in yen. The yen-dollar exchange rate in December 1986 averaged 160 yen per dollar and closed at 162.05.

[b]Seven-year yen term note bearing interest at 7.25 percent, to be amortized in six equal annual installments beginning at the end of 1988.

[c]Ten-year subordinated yen term note bearing interest at 9.5 percent, to be amortized by eight annual installments of ¥160 million ($1 million) each beginning at the end of 1988, with a ¥320 million ($2 million) balloon payment in 1996.

[d]Nonamortizing debt bearing interest at 1.25 percent over the yen commercial bills discount rate, currently 4.25 percent, i.e., gross 5.5 percent.

EXHIBIT 6 SCHEDULE OF INTEREST PAYMENTS AND PRINCIPAL AMORTIZATION FOR THE PROPOSED DEBT STRUCTURE (¥ MILLIONS)

	1987	1988	1989	1990	1991	1992	1993	1994	1995	1996
Seven-year term note, ¥										
Principal outstanding at start of year	¥960.0	¥960.0	¥800.0	¥640.0	¥480.0	¥320.0	¥160.0	—	—	—
Principal repayments	0.0	160.0	160.0	160.0	160.0	160.0	160.0	—	—	—
Pre-tax interest payments	69.6	69.6	58.0	46.4	34.8	23.2	11.6	—	—	—
Ten-year subordinated Term note, ¥										
Principal outstanding at start of year	¥1600.0	¥1600.0	¥1440.0	¥1280.0	¥1190.0	¥960.0	¥800.0	¥640.0	¥480.0	¥320.0
Principal repayments	0.0	160.0	160.0	160.0	160.0	160.0	160.0	160.0	320.0	
Pretax interest payments	152.0	152.0	136.8	121.6	106.4	91.2	76.0	60.8	41.8	30.4
Senior revolving credit*										
Principal outstanding at start of year	¥960.0	¥960.0	¥960.0	¥960.0	¥960.0	¥960.0	¥960.0	¥960.0	¥960.0	¥960.0
Principal repayments	—	—	—	—	—	—	—	—	—	—
Pre-tax interest payments	52.8	52.8	52.8	52.8	52.8	52.8	52.8	52.8	52.8	52.8

*Nonamortizing debt assumed to be fully utilized until term loans are repaid.

EXHIBIT 7   FIVE-YEAR PLAN FOR SIMMONS JAPAN LIMITED

	Year ending December 31 (millions)				
	1987	1988	1989	1990	1991
Domestic sales	¥2582	¥2960	¥3267	¥3610	¥4002
Exports	668	770	880	1034	1200
Total sales	3250	3730	4147	4644	5202
Gross profit	1092	1264	1465	1642	1842
Operating income*	537	642	726	812	911
Interest expense	(274)	(274)	(248)	(221)	(194)
Amortization[†]	(158)	(158)	(158)	(158)	(158)
Earnings before tax	105	210	320	433	559
Net income	44	88	134	182	235
Sales growth, %	9.7	14.8	11.2	12.0	12.0
Gross margin, %	33.6	33.9	35.3	35.4	35.4
Operating margin, %	16.5	17.2	17.5	17.5	17.5
Pre-tax margin, %	3.2	5.6	7.7	9.3	10.8
Net margin, %	1.4	2.4	3.2	3.9	4.5

	Year ending December 31 (thousands of U.S. dollars at ¥147 per dollar)				
	1987	1988	1989	1990	1991
Domestic sales	$17,565	$20,136	$22,224	$24,558	$27,224
Exports	4,544	5,238	5,986	7,034	8,163
Total sales	22,109	25,374	28,211	31,592	35,388
Gross profit	7,429	8,599	9,966	11,170	12,531
Operating income	3,653	4,367	4,939	5,524	6,197
Interest expense	(1,864)	(1,864)	(1,687)	(1,503)	(1,320)
Amortization[†]	(1,075)	(1,075)	(1,075)	(1,075)	(1,075)
Earnings before tax	714	1,429	2,177	2,946	3,803
Net income	299	599	912	1,238	1,599

*Pre-tax operating income includes depreciation charges of ¥35 million ($238,000) for each year beginning in 1987. Capital expenditures are expected to equal depreciation charges throughout the 5-year plan.

[†]Tax-deductible amortization of trademarks, patents, and technology. The anticipated annual amortization schedule for the items is ¥158 million ($1.075 million) for 1987–1991, ¥93 million ($632,000) for 1992–1996, and ¥12 million ($82,000) for 1997 and 1998.

EXHIBIT 8   EXCHANGE RATE AND INTEREST RATE DATA

Exchange rates (yen per dollar)	
Spot	162.05
Years forward	
1	157.15
2	152.50
3	148.00
4	143.60
5	139.35

Interest rates, %		
	Japan	United States
Domestic		
Treasury bills*	2.89	5.73
Long-term government bonds	4.61	7.79
Bank deposit rates	4.55	6.30
Corporate bonds[†]	5.93	8.88
Eurodeposits		
Three months	4.50	6.25
Twelve months	4.31	6.12

*Sixty-day, non-interest-bearing bills for Japan; 90-day bills for the United States.
[†]For Japan, the yield is that on NTT (Nypon Telephone and Telegraph) bonds maturing in March 1987; for the United States, it is the Salomon Brothers index of new issues yields for Aa industrial bonds with 5-year call protection.

NIPPON-WTI, LTD.

In the fall of 1985, Wafer Tools, Inc.'s board of directors was considering a proposal concerning the future operations of its Japanese joint venture, Nippon-WTI, Ltd. The proposal was to shift the joint venture's share of manufacturing Wafer Tools's chemical vapor deposition systems sold in Japan from 40 percent of the final product to 100 percent. Wafer Tools, by implication, would lose the profit contribution represented by its 60 percent share of the product's value added. This loss was to be compensated by an increase in the royalties received by Wafer Tools from the joint venture.

The proposal had come at a time when Wafer Tools was experiencing declining earnings and a languishing stock price, and when it was laying off workers in the United States. At the same time, it was targeting the Asian market in general as a major source of new growth for the company in the foreseeable future. In their deliberations, the directors had to determine if the proposal was financially acceptable in the short run while being consistent with Wafer Tools's Asian strategy in the long run.

BACKGROUND

Wafer Tools, Inc. (WTI), founded by Herman Westover in 1965, was an innovator and world leader in the silicon wafer fabrication and processing equipment industry. Its total revenues were $167 million and net income was $7.3 million in 1984. Historically, WTI had been a family-owned and -operated firm with a strong sense of

This case was prepared by Research Associate Glyn Ferguson under the supervision of Professor W. Carl Kester. Copyright © 1986 by the President and Fellows of Harvard College. Harvard Business School case 287-006.

commitment to its work force and to the quality of its products. Financial performance had become increasingly important since the company went public in 1972 and was listed on the American Stock Exchange in 1977.

Overseas operations accounted for 33 percent of WTI's sales and 51 percent of its operating profits in 1984. Exports from the United States constituted another 15 percent of sales in 1984 as well. **Exhibits 1** and **2** show recent financial statements for WTI and **Exhibit 3** presents a 5-year summary.

WTI described its fundamental business as the improvement of quality and productivity in the manufacture of semiconductors and semiconductor devices around the world. It sought dominance in this business through the development of innovative wafer fabrication equipment. WTI was a world leader in the production of a wide range of chemical vapor deposition (CVD) systems, which involve various techniques for thin-film deposition of conducting and insulating layers used to fabricate LSI/VLSI (Large Scale Integrations/Very Large Scale Integrations) bipolar and metal oxide semiconductor devices. Other products included wafer saws, wafer steppers (a basic tool used to transfer images onto silicon wafers), automatic sorter systems that measure wafer flatness, and automatic wire and die bonders.

Because the processes used by WTI's customers were highly sophisticated and complex, the equipment used therein had to perform with a high degree of accuracy and reliability. Hence, competition was based as much on product quality and service as on price.

WTI followed an aggressive distribution strategy in the Far East. It used local distributors in Korea, Singapore, Taiwan, and Hong Kong. The distributors purchased products directly from WTI and bore the inventory risks. In China, however, WTI sold products through representatives. A representative would find a customer and earn a commission only if and when a sale between WTI and the customer occurred. **Exhibits 4** and **5** provide some summary statistics for the worldwide market for wafer fabrication and processing equipment and for WTI's Asian markets, respectively.

Most of WTI's key competitors in Asia sold directly into these markets using neither distributors nor representatives. Only one other competitor used representatives in almost all of the Asian markets.

The years 1984 and 1985 were difficult ones for WTI due to the general slackening of worldwide demand for semiconductors. Semiconductor equipment manufacturers attributed the drop to the sluggish personal computer and computer peripherals market, which represented the largest portion of the consumer electronics market. Semiconductor sales in 1985 were estimated to have dropped by 19.5 percent from 1984 levels.

WTI reported a third-quarter loss in 1985 of $7.6 million compared to a $1.1 million loss in 1984. A loss of $1.2 million had also been posted in the second quarter of 1985. These losses were primarily due to drastic revenue declines. To control costs during this downturn, management sought to increase manufacturing efficiencies, improve manufacturing quality, and reduce the size of the work force. Two hundred fifty employees, or 15 percent of WTI's work force, were laid off in January 1985.

NIPPON SEMICONDUCTOR PRODUCTS, LTD.

In Japan, WTI followed a unique strategy through the establishment of a joint venture with Nippon Semiconductor Products, Ltd. In 1970 Nippon Semiconductor became WTI's sole Japanese distribution agent for CVD and wafer measurement systems. In 1979 a joint venture between the two companies was established, Nippon-WTI, Ltd., which manufactured a portion of the products sold by WTI in Japan. Nippon Semiconductor was the sole distributor of Nippon-WTI products in Japan.

Nippon Semiconductor was founded in 1964 by Ichiro Tanaka with financial backing from a major Japanese communications company. Nippon Semiconductor initially made its money from importing sophisticated semiconductor capital equipment from the United States and exporting low-technology Japanese electronics. In the 1960s, Nippon Semiconductor formed its first joint venture with Bipolar Technologies, a start-up U.S. manufacturer of integrated circuit devices. Bipolar agreed to transfer its technology to the Japanese joint venture and has since captured about 60 percent of the Japanese market for its devices. Nippon Semiconductor later repeated this arrangement with SK Industries, a U.S. producer of microtools used to assemble semiconductor equipment, and WTI. Thus, Nippon Semiconductor created its reputation by specializing in importing U.S. technology and creating joint ventures to help U.S. firms manufacture in Japan.

This specialization met with great success. Since 1980 Nippon Semiconductor's sales rose from $121 million to $333 million in 1984, while net income rose from $5.2 million to $20 million during the same period. About 10 percent of the Wafer Equipment Division's sales were generated by the Nippon-WTI joint venture in 1984.

THE JAPANESE JOINT VENTURE

Nippon-WTI was initially established in 1979 as a fifty-fifty joint venture to manufacture CVD systems. WTI had recognized the tremendous growth opportunities of the wafer equipment market in Japan and wanted to capture as large a share of this market as possible.

Although WTI's products faced relatively little Japanese competition in 1979, management did not believe this situation would persist indefinitely. They had observed other U.S. companies with large market shares in Japan ultimately fail due to the rise of small, aggressive local competitors. In light of this, and recognizing the Japanese cultural preference for purchasing from local vendors with customized products, WTI concluded that a Japanese partner would be a prerequisite to penetrating and holding the Japanese market.

The joint venture agreement followed a traditional pattern. The initial paid-in capital of the joint venture was ¥30 million, represented by 60,000 shares of common stock. The two parents each purchased 30,000 shares for ¥15 million in cash and were unable to sell, transfer, pledge, or dispose of any joint venture shares without the approval of the board of directors. The board consisted of three Nippon Semiconductor nominees and three WTI nominees. From the outset, it was anticipated that the joint venture would eventually become an independent business enterprise. It was also agreed that the profits generated in the first 2 years would be reinvested in the joint venture.

Nippon-WTI was granted the exclusive license to manufacture WTI's products in Japan using WTI's technology and in conformity with WTI's specifications. The products were to be sold exclusively by Nippon Semiconductor. The initial product series manufactured was the WTC 7500 CVD system. By 1984, this series had captured a 50 percent share of the market for such systems in Japan. WTI also started testing and evaluating procedures for manufacturing and selling other wafer fabrication and processing systems in Japan through the joint venture.

When the joint venture was established, WTI shipped the systems in kit form to Japan, where they were manufactured and assembled. Using this approach, WTI accounted for 60 percent of the product's standard manufactured value before Nippon Semiconductor's markup, and Nippon-WTI accounted for 40 percent. The standard contribution margins earned by WTI, Nippon Semiconductor, and the joint venture, given this manufacturing split, are shown in **Table 1**.

TABLE 1   STANDARD GROSS MARGIN CALCULATIONS*

	WTI	Nippon-WTI	Total U.S. list price	Nippon Semiconductor
Contribution to value added	60	40	100	115[†]
Internal discount (15%)[†]	(9)	(6)	(15)	—
Net price	51	34	85	115
Cost of goods sold	(24)	(16)	(40)	(85)
Gross margin	27	18	45	30

*Expressed as a percentage of U.S. list price.
[†]Nippon Semiconductor typically purchased systems from the joint venture at a 15 percent discount from U.S. list price and resold them at a 15 percent premium over U.S. list price. Although final sales prices were always negotiated between Nippon Semiconductor and the final customer, it was believed that 20 percent was the minimum gross margin that Nippon Semiconductor would be willing to accept.

In addition to earning a gross margin on shipments to Nippon-WTI, WTI received a royalty from the joint venture as well as having a claim on 50 percent of profits after tax. The royalty was set at 5 percent of the joint venture's net sales to Nippon Semiconductor. All sales from WTI to Nippon-WTI were billed in U.S. dollars, while the royalty payments were transferred in yen from the joint venture to WTI.[1] All profits were retained in the joint venture. Thus, the cash received by WTI was exclusively from the sale of kits and the payment of royalties. **Exhibit 6** shows WTI's quarterly sales to the joint venture and Nippon Semiconductor's final sales of CVD systems to Japanese customers. Nippon-WTI financial statements are shown in **Exhibits 7** and **8**.

[1]The royalty was subject to a 10 percent withholding tax in Japan. However, WTI could claim a credit for this tax in the United States.

THE PROPOSAL

Earlier in 1985, Nippon Semiconductor suggested to WTI that their joint venture be allowed to control 100 percent of CVD system production sold in Japan rather than just the 40 percent of value added to which they were presently limited. There was little in the way of productivity gains to prompt such a move. Rather, it was believed that complete local production would afford better control over quality, allow Nippon Semiconductor to respond better to the demands of Japanese end-users, and generally increase the marketability of the product within Japan. The local Japanese manager of Nippon-WTI reported that he felt hindered by the 60/40 split in producing a high-quality product, a problem that could be corrected if he had complete control.

The proposal came as no surprise to WTI since it had been understood from the outset that such a possibility would at least be studied at some point in the life of the joint venture. It was, however, somewhat earlier in its arrival than had originally been anticipated.

A change in the share of production held by WTI would necessitate a restructuring of the joint venture agreement. Specifically, WTI would need a higher royalty to compensate for its lost contribution on sales to the joint venture. This increase would have to be approved by the Japanese government (specifically, the Bank of Japan and the Japanese Fair Trade Commission), and the royalty itself would probably have to continue to be paid in yen (see **Exhibit 9** for recent trends in the yen-dollar exchange rate and other key economic variables). WTI's existing royalty of 5 percent was regarded as typical for most U.S. joint ventures in Japan.

EXHIBIT 1 WAFER TOOLS, INC., AND SUBSIDIARIES—STATEMENT OF CONSOLIDATED INCOME (THOUSANDS, EXCEPT PER SHARE DATA)

	Years ended		
	December 29, 1984	December 31, 1983	January 1, 1983
Net sales and service revenues	$166,384	$151,150	$125,409
Cost of products and services sold	76,353	65,619	58,110
Gross margin	90,031	85,531	67,299
Operating expenses			
Selling, general, and administrative	56,294	47,857	41,820
Research and development	27,492	20,812	16,120
Operating income	6,245	16,862	9,359
Other income (expense)			
Interest income	1,031	2,441	766
Interest expense	(1,421)	(1,306)	(2,717)
Other, net	826	(540)	145
Income from continuing operations before income taxes	6,681	17,457	7,553
Income taxes (benefit)	(651)	4,364	1,693
Income from continuing operations	7,332	13,093	5,860
Loss on disposal of discontinued division	—	—	(398)
Net income	$7,332	$13,093	$5,462
Per share amounts, $			
Income from continuing operations	$0.45	$0.83	$0.45
Loss on disposal of discontinued division	—	—	(0.03)
Net income	$0.45	$0.83	$0.42

Source: 1984 Annual Report.

EXHIBIT 2   WAFER TOOLS, INC., AND SUBSIDIARIES—CONSOLIDATED BALANCE SHEET
(THOUSANDS)

	December 29, 1984	December 31, 1983
Assets		
Current assets		
Cash and equivalents	$1,687	$18,465
Accounts receivable, less allowances		
of $1372 and $1015	54,140	50,340
Inventories	62,865	50,196
Refundable income taxes	894	3,370
Other current assets	7,184	5,149
Total current assets	126,770	127,520
Fixed assets		
Property and equipment, net	45,350	26,721
Other assets	4,942	4,040
Total assets	$177,062	$158,281
Liabilities and stockholders' equity		
Current liabilities		
Notes payable to banks	$6,671	$3,421
Trade accounts payable	9,339	13,035
Accrued liabilities	8,210	6,636
Accrued compensation and employee benefits	4,948	6,066
Income taxes payable	649	2,113
Current portion of deferred income taxes	53	3,828
Current portion of long-term debt and		
capital lease obligations	1,179	1,111
Total current liabilities	31,049	36,210
Long-term liabilities		
Long-term debt and capital		
lease obligations	19,318	6,122
Deferred income taxes	3,831	1,513
Accrued pensions	1,508	816
Total long-term liabilities	24,657	8,451
Stockholders' equity		
Common stock, $1 par value		
authorized 60,000,000 shares;		
issued and outstanding 10,584,000		
and 10,392,000 shares	10,584	10,392
Additional paid-in capital	62,508	60,009
Retained earnings	52,072	45,796
Equity adjustment from foreign-		
currency translation	(3,808)	(2,577)
Total stockholders' equity	121,356	113,620
	$177,062	$158,281

Source: 1984 Annual Report.

EXHIBIT 3   WAFER TOOLS, INC.—5-YEAR FINANCIAL SUMMARY

	Income data (millions)				
	1980	1981	1982	1983	1984
Revenues	$112	$113	$125	$151	$166
Operating income	11	8	9	17	6
Capital expenditures	16	6	7	10	26
Depreciation	3	5	6	5	6
Interest expense	2	5	2	1	1
Net income	7	2	5	13	7
Operating income as % of revenues	10%	7%	7%	11%	4%
Net income as % of revenues	6	2	5	9	4

	Balance sheet data (millions)				
Cash	$2	$2	$2	$19	$2
Current assets	75	79	77	127	127
Total assets	99	105	100	158	177
Current liabilities	23	24	27	36	31
Long-term debt	26	30	5	6	19
Common equity	50	50	66	114	121
Total capital	76	80	71	120	140
Current ratio	3.3	3.3	2.9	3.5	4.1
Long-term debt as % of capital	34%	38%	7%	5%	14%
Return on assets, %	7	2	5	8	4
Return on equity, %	14	4	8	11	6

EXHIBIT 4   WORLDWIDE PURCHASES OF WAFER FABRICATION AND PROCESSING EQUIPMENT (1983)

	Size of worldwide market: $865 million			
	United States	Western Europe	Japan	Rest of world
Size of geographic segment, millions	$500	$175	$150	$40
Historic market growth (1980–1983)	19.5%	5.5%	20.2%	35.4%
WTI revenue growth (1980–1983)	20.7%	4.4%	65.6%	66.8%

EXHIBIT 5 FAR EAST

	Japan	Korea	China	Singapore	Taiwan	Hong Kong
Population (1984—millions of people)	130	50	1100	2.5	19	5
Gross national product (1984—billions)	$1137	$63	$250	$13	$46	$25
Electronic equipment production (1984—billions)	$75.5	$4.3	$20.0	$2.4	$4.3	$2.9
Growth per annum (1981–1984)	23%	49%	12%	14%	2.7%	1%
Wafer Tools revenues (1984—millions)	$15.5	$3.2	$2.0	$1.5	$1.4	$1.2
Growth (1981–1984)	22%	93%	268%	185%	60%	187%

EXHIBIT 6 WAFER TOOLS, INC.'S SALES TO JOINT VENTURE (THOUSANDS)

Quarter ended	Gross sales	Discount	Net sales	Cost of sales	Gross margin	Nippon Semiconductor to end consumer gross sales
March 31, 1982	$2116	$315	$1801	$942	$859	$981
June 30, 1982	1836	308	1528	822	706	1645
September 30, 1982	2681	418	2263	1031	1232	1037
December 31, 1982	631	95	536	186	350	957
March 31, 1983	614	92	522	221	301	1341
June 30, 1983	542	81	461	175	286	504
September 30, 1983	1361	204	1157	477	680	2375
December 31, 1983	855	128	727	233	494	704
March 31, 1984	746	112	634	212	422	1723
June 30, 1984	723	109	614	183	431	1254
September 30, 1984	1371	205	1166	324	842	1587
December 31, 1984	721	108	613	205	408	1172
March 31, 1985	2027	304	1723	480	1243	2391
June 30, 1985	901	135	766	230	536	949
September 30, 1985	1052	157	895	237	658	2242

EXHIBIT 7 **NIPPON-WTI'S BALANCE SHEET (SEPTEMBER 30, 1985) (EXCHANGE RATE: ¥216.00/US$)**

	¥	US$
Assets		
Current assets		
Cash and deposit	¥96,260,293	$445,650
Accounts receivable—trade	124,887,011	578,181
Inventories	828,829,919	3,837,176
Prepaid expenses	6,904,572	31,966
Other current assets	1,101,617	5,100
Less: allowance for doubtful accounts	(980,490)	(4,539)
Total current assets	1,057,002,922	4,893,534
Fixed assets		
Tangible fixed assets		
Buildings	8,407,704	38,925
Machinery and equipment	16,136,592	74,706
Cars	1,671,694	7,739
Tools, furniture and fixtures	130,767,623	605,406
Intangible fixed assets	804,069	3,723
Long-term investments	395,000	1,829
Total assets	¥1,215,185,604	$5,625,862
Liabilities		
Current liabilities		
Accounts payable—trade	¥56,621,867	$262,138
Accounts payable—others	26,632,480	123,299
Loans payable (short-term)	667,000,000	3,087,963
Reserve for employees' bonuses	22,744,700	105,300
Income taxes payable	90,777,157	420,265
Other current liabilities	4,653,012	21,542
Total current liabilities	868,429,216	4,020,507
Fixed liabilities		
Reserve for retirement allowances	13,100,000	60,648
Capital stock		
Paid-in capital	30,000,000	138,889
Surplus		
Reserve for special depreciation	3,000,000	13,889
Unappropriated profit end of period	300,656,388	1,391,929
Total net worth	346,756,388	1,605,355
Total liabilities and capital	¥1,215,185,604	$5,625,862

EXHIBIT 8 **NIPPON-WTI'S INCOME STATEMENT FOR YEAR ENDED SEPTEMBER 1985 (AVERAGE EXCHANGE RATE: ¥229.92/US$)**

	¥	US$
Net sales	¥2,213,683,240	$9,628,059
Cost of goods sold	1,682,843,422	7,319,256
Gross margin	530,839,818	2,308,803
Operating expenses		
Research and development	60,000,000	261,184
Corporate, general, and administrative	185,093,739	805,035
Operating income	285,746,079	1,242,584
Nonoperating expenses/income		
Interest expense	31,816,191	138,379
Interest income	4,808,043	20,912
Income before tax	258,737,931	1,125,117
Extraordinary profits	12,147,529	52,834
Extraordinary losses	343,172	1,493
Taxes on income*	133,740,837	581,684
Net income	¥136,801,451	$594,774

*Assuming no dividend payout, the statutory marginal tax rate on Japanese corporations is typically 55 percent, consisting of a 42 percent corporate income tax rate and approximately 13 percent of various prefectual and other local taxes. Due to a high degree of tax conformity in accounting principles, essentially all reported taxes are current taxes in Japan.

EXHIBIT 9   EXCHANGE RATES AND SELECTED STATISTICS

	United States			
	1984 IV	1985 I	1985 II	1985 III
Interest rates				
Money market rates	9.27%	9.69%	7.92%	7.90%
Long-term government bond yields	11.74%	11.58%	10.81%	10.34%
Consumer price index (1982 = 100)	109.10	110.30	111.50	112.20
Real effective exchange rate*				
(1980–1982 = 100)	124.00	129.60	124.70	117.90
	Japan			
Interest rates				
Money market rates	6.39%	6.31%	6.35%	6.40%
Long-term government bond yields	6.42%	6.83%	6.39%	6.09%
Consumer price index (1982 = 100)	105.20	105.30	106.20	106.10
Real effective exchange rate*				
(1980–1982 = 100)	95.70	94.00	92.10	95.50
Nominal exchange rate, ¥/$	246.13	250.30	248.52	229.89
Premiums (against $) on 3-month				
forward exchange rates (annualized)	1.85	4.15	1.56	3.56

*Calculated on the basis of a trade-weighted basket of currencies. A rise in the index indicates appreciation of the real exchange rate and fall indicates depreciation.

Sources: *International Financial Statistics* (Washington, D.C.: International Monetary Fund, 1985); *World Financial Markets (New York: Morgan Guaranty Trust Company, 1986).*

MERCK-BANYU

On Wednesday, August 3, 1983, Merck & Co., Inc., of the United States announced that it had agreed to purchase a controlling interest in Banyu Pharmaceutical Co., Ltd. of Japan for ¥75.8 billion ($313.5 million). The transaction was to take the form of a new issue of 74 million Banyu common shares and a new issue of dollar-denominated bonds convertible between July 1, 1984, and September 25, 1998, into an additional 40 million Banyu common shares. Upon conversion of the bonds, Merck would own 50.02 percent of the company. Banyu was among the twelve largest pharmaceutical companies in Japan. Its acquisition by Merck represented the first acquisition by non-Japanese interests of a controlling stake in a firm listed on the prestigious First Section of the Tokyo Stock Exchange. Merck chairman John J. Horan stated that Merck planned to continue Banyu's Japanese style of management and had no immediate plans to merge Banyu with Merck's other Japanese interests.

MERCK & CO.

Merck was one of the world's largest manufacturers of ethical (prescription) pharmaceuticals. The company had worldwide sales in 1982 of $3.1 billion of which $140 million were generated in Japan. Net income in fiscal 1982 was $415 million. Merck's financial statements are given in **Exhibits 1** through **3**.

Merck had long been known for its commitment to research and new product development (R&D). During the 1970s, Merck's expenditures on research represented

This case was prepared by Professor Timothy A. Luehrman. Copyright © 1987 by the President and Fellows of Harvard College. Harvard Business School case 287-061.

about 8.5 percent of sales compared to an industry average of 5.8 percent. By 1982, the company had the most expensive R&D program of any U.S. pharmaceutical concern. Expenditures reached $330 million (9.4 percent of sales) in 1982 and were projected to rise to 11 percent of sales in 1983.

Merck's recently increased R&D effort reflected two strategic decisions: to commit the company's future to new product development and to redirect its emphasis in basic research from chemistry to applied life sciences. In 1975 Dr. P. Roy Vagelos, then chairman of the biochemistry department at Washington University in St. Louis, was hired to be president of Merck Sharp & Dohme Research Laboratories. Dr. Vagelos's objective was to direct Merck's research efforts toward applications of breakthroughs in biology, biochemistry, and computer technology to the development of commercial pharmaceutical products. By 1983, Merck had sixty-five new drug compounds in the clinical—or human—stage of testing that all new human pharmaceutical products had to undergo. Of these, eighteen to twenty were considered to be in the final 3 years of testing. (Industry analysts estimated that 25 percent to 30 percent of compounds that reach the clinical stage of testing eventually receive regulatory approval for sale.)

Merck's Japanese Operations

Like most of its major competitors, Merck had extensive international operations. These were grouped within its Merck Sharp & Dohme International (MSDI) division and accounted for 44 percent of Merck's total sales in 1982. The company's long-term goal was to be first or second in market share in each of the world's major ethical drug markets. In March 1983, Merck ranked first in North America, fifth in Europe, and thirtieth (30th) in Japan.

Merck's business interests in Japan consisted of various licensing agreements; a joint venture, Nippon Merck-Banyu (NMB); a wholly owned subsidiary, MSD Japan; and equity interests in two Japanese pharmaceutical companies, Banyu and Torii Pharmaceutical. NMB was formed in 1954 to manufacture and distribute Merck products. MSD Japan was formed in 1970 to perform administrative tasks and was not permitted to engage in manufacturing. During 1982, Merck purchased 5 percent of Banyu's common shares on the open market. In the same year, Merck purchased 30 percent of Torii, a much smaller firm (4 days after announcing its acquisition of Banyu, Merck announced that it had agreed to purchase an additional 20.5 percent of Torii).

THE U.S. PHARMACEUTICAL INDUSTRY

In 1983 the U.S. market for human pharmaceuticals was the largest in the world, with retail sales of $26.7 billion (37 percent of world retail sales). Of this total, $19.6 billion reflected prescription drugs and the remaining $7.1 billion over-the-counter preparations. Just over 15 percent of the (total) pharmaceuticals market was supplied by subsidiaries of non-U.S. concerns, most of which were based in Europe. See **Exhibit 4** for sales figures of the world's twenty largest pharmaceutical concerns.

The prescription drug segment of the pharmaceuticals market could be further subdivided into therapeutic classes according to the prescriptive decisions made by physicians. These classes included, for example, antiarthritics, antibiotics, antispasmodics, etc. Competition among products generally took place within rather than across these classes. Physicians were called upon by the sales representatives (''detailers'') of the pharmaceutical companies and relied on these representatives for information about a drug's therapeutic properties. Firms' greatest marketing efforts were directed at doctors, who prescribed specific drugs according to medical diagnoses. Patients then purchased these products from a retail pharmacist or from a hospital or clinic.

The profits of many large drug companies reflected to a great extent the success of a small number of products, generally protected by patents granted by the U.S. government for a term of 17 years. A successful product could result in annual worldwide sales of more than $100 million (SmithKline's Tagamet, a treatment for stomach ulcers, had estimated worldwide sales in 1981 of $640 million; Merck's largest seller was Aldomet, for high blood pressure, with estimated worldwide sales in 1981 of $278 million). Operating margins were large by conventional standards—60 percent to 70 percent before selling, general, and administrative (SG&A) and R&D expenditures was not unusual. These high margins compensated firms for investments in R&D and promotion and for long lags between investments and the realization of returns. Successful products attracted considerable competition as other companies tried to ''invent around'' the patent or prepared to offer generic substitutes as patent protection expired. Thus, most large companies maintained significant R&D programs to keep new, patentable products coming onstream.

The Product Development Process

A successful new drug had to pass through three phases: basic research and discovery; applied research and development; and manufacture and distribution. Basic research and discovery involved the search for advancements in general pharmacological knowledge and the synthesis of new substances. Newly discovered or invented compounds, called ''new chemical entities'' (NCEs), could be patented during this stage. Similarly, new uses for existing compounds could be discovered and were patentable as well.

Applied research and development involved biological (animal) and clinical (human) testing of a drug to establish pharmacological activity and determine adverse effects. At the same time, dosage and dosage forms were determined and manufacturing processes explored and evaluated. Applied research and development was estimated to require, on average, four times the money and time spent on basic research for a given compound.

Manufacturing and distribution was undertaken after regulatory approval was obtained. This phase included manufacturing, pricing, distribution to pharmacies, hospitals, and clinics, and the education of physicians about the drug's therapeutic benefits and side effects.

Worldwide, the resources devoted to the first two phases of new product development had risen steadily in real terms since the 1960s. This trend was especially evident in the United States (see **Exhibit 5A** and **B**) and was thought to reflect two major trends. First, the increase in research opportunities brought about by scientific advancements expanded the scope of drug research and required large expenditures on sophisticated laboratories, equipment, and personnel. Second, increased regulation of the drug approval process required more and more expensive testing.

The decision by Merck to redirect its research toward applied life sciences rather than applied chemistry reflected a move in this direction by several companies. Within the industry, this research strategy was described as relying on logic rather than serendipity. At worst it was thought to reduce the number of substances that had to be examined (working by trial and error, companies had to synthesize and screen an average of roughly 10,000 compounds in order to find one marketable drug); at best the approach would lead directly to new discoveries and inventions. Nevertheless, some analysts felt that this approach to new-product development was unproven and therefore risky. They argued that so far the total number of new drugs discovered using pure logic was two: Inderal and Tagamet, both discovered by Sir James Black of the United Kingdom's Wellcome Foundation and the University College London.

Regulation of the U.S. Market

New drug products had to be approved prior to sale in the United States by the Food and Drug Administration (FDA), an agency of the U.S. government. Pharmaceutical companies were required to submit to the FDA a New Drug Application (NDA), which was to contain data documenting a new product's safety and efficacy, as well as specifying dosages, dosage forms, and manufacturing processes. In addition, the FDA had broad authority to regulate many aspects of the clinical testing that led to submission of an NDA, including safety and quality control standards in manufacturing and laboratory facilities. Finally, U.S. law prohibited the export of products not approved by the FDA, regardless of whether such products had been approved by authorities in the importing country.

The FDA was subjected to lobbying pressure by two groups of critics. One group advocated tighter regulation as new drugs were increasingly powerful and new technologies, such as genetic engineering, were thought to be potentially dangerous. Another group, which included many drug companies, charged that the FDA's burdensome regulations made innovation slow and expensive, endangering U.S. leadership in biotechnology and the international competitiveness of U.S. pharmaceutical firms.

In 1980, the U.S. General Accounting Office estimated that the mean time between submission of an NDA and approval by the FDA was 23 months. The comparable figure for the United Kingdom was 5 months. Industry executives estimated that developing a major new drug in the United States required $70 million to $90 million and 7 to 9 years, about twice the time and money required in Japan. Some 80 percent of the time and expense was associated with the applied research and development phase of new product development. Industry executives argued that the lag between discovery and approval effectively cut the term of U.S. patent protection in half.

THE JAPANESE PHARMACEUTICAL INDUSTRY

In 1982, Japanese per capita consumption of pharmaceuticals was the highest in the world and the Japanese market was second in size, at $12 billion (1983 estimate), to the U.S. market. In some therapeutic classes, such as antibiotics, the Japanese market ranked first in size as well. Overall, Japan accounted for 25 percent of the world market for ethical drugs.

The Japanese market was served by some 2000 firms, none of which had a market share as high as 7 percent. This contrasted sharply with other major markets, in which one or more large firms each might claim as much as 10 percent to 15 percent of the market. In Japan, most foreign companies operated through joint ventures with Japanese partners, although, by 1983, some had begun to operate independently. (Prior to 1975, foreign companies were prohibited from manufacturing pharmaceuticals in Japan.) Most of these joint ventures relied on the Japanese partner for distribution and none of the ventures had a market share of more than 2 percent. In 1983, the total market share held by all foreign operations in Japan was less than 13 percent (see **Exhibit 6**).

Production and sales of pharmaceuticals were strictly regulated by an agency of the Japanese government, Koseisho, and were greatly affected by the mechanics of the government-administered National Health Scheme (NHI). Under this plan, physicians prescribed and sold drugs to their patients at official NHI prices set by Koseisho. Patients were reimbursed by the government for substantially all of the price of each prescription. Doctors purchased drugs from wholesalers and profited by the difference between the wholesale price of the drug and the official retail price paid by patients. For many drugs, this retail margin was significant and sales of pharmaceuticals often accounted for as much as half of doctors' incomes.

Pharmaceutical manufacturers in Japan employed sales representatives (''propas'') who called on physicians and wholesalers to sell the companies' product lines. Important customers might be visited daily; most accounts were called upon at least once per week. This frequency was roughly four times the typical rate in the United States. Distribution of drugs in Japan therefore required a large sales force of propas. Estimates of the sizes of some companies' forces are given in **Exhibit 7**.

Changes in the Japanese Regulatory Environment

Two major changes had recently occurred in the Japanese regulatory environment. Both were expected to encourage Japanese drug companies to be more innovative.

In 1975, Japanese patent law was revised. Prior to 1975, a Japanese firm could legally produce another company's patented drug if it could find a different manufacturing process for doing so. The law was changed to close this loophole and protect investments in research.

At the end of the 1970s, Koseisho introduced the practice of regularly reviewing the NHI prices of prescription drugs and began to lower some dramatically. Products which were older or viewed as less effective were subject to repeated downward revisions of their prices. Generic and ''me-too'' drugs were subjected to the same treatment. Newer, more innovative, or more promising drugs were able to command their traditional high markups. The policy, as announced by the Ministry of Health and Welfare, was intended to help control national health care costs by lowering expenditures on pharmaceuticals and encouraging the development of new drugs that could be substituted for more expensive types of health care, such as hospitalization.

The combined effects of these policy changes put intense pressure on smaller drug wholesalers and manufacturers, most of whom relied on narrow product lines of older products, often licensed from other major foreign and domestic pharmaceutical companies. Faced with declining profitability of established products, many of these firms also lacked the resources to develop major new products. At the same time, larger firms increased R&D expenditures dramatically; by 1982, these expenditures had reached 7 percent to 10 percent of sales, more than double the historical rate. By 1983, it was clear that these efforts were paying off as Japanese firms assumed world leadership in the invention of new substances. See **Exhibit 8** for figures on the introduction of new substances by country of inventor.

Further regulatory changes were possible. Many Japanese companies were eager to sell newly developed products abroad. At the same time, many foreign companies hoped to do business in Japan and complained that the Japanese market was effectively closed to outsiders. Both the U.S. FDA and Japan's Koseisho had long resisted accepting data from clinical tests performed outside their jurisdictions. In 1982, Koseisho agreed to accept clinical test data performed in the United States, but only if the test subjects were Japanese citizens living in the United States. Most U.S. drug companies considered this an unhelpful concession. Japanese companies familiar with FDA regulations judged them to be just as protective. Some firms had begun to lobby for the adoption of international standards for safety and efficacy and international recognition of clinical test results.

BANYU PHARMACEUTICAL CO., LTD.

Banyu was nearly as old as the modern pharmaceutical industry. It was founded in 1915 by Toru Iwadare, a chemistry graduate student at Tokyo University, to manufacture the drug Salvarsan after hostilities in Europe hampered imports into Japan. By the time World War II broke out, Banyu had become well established in Meguro, Tokyo, and Iwadare had developed many contacts abroad in the emerging pharmaceutical industry.

In 1945 Banyu was ordered to undertake the manufacture of penicillin as part of the war effort. The continued importance of penicillin after the war gave Banyu a high priority in the post-war allocation of capital and raw materials. The company was thus able to rebuild itself more quickly than many Japanese industrial concerns. In 1950, Iwadare visited the United States and renewed his contacts with the U.S. pharmaceutical industry. That same year, Banyu received from Merck a license to market streptomycin in Japan. Three years later the companies concluded a similar agreement for cortisone, Merck's promising new hormone.

A year later in 1954, Banyu and Merck established the joint venture Nippon Merck-Banyu (NMB). Merck and Banyu owned 50 percent and 49 percent of the venture, respectively. A private Japanese citizen (a Merck employee) owned the remaining 1 percent. NMB assumed ownership of a Banyu plant in Okazaki and began to manufacture Merck products, which were distributed through both Banyu's and NMB's own propas. Sales made by either organization were delivered through wholesalers affiliated with Banyu. By 1983, NMB had a propa force of roughly 450, all of whom were paid a straight salary.

In 1955 Banyu began licensing antibiotics from another U.S. firm, Bristol-Myers. This led to the establishment of Bristol-Banyu Research Laboratories in 1961, and a joint venture, Bristol-Banyu Pharmaceutical, in 1973 to manufacture Bristol-Myers products. Unlike Merck, Bristol-Myers had its own captive sales force in Japan and Bristol-Myers and Banyu marketed the products of their joint venture separately. In fiscal 1983, 35 percent of Banyu's sales were accounted for by Bristol-Myers products and its single largest seller was a Bristol-Myers oral antibiotic.

Banyu's Situation prior to Merck's Acquisition

Banyu originated the strategy among Japanese pharmaceutical companies of licensing products from abroad and importing the technology required to produce and distribute them through captive sales forces. Imports and joint venture products quickly came to account for more than half of Banyu's sales. While other Japanese firms spent as much as 5 percent of sales on R&D, Banyu typically spent less than 2 percent. This policy and conservative management led to very high net profit margins for nearly two decades. Although not a member of any of the Japanese industrial groups, Banyu was perennially among the top performers in the Japanese pharmaceutical industry and was virtually free of debt.

By 1975, growth in sales had slowed down. As energy became more expensive and as prices in Banyu's main business, antibiotics, were forced down by the government, pre-tax profit margins slipped from over 25 percent at the beginning of the decade to 18 percent in 1975 to 12 percent by 1980. Facing lower profitability than its major competitors, Banyu drastically raised R&D expenditures. The company spent ¥75 million on research in fiscal 1975; in the subsequent 5 years, annual expenditures averaged over ¥2 billion.

Despite these expenditures and the initiation in 1982 of a joint research effort with Kirin, Japan's largest brewer, Banyu still trailed the major Japanese drug companies in new-product introductions. Further, none of the company's new products during the decade 1973–1982 was developed in-house. Meanwhile, Banyu's existing product line suffered average price reductions of 20 percent in 1981 and 25 percent in 1983. Financial statements for Banyu at the end of fiscal 1983 are given in **Exhibits 9** through **11**. **Exhibit 12** gives comparative data for Banyu and other Japanese pharmaceutical companies.

THE ACQUISITION

In 1982, A. E. Cohen, president of MSDI, approached Koichi Iwadare, president of Banyu, and suggested that Merck would be interested in purchasing a significant stake in Banyu. At this time, Banyu's major shareholders were Dai-Ichi Kangyo Bank (6.3 percent), Fuji Bank (5.9 percent), Sumitomo Bank (5.6 percent), Tokai Bank (2.8 percent), and Koichi Iwadare (2.2 percent). Koichi Iwadare was 67 years old and the son of Banyu's founder. He had assumed the leadership of Banyu after his father's death in 1963. Like his father, Koichi Iwadare had studied chemistry at Tokyo University before joining the company. With promises from Merck that it would not interfere with his continued management of the company, Mr. Iwadare agreed to cooperate with Merck's efforts to acquire control of Banyu.

Seeking to avoid publicity that would have raised Banyu's stock price and engendered a political debate within Japan, Merck quietly began to accumulate Banyu shares on the Tokyo Stock Exchange. By the end of 1982, Merck held 6.04 million shares—nearly 5 percent of the outstanding equity, which was the legal maximum in the absence of government approval. (Industry observers later estimated that Merck had paid roughly $2.50 per share for its initial stake in Banyu.) Simultaneously, Banyu purchased $2 million worth of Merck's common stock. At the time, analysts interpreted the reciprocal share purchases as an effort by the two firms to forge closer ties, reinforcing their 30 years of cooperation.

The next steps, the issuance of new Banyu shares and convertible bonds and their purchase by Merck, required approval from the Japanese ministries of health and finance. The necessary approvals were obtained in 1983. Plans for the acquisition remained secret until Merck's announcement of the deal in August 1983, which took industry analysts in the United States and Japan completely by surprise. **Exhibit 13** gives selected contemporary stock market, interest, inflation, and exchange-rate data.

EXHIBIT 1 MERCK & CO., INC.—CONSOLIDATED BALANCE SHEET, DECEMBER 31
(THOUSANDS)

	1982	1981
Assets		
Current assets		
Cash and short-term investments	$313,242	$226,606
Accounts receivable	645,290	615,714
Inventories	628,615	647,610
Prepaid expenses and taxes	97,999	126,252
Total current assets	1,685,146	1,616,182
Property, plant, and equipment		
Land	42,822	37,604
Buildings	654,640	567,150
Equipment	1,509,540	1,340,742
Construction in progress	189,798	194,297
Accumulated depreciation	(839,310)	(743,226)
Net property, plant, and equipment	1,557,490	1,396,567
Investments maturing beyond 1 year	124,566	121,039
Other assets	288,179	176,212
Total assets	$3,655,381	$3,310,000
Liabilities and shareholders' equity		
Current liabilities		
Accounts payable and accrued liabilities	$400,214	$398,475
Income taxes payable	108,083	148,048
Dividends payable	51,726	51,795
Loans payable	264,754	272,939
Total current liabilities	824,777	871,257
Long-term debt	337,293	241,043
Deferred taxes and other liabilities	265,610	167,286
Minority interests in foreign subsidiaries	23,713	28,954
Shareholders' equity		
Common stock	2,109	2,109
Other paid-in capital	155,395	155,413
Retained earnings	2,046,484	1,843,938
Total liabilities and shareholders' equity	$3,655,381	$3,310,000

EXHIBIT 2   MERCK & CO., INC.—CONSOLIDATED STATEMENT OF INCOME, YEAR ENDED DECEMBER 31 (THOUSANDS, EXCEPT EARNINGS PER SHARE)

	1982	1981
Sales	$3,063,017	$2,929,455
Costs and expenses		
Materials and production costs	1,222,228	1,229,298
Marketing, administrative, and		
research expenses	1,212,387	1,111,460
Interest (net) and other	29,866	2,433
Income before taxes	598,536	586,264
Taxes on income	185,500	187,600
Minority interests	(2,121)	399
Net income	$415,157	$398,265
Earnings per share	$5.61	$5.36
Supplementary income statement information		
Research and development expenditures	$320,516	$274,168
Advertising expenses	86,351	80,931
Repairs and maintenance	95,321	95,697
Interest expense, net of amounts capitalized	51,599	35,286
Interest income	35,422	40,047

EXHIBIT 3 MERCK & CO., INC.—HISTORICAL FINANCIAL DATA (MILLIONS, EXCEPT AS NOTED)

	Year ended December 31									
	1982	1981	1980	1979	1978	1977	1976	1975	1974	1973
Revenues	$3063.0	$2929.5	$2734.0	$2384.6	$1981.4	$1724.4	$1561.1	$1402.0	$1260.4	$1104.0
Net income	415.1	398.3	415.4	381.8	307.5	277.5	255.5	228.8	210.5	182.7
Total assets	3647.7	3310.0	2900.5	2649.1	2278.1	1993.4	1759.4	1539.0	1243.3	989.0
Long-term debt	337.3	241.0	211.4	213.7	211.4	213.8	217.6	219.3	16.3	11.3
Equity	2204.0	2001.5	1863.3	1665.5	1455.1	1277.8	1102.2	950.0	822.8	709.6
Stock price, $/share	84.50	84.75	84.75	72.25	67.75	55.50	68.13	69.25	66.38	80.75
EPS (earnings per share)	5.61	5.36	5.54	5.06	4.07	3.67	3.38	3.03	2.79	2.43
Dividends, $/share	2.80	2.60	2.30	1.90	1.70	1.50	1.40	1.40	1.40	1.18
Price/earnings ratio	15.09	15.81	15.30	14.28	16.65	15.12	20.16	22.85	23.79	33.23
Return on sales	13.55%	13.60%	15.19%	16.01%	15.52%	16.09%	16.37%	16.32%	16.70%	16.55%
Return on beginning equity, %	20.74	21.38	24.94	26.24	24.06	25.18	26.89	27.81	29.66	29.48
Capital expenditures	$295.1	$322.8	$256.5	$170.1	$155.9	$177.2	$153.9	$249.0	$159.1	$90.2
Depreciation	121.1	105.0	91.3	80.6	74.3	65.8	57.0	51.1	45.1	39.5

EXHIBIT 4   1982 SALES OF TWENTY LEADING PHARMACEUTICAL MANUFACTURERS

Company	Country	Worldwide sales ($ billions)	
		Total	Pharmaceutical
Hoechst	West Germany	$14.79	$2.63
Bayer	West Germany	14.73	2.45
Merck & Co.	United States	3.06	2.21
American Home Products	United States	4.58	2.14
Ciba Geigy	Switzerland	6.95	2.05
Pfizer	United States	3.45	1.70
Eli Lilly	United States	2.96	1.54
Roche	Switzerland	3.57	1.51
Sandoz	Switzerland	3.04	1.42
Bristol-Myers	United States	3.60	1.36
SmithKline	United States	2.64	1.34
Abbott Labs	United States	2.60	1.30
Warner-Lambert	United States	3.25	1.29
Takeda	Japan	2.18	1.29
Upjohn	United States	1.83	1.21
B. Ingelheim	West Germany	1.49	1.21
Johnson & Johnson	United States	5.76	1.12
Squibb	United States	1.66	1.00
Glaxo	United Kingdom	1.66	0.98
Rhone-Poulenc	France	5.55	0.90

Note: Figures reflect sales at manufacturers' list prices.

EXHIBIT 5A   EXPENDITURES ON PHARMACEUTICAL R&D BY COUNTRY FOR 1964, 1973, AND 1978

Country	1964		1973		1978	
	Level, millions	Share,* %	Level, millions	Share,* %	Level, millions	Share,* %
United States	$282	59%	$640	35%	$1159	28%
West Germany	40	8	310	17	750	18
Switzerland	38	8	244	13	700†	17
Japan	27	6	236	13	641	15
France	28	6	166	9	328	8
United Kingdom	29	6	105	6	332	8
Italy	15	3	82	4	147	3
Sweden	9	2	33	2	72	2
Netherlands	9	2	26	1	72†	2

*Note: Shares denote percentage of world pharmaceutical R&D expenditures.
†Estimated.

EXHIBIT 5B   EXPENDITURES BY U.S. FIRMS FOR R&D PERFORMED ABROAD

Year	Total, millions	Foreign,* millions	% Foreign
1981	$2217.5	$494.7	22.31%
1980	1860.2	405.3	21.79
1979	1522.9	279.8	18.37
1978	1311.2	222.0	16.93
1977	1181.8	197.7	16.73
1976	1067.8	164.9	15.44
1975	973.5	144.9	14.88
1974	858.5	132.5	15.43
1973	752.5	108.7	14.45
1972	666.8	66.1	9.91
1971	628.8	52.3	8.32
1970	565.8	47.2	8.34
1969	505.8	41.7	8.24
1968	449.5	39.1	8.70
1967	412.4	34.5	8.37
1966	374.4	30.2	8.07
1965	328.6	24.5	7.46
1964	278.3	20.4	7.33
1963	267.1	18.9	7.08

*Denotes research undertaken by U.S. companies outside the United States.

EXHIBIT 6   1983 MARKET SHARES OF FOREIGN FIRMS OPERATING IN JAPANESE ETHICAL PHARMACEUTICAL MARKET

Firms operating joint ventures dependent on Japanese partner for distribution	Market share, %
Merck*	1.3%
Hoechst	1.2
Sandoz	1.2
Bristol-Myers[†]	1.1
Lederle	1.1
Bayer	1.0
Boehringer	0.9
SmithKline	0.9
Upjohn	0.8
Roussel Uclaf	0.6
Essex	0.5
Imperial Chemical	0.5
Searle	0.5
Abbott Labs	0.3
Syntex	0.3
Squibb	0.2
Travenol	0.2
Warner-Lambert	0.1
Wellcome	0.1
Astra	<0.1
American Home Products	<0.1
Eli Lilly	<0.1
Johnson & Johnson	<0.1
Rhone-Poulenc	<0.1
Rorer	<0.1
Wyeth	<0.1

Firms operating independently	Market share, %
Pfizer	2.2%
Ciba Geigy	1.3
Bristol-Myers[†]	1.1
Schering	0.5
Glaxo	0.3
Roche	0.3
Beecham	0.2

*Nippon Merck-Banyu had a 1.3 percent share. Following the acquisitions of Banyu and Torii, the Merck group had a combined share of 3.2 percent.

[†]Bristol-Myers operated both a joint venture and an independent sales force.

EXHIBIT 7   ESTIMATED SIZE OF "PROPA" (SALES) FORCES IN JAPAN, FISCAL 1982

Companies	Number of propas	Sales (¥ billions)
Japanese		
Takeda	1000	¥170.0
Sankyo	1100	160.0
Fujisawa	1400	150.0
Shionogi	800	85.0
Banyu	450	67.4
Torii	300	34.1
Foreign		
Pfizer	900	¥33.2
Bristol-Myers	500	23.4
Ciba Geigy	500	38.0
Hoechst	500	35.0
Merck (NMB)	450	22.7
Upjohn	400	17.9
Essex	375	10.0
Lederle	350	20.3
Schering	350	22.0
Boehringer	330	29.0
Sandoz	300	45.0
Bayer	285	30.0
Imperial Chemical	270	11.0
Beecham	200	10.0
Glaxo	200	16.0
Roche	200	25.0
Roussel Uclaf	150	9.0
Squibb	150	5.1

Note: Sales figures reflect estimates of fiscal 1982 prescription drug sales. Number of propas estimated by International Pharmaceutical Consulting (Japan), quoted in *IMS Pharmaceutical Marketletter,* February 21, 1983, p. 8.

EXHIBIT 8 **NUMBER OF NEW SUBSTANCES INTRODUCED, BY INVENTOR COUNTRY***

Country	1961–1983		1981–1983 only	
United States	377	(29.6%)	24	(21.8%)
France	284	(22.3%)	13	(11.8%)
West Germany	217	(17.0%)	16	(14.5%)
Japan	196	(15.4%)	41	(37.3%)
Switzerland	115	(9.0%)	6	(5.5%)
United Kingdom	84	(6.6%)	10	(9.1%)
Total	1273	(100%)	110	(100%)

*"Inventor country" denotes country where initial patent applications were filed.

EXHIBIT 9   BANYU PHARMACEUTICAL BALANCE SHEET, MARCH 31 (MILLIONS)

	1983	1982
Assets		
Current assets		
Cash and securities	¥26,816	¥24,760
Notes and accounts receivable*	34,645	31,875
Inventories	17,413	14,686
Other	1,383	1,412
Total current assets	80,257	72,733
Property, plant, and equipment		
Land	2,616	1,400
Depreciable assets (net)	3,252	2,920
Construction in progress	1	1
Total property, plant, and equipment	5,869	4,321
Investments		
Securities	7,923	7,108
Long-term loans	836	811
Total investments	8,759	7,919
Other assets	341	286
Total assets	¥95,226	¥85,259
Liabilities and equity		
Current liabilities		
Notes and accounts payable*	¥16,677	¥12,258
Short-term debt	426	1,426
Liability reserves	12,511	11,369
Other	3,112	2,589
Total current liabilities	32,726	27,642
Pension liability reserves	6,521	6,261
Shareholders' equity		
Paid-in capital	13,618	10,618
Retained earnings	42,361	40,738
Total liabilities and shareholders' equity	¥95,226	¥85,259

*Notes receivable in Japan are commercial instruments used in corporate transactions in lieu of cash. They are highly liquid and used as a kind of quasi currency among commercial enterprises.

†The pension liability reserve represents 40 percent of the liability that would be incurred in the form of lump sum severence settlements if all employees were to voluntarily leave the company on the balance sheet date.

EXHIBIT 10   **BANYU PHARMACEUTICAL STATEMENT OF INCOME, YEAR ENDED MARCH 31 (MILLIONS, EXCEPT EARNINGS PER SHARE)**

	1983	1982
Sales	¥71,529	¥67,439
Cost of goods sold*	39,792	40,187
Gross profit	31,737	27,252
SG&A expenses	25,292	21,552
Operating profits	6,445	5,700
Nonoperating income	2,857	2,694
Nonoperating expense	987	872
Profit before taxes	8,315	7,522
Provision for taxes	5,635	4,637
Net income	¥2,680	¥2,885
Dividends	926	1,152
Earnings per share	¥21.27	¥25.04

*Includes depreciation of ¥414 million and ¥388 million in 1983 and 1982, respectively.

EXHIBIT 11 BANYU PHARMACEUTICAL HISTORICAL FINANCIAL DATA (MILLIONS, EXCEPT AS NOTED)

Year ended March 31

	1983	1982	1981	1980	1979	1978	1977	1976	1975
Revenues	¥71,529	¥67,439	¥63,861	¥55,362	¥50,054	¥45,229	¥42,432	¥40,927	¥20,689
Net income	2,680	2,885	2,709	2,700	3,612	2,433	2,382	2,632	2,069
Total assets	95,226	85,259	84,881	79,200	75,386	63,032	61,218	57,563	54,564
Long-term debt	0	0	0	0	0	0	0	0	0
Short-term debt	426	1,426	1,026	426	436	436	436	436	436
Equity	55,979	51,356	49,652	48,123	46,507	37,662	36,034	34,459	32,589
Stock price, ¥/share	633	610	541	550	726	605	444	433	431
Earnings per share, ¥	21.27	25.04	23.51	23.43	31.35	29.02	29.83	34.61	55.78
Dividends per share, ¥	7.50	10.00	10.00	10.00	10.00	12.50	12.50	12.50	12.50
Price/earnings ratio	29.76	24.36	23.01	23.47	23.16	20.85	14.88	12.51	7.73
Return on sales, %	3.75%	4.28%	4.24%	4.88%	7.22%	5.38%	5.61%	6.43%	10.00%
Return on beginning equity, %	5.22	5.81	5.63	5.81	9.59	6.75	6.91	8.08	6.78
Capital expenditures	¥1,962	¥733	¥583	¥661	¥256	¥134	¥358	¥847	¥643
Depreciation charges	414	388	354	322	316	335	360	383	159

EXHIBIT 12   COMPARATIVE DATA ON JAPANESE PHARMACEUTICAL COMPANIES (MILLIONS, EXCEPT AS NOTED)

Company: Year ended:	Banyu 3/83	Chugai 12/83	Fujisawa 3/83	Shionogi 3/83	Takeda 3/83	31-Firm average* 3/83
Revenues	¥71,529	¥95,768	¥203,757	¥181,053	¥469,079	¥78,868
Net income	2,680	4,909	10,955	7,464	19,801	3,739
Total assets	95,226	105,114	242,575	164,468	471,829	89,702
Long-term debt	0	15,034	15,190	2,725	2,933	5,556
Equity	55,979	48,349	140,037	96,673	216,169	46,275
Stock price, ¥/share	633	973	1,070	808	806	
Earnings per share, ¥	21.27	31.15	49.22	27.71	25.89	
Dividends, ¥/share	7.50	7.50	7.50	7.50	7.50	
Price/earnings ratio	29.76	31.24	21.74	29.16	31.13	32.01
Payout ratio	0.35	0.21	0.14	0.27	0.26	0.28
Beta	0.54	0.50	1.09	0.85	1.15	0.99
Return on sales, %	3.75%	5.13%	5.38%	4.12%	4.22%	4.74%
Return on equity, %	4.79	10.15	7.82	7.72	9.16	8.08
Current ratio	2.45	2.22	1.67	2.12	1.97	2.25
Interest coverage	13.84	10.21	14.47	13.79	14.69	9.26
5-year growth rates, %†						
Revenues	9.60%	10.61%	11.72%	9.94%	6.86%	9.95%
Net income	1.95	10.31	4.90	3.75	22.36	11.95

*Thirty-one pharmaceutical firms traded on first section of Tokyo Stock Exchange.
†Growth rates are compounded annually.

EXHIBIT 13 SELECTED PRICES AND YIELDS

| Date | Closing stock prices | | | | 3-Month yields, % | | CPI* | | Exchange rates, ¥/$ | |
	Merck, $	Banyu, ¥	S&P Composite, $	TSE Index, ¥	Eurodollar	Euroyen	United States	Japan	Spot	3 months forward
3-81	$84.625	¥468	136.00	530.17	14.81%	7.62%	107.4	103.5	¥211.00	¥207.70
6-81	92.500	403	131.21	586.15	17.81	7.50	109.9	105.3	225.80	219.95
9-81	84.875	488	116.18	550.27	17.75	7.68	113.2	106.1	232.70	225.75
12-81	84.750	590	122.55	570.31	13.75	6.12	114.1	106.5	219.90	216.35
3-82	72.125	528	111.96	533.81	15.37	6.75	114.7	106.4	246.50	243.05
6-82	67.500	525	109.61	539.25	15.81	7.25	117.7	107.6	254.00	250.15
9-82	78.125	539	120.42	524.00	11.44	7.25	118.8	109.5	269.50	266.50
12-82	84.500	550	140.64	593.72	9.19	6.75	118.5	108.4	235.00	233.90
1-83	85.750	550	145.30	588.35	9.25	6.56	118.8	108.6	237.90	236.85
2-83	83.750	545	148.06	592.18	8.75	6.63	118.8	108.2	235.45	234.28
3-83	84.875	633	152.96	617.69	9.63	6.38	118.9	108.9	239.40	237.45
4-83	94.500	617	164.42	631.96	8.88	6.19	119.7	109.3	237.00	236.08
5-83	85.250	636	162.39	636.84	9.44	6.31	120.4	110.5	238.30	236.81
6-83	92.875	644	168.11	656.13	9.69	6.50	120.8	109.7	239.70	237.85
7-83	93.750	627	162.56	665.54	10.19	6.50	121.3	109.2	241.70	239.30

Notes: In August 1983, Merck had a price/earnings ratio of 15.5 and β = 0.80. On July 31, 1983, the annualized yields to maturity on 90-day government bills were 9.50 percent and 6.31 percent for the United States and Japan, respectively. S&P = Standard & Poor's; TSE = Tokyo Stock Exchange; CPI = consumer price index.
*1980 = 100.

NOTE ON U.S. TAXATION
OF FOREIGN-SOURCE
CORPORATE INCOME

Tax rules often have a very significant impact on the locations and capital structures of foreign operations, the nature of the entity through which foreign operations are conducted, the means by which foreign subsidiaries remit earnings to the parent, the times at which the earnings are remitted, and the locations of profits in a globally integrated system of manufacturing and distribution. Considerable value can be created by timely tax planning on a worldwide basis.

This note addresses one part of the much larger subject of international taxation. Its focus is on the income tax imposed by the United States on the profits of an American-owned corporation with foreign operations.

THE BASIC DILEMMAS: DOUBLE TAXATION/FOREIGN COMPETITIVENESS

To appreciate the basic dilemmas of foreign taxation, consider the following simple example. Assume that a corporation, U.S. Corp., does business in both the United States and the hypothetical country of Atlantus. It is posited, for the moment, that foreign business is conducted through a branch office in Atlantus, not through a separate but wholly owned subsidiary in Atlantus. Assume further that the branch earns $100 of profit in Atlantus and is exposed to a 40 percent tax rate there. Obviously, Atlantus will tax the $100 of profit earned by the branch. But should the United States include or exclude the Atlantus profit from U.S. gross income for tax purposes? If the

This note was prepared by Professor Henry B. Reiling. Copyright © 1992 by the President and Fellows of Harvard College. Harvard Business School note 292-101.

profit is included, should the United States give full credit, a deduction, or no credit or deduction for the taxes paid to Atlantus? Taxing all $100 could be punishing, as shown below:

Example 1

Atlantus corporate taxable income	$ 100.00
Atlantus tax @ 40%	−40.00
U.S. tax @ 34% on $100	−34.00
Dividend to U.S. shareholders	26.00
U.S. individual tax @ 28%	− 7.28
Net after tax	$ 18.72

Double taxation excites criticism. There is arguably little incentive for a company to undertake the presumably greater operating risks of foreign business if the result is higher risk and lower reward than limiting oneself to the more familiar domestic markets; to earn an acceptable return on the Atlantus operation, U.S. Corp. must raise prices or reduce costs and, as a consequence of the cost reduction, perhaps lower quality. Either way, the company's competitive position in Atlantus is injured.

Establishing a corporation in Atlantus and doing business there through this local Atlantus citizen clarifies matters a bit. It is a little easier to deal with allocations, and this two-corporation arrangement activates the very powerful and significant argument based on general principles of U.S. domestic taxation that one should only pay a tax in the United States when money is remitted to the shareholder as a dividend. More important may be nontax legal liability considerations. The second legal entity in Atlantus also may permit better "damage control" just in case Atlantus has or adopts unexpected rules dealing, for example, with the conditions under which people can sue for personal injury, environmental damage, or wrongful dismissal, and the amounts they can recover.

The two-corporation arrangement might produce taxes as follows:

Example 2

Atlantus taxable income	$ 100.00
Atlantus tax @ 40%	−40.00
Dividend to U.S. Corp.	60.00
U.S. tax @ 34% on $60	−20.40
Dividend to U.S. shareholders	39.60
U.S. individual tax @ 28%	−11.09
Net after tax	$ 28.51

This is an improvement over the prior possibility, but the company is still at a serious competitive disadvantage in Atlantus compared to the one national tax paid by a domestic Atlantus competitor with the same income [$18.72 or $28.51 versus $60 (see **Example 3**)]:

Example 3

Atlantus taxable income	$ 100.00
Atlantus tax @ 40%	−40.00
Dividend to Atlantus Corp.'s individual owners	$ 60.00

With its higher after-tax profit, a company paying only Atlantus taxes has a "war chest" it can use for such things as advertising, service, research and development, hiring more salespeople, capital investment for cost reduction, or price reduction.

If the United States and Atlantus have much business contact with each other, it is imperative that they reach an understanding as to how they will consistently deal with the other's businesses. Clearly one nation will not long be benevolent if its own corporations are treated more harshly than it treats guest companies. The United States and its trading partners have responded to these imperatives by adopting treaties. As common sense would suggest, uniformity is wise and the various U.S. tax treaties are very similar.

As noted, there are a variety of ways to try to deal equitably with the issues in this area. This note will focus on the choices made with brief statements of the reasons why. In short, it will focus on what *is* rather than exploring what *might have been*. Several key concepts dominate:

• *What* income is taxed in the United States? Answer: Worldwide income.

• *When* is the income taxed in the United States? The answer depends first on the entity through which one does business abroad. After that there are general rules with several exceptions. The general rules are:

> Divisions—when earned
> Subsidiaries—when dividends are remitted.

How is relief from double taxation afforded? The taxpayer has the choice of either a *credit* or a *deduction* for foreign taxes. The former is usually more valuable. However, foreign tax credits are subject to limitations. The credit cannot exceed the tax that would have been owed had the foreign income in fact been earned in the United States.

STANDARD STRATEGIES, BIASES, AND ABUSES

Higher Foreign-Country Tax Than in the United States

Frequently today U.S. corporate tax rates are lower than in other countries, as in the Atlantus example: 34 percent in the United States versus 40 percent in Atlantus. Where judgment and discretion permit, there is an obvious bias in the direction of maximizing expenses in Atlantus: Better if a given dollar of the chief executive officer's salary is offset against profits taxed at 40 percent rather than profits taxed at 34 percent. Consulting contracts and licensing agreements are among the ways companies fairly, and in going too far, unfairly, try to move U.S.-based costs to Atlantus for deduction there.

Tax Haven

Assume the small but climatically delightful nation of Tax Haven has a zero tax rate. The potential dividend of a subsidiary operating in Tax Haven is $100 (see **Example 4**).

Example 4

Tax Haven taxable income	$ 100.00
Tax Haven tax @ 0%	− 0.00
Potential dividend to U.S. Corp.	$ 100.00

Comparing the several examples, it is clear that tax effects would have a big impact on the business decision of whether to repatriate the potential dividend. Assuming no constraints in Atlantus or Tax Haven on repatriating dividends, and further assuming neutrality with regard to investment opportunities, the $60 dividend in **Example 2** could have been moved to the United States with no further tax effect provided, of course, that the United States gave credit for the Atlantus tax. Put another way, U.S. tax was not a factor in whether to leave the cash flow in Atlantus or move it to the United States. In the Tax Haven situation, there is a great incentive to leave the funds overseas. Repatriation leaves one with $66 of cash flow ($100 − $34), whereas leaving them in Tax Haven yields $100 to invest.

If one turns up the imagination a notch, several variations on deferred dividend repatriation occur. Instead of dealing with the risks of local work ethics and skill levels, why not merely place a portfolio overseas and invest from abroad, thus deferring the tax on dividends, interest, and capital gains? Moreover, if cash is needed in the United States, instead of repatriating the cash as a dividend, have the Tax Haven subsidiary lend it to U.S. Corp.

Transfer pricing preferences are a by-product of the tax deferral possible when a significant tax haven is involved. If one manufactures in a tax haven and ships to the United States or a moderate- or high-rate third country for sale, there is a great incentive to view manufacturing as the dominant value-added function rather than marketing. Assuming a manufacturing cost of $3 per unit, a retail price of $10, and a U.S. tax rate of 34 percent, one would prefer to sell to the U.S. company for $9 rather than $4 (see **Examples 5A** and **5B**).

	Example 5A	Example 5B
Tax Haven gross income	$ 9.00	$ 4.00
Tax Haven cost to manufacture	$ 3.00	$ 3.00
Tax Haven corporate taxable income	6.00	1.00
Tax Haven tax @ 0%	0.00	0.00
Cash flow in Tax Haven	6.00	1.00
U.S. gross income	$ 10.00	$ 10.00
U.S. cost of goods sold	9.00	4.00
U.S. corporate taxable income	1.00	6.00
Tax @ 34%	.34	2.04
Cash flow in United States	$ .66	$ 3.96
Total worldwide cash flow	$ 6.66	$ 4.96

Since the value added of the marketing or manufacturing function is a matter of judgment, much like the value of stock in an initial public offering, transfer pricing is a fruitful area of disagreement between taxpayers and the tax collector.

Controlled Foreign Corporations

The concept of the Controlled Foreign Corporation (CFC) was created to thwart some of the more flagrant instances of advantage being taken of the deferral of taxation until dividends are repatriated. A CFC is a foreign corporation owned more than 50 percent in terms of either voting power or market value by so-called "U.S. shareholder(s)." "U.S. shareholder" is a technical term that includes any U.S. person or corporation that owns more than 10 percent of the voting stock. Put the other way around, a U.S. corporation that owns less than 10 percent of a foreign corporation is *not* a "U.S. shareholder."

CFC status brings with it several probable disadvantages:

• Loss of the deferral on so-called Subpart F income (defined below), which is passive income, and other income from activities the U.S. Congress has concluded are too frequently and abusively shifted offshore for the purpose of deferring U.S. taxation.

• Loss of tax deferral on earnings and profits reinvested by the CFC in U.S. property (reinvestment in U.S. property is deemed to be repatriation of profits in substance, even though not so in form).

• Gains on the sale or redemption of stock, including redemptions in liquidation of a CFC, result in ordinary income rather than capital gain, subject, of course, to the standard tests of dividend characterization having to do with adequate earnings and profits.

Subpart F Income

An analogy to the domestic personal holding company rules is apt in the treatment of so-called Subpart F income. In the definition of personal holding company income, the U.S. Congress took rifle shots at several areas of perceived abuse. So too here. In this instance, the targets are subsidiaries in tax haven countries—i.e., low-tax countries—whose activities involve a substantial amount of paper pushing in contrast to manufacturing or the direct rendering of service. More specifically, the tax-hostility focus is on transactions that could essentially be performed in any stable country with good communications.

Subpart F has two main components:

• Income from the insurance of risks outside the country in which the CFC is organized

• Foreign base company income, which has five components as follows:

1. Foreign personal holding company income
2. Foreign base company *sales* income
3. Foreign base company *service* income
4. Foreign base company *shipping* income
5. Foreign base company *oil-related* income

The definition of foreign base company sales income is a good example of these components. Foreign base company sales income is derived from the purchase or sale of personal property where the property is manufactured outside the country of incorporation as well as sold to a user outside the country of incorporation. In short, the country of incorporation is typically one of convenience and minimal roots.

FOREIGN TAX CREDITS

Deemed Paid or Derivative Credit

For illustrative purposes, recall the above examples in which $100 was earned in Atlantus by a wholly owned subsidiary, $40 was paid in tax to Atlantus, and $60 was remitted to the U.S. parent. When business is conducted through a foreign subsidiary, the U.S. model for avoiding double taxation is triggered by the remittance of the $60 dividend. It would be simplest if the dividend was picked up as income and taxed at 34 percent. This would be **Example 2** above, where $39.60 is available after corporate taxes. Example 2 is not nearly so attractive to U.S. Corp. as **Example 3** in which $60 is available after U.S. corporate taxes.

The more competitive and equitable results of Example 3 are what U.S. law tries to accomplish. The foreign tax payment can be thought of as a down-payment on the domestic taxpayer's U.S. tax liability with respect to that income. Getting utility from that down-payment activates some complexity. We need two pieces of information: taxable income in Atlantus and the foreign tax for which we want credit. Happily, Atlantus's income can be derived by combining or "grossing up" the dividend and the credit, which is referred to as a *deemed paid* or *derivative credit:*

Example 6

Dividend received	$ 60.00
+ deemed paid credit	+40.00
= taxable income to U.S. Corp.	$ 100.00

The terminology "deemed paid" or "derivative credit" is at first perplexing. Bear in mind that U.S. Corp. did not pay the Atlantus tax of $40. A separate legal entity incorporated in Atlantus paid that tax. The fact that U.S. Corp. owns 100 percent of the Atlantus subsidiary does not change the fact that the Atlantus subsidiary is a separate legal entity. Some terminology was needed to convey the idea that U.S. Corp. is using, and eventually getting, tax utility from a tax paid by someone else. "Deemed paid," or alternatively "derivative," serves that purpose.

The deemed paid credit is not always 100 percent of the foreign tax paid. Quite properly, the credit is a function of the foreign subsidiary's dividend payout ratio. Thus:

$$\text{Deemed paid credit} = \frac{\text{foreign subsidiary's paid dividend}}{\text{foreign subsidiary's after-tax earnings}} \times \text{foreign tax paid}$$

i.e., $40 = $60/$60 \times $40.

Withholding Tax Credit

Just as domestic U.S. tax law requires employers to withhold taxes on salary and some dividends and interest, so do foreign governments frequently impose analogous requirements on dividends, interest, and other forms of income paid to the parent. Suppose a 10 percent withholding tax was imposed on dividends repatriated to U.S. Corp. in our example. The withholding tax would have been $6 ($60 $\times$ 10 percent), and the cash dividend received by U.S. Corp. would have been $54 ($60 − $6). In this circumstance, U.S. Corp.'s taxable income would have been computed as follows:

Example 7

Dividend received	$ 54.00
+ withholding tax	+ 6.00
+ deemed paid credit	+ 40.00
= taxable income to U.S. Corp.	$ 100.00

The Limitation in Operation

Given the concepts and examples previously discussed, the maximum credit available this year on $100 of Atlantus's income is $34, whereas U.S. Corp. has $40 of deemed paid credit and, assuming a 10 percent withholding tax was imposed, an additional $6 of withholding credit. The excess credits of $12 above the $34 limit are at risk of being lost. Some protection against loss is provided by a 2-year carryback and 5-year carryforward rule. As a fallback, the foreign tax might be taken as a deduction rather than a credit. While a credit, if usable, is worth 100 cents on the dollar and a deduction only 34 cents on the dollar (at a 34 percent marginal tax rate), a deduction is better than a potential credit that expires unused. This right to elect either a deduction or a credit arises each year and one or the other must always be elected. Neither can be claimed on a partial basis.

When a company does business in several foreign countries, the question arises as to whether the limitation functions on a per country or overall basis. The choice once resided with the taxpayer. Since 1987, choice has been eliminated. The limitation *must* be done on an overall basis. Another, and related, feature of the limitation is that foreign income must be separated into eight categories, called "baskets," with the limitation computed on a per basket basis. The purpose and workings of these limitations will be clearer if we assume that U.S. Corp. has foreign operations in both

Tax Haven and Atlantus. The former generates CFC "paper-pushing" income with current U.S. taxation on $100 and Tax Haven taxes of $0. Atlantus generates manufacturing income taxed, remitted, and grossed up as in **Example 6**. (To simplify, assume there is no withholding tax.)

Were there still a per country limitation, it seems that only $34 of Atlantus's $40 deemed paid credit could be used this year (limitation = $100 × 34 percent). In the past, U.S. Corp. would have opted for the now mandatory overall limitation where up to $68 of foreign taxes could be credited against U.S. taxes [($100 Tax Haven income + $100 Atlantus income) × 34 percent]. Thus, it tentatively appears that all $40 of the Atlantus taxes could be used. Here the baskets come into play. The Tax Haven paper-pushing profits go into one basket and the Atlantus manufacturing profits go into a different basket. The $100 of manufacturing profits would be taxed in the U.S. at 34 percent, giving a limitation of $34 versus taxes on foreign manufacturing of $40. Thus, $6 must be carried back or forward.

REFINEMENTS: DEFINITIONS OF INCOME; VALUE-ADDED TAX; POLICY CONFLICTS

Before leaving the mechanics of these provisions, it is important to anticipate some surprises and residual problems. First, despite treaties, fair-minded people can still differ—and do differ—about the definition of income in addition to such things as the proper mechanics for transfer pricing.

Second, the tax credit is available only for income taxes. This is significant since many European and Latin American countries have, and rely heavily upon, a value-added tax (VAT). This means that U.S. tax credits for foreign taxes will be less than they would have been if the foreign country used only an income tax to raise the money actually raised there by the income tax and the VAT. Naturally, there is no credit for foreign sales, property, and excise taxes.

Third, over the years, in the international area as domestically, tax law has been made the mechanism for accomplishing a number of secondary policy objectives. The result is added complexity, somewhat arbitrary compromise, and inconsistency. Examples of this intrusion include provisions relative to aiding the U.S. balance of payments and reducing the transfer of U.S. manufacturing and related jobs overseas. Less significant have been incentives to encourage development in less developed countries.

WHELAN PHARMACEUTICALS: TAX FACTORS AND GLOBAL SITE SELECTION

On March 15, 1991, the members of the Location and Sourcing Committee at Whelan Pharmaceuticals gathered for their usual semimonthly meeting held on the eighth floor of the corporate headquarters building in Maryland. The main item on their agenda was the examination of possible manufacturing sites for Whelan's newest product, which was about to enter the third stage of clinical trials in the United States. The locations under consideration were Maryland, Puerto Rico, Ireland, and several continental European sites. The meeting was chaired by John Neal, vice president for manufacturing and engineering. The other two members were Stefan Bischel, vice president for worldwide marketing and international planning, and Linda Gonzalez, executive director of taxes.

John Neal: You both look ready, so why don't we get started. As you know, we need to send a recommendation to the Executive Committee about where to source Varex. Clearly, in the past, tax has been the key player in sourcing decisions, and as I'm sure Linda will tell us, there are still ''big bucks'' in tax. In the last few years, several other factors have become increasingly important, so it is essential that we get these trade-offs right. In particular, we need to consider the importance of Whelan's presence in key markets for strategic and marketing reasons. We also must consider government regulation, duties, and our need for cash. And, finally, we would like to take advantage of any economies of scale in manufacturing.

This case was prepared by Research Associate Jane Palley Katz under the supervision of Professor G. Peter Wilson. It is a synthesis of several actual corporate location decisions. Copyright © 1991 by the President and Fellows of Harvard College. Harvard Business School case 192-066.

Before we really get going, I want to report that, as expected, the Executive Committee has accepted our earlier recommendation that Whelan locate all manufacturing stages at one site so that production will take place at one location for distribution and sale, worldwide.[1] I think that we were all in agreement that this configuration is in line with the conclusions of Whelan's recent reevaluation of long-term manufacturing strategy. It exploits potential economies of scale and makes it easier to meet government standards for good manufacturing practices and environmental regulations governing the transportation of hazardous materials.[2]

Well, I think we are ready to hear from each of you. Remember that this is initial fact-finding, so that while we want to know your first choice, we also want to hear about the benefits and drawbacks of all four options. Stefan, why don't you go first.

Stefan Bischel: Thanks, John. I am happy to report that all preliminary evidence indicates that Varex will be a very successful product. Varex is a cardiovascular drug; cardiovasculars are currently the largest segment of the domestic market, accounting for about 23 percent of domestic sales. They are the second largest segment of the foreign market, accounting for 19 percent of foreign sales. Phase II of the clinical trials went very well, so we are extremely optimistic about Varex's prospects. Of course, there is always uncertainty about efficacy until the testing on humans is done in Phase III. Nonetheless, we are currently projecting sales of $100 million in 1993, and we anticipate sales growing to a steady-state level of $400 million by 1996. By that time, Varex should be producing operating income of $160 million for the remainder of its patent life. By the end of 1997, we will have recovered our investment, including the $250 million on research and development. Once sales reach steady-state, Varex will provide approximately 8 percent of Whelan's revenues and 10 percent of our pre-tax operating income.[3]

Our marketing people feel that these are conservative estimates, and we have a high degree of confidence in them. There is always the chance that Varex will be a real blockbuster, but it is too early to be more confident.

John Neal: That's very interesting. If Varex sales exceed our current expectations, we will have to consider building more capacity.

Linda Gonzalez: Stefan, when are you assuming that Varex will be on the market?

Stefan Bischel: Right now, I'm assuming that Varex will be approved and will hit the market in fall 1993. That is what the scientists project, and so far everything has been right on schedule. That would mean we have 6 to 7 years until the patent expires.[4]

As far as each site goes, the marketing people have a strong preference for continental Europe. Many European countries regulate the price of the product once it is approved for sale. These price negotiations are very significant and can be very

---

[1]Pharmaceutical manufacture typically involves several stages: bulk chemical production; active ingredient production (turning the chemical compound into a specific drug); dispersion (diluting the active ingredient by granulating and mixing); tablet production; and fill/finishing (bottling, labeling, and boxing).

[2]In the past, Whelan's manufacturing facilities outside the United States, Puerto Rico, and Ireland were relatively small-scale operations, typically just fill/finishing plants. Each foreign site produced a variety of drugs which were intended to serve that local market.

[3]In 1990, Whelan reported $810 million of operating profit on slightly over $3 billion of sales.

[4]Vance C. Gordon, Ph.D., and Dale E. Wierenga, Ph.D., "The Drug Development and Approval Process," *New Drug Approvals in 1990* (Pharmaceutical Manufacturers Association, January 1991).

time-consuming. Our preliminary discussions with the pricing commissions of several European countries lead us to believe that we can get large price breaks, both on Varex and on our other products, if we agree to put our manufacturing facilities in one of those European countries.

John Neal: Stefan, what kind of numbers are we talking about here? And what kind of assurances do we have?

Stefan Bischel: In my meetings with the heads of several European pricing commissions, we discussed prices that should average at least 6 to 7 percent higher than what we'd get otherwise. It could even be a little better than this because there may be some additional room for bargaining, if a couple of countries really want to compete to get us. Also, we would probably be able to apply for subsequent price increases a little sooner. Look, as far as any guarantees go, I would characterize the results of these talks as an informal "handshake" type of agreement. I think we can reasonably count on these numbers, although any deal is not the kind of thing you can take into court. In the end, it comes down to the fact that these European governments want us; we have a good reputation in the industry, and we are planning to build a world-class, state-of-the-art facility.

And we want them as much as they want us. The European market is large, and we expect it to get even larger. In the pharmaceutical industry, foreign sales — particularly European sales — are increasing faster than sales in the United States. Whelan currently has a relatively weak presence in foreign markets; they account for only 30 percent of our sales, which is below the industry average. Increasing our long-term presence in Europe is a strategy very much in line with top management's recent push to improve our global position.

As for the other three sites, the marketing people are indifferent, although from our perspective, each is clearly inferior to continental Europe.

John Neal: Okay, that's good. Now, if there are no more questions for Stefan, Linda, you're up.

Linda Gonzalez: Great. Well, I am here to offer both the tax advantages and disadvantages for each site and also to present some related treasury issues. International tax and treasury issues can be complicated. Although you've both been through this kind of thing before, I thought it would be useful to review some of the basic features of Whelan's multinational tax environment. Please feel free to interrupt with questions.

Our worldwide tax bite is affected by numerous factors besides U.S. tax rates and rules. These include local tax rates and rules, withholding tax rates on distributions such as dividends and royalties, how we set our tax transfer prices, our repatriation policy, how we source our products (that is, how we use our excess capacity around the world), and our worldwide capital and legal structure. In particular, I would like to call your attention to two tax planning tools that have been important to Whelan: transfer prices and Puerto Rican tax benefits.

Flexibility in setting tax transfer prices has been a particularly useful tax planning tool for Whelan, although it is becoming more problematic. Section 482 requires that taxpayers that are owned or controlled by the same interests deal with each other at arm's length. Since many of our intermediate products and almost all of our final products are proprietary, we have had some discretion in setting tax transfer prices (there are no market prices available). This has allowed us leeway in allocating profits across our subsidiaries and provided Whelan with significant tax benefits. Nonetheless, we are subject to a great deal of IRS scrutiny in this regard. It is particularly noteworthy that Section 482 provides the IRS (but not taxpayers) with broad authority to allocate items of income, deduction, and credit among related parties if it determines that "such a distribution, apportionment, or allocation is necessary in order to prevent evasion of taxes or clearly to reflect the income of any of such organizations, trades, or businesses." In other words, the IRS may adjust our return, and any adjustment is presumed correct as long as it is reasonable.

In the past, Whelan's bottom line has also benefitted from tax breaks available in Puerto Rico. The United States Tax Reform Act of 1976 included Section 936, which has two major provisions.[5] One, it grants U.S. corporations a 100 percent credit equal to (and, therefore, fully offsetting) the U.S. tax on:

- Income earned in the active conduct of a trade or business in a possession, and

- Qualified possession source investment income, which is nonbusiness income derived from a trade or business in the possession and attributable to the investment of funds for use within the possession.

Two, Section 936 exempts the corporation from U.S. tax on any dividends remitted to the U.S. parent. For all practical purposes, these two provisions make Puerto Rico the only offshore location where we can obtain permanent forgiveness (as opposed to deferral) of federal taxes.[6] Combined with favorable Puerto Rican tax benefits, Section 936 can generate large tax savings.

John Neal: Linda, maybe you could comment on how these two tools have affected our tax planning in the past.

Linda Gonzalez: That is a good idea. In the 1960s and 1970s, we responded to Section 936 by manufacturing some of our most profitable drugs in Puerto Rico, and by transferring our product patents and proprietary manufacturing processes and other manufacturing intangibles to our Puerto Rican subsidiary. These were tax-free transfers, meaning that we did not pay taxes on the difference between the fair value of these intangibles at the transfer date and their development costs.[7] Our Puerto Rican subsidiary, Whelan P.R., sold the finished goods to Whelan U.S. for promotion and distribution throughout the world. The marketing intangibles, including product trademarks, remained in the United States.

---

[5]Section 936 replaced Section 931 of the Revenue Act of 1921, an earlier law that provided benefits to U.S. corporations in U.S. possessions. In the new Section 936, Congress sought to "assist the U.S. possessions in obtaining employment-producing investments by U.S. corporations, while at the same time encouraging those corporations to bring back to the United States the earnings of these investments to the extent they cannot be reinvested productively in the possession." See the *Report of the Committee on Ways and Means, U.S. House of Representatives, on H.R. 10612*, Report No. 94-658, and the *Report of the Committee on Finance, United States Senate, on H.R. 10612*, Report No. 94-938.

[6]While Section 936 benefits are available to corporations in other U.S. possessions such as Guam and the Virgin Islands, nearly all business conducted under its provisions occurs in Puerto Rico.

[7]The various tests under Section 351 would be met, and the transaction would be deemed a nonrecognition event.

Prior to 1982, and to a lesser extent until 1988, the IRS repeatedly challenged the transfer prices between Whelan P.R. and Whelan U.S. At issue was whether sufficient profit was being allocated to the marketing intangibles and whether a royalty should be paid to Whelan U.S. to compensate for research and development related to the patent and manufacturing intangibles. As you can imagine, there was considerable disagreement between Whelan and the IRS over this matter, and we became quite concerned about the potential costs in both time and money of protracted litigation. Ultimately, we negotiated a settlement without going to court, but some of our competitors were less fortunate. This increased litigation risk caused Whelan and our competitors to deemphasize Puerto Rico.

John Neal: What happened in 1982?

Linda Gonzalez: After several court cases, several years of uncertainty, and numerous Section 482 adjustments, Congress intervened in 1982 and established two ways that firms could elect to determine possession profits. One of these, the cost-sharing method, still required considerable judgment in setting transfer prices. The other, the profit-split method, required minimal discretion. Between 1982 and 1988, both of these methods were used. However, in 1988, the Treasury's now famous Section 482 white paper discouraged the use of cost-sharing. As a result, Whelan now uses the profit-split method for Puerto Rico, as do most other pharmaceutical companies. Overall, the new regulations are still complex and somewhat arbitrary, and we had hoped for a more favorable outcome from Congress, but at least the uncertainty about available tax benefits and the threat of expensive litigation have been significantly reduced.

John Neal: How does the profit split work?

Linda Gonzalez: Under the profit-split method, slightly less than 50 percent of the profit related to products produced in Puerto Rico is assigned to Whelan P.R. and the remainder is assigned to Whelan U.S. In this context, profit doesn't mean gross margin; sales and general administrative expenses including related product research and development costs must be allocated to Whelan P.R. Thus, while the tax bite for profits earned in Puerto Rico is low, there are virtually no transfer pricing games being played, and we don't run the risk of IRS adjustments or a lawsuit.

Now, let's consider each site, one at a time. The worst place for us would be one of the sites in continental Europe. Tax rates are the highest there, with several countries having rates above the U.S. rate of 34 percent. High European tax rates are complicated by the fact that we are getting uncomfortably close to the limit on our foreign tax credit (FTC). If we actually do go over the limit, we will not be able to credit additional foreign taxes against our U.S. taxes. Ideally, we would like to generate low-tax foreign source income so that we could fully use our credits. This makes Ireland an opportune place from a tax perspective.

John Neal: What about Puerto Rico?

Linda Gonzalez: Unfortunately, there is no U.S. foreign tax credit or deduction for foreign taxes paid on possession income. The taxes on our possession corporations are separate and distinct from our other consolidated taxes.

Stefan Bischel: Linda, as I recall, ever since U.S. tax rates fell in 1986, you tax folks have been warning us that Whelan might start to accumulate excess foreign tax credits. But so far you seem to have managed our way around this.

Linda Gonzalez: That's true, but it will get harder if we have a large increase in continental European profits. Manufacturing Varex there could make a lot of headaches for the tax department.

As for the Maryland location, manufacturing in the United States would be somewhat better than in continental Europe. Tax rates are lower, and we might be able to set up a Foreign Sales Corporation to garner tax benefits on exports, although those benefits are worth a lot less since 1986.[8] Plus, if we need the money at home for any reason, we have a guarantee that there will be no withholding tax. Getting money home from foreign locations can be troublesome; although we've been able to use tax treaties to reduce withholding taxes, we have not been able to avoid them altogether.

Stefan Bischel: It seems reasonable to me to assume that the differential between tax rates in the United States and continental Europe will narrow over the next decade. At some point, the U.S. is going to have to attack the large federal deficit and that will mean higher taxes.

Linda Gonzalez: Maybe, but this is far from certain. Every time new taxes are mentioned, there is vocal opposition from the American electorate. And there is a lot of opposition in Congress to any major new legislation so soon after the last overhaul and budget agreement. In addition, while Congress might raise tax rates, it is also under pressure to reinstate the investment tax credit, which would help us.

I believe that the bottom line here is this: For Whelan to get the "big bucks" from tax that John mentioned, we'd have to put Varex in either Ireland or Puerto Rico. The Irish tax rate is only 12 percent and is guaranteed until the year 2010.[9] Puerto Rico has a tax rate of approximately 17 percent, with no extra U.S. tax upon repatriation. There is an additional Puerto Rican withholding tax on money leaving the country. The current withholding tax rate is 10 percent if profits are repatriated immediately, with a sliding scale to zero if money is left for 10 years. Not surprisingly, we have a large pile of cash from our already established facilities in Puerto Rico; this is where we do a lot of our current production for the U.S. market. There is also a local Puerto Rican income tax, which is approximately 5 percent. Overall, the tax situation is still very favorable, although the exact effective tax rate depends on how long we hold our profits in Puerto Rico.

Stefan Bischel: Can we rely on the continued existence of Section 936? I've noticed a lot of articles in the press speculating on its imminent demise.

Linda Gonzalez: I agree that it is increasingly hard to predict what will happen to Section 936. Puerto Rico tries hard to protect these benefits by lobbying Congress. The

---

[8]In order to help U.S. companies compete in foreign markets, Congress created the Foreign Sales Corporation (FSC) legislation, which provides U.S. exporters the opportunity of excluding 15 percent of their net income generated from qualifying export sales from U.S. tax. In addition, distributions out of earnings and profits attributable to foreign trading gross receipts by the FSC to its U.S. parent are exempt from U.S. taxation. The Tax Reform Act of 1986 and subsequent legislation have significantly reduced the utility of FSCs.

[9]Actually, the Irish tax rate is 10 percent. However, Whelan Ireland is a branch of the subsidiary Whelan Switzerland, and there is an additional Swiss tax of 2 percent.

tax department puts a fair amount of energy into lobbying efforts, as do other interested companies. Nonetheless, the strength of the opposition appears to be growing. During the 1986 tax overhaul, Section 936 was targeted for extinction, but was saved after prodding by lobbyists for Puerto Rico, including Michael Deaver, a former Reagan White House aide.[10] Adding to this uncertainty is the increased support inside Puerto Rico for Puerto Rican statehood: With statehood, Section 936 benefits would be lost automatically. Recent polls indicate that statehood advocates, for the first time in history, slightly outnumber those who support the continuation of commonwealth status. Even President Bush supports statehood.[11]

Stefan Bischel: Obviously, Puerto Rico may present problems in the future. From a tax perspective, wouldn't we be better off in Ireland?

Linda Gonzalez: Ireland does offer advantages and disadvantages compared to Puerto Rico. The advantages center on the lower tax rate and potential to average foreign tax credits. On the other hand, recent transfer price regulations and enforcement mean that Irish profit might be lower. In particular, there is increasing pressure to have our subsidiaries, such as Ireland, pay larger royalties to the U.S. parent on patents and other intangibles. Note that the profit-split guidelines that are legislated for Puerto Rico are not applicable elsewhere. Keep in mind also that Ireland offers the opportunity for tax deferral, while Puerto Rico offers an exemption.

John Neal: Linda, I think it would be helpful to us if you could go through the procedures for FTC averaging again.

Linda Gonzalez: No problem. I can make this simple, or tell you the whole story. Which would you like?

John Neal: Why not keep it simple, for now.

Linda Gonzalez: Okay, here we go. When I calculate U.S. taxes each year, first I calculate total taxable income, which is the sum of both U.S. and foreign-source income for the year.[12]

John Neal: So if a European subsidiary reports $100 of income, does this count as foreign-source income?

Linda Gonzalez: It counts as foreign-source income only when the income is repatriated as a dividend (unless it is classified as Subpart F income).

Next, remember that we are taxed at the U.S. rate on our worldwide income. But to avoid double taxation, we can reduce our U.S. tax by taking a credit for the amount of income taxes paid to a foreign government.[13] However, there is a limit to the size

---

[10]Jill Abramson, "Plan for 1991 Referendum on Puerto Rico Status Spurs Rival Factions to Blitz Lawmakers in U.S.," *The Wall Street Journal,* October 10, 1989, p. 20.

[11]Jose De Cordoba, "Statehood Proponents Gain Favor in Puerto Rico as Debate over Island's Status Heats Up Again," *The Wall Street Journal,* April 13, 1990, p. 12.

[12]Foreign-source income includes, among other items: interest received from a foreign corporation; dividends received from a foreign corporation; compensation from services performed outside of the United States; 50 percent of income from inventory manufactured within the United States and sold with title passing outside the United States (the other 50 percent is U.S. source income); and royalties for the use of patents, copyrights, trademarks, trade names, and other intangible property used outside the United States.

[13]Alternatively, a U.S. taxpayer may deduct foreign taxes paid or accrued if they qualify as trade or business expenses incurred in the production of income. The foreign tax credit is generally preferable to the deduction because it reduces tax dollar for dollar as opposed to a reduction in taxable income.

of the credit that we are allowed.[14] Once we reach this limit, we cannot deduct any foreign taxes paid or accrued from our U.S. taxes, and our overall effective tax rate will tend to rise above 34 percent.

Perhaps a few examples would help. Suppose that our only foreign subsidiary was in a country with a 44 percent tax rate. Then, for every $1 of profit, we would have to pay $0.44 to the foreign authority. However, we would not pay additional tax to the United States upon repatriation, and we would accrue $0.10 of excess foreign tax credits for each dollar of profit.

Now suppose instead that our only foreign subsidiary is in Ireland. In this case, if we earn $1, we pay $0.12 to Ireland immediately, and we pay an additional $0.22 when we repatriate to the United States. Note that we have an incentive to defer repatriation, and that we would *not* have any excess foreign tax credits.

To complete the examples, suppose we generate $1 in each of these countries and repatriate immediately. In this case, $0.56 is paid in foreign taxes and can be credited against U.S. taxes. U.S. taxes before the credit would be $0.68 ($2 × 0.34), so an additional $0.12 must be paid to the United States. The pain of any additional taxes owed can be reduced by deferring repatriation. Now you can begin to see the problem if all of the $2 is earned in the high-tax country *and* we need to repatriate cash to the United States to support investments or dividends. Once we reach the FTC limit, income from high-tax countries such as the EC countries is very expensive! The way out is averaging: If we also have income from low-tax countries such as Ireland, we can effectively average the tax rate and take advantage of all of our foreign tax credits.

John Neal: Does this mean that we do not have to pay U.S. taxes or worry about excess credits as long as we do not repatriate?

Linda Gonzalez: This is complicated. But it is fair to say that you are correct, so long as we reinvest foreign earnings in projects abroad that generate "active" income.

Stefan Bischel: You mentioned some other nontax financial issues. What are they, and how do they figure in?

Linda Gonzalez: Well, there are two main issues that pertain to sourcing Varex. The first is customs and duties. Essentially, we have to pay duties on products entering the European Community, although once inside any EC country, products can be shipped to other member countries duty-free. On this issue, both Ireland and continental Europe would have an identical advantage over Maryland and Puerto Rico.

The second is a little more complicated and involves treasury questions. Namely, where is our cash? Is it safe? Where will we need cash? What does it cost to move cash? Right now we have nearly $300 million in cash and additional physical assets sitting in Puerto Rico. This makes a lot of sense from a tax perspective. I personally think the stuff is safe, but everything else being equal, top management would prefer not to add any more to the pile. We also have nearly $200 million in cash in Switzerland.

---

[14]FTC limitation = (foreign-source taxable income/total taxable income) × U.S. tax before credits. The FTC limit must also be computed separately for several categories of income, such as passive income, financial services income, shipping income, and others.

John Neal: [Interrupting] It seems to me that we have a tremendous need for cash at home. The board estimates that the new research facilities Whelan has planned will cost $1.2 billion over the next 10 years. Plus, if we stay at home we avoid the additional risks associated with having cash and assets outside the United States. There's political risk, exchange-rate exposure, and the possibility of natural disaster to think about.

Stefan Bischel: [Also interrupting] I was about to say just the opposite! We have a lot of "active" uses for money in continental Europe and other foreign markets where we want to expand our presence. With the increasing globalization of financial markets and the reduction of the restrictions on moving cash, wouldn't that favor production on the continent?

Linda Gonzalez: Actually, with our current legal structure, both our Irish and continental European operations are branches of our Swiss subsidiary. This means that Ireland would be just as good as continental Europe, if the point is to be able to move our cash around in Europe.

John Neal: Okay, I guess we won't settle this until our next meeting. Now, if there is nothing more on tax and finance, I'd like to turn to the estimates of the operations and engineering functions.

Probably neither of you will be surprised to learn that the manufacturing folks would like to be in Maryland. For one thing, our engineers and operations people are most comfortable in the United States. It is where we have the most experience, the labor force is excellent, and wages are comparable to continental Europe and only a little higher than in Puerto Rico. Also, from a public relations point of view, it would help to create more jobs in the United States, instead of sending them overseas. Human resources managers tell me that announcing new offshore jobs will cause some morale difficulties with the workers in Maryland and may stir up trouble with the unions at bargaining time. Certainly it doesn't help our image with the public at large, or our attempts to lobby Congress.

However, the biggest factor favoring Maryland is that we have excess capacity there, and could get up and running quickly and at the lowest cost. The other sites are greenfields. We need to start from scratch with environmental permits, buying land, all of that stuff. We figure that a greenfield site would cost one and a half times as much as the Maryland site and take 50 percent more time to be ready to go. As you know, Stefan, the extra time could cost us a lot if we get approvals and we don't have the product on the shelves.[15] Manufacturing cannot afford to be the bottleneck because our relative costs are too low!

Linda Gonzalez: But, John, when you figure the opportunity cost of the excess capacity into the calculations, don't the numbers for Maryland look higher? After all, just because we have the excess capacity doesn't mean that the capacity has no alternative use.

---

[15]Success in the pharmaceutical industry depends on a company's ability to discover new drugs, get them through the regulatory approval process in various countries, and market them quickly to harvest profits before their patents expire. For successful drugs, the lost revenues from delaying a product launch can be extremely high.

John Neal: Yes, that might be true. But that opportunity cost of existing capacity is not currently figured in when manufacturing is evaluated against its targets. To make us whole in choosing a greenfield site would require some specific decisions from top management to have the corporate office absorb some of our costs. Frankly, I think that this is unlikely given its current strategy emphasizing the global market. That noted, let me review the advantages and disadvantages of Ireland and continental Europe. Wages in Ireland are slightly lower than in continental Europe. On the other hand, I think that Europe has the edge in local suppliers and technical people. As far as Puerto Rico goes, we can operate well there. We have an experienced labor force and local managers, and wages are roughly comparable to the United States', maybe a little lower.

Stefan Bischel: Then is it fair to say that, by your calculations, manufacturing would be cheaper in continental Europe than in Ireland?

John Neal: Yes. I would give the edge to Europe, but by a small margin. Well, if there are no more comments or questions, I suggest that we spend the next 2 weeks mulling over what we have heard. The presentations and questions have been excellent. For the next phase of the process, I think that the three of us might look more closely at our assumptions and be prepared to change or defend them at our next meeting. At that time, we can have some additional discussion. Then I would like us to narrow the choice to two sites.

The next meeting of the Location and Sourcing Committee took place on March 29, 1991. John Neal, Stefan Bischel, and Linda Gonzalez were present.

John Neal: As you know, the main purpose of this meeting is to come to some preliminary recommendations about sourcing Varex. I would like us to narrow the choice to two sites, if possible, and to highlight any additional information that you have uncovered. If you'll indulge me, I would like to begin the discussion with a short summary of the last meeting and an opening recommendation.

It seems clear to me that the different functional areas preferred different sites for Varex. Manufacturing strongly supported Maryland, marketing saw enormous advantages in sourcing out of continental Europe, while the tax department favored Ireland, with Puerto Rico its second choice. My assessment is that the manufacturing numbers are relatively small compared to the potential additions to the bottom line due to tax or price breaks. I think manufacturing met its most important considerations with our initial recommendation to locate all production stages at one site. Therefore I propose that we vote to eliminate Maryland and discuss the remaining three sites with the purpose of eliminating at least one more. Any discussion?

Stefan Bischel: That would be fine with me.

Linda Gonzalez: I have no problems with that either.

John Neal: Well, if we are all agreed, why don't we begin with Puerto Rico. My next inclination is to eliminate Puerto Rico, mainly because the tax benefits which make it look so good are shaky. Manufacturing would be perfectly adequate there, but that is not a big enough plus to favor it over the other two sites if the tax breaks were to disappear. It also seems important that top management would really like to avoid accumulating more cash and assets in Puerto Rico, unless the advantages are absolutely compelling.

Linda Gonzalez: I really don't think the Puerto Rican tax benefits are as uncertain as all that. Besides, in our calculation of the tax benefits in Puerto Rico, we assumed that we would have the break for only 5 years. So anything after that would just be gravy on top of our figures.

Stefan Bischel: But, Linda, you don't have any guarantees on the withholding tax either. Puerto Rico can always change the rates. Anyway, I think that if it comes to taxes, Ireland is the best choice. It's in line with the global initiatives of top management, and it avoids the duties that we would have to pay by producing within the EC, it has the lowest tax rate, and it allows us to average foreign tax credits. If I might venture an opinion, I agree with John. Realistically, I think this decision comes down to Ireland versus continental Europe. Both sites are equally good for duties and for moving cash within the EC. Also, both are likely to be favorably viewed by top management. John noted that Europe is a little better than Ireland from his standpoint, but not by much. I propose that we also vote to eliminate Puerto Rico, so that we can focus on the merits of Ireland and Europe.

Linda Gonzalez: I have no objection.

John Neal: Good. Well, we can now proceed to consider Ireland and Europe. Linda, you raised several good points last time in response to Stefan's support of a continental European site.

Linda Gonzalez: [Interrupting] Actually, I have a few more things to add. After examining all the revenue projections, our tax position, and running all the numbers, I estimate that manufacturing in Ireland will give us continuing tax savings of $35 million a year by the fourth year that Varex is on the market. This savings is the average difference between the taxes that would be paid in Ireland and in the various sites in continental Europe.

By my calculations, we would need price breaks of 15 percent to match these tax breaks. Now it seems to me that a price break of 6 to 7 percent is more in line with other instances in the industry. Even then, I think that the price we can get for Varex will depend on its efficacy, and we cannot be sure of that until the end of clinical trials. The value of the price break will also depend on the number of units sold, and we can't really be sure about projected sales figures until the end of all clinical testing and government approvals. I don't need to remind you of past situations in other companies where sales projections collapsed when a problem with safety or efficacy was discovered late in the approval process. In light of all of this uncertainty, I think that the sales figures look optimistic. Also, political problems can arise unexpectedly which tie the hands of European pricing commissions, regardless of any previous ''handshakes.'' We can all cite instances in the industry where pricing or approval promises were made by foreign governments and facilities were built, then political considerations such as public outcries about safety blocked approval, or public concern about fairness kept prices down.

Anyway, I think that your projections about price differentials will go by the board after 1992. Won't the EC centralize price and regulatory approvals after that?

Stefan Bischel: Some people predict that this will happen eventually, but I believe that complete centralization is off in the future. For now, national authorities maintain their individual supervision over all approvals.

As for projected price breaks, I think that we can get at least 7 to 8 percent. Besides, continental Europe is one of our most important markets, not just for current sales but for the future as well. If the European market continues to grow faster than the U.S. market, as we expect, each percentage point that we can boost price will be multiplied by a lot of units sold. This is exactly the whole point of the big push that globalization is getting from top management.

Look, I have some of the same problems with your projections. How secure do you feel about the $35 million figure? How can you assume that pharmaceutical prices within the EC will harmonize after 1992 and not assume that taxes will also harmonize?

More important, what if we are audited and our transfer prices are adjusted? Ireland may not turn out to have such large tax benefits if the United States puts increased pressure on our tax transfer pricing policies. It seems to me that it is hard not to foresee stricter IRS interpretation and enforcement of all tax rules with the rising federal deficit combined with the political difficulties inherent in raising taxes. Linda, how do you assess these factors?

Linda Gonzalez: First, about EC and tax rate harmonization: There has already been a decision by EC members to emphasize removing sources of double taxation rather than pursuing the strict harmonization of corporate tax regimes. I really doubt that national governments will ever give up their independent power to set taxes. The EC has adopted uniform accounting practices, removed trade barriers and exchange controls, and banned hidden subsidies to particular companies or industries, which does suggest that there will be forces leading to the convergence of tax rates. There is already evidence that high-tax-rate countries in Europe are beginning to feel the pressure to lower their tax rates. But we'll already have significant tax savings on Varex by the time European tax rates converge.

However, I think your point about potential changes in the IRS interpretation is quite valid. Computers and greater cooperation between national tax authorities will allow ever greater scrutiny and sharing of company tax data, resulting in decreased flexibility for tax planning. For example, the IRS has instituted a new 40 percent penalty for transfer price adjustments over $20 million, although no penalty is imposed if the taxpayer can show reasonable cause and demonstrate that it acted in good faith.[16] The IRS has also announced plans to revise transfer pricing regulations, and I don't expect any new regulations to be in our favor!

Compared to our competitors, I believe that we are reasonably conservative. Our effective tax rate in 1990 was 30.6 percent, which was above the industry average. We've had good relations with our auditors the last few years. In addition, we have taken extra pains, hired economists—the whole nine yards—to make sure that our transfer prices are reasonable and defensible. On the other hand, no one can be entirely sure about the right transfer prices for proprietary products. If we are challenged, we may settle for a lower number, rather than risk litigation.

---

[16]See Section 6662 and Section 6664.

Stefan Bischel: What is your worst-case scenario?

Linda Gonzalez: I figure the worst-case scenario is a $15 million-per-year adjustment.

Stefan Bischel: If the tax breaks are only $20 million per year, I believe that the potential price breaks plus the manufacturing advantage in Europe will easily outweigh them. When you add some extra points for supporting top management's global strategy, there's no contest.

John Neal: Is there any more pertinent information that either of you would like to add? If not, I suggest we adjourn. We'll meet in 2 weeks for final discussion and a vote.

On April 12, 1991, the Location and Sourcing Committee met once more to consider the sourcing of Varex. Again, John Neal, Stefan Bischel, and Linda Gonzalez were present.

John Neal: I think that we have done a thorough job of examining all the factors and trade-offs involved in recommending where to produce Varex. Now it is time to vote. As I review all of the evidence and discussion, I find it difficult to come to a conclusion. Linda, you and the tax department clearly believe that Whelan would be better off in Ireland. Stefan, you and the marketing function feel equally strongly about continental Europe. As I review your presentations, the differences between you appear to result from the differences in your assumptions. You each make very different assumptions which lead you to divergent forecasts of the expected tax benefits and the likely price breaks. If Linda is correct about the tax breaks and Stefan is correct about the price breaks, the decision looks very close—although certainly some of the factors involved are hard to quantify. If either one of you is wrong, Whelan has a lot to lose if we make the wrong choice.

PART THREE

MANAGING EXCHANGE-RATE EXPOSURES

NOTE ON TRANSACTION
AND TRANSLATION
EXPOSURE

A company with subsidiaries in foreign countries faces various kinds of exposure when exchange rates change. The values of the company's assets, liabilities, and cash flows are all affected by movements in exchange rates. This note deals with two major forms of exposure, namely, transaction and translation. One of the important responsibilities of a company's financial officer is to understand the nature of these risks, what can be done to minimize their potentially adverse effects, and what the cost of such action may be.

TRANSACTION EXPOSURE

Transaction, or "contractual," exposure refers to the gains or losses that may be incurred when monetary transactions are to be settled in foreign currencies. This exposure arises when a company buys or sells on credit a good or service priced in a foreign currency, or when a company borrows or lends in a foreign currency.

A typical example of transaction exposure is when a company has a payable or receivable denominated in a foreign currency. If a British company buys cars from a German firm for DM2 million to be paid in 90 days, there is an exposure. If the exchange rate were DM4/£1, the British firm would owe the equivalent of £500,000. An exposure arises because the British firm would likely have to pay something other than £500,000 in 90 days. If the exchange rate changed to DM4.1/£1, then it would only cost the company £487,805 (2,000,000/4.1) for a savings of £12,195. But the rate

This note was prepared by Research Associate Richard P. Melnick and Professor W. Carl Kester. Copyright © 1987 by the President and Fellows of Harvard College. Harvard Business School note 288-017.

could change to DM3.9/£1, and then the cost would be £512,821, or £12,821 extra. Since this transaction was invoiced in deutsche marks, the British firm faces this risk of gain or loss. Had the transaction been invoiced in British pounds, the German firm would have faced the exposure.

Another major example of transaction exposure is when foreign currency is borrowed or loaned. In 1976 a British company incurred a devastating loss because of this risk. The Beecham Group borrowed SF100 million in 1971 when the British pound was worth approximately 10 Swiss francs. By 1976, when it repaid the loan, the pound only bought about 4.4 Swiss francs, requiring Beecham to come up with £22.7 million rather than £10 million. The increase in the sterling value of the Swiss franc loan *exceeded* Beecham's entire book value net worth. Because of the potential for such debilitating currency movements, firms generally try to manage their transaction exposure by using some form of cover.

Managing Transaction Exposure

In theory, losses and gains due to transaction exposures could be passed along to consumers through price increases or decreases. However, for competitive reasons, a company may not always want to pass transaction effects from exchange-rate movements straight through to prices. Instead, the company may wish to "cover" some or all of its transaction exposures, though covering imposes costs of its own. In the final analysis, companies must decide what costs are tolerable and strike a balance between foreign exchange (FX) risks and the costs of covering.

A company facing transaction exposure has several alternatives for covering. The most commonly used cover is a *forward-market hedge,* and the second most popular transaction is a *money-market hedge.* Less common choices are covering via currency options or leaving the position completely uncovered.

The best way to compare these alternatives is through an example. Suppose the French company LePoint sold $1 million of knives in January to NewKitchen, an American company. The invoice was denominated in dollars with payment due in July, 6 months later. At the time of the transaction, the rates prevailing in the foreign exchange and credit markets were as shown in **Table 1**. Though the forward-exchange rate "predicts" a future spot rate of FF5.115/$1, LePoint's foreign exchange forecasting service expects the rate will actually be FF5.235/$1.

TABLE 1	PREVAILING EXCHANGE RATES AND INTEREST RATES	
1. Spot rate		FF5.000/$1
2. Six-month forward rate		FF5.115/$1 (4.6% discount to the dollar)
3. FF 12-month interest rate		14.830%
4. U.S. 12-month interest rate		10.00%

If LePoint believed its forecasting service, it would expect to receive FF5,235,000 [$1,000,000 × (FF5.235/$1] in 6 months. But there is no guarantee what the spot rate will actually be at that time. The rate could fall to FF4.75/$1, in which case LePoint would receive only FF4,750,000, or the dollar could strengthen even more than LePoint's forecast service expects. If LePoint left its transaction exposure uncovered, it would incur the full effects of swings in the exchange rate over the next 6 months.

Forward Cover   An easy way for LePoint to hedge this exposure is to enter into a forward-market contract the day that it sells the knives to NewKitchen. If LePoint uses this method of coverage, it contracts in January to sell $1,000,000 six months forward for FF5.115/$1. In July, when LePoint receives $1 million from NewKitchen, it takes that money to the bank, executes its forward contract, and receives FF5,115,000. This is a ''covered'' or ''perfect'' hedge because LePoint is certain that it will receive exactly FF5,115,000 in 6 months (barring credit risk on the part of NewKitchen). Though this is less than the amount LePoint's forecasting service expects it could receive, it is a riskless amount. The ''cost'' of this hedge (actually a gain in this example) is measured by the franc's dollar premium or discount, which in this case is 4.6 percent.

Money-Market Hedge   An alternative form of cover is the money-market hedge. In such a hedge, the firm establishes a contract in the form of a loan. The company borrows in one currency, converts it to another, and invests that currency. When the loan comes due, the company will receive payment from its operations and uses that money to repay the loan.

This hedge works in a way similar to the forward hedge, except the spot rate rather than the forward rate is locked in, and the cost is measured by the difference in interest rates rather than the forward premium or discount. If markets are efficient and parity conditions hold (see the ''Note on Fundamental Parity Conditions'' in Part 1), then the costs for these two hedges should be comparable.

Using this hedge, LePoint borrows dollars in January, converts them into francs, and invests them. LePoint will repay the loan in July with the $1 million it received from NewKitchen. Therefore it needs to borrow enough so that its receivable will exactly offset its balance due. The number of dollars to borrow is $952,381 (at 10 percent for 6 months, this is $1,000,000/1.05). If this money is converted at the spot rate of FF5.000, LePoint receives FF4,761,905. These francs, invested for 6 months at an annual rate of 14.830 percent, or a 6-month rate of 7.415 percent, will yield FF5,115,000 (4,761,905 × 1.07415). Note this is exactly what LePoint would have received using a forward contract. This is an indication that the foreign exchange and credit markets are functioning properly. Not surprisingly, the cost of this hedge is also 4.6 percent on an annualized basis. This time, however, it can be measured using interest rates as follows: $[(1.07415/1.05) - 1] \times 200 = 4.6$ percent.

Options-Market Hedge   Yet another alternative for LePoint is an options-market hedge. Currency options give the holder of a contract the right to buy or sell a specific quantity of foreign currency for a fixed price on or before some predetermined date. The holder of an option is an option buyer, and that person acquires the option from an option seller, known as a writer. The option may be exercised at a predetermined exchange rate known as the ''exercise'' or ''strike'' price. Normally, this execution can take place any time on or before the expiration date (an American style option). A *call option* is the right to buy a fixed quantity of foreign exchange and a *put option* is the right to sell a fixed quantity of foreign exchange.

The usefulness of these contracts lies in the fact that they provide asymmetric risk protection. For the call-option holder, loss is limited to the price paid for the option (the premium) while the potential gain is unlimited. One implication of this asymmetry is that a holder will benefit if the currency is volatile because it will be more likely to exceed the exercise price and provide a gain at the time of maturity.

If LePoint wants to cover its exposure using options, it should purchase a put option giving it the right to sell dollars for French francs at a predetermined price. With a strike price of 5.115, an option premium of, say FF0.15/$1, and a standard contract size of $10,000, the cost of a single contract would be FF1,500. Brokerage fees of, say, FF125 would raise the total cost to FF1,625 per contract. Given a $1 million exposure, 100 such contracts would have to be purchased for a total cost of $162,500.

The amount of money LePoint will make depends on the spot rate at the settlement date in July. If the rate were above FF5.115 (i.e., the dollar strengthens considerably), then LePoint would not exercise the puts but would instead exchange at the spot rate. If, for example, the rate were the expected FF5.235/$1, there would be a small net profit of FF72,500 (FF5,235,000 − FF162,500 = FF5,072,500) on the entire covered transaction. Higher rates of exchange would lead to still higher French franc profits. The downside, however, is limited. If the spot rate were to fall below 5.115, LePoint would exercise its put, receiving FF5,115,000. Net of expenses, this would provide LePoint with FF4,952,500, capping its loss relative to the spot rate at the time of the commercial transaction to FF47,500.

Comparison   The four alternatives contain various degrees of risk and should be compared carefully. The unhedged position has an unlimited maximum and minimum, with an expected value around the prediction of FF5,235,000. The forward hedge and money-market hedge entail no risk and guarantee FF5,115,000. Finally, the options-market hedge allows for potentially unlimited profit (with a likely outcome of FF5,072,500) and a lower limit of FF4,952,500.

Some important differences between forward and option hedges should be noted. A forward contract is an agreement to pay or receive a certain amount of currency at some future date. The contract is not contingent on future events, and its execution is not open to the discretion of the parties involved. The execution of an option contract, in contrast, is discretionary and will depend on future conditions. This characteristic is useful when, for example, there is uncertainty about whether a cash inflow or outflow will take place (e.g., a contract may be broken). In such situations, a company wants the *right,* but not necessarily the obligation, to buy or sell currency. This is best accomplished through the vehicle of an option.

TRANSLATION EXPOSURE

Multinational corporations invariably have foreign subsidiaries with assets and liabilities denominated in many different currencies. Though the foreign subsidiaries may conduct business entirely in foreign currencies, their financial statements must be translated into the home currency before they can be included in the consolidated statements of the parent. If the exchange rate changes, the home-currency value of foreign subsidiaries' assets, liabilities, and cash flows will also change. For example, the German subsidiary of an American firm might deposit DM1 million in a German bank when the exchange rate is DM2/$1. This would be reflected in the company's consolidated accounts as $500,000. If the deutsche mark weakens to 2.5 per dollar by the next reporting period, then this must be recorded as $400,000. An unrealized translation loss of $100,000 would have been incurred. This type of foreign exchange risk that companies face is known as *translation exposure*. The example just given is fairly straightforward. However, when other types of assets or liabilities are involved, less clear-cut conceptual problems emerge about the true home-currency value of these items. Consequently, several different methods of measuring translation exposures have evolved.

Current/Noncurrent Method

The oldest translation method is the current/noncurrent method, which was used in the United States before 1976. According to this method, current assets and current liabilities are all translated at the current exchange rate on the date of financial statements. All noncurrent assets and liabilities are translated at historical rates, that is, the rates prevailing at the time they were acquired or incurred. Income statement accounts are generally translated at an average exchange rate for the reporting period or the actual rate, if known, on the dates transactions were incurred. Exceptions arise in the case of income statement items that are directly related to balance-sheet items (e.g., depreciation). Such items are translated at the same rate used for the corresponding balance sheet item.

Under this method, only current assets and liabilities are exposed to changes in exchange rates. Fixed assets are thought to be real assets whose value is independent of exchange rates. Similarly, because long-term liabilities do not have to be repaid at the current exchange rate, it is also thought that they do not require translation at current rates. This method is no longer allowed under generally accepted accounting principles in the United States, but is still used by many non-U.S. firms, including those in Germany.

Monetary/Nonmonetary or Temporal Method

The current/noncurrent method was replaced by the monetary/nonmonetary, or temporal, method in the United States in 1976. Accounting rules for foreign assets and liabilities were enumerated in the Statement of Financial Accounting Standards #8 (FASB #8). Under this method, financial assets and liabilities were translated at the exchange rate in effect on the balance-sheet date while fixed or real assets were translated at historical exchange rates. Income statement items were translated at the average exchange rate for the reporting period with the exception of accounts related to nonmonetary assets or liabilities, such as depreciation and cost of goods sold. In short, all monetary assets and liabilities were translated at current exchange rates, and everything else was not. The rationale behind this was that only monetary assets and liabilities were thought to be exposed to current-period currency fluctuations. The value of nonmonetary assets was thought to rise with local inflation, which, under the assumption of purchasing power parity, would mean that home-currency value would be maintained despite exchange-rate movements.

Under the temporal method, U.S. companies had to report translation losses or gains on their income statements each quarter. This was arguably the most controversial accounting rule in American history. There was tremendous opposition to this rule because most U.S. multinationals had to show large translation gains and losses, which led to large swings in quarterly earnings. Most companies did not believe such swings accurately reflected their actual performance. After many complaints about FASB #8, the Statement of Financial Accounting Standards #52 (FASB #52) was published in 1981 and took effect in fiscal year 1982.

All-Current Method

With the arrival of FASB #52, companies began using the all-current method of translation. According to this method, all assets and liabilities are translated at the current exchange rate on the balance sheet date. Equity accounts are translated at historical rates. Income statement items are translated either at the prevailing rate on the date that a sale or purchase occurred, or a weighted average of exchange rates for the appropriate period.

The most important change about FASB #52, however, is that translation gains and losses are not flowed through the income statement. Instead, they are lumped together and listed as a separate equity account, typically called a "cumulative translation adjustment" (CTA). Only when an asset is sold or liquidated does the realized gain move from the CTA to the income statement. Since there is no longer an automatic flow-through of these gains and losses, corporations do not feel the same pressure to hedge their positions completely in order to prevent volatile quarterly earnings. Though these translation gains and losses do not appear on the *income* statement until realized, they are still accounted for in the current quarter's statements.

An added component of FASB #52 is that companies must choose a *functional* currency for a foreign subsidiary. The functional currency is the primary operating currency of the subsidiary while the *reporting* currency is the currency of the parent's financial statements. These need not always be different currencies, however. If a foreign subsidiary is self-sufficient, buying material and selling its goods in a local foreign currency, than it should designate the local currency as its functional currency. However, if the foreign subsidiary buys materials in dollars and sells all its output back to its American parent, then the U.S. dollar will be both its functional and reporting currency, even though the subsidiary may be located outside the United States.

Finally, the FASB #52 rules contain special provisions for subsidiaries in countries where cumulative inflation over 3 years is 100 percent or more. In such situations, the foreign subsidiary must use FASB #8 rules. This is considered necessary to correct the distortion that arises when depreciation at historical cost is translated into current terms. Depreciation, plant, and equipment would all be increasingly understated if they were translated at current rates instead of historical rates in a hyperinflationary environment.

Exhibit 1 provides an illustration of the impact each translation method has on the reporting of a hypothetical German subsidiary of an American company in U.S. dollar terms. The example assumes the deutsche mark appreciates against the dollar over the reporting period. As can be observed, quite different results can be obtained depending upon the method chosen. Note that the subsidiary's net monetary liability exposure results in a reported foreign exchange *loss* for the subsidiary under the monetary/nonmonetary method (FASB #8), but its net current asset exposure results in a foreign exchange *gain* under the current/noncurrent method. No foreign exchange gain or loss is reported in the income statement under the all-current method (FASB #52).

Managing Translation Exposure

Balance-Sheet Hedge   Perhaps the most common means of covering translation exposure is a *balance-sheet hedge* in which the company has equal amounts of assets and liabilities in each currency that offset each other and leave the company without any translation exposure. Note that translation exposure at a consolidated corporate level is measured by *currency,* not country. Often, subsidiaries in different countries will have assets or liabilities in currencies other than their respective functional currencies, and these may net out on a consolidated basis. The balance-sheet hedge can be used for an indefinite period of time, though there may be distortions of debt policy or repayment of trade credit.

As an example of a balance-sheet hedge, consider Tirer, the French subsidiary of the American company Olympic. Using FASB #52 rules, Tirer has a net asset exposure of FF1 million (see **Table 2**). If the French franc were valued at FF6.0/$1 and depreciated 10 percent during the next accounting period to FF6.6/$1, there would be a translation loss of $15,151 [(FF1,000,000/6) − (FF1,000,000/6.6)].

TABLE 2   **TIRER'S BALANCE SHEET (FF)**

Current assets			Current liabilities
Cash	1,500,000	250,000	Payables
Receivables	500,000	1,750,000	Bank credit
Inventory	750,000		Long-term liabilities
Fixed assets		750,000	Long-term loan
Equipment	1,000,000	1,000,000	Equity
Total assets	3,750,000	3,750,000	Total liabilities and equity

Olympic has several choices to reduce this exposure. It can decrease Tirer's French franc assets by converting some cash into dollars and remitting them to the parent or using them to fund dollar requirements elsewhere in the corporation. Alternatively, Tirer can be instructed to increase French franc payables while investing the cash in dollar assets or remitting it to the parent. Or, if Olympic finds it more convenient and useful, it can borrow FF1 million. In principle, these francs could be borrowed by Olympic or Tirer, but in either case, they must be immediately exchanged for dollars to achieve the desired balance-sheet hedge.

Forward-Exchange Hedge   For a company to hedge translation exposure using a forward contract, it must buy or sell the exposed currency forward and then execute the contract in the spot market at the future balance-sheet date. A net asset exposure would require the forward sale of the exposed currency and a net liability exposure would require a forward purchase. This hedge can provide cover for up to 1 year. The size of the forward contract should be calculated as follows:

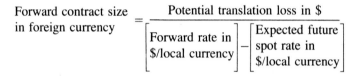

$$\begin{array}{c} \text{Forward contract size} \\ \text{in foreign currency} \end{array} = \frac{\text{Potential translation loss in \$}}{\left[\begin{array}{c}\text{Forward rate in} \\ \text{\$/local currency}\end{array}\right] - \left[\begin{array}{c}\text{Expected future} \\ \text{spot rate in} \\ \text{\$/local currency}\end{array}\right]}$$

In the case of Olympic, suppose the French franc were expected to depreciate from a level of FF6.0/\$1 as of the last balance-sheet date to a level of FF6.6/\$1 by the next balance-sheet date. If the forward-exchange rate were FF6.25/\$1, a forward contract to sell FF1,782,529 [\$15,151.5/(0.16 − 0.1515)] would be necessary to offset the anticipated translation loss. One problem with this hedge is that its success is completely dependent upon the accuracy of Olympic's exchange-rate forecast. Olympic could actually make considerably more or less money depending upon what happens to the rate. Despite its role as a translation-exposure hedge, this sort of activity does expose a firm to transaction exposure insofar as a foreign exchange contract has been entered into.

Money-Market Hedge   A money-market hedge, which is but a special case of the balance-sheet hedge, can also be used to cover translation exposure. A firm with a net asset exposure in a foreign currency borrows the foreign currency, exchanges it for dollars, invests the dollars, and later repays the loan out of the dollar investment, converting the dollars into the foreign currency at the future spot rate. If Olympic borrowed FF1 million at 12 percent, exchanged it for dollars at FF6.0/\$1, invested the dollars at 7.5 percent, and repaid the French franc loan from dollar proceeds at the expected future spot rate of FF6.6/\$1, the hedge would yield a profit of \$179,167 − \$169,697 = \$9,470. Though the assets and liabilities of Olympic would completely offset each other during this hedge period, the ultimate profit or loss from the total position would again be dependent upon the final spot rate and the ability to anticipate that rate. Like the forward hedge, this sort of protection can be used for up to 1 year, but creates a foreign exchange transaction exposure.

Swaps   Several types of swaps can be used to hedge foreign exchange exposures. Swaps are useful for covering an exposure over a number of years. In all such swaps, one party exchanges an amount of currency with a counterparty with an agreement to return the funds after some period of time. With *back-to-back* or *parallel loans,* two companies in different countries borrow each other's currencies. An example, diagrammed in **Fig. 1**, arises when a Japanese company wants to inject capital into its subsidiary operating in Italy. Instead of lending yen to the subsidiary, which would then convert them to lire, the Japanese parent might look for an Italian subsidiary operating in Japan that needed yen financing. If such offsetting needs could be matched, the Japanese parent could lend yen to the Italian subsidiary, and the Italian parent could lend lire to the Japanese subsidiary. (This transaction is executed completely outside the foreign exchange markets.) Because local financing would be used to acquire local assets, no translation exposure would be created by this arrangement. Similarly, because the respective liabilities incurred would be repaid by the borrowing subsidiaries in local currencies, no transaction exposure would be created either.

FIGURE 1   Back-to-back or parallel loan.

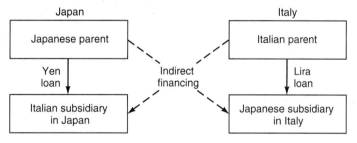

A related deal is called a *currency swap,* which is quite similar to the parallel loan except that no liabilities appear on the firms' balance sheets, and the swap is generally executed through a swap dealer (see the "Note on Foreign Currency Swaps" later in Part 3). Accountants regard this swap as a foreign exchange transaction and the future obligation is treated as a forward contract. Currency swaps of this type are also hedges for transaction exposures in that they eliminate foreign exchange risk associated with the periodic payment of foreign-currency interest and principal.

Finally, a *credit swap* is created when a firm exchanges currency with a bank or a central bank and agrees to reverse the transaction at some future date. This is illustrated in **Fig. 2** below. A British parent could finance its Mexican subsidiary by depositing pounds in the London office of a Mexican bank. In return, the bank would loan an equivalent amount of pesos to the Mexican subsidiary of the British firm. By doing so, the British parent could finance a weak-currency affiliate without creating a hard-currency exposure for it. This swap hedges only the principal involved, however, and not the interest on the loan or deposit.

FIGURE 2 **Credit swap.**

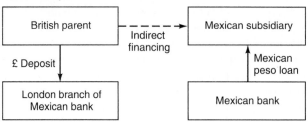

Leads and Lags Leading and lagging the movement of funds, for example, collecting foreign-currency receivables early or late, or repaying foreign trade credit early or late, is a common technique for achieving a hedged balance-sheet position that can be used for an indefinite period of time. This can be done within a corporation or among corporations. However, when this is done among firms, the benefit gained by one firm often comes at the expense of another. Consequently, incentives in the form of discounts to prepay receivables or interest to postpone payables may be needed to induce the desired leads or lags in funds flow. These costs should be compared to the forward discount on the currency in question or to the interest rate difference between two different currencies to determine the cost-effectiveness of leading and lagging versus other hedging techniques.

SUMMARY

When a company begins operating in international markets, it is invariably exposed to foreign exchange risk of various types. This note provides an introduction to two types of such exposure: transaction (or contractual) exposure and translation exposure. *Transaction exposure* arises whenever a firm enters into financial contracts requiring future settlement in some currency other than its reporting currency. Fluctuations in exchange rates between the date on which the contract was established and the settlement date introduce an element of risk into the firm's expected cash flows.

Translation exposure arises whenever a firm has assets or liabilities whose value is denominated in currencies other than the parent's reporting currency. The need to express the multinational firm's consolidated accounts in a common currency can give rise to fluctuations in reported results when exchange rates change between two reporting dates. Various sets of accounting rules have been devised to handle this problem with each providing a different—sometimes widely different—perspective on company performance within a given time period. Unfortunately, there is no worldwide agreement as to which set of rules should be used, although the all-current method has been increasingly accepted by many countries.

These two types of exposures can be controlled by any of several techniques. Among those discussed here are forward-market hedges, money-market hedges, balance-sheet hedges, various types of swaps, and leads and lags. Every one of these methods entails a cost of some type. Usually the explicit cost can be adequately measured in percentage terms as the forward premium or discount on a currency, or the difference in nominal interest rates on credit denominated in the two currencies. Other implicit costs related to the conduct and management of business locally may also exist if hedging activities result in, for example, a distortion in debt policy as a subsidiary tries to eliminate a net asset exposure, or an abuse of trade credit as a local manager tries to lag settlement of payables.

Given such explicit and implicit costs, an important but inherently unresolvable question is precisely how much attention should be paid to these two types of exposures. This question is complicated by the fact that eliminating one type of exposure sometimes comes at the expense of exacerbating another. For example, arranging a foreign-currency loan requiring periodic interest and principal payments in order to hedge a non-cash-generating asset denominated in the same currency may eliminate a translation exposure, but will create a transaction exposure in the process. Furthermore, actions designed to guard against one of these exposures could impede actions designed to address yet another type of foreign exchange exposure: *operating exposure* (see ''Note on Operating Exposure to Exchange-Rate Changes'' later in Part 3). Thus, a logically prior question for managers to address is which of several types of exposure deserves the highest priority.

Having answered this question, the issue of how much time, effort, and expense to devote to the elimination of foreign exchange exposures will turn on management's attitudes about risk and the efficiency of foreign exchange and credit markets. In general, the more risk-averse managers are (or the more difficult and costly it is for shareholders to engage in foreign exchange risk management on their own) and the more efficient markets are, the more likely companies are to engage in hedging activities. Unwanted risk can be disposed of at a fair price in such an environment. The less risk-averse managers are and the less efficient are markets, the less likely it is that companies will hedge completely. Under these conditions, the costs of hedging may be prohibitively high or the potential gains to be had from an unhedged position too tempting to give up.

EXHIBIT 1   COMPARISON OF TRANSLATION METHODS

Income Statement

	DM	All-current method (FASB #52)		Monetary/nonmonetary (FASB #8)		Current/ noncurrent	
		Rate	$	Rate	$	Rate	$
Sales	2,000,000	1.625*	1,230,769	1.625*	1,230,769	1.625*	1,230,769
Cost of sales	1,235,000	1.625	760,000	1.750†	705,714	1.750†	705,714
Depreciation	300,000	1.625	184,615	2.000‡	150,000	2.000‡	150,000
Other expenses	180,000	1.625	110,769	1.625	110,769	1.625	110,769
Taxes	142,500	1.625	87,692	1.625	87,692	1.625	87,692
Net income before exchange loss	142,500		87,692		176,594		176,594
Exchange loss	—		—		(54,912)		8,742
Net income	142,500		87,692		121,682		185,340

Balance Sheet

	DM	All-current method (FASB #52)		Monetary/nonmonetary (FASB #8)		Current/ noncurrent	
		Rate	$	Rate	$	Rate	$
Assets							
Cash and accounts receivable	200,000	1.500§	133,333	1.500§	133,333	1.500§	133,333
Inventory	337,500	1.500	225,000	1.625*	207,692	1.500	225,000
Net plant and equipment	1,000,000	1.500	666,667	2.000‡	500,000	2.000‡	500,000
Total	1,537,500		1,025,000		841,025		858,333
Liabilities and equity							
Current liabilities	200,000	1.500	133,333	1.500	133,333	1.500	133,333
Long-term debt	300,000	1.500	200,000	1.500	200,000	2.000	150,000
Capital stock	750,000	2.000‡	375,000	2.000	375,000	2.000	375,000
Retained earnings	287,500		165,025		132,692		200,000
Cumulative translation adjustment	—		151,642		—		—
Total	1,537,500		1,025,000		841,025		858,333

*Average exchange rate for the reporting period.
†Average historic exchange rate associated with the inventory sold.
‡Historic exchange rate prevailing when capital and fixed assets were acquired.
§Current exchange rate at the balance-sheet date.

HINTZ-KESSELS-KOHL A.G.

Kurt Wiesinger glanced over the wine list at a pleasant Viennese cafe across the street from his office. Today, however, he decided to pass up his favorite Johannesburg Riesling in favor of good, strong schnapps. He felt a need to reflect for a moment and consider some of the problems he was facing in his new position as treasurer of Hintz-Kessels-Kohl (HKK), Austria's largest auto manufacturer.

At the forefront of Wiesinger's concern today was a bid being prepared by HKK's Commercial Vehicles Division for a Costa Rican customer. HKK hoped to sell 180 four-wheel-drive trucks to San José Citronas, Ltda., the largest dealer of motor vehicles in Costa Rica. San José, jointly owned by several of Costa Rica's wealthiest families, was the exclusive automotive supplier to four government ministries. It was not unusual for a minister to be a cousin or in-law of a San José owner. (See **Exhibit 1** for financial information on San José Citronas.)

The proposed sale was expected to produce revenues of U.S. $17.75 million, or 300 million Austrian schillings (As) at the $/As exchange rate prevailing in early September 1981. It would also provide employment in HKK's plant in Austria. If San José accepted HKK's bid, it expected to pay for the trucks in U.S. dollars, with a 10 percent down payment and equal installments over a 5-year period.

Wiesinger, as head of the company's treasury department, had to consider the impact fluctuations in the value of the U.S. dollar might have on the proposed sale's profitability. The dollar had been appreciating substantially against the schilling, as a result of record-high interest rates in the United States and uncertainties about trade

This case was prepared by Professor Thomas R. Piper and Max Donner. Copyright © 1983 by the President and Fellows of Harvard College. Harvard Business School case 284-019.

relations with Eastern Europe, especially Poland. Earlier that year, Poland had suspended repayment of nonguaranteed loans to Austrian lenders. Wiesinger and his colleagues in the treasury department expected the value of the dollar to decline again, but not until U.S. interest rates fell at least 3 to 4 percentage points.

It was also Wiesinger's responsibility to see that all financing choices connected with the sale were executed at the lowest possible cost. There were a number of alternatives for reducing or eliminating the impact of fluctuations in the dollar's value. The proposed sale also involved a significant credit risk in a part of the world where HKK had had little experience—and in September 1981, Costa Rica sounded risky.

BACKGROUND

Hintz-Kessels-Kohl (HKK) was a leading manufacturer of two-wheeled vehicles (bicycles, motorcycles, and mopeds), trucks, buses, farm machinery, and ball bearings. Total revenues of As4845 million in 1978 placed HKK as Austria's third largest manufacturer and leading automotive firm.

HKK had held a leadership position in the Austrian domestic market since 1934, the year Hintz-Werke A.G. merged with Austro-Kessels-Kohl. Since the mid-1960s, the company had experienced rapid sales growth of 10 to 20 percent per year, following aggressive moves into select export markets. Its small, economical vehicles enjoyed great popularity in Eastern and Southern Europe, as well as some small Latin American countries such as Ecuador, Panama, and Costa Rica.

By 1975 exports alone accounted for over half of HKK's sales. In addition, the company had arrangements for its cars and trucks to be built in Poland, Hungary, and Yugoslavia. The company's management had anticipated that the fourfold increase in oil prices which occurred after 1973 would stimulate demand for its small fuel-efficient vehicles. But instead, growth in most export markets fell off.

Financial Administration

Hintz-Kessels-Kohl's rapid growth since the mid-1960s had prompted organizational decentralization. Seven responsibility centers, including the treasury department, reported to the management board. Creditanstalt, HKK's house bank and one of its important shareholders, and the company's labor unions had significant representation on the company's supervisory board.

Each division under the new organizational structure was set up as a profit center. The treasury department, for example, was held responsible for all foreign exchange transactions. Correspondingly, all profits and losses from foreign exchange operations were reported as net earnings of the treasury department. Thus, foreign exchange losses were not charged to the profits of the operating division which had conducted the underlying transactions.

Capital Structure

Since Kurt Wiesinger had joined HKK as an accounting trainee straight out of business college in 1962, the company's financial position had changed even more than its export markets. At that time, Wiesinger recalled, "Our balance sheet looked like a bank's. We had very little debt and were highly liquid." That liquidity had helped finance the rapid growth accompanying the export boom. Total short- and long-term debt, which had remained under As100 million during the 1960s, rose to As2463 million by 1979, or 40 percent of total capital. Concurrently, the company drew down its cash reserve. Wiesinger was now growing concerned about limits on the company's borrowing capacity and higher interest costs as U.S. dollar interest rates climbed to record-high levels, and Austrian, Swiss, and German borrowing costs rose as well. The interest coverage ratio had fallen to barely 2.0 in 1978. While new common stock issues of As200 million each had been sold in 1975 and 1977, this had only slowed the trend toward greater leverage within the company.

Wiesinger had recently met with an investment banker to discuss the feasibility of a private placement of debt.[1] The public capital markets did not appear large enough to satisfy HKK's future needs. In 1980 its total borrowings exceeded the combined lending limits of Austria's three largest commercial banks. Wiesinger doubted the Austrian equity markets could absorb more than As800 million in total new issues each year.

Foreign Exchange Exposure Management

As the proportion of export sales had grown, HKK increasingly purchased and invoiced goods in many foreign currencies. Over one-fifth of the company's short-term debt was also denominated in foreign currencies, primarily U.S. dollars, Swiss francs, and deutsche marks.

It had become routine practice for the four operating divisions to invoice foreign customers in local currency or U.S. dollars. The treasury department in Vienna had responsibility for managing any foreign exchange exposure that might result. In the company's judgment, centralized management of so many currency risks was most efficient.

Hedging had become the most common technique for managing foreign exchange exposure at HKK. However, forward markets for several of the currencies in which HKK invoiced were not well developed. Likewise, forward markets for the Austrian schilling were quite thin; at times, quotes on rates longer than 6 months were simply unavailable.

When hedging was chosen, HKK's policy was to hedge at least 50 percent of the value of the receivable. On average, 70 percent of the value of an item was hedged, if hedging was chosen.

---

[1]The investment banker had estimated HKK could place As300 million in 20-year debentures at a 12.5 percent coupon.

HEDGING THE COSTA RICAN EXPOSURE

Wiesinger knew that HKK's ability to make a competitive bid on San José's truck order and still make a profit would be affected by exchange-rate fluctuations. HKK could hedge its short-term assets or liabilities by "locking in" an exchange rate for a particular currency against the schilling. For example, if it expected to receive $500,000 from a customer in 3 months' time, it might sell those dollars forward against the schilling at a set rate, for delivery in 3 months. No cash would change hands, but HKK would be obligated to deliver $500,000 to the purchaser of its forward contract when it came due. At the end of 3 months, HKK's customer would pay the $500,000 it owed. The company would then deliver these dollars to the purchaser of its forward contract. For these dollars, HKK would receive schillings at the fixed rate agreed upon previously.

Unfortunately, the forward markets for the Austrian schilling were thin, especially for contracts extending beyond 1 to 2 years. Furthermore, the cost seemed unacceptable to Wiesinger. (See **Exhibits 2** and **3** for information on interest rates, forward exchange rates, inflation, and other macroeconomic data.)

The Situation in Costa Rica, September 1981

The attractiveness of the Costa Rican bid was complicated by the deteriorating economic and political situation in that country. The small nation of 2.2 million people had been a model of economic growth and stability within the Caribbean region. Real gross national product (GNP) had risen 6.5 percent annually between 1970 and 1980 while inflation averaged 10 percent. But the balance of trade showed chronic deficits. These reached 10 to 12 percent of GNP when commodity prices dropped sharply in 1979. Foreign borrowing bridged the gap at first, but by spring 1981 that source had all but disappeared. The inevitable fiscal crisis sent annual inflation soaring to 35 percent per annum. Costa Rica's finance minister resigned and the International Monetary Fund (IMF) stepped in with a $300 million facility contingent upon acceptance of an austerity program.

The IMF's main conditions were a reduction in the government deficit to 9 percent of gross domestic product (GDP), tax increases, a $350 million ceiling on foreign borrowing, and devaluation of the colon (C). The colon, which had traded between C10 and C11 per dollar during the 1970s, was devalued to C15 in May and C20 in July of 1981. On the black market, dollars were selling for as much as C35. The government instituted a tiered exchange-rate system, requiring exporters to sell their dollars to the Central Bank at C15 while importers had to pay C20.

Export-Import Bank Financing

Perhaps the most attractive choice for managing the country risk associated with a sale to Costa Rica was Austrian Export-Import Bank financing. Although it would increase HKK's foreign exchange exposure, the company would avoid hedging costs and obtain a generous concessionary financing rate. The Oesterreichische Kontrollbank Aktiengesellschaft (OKB) had available a pool of As91 billion to lend to Austrian banks for the purpose of providing medium- and long-term financing for export contracts.

OKB financing would be provided in two tranches (see **Table 1**). Tranche A would bear an interest rate that would float at a fixed spread over OKB's own cost of funds, which consisted mostly of long-term bonds with an average yield of 6.5 percent per annum. The shorter the maturity of the OKB financing, the larger would be the proportion charged a floating rate. For contracts with maturities of 8 years or more, as much as 85 percent of the funds would be made available in a second tranche, tranche B, at a fixed rate. In September 1981 that fixed rate was just 8.75 percent per annum. In contrast, the annual yield on long-term Austrian government bonds was 11.2 percent.

For transactions such as HKK's proposed sale to Costa Rica, those repayments due in the first year would be subject to the terms of credits less than 2 years. The stream of repayments due in years 2 to 5 would be subject to the terms of credits longer than 2 but less than 5 years.

The OKB facility covered commercial and political risk and was available in amounts up to 100 percent of a transaction. To the extent that it provided fixed-rate financing, it covered interest rate risk as well.

When compared to 12-month Austrian schilling borrowing costs of 12¾ percent plus a 1 percent spread, 9 percent financing from OKB seemed almost too good to pass up. And that was just the problem. OKB limited the amount it would lend any one exporter to 20 percent of the company's annual exports. HKK's 1981 export sales were expected to decline slightly to As2.5 billion, and the OKB facility had already been tapped to finance an As100 million sale of tractors to Yugoslavia and an As150 million sale of motorcycles to Pakistan's defense forces. Moreover, Wiesinger knew that

TABLE 1   AUSTRIA, STATUTORY EXPORT FINANCING SCHEME OPERATED BY OESTERREICHISCHE KONTROLLBANK AKTIENGESELLSCHAFT (INTEREST RATES, AS OF AUGUST 15, 1981)

Repayment period of the credit	Tranche A of the loan (floating-rate portion), %	Quarterly OKB export finance rate* (current), %/annum[†]	Tranche B of the loan (fixed-rate portion), %	Prevailing fixed interest, %/annum[†]	Blended rate (approx.), %/annum
Less than 2 years	85	9.00	15	8.75	8.96
2 years or more but less than 5 years	70	9.00	30	8.25	8.78
5 years or more but less than 8 years	40	9.00	60	8.50	8.70
8 years or more	15	9.00	85	8.75	8.79

*As of July 1, 1981.
[†]Interest is payable quarterly in arrears; the loan is denominated in schillings.

Burgenlander in the Commercial Vehicle Division had just sewn up HKK's first sale to Iran, helped by the absence of competition from American bidders. There was no practical way for HKK to cover the substantial political risk of that deal aside from the OKB facility.

Banker's Acceptance Financing

There was a chance that Wiesinger could partially reduce the risk of a U.S. dollar sale to Costa Rica by using a banker's acceptance facility. Banker's acceptances (B/As) are generally inexpensive means of financing export transactions, but they typically involve short maturities.

Wiesinger had placed a call to Creditanstalt to get some idea whether B/A financing would be possible. Under current conditions, banks like Creditanstalt did not want to take on any Latin American risks. Austrian banks did not have the capacity to evaluate such credits and were worried by press reports.

COMPETITION FOR THE SAN JOSÉ BID

While Wiesinger was preoccupied with the financing alternatives for the proposed sale to Costa Rica, his counterpart in the Commercial Vehicle Division, Claus Burgenlander, was most concerned with the possibility that American competitors might undercut HKK's price on yet another deal. Already beset by large losses, Ford and International Harvester had been shaving prices dramatically in an effort to win additional sales. In fact, HKK was one of the few automotive manufacturers outside Japan that was not losing large sums of money.

But in a world of highly volatile exchange rates, losses on foreign exchange could erase HKK's slim profit for the year. It was HKK's policy to value all monetary assets and liabilities at prevailing yearend exchange rates for reporting purposes. At the same time, the Operating Division was credited in Austrian schillings at the prevailing exchange rate on the date of the transaction. Thus, if the sale to Costa Rica were transacted today (September 4, 1981), HKK would book a receivable of As270 million. Treasury would have to borrow U.S. $16 million at prevailing exchange rates (As16.9 = $1) to employ a money-market hedge. Yet if the schilling declined to the level at which it had traded just 3 weeks ago (As18.1 = $1), the $16 million liability would appear on HKK's books as As289.6 million, and the treasury department would be charged an As19.6 million foreign exchange loss. Historically, treasury's losses had been offset by gains, but Wiesinger was reluctant to count on this in his first year as head of the treasury department.

The Confrontation with Burgenlander

As Wiesinger ordered his second drink, he recalled his meeting with Claus Burgenlander the previous day. Burgenlander was manager of export sales for the Commercial Vehicle Division. He had worked for the Austrian subsidiary of an

American soap company before coming to HKK. Burgenlander and Wiesinger disputed the economics of the proposed sale to San José Citronas.

Burgenlander: Kurt, I know there are financing costs, but with operating costs of just 200 million schillings, winning a bid for 300 million will make this one of the best deals I've pulled off this year.

Wiesinger: I agree, but we could still *lose* money if the exchange rates change, or if San José doesn't pay us, or if we pay our banks to take those risks for us.

Burgenlander: Impossible. There is no way in which we will take on a As100 million exchange loss.

Wiesinger: Claus, if we borrow dollars now to avoid foreign exchange risk, we'll have to pay more in interest on the dollars than we can earn investing it in Austrian government securities. Then that income has to be discounted. . . .

Burgenlander: The only thing you have to discount in this business is *price*. Your competitor charges $10,000, you sell it for $9995. Production makes up for it in volume. It seems to me you people in finance should start considering the competitive realities and the importance of keeping the plants running.

EXHIBIT 1   SAN JOSÉ CITRONAS, LTDA. [BALANCE SHEET AND INCOME STATEMENT (MILLIONS OF COSTA RICAN COLONS)]

	1977	1978	1979
Assets			
Cash and marketable securities*	49	46	51
Accounts receivable	170	193	235
Inventories	206	232	273
Total current assets	425	471	559
Real estate†	87	87	87
Investments in affiliated companies	16	16	12
Total assets	528	574	658
Liabilities and equity			
Bank borrowings	180	210	252
Accounts payable	52	59	78
Other short-term liabilities	24	31	39
Total current liabilities	256	300	369
Long-term debt‡	150	150	150
Total liabilities	406	450	519
Common stock	50	50	50
Retained earnings	72	74	89
Total liabilities and equity	528	574	658
Automobile sales	399	430	502
Services	67	64	78
Less: Cost of goods sold	348	377	410
Wages and salaries	64	77	95
Interest expense	25	27	40
Other expense	7	9	7
Gross profit	22	5	28
Taxes	10	2	13
Net profit	12	3	15

*The percentage of cash held in foreign currency was 23 percent, 19 percent, and 13 percent in 1977, 1978, and 1979, respectively.
†At cost.
‡Debentures held by Banco Quixote, San José's largest shareholder.

EXHIBIT 2   SELECTED MACROECONOMIC DATA

	1975	1976	1977	1978	1979	1980	First-half 1981
Industrial production							
Austria	100	106	110	113	122	125	124
United States	100	111	117	124	129	122	130
Employment							
Austria	100	101	103	104	104	105	105
United States	100	103	107	112	117	117	119
Earnings per employee in manufacturing							
Austria	100	109	118	125	132	143	152
United States	100	108	118	127	138	150	165
Money supply							
Austria	100	108	110	119	108	125	123
United States	100	106	115	121	127	135	135
Change in wholesale price index							
Austria		5.9%	2.9%	1.0%	4.2%	8.6%	8.1%
United States		5.0%	6.0%	8.1%	12.5%	14.1%	9.1%
Exchange rate (As/$)	18.5	16.8	15.1	13.4	12.4	13.8	16.9
Merchandise balance							
Austria ($ billions)	(2.0)	(2.6)	(3.8)	(3.3)	(4.3)	(6.4)	(2.2)
United States ($ billions)	(9.1)	(9.3)	(30.9)	(33.8)	(27.3)	(25.3)	(10.9)

EXHIBIT 3   SELECTED INFORMATION ON INTEREST RATES, INFLATION RATES, AND EXCHANGE RATES

I. Forward exchange rates (As/$)

Date	September 4, 1981	Bid	Offered	Cost per annum (bid),* %	Spread,† %
Spot rate (bid)	16.910				
Forward					
1 month		16.805	16.820	7.4	0.09
3 months		16.610	16.660	7.1	0.30
6 months		16.320	16.450	7.0	0.79
12 months		16.000	16.150	5.4	0.93

II. London interbank Eurodollar offer rates, September 4, 1981

	Short-term Eurodollars			Medium-term Eurodollars	
	Annualized rate (%)			Annualized rate (%)	
Maturity	Bid	Ask	Maturity, years	Bid	Ask
2 days	17.500	17.625	2	17.375	17.625
1 month	18.125	18.250	3	17.125	17.325
3 months	18.625	18.750	4	16.875	17.125
6 months	18.750	18.875	5	16.750	17.000
12 months	18.000	18.125			

III. Key interest rates in Austria, September 4, 1981 (annualized rates)

Central bank discount rate	6.75%
Prime rate	7.25
90-Day T-bill	7.75
90-Day time deposit	7.75
One-year Euroschilling deposit (bid)	11.75
Prime lending rate	13.50
Long-term government bonds	11.20

IV. Key interest rates in the United States, September 4, 1981 (annualized rates)

90-Day T-bill	15.45%
Prime lending rate	20.00
Long-term government bonds	15.40
Long-term AA corporate bonds	16.90

*The cost of a forward contract as a percent per annum is calculated as:

$$\frac{\text{Forward rate} - \text{spot rate}}{\text{Spot rate}} \times \frac{12}{\text{No. of months}} = \% \text{ per annum cost}$$

†The spread is calculated as:

$$\frac{\text{Offered} - \text{bid}}{\text{Bid}} \times 100 = \% \text{ per annum cost}$$

NOTE ON
FOREIGN CURRENCY
SWAPS

A foreign currency swap, in the simplest sense, is an agreement between two parties to exchange a given amount of one currency for another and to repay these currencies with interest in the future. Normally one counterparty—such as a corporation, bank, sovereign government, or supranational institution—borrows under specific terms and conditions in one currency while the other counterparty borrows under different terms and conditions in a second currency. The two counterparties then exchange the net receipts from their respective issues and agree to service each other's debt.

For instance, a U.S. company that has issued deutsche mark bonds with an annual all-in deutsche mark cost of 8 percent might enter into a foreign currency swap directly with a German company that has issued U.S. dollar bonds with an annual all-in dollar cost of 11 percent. The companies would exchange the initial receipts from their respective bonds. Meanwhile, the American company would agree to pay the interest and principal on the dollar bonds issued by the German company, and the German company would agree to pay the interest and principal on the deutsche mark bonds issued by the American company. From the American company's viewpoint, such an arrangement is beneficial if the German company is able to borrow dollars at a lower rate than the rate the American company would have been able to obtain. Likewise, the German company will find the swap attractive if the American company is able to borrow deutsche marks at a lower cost than the German company would have had to pay. Under the swap agreement, both companies know precisely their financing costs

This note is an abridged version of "Foreign Currency Swaps" (Harvard Business School note 286-073), originally prepared by doctoral student William B. Allen, Jr., under the supervision of Professor Scott P. Mason, abridged by Professor W. Carl Kester. Copyright © 1991 by the President and Fellows of Harvard College. Harvard Business School note 292-043.

in the desired currency. The all-in costs of the cash flows associated with the debt issues and the related foreign currency swaps are shown in a typical foreign currency swap diagram in **Exhibit 1**.

An alternative method for the American company to lock in the dollar cost of servicing its deutsche mark debt (or the German company to lock in the deutsche mark cost of servicing its dollar debt) would have been to use the forward-exchange market. However, long-dated outright forward-exchange rates are priced very conservatively by banks, and the bid-offer spreads tend to open quite wide. Banks are usually not eager to take on the risk of changes in the future level of spot exchange rates, and it is difficult for them to "square" their long-dated forward positions with offsetting future cash flows from other business or other forward trades in the market.

In contrast, a foreign currency swap typically results in an immediate matching of two counterparties with opposite hedging needs. The all-in costs of the cash flows in the desired currency using foreign currency swaps arranged directly between two counterparties are usually less than those using bank forward-exchange contracts. There is no need to build in an extra margin to cover exchange-rate risk from the standpoint of the bank, except to the extent that exchange-rate changes induce default by one of the counterparties. In the event of default, the bank would cease making swap payments to the defaulting party (the right of offset), but would continue making payments to the other counterparty.

THE DEVELOPMENT OF INTEREST RATE AND FOREIGN CURRENCY SWAP MARKETS

With the introduction of interest rate swaps in the spring of 1982, fixed-rate dollar obligations could be converted into floating-rate dollar obligations. This market developed from the needs of major European and Japanese banks to acquire competitively priced floating-rate dollar funding for their growing volume of floating-rate dollar assets. They had typically paid slightly higher spreads over the London Interbank Offer Rate (LIBOR) for Eurodollar bank borrowings than had their American counterparts. However, these banks had not been very active in the fixed-rate Eurodollar bond market and enjoyed a "scarcity" value in that market, resulting in low annual all-in dollar costs.

Many large, lower-credit American companies, however, were seeking fixed-rate American financing but were induced to use floating-rate loans with rates calculated as spreads over LIBOR because fixed-rate bonds seemed prohibitively expensive. Some European and Japanese banks began issuing fixed-rate Eurodollar bonds and entering into interest rate swaps in which they made floating-rate dollar LIBOR swap payments to the American companies. In return, these companies made fixed-rate dollar swap payments to the banks that covered the debt service on their Eurodollar bonds. These arrangements reduced the cost of floating-rate dollar funds for the banks to LIBOR and reduced the cost of fixed-rate dollar funds for the American companies to a level close to the more favorable dollar rates paid by the European and Japanese banks. In late 1982 and 1983, the tremendous volume of foreign bank fixed-rate Eurodollar bonds that were swapped into floating-rate dollars put pressure on these markets, and the savings resulting from this strategy were substantially reduced.

As the fixed-rate Eurodollar market became less hospitable to the European and Japanese banks, they sought fixed-rate funding in other currencies, such as the deutsche mark or Swiss franc, and swapped these liabilities for fixed-rate dollars. The fixed-rate dollar flows were then swapped into floating-rate dollars. Over time, the dollar interest rate swaps had become commodities that banks aggressively offered to their customers. An estimated $100 billion of notional principal amount of interest rate swaps was arranged in 1985.

Major international banks made a market in interest rate swaps by quoting bid-offer rates for various maturities and holding trading positions. The bid rate was the fixed dollar rate that banks were willing to pay in exchange for receiving 6-month dollar LIBOR, and the offer rate was the fixed dollar rate that they were willing to receive in exchange for paying 6-month dollar LIBOR. The fixed rates were typically quoted as spreads over benchmark Treasuries (see **Exhibit 2**). Thus, borrowers could easily exchange fixed foreign currency obligations into dollar LIBOR obligations by a combination of fixed-rate currency swaps and dollar interest rate swaps.

The practice of swapping fixed-rate foreign currency flows for dollar LIBOR was also attractive for sovereign borrowers and foreign state agencies that wanted fixed-rate foreign-currency liabilities but, because of the size of their needs or their lower credit, were forced to issue Eurodollar floating-rate notes. These borrowers were natural payers of fixed-rate foreign currency because they often wanted to establish liabilities in these currencies to hedge official reserves or match future foreign currency trade inflows.

DETERMINING FOREIGN CURRENCY SWAP FLOWS USING MARKET SWAP RATES

Foreign currency swaps are typically quoted as either the annual or semiannual fixed rate on the foreign currency flows against 6-month dollar LIBOR. By relating any two quotes to dollar LIBOR, banks can easily determine the fixed swap rate in one currency against the fixed swap rate in another currency. Major international banks make markets in foreign currency swaps, and quotes are generally available in several currencies for various maturities (see **Exhibit 3**).

An Illustration

To illustrate the mechanics of intermediated foreign currency swaps, which are structured using quoted market swap rates, consider a hypothetical currency generic swap between the World Bank (WB) and a company (Company) in which both parties agree to make swap payments that exactly cover the required future debt service of the counterparty. Assume their direct 5-year financing alternatives are as shown in **Table 1**.

TABLE 1   HYPOTHETICAL DIRECT FINANCING ALTERNATIVES

	World Bank	Company
Desired amount	SF100 million	$50 million
Target rate	SF8.1%	$16.7%
Direct borrowing all-in costs	SF8.38%*	$17.59%[†]
Alternative all-in borrowing costs	$16.58%[‡]	SF7.98%[§]
SF/$ spot rate (bid-ask)	SF1.9995–2.0005	

*7.75 percent coupon and front-end fees of 2½ percent.
[†]17 percent coupon and front-end fees of 1⅞ percent.
[‡]16 percent coupon and front-end fees of 1⅞ percent.
[§]7.35 percent coupon and front-end fees of 2½ percent.

Assume also that a bank has quoted the following annual foreign currency swap rates:

Swiss francs   7.70 to 7.80 percent against 6-month dollar LIBOR
Dollars   16.25 to 16.35 percent against 6-month dollar LIBOR

By virtue of its 16.25 percent dollar bid to receive 6-month dollar LIBOR, and its 7.80 percent Swiss franc asking price to pay 6-month dollar LIBOR, the intermediary has effectively offered to pay the WB dollars at 16.25 percent annually against receiving annual 7.80 percent in Swiss francs.

In this example, there are market swap rates for both the dollar and Swiss franc payments. Therefore, the 16.25 percent quoted annual dollar swap rate, which would be paid by the intermediary to the WB, was not the same as the 16.58 percent annual all-in cost on the bond. In regard to the cash flows, the intermediary agreed to pay to the WB in years 1 to 5 the exact amount of dollars needed to cover the annual interest and final principal payments on its bond. The WB also agreed to pay Swiss francs equal to the future required debt service on the Company's bond. Thus, the size of both initial swap exchanges in dollars and Swiss francs between the WB and the intermediary was adjusted to achieve the quoted swap rates.

The calculation of the WB's flows from the dollar bond and the swap with the intermediating bank are shown in **Exhibit 4**. Column (A) contains the flows from the dollar bond. In column (B), the WB's dollar swap receipts from the intermediary in years 1 through 5 exactly match its debt service. The amount of the initial dollar payment, which the WB must make to the intermediary, is $49.593 million—the present value of the required annual dollar flows from years 1 to 5 discounted at the 16.25 percent quoted dollar swap rate.

Similarly, column (C) of **Exhibit 4** shows the Swiss franc swap flows. The size of the WB's initial Swiss franc receipt is SF98.194 million—the present value of the required annual Swiss franc swap flows from years 1 to 5 discounted at the 7.80 percent quoted swap rate.

Note that the $49.593 million initial payment by the WB to the intermediary exceeds the $39.063 million net proceeds from its bond issue. The $0.531 million shortfall, shown in column (D) of **Exhibit 4**, is purchased by the WB in the spot foreign exchange market out of the initial Swiss franc proceeds received by the intermediary.

Thus, the initial Swiss franc swap inflow calculated above is effectively reduced by SF1.062 million—the amount of Swiss francs necessary to purchase $0.531 million at the spot offer rate. Column (F) shows the WB's effective Swiss franc cash flows after subtracting the amount of Swiss francs used to purchase dollars and cover the shortfall.

The effective annual all-in Swiss franc cost to the WB is 8.07 percent—the internal rate of return of the Swiss franc flows in column (F) of **Exhibit 4**. The quoted swap rates for the WB enabled it to reduce its annual all-in Swiss franc borrowing cost below its target rate of 8.10 percent by 3 basis points.

For the Company, the intermediary would pay Swiss francs at an annual rate of 7.70 percent against receiving dollars at an annual rate of 16.35 percent. The cash flows between the intermediary and the Company, calculated similarly to those between the intermediary and the WB, are shown in **Exhibit 5**. The cash flows to the intermediary from the swap, ignoring the foreign exchange transactions, appear in **Exhibit 6**.

Basis Point Conversion

In practice, intermediating banks often use another technique to structure swap flows. Notice that the quoted dollar swap rate paid to the WB is 16.25 percent compared with the 16.58 percent annual all-in cost of the bonds. This means that there is a shortfall of 33 basis points. The intermediary adjusted the swap terms so that the dollar swap rate paid to the WB would equal the 16.58 percent annual all-in cost of the bonds by adding 33 basis points to the 16.25 percent dollar swap rate. With a higher dollar swap rate paid to the WB, the Swiss franc swap rate that the intermediary received also had to be increased. However, 33 dollar basis points, paid annually over 5 years, are not equal to 33 Swiss franc basis points. Because the Swiss franc was at a forward premium to the dollar, the equivalent amount of Swiss franc basis points was smaller.

The calculation of the conversion of dollar basis points to Swiss franc basis points is often done by the following shorthand method. The excess basis points in one currency, expressed as an annual coupon on a hypothetical $100 par bond (see **Exhibit 7**), are discounted to the present at the appropriate term interest rate in that currency. This present value is then "reannualized" (i.e., a hypothetical level annual payment is computed) using the appropriate term interest rate in the second currency. In the WB example, the following calculations are made (see **Exhibit 7**):

1. The 33 dollar basis points are discounted for 5 years at 16.25 percent, the quoted dollar swap rate received by the WB. This results in a present value of 1.07425.

2. The 1.07425 present value calculated in step 1 is then reannualized at 7.80 percent, the quoted Swiss franc swap rate that the WB paid. That is, a level annual payment is computed such that the internal rate of return on the payments plus the present value is equal to 7.80 percent. This equals 0.2676, or approximately 27 Swiss franc basis points.

3. The quoted swap rates are then adjusted by adding 33 basis points to the 16.25 percent dollar rate and 27 basis points to the 7.80 percent Swiss franc rate (see **Exhibit 8**).

SUMMARY

Foreign currency swaps provide an attractive alternative to the use of long-dated forward foreign exchange contracts for currency hedging. The primary use of foreign currency swaps has been to hedge foreign currency debt. Many dollar-based borrowers have issued foreign currency debt: (1) to expand their investor base; (2) to avoid ratings revisions that are often triggered with new U.S. debt; or (3) to exploit arbitrage opportunities where it is less costly to issue debt denominated in foreign currencies and then swap into dollars.

Arbitrage opportunities can persist in an age of modern financial markets because of several factors. Markets sometimes become saturated with the paper of one borrower. This is often the situation with supranational institutions, sovereign borrowers, and state agencies seeking to issue debt in low-coupon currencies such as Swiss francs and deutsche marks. In this situation, lower all-in costs can be achieved by issuing in the more liquid dollar market, finding a surrogate foreign currency borrower—such as a high-credit U.S. company—and swapping liabilities.

Attractive opportunities to issue foreign currency debt and then swap this debt into a different currency are also created when investors in certain countries use different techniques of credit assessment, such as emphasizing name recognition and other qualitative factors. For example, Swiss investors are attracted to well-known corporate names, especially those that market high-quality consumer products, and are often willing to pay a premium on bonds from these issuers. Different credit norms in different markets can also cause borrowers to face different costs of debt. In many foreign capital markets, there is much less emphasis on quantitative analysis and credit ratings than in domestic U.S. markets. Also, foreign markets typically demand less spread differentials for lower credits. The resulting "spread compression" has enabled many U.S. BBB-rated firms to issue foreign debt swapped into dollars at attractive all-in costs.

Finally, regulations can also make borrowing in one currency more attractive than borrowing in another. For example, limitations on Japanese life insurance companies' purchases of foreign-issued bonds have led to a tremendous demand for the dollar-denominated bonds of Japanese resident companies (Sushi bonds), which are exempt from this regulation. Because of this demand, Japanese resident borrowers have issued U.S. dollar debt at below-market rates and have swapped into yen at very attractive all-in yen costs.

Foreign currency swaps have enabled borrowers to access debt markets that might otherwise have been difficult to tap. The World Bank, for example, can indirectly increase its Swiss franc and deutsche mark liabilities by issuing dollars and swapping into these currencies. Such swaps also allow the World Bank to preserve its access to these markets in the future. Other borrowers have used swaps to incur liabilities quickly in currencies for which there is a long queue of borrowers waiting to be given permission by local monetary authorities to issue securities in domestic capital markets.

Foreign currency swaps have proven to be flexible tools that need not be tied to newly issued securities. Many companies have also used swaps to transform the currency denomination of *existing* liabilities. The World Bank, for example, pursues a swap program to fine-tune its liability structure by actively swapping into and out of different currencies to achieve the lowest possible debt costs. Swaps can also be used to hedge anticipated future cash flows. This has led to "asset swaps" used by investors to transform the income on investments into different currencies.

Just as interest rate swaps have become a commodity, so too have foreign currency swaps. Banks frequently arrange deals before a matching counterparty can be found. While these open positions are on their books, banks generally hedge their exposure by buying government bonds in the currencies in which they are contracted to pay fixed rates, and selling government bonds in currencies in which they are contracted to receive fixed rates. It is easy to hedge swaps in U.S. dollars, Canadian dollars, British pounds sterling, and deutsche marks in this manner. In Swiss francs, where there are no adequate government bonds that can be used for hedging, banks have taken on unhedged positions because of the relative stability of Swiss franc interest rates and currency values. However, even when a counterparty is found, it is rare that the timing or the amount of future swap flows will exactly match. Therefore, the bank usually has future cash flow mismatches that also must be hedged. As these hedging techniques are perfected, an important barrier to continued strong growth of the foreign-currency swap market—namely, the ability to find a matching counterparty—will be overcome.

EXHIBIT 1   ANNUAL ALL-IN COSTS OF CASH FLOWS ASSOCIATED WITH A FOREIGN CURRENCY SWAP BETWEEN A U.S. AND A GERMAN COMPANY

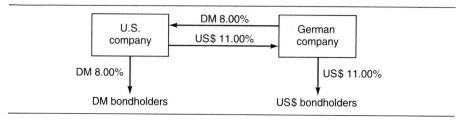

EXHIBIT 2   INTEREST RATE SWAP INDICATIONS ON DECEMBER 16, 1985, FIXED DOLLAR PAYMENTS AGAINST 6-MONTH DOLLAR LIBOR

Year	Semiannual quotations*		Benchmark U.S. Treasuries, %	Semiannual rates, %		Annual rates, %	
	Bid	Offer		Bid	Offer	Bid†	Offer
3	T+55	T+73	8.24	8.79	8.97	8.98	9.17
5	T+55	T+70	8.66	9.21	9.36	9.42	9.58
7	T+45	T+60	9.03	9.48	9.63	9.70	9.86
10	T+45	T+60	9.21	9.66	9.81	9.89	10.05

*Semiannual basis point spread over benchmark Treasuries.
†Rates are quoted from the bank's perspective: The bank will pay annual 8.98 percent against receiving 6-month dollar LIBOR, or the bank will receive annual 9.17 percent against paying 6-month dollar LIBOR.
Source: Morgan Guaranty, Ltd, London.

EXHIBIT 3   FOREIGN CURRENCY SWAP INDICATIONS ON DECEMBER 16, 1985

| | Semiannual quotations* | | | | | | | |
| | 3 Years | | 5 Years | | 7 Years | | 10 Years | |
Currency	Pay†	Receive	Pay	Receive	Pay	Receive	Pay	Receive
U.S. dollars	8.79%	8.97%	9.21%	9.36%	9.48%	9.63%	9.66%	9.81%
British sterling	11.18	11.38	11.14	11.34	11.08	11.28	11.20	11.40
Canadian dollars	9.46	9.66	9.81	10.01	9.97	10.17	10.13	10.33
Japanese yen	7.00	7.15	6.90	7.05	7.00	7.15	7.00	7.15
Swiss francs	5.04	5.28	5.28	5.52	5.48	5.72	5.57	5.82
Deutsche marks	5.72	6.01	6.35	6.64	6.59	6.88	6.83	7.07
French francs	11.50	11.50	11.50	11.50	11.50	11.50	11.50	11.50

| | Annual quotations* | | | | | | | |
| | 3 Years | | 5 Years | | 7 Years | | 10 Years | |
Currency	Pay†	Receive	Pay	Receive	Pay	Receive	Pay	Receive
U.S. dollars	8.98%	9.17%	9.42%	9.58%	9.70%	9.86%	9.89%	10.05%
British sterling	11.49	11.70	11.45	11.66	11.39	11.60	11.51	11.72
Canadian dollars	9.68	9.89	10.05	10.26	10.22	10.43	10.39	10.60
Japanese yen	7.12	7.28	7.02	7.17	7.12	7.28	7.12	7.28
Swiss francs	5.10	5.35	5.35	5.60	5.56	5.80	5.65	5.90
Deutsche marks	5.80	6.10	6.45	6.75	6.70	7.00	6.95	7.19
French francs	11.83	11.83	11.83	11.83	11.83	11.83	11.83	11.83

*All rates are against 6-month dollar LIBOR.
†Rates are quoted from bank's perspective: The bank will pay semiannual 8.79 percent against receiving 6-month dollar LIBOR, or the bank will receive semiannual 8.97 percent against paying 6-month dollar LIBOR.
Source: Morgan Guaranty, Ltd, London.

EXHIBIT 4   CASH FLOWS OF THE WORLD BANK IN A HYPOTHETICAL SWAP USING
QUOTED SWAP RATES (MILLIONS)*

		World Bank receipts (− payments)				
	From	Swap flows with intermediary		Dollar	Swiss franc	Effective SF low
Year	dollar bond	$	SF	shortfall	equivalent	for WB
	(A)	(B)	(C)	(D)	(E)	(F)
0	49.063	(49.593)	98.194	(0.531)	(1.062)	97.132
1	(8.000)	8.000	(7.350)			(7.350)
2	(8.000)	8.000	(7.350)			(7.350)
3	(8.000)	8.000	(7.350)			(7.350)
4	(8.000)	8.000	(7.350)			(7.350)
5	(58.000)	58.000	107.350			(107.350)
All-in cost	16.58%	16.25%	7.80%			
Quoted swap rates		16.25%	7.80%			
Effective all-in cost						8.07%

*Note: Column head explanations: (A) Flows from dollar bond. (B) Dollar swap flows with intermediating bank. Initial dollar payment is the present value of required debt service discounted at 16.25 percent quoted swap rate. (C) Swiss franc swap flows with intermediating bank. Initial Swiss franc receipt is the present value of required annual Swiss franc debt service of counterparty discounted at 7.8 percent quoted swap rate. (D) Difference between net dollar proceeds from bond issue in column (A) and initial dollar swap payment in column (B). (E) Dollar shortfall in column (D) purchased with Swiss francs at offered rate of SF2.0005/$1. (F) Effective Swiss franc flows for WB after adjusting for FX purchase of initial dollar shortfall.

EXHIBIT 5   CASH FLOWS OF THE COMPANY IN A HYPOTHETICAL SWAP USING
QUOTED SWAP RATES (MILLIONS)*

		U.S. Company receipts (− payments)				
	From	Swap flows with intermediary		Swiss franc	Dollar	Effective dollar
Year	SF bond	$	SF	shortfall	equivalent	flow for Co.
	(A)	(B)	(C)	(D)	(E)	(F)
0	97.500	49.432	(98.591)	(1.091)	(0.546)	48.886
1	(7.350)	(8.000)	7.350			(8.000)
2	(7.350)	(8.000)	7.350			(8.000)
3	(7.350)	(8.000)	7.350			(8.000)
4	(7.350)	(8.000)	7.350			(8.000)
5	(107.350)	(58.000)	107.350			(58.000)
All-in cost	7.98%	16.35%	7.70%			
Quoted swap rates		16.35%	7.70%			
Effective all-in cost						16.69%

*Note: Column head explanations: (A) Flows from Swiss franc bond. (B) Dollar swap flows with intermediating bank. Initial dollar receipt is the present value of required annual Swiss franc debt service of counterparty discounted at 16.35 percent quoted swap rate. (C) Swiss franc swap flows with intermediating bank. Initial Swiss franc payment is the present value of required debt service discounted at 7.7 percent quoted swap rate. (D) Difference between net Swiss franc proceeds from bond issue in column (A) and initial Swiss franc swap payment in column (C). (E) Swiss franc shortfall in column (D) purchased with dollar at bid rate of SF1.9995/$1. (F) Effective dollar flows for Company after adjusting for FX purchase of initial Swiss franc shortfall.

EXHIBIT 6   CASH FLOWS TO (− FROM) THE INTERMEDIATING BANK (MILLIONS)*

Year	Swap flows with WB		Swap flows with Company		Net flows to bank	
	$	SF	$	SF	$	SF
	(A)	(B)	(C)	(D)	(E)	(F)
0	49.593	(98.194)	(49.432)	98.591	0.161	0.397
1	(8.000)	7.350	8.000	(7.350)	0.000	0.000
2	(8.000)	7.350	8.000	(7.350)	0.000	0.000
3	(8.000)	7.350	8.000	(7.350)	0.000	0.000
4	(8.000)	7.350	8.000	(7.350)	0.000	0.000
5	(58.000)	107.350	58.000	(107.350)	0.000	0.000

Note: column head explanations: (A) Flows are equal and opposite to those in Exhibit 4, column (B). (B) Flows are equal and opposite to those in Exhibit 4, column (C). (C) Flows are equal and opposite to those in Exhibit 5, column (B). (D) Flows are equal and opposite to those in Exhibit 5, column (C). (E) Column (A) − column (C). (F) Column (B) − column (D).

EXHIBIT 7   CONVERSION OF 33 DOLLAR BASIS POINTS TO SWISS FRANC BASIS POINTS

Year	Dollar basis points	Swiss franc basis points
Present value*	1.07425	1.07425
1	(0.33000)	(.26760)
2	(0.33000)	(.26760)
3	(0.33000)	(.26760)
4	(0.33000)	(.26760)
5	(0.33000)	(.26760)
Internal rate of return	16.25%	7.80%

*The present value is computed using the 16.25 percent dollar discount rate.

EXHIBIT 8   CALCULATION OF EFFECTIVE SWAP RATES

	U.S. dollar	Swiss franc
Quoted swap rates	16.25%	7.80%
Add		
Dollar basis points	0.33	
SF basis points	—	0.27
Effective swap rates	16.58%	8.07%

THE WALT DISNEY COMPANY'S YEN FINANCING

In early July 1985, Rolf Anderson, the director of finance at The Walt Disney Company, was concerned about possible foreign exchange exposure due to future yen royalty receipts from Tokyo Disneyland. Tokyo Disneyland, open for just over 2 years, was operated by an unrelated Japanese company and paid royalties on certain revenues to Walt Disney Productions. These yen royalties had increased significantly during the last year and Mr. Anderson foresaw further growth in the years ahead. Given the recent depreciation of the yen against the dollar, he was considering various ways of hedging this exposure.

Mr. Anderson had considered hedging techniques using foreign exchange options, futures, and forwards. Also, he had thought about swapping out of existing dollar debt into a yen liability. But these choices did not appear particularly attractive, and he had focused his attention on a possible ¥15 billion, 10-year term loan with interest of 7.50 percent paid semiannually.

However, Goldman Sachs, which had been working with Disney on this problem, proposed a rather unusual solution. Disney could issue 10-year ECU Eurobonds with a sinking fund that would then be swapped into a yen liability at an attractive all-in yen cost. Although this seemed a rather roundabout way to create yen financing, Mr. Anderson was delighted at the prospects of costs below the yen loan. Furthermore, he

This case was prepared by doctoral student William B. Allen, Jr., under the supervision of Professor W. Carl Kester. The Walt Disney Company is not responsible for the accuracy of any information contained in the case. The case is not intended as a recommendation or endorsement by The Walt Disney Company of any particular type of financing. Copyright © 1987 by the President and Fellows of Harvard College. Harvard Business School case 287-058.

could not help but wonder what factors in the international capital markets would make a deal such as this work.

THE WALT DISNEY COMPANY

The Walt Disney Company, a diversified international company headquartered in Burbank, California, operated entertainment and recreational complexes, produced motion picture and television features, developed community real estate projects, and sold consumer products. The company was founded in 1938 as successor to the animated motion picture business established by Walt and Roy Disney in 1923. These early films had immortalized cartoon characters created by the Disney brothers such as Mickey Mouse and Donald Duck.

The company operated the Disneyland amusement theme park in Anaheim, California, and the Walt Disney World destination resort in Orlando, Florida. The Disneyland Park was renowned for its rides and attractions in addition to the seven principal theme areas: Fantasyland, Adventureland, Frontierland, Tomorrowland, New Orleans Square, Main Street, and Bear Country. In each area there were restaurants, refreshment stands, and souvenir shops in keeping with the surrounding theme. The Walt Disney World Complex included the Magic Kingdom amusement theme park (similar in concept to Disneyland Park) and Epcot Center (an acronym for Experimental Prototype Community of Tomorrow); three hotels; camping, golfing, and other recreational facilities designed for the whole family; a shopping village; a conference center; and other lodging accommodations.

In addition to the domestic entertainment and recreation revenues from Disneyland and Walt Disney World, the company received royalties, paid in yen, on certain revenues generated by Tokyo Disneyland. Similar in concept to the other Disney centers, this amusement theme park was located just 6 miles from downtown Tokyo, Japan. Owned and operated by an unrelated Japanese corporation, Tokyo Disneyland was opened to the public on April 15, 1983.

Disney produced motion pictures for the theatrical, television, and home video markets for audiences around the world. Although most of Disney's best-known films were fully or partially animated and were targeted at younger audiences, the company also made films designed to appeal to teenagers and young adults. In addition, Disney developed and produced television programs, such as *Disney's Wonderful World* and The Disney Channel, for network, syndicated, and pay television markets.

Through its real estate subsidiary, Arvida Corporation, acquired in 1984, the company planned and developed distinctive resort and home communities, primarily in Florida. Commercial and industrial properties, such as neighborhood shopping centers and office buildings, were also developed within or near the planned communities. In its consumer products segment, Disney licensed its name, its characters, its literary properties, and its songs and music to various manufacturers, retailers, printers, and publishers. The company also produced a variety of educational materials and teaching aids.

Consolidated revenues for The Walt Disney Company and its subsidiaries increased by almost 27 percent in 1984 to $1.7 billion (see **Exhibit 1**). Total entertainment and recreation revenues, including royalties from Tokyo Disneyland, increased 6 percent to $1.1 billion in the fiscal year ended September 30, 1984. Although theme park attendance in the United States was down 5 percent to 31 million in 1984, the increased revenues for 1984 reflected admission price increases, higher per capita spending at the parks, and the inclusion of a full year of royalties from Tokyo Disneyland. Filmed entertainment revenues increased 48 percent to $245 million in 1984 due to strong domestic theatrical film rentals. Community development and consumer products revenues added another $204 million and $110 million, respectively.

Net income totaled $97.8 million in 1984, an increase of 5 percent from 1983. This growth was due primarily to the operating profits before corporate expenses contributed by the recently acquired real estate subsidiary and a turnaround in the filmed entertainment segment. Operating profits before corporate expenses for the entertainment and recreation segment actually decreased by 2 percent in 1984. Corporate expenses increased substantially due to $20 million nonrecurring costs associated with the acquisition of Arvida and increased interest costs on high levels of borrowing. The company also provided for $166 million in unusual charges to write down the values of several motion pictures and various development projects.

Total assets grew 15 percent to $2.7 billion at the end of fiscal 1984 (see **Exhibit 2**), due primarily to the addition of real estate inventories as part of the acquisition of Arvida. Borrowings more than doubled to $862 million in 1984 because of the $215 million of Arvida debt assumed upon its acquisition and the $328 million expenditure for the repurchase of 4.2 million shares of the company's common stock from Reliance Insurance Company, which had launched a hostile takeover bid for the company. The ratio of debt to total capitalization jumped to 43 percent at September 30, 1984, from 20 percent at the end of the previous fiscal year, a level since reduced to 32 percent. Two-thirds of borrowings at the end of 1984 consisted of relatively high interest rate short-term bank loans and commercial paper **(Exhibit 3)**. The company had two separate Eurodollar note issues outstanding, rated single A, totaling $175 million. However, $50 million of the $75 million issue due in 1989 had been swapped into a yen liability at a yen cost of 7.40 percent. Also, the company had a yen term loan at 8.60 percent that required semiannual principal and interest payments over the next 8 years.

By March 31, 1985, Disney had succeeded in reducing its short-term bank borrowings to $168.7 million. At the same time, commercial paper outstanding had grown to $352.2 million. Also, the 15.75 percent Eurodollar notes due in 1986 had been called and replaced with 2-year Eurodollar notes at a significantly lower coupon.

THE ECU AND THE ECU EUROBOND MARKET

The European Currency Unit (ECU) was officially accepted in 1978 as the unit of account for the countries that formed the European Monetary System (EMS). It was used as the basis for monitoring exchange-rate divergence among member nations and was an officially sanctioned reserve currency within the EMS. The ECU, a composite currency, was defined as a trade-weighted basket of European currencies. In mid-1985, the ECU consisted of the following amounts of currencies:

0.719	West German deutsche marks	3.71	Belgian francs
0.0878	British pounds sterling	0.14	Luxembourg francs
1.31	French francs	0.219	Danish kroner
140.00	Italian lire	0.00871	Irish pounds
0.256	Dutch guilders	1.15	Greek drachmas

This weighting was scheduled for its next official 5-year review in 1989. With the likely admission of Spain and Portugal to the European Economic Community, market participants expected the currencies of these countries to be incorporated within the ECU at that time.

The ECU was traded in the foreign exchange markets like any other currency, with both spot and forward transactions. However, the forward market was relatively thin, and long-dated forwards were not readily available. Banks in most European countries (with the notable exception of West Germany) freely accepted ECU deposits and made ECU loans. Other financial instruments included ECU certificates of deposit, ECU Eurobonds and floating-rate notes, and ECU bonds in the domestic U.S. ("Yankee") bond market. Interest rates in ECU were, theoretically, the weighted average of the interest rates in the component currencies. However, since it was difficult for nonresidents to access the money markets in some of these countries and long-term interest rates were often nonexistent, ECU interest rates tended to have a life of their own. ECU interest rates historically exceeded the theoretical rate by 1 to 1½ percent. Still, ECU interest rates were generally higher than those of the strong component currencies but lower than those of the weak component currencies.

The first ECU Eurobond, ECU35 million issued by an Italian state agency in April 1981, had a 6-year life and a coupon of 13 percent. Following that issue, the ECU Eurobond market grew impressively and by mid-1985 was the third largest Eurobond market in terms of new-issue volume behind dollars and marks. As of mid-1985, there were about 175 fixed-rate ECU Eurobonds totaling over ECU9.5 billion listed as outstanding by the Association of International Bond Dealers. (In addition, there were seven floating-rate notes totaling ECU450 million.) ECU Eurobonds had historically averaged ECU30 to ECU50 million in size although, more recently, it was not uncommon to see issues of ECU100 million or more. Three-quarters of ECU Eurobonds were offered with original maturities of 6 to 10 years, and the majority of the fixed-rate coupons ranged from 11 to 9 percent.

In the early years, ECU Eurobond issuers were primarily European supranationals, banks, and state agencies. The dearth of non-European and nonfinancial corporate borrowers was explained by the scarcity of attractive foreign-currency swaps. However, by mid-1985 nonfinancial corporate borrowers accounted for over a quarter of new issues, while supranationals, sovereigns, and state agencies represented only one-third and banks another one-third. Although three-quarters of the borrowers were still European, U.S. and Canadian borrowers accounted for 10 percent and Far Eastern borrowers accounted for an additional 7 percent. Market participants attributed most of the growth of this market and the increasing diversity of issuers to the development of the ECU/dollar swap market.

ECU Eurobonds had been traditionally sold to individuals in France, Belgium, Luxembourg, and Switzerland who had established ECU bank accounts. These

Eurobond investors were attracted by the high coupons and relative stability of the ECU to their domestic currencies. Because of this historical concentration of demand, new issues were usually lead-managed by major French or Belgian banks. However, there were signs in mid-1985 of increased institutional demand, not only from European institutions, but also from Japanese and U.S. funds wishing to diversify their portfolios away from dollars.

THE PROBLEM FACING DISNEY

With the opening of Tokyo Disneyland in April 1983 and the inflow of yen royalty receipts, Mr. Anderson was concerned about the possible exposure of Disney to future fluctuations in the yen/dollar spot rate. The current spot rate of ¥248/$1 represented almost an 8 percent depreciation in the value of the yen from 229.70 just over a year ago (see **Exhibit 4**). During fiscal 1984, yen royalty receipts had been just over ¥8 billion. However, Mr. Anderson expected these receipts to grow at 10 to 20 percent per year over the next few years as the new theme park attracted the interest of Japanese vacationers and foreign tourists traveling to Tokyo.

Mr. Anderson had considered various ways of hedging a portion of the expected future yen receipts, including foreign exchange (FX) options, futures, and forwards. One issue that confronted him immediately was how far into the future he should attempt to hedge. Liquid markets for options and futures contracts existed only for maturities of 2 years or less. A similar problem appeared to exist with bank FX forward contracts, although Disney had obtained an indication of long-dated FX forward rates from its banks (see **Exhibit 5**). However, the banks would consider the FX forwards as a part of their total exposure to Disney, thus tying up valuable credit lines.

As an alternative, Disney could enter into another foreign-currency swap, as it had done a year earlier, converting more of its existing dollar debt into a yen liability. This type of a hedge would also be short-term since Disney's Eurodollar note issues matured in 1 to 4 years. Mr. Anderson also knew that attractive yen swap rates for maturities less than 4 years were hard to find. Moreover, this arrangement would not provide any additional cash, and Disney was interested in reducing further its short-term debt. For the moment, Mr. Anderson had ruled out a longer-maturity Eurodollar debt issue, which could be more effectively swapped into yen, because of Disney's recent Eurodollar note issue and the company's temporarily high debt ratio. Euroyen bonds were also out of the question. Despite the recent liberalizations in the Euroyen bond market, Disney was ineligible to issue Euroyen bonds under the current Japanese Ministry of Finance guidelines.

Thus, should Disney wish to hedge much beyond 3 or 4 years, it appeared that its only viable choice was to create a yen liability through a term loan from a Japanese bank at the Japanese long-term prime rate. Disney was considering a ¥15 billion 10-year bullet loan, with principal repaid at final maturity, which required interest of 7.50 percent paid semiannually and front-end fees of 0.75 percent.

However, Goldman Sachs, which had been working with Disney on this matter, proposed a rather unusual solution. Goldman suggested that Disney issue 10-year ECU Eurobonds that would be swapped into a yen liability at a potentially more attractive all-in yen cost than a yen term loan. Specifically, Goldman was prepared to underwrite ECU80 million 10-year Eurobonds at 100.25 percent of par, with a coupon of 9⅛ percent, and underwriting fees of 2 percent. Additional expenses to be paid by Disney were capped at $75,000. The ECU Eurobonds would have an annual sinking fund payment of ECU16 million beginning in the sixth year and continuing until maturity. (The cash flows for the ECU Eurobond are shown in **Exhibit 6**.) If the ECU Eurobonds were launched, Disney would be only the second U.S. corporation to access this market. Also, it would be the first ECU bond incorporating an amortization schedule to repay the bond's principal. Thus, Mr. Anderson was concerned about the market reception of such an issue.

Goldman could also arrange an ECU/yen swap intermediated by Industrial Bank of Japan (IBJ), a powerful Japanese commercial bank rated AAA. In this arrangement, Disney would exchange its ECU Eurobond net proceeds in exchange for IBJ making future ECU payments to Disney that exactly matched the coupons and principal payments of the Eurobonds (see **Exhibit 7**, column A). At the same time, Disney would receive the yen equivalent of the net ECU proceeds from the Eurobond, converted at the spot rate, and would make future semiannual yen swap payments according to a fixed schedule (see **Exhibit 7**, column B). Disney could then exchange the initial yen proceeds for dollars at the spot rate in order to reduce its short-term borrowings. At the time of the proposal, the ECU spot exchange rate was $0.7420/ECU1, and the yen/dollar exchange rate was ¥248/$1.

THE COUNTERPARTY TO THE SWAP

Goldman Sachs was aware that a French state-owned utility was interested in swapping some of its yen debt for ECU debt. The utility was a major borrower in the world capital markets because its financing needs were far too large to be supplied by either the domestic French franc debt market or the fledgling Euro-French franc bond market (reopened only recently, in April 1985, after being closed for 5 years). Rated AAA, it had issued numerous public Eurobonds in dollars, ECU, yen, and deutsche marks (see **Exhibit 8**) in addition to various domestic borrowings, private placements, and term loans. Like many European state agencies, it preferred ECU liabilities since the ECU most closely matched its natural currency flows. However, European sovereigns and state agencies, including the French utility, were often perceived by the markets as borrowing ECU too frequently and wearing out their welcome among the retail purchasers of ECU bonds.

At the time of Disney's financing, the French utility wished to swap out of a 10-year yen term loan with sinking fund payments that began in 5 years. Thus, Goldman could arrange for Disney and the utility to enter into a swap, intermediated by IBJ, in which the utility would take on an ECU liability in exchange for future yen receipts, and Disney would take on a yen liability in exchange for future ECU receipts. Specifically, IBJ would pay semiannually to the utility an amount equal to its debt service on the yen term loan. In return, the utility would make ECU payments to IBJ more than sufficient to cover the payments IBJ had to make to Disney (see **Exhibit 7**, column C). The ECU principal to be ''received'' by the utility in the swap was strictly notional and would be determined by the size of Disney's financing and the ECU/yen exchange rate; no new funds would actually be received by the utility. Goldman believed that the all-in cost of the utility's ECU flows after the swap would be less than that prevailing in the ECU Eurobond market. Moreover, the utility would be able to structure the swap flows to accomplish its objective of perfectly matching future yen payments on this loan and reducing its yen exposure.

As he sat down in his office in California and began to analyze the Goldman proposal, Mr. Anderson could not help but be impressed at the combination of factors in the international capital markets from New York to Europe to Tokyo that made such a deal possible. It required considerable ingenuity on Goldman's part to put the deal together. However, he needed to determine if this arrangement made sense for Disney before giving the go-ahead.

EXHIBIT 1 THE WALT DISNEY COMPANY AND SUBSIDIARIES CONSOLIDATED STATEMENT OF INCOME, YEAR ENDED SEPTEMBER 30 (IN THOUSANDS, EXCEPT PER SHARE DATA)

	1984	1983	1982
Revenues			
Entertainment and recreation	$1,097,359	$1,031,202	$ 725,610
Filmed entertainment	244,552	165,458	202,102
Community development	204,384	—	—
Consumer products	109,682	110,697	102,538
	$1,655,977	$1,307,357	$1,030,250
Costs and expenses			
Entertainment and recreation	$ 904,664	$ 834,324	$ 592,965
Filmed entertainment	242,303	198,843	182,463
Community development	162,158	—	—
Consumer products	55,819	53,815	54,706
	$1,364,944	$1,086,982	$ 830,134
Income (loss) before corporate expenses and unusual charges			
Entertainment and recreation	$ 192,695	$ 196,878	$ 132,645
Filmed entertainment	2,249	(33,385)	19,639
Community development	42,226	—	—
Consumer products	53,863	56,882	47,832
	$ 291,033	$ 220,375	$ 200,116
Corporate expenses (income)			
General and administrative	$ 59,570	$ 35,554	$ 30,957
Design projects abandoned	7,032	7,295	5,147
Net interest expense (income)	41,738	14,066	(14,781)
	$ 108,340	$ 56,915	$ 21,323
Income before unusual charges, taxes on income, and accounting change	$ 182,693	$ 163,460	$ 178,793
Unusual charges	165,960	—	—
Income before taxes on income and accounting change	$ 16,733	$ 163,460	$ 178,793
Taxes on income (benefit)	(5,000)	70,300	78,700
Income before accounting change	$ 21,733	$ 93,160	$ 100,093
Cumulative effect of change in accounting for investment tax credits	76,111	—	—
Net income	$ 97,844	$ 93,160	$ 100,093
Earnings per share			
Income before accounting change	$ 0.61	$ 2.70	$ 3.01
Cumulative effect of change in accounting	2.12	—	—
	$ 2.73	$ 2.70	$ 3.01
Average number of common and common equivalent shares outstanding	35,849	34,481	33,225

EXHIBIT 2   THE WALT DISNEY COMPANY AND SUBSIDIARIES CONSOLIDATED BALANCE SHEET, YEAR ENDING SEPTEMBER 30 (IN THOUSANDS)

	1984	1983
Assets		
Cash	$ 35,346	$ 18,055
Accounts and notes receivable (net)	172,762	104,746
Taxes on income refundable	60,000	70,000
Merchandise inventories	83,467	77,945
Film production costs	102,462	127,010
Real estate inventories	229,424	—
Entertainment attractions and other property	2,413,985	2,251,297
Less accumulated depreciation	(600,156)	(504,365)
	$1,813,829	$1,746,932
Construction and design projects in progress	94,710	108,190
Land	28,807	16,687
	$1,937,346	$1,871,809
Other assets	118,636	111,630
Total assets	$2,739,443	$2,381,195
Liabilities and stockholders' equity		
Accounts payable, payroll, and other accrued liabilities	$ 239,992	$ 182,709
Taxes on income payable	24,145	13,982
Borrowings	861,909	352,575
Unearned deposits and advances	178,907	109,556
Deferred taxes on income	279,005	321,845
Commitments and contingencies		
Stockholders' equity		
Common shares, no par Issued and outstanding—33,729 and 34,509 shares	359,988	661,934
Retained earnings	795,497	738,594
	1,155,485	1,400,528
Total liabilities and stockholders' equity	$2,739,443	$2,381,195

EXHIBIT 3   ANALYSIS OF OUTSTANDING BORROWINGS (MILLIONS)

	3/31/85	9/30/84	9/30/83
Unsecured borrowings under revolving line of credit and bank term loans	$168.7	$408.0	—
Commercial paper	352.2	200.2	$118.2
15.75% Eurodollar notes, due 9/1/86*	—	100.0	100.0
12.50% Eurodollar notes, due 1/10/87	150.0	—	—
12.50% Eurodollar notes, due 3/15/89†	75.0	75.0	75.0
8.60% Yen term loan, due 2/1/93‡	50.0	53.1	59.4
Other	58.4	25.6	—
	$854.3	$861.9	$352.6

*Called on October 17, 1984.
†Of the $75 million outstanding, the company swapped $50 million into yen liabilities of approximately ¥12 billion. This synthetic yen borrowing was due 3/14/89 and had a cost of 7.40 percent payable annually.
‡Outstanding yen principal at March 31, 1985, was ¥12.5 billion, with semiannual yen principal payments of ¥765 million.

EXHIBIT 4   HISTORICAL SUMMARY OF AVERAGE YEN/DOLLAR EXCHANGE RATES AND CONSUMER PRICE INDEXES

Year	Yen/dollar	U.S. CPI	Japan CPI
1980	225.70	100.0	100.0
1981	220.10	110.4	104.9
1982	248.30	117.1	107.8
1983	237.40	120.9	109.9
1984			
I	230.80	125.0	111.4
II	229.70	125.6	112.3
III	243.60	126.6	112.2
IV	246.10	128.3	113.5
Average 1984	237.30	126.1	112.3
1985			
I	257.50	128.6	113.7
II	250.80	130.2	114.7

EXHIBIT 5   YEN LONG-DATED FOREIGN
EXCHANGE FORWARDS

| Years | Outright forward quotes | |
	Bid	Offer
Spot	247.95	248.05
1	242.05	242.65
2	235.95	239.05
3	227.95	231.55
4	217.95	222.55
5	208.95	213.55
6	200.95	210.55
7	192.95	204.05
8	185.95	199.05
9	178.95	192.55
10	172.95	189.05

EXHIBIT 6   CASH FLOWS OF 10-YEAR ECU
EUROBOND WITH SINKING FUND

Par	ECU80 million
Price	100.250%
Coupon	9.125%
Fees	2.000%
Expenses	$75,000
Dollar/ECU	0.7420

Year	Cash flows (ECU millions)
0	78.499
1	(7.300)
2	(7.300)
3	(7.300)
4	(7.300)
5	(7.300)
6	(23.300)
7	(21.840)
8	(20.380)
9	(18.920)
10	(17.460)

EXHIBIT 7	ECU/YEN SWAP FLOWS, IN MILLIONS (ASSUMING $/ECU OF 0.7420 AND YEN/DOLLAR OF 248)*			

	Disney's swap flows: Received from/(paid to) IBJ		French utility's swap flows: Received from/(paid to) IBJ	
Year	ECU	Yen	ECU	Yen
	(A)	(B)	(C)	(D)
0.0	(78.499)	14,445.153[†]	80.000[‡]	(14,445.153)[†]
0.5		(483.226)		483.226
1.0	7.300	(483.226)	(7.350)	483.226
1.5		(483.226)		483.226
2.0	7.300	(483.226)	(7.350)	483.226
2.5		(483.226)		483.226
3.0	7.300	(483.226)	(7.350)	483.226
3.5		(483.226)		483.226
4.0	7.300	(483.226)	(7.350)	483.226
4.5		(483.226)		483.226
5.0	7.300	(1,808.141)	(7.350)	1,808.141
5.5		(1,764.650)		1,764.650
6.0	23.300	(1,721.160)	(23.350)	1,721.160
6.5		(1,677.670)		1,677.670
7.0	21.840	(1,634.179)	(21.880)	1,634.179
7.5		(1,590.689)		1,590.689
8.0	20.380	(1,547.199)	(20.410)	1,547.199
8.5		(1,503.708)		1,503.708
9.0	18.920	(1,460.218)	(18.940)	1,460.218
9.5		(1,416.728)		1,416.728
10.0	17.460	(1,520.450)	(17.470)	1,520.450

*Note: These cash flows exclude fees paid to either IBJ or Goldman Sachs.

[†] The initial yen principal received by Disney from IBJ is relevant only to the swap transaction and the calculation of an all-in yen financing cost. By exchanging the initial yen for dollars in the spot market, Disney would eventually obtain new dollar financing.

[‡] The principal amounts for the French utility are strictly notional; no net new funding would be obtained by the utility as a result of the swap.

EXHIBIT 8   SUMMARY OF THE FRENCH UTILITY'S OUTSTANDING PUBLICLY TRADED EUROBONDS—AS OF MID-1985 (EXCLUDING DOMESTIC ISSUES, PRIVATE PLACEMENTS, AND TERM LOANS)

Currency	Amount (millions)	Issue date	Maturity	Life, years Original	Life, years Remaining	Coupon, %	Yield to maturity, %
Dollars	20	May-71	May-86	15	0.8	8.500	9.32
Dollars	50	Jun-77	Jun-87	10	1.9	8.500	9.30
Dollars	100	Aug-76	Sep-86	10	1.2	8.900	9.08
Dollars	100	Apr-79	Apr-86	7	0.8	9.625	9.09
Dollars	125	Jun-80	Jul-88	8	3.0	10.000	10.09
Dollars	225	Jun-85	Jul-95	10	10.0	10.000	10.80
Dollars	100	Apr-83	May-93	10	7.8	11.125	10.76
Dollars	100	May-80	May-90	10	4.9	11.250	10.84
Dollars	150	Oct-82	Oct-87	5	2.3	12.750	9.57
Dollars	200	Apr-82	Apr-89	7	3.8	14.375	10.45
Dollars	500	Sep-84	Sep-94	10	9.2	0.000	11.44
Dollars	300	Mar-85	Mar-97	12	11.7	LIBOR+¼	9.66
Dollars	400	Feb-84	Feb-99	15	13.7	LIBOR+⅛	9.70
ECU	75	Feb-85	Mar-95	10	9.7	9.750	9.37
ECU	60	Dec-82	Jan-93	10	7.5	12.500	10.00
Yen	20,000	Jan-85	Jan-95	10	9.6	6.875	6.83
DM	200	Sep-83	Oct-93	10	8.3	8.375	7.12
DM	100	Sep-82	Sep-92	10	7.2	8.875	7.38

Source: The Association of International Bond Dealers.

GAZ DE FRANCE

In the summer of 1986, M. Jean Reboul, a former French Treasury official who became the director of the legal and finance division of Gaz de France (GDF), was reflecting on the successes of GDF's liability-management program. The profits from this program—especially the swap activities—had topped FF1 billion (about $143 million) over the past three years. About one-fourth of these profits had been realized, adding directly to the net income of GDF.

M. Reboul used currency and interest rate swaps, forwards, futures, and options to transform a significant portion of GDF's nonfranc debt. In particular, he had entered into numerous swap transactions to receive U.S. dollars against paying either French francs or European Currency Units (ECUs). He had also used swaps in other currencies such as the deutsche mark, Japanese yen, Canadian dollar, and Dutch guilder. Furthermore, M. Reboul was not averse to unwinding profitable positions to take trading profits for the treasury group.

However, the continued appreciation of the franc against the dollar since the franc's low levels of 1985 raised questions as to what GDF should do about its liability structure in the future. GDF had already begun to make accounting provisions for possible losses from some of its swaps. At the same time, the franc was struggling against the deutsche mark, which raised concerns about the possibility of realignment of the European Monetary System (EMS) and the subsequent effects on GDF's ECU liabilities. This changing foreign exchange environment and its potential impact on GDF's debt provided the impetus for reflection on the appropriateness of GDF's

This case was prepared by doctoral student William B. Allen, Jr., under the supervision of Professor W. Carl Kester. Copyright © 1988 by the President and Fellows of Harvard College. Harvard Business School case 288-030.

proactive liability-management program. Furthermore, GDF planned to undertake a thorough review of the risks involved in such a program.

THE NATURAL GAS INDUSTRY

Natural gas, a lighter-than-air mixture of gases composed principally of methane, was a popular fuel because it was cleaner, more powerful, less toxic, and safer relative to substitutes such as coal and oil. The exploration and production of natural gas was pioneered in the 1930s in the United States by oil exploration companies. Initially, the discovery of natural gas while drilling for oil was considered a nuisance. Later, as consumers grew to appreciate the value of natural gas, distribution technologies were developed to utilize these discoveries. In the 1960s, production fields in Western Europe, the Soviet Union, and North Africa came on-line and began to supply more and more of the world's needs. By the mid-1980s, the Soviet Union produced almost 35 percent of total natural gas, the United States produced about 30 percent, and Western Europe produced just under 10 percent (see **Exhibit 1**). France produced less than one-half of 1 percent of the world supply. Worldwide reserves of natural gas are shown in **Exhibit 2**.

Since 1950, the importance of natural gas as a percentage of total energy demands has increased substantially. The share of natural gas in world primary energy consumption (excluding electricity) nearly doubled from 10 percent in 1950 to almost 20 percent in 1984 while the share of petroleum increased 150 percent and that of coal decreased by 50 percent. The growth of natural gas consumption in France was even more dramatic during this period, increasing over thirtyfold from 0.4 to 12.3 percent of total primary energy consumption. Petroleum usage jumped from 17 to 45.3 percent, and coal usage decreased substantially from 75 to 13.2 percent.

Transportation and distribution of natural gas was accomplished through pipelines or liquid natural gas (LNG) carriers such as trucks, railcars, or tanker ships. Substantial investments had been made around the world to build extensive pipeline networks. However, the marginal cost for pipeline transportation of natural gas was quite small.

As natural gas became more popular, the fluctuating demands relative to constant supplies created a storage problem. In France, for example, gas demand in January was typically three times larger than that in August. It was estimated that an additional 6 million cubic meters would need to be supplied to all of France when the outdoor temperature decreased by 1 degree centigrade. The primary storage vessel was the transportation system itself (i.e., the pipeline) which contained large quantities of gas at high pressures that could act as a buffer against sudden increases in demand. Substantial underground storage was also used by hollowing out cavities in sand or salt beds. By 1986 France had developed thirteen underground storage sites capable of holding up to 72.8 billion kilowatt-hours (kWh) of natural gas.

Natural gas, a substitute for oil and electricity, was quoted at a world price in dollars (see **Exhibit 3**). Gas supply contracts between distributors such as GDF and their producers were typically long-term, ranging from 20 to 25 years. This was considered necessary to ensure the payback on the substantial investments in production and transmission facilities. These contracts typically provided for a formula that determined the exact price paid relative to the world price, depending upon the quality of the gas and the location where it was supplied.

HISTORY AND OVERVIEW OF GAZ DE FRANCE

Formed under the April 8, 1946, act nationalizing the gas and electricity industry in France, Gaz de France (GDF) was chartered to produce, transport, distribute, import, and export gas. Over the years, GDF became primarily a buyer and distributor of natural gas. By 1986 GDF and its subsidiaries had 8.6 million subscribers and sold 307.4 billion kilowatt-hours of gas to residential, commercial, and industrial customers through an extensive transport and distribution network covering all of France (see **Exhibit 4**).

When the French gas industry was nationalized, gas was manufactured from coal in small plants owned by more than 500 utilities spread throughout France. This gas was distributed locally within a range that rarely exceeded 30 kilometers. GDF first attempted to modernize and concentrate gas production by building several large plants. A 300-kilometer gas transmission pipeline was built in 1954 to supply Paris with gas manufactured in coke oven plants in Lorraine and Saarland. At about the same time, liquefied petroleum gases were introduced to supplement coal gas.

The discovery of a substantial natural gas field in Lacq in the eastern French Pyrenees drastically changed the situation before the end of the decade. The state enterprise Société Nationale des Pétrole d'Aquitaine (now known as the Société Nationale Elf Aquitaine, or SNEA) was commissioned in 1957 to produce this gas for GDF. Other production facilities were opened in nearby Meillon and St. Faust. Over a period of 4 years, GDF laid some 4000 kilometers of pipelines to transport this gas from the production sites and supply Brittany, mideastern France, and the Paris area. By 1965, approximately half of France was supplied with natural gas.

However, the production from Lacq and other domestic fields could no longer keep up with the growing demand, and GDF was forced to begin what was to become a substantial program of gas importation. That year, the first cargo of gas liquefied at Arzew, Algeria, was transported via a GDF-owned LNG carrier ship to Le Havre on the French Atlantic coast and regasified there for further distribution through GDF's domestic pipelines. In 1967 natural gas from the Groningen, a field in the Netherlands, was piped across the border into France. A second LNG link was opened in 1973 between Skikda, Algeria, and Fos-sur-Mer (a small town on the French Mediterranean coast near Marseille). In 1977 the first contract for the import of natural gas from the Soviet Union was signed. That same year gas from the Ekofisk field off the North Sea coast of Norway first entered France. A third LNG chain was opened in 1982 linking Algeria and Montoir-de-Bretagne, near Saint-Nazaire on the northern French Atlantic coast.

THE ECONOMIC AND POLITICAL ENVIRONMENT IN FRANCE

The early 1980s were difficult times for France and GDF. Large government budget deficits and trade deficits led to inflation and high interest rates. Shortly after the election of the socialist François Mitterrand as president in 1981, France nationalized six big industrial corporations and sixty-six banks. Official reserves were drained as the balance of payments worsened (see **Exhibit 5**). In the wake of these problems, GDF was not allowed to increase its prices to cover higher costs. Consequently, it incurred substantial losses for several years running.

A change in the economic climate coincided with the election in 1986 of conservative premier Jacques Chirac. Believing that France's future competitiveness depended upon the efficiency of the private sector, he proposed a program of economic reforms including the return to the private sector of a number of the firms that had only recently been nationalized. By the spring of 1986, the economy in France appeared to be improving. Inflation and interest rates were under control. The French franc appreciated against the dollar, although it struggled to keep up with the deutsche mark (see **Exhibit 6**). This led to fears of a realignment of the European Monetary System which might devalue the French franc relative to the deutsche mark.[1]

In mid-1986 the French government was circulating a list of companies to be privatized within the next few years. Although this list did not include GDF, it did include CGE (Compagnie Générale d'Electricité), Elf Aquitaine (SNEA), and Compagnie Française des Pétroles. In contrast, the United Kingdom—whose privatization program had begun several years earlier with the sale of several profitable industrial corporations—had recently completed the sale of the state-owned utility British Telecom and was planning to sell British Gas within a few months.

THE OPERATIONS OF GAZ DE FRANCE

For the year 1985, GDF showed a profit of FF485 million—its first since 1980 (see **Exhibit 7**). This represented a considerable turnaround from the prior year's loss of FF3020 million. The results were attributed to streamlining company management, renegotiating gas purchase contracts, and instituting more stringent liability management. In addition, domestic gas prices for industrial customers were deregulated, and tariff increases were obtained for other users.

Total revenues from gas sales increased almost 18 percent to FF54.1 billion. Overall French primary energy consumption rose 0.5 percent (after temperature correction) in 1985. The share of natural gas as a percentage of all usage of primary energy fell to 12.3 percent due to lower sales to large industrial customers. Gas sales were predominantly domestic and were billed in French francs.

GDF's gas deliveries rose 9.6 percent to 304 billion kilowatt-hours and the number of customers increased 0.7 percent to 8.5 million. Gas sales broke down as follows:

---

[1]The European Monetary System constrained the fluctuations of the currencies of member countries (except Britain) relative to one another. Cross rates were defined from which no currency could deviate more than 2¼ percent (the Italian lira was permitted a larger divergence band). Since its formation in 1979, the EMS had been realigned seven times. The most recent realignment was on April 6, 1986, when the French franc was devalued 3 percent.

	1985	1984	1983
Residential and commercial	52.4%	52.3%	54.1%
Industrial	37.2	40.0	38.9
Other	10.4	7.7	7.0

Residential and commercial prices were regulated by the French government. Residences used gas for cooking and hot water and dwelling heating. The commercial sector covered customers such as wholesale and retail businesses that had similar usages for gas. During 1985 a 4.5 percent rate increase was approved by the state for these customers, followed by a 2 percent rate decrease in October and December. For the year, these rates averaged 0.4 percent higher than in 1984.

In April 1985 industrial gas prices in France were deregulated, allowing GDF independence and flexibility in its pricing policy for these customers. GDF immediately increased industrial rates an average of 6 percent but then lowered them by 3 percent on May 8 and 6.5 percent on October 1. For the year, industrial rates averaged 1.9 percent higher than in 1984.

Industries that were major users of gas in France included metallurgy, cement, ceramics, chinaware, glass, textiles and agriculture-based food industries. In addition, gas was used as a feedstock in the chemical industry to manufacture synthetic products such as nitrate fertilizers, ammonia, and plastics. Pricing flexibility was deemed a necessity because most of these customers were equipped to switch quickly and easily (in some cases, on a daily basis) from one source of primary energy to another. With the volatility in oil prices, gas prices needed to adjust quickly in order to retain industrial customers with high elasticities of demand.

Total natural gas purchased by GDF rose 11.8 percent to 313 billion kilowatt-hours. Gas purchased from domestic suppliers settled in 1985 at 14.3 percent of total purchases compared to 22.1 percent in 1984 and 22.4 percent in 1983. Imports (in volume terms) broke down as follows:

	1985	1984	1983
Netherlands	28.8%	30.5%	30.1%
Norwegian North Sea	10.4	10.7	11.0
U.S.S.R.	27.0	20.3	15.9
Algeria	33.6	38.2	36.4
Other	0.2	0.3	6.6
Total	100.0%	100.0%	100.0%

In light of the world energy glut, GDF renegotiated several of its long-term gas contracts during 1985. Renegotiations with the Dutch suppliers resulted in a price reduction retroactive to October 1984. This agreement also specified that the ECU would be used as the currency for billing and payment. Renegotiations with Soviet suppliers resulted in price reductions retroactive to January and October 1985. These renegotiations had an overall positive impact of approximately FF2 billion in the 1985 financial statements. Renegotiations were ongoing with Norway and other suppliers.

GDF's LIABILITY MANAGEMENT

In the early 1980s, GDF had substantial borrowing needs, requiring M. Reboul to initiate a program of innovative and opportunistic liability management. Since the domestic French franc debt market was relatively small, GDF was forced to turn to the international markets. This meant substantial offshore and nonfranc borrowings—something that was also encouraged by the government to help ease balance-of-payments pressures.

In April 1985 GDF reopened the Euro-French franc market, which was effectively closed in 1981 after the Socialist party came to power, with a FF489 million issue. GDF was also an active issuer of dollar-denominated commercial paper in the U.S. market. Standby credit facilities, averaging FF230 million in the domestic French franc market and $700 million in multicurrency Eurocredit facilities, provided extra liquidity, if needed, and inexpensive backing for the U.S. commercial paper program.

In July 1985 GDF substantially altered its capital structure (see **Exhibit 8**) by issuing a total of FF3.2 billion of perpetual participating bonds, known as "titres participatifs" (TPs). Of this amount, FF1.2 billion represented an exchange of outstanding GDF bonds issued in 1971 and 1972. The TPs were a popular instrument in the French market, issued previously by other state-owned entities such as Saint-Gobain, Rhone-Poulenc, and Thomson Brandt. TPs paid a variable return that was "collared" by predetermined benchmarks. Usually, they provided for a minimum return below prevailing bond yields but contained provisions that allowed the investor to share in profits of the enterprise. GDF had issued two tranches (A and B) of TPs. The minimum return for both was set at 85 percent of the taux moyen mensuel du marché obligataire (TMO), an average of medium- and long-term "first-category" bond yields.[2] A certain percentage of GDF's annual value added (roughly sales less costs plus or minus inventory changes) increased the potential return up to a maximum of 130 percent of the TMO for tranche A TPs and 125 percent of the TMO for tranche B TPs (see **Exhibit 9** for the coupon calculations for both tranches of TPs). Although GDF had the right to call the TPs, there were no fixed maturity dates.

By the end of 1985, borrowing requirements slackened. At that time, only 51.5 percent of the outstanding debt had originally been raised and denominated in French francs. Most of the debt had been raised internationally, with dollar debt making up the greatest share. However, through the use of currency swaps and forward contracts, GDF increased its actual French franc exposure to 73.4 percent. Of the remaining portion, ECU debt represented over 50 percent of the outstanding amounts, and dollar-denominated debt was about 2 percent (see **Exhibit 10**).

GDF was particularly proud of its swap activities as a feature of its liability management. Concerned about the growth of nonfranc debt—especially dollar-denominated debt—in 1982 and 1983, it began using swaps to hedge against a depreciation of the franc. GDF sought swaps in which it received dollars against paying

---

[2]All bonds issued in the French domestic market were differentiated according to the quality of the borrower and defined within two categories. First-category bonds were issues made by the Republic, government agencies, or public sector corporations that might or might not have been guaranteed by the state. Second-category bonds were issued by private corporations.

French francs. Also, since French francs were not always available, GDF swapped into ECU because, with EMS constraints, the ECU would not likely appreciate substantially against the franc. Also, ECU interest rates reflected the low levels available in the Netherlands and Germany. In conjunction with the swaps, M. Reboul also used currency futures, interbank forwards, and currency options to transform GDF's liability structure.

Although the swap activities were designed as long-term hedges rather than short-term arbitrage, GDF was not committed to holding swaps for their entire lifetime. With the appreciation of the dollar since 1982 and the fall in dollar interest rates, swap positions in which GDF had negotiated to receive fixed-rate dollars became quite valuable. Out of almost 300 swap transactions representing over $10 billion executed over the last few years, approximately 25 percent had been unwound to realize profits. This was usually accomplished by negotiating a cash settlement reflecting the value of the swap with the original counterparty. Another method, with similar results, was to enter into an offsetting swap with another counterparty.

Quotes on the value of unwinding a swap could be obtained directly from market makers. A method for calculating such a value is described in the appendix to this case. GDF's staff had developed a computer model which enabled GDF to do these calculations quickly and monitor the profit or loss for each swap. The profits from swap-unwind transactions—estimated to be about $40 million for 1985—added directly to net income. Total profits on all swap activities (realized and unrealized gains) topped FF1 billion ($143 million) through the spring of 1986.

M. Reboul believed that GDF was the second most active swapper after the World Bank. In many cases, his staff negotiated swaps directly with counterparties such as a major Swedish corporation, a sovereign European debtor, and a small number of French companies, effectively eliminating banks altogether. However, he noted that GDF would never swap directly with any nonfinancial counterparty with a credit rating below AAA. Using banks to intermediate swaps also allowed GDF to negotiate "stop loss limits" on the value of the swaps at little or no extra cost. This provided an asymmetric liability position that allowed GDF unlimited gains while fixing its losses. Typically, the loss limit was set at the price of a 6-month currency option on the French franc/dollar exchange rate. Thus, a bank would commit to unwind automatically GDF's swap if it hit the pre-agreed loss limit in exchange for a cash payment from GDF of this amount.

CONCERNS FOR THE FUTURE

The success of GDF's liability management had generated considerable publicity in France and the international banking community. However, the reaction to this publicity was not always positive. Some market participants wondered if French government officials fully understood GDF's liability-management program and the risks involved. Moreover, some financial managers at other French state-owned enterprises had expressed reservations about this type of program. France's largest borrower, Electricité de France (EDF), also had substantial nonfranc debt but was not a major user of swaps. Pierre Goldité, M. Reboul's counterpart at EDF, considered swaps to be a "marginal activity" for EDF.[3] Credit National, the French state-owned bank that helped finance domestic industrial growth, was fortunate in that the French government gave it forward foreign exchange rate guarantees to hedge the costs of its nonfranc debt. Still, Pierre Poplu, the head of the financial department at Credit National, was somewhat skeptical of the swaps market. "It's rather like betting," he once remarked.[4]

Despite past successes in liability management, there was reason for M. Reboul to be concerned about the future. During the spring of 1986, the French franc continued to appreciate against the dollar. It was approaching 7 francs per dollar, considerably stronger than the 10-franc level it had reached over a year ago. GDF had already begun to make accounting provisions for possible losses from some of its swaps. At the same time, the franc was under pressure relative to the deutsche mark. If this resulted in a realignment in the European Monetary System, it would clearly affect the cost of GDF's ECU debt.

There was also reason to be concerned about the increasing complexity of managing the risks associated with GDF's growing swap book. GDF's finance staff was executing over 100 swap transactions per year and the task of monitoring and controlling these positions had become formidable. Despite the computer model used to price these swaps, other factors such as credit exposure and liquidity had to be considered as well. As a result, GDF planned to undertake a thorough review of the risks involved in these activities.

Last, the very success of GDF and M. Reboul in liability management had given rise to a considerable amount of publicity and public scrutiny. The reservations about swap transactions expressed by other finance executives in France could be interpreted as implicit challenges to the wisdom of such a proactive management program. Should it become necessary to realize losses on some of GDF's swap positions, GDF's finance staff would have to articulate sound justifications for their policies and decisions.

[3] *Euromoney,* January 1984, p. 21.
[4] Ibid., p. 27.

EXHIBIT 1   NATURAL GAS PRODUCTION BY COUNTRY

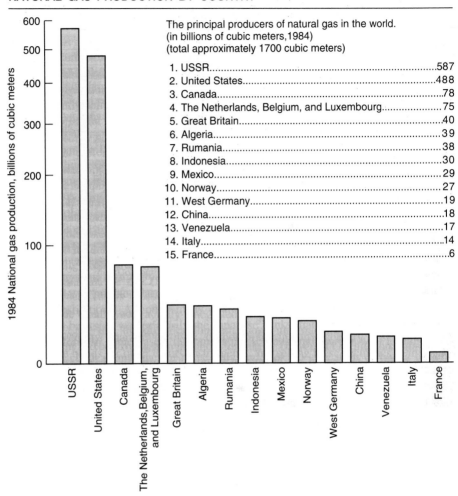

The principal producers of natural gas in the world.
(in billions of cubic meters,1984)
(total approximately 1700 cubic meters)

1. USSR...587
2. United States..488
3. Canada...78
4. The Netherlands, Belgium, and Luxembourg....................75
5. Great Britain...40
6. Algeria..39
7. Rumania...38
8. Indonesia..30
9. Mexico..29
10. Norway..27
11. West Germany...19
12. China...18
13. Venezuela..17
14. Italy...14
15. France...6

1984 National gas production, billions of cubic meters

Producers

EXHIBIT 2   THE LARGEST NATURAL GAS RESERVES IN THE WORLD (IN BILLIONS OF CUBIC METERS)

Eastern Europe		Middle East		Americas	
Total	38,000	Total	25,600	Total	13,700
U.S.S.R.	37,500	Iran	13,500	United States	5,600
		Qatar	4,300	Canada	2,600
		Abu Dhabi	2,600	Mexico	2,100
		Saudi Arabia	2,350	Venezuela	1,600
		Kuwait	980	Argentina	670
		Iraq	760		

Far East and Australia		Africa		Western Europe	
Total	7,200	Total	5,800	Total	5,600
Australia	1,500	Algeria	3,000	Norway	2,200
Malaysia	1,400	Nigeria	1,300	Low Countries	1,900
Indonesia	1,100	Libya	570	Great Britain	700
China	850			Italy	250
Pakistan	600			West Germany	190
India	500			France	40
Thailand	200				

EXHIBIT 3   GAS, PETROLEUM, AND ELECTRICITY PRICES FOR FRANCE

	1980	1981	1982	1983	1984
Natural gas, $/1000 cubic feet	4.19	4.46	4.48	4.22	3.97
Petroleum, $/barrel	27.39	30.07	28.59	27.49	29.72
Electricity, ¢/kilowatt-hour	5.58	4.43	4.10	3.98	na

EXHIBIT 4   FRENCH NATURAL GAS DISTRIBUTION NETWORK AS OF JANUARY 1, 1986

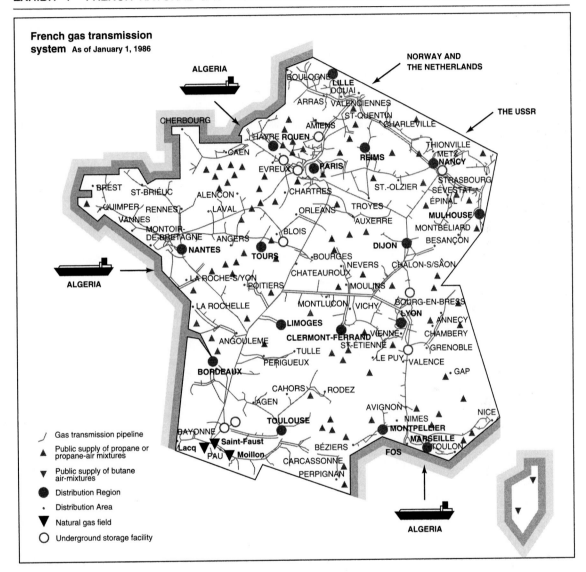

French gas transmission system As of January 1, 1986

Legend:

⌐ Gas transmission pipeline

▲ Public supply of propane or propane-air mixtures

▼ Public supply of butane air-mixtures

● Distribution Region

· Distribution Area

▼ Natural gas field

○ Underground storage facility

EXHIBIT 5   ECONOMIC INDICES FOR FRANCE

	1980	1981	1982	1983	1984	1985	First-quarter 1986
Gross domestic product, billions of francs	2,808.3	3,164.8	3,626.0	4,006.5	4,364.9	4,692.5	4,895.2
Government budget surplus/(deficit), billions of francs	(1,000)	(85,600)	(111,400)	(142,400)	(132,600)	(140,900)	(110,100)
Current account surplus/(deficit), millions of dollars	(4,208)	(4,811)	(12,082)	(5,166)	(876)	907	(416)
Foreign exchange reserves, millions of dollars	25,338	19,976	14,594	18,057	19,102	24,319	24,135
Money supply, billions of francs	671	778	862	970	1,057	1,072	1,039
Short-term interest rates, %	11.85	15.30	14.87	12.53	11.74	9.93	8.71
Government bond yield, %	13.03	15.79	15.69	13.63	12.54	10.94	9.53
Consumer price index	100.0	113.4	126.8	139.0	149.3	157.9	160.3

EXHIBIT 6   EXCHANGE RATES (UNITS OF FOREIGN CURRENCY PER DOLLAR, EXCEPT FOR POUND)

	French franc	German deutsche mark	United Kingdom pound	Japanese yen	Swiss franc	ECU
1980	4.2205	1.8152	2.3258	225.68	1.6751	0.7189
1981	5.4086	2.2542	2.0243	220.11	1.9598	0.8948
1982	6.5389	2.4251	1.7480	248.24	2.0254	1.0191
1983	7.5855	2.5487	1.5159	237.37	2.0982	1.1221
1984	8.7154	2.8385	1.3356	237.31	2.3432	1.2675
1985						
I	9.9502	3.2544	1.1152	257.49	2.7524	1.4618
II	9.4197	3.0883	1.2556	250.79	2.5930	1.3774
III	8.6738	2.8440	1.3763	238.23	2.3540	1.2740
IV	7.8827	2.5827	1.4353	207.03	2.1342	1.1713
1986						
I	7.2036	2.3456	1.4405	187.34	1.9757	1.0935

Source: Economic Report of the President (Washington, DC: U.S. Government Printing Office, 1987), p. 365.

EXHIBIT 7   INCOME STATEMENTS (MILLIONS)

	1985	1984	1983
Revenues			
Gas sales			
Domestic	FF53,703	FF 45,767	na
Outside France	383	214	na
Other operating revenues	3,772	3,561	na
Total operating revenues	57,858	49,542	FF 44,281
Interest and dividends	1,901	1,244	1,228
Other revenues	256	295	304
Total revenues	60,015	51,081	45,813
Expenses			
Operating charges			
Cost of inputs	42,102	37,578	32,574
Staff costs	6,696	6,190	5,757
Depreciation, amortization, and allowances	4,377	4,460	4,024
Other	897	755	568
Total operating charges	54,072	48,983	42,923
Financial charges	5,174	4,999	5,114
Other expenses	284	119	160
Total expenses	59,530	54,101	48,197
Profit (loss)	FF 485	FF (3,020)	FF (2,384)

EXHIBIT 8   BALANCE SHEETS (MILLIONS)

	1985	1984	1983
Assets			
Current assets			
Cash	FF 1,557	FF 1,494	FF 1,814
Customer receivables	10,229	8,407	7,849
Gas stocks	5,780	5,538	5,237
Other	2,340	1,582	1,846
Total current assets	19,906	17,021	16,746
Net fixed assets	36,967	34,772	33,166
Other assets	2,730	5,876	5,706
Total assets	FF59,603	FF57,669	FF55,618
Liabilities and equities			
Trade payables	FF 6,214	FF 4,693	FF 4,397
Other payables	2,699	2,088	2,397
Borrowings			
Debenture loans	17,782	19,337	17,534
Bank loans	8,430	12,335	9,495
Other	4,911	4,369	5,860
Total borrowings	31,123	36,041	32,889
Total liabilities	40,036	42,822	39,683
Provisions for liabilities and			
other charges	6,632	6,438	5,372
Donated franchises	12,918	12,000	11,074
Irredeemable bonds	3,185	—	—
Equity			
Special fund	5,785	5,785	5,785
Retained earnings	(9,947)	(10,431)	(7,411)
Other	994	1,055	1,115
Total equity	(3,168)	(3,591)	(511)
Total liabilities and equity	FF59,603	FF57,669	FF55,618

EXHIBIT 9	COUPON CALCULATIONS FOR GDF'S TITRES PARTICIPATIFS

Tranche A
1. Fixed portion = 63% of TMO.
2. Variable portion = 29% of the principal amount adjusted by the coefficient of remuneration (CR_t) for that year.
3. The $CR_t = CR_{t-1} \times \dfrac{\text{(value added in year } t-1)}{\text{(value added in year } t-2)}$
4. The total coupon consists of the sum of the fixed and variable portions.
5. The total coupon shall never fall below 85% or exceed 130% of the TMO.

Tranche B
1. Fixed portion = 43% of the TMO.
2. Variable portion = 34% of the TMO adjusted by the coefficient of remuneration for that year (CR_t).
3. The $CR_t = CR_{t-1} \times \dfrac{\text{(value added in year } t-1)}{\text{(value added in year } t-2)}$
4. The total coupon consists of the sum of the fixed and variable portions.
5. The total coupon shall never fall below 85% or exceed 125% of the TMO.

Note: The CR for the first coupons for both tranches, paid in October 1986, was 1.2058. This was the value added in 1985 divided by the value added in 1984.

EXHIBIT 10   DEBT STRUCTURE BEFORE AND AFTER SWAP AND FORWARD EXCHANGE CONTRACTS—YEAR ENDED DECEMBER 31, 1985 (THOUSANDS)

	Debt structure before swaps and forward-exchange contracts				Decommitment (−) French francs	Commitment (+) French francs	Debt structure after swaps and forward-exchange contracts			
	Foreign currencies	French francs	%	%	French francs	French francs	Foreign currencies	French francs	%	%
Domestic	—	12,136,175	46.1			5,901,980	—	18,038,155		68.0
Outside France										
Eurofrancs*	1,426,971	1,426,971	5.4				1,426,971	1,426,971		5.4
Other currencies										
Canadian dollar	152,145	821,583		6.4	405,000		77,145	416,583	5.9	
Deutsche mark	300,718	923,205		7.2	301,935		202,368	621,270	8.8	
ECU	99,763	667,414		5.2		2,912,344	535,091	3,579,758	50.7	
Japanese yen	30,000,000	1,128,000		8.8	704,427		11,265,248	423,573	6.0	
U.S. dollar	1,033,802	7,815,547		61.2	7,663,804		20,071	151,743	2.1	
Other	—	1,418,327		11.1	735,178	1,190,236	—	1,873,385	26.5	
Subtotal (other currencies)		12,774,076	48.5	100.0	−5,707,764			7,066,312	100.0	26.6
Total outside France		14,201,047			−5,707,764			8,493,283		
Grand total		26,337,222	100.0		+194,216			26,531,438		100.0

*Includes the French franc share of multicurrency loans.

APPENDIX: UNWINDING SWAPS

Assume GDF wished to unwind a $100 million swap into which it had entered 1 year earlier. The terms of the original swap were to receive fixed-rate dollars at 8 percent against paying fixed-rate French francs at 10 percent for 5 years with principal paid in full at maturity. One year later, assume the terms available for an offsetting swap to unwind the original swap were to pay fixed-rate dollars at 6 percent against receiving fixed-rate French francs for 9 percent for 4 years. Assume also that the spot exchange rate was FF5/$1 at the time of the original swap, but had increased to FF10/$1 after 1 year. The cash flows associated with the original swap are shown in panel A of **Exhibit A.1**.

The gain from unwinding the original swap can be determined in a three-step process. First, GDF would exactly "neutralize" its future dollar receipts on the original swap by paying these same amounts over the remaining 4 years. (This is shown in the right-hand column of panel B in **Exhibit A.1** entitled "Dollars paid"). The present value of this offsetting position can be found by discounting the required future cash outflows at the new market rate for paying fixed dollars in a 4-year swap. Discounting these future cash outflows at 6 percent gives a present value of $106.93 million.

Second, the size of the corresponding offsetting French franc swap is scaled by multiplying the present value of $106.93 million times the new exchange rate of FF10/$1. Therefore, the notional principal amount of the offsetting French franc swap is FF1,069.3 million. GDF's French franc receipts, based upon this notional principal amount and the new market rate of 9 percent for receiving fixed francs in a 4-year swap, are shown in the left-hand column of panel B in **Exhibit A.1** entitled "French francs received."

Finally, the difference between the French franc receipts in the offsetting swap and the French franc payments in the original swap constitute incremental cash inflows associated with the decision to unwind the position (see panel C in **Exhibit A.1**). Discounting these incremental cash inflows at the 9 percent French franc 4-year swap rate yields a net present value of FF553.1 million. This value would be the price that a swap dealer operating in a competitive market should quote GDF to take it out of its original swap.

EXHIBIT A.1   INCREMENTAL CASH FLOWS FROM UNWINDING A SWAP ($ THOUSANDS)

A. Original currency swap (FF5/$1)

Year	Dollars received	French francs paid
1	$ 8,000	FF50,000
2	8,000	50,000
3	8,000	50,000
4	8,000	50,000
5	108,000	550,000

B. Reverse swap 1 year later (FF10/$1)

Year	French francs received	Dollars paid
2	FF96,237	$ 8,000
3	96,237	8,000
4	96,237	8,000
5	1,165,539	108,000

C. Incremental cash flows

Year	French francs amount
2	FF46,237
3	46,237
4	46,237
5	615,539

GENERAL CINEMA
CORPORATION—1987

In May 1987, J. Atwood Ives, vice chairman and chief financial officer of General Cinema Corporation, was considering the issuance of a debenture exchangeable into the common stock of Cadbury Schweppes. General Cinema, the largest independent bottler of Pepsi-Cola in the United States and a major motion picture exhibitor, was quite familiar with this type of instrument, having previously issued three similar debentures: one in 1980 exchangeable into the common stock of Columbia Pictures, and two others in 1983 and 1984 exchangeable into the common stock of RJR Nabisco. However, the new exchangeable debenture under consideration would be General Cinema's largest to date and would differ in several other important respects from the previous issues. The board of directors would undoubtedly have many questions for Mr. Ives concerning the proposed debentures before voting for approval.

BACKGROUND

General Cinema grew from a company first organized by Philip Smith in 1922 to build and operate movie theaters. Mr. Smith was credited with opening the first open-air theater in 1935. The company was eventually incorporated in Delaware in 1950. At the end of 1986, Richard Smith, the current chairman and CEO of General Cinema, and his family owned approximately a third of the outstanding shares of General Cinema. Other officers and directors of the company, excluding Mr. Smith, owned about 3 percent of the company's stock.

This case was prepared by Research Associate Richard P. Melnick and Professor W. Carl Kester. Copyright © 1988 by the President and Fellows of Harvard College. Harvard Business School case 288-061.

In 1968 General Cinema entered the soft drink bottling industry by acquiring American Beverage Corporation for $18 million. The soft drink bottling industry was attractive because of its record of sustained long-term growth that was expected to continue for some time. Within the industry, Pepsi-Cola was generally thought to be the best opportunity for future growth. Accordingly, General Cinema acquired groups of family-dominated franchises that sold Pepsi, 7-Up, Dr Pepper, Sunkist, and other brands. General Cinema's soft drink bottling diversification took place with very little dilution of equity ownership, for its acquisitions were usually financed by internally generated funds, borrowings, or sale-and-leaseback transactions.

The other major business of General Cinema was its theater operations. As of January 1987, General Cinema operated 1257 screens at 332 locations in 36 states and the District of Columbia. Most theaters were leased, multiscreen units located in or near shopping centers. Historically, the theater business had generated substantial excess cash that had been used to fund diversification into bottling. As General Cinema's beverage business became more profitable, however, the theater division accounted for less of General Cinema's total earnings. Theater sales and earnings as a percentage of General Cinema's total were 46 percent and 31 percent in 1977, and 35 percent and 22 percent in 1986, respectively.

General Cinema also acquired a substantial equity holding in Carter Hawley Hale Stores in 1984 and 1987. General Cinema owned 1 million shares of Carter Hawley Hale cumulative convertible preferred stock and 3,555,000 shares of Carter Hawley Hale common stock. These holdings had a cost basis to General Cinema of $473.3 million as of May 1, 1987, and represented 49 percent of Carter Hawley Hale's outstanding equity, assuming full conversion. The Carter Hawley Hale board of directors approved a major restructuring in December 1986 that would split the company into its specialty store business ("The Neiman-Marcus Group") and its department store operations ("Carter Hawley Hale").[1] The Neiman-Marcus Group would own the Neiman-Marcus, Bergdorf Goodman, and Contempo Casuals stores. Constituted as such, the Neiman-Marcus Group would represent a $1.2 billion company facing attractive prospects for the future, but also requiring substantial new investment at first. General Cinema would eventually own 61.14 percent of the Neiman-Marcus Group, though it would control only 44 percent of its voting shares until 1993. Richard Smith would also become the chairman and CEO of the Neiman-Marcus Group. General Cinema's other top executives would join Mr. Smith in its management. Subsequent to the restructuring, General Cinema would own none of the new Carter Hawley Hale group.

SOFT DRINK BOTTLING INDUSTRY

In the early 1900s, Coca-Cola and Pepsi began granting franchises for the right to bottle their soft drinks. The franchise system allowed their product lines to be distributed nationally with only minimal investment requirements from the parent companies. The franchise granted the bottler an exclusive right, in perpetuity, to

---

[1] As of the spring of 1987, shareholders of Carter Hawley Hale had yet to approve the restructuring.

manufacture, distribute, price, and sell the producer's product in a defined territory as long as the bottler abided by certain conditions. Requirements included purchasing concentrate from a particular franchisor, following specific formulas in production, meeting quality control standards, and vigorously promoting sales in a given region.

Though a bottler could not market a directly competitive brand (e.g., a Pepsi bottler could not also sell Coke), the same bottler could elect to bottle a secondary product line of another producer. The exclusive-territorial-rights clause contained in franchise agreements prompted the Federal Trade Commission to charge the eight major concentrate producers with illegally preventing interbrand competition. However, in 1980, Congress enacted the Soft Drink Interbrand Competition Act, maintaining exclusive territorial rights for bottlers.

There were four basic types of bottlers in the soft drink industry. Privately owned franchise bottlers were generally small companies marketing only Coke or Pepsi, though some grew by purchasing many different franchises. Between 1974 and 1984, the number of such independent bottling franchises declined by 15 percent, and the number of bottling plants under their control fell about 40 percent from 2613 to 1522. Large, publicly owned, multibrand franchising firms, generally based in metropolitan areas, constituted a second type of bottler. Performance in this group varied. Coca-Cola Bottling of New York, for example, had an average return on equity of 10 percent over 5 years before it went private in 1982. However, the MEI Corporation, an owner of Pepsi franchises in nineteen states, had an average return on equity of 23 percent between 1981 and 1986. Comprising a third group were the major soft drink producers themselves, which owned some, but not many, of their own bottlers. Before 1985, Pepsi owned about 25 percent of its bottlers, Coke owned 11 percent, and 7-Up and Royal Crown each owned about 5 percent. Finally, diversified companies such as General Cinema, Beatrice Foods, and Procter & Gamble made up the fourth group.

INDUSTRY CHANGES IN THE 1980s

Beginning in the 1980s, consolidation of the soft drink bottling industry began to take place as the major producers strived to increase their bottling holdings. Economies of scale became an increasingly important factor because of pressure from retailers for discounts, as well as rising costs of ingredients and production. While manufacturing syrup and concentrate was a low-cost activity, the bottling operation was so expensive that even a small franchise required at least $5 million in capital equipment. Discounts and rising costs caused bottlers' margins to fall from a level of 10 to 12 percent in 1975 to 7 to 8 percent by 1985. Notably, however, large bottlers realized margins averaging 13 percent while small, third-tier operations averaged only 1.7 percent.

Another problem that small bottlers faced was the large increase in cost of operations as they attempted to bottle new lines of soda. New products were expensive for bottlers, who had to buy new packages and labels as well as make space on their shelves. Because many small bottlers were not able to handle the increasing pressures of the industry, they sold out to larger franchises or to the producers themselves. By buying bottlers, Coke and Pepsi increased their control over the bottling process and thereby improved their ability to introduce new products quickly.

Bottling franchises, however, were very expensive. For example, in 1986 Coke acquired the Lupton family franchise for $1.4 billion and the Coke bottling operations of Beatrice for $1 billion. These acquisitions increased Coke's bottler ownership from 11 percent to 31 percent. Pepsi increased its bottler holdings from 25 percent to 33 percent in 1985 when it acquired the bottling operations of MEI Corporation for $600 million. Despite the benefits brought to a company by owning its own bottlers, the profit margin for Pepsi's company-owned bottling operations were expected to be only 5.3 percent in 1986, down from 9.1 percent in 1981.

GENERAL CINEMA IN THE 1980s

General Cinema's bottling operations continued to grow during the period of consolidation and, by the mid-1980s, it owned seventeen production facilities and thirty-eight distribution centers in California, Florida, Georgia, Indiana, Maryland, North Carolina, Ohio, Virginia, and West Virginia. The Beverage Division contributed an increasingly large part of General Cinema's sales and profits. In 1986 sales and profits of the division accounted for 65 percent and 76 percent of total sales and profits, respectively. (See **Exhibits 1**, **2** and **3** for recent financial statements and a 5-year financial history for General Cinema.) General Cinema's success resulted from its economies of scale in operations, but also from the profitable geographic areas in which the company chose to operate. Although Coke outsold Pepsi nationally, in most of the markets served by General Cinema, Pepsi was well ahead of all its competitors, and ahead of the Pepsi national average. In 1975 General Cinema's average share in its markets was 37.7 percent, compared to Coke's 29.3 percent average share.

In another major investment, General Cinema spent £89.7 million between September 1986 and January 1987 to acquire 46.5 million shares, or approximately 8.5 percent, of Cadbury Schweppes, a major U.K. food products company. Subsequently, General Cinema filed for and received permission under the U.S. antitrust law to buy more than 15 percent, but less than 25 percent, of Cadbury Schweppes. General Cinema made it clear that its Cadbury Schweppes holdings were for investment purposes only. As the company explained in a public offering document, "General Cinema has no intention of making an offer [for all of Cadbury Schweppes]; to avoid any doubt, we accept that the significance of our statement of intention is that we will be precluded from making an offer for the remaining shares of Cadbury Schweppes for at least one year, barring any material change in circumstances affecting our investment." Such pronouncements notwithstanding, Cadbury Schweppes was wary of a takeover bid and expressed reservations concerning General Cinema's motives.

CADBURY SCHWEPPES

Cadbury Schweppes was the largest British-owned branded food products company that was primarily involved in manufacturing and marketing confectionery and soft drinks. Incorporated in 1897, the company sold its brands in more than 100 countries, with a concentration of its business in the United Kingdom, North America, and Europe. In the mid-1980s Cadbury Schweppes rationalized its business by selling off those entities not viewed as core businesses and simultaneously acquiring other companies. Important brands in its confectionery division included Cadbury's Dairy Milk and Crunchie and Creme Eggs. The confectionery division accounted for 46 percent of Cadbury Schweppes's sales and 47 percent of its profits in 1986.

In May of 1986 Cadbury Schweppes bought Canada Dry and Sunkist from the RJR Nabisco corporation for $230 million. (RJR had itself just bought Canada Dry from Dr Pepper, and Sunkist from General Cinema, in 1984.) Together, these two brands raised Cadbury Schweppes's share of the worldwide soft drink market to 3.5 percent, and of the U.S. soft drink market to 3.5 percent. Later that year it acquired a 30 percent stake in Dr Pepper, which held a 2.4 percent share of the U.S. soft drink market. By 1987, Cadbury Schweppes had become the third largest soft drink company in both North America and the world.

Approximately 20 percent of Cadbury Schweppes's sales came from the United States, but Cadbury Schweppes hoped to increase that to 30 percent over the next 4 years through sales of "adult tonics" and colas. Cadbury Schweppes also participated in a joint venture with Coca-Cola that bottled and sold both companies' brands in the United Kingdom and had projected sales of $1 billion. The drinks division of Cadbury Schweppes accounted for 44 percent of total sales and 47 percent of total profits in 1986. (See **Exhibits 4** and **5** for recent financial statements for Cadbury Schweppes, and **Exhibit 6** for a breakdown of operations by geographic area.)

THE EXCHANGEABLE DEBENTURE PROPOSAL

Exchangeable debenture issues, while not as common as ordinary convertibles, nevertheless appear regularly in the U.S. and Euro-capital markets. They are similar to convertible subordinated debentures in many respects except that, as their name suggests, they are exchangeable into the common stock of some corporation *other* than the issuing company. This difference has some tax implications for the issuer. If the debentures mature without being exchanged, then, like a convertible note, they will be redeemed at par with no tax consequences for the issuing corporation. But if an exchange does take place, the difference between the exchange price of the third-party stock and the issuer's tax basis in that stock will constitute a taxable gain or loss.[2] Subsequent to tax reforms in 1986 and 1987, the corporate exclusion from taxable income of dividends received after December 31, 1987, on the third-party stock was reduced to 70 percent (from 85 percent prior to the reforms) in the case of ownership of less than 20 percent of the equity of the third-party stock, and to 80 percent in the case of ownership of 20 percent or more. In addition, the tax deductibility of interest paid on any debt used to fund an equity position (such as exchangeable debentures) was subject to limitations unless the position was acquired prior to October 1984. As had always been true, dividends received by American corporations on foreign stock holdings were not subject to any exclusions for U.S. tax purposes. Rather, they were taxed as foreign-source income on which a foreign tax credit could be claimed.

---

[2]Prior to the 1987 tax year, the taxable gain or loss on the third-party stock may have qualified for long-term tax treatment depending upon the holding period involved.

General Cinema's first exchangeable debenture, issued in 1980, was a $17,329,000 offering of 8.25 percent notes exchangeable into the common stock of Columbia Pictures Industries, Inc., at the rate of 24.69 shares per $1000 face value.[3] The shares needed to redeem the bonds in the event of exchange by bondholders were deposited in an escrow account. This relatively small issue was called by General Cinema in 1982 and exchanged for Columbia Pictures's common stock.

The next General Cinema exchangeable debentures were issued in 1983 and 1984. They were exchangeable into shares of RJR Nabisco.[4] The 1983 issue was for $100,000,000 of 10 percent subordinated debentures due 2008 and (after adjusting for splits) exchangeable into 3,984,000 shares of RJR. In 1985 and 1986 principal amounts of $213,000 and $4,654,000, respectively, of the 2008 debentures were exchanged for RJR stock. The 1984 issue was for $78,167,000 of 10 percent subordinated debentures due 2009 and (also after adjusting for splits) exchangeable into 2,605,568 shares of RJR. During 1985 and 1986, $2000 and $4,464,000 principal amounts of the 2009 debentures were exchanged for RJR stock, respectively. Further details regarding these debentures are shown in **Exhibit 7**. Stock price and dividend information for Columbia Pictures and RJR Nabisco is provided in **Exhibit 8**. General Cinema considered all of these exchangeable issues to have been quite successful.

The proposed terms of a new debenture exchangeable into Cadbury Schweppes stock are shown in **Exhibit 9**. The proposed debenture differed from General Cinema's previous exchangeable issues in several important respects: General Cinema would now be issuing securities exchangeable into the stock of a foreign corporation; the issue itself would be denominated in a foreign currency, namely, pounds sterling (see **Exhibits 10** and **11** for a recent history of Cadbury Schweppes's stock prices and the sterling/dollar exchange rate); and the debentures were to be issued in the Euromarkets rather than the U.S. domestic market.

In addition, the new exchangeable debentures were to have a "cash option," which would permit General Cinema to settle in cash rather than stock in the event investors

---

[3]General Cinema acquired 4.6 percent of Columbia Pictures's common stock on the open market in late 1978 at a direct cost of $9,659,000. Between 1978 and 1980, a struggle for control of Columbia Pictures took place that resulted in the company repurchasing 25.5 percent of its own stock from Kirk Kerkorian and his investment firm, Tracinda Investment Corporation (Mr. Kerkorian held a 48 percent controlling interest in MGM, and it was speculated at the time that he wished to merge the two companies). The repurchase took place at a value of $50 per share, a 253 percent gain over Mr. Kerkorian's average purchase price. Shortly after its open-market purchase, General Cinema entered discussions with Columbia to explore the possibility of increasing its stake in Columbia to 25 percent, putting it in competition with Mr. Kerkorian. Stock analysts were puzzled by the discussions since General Cinema had not historically held minority positions, and they did not see Columbia as the correct "third leg of activity that General Cinema's been looking for" (*The Wall Street Journal*, January 3, 1979). In any event, the discussions did not result in an increase in General Cinema's stake in Columbia Pictures.

[4]RJR common stock was acquired in 1982 when Heublein, Inc., was merged into a wholly owned subsidiary of RJR. In the early 1980s, General Cinema invested $159,982,000 to acquire an 18.9 percent interest in Heublein and indicated its desire to participate in the company's strategic planning. Heublein's resistance to this offer concluded in a merger with RJR. As a result of the merger, 4,092,900 shares of Heublein common stock owned by General Cinema were automatically converted into 2,635,827 common shares of RJR Nabisco and 1,023,225 shares of Reynolds series B $11\frac{1}{2}$ cumulative preferred stock. Subsequent stock splits increased the number of RJR's outstanding common shares 2.5 times, resulting in a rise in General Cinema's RJR share holdings to 6,589,568 common shares.

elected to exchange their securities, and a so-called ''Swiss put'' that gave holders the option of redeeming their debentures for cash at a substantial premium above par (see **Exhibit 9**). These differences made the debentures somewhat unusual, even for General Cinema, requiring care in the execution of their offering.

Mr. Ives weighed the pros and cons of the proposed deal carefully as he prepared to respond to questions from General Cinema's board of directors. The purpose of the proposed offering would have to be explained in light of General Cinema's 13d filing with the Securities and Exchange Commission (SEC) in January of 1987, in which the company stated its intention to acquire more than 15 percent, but less than 25 percent, of Cadbury Schweppes's stock.

EXHIBIT 1   **BALANCE SHEET FOR GENERAL CINEMA CORPORATION (IN THOUSANDS)**

	October 31	
	1986	1985
Assets		
Current assets		
Cash and short-term investments—at cost (which approximates market)	$ 19,343	$ 6,845
Notes and accounts receivable—trade, less allowance for doubtful accounts of $2459 and $1951	47,790	43,246
Sundry deposits and receivables	20,505	19,834
Inventory	29,351	28,869
Other current assets	27,039	20,716
Total current assets	144,028	119,510
Property, plant, and equipment		
Land, buildings, and improvements	218,837	190,473
Equipment, fixtures, and vehicles	356,967	328,096
	575,804	518,569
Less accumulated depreciation and amortization	262,773	240,193
Total net property, plant, and equipment	313,031	278,376
Investments		
Carter Hawley Hale Stores, Inc.	295,375	295,375
RJR Nabisco, Inc.	150,175	154,578
Other	63,945	14,639
Total investments	509,495	464,592
Other assets	21,356	30,848
Intangibles, principally beverage franchises	54,479	51,887
	$1,042,389	$945,213

EXHIBIT 1 **BALANCE SHEET FOR GENERAL CINEMA CORPORATION (IN THOUSANDS)**
(Continued)

	October 31	
	1986	1985
Liabilities and shareholders' equity		
Current liabilities		
Long-term liabilities—due within 1 year	$ 8,993	$ 11,296
Note payable to shareholder	—	43,214
Accounts payable and other current liabilities	104,362	113,854
Taxes payable	48,389	26,147
Total current liabilities	161,744	194,511
Long-term liabilities		
Senior debt	81,211	54,606
Subordinated debt	227,417	233,922
Other	4,620	5,660
Total long-term liabilities	313,248	294,188
Unearned exchange income	36,526	40,270
Deferred income taxes	36,476	29,991
Commitments and contingencies	—	—
Shareholders' equity		
Preferred stock; authorized—40,000,000 shares		
Series A Cumulative Convertible—$1.00 par value		
Issued—2,532,513 and 3,154,107 shares	2,533	3,154
Common stocks		
Class B stock—$1.00 par value		
Authorized—40,000,000 shares		
Issued—11,098,554 and 11,116,619 shares	11,099	11,117
Common stock—$1.00 par value		
Authorized—80,000,000 shares		
Issued—22,834,873 and 22,090,439 shares	22,835	22,090
Paid-in capital	925	—
Retained earnings	457,003	349,892
Total shareholders' equity	494,395	386,253
	$1,042,389	$945,213

**EXHIBIT 2 INCOME STATEMENT FOR GENERAL CINEMA CORPORATION
(IN THOUSANDS EXCEPT FOR PER SHARE DATA)**

	Years ended October	
	1986	1985
Revenues		
Beverage operations	$638,792	$599,291
Theater operations	349,432	341,383
Other	9,613	2,170
	997,837	942,844
Operating costs and expenses		
Costs applicable to revenues		
Beverage operations	378,045	352,083
Theater operations	292,525	282,624
Other	8,028	2,175
	678,598	636,882
Selling, delivery, and general and administrative expenses	206,577	193,411
	885,175	830,293
Operating earnings	112,662	112,551
Corporate activities		
Interest expense—net of interest income of $5492, $8201, and $9608	34,709	34,941
Net administrative and other expenses	7,836	7,353
Dividend income	(51,391)	(51,059)
Total corporate activities	(8,846)	(8,765)
Earnings from continuing operations before income taxes	121,508	121,316
Income taxes	31,470	34,843
Earnings from continuing operations	90,038	86,473
Discontinued operations		
Earnings from discontinued operations net of taxes of $915, $1158, and ($334)	880	1,758
Gain on disposal—net of income taxes of $12,500 and $16,000	34,902	—
Net earnings	$125,820	$ 88,231
Net earnings per common and common equivalent share		
From continuing operations	$2.45	$2.29
From discontinued operations	0.98	0.04
Net earnings	$3.43	$2.33

EXHIBIT 3   FIVE-YEAR SUMMARY OF GENERAL CINEMA CORPORATION
(IN THOUSANDS EXCEPT FOR PER SHARE DATA)

	1986*	1985	1984	1983	1982
Revenues					
Beverage operations	$638,792	$599,291	$512,736	$473,140	$451,462
Theater operations	349,432	341,383	350,659	353,099	343,914
Other	1,914	2,170	2,205	2,084	1,837
Total	990,138	942,844	865,600	828,323	797,213
Operating earnings					
Beverage operations	89,821	83,599	66,673	63,121	61,229
Theater operations	25,755	29,094	37,610	35,505	32,219
Other	980	(142)	1,681	99	3,708
Total	116,556	112,551	105,964	98,725	97,156
Corporate activities					
Interest—net	34,709	34,941	30,031	20,746	24,222
Administrative and other	11,905	7,353	9,612	9,582	10,225
Dividend income	(51,391)	(51,059)	(39,932)	(19,370)	(5,476)
	(4,777)	(8,765)	(289)	10,958	28,971
Earnings from continuing operations before nonoperating income and income taxes	121,333	121,316	106,253	87,767	68,185
Nonoperating income	4,069	—	1,992	—	6,915
Earnings from continuing operations before income taxes	125,402	121,316	108,245	87,767	75,100
Income taxes	33,262	34,843	36,919	33,942	28,505
Earnings from continuing operations	92,140	86,473	71,326	53,825	46,595
Net earnings	$125,820	$ 88,231	$110,959	$ 98,519	$ 48,036

**EXHIBIT 3   FIVE-YEAR SUMMARY OF GENERAL CINEMA CORPORATION
(IN THOUSANDS EXCEPT FOR PER SHARE DATA)** *(Continued)*

	1986*	1985	1984	1983	1982
Cash flow	$140,915	$135,809	$111,815	$ 97,167	$ 85,180
Depreciation and amortization of capital assets	47,581	39,098	36,592	37,571	38,098
Capital expenditures	86,962	69,000	52,181	53,992	42,741
Cash dividends paid	18,709	15,843	13,596	11,220	9,861
Total assets	1,042,389	945,213	991,448	619,157	592,809
Total long-term debt	313,248	294,188	407,865	140,563	283,217
Shareholders' equity	494,395	386,253	355,922	259,096	169,157
Long-term debt to shareholders' equity	0.63 to 1	0.76 to 1	1.15 to 1	0.54 to 1	1.67 to 1
Number of shares outstanding[†]	73,420	75,616	75,402	75,232	80,732
Per share data[‡]					
Earnings from continuing operations	$1.25	$1.14	$0.95	$0.72	$0.58
Net earnings	1.71	1.17	1.47	1.31	0.60
Common dividends paid	0.26	0.21	0.17	0.14	0.13
Book value	6.78	5.31	4.73	3.46	2.28
Market price					
High	59.000	42.500	28.000	45.500	30.500
Low	36.625	24.500	16.500	27.750	14.875
Close	43.875	38.625	26.750	45.000	29.125

	High	Low	Close
1987: January	51.500	44.000	51.250
1987: February	56.000	51.000	55.500
1987: March	55.375	50.000	51.250
1987: April	53.625	45.625	47.250

*Restated to reflect discontinued operations.
[†]Weighted average number of shares and common share equivalents outstanding adjusted to reflect stock splits and stock dividends.
[‡]Assuming full conversion of Series A shares into common stock.

EXHIBIT 4   CADBURY SCHWEPPES'S BALANCE SHEET (MILLIONS)

	1986	1985
Assets		
Current assets		
Stock	£ 237.1	£ 256.6
Debtors	308.9	315.2
Investments—short-term loans and		
deposits	140.4	17.6
Cash at bank and in hand	37.0	29.5
Total current assets	723.4	618.9
Fixed assets		
Tangible assets	539.2	570.9
Investments	16.2	23.1
Total fixed assets	555.4	594.0
Total assets	£1278.8	£1212.9
Liabilities		
Current liabilities		
Borrowings	£ 79.9	£ 70.2
Other	456.8	409.1
Total current liabilities	536.7	479.3
Long-term liabilities		
Borrowings	185.6	195.4
Other	23.8	11.0
Provision for liabilities and charges	16.5	14.8
Capital and reserves		
Called up share capital	142.9	132.9
Share premium account	167.2	118.3
Revaluation reserve	41.1	48.8
Profit and loss account	112.0	171.0
Minority interests	53.0	41.4
Total liabilities	£1278.8	£1212.9

EXHIBIT 5 CADBURY SCHWEPPES'S GROUP PROFIT AND LOSS ACCOUNT (MILLIONS EXCEPT WHERE NOTED)

	1986	1985
Sales	£1839.9	£1873.8
Cost of sales	(1100.2)	(1190.8)
Gross profit	739.7	683.0
Distribution costs, including marketing	(435.9)	(431.4)
Administration expenses	(168.1)	(143.8)
Other operating income	4.7	5.2
Trading profit	140.4	113.0
Share of profits of associated companies	4.7	8.0
Other investment income and interest receivable	20.5	11.8
Interest payable and similar charges	(34.9)	(39.5)
Profit on ordinary activities before taxation	130.7	93.3
Tax on profit on ordinary activities	(44.7)	(37.3)
Profit on ordinary activities after taxation	86.0	56.0
Profit attributable to minority interests	(9.9)	(8.2)
Profit before extraordinary items	76.1	47.8
Extraordinary items	25.9	(5.9)
Profit attributable to shareholders	102.0	41.9
Dividends	(37.6)	(30.7)
Profit retained for the year	£ 64.4	£ 11.2
Number of ordinary shares outstanding (year-end)	558.3	518.7
Earnings per ordinary share of 25p*:		
Net basis	15.40p	10.80p
Pretax basis	23.41p	17.99p
Dividends per ordinary share[†]:	6.73p	5.92p

*Based upon profit on ordinary activities after taxation.

[†]Under U.K. tax law prevailing in 1987, companies paying cash dividends are obligated to pay an advance corporation tax ("ACT") to the United Kingdom Inland Revenue at a rate of 27/73rds of the dividend paid (effectively, 27 percent of the sum of the dividend and the ACT). Individual U.K. resident shareholders could then be entitled to a tax credit equal to 27/73rds of the dividends received.

EXHIBIT 6	CADBURY SCHWEPPES'S SALES AND PROFITS BY GEOGRAPHIC AREA				
	Group profit and loss accounts, million				
	1986	1985	1984	1983	1982
Sales					
United Kingdom	£ 766.1	£ 951.2	£ 920.8	£ 823.9	£ 771.7
Europe	293.1	253.2	232.1	196.2	172.6
North America	415.0	357.9	486.0	374.8	279.6
Rest of the world	365.7	311.5	377.3	307.9	270.3
	£1839.9	£1873.8	£2016.2	£1702.8	£1494.2
Trading profit					
United Kingdom	£ 76.2	£ 65.6	£ 62.3	£ 57.3	£ 51.5
Europe	23.4	20.6	16.5	10.6	9.4
North America	6.0	(5.6)	36.9	26.9	19.6
Rest of the world	34.8	32.4	38.7	30.8	24.3
	£ 140.4	£ 113.0	£ 154.4	£ 125.6	£ 104.8

EXHIBIT 7   SUMMARY OF TERMS FOR GENERAL CINEMA'S PRIOR EXCHANGEABLE DEBENTURES

Debentures exchangeable into Columbia Pictures common stock

Issue date	September 9, 1980
Principal amount	$17,329,000
Issue price	$1000 per debenture
Par value	$1000 per debenture
Coupon	8.25% per annum
Maturity	20 years
Exchange rights	24.69 ordinary shares of Columbia common stock for each $1000 principal amount of debentures
Conversion premium	20.9%
Redemption at General Cinema's option	The debentures are redeemable at any time, at the option of General Cinema, at 108.25% of the principal amount prior to September 15, 1981, and thereafter at prices declining annually to 100% of the principal amount on and after September 15, 1995.

Debentures exchangeable into RJR Nabisco common stock, due 2008

Issue date	March 29, 1983
Principal amount	$100,000,000
Issue price	$1000 per debenture
Par value	$1000 per debenture
Coupon	10% minimum interest rate per annum, payable semiannually. Semiannual interest payments per $1000 principal amount of debentures shall be equal to the greater of (a) $50 (reflecting the minimum annual interest rate of 10%) or (b) $5 plus the amount of dividends paid during the preceding 6 months on the shares of RJR common stock for which the debentures are exchangeable. In no event, however, will the annual rate of interest exceed 20%.
Maturity	25 years
Exchange rights	15.936 shares of RJR common stock for each $1000 principal amount of debentures (39.84 shares following a 5/2 split in 1985)
Conversion premium	20%
Redemption at General Cinema's option	The debentures are redeemable at any time after March 14, 1986, at the option of General Cinema, at 107% of the principal amount prior to March 15, 1987, and thereafter at prices declining annually to 100% on and after March 15, 1993.

EXHIBIT 7   SUMMARY OF TERMS FOR GENERAL CINEMA'S PRIOR EXCHANGEABLE DEBENTURES *(Continued)*

Debentures exchangeable into RJR Nabisco common stock, due 2009

Issue date	January 12, 1984
Principal amount	$78,167,000
Issue price	$1000 per debenture
Par value	$1000 per debenture
Coupon	10% minimum interest rate per annum, payable semiannually. Semiannual interest payments for the debentures shall be equal to the greater of (a) $50 (reflecting the minimum annual interest rate of 10%) or (b) $5 plus the amount of cash dividends paid during the 6-month period preceding the record date for the next previous interest payment, on the shares of RJR for which such debentures are exchangeable, together with any other cash income attributable to such shares and received by the escrow agent during such period. In no event, however, will the annual rate of interest exceed 20% per year.
Maturity	25 years
Exchange rights	13.33 ordinary shares of RJR for each $1000 principal amount of debentures (33.325 shares following a 5/2 split in 1985)
Conversion premium	20%
Redemption at General Cinema's option	The debentures are redeemable at any time, at the option of General Cinema, at 110% of the principal amount prior to January 15, 1985, and thereafter at prices declining annually to 100% of the principal amount on and after January 15, 1994; provided, however, that the debentures may not be redeemed prior to February 1, 1986, unless the average closing price of RJR during a specified 30-day period shall have equaled or exceeded 150% of the exchange price then in effect.

EXHIBIT 8 **STOCK PRICES AND DIVIDENDS FOR COLUMBIA PICTURES AND RJR NABISCO**

| | Stock price, $/share | | | |
	High	Low	Close	Dividends per share
		Columbia		
1979	$37.500	$18.500	$34.125	$0.800*
1980	44.500	27.000	43.375	0.375
1981	47.500	31.500	44.375	0.575
1982†	72.375	41.750	72.000	
		RJR Nabisco‡		
1982	$22.875	$16.000	$20.500	$1.140
1983	25.500	18.125	24.400	1.220
1984	29.000	21.125	29.000	1.300
1985	35.000	24.750	31.375	1.410
1986	55.125	31.000	49.500	1.510
1987: January	64.250	50.000	62.625	
1987: February	63.375	58.125	60.250	
1987: March	62.000	56.250	56.750	0.400§
1987: April	58.000	51.250	53.000	

*Includes a $0.40 special fiscal 1978 yearend dividend declared and paid in fiscal 1979.
†Coca-Cola acquired Columbia Pictures for $336.7 million in cash and $414.9 million in stock for a total of $751.6 million on June 21, 1982.
‡Prices and dividends are adjusted for the 5/2 stock split on June 18, 1985.
§First-quarter dividend for 1987.

EXHIBIT 9   SUMMARY OF PROPOSED TERMS FOR GENERAL CINEMA'S DEBENTURES EXCHANGEABLE INTO CADBURY SCHWEPPES COMMON STOCK

Principal amount	£110,000,000
Issue price	£1000 per debenture
Par value	£1000 per debenture
Coupon	5% per annum, payable semiannually
Maturity	15 years
Exchange rights	333 ordinary shares of Cadbury Schweppes for each £1000 principal amount of debentures
Conversion premium	19%
Redemption at the holder's option	At the option of the holder, debentures may be redeemed by General Cinema on June 9, 1992, at 122.375% of their principal amount, plus accrued interest.
Redemption at General Cinema's option	The debentures may be redeemed by General Cinema at its option, in whole or in part, on or after the distribution of the debentures, at 106% of their principal amount, plus accrued interest, prior to June 9, 1988, and at declining prices thereafter, but are not redeemable prior to June 9, 1992, unless the market value of the exchange property exceeds £1300 per £1000 principal amount of debentures for a specified period. In the event of certain developments affecting U.S. taxation or the imposition of certain certification, information, or other reporting requirements, the debentures may also be redeemed, in whole, at 100% of their principal amount, plus accured interest.
Cash option	At the option of General Cinema, holders of the debentures electing to exchange their debentures for shares may, in lieu thereof, be given the cash equivalent, in pounds sterling, of the market value of such shares.

EXHIBIT 10   CADBURY SCHWEPPES STOCK PRICES AND DIVIDENDS

	Stock price (in pence)			
	High	Low	Close	Dividend, pence
1982	133p	95p	117p	4.9
1983	133	95	117	5.4
1984	161	113	161	5.9
1985	178	128	158	5.9
1986	198	141	187	6.7
1987: January	228	187	225	
1987: February	263	224	257	
1987: March	259	227	243 xd*	
1987: April	253	229	253	

*xd: ex dividend price.

EXHIBIT 11 $/£ EXCHANGE RATES AND INTEREST RATE DATA

	Spot exchange rate, $/£	One-year forward exchange rate, $/£	Long-term government bond yields	
			U.S.	U.K.
1982	1.6170	1.6083	10.61%	10.62%
1983	1.4510	1.4608	12.00	9.94
1984	1.1585	1.1547	11.61	10.25
1985	1.4450	1.3982	9.49	10.35
1986	1.4820	1.4185	7.79	10.17
1987: January	1.5130	1.4500	7.47	10.64
1987: February	1.5455	1.4930	7.48	9.51
1987: March	1.6045	1.5621	7.81	9.15
1987: April	1.6600	1.6410	8.45	8.87

UNIVERSAL CIRCUITS, INC.

Pierre Bourquin, manager of international finance of Universal Circuits, was troubled by problems confronting the Irish subsidiary. The strong U.S. dollar had contributed to excellent profitability for the plant located near Limerick, but today's good news could be tomorrow's problem. The controller of the Irish plant estimated that the profit margin was highly vulnerable to any weakening of the dollar against the Irish punt. A telex had been received from the controller pointing out the severity of the risk and urging that he be allowed to buy the punt forward to protect his 1985 budgeted profit. He felt certain that the huge American trade deficits, running at an annual rate in excess of $100 billion, would crater the dollar.

Bourquin felt caught in the middle. There was no question that the Irish operation was exposed, but the pessimism about the dollar was far from shared. Universal Circuits's chief financial officer, Joe Merrill, had recently pointed out that the dollar was in the middle of its 20-year range (see **Exhibit 1**): "Anyone who can forecast which way it is going to move shouldn't bother being in the manufacturing business; he could make a fortune speculating on currencies." Speculation was of no interest to senior management.

COMPANY BACKGROUND

Universal Circuits, Inc., is a leading supplier of components for the measurement and control industry. The function of a computerized measurement and control system is to

This case was prepared by Professor Thomas R. Piper. Copyright © 1985 by the President and Fellows of Harvard College. Harvard Business School case 286-006.

acquire physical information from the real world, to measure this information, and then to control the physical process. The physical information to be measured can be temperature, pressure, light, weight, velocity, thickness, density, etc. Applications include medical instruments, such as blood analyzers and computerized axial tomography (CAT) scanners, industrial automation systems, process controls, environmental controls, instruments for energy conservation, pollution control, cancer research, oil exploration, radar systems for missile detection, aircraft navigation systems, and fire control systems.

Universal Circuits's products are sold through an extensive field sales force. The company's U.S. sales organization consists of approximately 170 sales engineers and sales managers, and 37 manufacturers' representatives. Outside the United States, Universal Circuits maintains wholly-owned sales subsidiaries in eleven countries, with approximately 120 sales engineers and sales managers. In addition, the company is represented by independent sales representatives in seventeen other countries. Foreign sales account for 40 percent of total sales.

Universal Circuits has many competitors within each of its industry segments. Some offer a broad range of other electronic products, and some have substantially larger financial resources. The principal competitors are U.S.-based companies that supply their worldwide operations almost entirely from U.S. plants. Several Japanese manufacturers including Fujitsu, Hitachi, Toshiba, Matsushita, and NEC have introduced products that compete at least marginally with Universal Circuits. However, competition from Japanese products is not significant.

Relative competitive strength is dependent upon technical innovation, quality, and reliability; product availability; technical service and support; and range of products. While price is the most important competitive factor when all other considerations are equal, and price reductions frequently accompany improvements in manufacturing techniques, users are willing to pay a higher price for superior performance and reliability.

In general, Universal Circuits uses standard supplies and materials in the manufacture of its products. Most of the raw materials and components are generally available from a number of suppliers in the United States and Europe. Approximately 25 percent of Universal Circuits's manufacturing is conducted in Ireland, the United Kingdom, the Philippines, and Japan. Ireland is by far the largest of the offshore facilities.

Management's goals include annual sales growth of 25 to 35 percent, nearly twice the growth rate of the broad markets served. The growth is largely self-financed, based on a target return on capital of 19 percent, a willingness to use debt, and a policy of paying no cash dividend.

Universal Circuits's record since 1978 had been outstanding. Sales had more than tripled to $214 million in fiscal 1983 as the company pursued its goal of increased market share. Net income quadrupled to $18.4 million, and the share price increased tenfold (see **Exhibits 2**, **3**, and **4** for financial information). This strong performance made equity sales possible at attractive prices. A $37 million issue in 1983 was placed at a price of $35½ per share.

THE IRISH OPERATION

Several factors prompted Universal Circuits to establish operations in Ireland in 1976. First, the Irish Development Authority provided a capital grant and very attractive tax inducements and authorized full repatriation of profits. Manufacturing profits would be taxed at an effective rate of 0 percent until 1990 and at a 10 percent rate thereafter. The low rate resulted from the special treatment of profits on goods that provided Ireland with export earnings. Second, location within the European Economic Community (EEC) would save the 17 percent duty on all sales within the EEC. This would be only partially offset by a 4.2 percent tariff on goods shipped from the plant to the United States. Third, a well-educated, young population would provide a technically skilled work force.

To facilitate intercompany funds transfers, the Irish operation was established as a branch of a Dutch holding company, UCNV Netherlands. Had it been established as a separate legal entity, all remittances to the Dutch holding company would have been subjected to Irish withholding taxes. The manufacturing profits of the Irish branch would not be taxed in the Netherlands as they were already subject to taxation in Ireland. All dividends paid to the U.S. parent would be taxed at the full U.S. tax rate. Alternatively, funds could be invested by the Dutch holding company in other operations outside of the United States, although this could result in a currency exposure.

The Irish branch was a fully integrated research and manufacturing operation, responsible for the design, development, and manufacturing of all computer measurement and control system products for sale by Universal Circuits throughout the world. Labor and locally sourced supplies accounted for 30 percent of direct cost of sales; raw materials and supplies, most of which were sourced from the United States and Europe, accounted for the balance (see **Exhibit 5**). Operating and other expenses were incurred virtually entirely in Irish punt.

The plant's output was exported to Universal Circuits's foreign sales affiliates, the U.S. sales force, and the independent manufacturers' representatives. Transfer prices were based on the U.S. dollar price list, with some modification to meet competitive pressures. All sales were invoiced in U.S. dollars, with payment made in 0 to 90 days. On average, the affiliates paid the Irish branch in 55 days.

Operations in Ireland were profitable. In fiscal year 1984, both the pre-tax return on assets and the pre-tax contribution margin were above the targets set for all Universal Circuits's divisions (see **Exhibit 5**). These performance evaluations measures, along with all budgets, were made in U.S. dollars, the functional currency of the branch.

THE SALES AFFILIATES

In addition to its U.S. sales force, Universal Circuits had wholly-owned sales affiliates, established as separate legal entities, in Great Britain, France, West Germany, Belgium, Denmark, the Netherlands, Sweden, Italy, Japan, Israel, and Switzerland. The company was also represented by independent sales representatives in seventeen other countries. The sales affiliates reported to the vice president of sales and were evaluated on the basis of (1) sales growth, measured in U.S. dollars and in the local currency; (2) return on assets; (3) change in market share; (4) direct contribution margin; and (5) growth of operating profits. The measures were calculated before interest and before currency gains and losses.

Customers often asked for quotes several weeks prior to committing to purchase. Quotes were made in the local currency, based on the standard U.S. transfer price plus shipping costs from the United States plus the duty on goods imported from the United States plus the target sales mark-up to cover local costs of doing business in the various countries. The local currency quote was based on the spot rate with the provision that the final price would be based on the spot rate at the time of shipment to the customer. Thus, Universal Circuits was theoretically insulated from any change in the local currency/U.S. dollar exchange rate between the quotation date and the date of shipment. (See **Exhibit 6** for a portrayal of the flow of goods from manufacturing to the customer.)

In fact, Universal Circuits's recent experience indicated that local currency prices could be increased on 60 to 90 percent of foreign sales, to offset a weakening of the local currency after the initial quotation. Approximately 10 to 20 percent of foreign sales were made on long-term contracts at fixed local-currency prices. Another 10 to 20 percent were priced in U.S. dollars.

Customers were invoiced in the local currency, with credit terms based on local regulations and competitive patterns. Collection periods in the various countries ranged from 28 days to 100 days. (See **Exhibit 7** for the financial statements of a typical sales affiliate.)

THE INTERNATIONAL FINANCE FUNCTION

The organization of the international finance function reflected Universal Circuits's strong commitment to decentralization. The markets served by each of the divisions were characterized by rapid technological advances. The company's growth was driven by a continuing flow of new products. It seemed essential to maintain a strong entrepreneurial mentality at the divisions by granting them full managerial responsibility.

However, some members of senior management felt that responsibility for exchange-rate exposure should be centralized. "We want manufacturing to focus on operations and sales to work on pricing and sales margins, rather than mess around with currencies," stated the chief financial officer. "It's treasury's responsibility to manage the financial structure and the net consolidated currency exposure."

Pierre Bourquin was confident that no one at Universal Circuits focused on the balance-sheet account for currency gains and losses, stating: "Our focus is on economic exposure. . . . We're not going to worry about what we think are accounting fictions. . . . In terms of profit and loss exposure, we take a one-month time horizon, estimate the exposure, and then decide whether to hedge based on trends in the market for the currency and current market inputs. . . . Management of exposure is clearly our responsibility but it requires the active participation and cooperation of the controllers at the sales affiliates who report to their local managers and on a dotted line to the controller of corporate sales.'' (See **Exhibit 8**.)

The treasurer of Universal Circuits, Jon Kriesler, supported the policy of selective hedging: ''We review regularly our exposure position, hedging exposure and market conditions with the belief that we can do a little better in terms of long-run economic value by actively managing the exchange rate exposure.''

But what should be done about the telex from the controller of the Irish operation?

EXHIBIT 1   INFORMATION ON SELECTED COUNTRIES

	1977	1978	1979	1980	1981	1982	1983	1984-II
France								
Consumer prices	73	79	88	100	113	127	139	149
Industrial prices	78	81	92	100	111	123	137	155
Money supply	75	84	94	100	116	129	145	na
Gross domestic product*	92	96	99	100	100	102	103	na
Trade balance[†]	(3.3)	0.1	(3.2)	(13.4)	(10.0)	(15.8)	(8.1)	na
Government (deficit)[‡]	(14)	(17)	(3)	0	(33)	(84)	(159)	na
Government bond yields	9.6	9.0	9.5	13.0	15.7	15.6	13.6	13.0
FF/$ (end of period)	4.7	4.2	4.0	4.5	5.7	6.7	8.3	8.5
Japan								
Consumer prices	86	89	93	100	105	108	110	112
Wholesale prices	81	79	85	100	101	103	101	100
Money supply	87	99	102	100	110	116	116	118
Gross domestic product*	86	91	95	100	104	107	111	na
Trade balance[†]	17	26	2	2	20	18	31	na
Government bond yields	7.3	6.1	7.7	9.2	8.7	8.1	7.4	6.6
¥/$ (end of period)	240	195	240	203	220	235	232	238
United Kingdom								
Consumer prices	69	75	85	100	112	122	127	133
Manufacturing prices	72	79	88	100	110	118	125	132
Money supply	76	89	97	100	117	131	147	153
Gross domestic product*	96	100	102	100	99	101	104	na
Trade balance[†]	(4)	(3)	(7)	4	8	4	(1)	na
Government (deficit)[‡]	(4)	(8)	(10)	(11)	(10)	(8)	(14)	na
Government bond yields	12.7	12.5	13.0	13.8	14.7	12.9	10.8	11.2
£/$ (end of period)	0.52	0.49	0.45	0.42	0.52	0.62	0.69	0.74
United States								
Consumer prices	74	79	88	100	110	117	121	126
Industrial prices	71	76	86	100	111	114	115	118
Money supply	81	88	94	100	107	115	127	132
Gross domestic product*	93	98	100	100	102	100	104	na
Trade balance[†]	(31)	(34)	(28)	(26)	(28)	(36)	(61)	na
Government (deficit)[‡]	(51)	(44)	(28)	(69)	(73)	(131)	(190)	na
Government bond yields	7.7	8.5	9.3	11.4	13.7	12.9	11.3	13.5
West Germany								
Consumer prices	89	91	95	100	106	112	116	119
Industrial prices	88	89	93	100	108	114	116	119
Money supply	82	93	96	100	99	106	114	114
Gross domestic product*	91	94	98	100	100	99	100	na
Trade balance[†]	20	25	17	9	17	25	22	na
Government (deficit)[‡]	(22)	(26)	(26)	(29)	(40)	(36)	(31)	na
Government bond yields	6.2	5.8	7.4	8.5	10.4	9.0	7.9	8.1
DM/$ (end of period)	2.1	1.8	1.7	2.0	2.3	2.4	2.7	2.8

*Gross domestic product in 1980 prices.
[†]Trade balance in billions of U.S. dollars.
[‡]Government surplus (deficit) in billions of local currency.

EXHIBIT 1   INFORMATION ON SELECTED COUNTRIES *(Continued)*

Relative industrial prices	1960	1970	1980	1984	
U.S. ÷ France	100	88	98	73	
U.S. ÷ Ireland	100	80	53	41	
U.S. ÷ Japan	100	102	121	139	
U.S. ÷ United Kingdom	100	86	59	51	
U.S. ÷ West Germany	100	102	151	147	

Exchange rates	1960	1970	1980	1984	Range 1960–1980
French franc/dollar	4.90	5.52	4.52	8.50	4.02–5.56
Irish punt/dollar	0.36	0.42	0.53	1.01	0.36–0.53
Japanese yen/dollar	360	358	203	238	195–362
British pound/dollar	0.36	0.42	0.30	0.74	0.36–0.59
Deutsche mark/dollar	4.17	3.65	1.96	2.85	1.73–4.17

EXHIBIT 2   SELECTED FINANCIAL INFORMATION*

	1978	1979	1980	1981	1982	1983
Sales, $ millions	66	100	136	156	174	214
Net income, $ millions	4.5	7.0	9.3	4.6	9.9	18.4
% of sales	6.8	7.1	7.0	2.9	5.7	8.6
Earnings per share, $	.32	.47	.59	.27	.55	.97
Dividends per share	0	0	0	0	0	0
Book value per share, $	1.72	2.23	3.05	4.02	4.69	7.79
Share price, high, $	4½	8½	16½	15⅜	19¾	41¾
low, $	2¼	3¼	6½	8⅜	8¾	17½
Price/earnings ratio	7–14	7–18	11–28	31–57	16–36	18–43
Return on assets, %	9	10	9	3	6	9
Return on capital, %	14	15	15	8	10	13
Return on equity, %	21	25	23	8	13	16
Long-term debt ÷ capital, %	38	45	51	42	37	15
EBIT ÷ interest	5×	5×	3×	3×	3×	6×
Shares outstanding (millions)	13.2	15.0	15.8	17.2	18.0	19.0

*The data in the case have been disguised. EBIT = earnings before interest and taxes.

EXHIBIT 3   CONSOLIDATED STATEMENT OF INCOME, YEAR ENDING OCTOBER 30 (MILLIONS)*

	1981	1982	1983
Sales	$156	$174	$214
Cost of sales	81	84	99
Gross margin	75	90	115
Research, development, and engineering	12	15	20
Marketing	9	10	11
Selling	23	26	32
General and administrative	14	16	20
Interest expense	10	8	5
Other	1	1	0
Income before taxes	6.7	14.5	27.1
Provision income taxes†	2.2	4.6	8.7
Net income	$4.6	$9.9	$18.4

*The data in the case have been disguised.

†The company's practice is to reinvest the earnings of its international subsidiaries in those operations, and repatriation of such earnings occurs only when it is advantageous to do so. Applicable taxes are provided only on amounts planned to be remitted. Accordingly, no income taxes have been provided for approximately $20 million of unremitted earnings of international subsidiaries, principally the company's Irish operation. For tax purposes, the company has available approximately $2.4 million of foreign tax credit carry-forwards expiring in 1984 and 1988.

EXHIBIT 4 CONSOLIDATED BALANCE SHEET (MILLIONS)*

	1982	1983
Assets		
Cash	$ 1	$ 24
Accounts receivable	34	42
Inventories	47	56
Other	5	6
Total current	87	128
Net property, plant, and equipment	61	70
Investments	8	15
Other	7	10
Total assets	$163	$223
Liabilities and equity		
Short-term borrowings	$ 1	$ 2
Obligations under capital leases	1	2
Accounts payable	11	15
Income taxes payable	1	8
Accrued liabilities	9	11
Total current	23	38
Long-term debt	48	23
Obligations under capital leases	4	5
Deferred income taxes	4	5
Common equity	86	154
Cumulative translation adjustment	(2)	(2)
Total	$163	$223

*(1) The consolidated financial statements included the accounts of the company and all its subsidiaries. (2) In the first quarter of 1982, the company adopted Statement of Financial Accounting Standards No. 52, "Foreign Currency Translation." (3) At year end 1983, foreign-currency debt totaled $13.7 million and was made up almost entirely of yen, French franc, and deutsche mark borrowings. (4) The data in the case have been disguised.

EXHIBIT 5 PROFIT AND LOSS STATEMENT OF THE IRISH OPERATIONS (% OF SALES)*

Sales	100%
Direct cost of sales	48
Direct margin	52
Operating expenses	34
Contribution margin	18
Other income/expense	3
Profit before tax	15%

*The data in the case have been disguised.

EXHIBIT 6   FLOW OF GOODS THROUGH SYSTEM

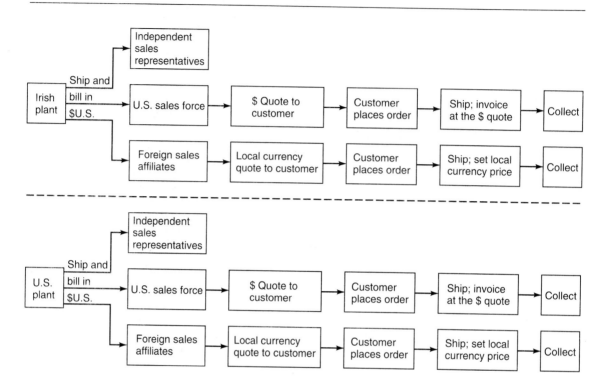

EXHIBIT 7 SUMMARY FINANCIALS FOR A TYPICAL SALES AFFILIATE*

Balance sheet—% of total

Cash	0%	Bank debt	59%
Receivables	75	Accounts payable	19
Inventory	15	Intercompany payables	7
Other	6	Total current	85
Total current	96	Equity	15
Fixed assets	4	Total	100%
Total	100%		

Profit and loss—% of sales

Trade sales	100%
Cost of sales	75
Gross margin	25
Operating expenses	15
Other expense	5
Net income	5%

*The data in the case have been disguised.

EXHIBIT 8   ABBREVIATED OPERATIONAL ORGANIZATION CHART

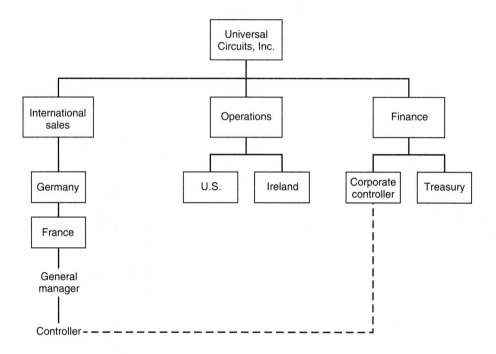

NOTE ON OPERATING EXPOSURE TO EXCHANGE-RATE CHANGES

This note examines operating exposure: the effect of a change in exchange rates on the expected value of a firm's future operating cash flows. It is useful to begin with a comparison of this phenomenon to another, similar one. Consider the oil shocks of the 1970s. When oil prices changed abruptly, the price of oil relative to other goods rose sharply. Many firms' expected future cash flows changed dramatically as a result, because manufacturing costs changed, consumption patterns changed, some technologies changed, etc. This change in the relative price of oil represented a real macroeconomic shock and most firms were exposed to it, some positively and others negatively, and each to a greater or lesser degree depending on many firm-specific factors. Similarly, large unexpected changes in exchange rates may represent real macroeconomic shocks and can result in changes in the value of firms' expected future operating cash flows. Operating exposure, sometimes referred to as "economic exposure," should be thought of as the response of operating cash flows to a real exchange-rate shock.

This definition of operating exposure immediately distinguishes it from two other types of foreign exchange exposures: contractual exposure (often referred to as "transaction exposure") and translation exposure. The former denotes the exposure of contracts *denominated* in a foreign currency; for example, firms may have cash deposits or debt obligations that carry a specified foreign-currency denomination. With a few exceptions, it is easy to calculate the effect on these instruments of a change in the exchange rate. It is also easy to hedge this type of contractual exposure. Translation

This note was prepared by Professor Timothy A. Luehrman. Copyright © 1991 by the President and Fellows of Harvard College. Harvard Business School note 288-018.

exposure, in contrast, denotes the change in a firm's reported results and financial condition brought about by changing exchange rates. For accounting purposes, it is necessary to express the firm's financial statements in a common currency, regardless of economic reality. Obviously, the particular rules adopted for effecting this translation will play an important part in determining translation exposure. Thus, contractual and translation exposures differ from operating exposure, first because they do not pertain to expected future operating cash flows, and second because the contemplated change in the exchange rate may or may not constitute a real shock.[1]

PURCHASING POWER PARITY AND REAL EXCHANGE RATES

The oil shock mentioned above was a real shock because oil prices rose *relative* to the prices of other goods. In the same way, a *real* change in exchange rates is one that changes the relative prices of the goods and services consumed and produced by firms. To see the importance of this distinction, suppose instead that oil prices rose no more or less than the prices of all goods and services. In such a case the general price level rises (''inflates''), but relative prices remain the same and firms and consumers have no reason to change their decisions about production and consumption. Similarly, if a change in a given exchange rate only reflects the difference in inflation rates associated with two currencies, then relative prices do not change and the shift in the exchange rate is said to be nominal rather than real.

To the extent that changes in exchange rates reflect only the differences in inflation rates among currencies, they are consistent with purchasing power parity (PPP). PPP implies that the rate of change of an exchange rate should be equal to the difference between inflation rates for the two currencies. If PPP always held, changes in exchange rates would be nominal rather than real and would not give rise to operating exposure. However, empirical evidence indicates that PPP is not a good explanation of exchange-rate movements, except in the very long run, and it has done especially poorly during the 1980s. Some of this evidence, for the specific case of the yen/dollar exchange rate, is presented in **Exhibit 1** and described in the appendix to this note.[2]

When PPP fails to hold, for whatever reason, changes in exchange rates may be associated with changes in relative prices. For example, the relative prices of manufacturing inputs, such as labor in the United States versus labor in Japan, may change in response to a real change in the yen/dollar exchange rate. When this happens, cost structures change and firms may change their pricing and output decisions; as a result, expected future cash flows change.

Two final points should be noted. First, it is possible to have a real exchange-rate shock even if observed nominal exchange rates are constant. If two countries have different inflation rates, PPP says that the *nominal* exchange rate between their currencies should change. If it does not, then the *real* exchange rate does change; i.e.,

---

[1] For more on these other types of exposures, see ''Note on Transaction and Translation Exposure,'' earlier in Part 3.

[2] For more on PPP and why it breaks down, see ''Note on Fundamental Parity Conditions,'' Harvard Business School note 288-016, in Part 1; or M. Levi, *International Finance*, 2nd ed., McGraw-Hill, New York, 1990.

relative prices change and this will affect firms' cash flows (note this implies that firms have operating exposures even under fixed exchange-rate regimes). Second, it should be obvious that relative prices can change for reasons other than shifts in exchange rates (e.g., technological or demographic changes) and firms' operating cash flows are also exposed to these types of real phenomena.

THE RESPONSES OF OPERATING CASH FLOWS

Estimating a firm's operating exposure requires an assessment of the responsiveness of operating cash flows to a given real change in exchange rates. The major categories of inflows and outflows are revenues and costs, respectively, and these are addressed first.

Consider a U.S. firm whose primary activity is manufacturing a product in the United States for sale in the United States and Germany. It imports none of its inputs, a large fraction of which is labor, and it exports roughly half of its output. Suppose now that the dollar unexpectedly appreciates against the mark and that this change is real, i.e., it represents a deviation from PPP. What happens to the cash flows of the U.S. firm?

First, a currency must be chosen to measure cash flows. Since the firm is from the United States, the dollar is the likely candidate, though this is not required. Next, consider the effect on the dollar costs of the U.S. firm. Since inputs are all sourced in the United States, their prices, measured in dollars, may be unaffected by the exchange-rate change. Assume for the moment that this is the case and that the firm need worry only about revenues. In particular, let dollar prices and unit volume remain the same in the United States and focus instead on revenues from the German market.

When the firm exports to Germany, it must set a price in deutsche marks for its products because the German consumers have deutsche mark cash to spend (even if the firm quoted prices in U.S. dollars, consumers would have to sell their deutsche marks and buy dollars at the prevailing exchange rate, so the firm would still be exposed to the deutsche mark/dollar rate). When the dollar appreciates, the firm must decide what to do with the deutsche mark price it has quoted. To pick two extremes, it can either leave the deutsche mark price constant or it can raise the deutsche mark price to offset fully the deutsche mark depreciation.

In the first case, with deutsche mark prices constant, German consumers may continue to purchase the product as if nothing had happened: Unit volume remains constant, as does deutsche mark revenue. But the firm's shareholders measure their returns in U.S. dollars; because the deutsche mark has depreciated (the dollar has appreciated), the same deutsche mark revenue represents a lower dollar revenue and, because dollar costs are unchanged, lower dollar cash flow. In the second case, the firm raises deutsche mark prices in order to keep dollar-equivalent prices the same as before the exchange-rate shock. German consumers are bound to notice the deutsche mark price rise and can be expected to either lower their consumption of the product or purchase it from other (presumably German) producers. Either way, the consequence is a drop in unit volume for the U.S. firm and hence, again, a drop in dollar cash flow.

In the simple example just described, the dollar cash flow of the firm is *negatively exposed* to the real deutsche mark/dollar exchange rate. When the real deutsche mark/dollar rate goes up, corresponding to a dollar appreciation, the dollar cash flows of the firm decline, regardless of how the firm adjusts its deutsche mark prices. This illustrates the traditional view of operating exposure, namely, that a real home-currency appreciation reduces the cash flow of home-country firms engaged in exporting or competing at home with imports. This is because a home-currency appreciation makes exports from the home country relatively more expensive for consumers abroad while making imports into the home country relatively cheaper. While it is important to understand this fundamental concept, it is also important to realize that it is quite simplistic and therefore may be very misleading.

Important Extensions

To consider the factors that complicate the traditional view of operating exposure, it is helpful to return to the example of the oil shock. When the relative price of oil rose dramatically in the 1970s (and when it subsequently fell) many economic actors changed their behavior. Energy users changed their consumption habits, primarily by conserving. Consumers changed their buying habits, for example, by buying smaller cars instead of bigger ones. Firms designed new products, modified manufacturing processes, and developed new technologies. Governments introduced new taxes and new tax incentives. The business cycle changed; some economies expanded and others fell into recession, with important implications for inflation and interest rates.

While the oil shocks may seem an overly dramatic example of changes in economic behavior, they illustrate the important point that people respond, sometimes very quickly and dramatically, to real macroeconomic shocks. Further, the recent changes in exchange rates have also been very dramatic; since 1980 the yen/dollar rate has been both over ¥270/$1 and under ¥140/$1. Changes of this magnitude can be expected to have great impact on the world economy, principally because consumers, managers, and government officials all react to them.

Consumer Reactions   One aspect of the problem frequently overlooked is the direct effect of a real exchange-rate shock on consumers. Returning to the example above of a real appreciation of the dollar against the deutsche mark, note that, because the change is real, the deutsche mark loses purchasing power relative to the dollar. Consumers in both countries are affected directly by the change, regardless of what any particular firm decides to do. German consumers may cut back their purchases of many goods, including those of the U.S. exporter, even if the U.S. firm decides to keep deutsche mark prices constant. At the same time, U.S. consumers are better off because the relative purchasing power of the dollar has risen; they may demand more of many goods. So the firm may experience *both* an increase in U.S. demand and a decrease in German demand. How these effects net out depends on the behavior of German and U.S. consumers and on the relative importance to the firm of the two markets. If the U.S. market contributes significantly more to the firm's cash flow, the dollar appreciation may help the firm more than hurt it.

An example of this phenomenon is the rise of the dollar in the early 1980s. The traditional view is that such a rise is bad for U.S. producers, which have to compete with imports. However, by 1984 the real increase in the dollar's value had put such purchasing power into the hands of the huge pool of U.S. consumers that the general economic expansion in the United States may have helped many firms more than imports hurt them. While the rise of the dollar should not be viewed as the sole cause of the expansion, such currency movements can clearly be good for consumers and at least some firms will benefit from this direct effect on their customers.

Competitor Reactions   Another important determinant of operating exposure is the nature of a firm's competition. Just as consumers respond to exchange-rate changes, so do competitors. A U.S. firm's exposure to the depreciation of the deutsche mark described above may be very different if its competitors in Germany are other U.S. exporters as opposed to German firms. If they are German, the competition may find themselves with a new cost advantage (e.g., German labor may have become relatively cheaper than U.S. labor). If competition is price-based, they may exploit this cost advantage to increase market share; alternatively, they may choose to keep deutsche mark prices and margins up, thereby increasing deutsche mark profits. On the other hand, if the competition comes from other U.S.-based exporters, it may be that none of them will obtain a relative cost advantage from the deutsche mark/dollar shift.

Note that even the U.S. business of a U.S. firm is exposed if it faces competition from non-U.S. producers. In the present example, the U.S. firm may find dollar prices changing in the U.S. market as (foreign) competitors react to the new level of the deutsche mark/dollar exchange rate. Other good examples of this sort of competitive exposure are the steel, textile, and machine tool industries in the United States. Producers in these industries have found themselves significantly exposed to real exchange rates even though they may have no foreign operations themselves, because they compete with firms producing abroad.

Supplier Reactions   A third complication is the behavior of a firm's suppliers in the face of an exchange-rate shock. In general, they also are exposed to changes in relative prices and their reactions to an exchange-rate shock will be felt by firms using their products as inputs. An obvious example is imported inputs. If two U.S. firms are competing with each other and one imports more raw materials than the other, then a shift in the real value of the dollar may give one or the other a relative cost advantage, even if neither of them exports and neither faces product market competition from imports. How large an advantage is realized by which firm depends on how the firms' suppliers react to the exchange-rate change.

The nature of competition among suppliers also must be examined. For example, suppliers competing on the basis of price will respond differently to an exchange-rate change than if they competed on quality, service, or delivery. In general, the location of suppliers, their cost structures, and the types of demand they face will affect their customers' exposures. This is clearly true for traded inputs such as steel or energy, and it may be true for nontraded ones as well, such as labor. Recall from above that a real appreciation of the dollar relative to the deutsche mark appeared to make German labor relatively cheaper than U.S. labor. However, this simple conclusion ignores the fact that laborers are affected directly by the exchange-rate shock; i.e., it ignores the impact of the suppliers' (laborers') exposures. If a lower real deutsche mark lowers the relative cost of German labor, both employers and employees feel the effect of this, and the latter may be expected to demand higher pay if they are in a position to do so. Once again, the nature of the relationship between the firm and its suppliers and between competing suppliers will help determine the outcome.

Public Sector Reactions   Finally, politicians and governments react to real macroeconomic shocks and this is no less true for exchange-rate changes than for oil price changes. Following the oil shocks, governments taxed ''windfall'' profits on ''old'' oil, introduced incentives for exploration and conservation, and invested in the development of alternative energy sources. These actions had significant effects on firms' expected cash flows. Similarly, real changes in exchange rates induce governments to contemplate protectionist trade legislation, to offer tax breaks as incentives to new (possibly foreign) investment, to control currency flows and capital transactions, etc. While the timing of governmental policy changes may be difficult to predict, it is often easy to observe a political consensus developing for one action or another as real exchange rates change. For example, during 1985–1986 the value of the dollar against a number of currencies, primarily the yen, was widely regarded as a barometer of the likelihood of protectionist trade legislation in the United States. While it may be argued that changes in expected cash flows resulting from shifts in government policies are really ''political exposure'' more than exchange-rate exposure, this distinction seems academic if the policy changes were motivated by the exchange-rate shock and were, to some degree, predictable.

So far, two basic points have been made about the responsiveness of operating cash flows to real exchange-rate changes. First is the fundamental notion that, all other things being equal, a real appreciation of the ''home'' currency makes exports from the home country more expensive for consumers abroad and makes goods from abroad relatively cheaper for consumers in the home country. This characteristic of relative prices is at the root of changes in corporate cash flows. Second, the traditional view that a home-currency depreciation helps home-country firms is complicated by changes in behavior by consumers, suppliers, competitors, governments, and firms themselves. Thus, understanding operating exposure requires a thorough understanding of how a business works; namely, where output is produced and sold; where competitors produce and sell; where suppliers produce and sell; and how each of these actors will respond to a real exchange-rate shock.

Some Further Extensions

In addition to the considerations described above, there are some which may be less obvious. First among these are the macroeconomic relationships among interest rates, inflation rates, and exchange rates. Recent empirical evidence from the United States and Japan suggests that changes in real exchange rates tend to be accompanied by changes in real interest rates. This implies that while a real exchange-rate shock changes expected future operating cash flows, a concurrent shift in real interest rates changes the discount rate applicable to those cash flows. To the extent that real exchange rates and real interest rates move together, effects on cash flows should not be viewed in isolation; some decisions are made on the basis of present values rather than cash flows per se, so discount rates need to be examined.

Though there are no hard and fast rules, existing evidence indicates that if currency A is appreciating (in real terms) relative to currency B, then A's real interest rate tends to decline relative to B's real interest rate. For example, suppose the U.S. exporter described above realizes a decrease in its expected dollar cash flows following a real rise in the dollar versus the deutsche mark. It may also be the case that the real dollar interest rate has declined relative to the real deutsche mark interest rate, and that the discount rate applicable to future dollar cash flows has decreased. If so, then the decrease in cash flows is offset to some extent (perhaps even more than offset) by the decrease in the discount rate. In this sense, the exposure of the *value* of the cash flows depends on their timing and on the relationship between real interest and exchange rates in addition to the factors outlined above.

Next, as the foregoing discussion made clear, the reactions of various economic actors are important determinants of a firm's exposure. Such reactions are often very difficult to anticipate. It is usually helpful to bear in mind that the response of, say, a competitor to an exchange-rate shock depends not on the exposure of the competitor's *total* cash flows, but rather on the exposure of its *marginal* cash flows. The distinction is an important one because total exposure and marginal exposure can have opposite signs. For example, revenues may be slightly positively exposed to a given exchange rate and costs highly negatively exposed, resulting in an overall negative exposure; however, if a substantial portion of costs are fixed, marginal cash flows may be positively exposed. The firm will respond differently depending on whether marginal cash flows are positively or negatively exposed. In short, to determine the effect of an exchange-rate shock on a firm's value (its operating cash flows), one looks at (total) operating exposure; to anticipate what the firm will *do* about it, i.e., what actions it will take in response to the shock, one looks at the exposure of marginal cash flows. Note that, as a result, a given firm's total operating exposure depends on its *competitors'* (and suppliers') *marginal* exposures.

These competitive relationships are especially important and difficult to analyze in a setting of global competition. Global competitors pursue business strategies designed to coordinate and optimally exploit interdependent positions in multiple markets. As a result, actions taken by a firm in one market have significant spillover effects on both its own and its competitors' operations in other markets. Hence, a U.S. firm exporting to Germany and facing global competitors will find that the exposure of its dollar cash flows depends on the exposure of its suppliers and competitors' marginal cash flows, not only in Germany, but also in the United States and other markets.

Finally, it should be pointed out that by focusing on revenues and costs, the foregoing discussion has largely neglected another type of cash flow, namely, investment. While capital budgeting analyses may take into account changes in net working capital and net fixed assets when computing a project's free cash flows, these types of investments are not typically considered cash flows from operations. Nevertheless, they affect future operating cash flows. A firm's expected future operating cash flows may be thought of as follows:

Total operating = Operating cash flows from assets already in place
cash flows   + Operating cash flows from future discretionary investments

"Operating cash flows from future discretionary investments" refers to cash flows the firm is expected to realize, but for which the necessary investments have not yet been made. For example, IBM is expected to have access in the future to projects that have positive net present values. Access to such projects is valuable and comprises part of IBM's value now. The access may arise from IBM's position as a market leader, from new technologies in the computer business, etc. Essentially, IBM owns a call option on some operating assets. At some future date, the option may be exercised by making the necessary investment, in return for which IBM would receive the assets, which then have a value equal to the present value of the cash flows they are expected to produce. Alternatively, the option may never be exercised, but it is still valuable until it expires.

A real exchange-rate shock may change the terms on which a firm can make such investments in the future, i.e., the terms on which the "option" may be exercised. This may affect the firm's decision about when or even whether to exercise the option. Thus, operating cash flows from assets not yet in place, i.e., from future discretionary investments, are subject to this additional effect of the exchange-rate change, and it forms part of their exposure.

Once again, competition further complicates the possibilities. Just as competitors' pricing and output behavior affects exposure, so does their investment behavior. Many investments have a competitive aspect to them; for example if one firm invests in a new technology, its competitor may be forced to follow or, alternatively, may be prohibited from following by patents. Either way, one firm's investment expenditures affect another's. A shift in real exchange rates changes the terms on which firms compete for some kinds of investments. When a firm's home currency appreciates, it may be able to make investments (exercise options) on more favorable terms than a particular competitor because the relative purchasing power of its currency has increased. This can be so even if cash flows from assets already in place are reduced, and even if the future cash flows from newly acquired assets are reduced. The same exchange-rate shock may also speed up or slow down investment plans and it may cause some investments to be undertaken which previously seemed unattractive. A good recent example of this phenomenon is the greatly increased pace of investment by Japanese firms following the rapid appreciation of the yen in 1985–1986.

MANAGING OPERATING EXPOSURE

There are three steps to managing operating exposure: understanding how it works; estimating its signs and magnitudes; and doing something about it. This note has emphasized the first of these and has comparatively little to say about the other two. Estimating exposures is very difficult, because they are complex, because they may change from year to year or even quarter to quarter, and because they depend on variables that are largely unobservable.

One approach to the estimation problem is strictly qualitative and takes the form of an exposure "audit." An audit consists of a careful examination of the separate elements of a firm's operating cash flows, and an attempt to anticipate the effects of a particular type of real exchange-rate change. This exercise is especially useful to line managers whose responsibility it will be to respond to an exchange-rate shock when it arrives.

A second approach is to appeal to the judgment of the capital markets. When exchange rates change, investors are faced with the task of assessing the effects on the value of firms' public securities. A regression of changes in firm value on changes in exchange rates gives a statistical estimate of operating exposure. The advantages of this approach are that all the necessary variables are observable, the data are of reasonably high quality for many firms, and securities prices respond very quickly to shocks, which makes it unnecessary to worry about the nature of the lag between an exchange-rate change and its effect on cash flows. The primary drawback of this statistical approach is that it measures aggregate exposure and so does not afford a view of the different elements of operating exposure the way an audit does.

Once a firm has an estimate of its operating exposure, what should be done about it? This is a question on which there is little agreement among either academics or managers. Much of the debate concerns whether or not exposures should be hedged, and if so, by whom. On the one hand, such exposures are very difficult to measure and hedge and, in any event, could be hedged by investors rather than firms to the extent that hedging is desirable. On the other hand, firms should have much better information about their operations, and hence about the nature of the exposure, than do individual investors. Firms also may be able to hedge at a lower cost than investors could.

By comparison, there is less debate about how a firm should respond internally to an exchange-rate shock. In short, it should continue to maximize value. This requires certain operating responses, including, for example, changes in pricing, sourcing, and product mix. One way to train managers to take such actions in a timely fashion is to conduct "rehearsals." This involves asking line managers to walk through the specific steps they would expect to take in response to a hypothetical exchange-rate change. It provides potentially valuable information about how the organization as a whole is likely to perform, and where bottlenecks and misunderstandings are most likely to appear. The direct involvement of line, as opposed to staff, managers makes such rehearsals a useful training exercise within firms that have significant operating exposures.

SUMMARY

Operating exposure should be thought of as the response of a firm's expected future operating cash flows to a real macroeconomic shock, i.e., a real change in exchange rates. Real exchange rates change when changes in nominal exchange rates fail to reflect purchasing power parity. As a result, the relative prices of goods and services change, and consequently so do firms' operating cash flows.

A real change in exchange rates leads to the following fundamental type of change in relative prices: the real appreciation of a currency, say, the dollar versus the deutsche mark, makes exports from the United States to Germany relatively more expensive for German consumers and imports from Germany to the United States relatively less expensive for U.S. consumers. Under many plausible scenarios, this results in a reduction of dollar cash flows to a firm producing goods in the United States for sale in Germany. The dollar operating cash flows of the firm are said to be negatively exposed to the deutsche mark/dollar exchange rate. The magnitude of the exposure is equal to the amount by which the value of the cash flows changes following a given shift in the exchange rate, and it is typically measured in the foreign (in this case deutsche mark) currency. This simple relationship underlies the traditional view of operating exposure, namely, that a home-currency appreciation reduces the cash flows of home-country firms engaged in exporting or competing with imports.

There are many complicating factors which can make this traditional conclusion misleading. A significant change in relative prices represents a real macroeconomic shock to which many people will respond. It is important to examine the reactions of consumers, suppliers, competitors, and governments and to assess the impact of these reactions on the particular firm's operating cash flows. It is also necessary to consider possible changes in the investment behavior of a firm and its competitors in addition to the more obvious changes in production and consumption decisions. Finally, the effects of real exchange-rate changes should not be taken out of their proper macroeconomic context. In particular, if real interest rates change simultaneously, the appropriate discount rate for future operating cash flows may change as well. The complications just described are capable, separately or together, of either offsetting or reinforcing the firm's basic operating exposure. Note that if they completely offset it, the traditional view predicts both the wrong sign and the wrong magnitude of actual operating exposure.

APPENDIX: PURCHASING POWER PARITY AND REAL EXCHANGE-RATE CHANGES

The term "real exchange rate" is widely used in business and economics, but unfortunately is not very precise. It typically refers to a nominal exchange rate that has been adjusted to reflect deviations from purchasing power parity. However, this still leaves some doubt about its meaning.

PPP can be stated in two forms: absolute and relative. Its absolute form is given by the following:

$$S = \frac{P_f}{P_d}$$

where S denotes an equilibrium exchange rate stated in terms of foreign currency per unit of domestic currency and P_f and P_d denote price levels in the foreign and domestic country, respectively. The condition simply states that a given unit of currency should have the same purchasing power around the world. If a certain value for an exchange rate is accepted as an "equilibrium" or "parity" value, then subsequent changes in price levels in the two countries imply a new level for the exchange rate in accordance with PPP. To the extent that this level is not realized, PPP is violated and the *real* exchange rate is said to change. Note that this conception of a real exchange rate depends on the particular value chosen to represent parity.

Exhibit 1 presents data from the period 1974–1990 for the yen/dollar exchange rate and for consumer prices (CPI) in the United States and Japan. The exchange rates predicted by PPP and the price level data are shown in columns 5 and 6 of the exhibit, using base (''parity'') years of 1974 and 1984-I, respectively. For example, using the 1974 value of ¥300.95/$1 as a base, absolute PPP suggests that the dollar was undervalued for most of the decade 1974–1983, returned to parity in mid-1984, was briefly overvalued in 1985, and has been undervalued since. By comparison, if 1984-I is deemed to represent equilibrium for the yen/dollar rate, a somewhat different story emerges (column 6): The dollar appears to have been overvalued until the third quarter of 1985, and has been undervalued since, though less seriously than if 1974 is used as a base.

A real exchange rate may be formally defined and computed as the ratio of the actual exchange rate and the rate predicted by absolute PPP for a given base value. So for example, if column 4 is divided by column 6, the result is a ''real'' exchange rate, which is equal to 1.0 when PPP holds. If it is greater than 1.0, the dollar is overvalued (the actual yen/dollar is higher than PPP predicts); if less than 1.0, the dollar is said to be undervalued.

Because it is difficult to decide whether a given level of the exchange rate represents parity, a *relative* form of PPP is commonly used. Relative PPP applies to changes in the exchange rate rather than absolute levels of the rate. It states that regardless of the level of the exchange rate, changes in the rate should be driven by differences in inflation rates. This can be expressed as:

$$\frac{S_{t+1}}{S_t} = \frac{(P_{f,t+1}/P_{f,t})}{(P_{d,t+1}/P_{d,t})}$$

where the subscripts t and $t + 1$ refer to time periods t and $t + 1$. In words, the fractional change (from t to $t + 1$) in the exchange rate is equal to the fractional change in foreign prices divided by the fractional change in domestic prices. Note that the numerator and denominator of the right-hand side of this expression are just {1 + inflation rate} for the foreign and domestic countries, respectively.

The exchange rates predicted by relative PPP are given in column 7 of **Exhibit 1** and they tell yet a different story about real movements in the yen/dollar rate. In particular, they suggest that the dollar was mostly overvalued from 1981 through 1985-I, but since then it has not deviated from relative PPP one way or the other for more than three quarters in a row. Note that the 1990-IV level of ¥133.55/$1 is close to the level predicted by relative PPP and that, in general, all of the figures in column 7 are closer to actual exchange rates than are the predictions in columns 5 and 6. This is because relative PPP does not rely on a particular base as an equilibrium value for the exchange rate.

It is not possible to state with confidence that any one of these conflicting sets of predictions is "right." It depends on what version of PPP (if any) is deemed most appropriate and what level of the exchange rate is adopted as an equilibrium value. The conflicting data clearly illustrate the difficulty of defining "the real exchange rate" in a useful way.

Fortunately, for the purpose of analyzing operating exposure, it is not necessary, and may even be misleading to focus on "the real exchange rate." Firms cannot observe a real exchange rate per se; they can observe changes in currency values and try to determine whether these have effected changes in relative prices of goods and services. "The real exchange rate" as conventionally defined is an artificial construct devised by economists to measure the extent to which PPP holds. This does not make it a perfect way to determine the extent to which relative prices have changed for a given firm.

As stated in the text of this note, operating exposure should be thought of as the response of operating cash flows to a real exchange-rate shock, where "real" refers more properly to "shock" than to "exchange rate." In other words, cash flows are exposed to real macroeconomic shocks, meaning shocks that change relative prices. Sometimes, changes in exchange rates are "real" in this sense. Violations of PPP give an indication of whether a given change in exchange rates merely reflects changes in price levels or whether relative prices have changed as well. It is still necessary for the firm to understand which relative prices have changed, how they have changed, and how the changes affect expected cash flows.

EXHIBIT 1   THE YEN/DOLLAR EXCHANGE RATE AND VIOLATIONS OF PPP

| | | | | Exchange rate predicted by | | |
| | | | | Absolute PPP | | |
Year/ quarter	Japan CPI	U.S. CPI	Actual exchange rate, ¥/$	1974 base	1984-I base	Relative PPP
(1)	(2)	(3)	(4)	(5)	(6)	(7)
1974	100.00	100.00	300.95	300.95		300.95
1975	111.85	109.14	305.15	308.42		308.42
1976	122.23	115.44	292.80	318.66		315.28
1977	132.07	122.88	240.00	323.43		297.19
1978	137.12	132.30	194.60	311.92		231.46
1979	142.01	147.19	240.30	290.36		181.15
1980	153.42	167.10	203.00	276.33		228.69
1981	160.98	184.43	219.90	262.68		192.98
1982	165.27	195.73	235.00	254.11		212.72
1983	168.32	202.03	232.20	250.73		231.87
1984-I	172.01	210.63	224.70	245.77	224.70	227.61
1984-II	173.40	213.01	237.50	244.99	223.99	223.99
1984-III	173.25	215.38	245.50	242.07	221.32	234.67
1984-IV	175.25	216.91	251.10	243.15	222.31	246.60
1985-I	175.56	218.27	252.50	242.07	221.32	249.98
1985-II	177.11	220.98	248.95	241.20	220.52	251.59
1985-III	177.42	222.51	217.00	239.96	219.39	247.67
1985-IV	178.03	224.55	200.50	238.61	218.15	215.78
1986-I	178.19	225.06	179.60	238.28	217.85	200.22
1986-II	178.65	224.55	165.00	239.44	218.91	180.48
1986-III	177.72	226.24	153.60	236.41	216.14	162.91
1986-IV	177.72	227.43	159.10	235.17	215.01	152.80
1987-I	176.18	229.98	145.80	230.55	210.78	155.97
1987-II	178.96	233.03	147.00	231.12	211.30	146.16
1987-III	178.61	235.69	146.35	228.07	208.51	145.06
1987-IV	178.96	237.69	123.50	226.59	207.16	145.40
1988-I	178.07	239.24	125.40	224.00	204.80	122.09
1988-II	179.31	242.12	132.40	222.88	203.77	124.77
1988-III	179.67	245.45	134.55	220.30	201.41	130.87
1988-IV	180.91	247.89	125.85	219.63	200.80	134.15
1989-I	180.02	250.77	132.05	216.04	197.52	123.79
1989-II	184.27	254.76	144.10	217.68	199.02	133.05
1989-III	184.45	256.98	139.30	216.01	197.49	142.99
1989-IV	185.69	259.41	143.45	215.43	196.90	138.92
1990-I	186.04	263.85	157.20	212.20	194.01	141.30
1990-II	188.70	266.51	152.90	213.08	194.32	157.86
1990-III	189.53	271.17	137.80	210.40	192.36	150.97
1990-IV	189.08	271.17	133.55	209.84	191.86	137.44

Source: International Financial Statistics (Washington, DC: International Monetary Fund, 1978, 1982, 1987, 1991).

JAGUAR PLC, 1984

In July 1984, the British government was preparing to return ownership of Jaguar plc, a manufacturer of luxury automobiles, to the private sector through a public offering of stock. After a difficult decade in the 1970s, Jaguar had experienced a dramatic return to profitability in the 1980s, but the offering was not without its risks. The company was on the verge of a critical new product introduction, its model XJ40. The labor market upon which Jaguar would rely to produce it was notoriously volatile. Finally, as the prospectus for the offering noted, Jaguar was exposed to exchange-rate volatility: ". . . there could come a point where the weakening of the Dollar would have a severe effect on Jaguar's profitability and cash flow."[1] At the time, many analysts felt the dollar was overvalued at \$1.35/£1 and predicted a significant rise in the dollar/sterling exchange rate. It was amid these uncertainties that the new Jaguar shares had to be priced.

JAGUAR CARS LTD.

In 1922, 20-year-old William Lyons formed a partnership with William Walmsley called Swallow Chairs, to produce sidecars for motorcycles and some car trimmings. In 1926 the owners decided to produce motor cars and renamed the firm Swallow Sidecar and Coach Building Company. Swallow Coach Building became a public company in 1935 under the name SS Cars Limited. Later that year the Jaguar name was first used, on the company's SS Jaguar 100.

[1]*Jaguar plc Offer for Sale,* 1984, p. 16.

This case was prepared by Research Associate William T. Schiano and Professor Timothy A. Luehrman. Copyright © 1989 by the President and Fellows of Harvard College. Harvard Business School case 290-005.

In 1945 SS Cars Ltd. became Jaguar Cars Ltd. The following year, Jaguar produced 1132 cars and reported a profit of £22,852. By 1965, Jaguar produced 24,601 cars for a profit of £1,663,180. In July 1966, Chairman and Managing Director Sir William Lyons announced that Jaguar would merge with the British Motor Corporation to form British Motor Holdings (BMH). Two years later, BMH merged with the Leyland Motor Corporation to form British Leyland (BL). Mr. Lyons supported both mergers because he felt that a unified British motor industry would be better positioned to compete in the international automobile market. He was adamant, however, about maintaining Jaguar's autonomy, a position future Jaguar management would continue to hold.

In late 1974, with BL incurring significant losses, the government commissioned a team led by Sir Don Ryder to study BL and propose a course of action. The commission reported in mid-1975 that BL was in serious financial trouble and did not rule out the possibility of its collapse. As recommended by the report, the government decided to acquire nearly all of BL's equity and, over the following 5 years, provided over £1 billion to BL.[2] The funds were used for plant expansion and modernization and retooling for new models. The report further recommended that Jaguar Cars not continue as a separate entity, but be integrated into Leyland Cars. In a subsequent reorganization in 1978, Jaguar operations became part of Jaguar Rover Triumph, BL's specialist cars division.

TURNAROUND IN THE 1980s

During the 1970s, Jaguar had developed a reputation for outstanding design but poor production quality. In April 1980, Mr. John Egan was named Chairman and Managing Director of Jaguar Cars, the first full-time Jaguar chief executive in 5 years. Mr. Egan, brought in from Massey-Ferguson, made it clear that his top priority was to improve quality, asserting, "Jaguar must be not as good as the Germans and Japanese, but better."[3] He initiated "action this day" inquiries, driving cars home off the assembly line and demanding explanations for imperfections the next morning. Many problems were traced back to faulty purchased parts. In his first year, Mr. Egan sacked six parts suppliers for not meeting quality standards, and made clear that Jaguar would not be afraid to go outside the United Kingdom for parts if necessary. Within government-owned BL, this would have been viewed as a drastic measure.

As Jaguar re-established itself as a quality producer, productivity, sales, and profits began to climb. Average output per employee increased from 1.4 cars per person in 1980 to 3.4 cars per person in 1983. Revenues grew at an average annual rate of over 40 percent from 1980 to 1983, and the company's operating margin went to 11 percent in 1983 from −27 percent in 1980.

Jaguar's relations with its work force also improved. Despite Mr. Egan's assertion that Jaguar's goal must be a satisfied customer, not worker, Jaguar workers did not become more alienated. On the contrary, they appeared to take pride in the quality that

[2]In 1984, the government owned 4.2 billion shares of BL, representing 99.7 percent of all shares.
[3]*The Times* (London) July 13, 1983, p. 8a.

had been restored to Jaguar automobiles. Morale within the "family" of Jaguar workers was further boosted by company picnics, newsletters, quality circles, and, most publicly, the revitalization of the Jaguar racing team and its return to international races such as Le Mans. The racing program also heightened public awareness of Jaguar's recovery, as Jaguars once again entered the winner's circle at major race tracks around the world.

Another feature of Mr. Egan's strategy was for Jaguar to increase its exports, primarily to the United States. Sales goals in the United States for 1981 and 1982 were increased by 50 percent per year, and dealers were urged to emphasize customer service. Early in 1984, a dealer buyout program was instituted to reduce the number of U.S. dealers by 20 percent through the purchase of marginal dealerships. In response to these measures, sales in the United States rose from £37 million in 1980 to £294 million in 1983.

By the end of 1983, Jaguar's fortunes had turned around completely. Revenues had nearly tripled from £166 million in 1980 to £473 million in 1983. Operating profit was £57 million in 1983, from a loss of £44 million in 1980. Already in 1984, profit before taxes and extraordinary items was estimated to be £41 million for the 6 months ended June 30. The company anticipated sales of 32,000 cars in 1984 and many analysts expected volume gains to continue during the rest of the decade. **Exhibits 1** through **3** summarize certain operating and financial results for the period 1980–1983.

THE SITUATION IN 1984

In 1984, Jaguar produced a narrow line of cars, consisting primarily of the Series III saloons and XJ-S sports coupes (see **Exhibit 4**). In markets outside the United Kingdom, the saloon range consisted of two models, the XJ6 and the Vanden Plas, both powered by the 4.2-liter XK engine. In the United Kingdom, there were additional variations within the Series III line. The XJ-S sport coupes, with either the company's new six-cylinder AJ6 engine or the established twelve-cylinder engine, were available in all of Jaguar's markets. Worldwide, as shown in **Exhibit 3**, Jaguar sold 23,413 saloons, which accounted for 82 percent of 1983 sales, while coupes accounted for 17 percent. The remaining 1 percent represented sales of Daimler limousines.

Jaguar produced all of its cars in and around Coventry, England. At Browns Lane, Coventry, Jaguar manufactured trim and assembled vehicles. At Radford, Coventry, the company produced its full range of engines, suspensions, and axles. Finally, at Castle Bromwich in Birmingham, 15 miles from Browns Lane, car bodies were assembled and painted. Relatively few parts were imported; some exceptions were certain gearboxes produced by General Motors in the United States and various components produced by West German suppliers.

Jaguar's engineering department was among the most respected in the industry, but it was also among the smallest: BMW had 2000 engineers, Daimler-Benz 5000, and even Porsche had 1400, compared to Jaguar's 450. In the 1980s, most of Jaguar's research and development resources had been concentrated on a new model, code-named the XJ40. The XJ40 was to replace the XJ6 and was approaching the final stages of testing by July 1984. Although mechanical design success seemed assured, consumer acceptance and production success were not guaranteed. Should the XJ40 fail to meet expectations, Jaguar did not have the resources to redevelop it quickly.

In 1984, the United States was the world's largest market for luxury automobiles costing $30,000 or more. Segment volume in the United States was 91,200 units in 1983. Jaguar's share of the U.S. market was 17.3 percent in 1983, up from 5.3 percent in 1980. Most analysts considered the U.S. luxury car market to be stable and somewhat price-insensitive, but a severe recession or fuel shortage would likely reduce demand. Although the Reagan administration supported free trade, import restrictions were a potential issue in the 1984 U.S. presidential campaign. In addition, "gas guzzler" taxes and penalties arising from Jaguar's failure to meet government-mandated fuel economy restrictions were already raising the prices of Jaguars in the United States.

West Germany was the largest European market, accounting for two-thirds of all Continental European luxury car sales. Sixty thousand such vehicles were sold in Germany in 1983, but Jaguar's market share was only 2 percent. In contrast, in the United Kingdom Jaguar's share was 49 percent of 14,333 units, including a very strong position in company cars for executives.

In most of its markets, Jaguar's primary competitors were the German automakers BMW, Daimler-Benz, and Porsche. Several Japanese manufacturers were expected to move into this market segment, but were not yet major competitors to Jaguar and the German producers.

Daimler-Benz was the largest producer in the luxury market, with revenues of DM40 billion and profits of DM355 million (see **Exhibit 5**). Daimler-Benz also had the most even geographic distribution of sales, as shown in **Exhibit 6**. Although the Mercedes 300 series was considered the primary competitor for Jaguar cars, it was not yet a major part of Daimler-Benz's line. Nevertheless, were Jaguar's sales to expand primarily at the expense of the 300 series, industry observers expected Daimler-Benz to respond to the competitive threat.

Although not as large as Daimler-Benz, BMW was planning a significant capacity expansion to meet the demand for its cars. Some of BMW's line, the 3 and 5 series, did not compete directly with Jaguar. However, the 6 and 7 series competed directly in both Germany and the United States, which were also BMW's major markets. BMW's production of 6 and 7 series cars was roughly as large as Jaguar's total output.

In size and geographic distribution, Porsche was the most similar to Jaguar. Porsche had just completed its first equity offering in mid-May 1984. The shares offered were nonvoting, and the funds raised were being used to expand production. Earlier in 1984, Porsche had announced it would break its ties with the Audi distribution network in the United States, and set up its own U.S. dealer network in 1985. This prompted legal challenges from a number of dealers. The resulting turmoil in Porsche's U.S. distribution was expected to continue for several more years.

Finally, in 1984, it was well known that several major Japanese auto manufacturers would be entering at least the low end of the luxury car market by the end of the decade. This could eventually affect Jaguar directly and might have the immediate effect of pushing the German manufacturers further upscale, creating more competition in Jaguar's market niche.

PRIVATIZATION

By January 1984, the U.K.'s conservative Thatcher government had decided to privatize at least part of BL as part of its continuing effort to reduce the number of state-owned companies. Just as Jaguar had desperately needed a successful turnaround in 1980, so the government needed a successful privatization in 1984. The Jaguar offering would come on the heels of the disastrous privatization of Enterprise Oil.[4] The Enterprise Oil affair had resulted in considerable bad press for the Thatcher government, which was anxious to ensure the success of the Jaguar offering. Moreover, British Telecom, a £4 billion company, was to be privatized some months later, and a successful sale of Jaguar could be expected to make the British Telecom offering easier.

In February, BL management announced that it wished to retain a 25 percent interest in Jaguar after the privatization. Some weeks later, the government announced that it, and therefore BL, would retain no interest in Jaguar. The government did decide, however, to retain a Special Share. The Special Share, together with certain provisions of the bylaws, enabled the government to prevent anyone from accumulating more than 15 percent of the company and to prevent any substantial sale of assets by the company. This helped quell fears that England would lose its only home-owned private auto manufacturer, at least until the end of 1990, when the Special Share would expire.

The terms of the offering provided that nongovernment BL shareholders would receive preferential treatment in terms of allocations, but would pay the full offer price. The 7000 Jaguar employees who had been with the company prior to January 1983 would receive a bonus of shares worth £450. Another 1000 hired since that time would receive shares worth £105.

EXCHANGE-RATE EXPOSURE AND PRICING JAGUAR SHARES

Among the major uncertainties facing Jaguar at the time of its public offering was the future course of the dollar-sterling exchange rate. In 1983, Jaguar exported 75 percent of its production, primarily to the United States. A significant fraction of Jaguar's output would continue to be exported for the foreseeable future. As a result, the company's profitability would be significantly affected by real changes in the dollar value of sterling.

---

[4]Enterprise Oil was the target of a controversial hostile takeover by Rio Tinto-Zinc (RTZ) even before the stock was publicly traded. The July 1984 public offering was undersubscribed (only two-thirds of the shares offered were applied for), and RTZ attempted to buy all remaining shares. The government blocked RTZ's purchase, and pledged to prevent any takeover in the near future.

Jaguar management felt that it had some alternatives for responding to dramatic changes in currency values. These included adjusting market mix, pricing, and sourcing policies. However, such flexibility was quite limited and a significant weakening of the dollar would undoubtedly harm the company's large export business.

In mid-1984, the dollar-sterling exchange rate was \$1.35/£1 compared to \$2.39/£1 at the beginning of 1981. Many analysts felt the dollar was significantly overvalued against all major currencies and predicted a sharp decline in its value. On June 29, the dollar was at a forward discount to both the British pound and German mark. Data on spot exchange rates and inflation rates are presented in **Exhibits 7** and **8**, respectively. Forward rates for the dollar against British sterling and German marks are presented in **Exhibit 8**.

It was in this environment that the new Jaguar shares were to be priced. Following the offering, Jaguar management would have to decide how the newly independent company ought to cope with its exchange-rate exposure. Of particular importance was whether and how such exposure could be hedged.

EXHIBIT 1   BALANCE SHEETS (MILLIONS)

	March 31, 1984	December 31		
		1983	1982	1981
Fixed assets				
Tangible assets	£118.6	£112.0	£87.3	£55.7
Investments in related company	0.4	0.4	—	—
	119.0	112.4	87.3	55.7
Current assets				
Stocks	76.5	62.7	68.8	56.3
Debtors	42.5	33.8	29.6	26.3
Cash and short-term deposits	11.5	29.5	6.9	1.3
	130.5	126.0	105.3	83.9
Creditors: amount falling due within one year	127.5	128.8	81.1	51.3
Net current assets (liabilities)	3.0	(2.8)	24.2	32.6
Total assets less current liabilities	122.0	109.6	111.5	88.3
Creditors: amounts falling due in more than 1 year*	58.0	43.9	17.6	1.2
	64.0	65.7	93.9	87.1
Capital and reserves				
Called up share capital	45.0	—	—	—
Other reserves	2.8	10.3	—	—
Profit and loss account	16.2	55.4	—	—
BL Group funding balance†	—	—	93.9	87.1
	£ 64.0	£ 65.7	£93.9	£87.1

*These obligations consisted primarily of capitalized leasing obligations and warranty expense accruals.
†The BL Group funding balance was made up of certain loans from BL Group which represented the capital and reserves of the Jaguar business before the Jaguar Group acquired that business with effect from January 1, 1983.
Source: Jaguar plc Offer for Sale, 1984.

EXHIBIT 2   INCOME STATEMENTS (MILLIONS)*

	Quarter ended March 31, 1984	Years ended December 31			
		1983	1982	1981	1980
Turnover					
Continuing activities	£143.3	£472.6	£305.6	£195.2	£166.4
Discontinued activities	—	—	4.3	48.3	83.6
	143.3	472.6	309.9	243.5	250.0
Cost of sales†	(108.8)	(369.7)	(258.4)	(245.6)	(273.7)
Gross profit/(loss)	34.5	102.9	51.5	(2.1)	(23.7)
Distribution costs	(4.4)	(13.3)	(13.8)	(7.8)	(7.3)
Administrative expenses	(6.2)	(22.0)	(14.8)	(11.2)	(8.1)
Research and development cost	(5.7)	(16.5)	(12.8)	(9.8)	(5.2)
Operating profit/(loss)	18.2	51.1	10.1	(30.9)	(44.3)
Interest	(0.2)	(1.1)	(0.5)	(0.8)	(3.0)
Profit /(loss) on ordinary activities before taxation	18.0	50.0	9.6	(31.7)	(47.3)
Taxation on ordinary activities	(0.5)	(0.5)	(0.1)	—	1.3
Profit/(loss) on ordinary activities after taxation	17.5	49.5	9.5	(31.7)	(46.0)
Extraordinary items	(14.2)	—	(3.0)	(4.6)	(6.2)
Profit/(loss) for the financial period	£ 3.3	£ 49.5	£ 6.5	£ (36.3)	£ (52.2)

*In regard to rates of exchange, realized profits on exchange, together with losses on exchange, whether realized or unrealized, which arise on settlement of overseas liabilities are included in trading results. Profit and loss account items of foreign subsidiaries are translated into sterling at the average rate of exchange for each monthly accounting period. Assets and liabilities, including outstanding forward exchange contracts, are translated into sterling at the rates of exchange ruling at the end of the financial period.

†Includes depreciation charges of £5.6 million in 1980, £7.3 million in 1981, £7.2 million in 1982, £8.6 million in 1983 and £2.5 million for the first quarter of 1984.

Source: Jaguar plc Offer for Sale, 1984.

EXHIBIT 3   JAGUAR SALES BY MODELS AND MARKETS; DECEMBER 31 OF EACH YEAR (IN NUMBER OF VEHICLES AND % OF TOTAL JAGUAR MARKET)

	1983	1982	1981	1980
Model range				
Series III saloons	23,413	17,733	12,666	13,851
XJ-S sports cars	4,886	3,131	1,108	1,526
Limousines	168	143	159	92
Total Jaguar	28,467	21,007	13,933	15,469

Geographical area	1983	%	1982	%	1981	%	1980	%
United States	15,260	54	9,971	47	5,154	37	2,518	16
United Kingdom	7,236	25	6,415	31	5,196	37	6,135	40
West Germany	1,164	4	839	4	479	3	1,612	10
Rest of Europe	1,845	6	1,742	8	1,229	9	3,539	23
Australia	579	2	582	3	654	5	140	1
Canada	563	2	280	1	375	3	305	2
Rest of world	1,820	6	1,178	6	846	6	1,220	8
Total Jaguar	28,467	100	21,007	100	13,933	100	15,469	100

Source: Jaguar plc Offer for Sale, 1984.

EXHIBIT 4   SELECTED MANUFACTURERS' PRODUCT LINES AND PRICES FOR THE U.S. MARKET, MARCH 1984

Manufacturer	Price, $
Jaguar	
XJ-6 Series III 4-door sedan	31,000
Vanden Plas 4-door sedan	34,200
XJ-S (V-12) Sport coupe	34,700
Automatic transmission, power steering, power disk brakes and air-conditioning standard on all models.	
BMW	
318i 2-door sedan (5 speed)	16,430
520e 4-door sedan (5 speed)	24,565
533i 4-door sedan (5 speed)	30,305
733i 4-door sedan (5 speed)	36,335
633CSi coupe (5 speed)	40,705
Power steering, power disk brakes, and air-conditioning standard on all models. Radio standard on all models except 318i. Automatic transmission $495 on 318i and $795 on all other models.	
Mercedes-Benz	
190-E 4-door sedan (5 speed)	22,850
(automatic)	23,430
(diesel 5 speed)	22,930
(diesel automatic)	23,510
300-D 4-door sedan (automatic)	31,940
300-TD 4-door wagon (automatic)	35,310
300-CD coupe (automatic)	35,220
300-SD 4-door sedan (automatic)	39,500
380-SE 4-door sedan (automatic)	42,730
380-SL coupe-roadster (automatic)	43,820
500-SEL 4-door sedan (automatic)	51,200
500-SEC coupe (automatic)	56,800
Power steering, power disk brakes, radio, and air-conditioning standard on all models.	
Porsche	
944 coupe (5-speed)	21,440
(automatic)	21,940
911 Carrera coupe	31,950
Targa coupe	33,450
Cabriolet	36,450
928-S coupe (automatic)	44,000
Power steering and power disk brakes are standard on 944 and 928-S. Air-conditioning standard on all models.	

Source: Automotive News Market Data Book 1984 (Detroit: Crain Communications, Inc, 1984).

EXHIBIT 5 COMPARATIVE DATA ON SELECTED MANUFACTURERS

	BMW, DM millions	Daimler-Benz, DM millions	Porsche, DM millions	Jaguar, £ millions
Year ended	Jul. 31, 1983	Dec. 31, 1983	Dec. 31, 1983	Dec. 31, 1983
Revenues	DM11,943.0	DM40,004.8	DM2,133.6	£472.6
Operating profit	916.1	3,665.8	194.5	51.1
Profit after taxes	291.7	987.9	69.6	49.5
Depreciation charges	733.2	2,604.1	71.1	5.6
Interest expense	85.3	388.5	3.6	1.1
Total assets	5,799.6	24,826.7	866.6	249.5
Equity	2,169.3	7,547.6	220.7	—
Debt				
Long-term	652.7	7,534.0	15.7	43.9
Short-term	207.1	1,100.9	34.1	128.8
Stock price (6/29/84)	DM343.88	DM467.90	DM1003.00	—
Shares outstanding (thousands)	15,000	42,313	700	—
Earnings/share	DM19.45	DM8.40	DM99.43	—
Dividends/share	DM10.00	DM10.50	—	—
Manufacturing volume (units)	407,507	483,359	48,288	28,041
Employees	50,158	184,877	5,883	8,606
Engineers	2,000	5,000	1,400	450

EXHIBIT 6   1983 NEW-CAR REGISTRATIONS FOR UNITED STATES AND EUROPE BY MANUFACTURER (PIES ARE PROPORTIONAL TO TOTAL SALES)

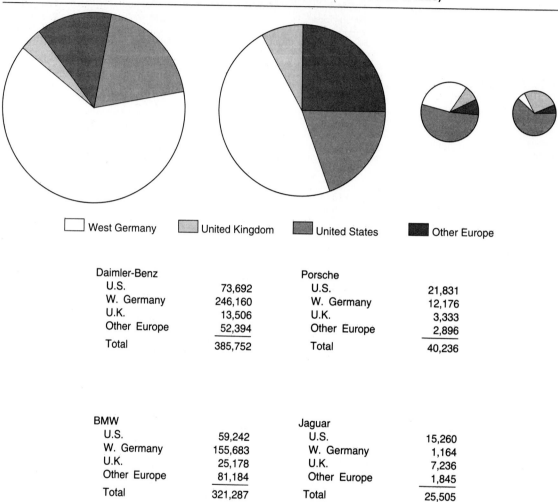

| West Germany | United Kingdom | United States | Other Europe |

Daimler-Benz		Porsche	
U.S.	73,692	U.S.	21,831
W. Germany	246,160	W. Germany	12,176
U.K.	13,506	U.K.	3,333
Other Europe	52,394	Other Europe	2,896
Total	385,752	Total	40,236

BMW		Jaguar	
U.S.	59,242	U.S.	15,260
W. Germany	155,683	W. Germany	1,164
U.K.	25,178	U.K.	7,236
Other Europe	81,184	Other Europe	1,845
Total	321,287	Total	25,505

Source: 1984 Automotive News Market Data Book (Detroit: Crain Communications, Inc., 1984).

EXHIBIT 7   QUARTERLY NOMINAL SPOT EXCHANGE RATES, 1975–1984

Quarter	$/£	DM/$	Quarter	$/£	DM/$
1975–I	$2.418	DM2.319	1980–I	$2.154	DM1.957
II	2.280	2.340	II	2.359	1.763
III	2.084	2.618	III	2.384	1.814
IV	2.022	2.622	IV	2.391	1.974
1976–I	1.943	2.560	1981–I	2.237	2.111
II	1.764	2.578	II	1.923	2.396
III	1.727	2.489	III	1.801	2.323
IV	1.678	2.383	IV	1.913	2.237
1977–I	1.717	2.392	1982–I	1.784	2.413
II	1.719	2.356	II	1.733	2.468
III	1.743	2.324	III	1.693	2.531
IV	1.904	2.110	IV	1.618	2.374
1978–I	1.863	1.998	1983–I	1.483	2.429
II	1.860	2.072	II	1.528	2.544
III	1.974	1.940	III	1.495	2.631
IV	2.043	1.820	IV	1.445	2.728
1979–I	2.062	1.868	1984–I	1.445	2.603
II	2.178	1.837	II	1.353	2.783
III	2.204	1.741			
IV	2.209	1.725			

Quarterly Nominal Spot Exchange Rates

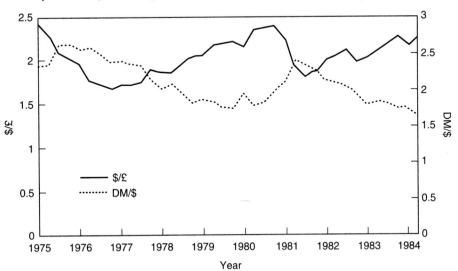

EXHIBIT 8   CONTEMPORARY FINANCIAL MARKET DATA

INFLATION RATES*

	U.S., %	U.K., %	Germany, %
1975	9.2	24.1	5.9
1976	5.8	16.6	4.3
1977	6.4	15.7	3.8
1978	7.6	8.4	2.6
1979	11.4	13.4	4.1
1980	13.5	17.9	5.5
1981	10.3	11.9	6.4
1982	6.2	8.6	5.2
1983	3.2	4.5	3.3
1984-I	2.7	2.7	1.8
1984-II	1.1	2.1	0.5

*Rates for 1975 through 1983 are annualized. 1984 rates are quarterly.
Source: International Financial Statistics (Washington, DC: International Monetary Fund, 1975–1984).

STERLING EXCHANGE RATES, JUNE 29, 1984

	Spot	Forward			
		1 month	3 month	6 month	12 month
U.S. dollar	1.3568	1.3600	1.3659	1.3752	1.3940
German mark	3.7725	3.7620	3.7394	3.7047	3.6438
Japanese yen	322.0	321.2	319.4	316.5	310.2

Source: Financial Times, July 1, 1984, p. 32

INTEREST RATES, END OF JUNE 1984

	Domestic government bonds (long-term), %	Domestic corporate bonds (long-term),[†] %	Treasury bills, %	Domestic money market, %
U.S., $	13.75	14.50	10.29	11.63
Germany, DM	8.25	8.00	na	6.10
U.K., £	10.81	12.69	9.08	9.44
Japan, ¥	7.46	7.13	4.91	6.40

[†]Domestic corporate bonds are of various terms not necessarily identical to corresponding domestic government issues.
Source: World Financial Markets (New York: Morgan Guaranty Trust Company, July 1984).

FOUR

GLOBAL FINANCING

ALCOA OF AUSTRALIA, LTD.

On August 6, 1980, Mr. Norman Perry, a financial advisor to the board of Alcoa of Australia, Ltd., was weighing alternatives for long-term financing. Crédit Suisse First Boston (CSFB), Alcoa's investment bankers, had recommended a unique deferred-payment bond to be sold in the Eurobond market. This $80 million (approximately A$68 million) financing would be the first offering of such an issue in the Eurobond market. Concern about the future direction of interest rates had considerably dampened investors' enthusiasm for long-term bonds, but CSFB felt the deferred-payment feature would increase the marketability of an Alcoa issue.

In spite of the unsettled market, Mr. Perry felt that Alcoa should actively consider adding some long-term debt to its capital structure. The company had embarked on an ambitious A$780 million capital spending program over the next 3 years. A US$510 million borrowing facility with several Australian and American banks had already been arranged, but Mr. Perry felt that, sooner or later, some long-term debt would be needed to help support the capital spending program.

COMPANY BACKGROUND

Alcoa of Australia was formed in 1961 by Alcoa USA, which still retained 51 percent ownership of the company. The two companies continued to share processes and technology, but operated independently. For example, the U.S. parent provided no

This case was prepared by Research Associate Elaine Ide under the supervision of Professors Dwight B. Crane and Samuel L. Hayes, III. Copyright © 1981 by the President and Fellows of Harvard College. Harvard Business School case 281-047.

financial guarantees for the Australian company. The stock of Alcoa of Australia was not listed on any exchange since the remaining 49 percent of the shares were held by a small number of Australian companies.

The company was a fully integrated aluminum producer operating in Western Australia. Its operations included the annual mining of 13.5 million tons of bauxite at three mines in Jarrahdale, Del Park, and Huntly, Australia (see **Exhibit 1**). The bauxite was then refined to alumina at the company's two refineries in Kwinana and Pinjarra. A portion of the alumina was sold and the remainder was converted to aluminum at a smelter in Point Henry. The aluminum was then either sold in its primary form or manufactured into semifinished aluminum products at a plant near the Point Henry smelter.

Alcoa of Australia was strongly export-oriented, with 80 percent of its sales revenue coming from exports. As shown in **Exhibit 2**, alumina was the major product, accounting for 55 percent of sales in 1979. Ninety percent of the alumina was shipped under long-term contracts, with the majority of these having more than 10 years to run. As is customary in the international aluminum trade markets, these contracts were denominated in U.S. dollars. Customers in the United States and Japan accounted for two-thirds of the total alumina sales, including a subsidiary of Alcoa USA that took 800,000 tons each year.

The company had performed well over the past 5 years, growing much faster than its major competitor, Comalco. In 1973 Alcoa had been only half the size of Comalco; but by 1979 Alcoa had become the larger of the two companies. Alcoa's capacity expansions (see **Exhibit 3**) had supported a growth in sales from A$205 million in 1975 to A$650 million in 1979. Profits grew more rapidly from A$17 million to A$95 million during the same time period, so that the net income to sales ratio improved from 8.4 percent to 14.6 percent. The company's financial statements and comparative data about Comalco are shown in **Exhibits 4** through **7**.

In spite of the company's capacity expansions during the 1970s, the additions were not sufficient to keep pace with growing world demand for alumina and aluminum. During 1979 the two alumina refineries and the Point Henry aluminum smelter operated in excess of capacity and inventory stocks were reduced. The shortage of aluminum had been especially acute in Australia, where demand had grown 17 percent in 1979 to reach 220,000 tons per year. Alcoa's management had to monitor closely the company's limited aluminum supply to ensure that long-term customers were treated equitably. The company gave domestic customers priority except when meeting contract commitments to export customers. However, this prevented Alcoa from benefiting from the higher prices for aluminum outside Australia. The Australian price for aluminum ingot had remained at $0.69 per pound in 1979 while the official international price had risen from $0.56 per pound to $0.73 per pound. The actual world spot price was even higher, ranging between $0.75 per pound and $0.83 per pound.

The company's management predicted that demand for alumina and aluminum would remain strong during the 1980s. It was determined to retain Alcoa's position as an important supplier of these two products to Australian and world markets. It planned several capacity expansions to prepare for this expected growth and to relieve the strain and inefficiencies of continually operating above capacity.

Company plans included increasing alumina refining capacity by 500,000 tons per year with the construction of a new refinery at Wagerup. Half the output of the new refinery was planned for export and half was to supply Alcoa's own aluminum smelters. Site preparation for the refinery had already begun in January 1979 and would be completed in 1982. Management estimated the Wagerup project would cost A$320 million.

In addition, Alcoa planned two projects that together would increase total aluminum smelting capacity to 297,000 tons per year. The first of these projects, already under way, was a 65,000-tons-per-year expansion of the Point Henry smelter. The expansion was to be completed before the end of 1980 and was estimated to cost A$100 million. The second aluminum project was a completely new smelter facility in Portland, Victoria, which Alcoa expected to cost A$360 million. Construction was to begin in late 1980. By 1983, the Victoria smelter would produce 132,000 tons per year of aluminum.

A considerable amount of time had gone into forecasting the capital expenditures required by the three projects. So many variables affected construction of this magnitude that it was always difficult to judge exactly when a project would be on line and what its total cost would be. There were many opportunities for delays and design changes, and, of course, the rate of inflation, averaging 11 percent in Australia in recent years, added to the uncertainty of cost figures. But Alcoa planners, who had proven their ability to predict the costs and timing of such projects fairly accurately, put together likely estimates. **Exhibit 8** shows one estimate of the projected cash flow assuming no inflation. The other assumptions used in calculating these figures are explained in the footnotes of the exhibit.

The A$780 million expansion plan was ambitious when compared to Alcoa's present size and capital structure. In 1979 the company had net plant of A$908 million (at replacement cost) and total long-term capital funds of A$945 million. Of the capital funds, A$226 million was long-term debt. Alcoa planned to finance the expansion program with internally generated funds and additional borrowings. The first step was taken in June 1979, when $60 million (equivalent to A$53.4 million at the time of the issue) was raised in the Eurobond market. In an unusual departure from market practices, Crédit Suisse First Boston managed the issue alone without a comanager. Before that time, all Eurobond issues had been managed by at least two investment banks.

In addition to its already outstanding bank debt, the company had also negotiated $510 million (equivalent to A$434 million at August 1980 exchange rates) in borrowing facilities from Australian and foreign banks. The facility provided a revolving line of credit for 4 years, convertible at that point to a term loan of another 6 years. Alcoa would have the right to cancel the credit line at any time. Mr. Perry hoped the company would gradually be able to replace it with long-term fixed-rate financing, since the cost of the facility floated with current short-term rates and was, therefore, unpredictable.

THE EUROBOND MARKET ENVIRONMENT

The Eurobond market was a unique financial market in that it was international and was not under the supervision of any national, international, or supranational authority. The issuers and the investors in the market were international as well, representing a broad variety of investment needs and preferences. This often made the Eurobond market a difficult one to predict or understand, for it reflected the events of many nations and the psychology of many cultures.

The market evolved in the early 1960s when a sizable pool of U.S. dollar deposits had accumulated in European banks. These deposits originated from U.S. balance-of-payments deficits that began in the late 1950s and extended into the early 1960s when the United States was paying out more dollars for imports than it was receiving back for exports. U.S. companies' foreign investments in Europe, as well as the purchase of dollars by Europeans who saw the dollar as a stable currency for their savings, were other sources of dollar deposits. When the U.S. government enacted the Interest Equalization Tax in 1963 to discourage foreign borrowers from raising debt in the U.S. domestic market, non-American borrowers wanting funds turned to this European source for their debt issues.

The Euromarket grew quickly over the next two decades. This growth was strongly encouraged by the Euromarket's freedom from regulation. The lack of binding regulations and reporting requirements made it possible to raise money more quickly in this market relative to national markets. As the market grew, it came to encompass the international deposits of national currencies other than the U.S. dollar. These resources became an important source of international loans, syndicated intermediate-term loans, and the bond market. By 1980 the equivalent of $93 billion had been raised in the bond sector alone since its inception in 1963. The amount of U.S. dollar bonds issued in 1979 reached $12.6 billion, an amount almost one-half the size of the $26 billion U.S. domestic bond market, the world's largest market. Over 50 percent of the bonds were still denominated in U.S. dollars, but German deutsche mark and Swiss franc issues also had become significant in recent years.

It was estimated that one-quarter of the total Eurobonds outstanding was held by institutions such as pension funds, insurance companies, and central banks. These three types of institutions were quality-conscious and sought to preserve capital. However, some pension fund managers were performance-oriented as well. They often traded their portfolio positions, swapping investments to try to improve performance. The majority of the Eurobonds were purchased by banks that managed the investment portfolios of their private customers. Swiss banks alone were believed to hold as much as 40 percent of the total Eurobond market in their trust portfolios. These bank trust departments usually traded less frequently than pension funds, being more conscious of long-term return than short-run performance.

Little was known about the individual investors who owned the bulk of the funds invested in the Eurobond market. They were noted for their secrecy and their desire to keep their investments confidential. For this reason, the Eurobond market had developed almost entirely as a bearer-bond market in which the owner of the bond was never registered. This made characterizing an investor profile difficult, but German,

Italian, Swiss, and Middle Eastern investors were rumored to play a large role. Often they invested money that was unreported, untaxed income that they did not want revealed. Liquidity and the ability to move money quickly were frequently important objectives.

For the most part, then, individual and institutional investors in the Eurobond market were concerned about liquidity and capital preservation. This meant they would tend to desert the market when terms were considered unfavorable or interest rates were expected to rise. They also preferred bonds of shorter maturities. Eurobond issues matured in 7 to 8 years on average, whereas issues in the U.S. bond market typically matured in 20 to 25 years.

Interest Rate Trends

Interest rates in the Eurobond market have historically reflected international inflation expectations and money supply trends. In particular, U.S. interest rates and monetary policies have had a significant impact on Euromarket interest rates as U.S. dollars make up such a large portion of the Eurobond market.

In the period after the 1974 recession through 1977, annual Eurobond market issues grew eightfold, reaching $17.8 million. Dollar supply was high as a result of the large monetary surpluses of Middle Eastern oil exporters, whose oil receipts were denominated in U.S. dollars. This large pool of oil dollars created an excess supply of funds great enough to hold down interest rates, even though inflation rates were high (see **Exhibit 9**).

The period of stable interest rates ended in 1978, though, as issue volume declined, short-term dollar interest rates began to rise, and dollar exchange rates were uncertain. Interest rates stabilized in early 1979 and issue volume grew again as market reception improved (see **Table 1**). However, interest rates rose sharply later in the year as the result of rising inflation and a tightening of monetary policy in the United States (see **Exhibit 10**).

In March 1980 the industrialized nations reported record rates of inflation and the Organization of Petroleum Exporting Countries (OPEC) announced an unexpected oil price hike. The Euromarket reacted with still higher bond rates that finally peaked at an unprecedented 13 percent.

The U.S. Federal Reserve Board announced several significant credit tightening measures in mid-March. This seemed to serve as a signal to the bond markets that U.S.

TABLE 1   TRENDS IN EUROBOND INTEREST RATES AND VOLUME

	1977	1978	1979
Eurobond issues, $ billions	17.8	14.1	18.7
Corporate Eurodollar bond interest rates (yearend), %	8.4	9.2	10.9

inflation would be brought under control. In addition, demand for credit slowed as most industrialized countries began heading into economic recession. Thus, Eurobond interest rates fell through the spring to a level of 10.5 percent in June (see **Exhibit 10**).

Then, unexpectedly, interest rates began edging up again in July and stood at 11.0 percent on August 5, 1980. Market participants were surprised at what they felt was an unwarranted upturn. Never before had interest rates turned up before the general economic recovery began. The confusion was compounded by the recent trend of leading indicators, which hinted the recession in the United States would be slight and could end prematurely. Investors had to speculate on whether the upturn would be temporary, leading to a second, more severe economic slump. They also wondered how much longer U.S. monetary authorities could pursue their tight money policies in light of growing political pressure to release their grip in order to allow a sustained economic recovery.

Future interest rates appeared more uncertain still as economic experts disagreed about world economic and inflation trends for the early 1980s. One opinion held that inflation rates in Western industrial countries would settle below an average of 10.0 percent by early 1981. Proponents of this outlook felt that recovery from the recession would be mild and that most Western economies would not heat up enough to cause another inflationary cycle of the same magnitude as in the late 1970s. They also felt that the U.S. Federal Reserve Board would continue its tight monetary policy in an effort to reduce inflation in the United States and that this would have an ameliorating effect on the international economic picture as well.

The opposing viewpoint maintained by many economists warned that the low interest rates of June had been unrealistic since there had been no real impact on the base rate of inflation. They cited the July figures on the U.S. economy as an indication that the next round of inflation in the United States had already begun. They also argued that, as unemployment rose, constituents would force governments to increase the money supply and encourage economic expansion. The result would be a return to prerecession inflation rates.

Eurobond underwriting activity had become unpredictable as investors exhibited reluctance to commit capital to this volatile market. Short-term rates were currently higher than long-term rates so that investors had little incentive to buy bonds until they believed long-term rates had stabilized.

ALCOA'S FINANCING ALTERNATIVES

At this time of investor uncertainty, Mr. Perry was trying to decide on Alcoa's best strategy for raising long-term debt for the proposed expansion. He had sought the advice of Alcoa's investment bankers, Crédit Suisse First Boston, which recommended Alcoa raise $80 million in long-term debt. The bank had looked at several options for raising these funds. One alternative was to make a straight bond issue in the Eurobond market immediately. CSFB felt Alcoa would have to pay a significant premium to make the bonds salable in the current marketplace because the kinds of investors attracted to multinational bonds were no longer in the market. Even though the most recent Eurodollar bond, an issue of the European Coal and Steel Community, had been issued at 11.25 percent, CSFB estimated that, at this time, an Alcoa issue would have to bear a 12.5 percent coupon. Even with this premium, they warned that the issue might not be fully subscribed because of a lack of investor interest.

Another alternative was to wait, perhaps 6 months, before raising long-term debt in hopes that market conditions would be more favorable. Mr. Perry knew the company could, in the interim, finance necessary project costs by drawing down part of the $510 million (A$434 million) commercial bank facility and the nearly A$100 million liquid assets Alcoa had recently accumulated.

CSFB had also considered some of the innovative bonds that had recently been tried in the market in an effort to coax reluctant investors into long-term instruments. These innovations usually offered investors the sweetener of high early interest payments comparable to current short-term rates. The interest payments later decreased to a more normal long-term bond rate. The innovations varied in how the interest payments dropped from the initial rate to the permanent, lower rate. One design was called the "step-down" bond. This bond was issued at an initial coupon rate that later dropped to a lower rate for the remaining life of the bond. For example, the bond might bear a 10 percent coupon for the first 2 years, then step down to 9 percent for all following interest payments. The graduated-rate bond, a variation of the step-down bond, was issued at a coupon rate that was gradually reduced as each coupon came due. At some point, the coupon reached a base rate that was maintained for the remaining life of the bond.

There were also "drop-lock" bonds, an innovation introduced by CSFB, in which the bonds bore coupons that floated with current interest rates. However, the issuer stated a predetermined base rate below which the coupon would not fall. Once the base rate was hit, it was locked in for the life of the bond. The drop-lock gave investors an even greater incentive than the step-down or the graduated-rate bonds because it allowed the investor to participate in any short-term rate increases that occurred after its purchase.

Deferred-Payment Feature

After considering these innovations, Crédit Suisse First Boston decided to recommend a deferred-payment approach that was new to the Eurobond market. The general idea was that investors would pay for the bonds in two installments, a down payment at the time of the offering in August, and the remaining amount in January 1981. This approach would allow investors to guarantee access to bonds bearing current bond rates, but postpone their full payment for several months.

Although the deferred-payment design was new to the Eurobond market, it resembled an approach that the British government had employed since 1977 in the U.K. gilt (government debt) market. The government issued securities called "partly paid gilts" that were purchased over time via installment payments. The specific design of a partly paid gilt differed with each issue, but the initial payment could equal as little as 10 percent of the face value of the bond, with partial payments being required on predetermined dates until all the principal had been paid. Total payment was usually completed within several weeks of the first installment. The partly paid gilts were registered in the owner's name so that holders of the partially paid outstanding bond were liable for each successive payment.

The British government's stated purpose for issuing the partly paid gilts was to smooth its use of the financial markets by drawing funds out in several scheduled smaller amounts rather than in less frequent large amounts. This innovation originated during a time when high inflation, which made fixed-income gilts unattractive, coincided with greatly increased government borrowing requirements. Thus some observers felt the partly paid idea had been created to get issues off the ground by encouraging speculators into the market.

Speculators were attracted to partly paid gilts because they were able to leverage their position. For example, if the first payment were equal to 10 percent of the face value of the bond, an investor could get in at one-tenth the cost of the bond or, conversely, could take a position equal to ten bonds for the cost of one bond. If interest rates then changed, the investor could significantly benefit or lose from the change in value of the partially paid bond.

For the most part, the partly paid gilts had been a successful instrument. The British government had used them for 3 years as an effective means of raising public debt. However, market participants noted some problems. They felt the securities had caused more volatile markets as the gearing led investors to buy positions for which they could not afford the next installment. As the installment came due, they would have to sell their partly paid gilts. The market price of partly paid gilts could therefore drop dramatically as payment dates approached. Institutional investors had responded by staying out of the early market until speculators' dumping provided the opportunity to pick up cheap bonds. To curb the volatility of the market, the government had gradually increased the size, as a percent of face value, of the initial payment in order to reduce the partly paids' leveraging opportunities.

The Crédit Suisse First Boston Proposal

Because of current market conditions and the magnitude of Alcoa's expansion, the bankers at CSFB believed that a deferred-payment bond would be successful and would fit Alcoa's needs. They felt that an $80 million issue could be sold with a 12 percent coupon rate and a maturity of January 15, 1988. Certificates representing a percentage of the face value of the bond would be sold in August 1980, and the remaining share of the capital would come due on January 15, 1981. These bonds would have one important difference from partly paid gilts in that the bond would be unregistered and certificate holders could *not*, therefore, be forced to make the second capital payment. The details of the proposal were quite complicated, but the timetable would work as shown in **Table 2**.

CSFB saw two potential advantages of the deferred-payment bond for investors. First, some investors might be expecting cash inflows from bond maturities or other sources over the next several months. These individuals or institutions would be able to "lock in" the current bond rate, but would not have to purchase the bonds completely until a later date. The second feature that would appeal to some investors was the leveraging possibility available with the certificates. Assume, for example, that

TABLE 2	TIMETABLE OF THE PROPOSED DEFERRED-PAYMENT BONDS
August 1980	Certificates representing a percentage of the face value of the bond issue would be sold to investors. During this period, bankers would maintain a secondary market so that these down-payment certificates could be freely traded.
January 15, 1981	Interest would be paid on the capital represented by the certificates for its use from August to January at a 12% annual rate. The second installment to purchase the remaining share of the face value of the bond would come due. No further secondary market for the down-payment certificates would be maintained. After this date, only fully-paid bonds could be traded on the open market.
	A 2-week period would follow during which Alcoa must accept the second installment, but the investor would have to pay a late fee on the overdue capital equal to a 15%-per-year interest charge.
January 29, 1981	At any time after this date during the life of the bond, Alcoa would have the option to refuse additional second-installment payments. Should the company exercise this option, it would retain the initial capital received from the sale of any first-down-payment certificates that were not yet fully paid. Any investor who had not yet made the second-installment payment would forfeit the capital represented by the certificate and receive no further interest. So long as Alcoa did not exercise this option, holders of first-down-payment certificates could make the second installment at any time during the life of the bond as long as the late penalty of 15% per year on the overdue capital was paid.

certificates were sold on August 15, 1980, representing a 20 percent down payment. Investors could then purchase a $2000 certificate that would entitle them to purchase the remainder of a $10,000 bond on January 15, 1981. The return they would receive would include some interest on January 15; 5 months of interest at 12 percent would equal $100.

More importantly, there was also the possibility of a significant capital gain or loss. The amount of the gain or loss would depend on changes in Eurobond interest rates that occurred between August and January. These changes would affect the market value of the bond to be received on January 15. As an example, assume that the 7-year Eurobond rate for borrowers similar to Alcoa had fallen to 10 percent on January 15, 1981. Since the Alcoa bond coupon interest was 12 percent, the market value of a $10,000 bond would increase $990 to $10,990. As a result, the value of the certificate would also rise $990, providing a 49.5 percent gain in 5 months. The entire increase of the bond's value would accrue to the certificate holder because an investor who bought the certificate would then have the option to purchase the bond for another $8000. If the bond's total value were $10,990, an investor should be willing to pay up to $2990 for this option. Of course, if bond yields rose by January, the bond's value would fall and the investors' leverage would work to their detriment, causing a large percentage loss. **Exhibit 11** indicates the return to investors for several future bond yields and a variety of down payment amounts.

CONCLUSION

As Mr. Perry reviewed the proposed bond issue, he felt that it offered some advantages for Alcoa. If the investment bankers' assessment was correct, it offered an opportunity to get some long-term capital in the currently unfavorable market, while paying a lower interest rate than would normally be required. This would look especially attractive if long-term rates moved up in the next few months. On the other hand, if rates decreased significantly, it naturally would have been better to have postponed the issue. Thus, he did not want to rush ahead without thinking carefully about the future direction of bond yields.

Mr. Perry also had some concerns about the deferred-payment concept. Some colleagues felt that the certificates would appeal primarily to speculators rather than major institutional investors whose support Alcoa might need in the longer run. A related issue was that certificate holders did not have to put up the second payment. What was the likelihood that the 12 percent bond coupons would be so unattractive by January that investors would sacrifice their certificate rather than invest the additional money that Alcoa needed? Were interest rates likely to rise so much by January 1981 that the certificates would have no value? Could the deferred-payment feature be designed to reduce this possibility while retaining its basic appeal? Given an unreceptive, unsettled market, was it better to reach out with an untested innovation, offer a standard product at a slightly higher price, or wait for better times?

EXHIBIT 1   ALCOA OF AUSTRALIA OPERATING LOCATIONS

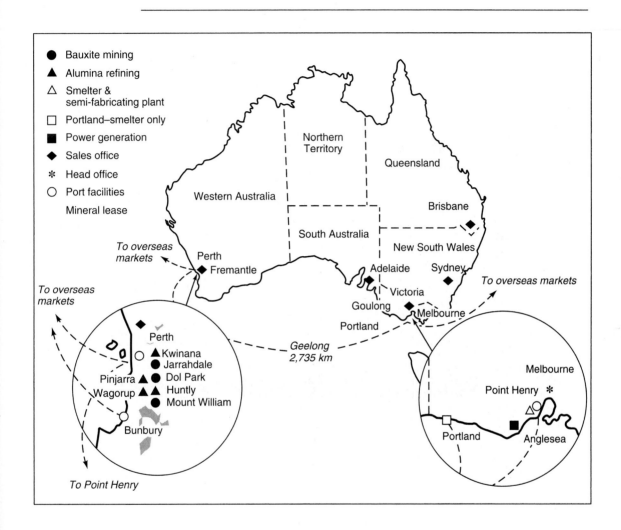

EXHIBIT 2   SALES REVENUES BY PRODUCT: YEAR ENDED DECEMBER 31 (A$ MILLIONS)

	1979	1978	1977	1976	1975
Sales revenues					
Alumina	358	260	255	187	125
Primary aluminum	65	35	31	24	12
Semifinished aluminum					
products	99	63	59	46	33
Tolling*	125	112	91	79	34
Other	3	2	2	3	1
	650	472	438	339	205

*Tolling income is income earned on leased mining rights.

EXHIBIT 3   PRODUCTION CAPACITY: YEAR ENDED DECEMBER 31 (THOUSANDS OF TONS PER ANNUM)

	1979	1978	1977	1976	1975
Rated capacity					
Alumina					
Kwinana refinery	1400	1400	1400	1400	1400
Pinjarra refinery	2400	2200	2000	2000	1500
	3800	3600	3400	3400	2900
Aluminum					
Point Henry smelter	100	100	91	91	91

EXHIBIT 4   ALCOA OF AUSTRALIA, LTD., AND SUBSIDIARY COMPANIES: CONSOLIDATED STATEMENT OF EARNINGS (YEAR ENDED DECEMBER 31; A$ THOUSANDS)

	1979	1978	1977	1976	1975
Sales revenue	659,780	476,429	441,733	340,057	206,425
Cost and expenses					
Cost of goods sold	385,542	287,258	254,372	199,743	127,405
Net loss on currency fluctuations	5,793	—	3,477	1,150	—
Depreciation expense	49,020	46,021	31,305	28,861	23,931
Interest expense	30,949	26,154	28,498	28,953	23,932
Other expense	887	835	1,719	686	2,687
	472,191	360,268	319,371	259,393	177,955
Income from operations	187,589	116,161	122,362	80,664	28,470
Provisions for taxes	93,846	56,604	58,062	31,357	12,059
Income from operations after taxes	93,743	59,557	64,300	49,307	16,411
Income from associated companies					
Dividends received	440	213	566	228	450
Equity in retained earnings	751	1,120	350	939	362
	1,191	1,333	916	1,167	812
Income before extraordinary item	94,934	60,890	65,216	50,474	17,223
Extraordinary item	—	—	—	(7,777)	—
Net income	94,934	60,890	65,216	42,697	17,223
Retained earnings at beginning of year	156,623	129,208	102,802	73,355	58,442
Transfer to trading stock valuation adjustment reserve	5,785	(225)	(5,560)	—	—
Ordinary dividends declared and paid	(40,000)	(33,250)	(33,250)	(13,250)	(2,310)
Retained earnings at end of year	217,342	156,623	129,208	102,802	73,355

EXHIBIT 5 ALCOA OF AUSTRALIA, LTD., AND SUBSIDIARY COMPANIES: CONSOLIDATED BALANCE SHEET (YEAR ENDED DECEMBER 31; A$ THOUSANDS)

	1979	1978
Assets		
Cash and equivalents	101,746	12,993
Accounts receivable	82,974	85,387
Inventories	128,181	112,222
Due from related companies	16,979	5,616
Prepared expenses and other items	1,598	1,976
Total current assets	331,478	218,194
Investments in associated companies	7,698	6,971
Other assets and deferred charges	23,088	19,094
Property, plant, and equipment	907,994	743,794
Secret processes and technical information	10,712	11,178
Total assets	1,280,970	999,231
Liabilities		
Bank overdrafts and short-term loans	11,786	6,881
Prepaid export alumina sales	16,468	5,013
Accounts payable, trade	70,240	33,954
Accrued expenses	26,611	19,122
Provision for current taxes	52,782	45,129
Long-term unsecured debt due within 1 year	22,325	27,588
Total current liabilities	200,212	137,687
Long-term unsecured debt, less amounts due within 1 year:		
Eurodollar bonds	52,719	—
Related companies	19,205	24,657
Acceptance credit facilities	—	20,154
Banks	154,138	167,558
	226,062	212,369
Noncurrent liabilities		
Provision for taxes	131,052	89,183
Prepaid export alumina sales	—	16,917
Other	4,936	3,948
	135,988	110,048
Shareholders' equity		
Authorized−320 million shares of A$1 each, issued 200 million shares fully paid	200,000	200,000
Asset revaluation reserve	301,366	182,504
Retained earnings	217,342	156,623
Total shareholders' equity	718,708	539,127
Total liabilities and shareholders' equity	1,280,970	999,231

EXHIBIT 6   ALCOA OF AUSTRALIA, LTD., AND SUBSIDIARY COMPANIES: CONSOLIDATED STATEMENT OF SOURCE AND USES OF FUNDS (YEAR ENDED DECEMBER 31; A$ THOUSANDS)

	1979	1978	1977	1976	1975
Source of funds					
Net income for year	94,934	60,890	65,216	42,697	17,223
Depreciation and amortization	49,020	46,021	31,305	28,861	23,931
Other expenses not involving funds	93,095	55,484	57,712	30,418	11,697
Funds derived from operations	237,049	162,395	154,233	101,976	52,851
Long-term borrowings (net)	8,430*	—	—	—	64,049
Other	2,490	20,386	3,578	8,487	13,950
Total funds available	247,969	182,781	157,811	110,463	130,850
Application of funds					
Increase in working capital†	53,149	23,596	15,313	48,885	24,021
Payment of income tax	44,324	36,012	—	—	—
Dividends paid	40,000	33,250	33,250	13,250	5,000
Repayment of long-term debt (net)	—	35,310	68,461	6,767	—
Expenditure on purchase of property, plant, and equipment	90,597	52,960	40,450	35,258	100,624
Other	19,899	1,653	337	6,303	1,205
Total funds applied	247,969	182,781	157,811	110,463	130,850

*Net borrowings = Eurobond issue less repayment of long-term debt, or $8,430 = $53,386 − $44,956.
† Working capital excludes the current portion of long-term debt and the current portion of the provision for income taxes.

EXHIBIT 7   COMPARABLE COMPANY DATA (A$ MILLIONS, EXCEPT PERCENTAGES)

Alcoa of Australia	1979	1978	1977	1976	1975	1974	1973
Sales	650	472	438	339	205	163	115
Net income	95	61	65	43	17	15	12
Long-term debt	248	240	275	348	355	283	260
Equity*	719	539	511	178	148	124	101
Long-term debt as a percent of total capitalization,[†]	25.6	30.8	35.0	66.2	70.6	69.5	72.0
Return on equity, %	13.2	11.3	12.7	24.2	11.5	12.1	11.9
Comalco[‡]							
Sales	574	507	403	331	288	232	227
Net income	58	37	40	26	7	17	18
Long-term debt	172	157	174	180	153	123	105
Equity	319	288	211	189	176	153	144
Long-term debt as a percent of total capitalization[†]	35.0	35.3	45.2	48.8	46.5	44.6	42.2
Return on equity, %	18.2	12.8	19.0	13.8	4.0	11.1	12.5

*Includes effects of two asset revaluations in 1977 and 1979 equal to a total of A$302 million.
[†]Long-term debt as a percent of total capitalization = (long-term debt) ÷ (long-term debt + net worth).
[‡]Comalco is a fully integrated aluminum producer that mines bauxite, produces alumina and aluminum, and fabricates a variety of aluminum products.

EXHIBIT 8 ALCOA OF AUSTRALIA PROJECTED CASH FLOW, 1980–1984* (A$ MILLIONS; ASSUMES NO INFLATION)

	1984	1983	1982	1981	1980	1979
1. Revenue	1369	1140	950	792	660	660
2. Profit after taxes	219	179	144	116	94	94
3. Dividends	(94)	(77)	(62)	(50)	(40)	(40)
4. Addition to retained earnings	125	102	82	66	54	54
5. Depreciation	88	79	62	54	49	49
6. Other noncash items: provision for taxes	8	32	57	42	16	42
7. Capital expenditures on existing fixed assets	(88)	(79)	(62)	(54)	(49)	(49)
8. Capital expenditures on proposed projects	0	(140)	(290)	(210)	(140)	0
9. Net change in working capital	(46)	(38)	(32)	(26)	0	(51)
10. Repayment of current outstanding debt	(26)	(26)	(26)	(21)	(21)	(28)
Projected corporate cash flow	61	(70)	(209)	(149)	(91)	17
Cumulative funds need	(441)	(502)	(432)	(223)	(74)	17

Assumptions
1. Due to capacity constraints, sales do not grow during 1980 and then grow, thereafter, at 20% per year.
2. Profit after tax remains at 14.2% of sales in 1980, then gradually increases to 16% of sales as added capacity results in higher operating efficiencies.
3. Dividends are 43% of profits after tax.
4. Addition to retained earnings profit after taxes (line 2) minus dividends (line 3).
5. Depreciation figures include the writedown of the new projects, beginning in the quarter after completion. The new assets are depreciated on a straight-line basis over 20 years.
6. Tax provisions include an estimated investment tax credit on each year's new capital expenditures plus a small amount due to the timing of the tax payment on a growing level of earnings.
7. Capital expenditures to maintain existing fixed assets are assumed to equal depreciation.
8. The timing of the $780 million outlay is based upon general industry experience.
9. Net working capital is assumed to increase $1.00 for each $5.00 increase in sales.
10. Derived from footnote 11, page 19, of the company's 1979 annual report.

*Based on case-writer's estimates.

EXHIBIT 9   AVERAGE YIELDS ON U.S. DOLLAR EUROBONDS

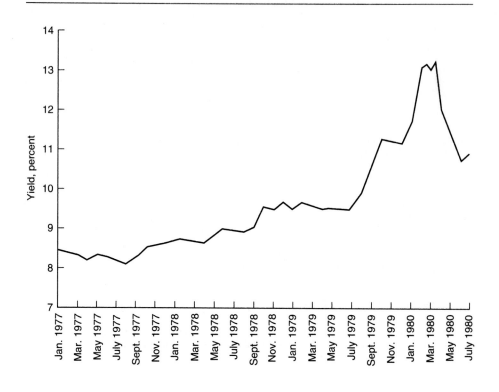

EXHIBIT 10   AVERAGE 6-MONTH EURODOLLAR INTEREST RATES

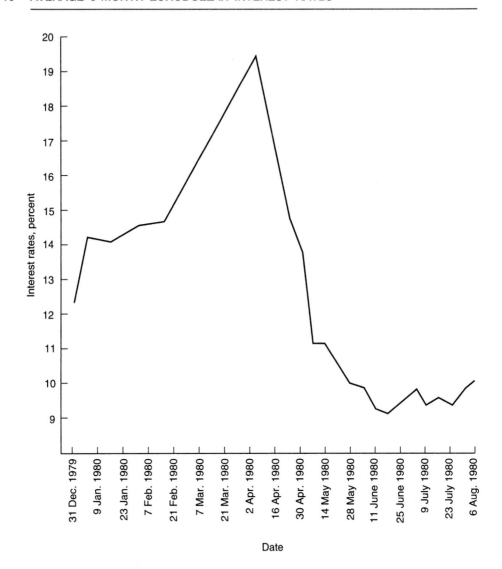

EXHIBIT 11 RETURNS TO PURCHASERS OF CERTIFICATES: IMPLICATIONS OF DOWN PAYMENT SIZE AND JANUARY BOND YIELDS*

Assumed yield on 7-year bonds, %	Market value of 7-year 12% bonds, $	Five-month change in value of certificate, $	Hypothetical results as of January 15, 1981					
			$1000 certificate (10% down)		$2000 certificate (20% down)		$3000 certificate (30% down)	
			Market value of certificate, $	% Return to original purchaser	Market value of certificate, $	% Return to original purchaser	Market value of certificate, $	% Return to original purchaser
9%	$11,533	$ 1533	$2533	158%	$3533	82%	$4533	56%
10%	$10,990	$ 900	$1990	104%	$2990	55%	$3990	38%
11%	$10,479	$ 479	$1479	48%	$2479	29%	$3479	21%
12%	$10,000	$ —	$1000	5%	$2000	5%	$3000	5%
13%	$ 9,549	$ (451)	$ 549	(40)%	$1549	(18)%	$2549	(10)%
14%	$ 9,125	$ (875)	$ 125	(83)%	$1125	(39)%	$2225	(24)%
15%	$ 8,727	$(1273)	$ —	(95)%	$ 727	(59)%	$1727	(37)%

*Note: The % return columns all include a 5 percent return from interest received on January 15, 1981. Note that these returns are received over a 5-month period from August 15 to January 15. They are not annualized returns.

R.J. REYNOLDS INTERNATIONAL FINANCING

In August 1985 Earl Hall, the director of corporate finance at R.J. Reynolds Industries, Inc. (RJR), had requested from the company's various bankers proposals for financing a portion of its recent $4.9 billion acquisition of Nabisco Brands, Inc. As part of the acquisition agreement, Reynolds would issue $1.2 billion of 12-year notes and $1.2 billion of preferred stock in the U.S. domestic markets within the next few weeks. It had already funded $1.5 billion of the Nabisco acquisition, leaving $1 billion more to finance.

Responding to this request, a financing team at Morgan Guaranty Trust Company in New York, along with their colleagues at Morgan Guaranty Ltd (MGL) (the merchant banking affiliate), in London, had spent the last few weeks analyzing the terms of potential deals Reynolds could issue in the Eurobond market. One interesting idea was a 5-year yen/dollar dual currency Eurobond. The New York team had been told by London that Reynolds could issue ¥25 billion of noncallable bonds at a price of 101.50 percent of par, with an annual coupon of 7¾ percent paid in yen and fees of 1⅞ percent. However, the final principal payment would be $115.956 million rather than the ¥25 billion face amount. Reynolds might want some 5-year debt, and the coupon seemed attractive. However, the team was concerned about the foreign exchange risks presented by such a hybrid structure and whether this transaction made sense for R.J. Reynolds. Thus, the team would also need to consider ways to hedge the dual-currency bond.

This case was prepared by Research Associate William B. Allen, Jr., under the supervision of Professor W. Carl Kester. Copyright © 1987 by the President and Fellows of Harvard College. Harvard Business School case 287-057.

Furthermore, the group in New York thought it was appropriate to evaluate the costs of this structure in light of the terms on other potential deals mentioned by London. One alternative would be 5-year Eurodollar bonds and another was 5-year Euroyen bonds. The team realized that they would also need to evaluate the Eurodollar bonds in terms of the all-in cost of hedging or swapping the Euroyen bonds into a dollar liability.

R.J. REYNOLDS

R.J. Reynolds Industries, Inc. (RJR), a major international consumer products company based in Winston-Salem, North Carolina, operated tobacco products and food and beverage businesses throughout the world. RJR sold tobacco products to more than 160 markets around the world. Popular cigarette brands in the United States included Camel, Winston, Salem, and Vantage, all four of which ranked among the top ten best-selling domestic brands in 1984. Food and beverage operations were conducted through Del Monte, Heublein, and Kentucky Fried Chicken subsidiaries. Del Monte was the largest canner of fruits and vegetables in the world. Its other product lines included Canada Dry and Hawaiian Punch beverages, Sunkist soft drinks, Morton frozen foods, and Chun-King oriental-style foods. Heublein was the largest producer of vodka and premixed cocktails in the United States and one of the nation's largest producers of wine. Kentucky Fried Chicken was the largest chicken chain in the United States and ranked second in worldwide fast food sales.

RJR's strategy was to focus on high-margin consumer-related businesses with a dominant or leading position in their respective industries. This led to an active program of acquisitions and divestitures, which began with the purchase of Del Monte in 1979, followed by the purchase of Heublein in 1982. During 1983 RJR acquired Canada Dry and Sunkist as part of its Del Monte subsidiary. This consumer focus was further refined in 1984 with the spin-off of Sea-Land, the world's largest container shipping company, and the sale for cash of Aminoil, the second largest independent oil and gas exploration company in the United States. The acquisition of Nabisco in mid-1985 (discussed below) fit neatly within the company's overall strategic plan.

RJR, which ranked twenty-third in 1984 on the *Fortune* 500 list of companies, had sales of almost $13 billion and net income of $1.2 billion for that year (**Exhibit 1**). Tobacco-related sales accounted for 58 percent of revenues and 75 percent of income, with food and beverage sales accounting for another 36 percent of revenue and 22 percent of income. Although tobacco products sales had grown at an annual rate of approximately 8 percent over the last few years, food and beverage sales had grown at an annual rate of 22 percent.

Total assets were $9.3 billion at the end of 1984 (**Exhibit 2**). With the sale of its energy operations, cash and short-term investments more than tripled to $1.3 billion in 1984 from $363 million in 1983. Total long-term debt of $1.3 billion was 14 percent of total assets—a slight decrease compared to 15 percent in 1983. In November 1984 RJR purchased and retired 10 million shares of its common stock at an aggregate cost of $738 million. In May 1985 common stock was split 2.5 for 1. By August 1985 RJR had repurchased an additional 7.9 million of its common shares at an aggregate cost of

$248 million. As of mid-1985, the stock was selling for around $27 per share, and RJR was in the process of listing its shares on several major foreign stock markets.

The majority of RJR's sales and manufacturing was in the United States, although Europe, Canada, Australia, and parts of Asia were important markets (**Exhibit 3**). RJR's various foreign subsidiaries hedged nondollar operating cash flows through its Swiss banking subsidiary, which, in turn, selectively hedged the global currency exposure of RJR. Foreign subsidiaries with substantial manufacturing operations, such as Germany, financed these assets in part by borrowing in local markets. RJR's Japanese operations consisted primarily of its Kentucky Fried Chicken chain. Fixed assets were minimal, and yen cash flows were used to support expansion within Japan.

THE NABISCO ACQUISITION

In June 1985 RJR announced the acquisition of Nabisco Brands, Inc., for $4.9 billion. Nabisco, one of the largest food companies in the United States, manufactured and sold cookies, crackers, nuts and snacks, confectionery desserts, margarines, hot cereals, pet snacks, and consumer yeast. Nabisco products were also produced and marketed in Canada, the United Kingdom, continental Europe, Latin America, and the Asia/Pacific region.

Nabisco's sales grew 5 percent during 1984 to $6.3 billion while net income decreased to $309 million from $323 million (**Exhibit 4**). Total assets at the end of 1984 were $3.8 billion, and the balance sheet showed little change from the previous year (**Exhibit 5**). Over 60 percent of sales and 75 percent of earnings were in the United States (**Exhibit 6**). Assets in the United States, including corporate headquarters, represented about 60 percent of the consolidated total. Significant foreign operations were located in both Europe (including the United Kingdom) and Canada. In 1984 European sales and earnings were 18 percent and 10 percent, respectively, of the consolidated total. Products marketed in Europe were primarily brand-name biscuits, crackers, and desserts. Identifiable assets in Europe of $373 million represented 21 percent of the world total. In Canada, manufacturing plants in various provinces supported sales of brand-name cookies, crackers, and other food products. Sales in Canada were 12 percent and earnings 10 percent of the consolidated total.

The first step of the acquisition was a tender offer for 51 percent of Nabisco's stock for $2.5 billion in cash. The remaining 49 percent of the outstanding stock, valued at an additional $2.4 billion, would be acquired in a few weeks by an exchange of both RJR preferred stock and 12-year U.S. domestic notes, each with a value of $1.2 billion at the time of the exchange.

The $2.5 billion cash paid at the conclusion of the tender offer was obtained from $500 million of cash on hand and $2 billion of bank borrowings and commercial paper. RJR decided to retain only $500 million of this amount as short-term floating-rate debt and to seek alternative funding for the remaining $1.5 billion. The company analyzed the maturity spectrum of its existing debt and targeted amounts for various maturities ranging from 4 to 30 years. The entire financing operation was further complicated by the fact that RJR's debt had been downgraded to single A following the announcement of the acquisition. The company was not sure how this decision would affect its financing operation.

By the end of July, RJR saw windows in the domestic bond market and quickly issued $500 million of bonds: $250 million of 30-year debentures and $250 million of 8-year notes. The all-in costs of these issues were 11.857 percent, or Treasuries plus 99 basis points, for the 30-year debentures and 10.90 percent, or Treasuries plus 54 basis points, for the 8-year notes. Sourcing the remaining $1 billion remained problematic, however. RJR did not wish to jeopardize the reception of either the $1.2 billion of domestic 12-year notes or the $1.2 billion of preferred stock that it was committed to exchange for the remaining portion of Nabisco stock.

DUAL-CURRENCY BONDS

Dual-currency bonds were denominated and paid interest in one currency but were redeemable in another. Typically, the denominations and interest payments were in low-interest-rate foreign currencies, such as Swiss francs or Japanese yen, while redemption was in U.S. dollars. The coupons were usually set above the yields prevailing in the foreign currency but below the rates on dollar bonds. Also, the implied exchange rate at redemption, determined by dividing the foreign-currency denomination amount by the dollar redemption amount, provided for some appreciation of the foreign currency against the dollar.

The first dual-currency bonds were launched by American Medical International N.V. in the Swiss market in 1982. This was followed by a slow but steady stream of Swiss franc/dollar dual-currency issues over the following years. By mid-1985 there were just over twenty dual-currency bonds listed on the Zurich stock exchange totaling almost SF2 billion. Most of these bonds had 8- to 10-year maturities, although some of the earlier issues had 12- and 15-year maturities. The coupons were typically 7 to 7½ percent—perhaps 100 to 200 basis points higher than comparable regular Swiss franc bonds. However, the implied exchange rate at maturity was often SF1.60 to 1.90 per dollar compared to spot rates that averaged above SF2.00 from 1982 to 1985. With a favorable exchange rate at redemption relative to prevailing spot rates, Swiss franc dual-currency bonds were targeted to small retail investors to provide a convenient way to speculate in future Swiss franc/dollar exchange rates.

Although there had been some interest in dual-currency bonds in other currencies, the real growth potential in the market appeared to be in yen/dollar bonds. With the liberalization in May 1985 of the Euroyen market, several yen/dollar issues had been launched during the summer of 1985. The standard for these issues was set by the Ford Motor Credit yen/dollar dual-currency bonds launched in July 1985. This 10-year, ¥25 billion issue was offered at a price of 100¹¹⁄₁₆ percent of par with a coupon of 8 percent and an effective redemption exchange rate of ¥208. Coupons on comparable Euroyen bonds were 100 to 150 basis points lower than this, and new 10-year Japanese government bonds had coupons of only 6.2 percent.

The yen/dollar dual-currency bonds were targeted primarily at Japanese institutions wishing to lock in high coupon yields and that were willing to assume the foreign exchange risk at redemption. Many Japanese investment funds, such as those managed by the life insurance companies, were evaluated in light of current yields, while foreign exchange and capital gains and losses were booked to reserve accounts. These and other institutions wanted to replace the substantial amounts of maturing 10-year Japanese government bonds, issued in the turbulent years following the oil crisis in 1974–1975, which bore coupons of 8 percent or more.

An important part of many of these deals was the attractive foreign exchange forward rates Japanese banks would often offer to borrowers. A host of U.S. corporations and some European sovereigns and corporations were able to hedge the yen liabilities into other currencies — primarily dollars — at extremely favorable rates. Market participants wondered if these off-market forward rates were economical deals for the Japanese banks, perhaps offset by the likes of Japanese oil importers who needed to buy dollars forward to pay for future oil supplies, or whether they were ambitious attempts to buy into the Eurobond business by winning the attention of prestigious borrowers.

Despite their popularity with borrowers, yen/dollar dual-currency bonds were not without their critics. Many investors, noting the exchange rates indicated in the long-dated forward foreign exchange market, believed either the coupon was too low for the implied redemption exchange rate or the redemption exchange rate did not allow enough appreciation of the yen against the dollar. Other market participants compared these bonds to private placements because they were usually presold to Japanese financial institutions. Although many of these deals were arranged by non-Japanese investment banks, it was primarily the Japanese banks that had strong placing power with investors. In some cases, the non-Japanese bank underwriter who arranged the deal was a co–lead manager in name only and took no allocation of bonds to sell. Yen/dollar dual-currency bonds typically disappeared from dealers' screens just a few days after they were launched, and there was virtually no secondary market trading.

Neither the stipulation by the Japanese Ministry of Finance (MOF) that no more than 10 percent of a Japanese firm's assets be held in foreign securities nor the requirement that Eurobonds be held for 180 days outside Japan prevented most of these bonds from ultimately finding their way back to Japan. Many observers believed that the offshore subsidiaries of cash-rich Japanese life insurance and trust companies warehoused these bonds for 6 months until they could be sold in Japan. During the summer of 1985, suspected hedging activities associated with temporarily warehousing the large rush of issues caused the yen/dollar 6-month forward foreign exchange market virtually to dry up. With such apparent disregard for the guidelines, many market participants wondered if the MOF would soon crack down.

ANALYZING THE YEN/DOLLAR DUAL-CURRENCY EUROBONDS

Before making a proposal to Mr. Hall at RJR, the Morgan team in New York wanted to consider carefully the terms of the various deals supplied by their colleagues at Morgan Guaranty Ltd in London. Based on its close relationships with various Japanese financial institutions, MGL felt confident it could arrange a ¥25 billion issue of 5-year noncallable yen/dollar dual-currency Eurobonds at 101.50 percent of par. The annual coupons of 7¾ percent would be paid in yen, but the final principal repayment would be $115.956 million rather than the yen face amount. (See **Exhibit 7** for a summary of financing terms for various structures available to RJR.) The team realized that dual-currency bonds might present RJR with additional foreign exchange exposure risks and, therefore, would require careful analysis. Furthermore, they wanted to be prepared for questions about the relative cost of this issue and how the markets would receive this structure.

The team would first need to determine whether it made sense for RJR to take on a yen liability. If so, they would then need to determine whether RJR would be better off leaving the cash flows of the dual-currency bond as proposed, thus exposing RJR only to the annual yen coupons, or modifying the cash flow structure. The yen/dollar dual-currency Eurobond could, for example, be converted into a regular yen liability by buying dollars for 5-year forward delivery against the yen in the interbank foreign exchange (FX) forward market. If a yen liability did not make sense, a regular dollar liability could be created by buying yen forward against dollars to cover the annual yen coupons over the next 5 years. The group in New York was aware that MGL had negotiated special yen/dollar FX forward rates for RJR **(Exhibit 8)** through Nikko Securities, Ltd., which would likely participate in the management group for this deal. These forwards might make the all-in dollar cost of this alternative quite attractive.

The all-in costs of the modified yen/dollar dual-currency bonds could then be compared with the all-in costs of other potential deals. With $1.2 billion of 12-year notes scheduled to be launched in the domestic debt market in just a few weeks, it seemed prudent to restrict other financing choices to the offshore markets. One relatively straightforward alternative would be to issue 5-year Eurodollar bonds. RJR could issue $100 million of 5-year noncallable Eurodollar bonds at 100.125 percent of par, with an annual coupon of 10⅛ percent and fees of 1⅞ percent. The all-in cost of this deal would provide a benchmark spread over comparable Treasury securities that could be used in comparing the various financing alternatives under consideration. Five-year U.S. Treasuries were trading at a yield of 9.88 percent.

RJR could also issue ¥25 billion 5-year noncallable Euroyen bonds at a price of 100.25 percent of par, with an annual coupon of 6⅜ percent and fees of 1⅞ percent. The team wondered how the all-in yen cost of this deal would compare to the yen/dollar dual-currency bond completely hedged into yen. They also wondered how the all-in *dollar* costs of the Euroyen bonds (either hedged or swapped into a dollar liability) compared to the all-in cost of the straight Eurodollar bonds. The Euroyen bonds could be hedged into dollars using FX forwards in a manner similar to that used to hedge the yen/dollar dual-currency bonds into dollars.

As an alternative to using FX forwards, RJR could convert a Euroyen liability to a dollar liability with a currency swap. MGL indicated that it could arrange swaps in which it would pay to RJR fixed yen cash flows with an annual internal rate of return of 7.10 percent in exchange for receiving from RJR a stream of cash providing a yield equal to 6-month dollar LIBOR (the London Interbank Offered Rate). Similarly, MGL would agree to pay 6-month dollar LIBOR to RJR in exchange for receiving from RJR fixed dollar cash flows with an annual internal rate of return of 10.92 percent **(Exhibit 9)**. Since the LIBOR payments and receipts offset each other, RJR could effectively contract to receive from MGL fixed yen cash flows in exchange for paying fixed dollar cash flows.

To calculate the all-in dollar costs of the Euroyen bond swapped into dollars, the quoted yen swap rate would be adjusted to make it equal the all-in cost of the Euroyen bond. The team suspected that the 7.10 percent quoted yen swap rate paid to RJR would exceed the all-in cost of the Euroyen bonds; thus, there would be extra yen basis points left on the table. These extra yen basis points could be converted to dollar basis points (see the ''Note on Foreign-Currency Swaps''). The equivalent amount of dollar basis points would then be subtracted from the dollar swap rate in order to determine the all-in cost of the dollar cash flows from the swap. Before making the calculations, the team drew a simple swap diagram to illustrate the all-in costs of the various cash flows from the Euroyen bond and the currency swap **(Exhibit 10)**.

The team also wanted to be prepared to discuss the best way to structure the cash flows of the swap transaction. MGL was willing to make future yen swap payments to RJR that perfectly coincided with the yen coupon and principal payments in order to eliminate any yen exposure. The initial yen payment from RJR would be the present value of these future yen swap payments to RJR discounted at the swap rate. One way to structure the dollar swap flows was to ''scale'' the initial dollar swap ''principal'' RJR would receive using a negotiated spot exchange rate and calculate RJR's future annual dollar payments by multiplying the dollar swap rate times this principal. In the final year, the total dollar payment made by RJR would consist of both the annual payment and the repayment of the swap principal.

As they began their evaluation of the dual-currency structure, the Morgan team realized the complexity of the analysis they would need to make. Furthermore, like most Eurobond proposals, the terms were probably good for a few hours only. Given RJR's tremendous need for financing, they certainly did not want to miss a potentially attractive opportunity.

EXHIBIT 1 CONSOLIDATED STATEMENTS OF EARNINGS AND EARNINGS RETAINED
(MILLIONS EXCEPT PER SHARE AMOUNTS)

	1984	1983	1982
Net sales	$12,974	$12,312	$10,160
Costs and expenses			
Cost of products sold	8,282	8,226	6,719
Selling, advertising, administrative, and general expenses	3,073	2,689	2,219
Earnings from continuing operations	1,619	1,397	1,222
Interest and debt expense (net of capitalized amounts of $29, $9, and $4, respectively)	(187)	(196)	(186)
Other income (expense), net	120	87	61
Earnings from continuing operations before provisions for income taxes	1,552	1,288	1,097
Provision for income taxes	709	586	513
Earnings after taxes	843	702	584
Extraordinary items	311	117	250
Net earnings applicable to common stock	1,154	819	834
Earnings retained at beginning of year	4,461	3,987	3,457
Less			
Cash dividends on common stock	360	345	304
Distribution of Sea-Land stock	540	—	—
Retirement of common stock	681	—	—
Earnings retained at end of year	$ 4,034	$ 4,461	$ 3,987
Net earnings per common share			
Continuing operations	$ 7.00	$ 5.66	$ 5.14
Discontinued operations	3.27	1.59	2.68
	$ 10.27	$ 7.25	$ 7.82
Average number of common shares outstanding (in thousands)	112,375	112,997	106,706

EXHIBIT 2   CONSOLIDATED BALANCE SHEETS—DECEMBER 31 (MILLIONS)

	1984	1983
Assets		
Current assets		
Cash and short-term investments	$1323	$ 363
Accounts and notes receivable (net)	1226	1344
Inventories	2493	2690
Prepaid expenses	72	64
Total current assets	5114	4461
Property, plant, and equipment—at cost	3760	3001
Less depreciation and amortization	(944)	(794)
Net property, plant, and equipment	2816	2207
Other assets	1342	2549
Total assets	$9272	$9217
Liabilities and stockholders' equity		
Current liabilities		
Note payable	$ 101	$ 132
Accounts payable and accrued accounts	1459	1205
Current maturities of long-term debt	227	38
Income taxes accrued	463	124
Total current liabilities	2250	1499
Long-term debt (less current maturities)	1257	1420
Other noncurrent liabilities	265	168
Deferred income taxes	523	276
Redeemable preferred stocks	499	631
Common stockholders' equity		
Common stock	255	280
Paid-in capital	344	585
Cumulative translation adjustments	(155)	(103)
Earnings retained	4034	4461
Total common stockholders' equity	4478	5223
Total liabilities and stockholders' equity	$9272	$9217

EXHIBIT 3   R.J. REYNOLDS GEOGRAPHIC DATA (MILLIONS)

	1984	1983	1982
Net sales			
United States	$10,216	$9,584	$7,753
Canada	628	566	548
Europe	1,336	1,383	1,146
Other geographic areas	1,194	1,117	1,038
Less transfer between geographic areas	(400)	(338)	(325)
Consolidated net sales	12,974	12,312	10,160
Earnings from continuing operations			
United States	1,464	1,297	1,172
Canada	53	44	44
Europe	46	37	32
Other geographic areas	150	110	50
Other (principally corporate expense)	(94)	(91)	(76)
Consolidated earnings from continuing operations	$ 1,619	$ 1,397	$ 1,222
Assets			
United States	$ 5,203	$ 4,443	$ 4,641
Canada	399	337	304
Europe	511	451	413
Other geographic areas	594	560	515
Corporate	2,565	1,977	1,517
Net assets of discontinued operations	—	1,449	1,850
Consolidated assets	$ 9,272	$ 9,217	$ 9,240
Liabilities of company's continuing operations located in foreign countries	$ 832	$ 844	$ 729

EXHIBIT 4 NABISCO BRANDS, INC.–CONSOLIDATED STATEMENT OF INCOME
(MILLIONS EXCEPT PER SHARE DATA)

	1984	1983	1982
Net sales	$6253	$5985	$5871
Cost of sales	3939	3730	3700
Gross profit	2314	2255	2171
Selling, general, and administrative expenses	1735	1627	1597
Operating income	579	628	574
Interest expense	77	77	90
Miscellaneous (income) expense, net	(27)	(15)	(39)
Income before income taxes	529	566	523
Income taxes			
Current			
United States	86	90	75
Foreign	75	78	74
State and local	19	13	20
Deferred	40	62	39
Total income taxes	220	243	208
Net income	$ 309	$ 323	$ 315
Net income per common share	$ 5.03	$ 4.87	$ 4.84
Dividends declared per common share	$ 2.48	$ 2.28	$ 2.05
Average common shares outstanding (in thousands)	61,486	66,310	65,026

EXHIBIT 5   NABISCO BRANDS, INC.—CONSOLIDATED BALANCE SHEET–DECEMBER 31 (MILLIONS)

	1984	1983
Assets		
Current assets		
Cash and short-term investments	$ 268	$ 251
Accounts receivable (net)	604	621
Inventories	766	766
Prepaid expenses	29	25
Total current assets	1667	1663
Property, plant, and equipment	2459	2376
Less depreciation	(913)	(868)
Other assets (net)	548	455
	$3761	$3626
Liabilities and stockholders' equity		
Current liabilities		
Notes payable	$ 27	$ 39
Accounts payable and accrued expenses	923	924
Current maturities of long-term debt	33	42
Income taxes accrued	54	74
Total current liabilities	1037	1079
Long-term debt	682	482
Other liabilities and minority interests	205	110
Deferred income taxes	292	244
Redeemable preferred stocks	2	2
Common stockholders' equity		
Common stock	139	139
Paid-in capital	277	276
Cumulative translation adjustments	1837	1680
Earnings retained	(215)	(151)
Less treasury stock at cost	(495)	(235)
Total common stockholders' equity	1543	1709
	$3761	$3626

EXHIBIT 6   NABISCO GEOGRAPHIC DATA (MILLIONS)

	1984	1983	1982
Net sales			
United States	$3950	$3622	$3491
Canada	721	732	639
Europe	1102	1138	782
Latin America	290	298	374
Asia/Pacific	190	195	178
Other			407
Consolidated net sales	6253	5985	5871
Earnings from continuing operations			
United States	451	475	438
Canada	61	67	60
Europe	78	81	67
Latin America	53	58	57
Asia/Pacific	10	13	12
Other (principally corporate expense)	(63)	(66)	(60)
Consolidated earnings from continuing operations	$ 590	$ 628	$ 574
Assets			
United States	$1730	$1659	$1541
Canada	373	376	415
Europe	791	822	819
Latin America	197	191	259
Asia/Pacific	119	136	120
Corporate	551	442	770
Consolidated assets	$3761	$3626	$3924

EXHIBIT 7   SUMMARY OF 5-YEAR EUROBOND TERMS AVAILABLE TO R.J. REYNOLDS

	Dollar Eurobonds	Yen Eurobonds	Yen/dollar dual-currency Eurobonds
Face value	$100 million	¥25 billion	¥25 billion
Price	100.125%	100.250%	101.500%
Fees	1.875%	1.875%	1.875%
Coupon (paid annually)	10.125%	6.375%	7.750%
Final redemption	Par	Par	$115.956 million

EXHIBIT 8 LONG-DATED YEN/DOLLAR FORWARD EXCHANGE RATES (FORWARDS ARRANGED BY NIKKO SECURITIES)

Year	Outright Rates	
	Bid	Offer
0	236.80*	236.90
1	231.30	231.70
2	223.90	225.90
3	215.60	218.70
4	207.10	211.20
5	197.60	202.70

*Bid and offer rates are quoted from the perspective of the market-making dealer. For example, a dealer bank would buy a dollar from a corporation in exchange for selling to it 236.80 yen. Similarly, the bank would sell a dollar to a corporation in exchange for buying from it 236.90 yen.

EXHIBIT 9 CURRENCY AND INTEREST RATE SWAP INDICATIONS (ALL RATES ARE AGAINST 6-MONTH DOLLAR LIBOR)

	Semiannual quotations		Benchmark U.S. Treasury, %	Semiannual fixed rates against 6-month dollar LIBOR, %		Annual fixed rates against 6-month dollar LIBOR, %	
	Pay	Receive		Pay*	Receive	Pay	Receive
5-Year dollar rates†	T+60	T+76	9.88%	10.48%	10.64%	10.75%	10.92%
5-Year yen rates				6.98%	7.22%	7.10%	7.35%

*All rates are quoted from the perspective of the bank offering the swap—that is, a bank would agree to pay semiannual fixed dollars at 10.48 percent against receiving semiannual 6-month dollar LIBOR. Similarly, the bank would agree to receive semiannual fixed dollars at 10.64 percent against paying semiannual 6-month dollar LIBOR.
†T represents the semiannual yield on 5-year U.S. Treasury securities.

EXHIBIT 10   ANNUAL ALL-IN COSTS ON CASH FLOWS FROM 5-YEAR EUROYEN BOND WITH YEN/DOLLAR SWAP*

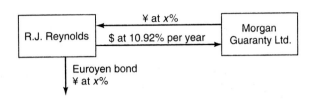

*The internal rate of return of the yen cash flows from both the Euroyen bond and the yen swap is represented by x and the dollar equivalent of the excess yen basis points is represented by y.

INTERNATIONAL PHARMACEUTICALS INCORPORATED

John Smiley, assistant treasurer of International Pharmaceuticals Incorporated (IPI), sat in his Manhattan office following a meeting with representatives of the Morgan Guaranty Trust Company in September 1986. IPI had decided in January 1986 to expand the plant facility of La Compañía de Píldora, S.A., a subsidiary based in Mexico City. Traditionally Mr. Smiley's company would have used intercompany trade credit to finance the project. Morgan, however, suggested that IPI might save as much as $1,580,000 on a $5,000,000 project if they financed the expansion through a debt-for-equity swap. The swap involved buying Mexican government external dollar debt at a discount, redeeming the debt at the Mexican Central Bank for pesos (MP), and investing these pesos in the subsidiary.

As he thought about his decision, Mr. Smiley could not help but recall what Richard L. Huber, a group executive at Citibank, had said about these deals: "We think everybody ends up a winner. The country has its total foreign debt reduced. Investment funds are pumped into the economy. And the seller of the debt gets liquidity."[1] Mr. Smiley had to decide within the week which form of financing best fit IPI's needs.

COMPANY BACKGROUND

International Pharmaceuticals Incorporated, founded in 1933, produced a wide array of pharmaceuticals and consumer household products. Incorporated in New York, IPI

---

[1]*The New York Times,* September 11, 1986, p. D5.

This case was prepared by Research Associate Richard P. Melnick and Professor W. Carl Kester. Copyright © 1987 by the President and Fellows of Harvard College. Harvard Business School case 288-011.

was the parent company of numerous subsidiaries that manufactured products in thirty-nine countries for distribution and sale throughout the world. The company typically had little leverage and was characterized by a conservative corporate culture and centralized financial management. IPI's success over a period of years was demonstrated in its recent financial statements, which appear in **Exhibit 1**.

The corporation was divided into ten domestic/international divisions and four separate international divisions. IPI had been in Mexico since 1951, where several of its divisions had subsidiaries. La Compañía de Pildora, S.A. was a 100-percent-owned subsidiary that reported to the Rolan International Division. Based in Mexico City, La Compañía de Pildora had a plant that manufactured oral contraceptive products, nutritional products, and veterinary products, all for domestic consumption. The subsidiary had expected 1986 sales of MP10 billion, or about $10 million.

THE LATIN AMERICAN DEBT PROBLEM

The debt-for-equity swap proposed by Morgan had its roots in the broader Latin American debt problem. This, in turn, had its origin in the 1973 oil shock. Following the surge in the dollar price of oil, many OPEC (Organization of Petroleum Exporting Countries) nations deposited their dollar surpluses in Western money-center banks. This influx of deposits made credit a borrower's market, prompting many major banks to turn to the less developed countries (LDCs) to increase profitability. Banks had lost few loans to the LDCs since the 1930s, spreads on loans to the LDCs were more attractive than on loans to developed countries, and new funds in the LDCs would support export-oriented growth that began in the 1960s. During the recovery from the 1973 shock, LDC exports rose to the point where, in 1978, current account deficits decreased in borrowing countries.

When the second oil shock hit in 1979, the situation was quite different. Billions of dollars flowed into Western banks, but by this time, the LDCs already had multibillion-dollar debts. Most post-1979 borrowing was short-term, which contributed substantially to the subsequent LDC debt problems. Many country officials in the LDCs believed inflation would increase commodity prices while decreasing real interest rates, thus lowering the cost of their dollar debt. To their dismay, the reverse scenario ensued. While inflation dropped, U.S. interest rates remained relatively high, attracting capital and driving up the value of the dollar. The combination of expensive dollar-denominated loans and low commodity prices drove the debt-service ratios for average Latin American borrowers to 125 percent of exports in 1982. This scenario placed enormous pressures on the LDCs and finally, in 1982, Mexico announced that it could not make its debt-service payments.

By 1984 Latin American debt totaled $450 billion. About 15 percent of this was short-term trade financing, 30 percent was owed to governments or international organizations, and commercial banks held the remaining 55 percent. As the problem spread, banks began to search for solutions. Restructuring instead of rescheduling loans might give the LDCs enough flexibility to stimulate their exports. Some analysts recommended increased funding from the IMF or other international agencies, which would then allow a transfer of some debt from private to public sources.

EVOLUTION OF DEBT-FOR-EQUITY SWAPS

While banks searched for a solution to the LDC-debt problem, an interbank swap market for LDC debt emerged in 1983 as one private-sector means of controlling exposure to LDC debt. Bankers Trust was one of the most active players in this market, executing twelve deals that year. In their largest deal, Bankers Trust traded $90 million in cash and $100 million in Brazilian debt for $190 million in Mexican debt from the Brazilian Banco Real. With this deal, illiquid sovereign credits of international banks began trading in a secondary market. There were many incentives stimulating these transactions. One incentive was to increase or decrease exposure to a particular country. Bankers Trust, for example, reduced its loans to Brazil by $149 million and increased its loans to Mexico by $235 million in the third quarter of 1983. Occasionally banks were willing to leverage down their loans by swapping higher-quality public loans for private paper and cash. These deals also allowed banks to improve their balance sheets by trading up or consolidating positions without taking the write-downs on the loans that Congress and regulators demanded if the loans were actually sold. In addition to Latin American and American banks, Middle Eastern and European banks also put some of their loans up for swaps (see **Exhibit 2** for major U.S. banks' exposure to Mexico).

These deals, however, raised banking, accounting, and regulatory questions. Perhaps the most important issue was valuation. The banks' loan portfolios were accounted for under the assumption that loans would mature at full face value. In 1983 the U.S. comptroller of the currency and the Federal Reserve Board decreed write-offs for certain loans ranging from 10 percent to 75 percent. When a loan was sold or swapped, the difference between historical and market values had to be recorded as a gain or loss. Swaps posed a problem because it was difficult to value an exchange of, say, Chilean for Brazilian debt. If, for example, a bank sold 30 percent of its Mexican debt at a 20 percent discount, should that bank have to write down the remaining 70 percent? Such concerns discouraged banks from doing these deals on a larger scale. Moreover, the interbank swapping of loans only helped individual banks to optimize their portfolios. Swapping did not reduce the overall exposure of the banking system as a whole to LDC debt, nor did it do much to solve the LDC-debt problem itself.

A novel idea for tackling the LDC-debt problem, and an early precursor to the modern debt-for-equity swap, emerged when Congress passed the 1982 Export Trading Companies Act (ETC). This act gave banks the ability to own equity in export trading companies that took title to goods for resale. Once a bank created an ETC, it could place its outstanding loans to an LDC company in the ETC at par value. In exchange, the ETC would be entitled to receive a percentage of the LDC company's exports, which the ETC would sell in the United States and the international market. Principal would be repaid from profits from the sales. Yet, because of their complexity and bank inexperience with commodity trading, these deals were never very popular.

In 1983 the Brazilian government established a debt conversion plan in which $1.8 billion was converted into equity invested locally. This plan differed from subsequent developments in other countries in that it was unofficial and only added capital to existing projects. No new projects were stimulated by the plan. By 1984 Brazil terminated this plan reportedly because it was embarrassed to be dealing in its own debt, which was selling at a deep discount.[2]

THE MODERN DEBT-FOR-EQUITY SWAP PROGRAMS

Debt-for-equity swaps of the type proposed to Mr. Smiley were among the most popular deals being executed in 1986. Chile's program appeared to be the most successful on the basis of the extent to which it was imitated by other LDCs, though Mexico's was the biggest. Mexico's first deal involved the Nissan Motor Company's purchase of $60 million worth of Mexican government debt for $40 million, resale of the debt to the Mexican central bank for $54 million worth of pesos, and the investment of the pesos in its Mexican subsidiary. These capitalization schemes seemed popular with everyone. From the debtor country's perspective, it retired hard-currency debts at a discount while promoting local investment. Commercial banks could take some bad loans off their books while investment banks or commercial banks could earn substantial fees (generally 1 percent of original face value) acting as financial intermediaries in these deals. Multinationals liked them because they could increase their equity stake in the LDCs at greatly reduced cost.

LDC nationals who repatriated flight capital were another group that benefited from these swaps. Residents withdrew significant capital during the early 1980s, and this "flight capital" continued during the 1983 to 1985 period of "involuntary lending." Creditors hesitated to lend new funds until debtor nations stopped capital flight. The data shown in **Exhibit 3** indicate the potentially favorable impact that repatriation might have on the capital flows of various debtor nations. If aggregate foreign assets of residents were repatriated and yielded 6 percent, the earnings would generate enough foreign exchange to pay the interest on one-third of total LDC external debt.[3] The discount these swaps provided enticed locals, particularly in Chile, to repatriate flight capital.

The basic plan underlying these deals was straightforward. A financial intermediary acting on behalf of a multinational bought LDC debt from a commercial bank (usually an American or European) at a discount, paying, say, 65 cents on the dollar (see **Exhibit 4** for discount prices for LDC debt). After presenting the debt certificate to the LDC central bank for redemption, the intermediary would receive, say, 85 cents worth of local currency for each dollar. The central bank, representing the government of the LDC, retired the debt. The intermediary then had to turn the money over to the

[2]*Institutional Investor,* February 1987, p. 180.
[3]*World Financial Markets* (Morgan Guaranty Trust Company, New York, September 1986), p. 6.

multinational that would invest it in the local economy. Though the intermediary could use cash for the initial debt purchase, the intermediary usually started a chain of deals that involved swapping other foreign debt with banks from other countries. Thus, these swaps were seldom as simple and straightforward as they appeared on paper.

The Chilean Program

The rules governing swaps varied from one country to the next. Chile's conversion program was the most active because it had the fewest restrictions and the clearest regulations. By September 1986 Chile had executed twenty-six swaps totaling $280 million. Finance Minister Hernán Buchi was aiming for $2 billion by the middle of 1987, which would represent 10 percent of Chile's $21 billion debt. Chapter 19 of Chile's foreign debt compendium placed a 4-year deferral period on dividends for equity that had been converted from debt. After 4 years, dividends could still only be remitted at 25 percent of net profits.

The Mexican Program

As of September 1986, Mexico had executed twenty-three deals worth $300 million, with the expectation of doing $1.2 billion more in the next 12 months. A major reason for Mexico's success was that the government dismantled many important obstacles to foreign investment. The regulation of the capitalization plan appeared in Clause 5.11 of the Agreement on the Restructure of Foreign Debt (the text of Clause 5.11 appears in **Exhibit 5**). Whereas investors previously had to win approval from various ministries before they could start operating in Mexico, now approval from the Ministry of Finance (Hacienda) was sufficient. Mexico usually redeemed debt at between 70 percent and 100 percent of face value. The redemption rate depended upon how the pesos were to be used and the difference between the free and controlled exchange rates (see **Exhibit 6**). The best redemption prices were given for new investments or capital expansions that created jobs and helped the trade balance. Analysts expressed some reservations about these swaps because the approval process for each deal was often cumbersome and arbitrary.

The Argentine and Philippine Programs

Under pressure to allow swaps, the Argentine government reluctantly announced a swap program that required investors to bring in additional foreign exchange equal to the face value of the debt being converted. This restriction and other regulations were likely to keep swaps limited in Argentina.

Debt-for-equity swap programs were also becoming popular outside Latin America. The Philippine government approved a comprehensive and attractive swap program under which it hoped to reduce its debt by $1.5 billion. Investment was allowed in almost every sector of the economy. Debt traded at discounts between 20 percent and 35 percent and was redeemed at face value less a conversion charge of 5 percent to 10 percent.

Nobody saw debt-for-equity swaps as a panacea for the LDC debt problem. Optimists hoped that the program could eliminate 15 percent of the global debt. Shearson senior vice president Christine Bindert concluded, ''If nearly $50 billion can be done through debt-equity [swaps] over the next 10–15 years, which could happen if full-scale privatization programs take place, the debt mess could be that much easier.''[4]

MEXICO AND THE CLIMATE FOR INVESTMENT

The Mexican peso was devalued in 1954 from MP8.65 to MP12.50 per U.S. dollar and remained at that level until 1976. A combination of confidential bank accounts and political stability in the 1960s maintained the solid peso and led to economic growth. Mexico avoided the currency crises of the early 1970s and, at times, the IMF actually used the stable peso to support other major currencies.

Problems began shortly after the discovery of major oil deposits. In 1973 the Foreign Investment Law was passed, which placed restrictions on foreign investment and led to reductions in investment and economic expansion. Consumer prices rose 76 percent between 1970 and 1975 as massive foreign borrowing kept the country solvent. By 1976 the peso was devalued by 43 percent, prompting capital flight. Mexico abandoned fiscal restraint in 1979 in an effort to expand production and create jobs. With the help of large foreign loans in 1980, the economy expanded. In 1981, however, inflation was out of control and the economy dependent upon sagging oil prices, and in 1982 the deficit- and debt-ridden economy collapsed. Massive capital flight emptied the Mexican treasury's foreign exchange coffers. International banks assembled a $10 billion rescue package when Mexico declared a moratorium on foreign debt payments.

Despite Mexico's drastic austerity program and an 80 percent devaluation of the peso in 1982, the economy's problems continued. By 1986 the central problems facing Mexico were the declining oil industry, a foreign debt that grew from $15 billion to $96 billion in 10 years, and rapid 2.5 percent population growth. Oil sales, representing 70 percent of Mexico's export income, dropped in half because of falling oil prices. The devastating Mexico City earthquake of 1985 took 10,000 lives and left 150,000 more people unemployed. Data Resources, Inc., said at the start of 1986 that conditions in Mexico ''. . . were somewhat similar to [those of] 1982. Now, as then, the foreign sector is in disarray, inflation has escalated rapidly, and the budget deficit has escalated to record levels.''[5] Both inflation and interest rates were expected to reach 100 percent by the end of 1986. Though the peso's value fell from MP27 per dollar in January 1982 to MP250 per dollar in June 1985, the next 12 months saw it fall even further. By November 1985 there were MP500 to the dollar, and in June 1986 the peso fell 30 percent in 6 days until it stood at MP727.[6]

---

[4]*Institutional Investor,* February 1987, p. 180.

[5]*American Banker,* January 9, 1986, p. 2.

[6]The plunge occurred in the ''free'' exchange rate, which represented only 20 percent of Mexico's currency transactions. The regulated floating rate, used for imports and exports, accounted for the other 80 percent. This rate was set by the central bank and stood at MP545.70.

As a response to the chronic devaluation, the government provided monetary investments that could be used as a hedge. Companies could keep their money in short-term Treasury Certificates (Cetes), which paid close to 100 percent interest by mid-1986 (see **Exhibits 7** and **8** for Cetes rates and other economic data for Mexico). Another option was Federation Treasury Bills (Pagafes), created by the government in July 1986. These 6-month instruments were denominated in dollars and yielded "dollar" interest, but were actually bought and redeemed in pesos, and paid interest in pesos, using a controlled exchange rate (see **Exhibit 8**). In effect, they were Mexican peso instruments designed to provide a total annual peso yield equivalent to the peso's percentage devaluation against the dollar plus some market-determined dollar interest rate appropriate for Mexican government debt.

FINANCING LA COMPAÑÍA DE PILDORA'S PROJECT

By early 1986, La Compañía de Pildora's plant operated at capacity. With demand expected to grow, IPI had the choice of expanding its capacity in Mexico or allowing market share to erode. The company eventually decided to expand its facility in Mexico City by building a new floor covering 2500 square meters and renovating the main floor.

Mr. Smiley's responsibility was to determine the best means of financing the project. IPI's traditional means of financing subsidiaries was intercompany trade credit. La Compañía de Pildora would record its purchases from IPI as an account payable, while IPI would record the transaction as an account receivable. Although ostensibly short-term, the payable owned to the parent could, in fact, remain outstanding until the subsidiary had enough cash to repay IPI. Other alternatives included intercompany dollar debt at prime plus 2 percent (the prime rate in September 1986 was 7.5 percent), a revolving credit arrangement (from either a foreign or local bank), and straight equity from the parent to be invested as required.

As in any subsidiary financing, tax considerations were also a factor in Mr. Smiley's choice of financing methods. The prevailing tax rates were those shown in **Table 1**. Though profitable, La Compañía de Pildora had not remitted a dividend to the parent since 1982.

TABLE 1	MEXICAN TAX RATES	
Mexican corporate tax rate		42%
Mexican withholding tax rate on dividends		55%
Mexican withholding tax rate on intercompany loan interest		42%
Mexican withholding tax rate on bank loan interest		15%
Parent tax rate		46%

A representative of the Morgan bank had recommended that IPI finance La Compañía de Pildora's expansion through a Mexican debt-for-equity swap. Mr.

Smiley met his Morgan counterpart on several occasions and thought he understood how the process worked. With the help of Morgan, La Compañía de Pildora would submit an application to Hacienda to finance the project through the swap. Upon approval of the application (which could be granted if Hacienda were satisfied with La Compañía de Pildora's profit and performance forecasts), IPI would have Morgan purchase $5,700,000 face value of Mexican government debt from a commercial bank at a discount of approximately 40 percent, or $3,420,000 net cost. La Compañía de Pildora would present the $5,700,000 debt certificates to the Mexican central bank for redemption at approximately 88 percent of the face value or $5,000,000 in pesos, converted at the free rate on that day. The discount the Mexican government would offer would depend upon the expected contribution of the project to the economy (refer to **Exhibit 6** for a description of discounts from face value by type of project).

Since the proposed project spanned 18 months, the government would set up a peso deposit for the subsidiary at the central bank. Instead of receiving all the pesos up front, La Compañía de Pildora would submit receipts and pro formas allowing it to draw down the pesos as needed (the schedule of planned expenditures for the capitalization program appears in **Exhibit 9**). To offset potential losses from devaluation, the central bank would pay a substantial interest rate on the funds in the account. Money in the account would either earn the Cetes rate (i.e., Mexican T-bill) or the Pagafe rate (i.e., the Mexican peso's annualized rate of devaluation against the dollar plus an appropriate dollar yield for Mexican government debt). Once La Compañía de Pildora received the peso payment from the central bank, Clause 5.11 stipulated that La Compañía de Pildora had to issue "Qualified Capital Stock" to IPI. The restrictions on Qualified Capital Stock appear in **Exhibit 5** along with the text of Clause 5.11.[7]

Mr. Smiley sent a description of this swap to IPI's legal department. Ray Edwards, an IPI lawyer who had studied Latin American problems for 25 years, urged Mr. Smiley *not* to undertake the proposed deal. Mr. Edwards had two major concerns. First he feared that the Mexican government might renege on the deal. A new government that might not recognize debts of the previous administration could come to power at any time. Furthermore, he expressed uncertainty about this program because it was implemented by an agency of the Mexican government rather than being enacted through the legislative process.

Another factor mitigating enthusiasm for the proposed deal was the sheer complexity of the transaction. Besides IPI and Morgan, other parties such as a foreign creditor bank and a Mexican bank would have to be involved. Ultimately, as many as eight separate parties would have to be signatories to the swap. This complexity is reflected in the schematic diagram shown in **Exhibit 10**.

---

[7]IPI had two accounting alternatives for this transaction. It could credit $3.42 million from cash and debit $3.42 million to fixed assets. Alternatively, IPI could credit cash $3.42 million, debit fixed assets $5 million, and recognize a $1.58 million gain on the transaction. For its part, under either alternative, La Compañía de Pildora would debit fixed assets $5 million and credit $5 million to Qualified Capital Stock.

THE DECISION

The debt-for-equity swap was attractive for many reasons, but particularly because of the expected savings of more than a million dollars for IPI. Yet the legal department's concerns and other complicating factors gave Mr. Smiley pause for thought. He had only a short time in which to weigh the conflicting advice and decide which financing method to use.

EXHIBIT 1   RECENT FINANCIAL HISTORY (MILLIONS, EXCEPT RATIOS AND PER SHARE DATA)

	1980	1981	1982	1983	1984	1985
Sales, $	2532.3	2754.1	3054.7	3237.7	2990.3	3123.1
Operating margin, %	22.0	23.1	23.9	24.8	26.4	26.7
Depreciation, $	32.9	35.9	48.5	63.7	62.4	64.5
Net profit, $	297.3	331.5	386.7	418.1	437.2	478.1
Income tax rate, %	46.1	47.4	45.7	44.8	44.2	40.8
Common shares outstanding	155.54	155.07	155.86	155.87	152.00	150.89
Earnings per share, $	1.91	2.14	2.48	2.68	2.88	3.17
Dividends declared per share, $	1.13	1.27	1.43	1.60	1.76	1.93
Working capital, $	783.4	892.7	757.5	905.3	959.8	1075.8
Long-term debt, $	0	0	0	0	0	0
Net worth, $	981.9	1103.0	1229.1	1365.9	1392.4	1527.9
Net profit margin, %	11.7	12.0	12.7	12.9	14.6	15.3
Earned net worth, %	30.3	30.1	31.5	30.6	31.4	31.3
Dividend payout, %	59.8	59.9	59.8	59.9	62.0	61.7

EXHIBIT 2   MAJOR U.S. BANKS' EXPOSURE TO MEXICO IN 1985 (MILLIONS, EXCEPT RATIOS)

Bank	Total assets	Net worth	Return on net worth	Total loans to Mexico 1985	Mexican loans/ total assets	Mexican loans/ net worth
BankAmerica	$118,541	$4547	(7.4)%	2700	2.3%	59%
Bankers Trust	50,581	2495	14.9	1277	2.5	51
Chase Manhattan	87,685	3795	14.9	1700	1.9	45
Chemical Bank	56,990	2820	13.8	1500	2.6	53
Citicorp	173,597	7765	12.9	2800	1.6	36
Manufacturers Hanover	76,526	3547	11.5	1800	2.4	51
Morgan Guaranty	69,375	4392	16.1	1152	1.7	26

Sources: The New York Times, July 23, 1986, p. D1, and bank annual reports.

EXHIBIT 3   POTENTIAL IMPACT OF CAPITAL REPATRIATION

External Assets and Debt of Selected Debtor Nations (billions, at end 1985)

	Assets			Gross debt
	Total	Banking system*	Other	
Argentina	$33	$ 7	$26	$ 49
Brazil	30	19	11	106
Mexico	60	6	54	97
Venezuela	54	19	35	38
Philippines	10	3	7	26
Nigeria	12	2	10	20

*Official reserves (including gold) and foreign assets of domestic banks.

Potential Contribution of Earnings Repatriation to Debt Service (Billions and percent)

	Earnings at 6% on nonbanking foreign assets	1986 interest payments on external debt	Earnings as a % of payments
Argentina	$1.6	$ 4.3	37%
Brazil	0.7	8.9	8
Mexico	3.2	8.3	39
Venezuela	2.1	2.9	73
Philippines	0.4	2.0	22
Nigeria	0.6	1.1	53
Total	$8.6	$27.5	31

Source: World Financial Markets (New York: Morgan Guaranty Trust Company, September 1986), p. 6.

EXHIBIT 4   DISCOUNT PRICES FOR DEBT ISSUED
BY LESS DEVELOPED COUNTRIES
(AS OF JULY 1986; NUMBERS ARE A
PERCENTAGE OF FACE VALUE)

Poland	45%
Mexico	56
Ecuador	65
Argentina	66
Chile	67
Venezuela	75
Brazil	76
Yugoslavia	80
Colombia	83
Romania	90

Source: Euromoney, August 1986, p. 71.

EXHIBIT 5   EXCERPTS FROM THE AGREEMENT ON THE RESTRUCTURE OF FOREIGN DEBT

SECTION 5.11. Capitalization of Credits. (a) General. Subject to written agreement between the Obligor and any Bank and subject to all required Mexican governmental authorizations, including authorization by the Ministry of Finance and Public Credit, the National Commission on Foreign Investment and the Ministry of Foreign Relations of the United Mexican States, all or a portion of the Credits held by such Bank may be exchanged for Qualified Capital Stock. The Obligor and such Bank will promptly notify the Servicing Bank in writing of any such agreement that has been so authorized, which notice shall specify each Credit (or portion thereof) to be exchanged for such Qualified Capital Stock. Upon delivery of such Qualified Capital Stock by or on behalf of the Obligor to such Bank or its designee, (i) each Credit (or portion thereof) in respect of which such Qualified Capital Stock is delivered shall cease to be a "Credit" and "External Indebtedness" for all purposes of this Agreement and the Obligor shall have no further obligations in respect of any such Credit (or portion thereof) and (ii) the Obligor and such Bank shall deliver to the Servicing Bank a Correction Notice reducing the principal amount of each such Credit by the principal amount exchanged for such Qualified Capital Stock.

(b) Qualified Capital Stock. For purposes of this Section, "Qualified Capital Stock" means capital stock of any Mexican public sector entity or Mexican private sector company (i) which is issued in registered, certificated form in the name of such Bank or a Person designated by such Bank which is not a Mexican Entity (as defined below), (ii) which is not transferable on the registration books of such public sector entity or private sector company before January 1, 1998 to any Mexican Entity and the Certificate of which bears a legend with such restriction, (iii) which is not by its terms subject to redemption on a basis more favorable to such Bank or its designee than the amortization of the Credit or Credits exchanged for such capital stock, (iv) which is not entitled to guaranteed dividends payable irrespective of earnings and profits, except as expressly contemplated by Article 123 of the Ley General de Sociedades Mercantiles, and (v) which is not convertible into any instrument or security other than Qualified Capital Stock. As used herein, the term "Mexican Entity" means any Person who, in the case of an individual, is a resident of or, in the case of an entity, has its principal place of business in the United Mexican States.

Source: Operating Manual for Capitalization of Liabilities and Substitution of Public Debt by Investment (Mexico City: Mexican Ministry of Finance and Public Credit, and the National Commission of Foreign Investment, 1986).

EXHIBIT 6   MEXICAN DISCOUNTS FOR DEBT/EQUITY SWAPS

Category	Discount, %	Conditions
0	0	Buy government corporations that Mexico wants to sell.
1	5	New corporations, expansions, or activities in which 80% of production is exported. Corporations located within certain locations. New firms with state-of-the-art technology.
2	8	New corporations or expansions where 50% of production is exported. Firms working in priority sectors of the economy, and generating foreign exchange. Projects with national integration levels comparable to similar firms'.
3	12	Firms with state-of-the-art technology. Projects at a late stage of development. New firms or product lines with at least 30% exports.
4	13	Buy corporation with balance-of-payments deficit. Corporation is self-sufficient in foreign exchange.
5	14	Project that improves the negative trade balance of a firm. Expansion reduces liabilities to domestic suppliers.
6	15	Incomplete capitalization or prepayment to FICORCA* of local debt.
7	16	Full payment to FICORCA* of local debt.
8	25	No foreign exchange generation.

*Fideicomiso para la Cobertura de Riesgos Cambiarios, that is, the Mexican Trust for Coverage of Foreign Exchange Risks.

EXHIBIT 7   MEXICAN ECONOMIC DATA (BILLIONS, EXCEPT RATIOS AND INDEXES)

	1980	1981	1982	1983	1984	1985
Gross domestic product						
(1980 prices), $	186.3	201.1	200.1	189.6	196.2	202.0
Wholesale price index (WPI)	100.0	124.4	194.2	402.7	686.0	1053.4
Consumer price index (CPI)	100.0	127.9	203.3	410.2	679.0	1071.2
Relative prices, Mexican/U.S.:						
WPI	1.00	1.16	1.74	3.57	5.94	9.17
CPI	1.00	1.16	1.74	3.39	5.38	8.21
Treasury bill rate, %	22.46	30.77	45.75	59.19	49.47	63.36
Exports, $	23.9	29.4	26.1	27.1	30.4	26.6
−% oil and related, %	43.6	49.5	63.0	59.0	54.6	55.7
Imports, $	26.3	34.4	20.2	12.8	16.2	18.6
Trade balance, $	(2.4)	(5.0)	5.9	14.3	14.2	8.0
Total external debt, $	41.0	52.9	59.5	82.3	87.5	98.0
Debt service/exports, %	33.1	34.8	44.3	43.7	48.6	54.7
Exchange rates, MP/$:						
Controlled rate	23.26	26.23	96.48	143.93	192.56	371.70
Floating rate	na	na	149.25	161.35	209.97	450.75

Sources: *International Financial Statistics,* World Bank data, and *The Economist Quarterly Review of Mexico.*

EXHIBIT 8   CETES AND PAGAFE YIELDS (ANNUALIZED RATES OF RETURN)

Cetes

Month (1986)	Annualized MP yield
January	73.80%
February	75.70
March	78.47
April	80.52
May	80.46
June	84.00
July	91.11
August	94.70
September	98.37

Pagafes*

Issue	Maturity date	Annualized dollar yield†	Total issued, $ thousands	Sold to public, $ thousands
8/21/86	2/19/87	8.64%	$70,000	$40,000
8/28/86	2/26/87	13.66	45,000	39,510
9/04/86	3/05/87	15.96	18,000	3,910
9/11/86	3/12/87	16.66	19,000	8,770
9/18/86	3/19/87	18.78	23,000	12,820
9/25/86	3/26/87	21.94	21,000	1,070

*The controlled exchange rate averaged MP665 for the month of August and ended at MP695.7. In the month of September, the controlled rate averaged MP725 and ended at MP751.6. The freely floating rate for August averaged MP682 and ended at MP714.5, and for September, averaged MP743 and ended at MP765.5.

†Annualized 6-month yields on U.S. T-bills at each corresponding issue date are as follows:

Date	Yield
8/21/86	5.44%
8/28/86	5.32
9/04/86	5.26
9/11/86	5.43
9/18/86	5.43
9/25/86	5.34

EXHIBIT 9

LA COMPAÑÍA DE PILDORA, S.A., SCHEDULE OF PLANNED EXPENDITURES UNDER CAPITALIZATION OF CREDITS PROGRAM*

	Project cost, $	Peso equivalent at estimated MP900/$1.00	Paid prior to Oct. 1, 1986	Oct. 1986	Nov. 1986	Dec. 1986	Jan. 1987	Feb. 1987	Mar. 1987	Apr. 1987	May 1987	Jun. 1987
				Monthly outlays, MP thousands								
Engineering and construction management†	154,000	138,600	20,000	—	—	—	27,600	2,600	27,600	2,600	24,400	2,600
Building construction‡	1,409,500	1,268,550	34,000	—	450,000	35,000	35,000	35,000	155,550	35,000	35,000	35,000
Building equipment§	2,339,400	2,105,460	10,000	—	800,000	100,000	60,000	155,460	55,000	55,000	55,000	155,000
Manufacturing equipment¶	1,097,100	987,390	—	—	—	—	—	—	329,390	329,000	329,000	—
Total project cost	5,000,000	4,500,000	64,000	—	1,250,000	135,000	122,600	193,060	567,540	421,600	443,400	192,600

	Jul. 1987	Aug. 1987	Sep. 1987	Oct. 1987	Nov. 1987	Dec. 1987	Jan. 1988	Feb. 1988	Mar. 1988	Apr. 1988	May 1988	Jun. 1988
	Monthly outlays, MP thousands											
Engineering and construction management†	2,600	2,600	2,600	2,600	2,600	2,600	2,600	2,600	2,600	2,600	2,600	2,600
Building construction‡	35,000	35,000	35,000	35,000	35,000	35,000	35,000	35,000	35,000	35,000	35,000	35,000
Building equipment§	55,000	55,000	55,000	55,000	55,000	55,000	55,000	55,000	55,000	55,000	55,000	55,000
Manufacturing equipment¶	—	—	—	—	—	—	—	—	—	—	—	—
Total project cost	92,600	92,600	92,600	92,600	92,600	92,600	92,600	92,600	92,600	92,600	92,600	92,600

*The Schedule of Planned Expenditures includes allowances for estimated cost inflation during the construction period. The exchange rate of MP900/$1.00 represents the average expected controlled rate at which dollars could be exchanged for pesos over the anticipated construction period.
†Fees for design and layout, drawings, and on-site management.
‡Cost of physical construction including demolition and land improvement.
§Air-conditioning, electrical, water treatment, plumbing, and related building services.
¶Pharmaceutical manufacturing equipment.

EXHIBIT 10   SCHEMATIC DIAGRAM OF DEBT/EQUITY SWAP

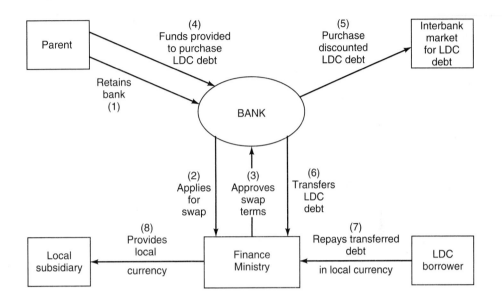

FIAT—1986

On September 23, 1986, executives of Deutsche Bank Capital Markets (DBCM) in London and Mediobanca in Italy were preparing to sell $2.1 billion of Fiat S.p.A. stock in the largest Euro-equity offering to date. Mr. Giovanni Agnelli, chairman of Fiat and a member of the family that controlled 32 percent of the company, had announced that day that Colonel Qaddafi's Libyan government had agreed to sell its 15.2 percent holding in Fiat. The sale was important to Mr. Agnelli because the presence of two Libyans on his board of directors had stigmatized the company in some circles and prevented Fiat from bidding for Strategic Defense Initiative (SDI) contracts in the United States.

The total sale of shares by Libya amounted to $3.2 billion. Istituto Finanziario Industriale (IFI), a private company controlled by the Agnelli family, was the initial buyer of the Libyan package. However, as became clear on September 24, IFI intended to retain only $1.1 billion of the common shares. Of the balance, $1.6 billion of various classes of stock was to be bought and resold by Deutsche Bank and $500 million by Mediobanca. Deutsche Bank had set up a syndicate of ten co–lead managers who would each sell $100 million worth of shares, while Mediobanca had enlisted seven Italian banks to help distribute its shares. Excitement abounded as the syndicate members prepared to test the Euro-equity markets when they started selling stock the following morning.

This case was prepared by Research Associate Richard P. Melnick and Professor W. Carl Kester. Copyright © 1987 by the President and Fellows of Harvard College. Harvard Business School case 288-003.

THE LIBYAN CONNECTION

Fiat S.p.A. was Italy's largest listed company with 1985 sales in lire (Lit) of Lit27,101 billion and net income of Lit1326 billion. The diversified company had 53 percent of its 1985 sales in automobiles; 31 percent in agricultural, commercial, and construction vehicles; and the rest in activities such as publishing, telecommunications, and bioengineering. A 5-year financial summary is provided in **Exhibit 1**.

Fiat's performance suffered during the energy and Italian currency crises that began in 1973. A poor economic environment made 1975 Fiat's worst year for auto sales since World War II. Labor costs rose 21 percent that year while demand for cars in the Italian market decreased dramatically. By 1976 demand for Fiat's cars still remained significantly below the 1972–1973 level. It was at this juncture, when Fiat was badly in need of new capital, that its Libyan connection began. In 1976 the Libyan government invested $400 million in the company and received 15.2 percent of the ordinary voting shares, 13 percent of the preference shares (with limited voting rights), and 13 percent of the "savings" shares (no voting rights, but slightly higher dividends and warrants to buy shares of a Fiat affiliate). This infusion of new equity made Libya the second largest holder of Fiat's shares, the Agnelli family still being the largest. Because of its substantial ownership position, Libya had two representatives, Mohammed Siala, a banker, and Ali Elgheriani, an official in the Libyan industry department, on Fiat's board of directors. Fiat's equity ownership structure in 1986 is shown in **Exhibit 2**.

After the difficult period in the 1970s, Fiat began to recover in 1979. Between 1983 and 1986 profits doubled each year, and Fiat's improved condition was reflected in its stock price. **Exhibits 3** and **4** show Fiat's stock price and an index for the Milan Exchange for the period immediately preceding and following the announced sale.

While 10 percent of Fiat's sales already came from defense-related products such as rockets and explosives, Mr. Agnelli sought new defense contracts in an effort to diversify Fiat away from the cyclical auto and construction industries. This effort had been frustrated to some extent by the Libyan presence on Fiat's board, for this disqualified Fiat from bidding for U.S. SDI contracts. The prospects for change grew dim in June 1986 when Libya's Colonel Qaddafi indicated his unwillingness to dispose of the Fiat shares. In response to this indication, Mr. Agnelli hired Abdullah Saudi, president of the Arab Banking Corporation and an influential man in the Arab world, to retrieve the shares.

To the surprise of most observers, Colonel Qaddafi changed his mind. An agreement to sell Libya's shares to Fiat evidently was reached roughly a week or so before the September 23 announcement: Mr. Agnelli met privately with Italian Prime Minister Bettino Craxi on September 17, reportedly to inform him of the Libyan agreement. News of the meeting's purpose, however, was not revealed publicly until after September 23.

Reasons for Libya's turnaround were unclear. Some speculated that declining oil prices had created a need for revenues by the Libyan government. In addition, a Milan court froze $5 million worth of Libyan assets in August 1986. Although the amount was insignificant, Libya might have decided to liquidate its position before any further similar actions were taken.

STRUCTURING THE REPURCHASE

IFI funded its $1.1 billion Libyan share repurchase by issuing bonds convertible into the equity of three of its financial subsidiaries: Toro, Saes, and Mito. Because other Fiat-controlled companies were expected to buy these bonds, Fiat was effectively able to regain control of its own shares without obtaining a special vote of its shareholders.

Once IFI bought the Libyan package, it had to move forward quickly and quietly. Libya wanted its entire cash payment on a date in the near future, and the deal seemed too politically delicate to initiate open competitive bidding. Fiat reportedly first offered the deal to Italian banks, which declined the invitation on the grounds that they could not successfully place such a large block of stock. Deutsche Bank was the next obvious choice. Fiat preferred to deal with a European bank, and Deutsche Bank had worked with Fiat in various capacities over a number of years. The Libyan Arab Foreign Investment Corporation was also satisfied with Deutsche Bank. Finally, Deutsche Bank had been very successful in the distribution of Eurobonds and Euro-equities. Deutsche Bank preferred to do big deals rather than a large number of smaller deals. The bank's most substantial accomplishment in the Euro-equity market was its $1.52 billion offering for Daimler-Benz AG the previous December, suggesting that it could handle a large equity deal like Fiat's.

THE EURO-EQUITY MARKET

The Euro-equity market involves corporations in one country issuing shares, convertible bonds, or other equity instruments, and selling these securities to investors throughout the world. Though Euro-equities have in some sense been around since the 1920s, when American Depository Receipts (representing non-U.S. shares) began being traded in New York, the market's rapid growth in its modern form did not begin until 1983. In that year, issues of straight Euro-equity totaled $200 million, and by 1986 the total was expected to be about $8 billion. Euro-equities were becoming a significant component of the international capital markets (see **Exhibit 5** for a list of the largest Euro-equity issues).

Most issuers in this market were outside the United States and Japan, which had the two largest equity markets. According to a *Euromoney* study, Swiss, German, British, and French companies had accounted for more than two-thirds of the Euro-equity offerings between 1983 and 1986.[1] Though primary issues dominated this market, there were also notable initial public and secondary offerings. Data on the volume of underwritings by bookrunner are provided in **Exhibit 6**.

Once a company decided to issue stock abroad, it could choose one of three basic methods of selling shares to investors. A Euro-equity offering generally involved a separate syndicate placing shares outside the issuer's home market. European banks preferred this system where a lead manager directed the regional subsyndicates to place the issue with their local customers. Another option was a combined offering in which a single syndicate placed shares both abroad and in the issuer's home market.

[1]*Euromoney,* May 1986, p. 197, and May 1987, p. 167.

American investment banks preferred this system because the lead manager had tighter control of the underwriters. The last choice was a private placement involving one or a small group of financial institutions. Corporations used this method when they wanted to issue shares quickly and with tight control. These deals did not significantly increase the shareholder base, but they did place the shares with known end-buyers.

ITALIAN STOCK MARKET

Although Fiat stock was traded on exchanges in Milan, Frankfurt, Zurich, and Paris, it was the Milan center that mattered most to Fiat's investors, for it was here that the greatest liquidity in Fiat shares could be found. However, in order for shares to be traded in Milan, they had to be registered and physically held within Italy. Other pertinent regulations of the Italian market included the prohibition of short sales by nonresidents and a required 30 percent withholding tax on dividends paid to foreign shareholders. The Italian market was complicated by its registration laws, and historically there had been long settlement delays in which foreign investors experienced significant problems. As **Exhibit 7** demonstrates, the Italian market as a whole was not nearly as large nor as liquid as the markets in the United States, the United Kingdom, and Japan. Indeed, by itself, the Fiat offering would have represented more than 10 percent of the Milan Exchange's total turnover in 1985.[2]

THE EQUITY OFFERING

On September 23, Fiat announced publicly that IFI would retain 90 million of the 205.1 million ordinary shares repurchased from Libya. The breakdown of the Libyan share repurchase is shown in **Table 1**. At the time of the announcement, Fiat had 1.35 billion ordinary shares outstanding. By 5:00 p.m. that same day, Deutsche Bank officials in London started calling to line up co–lead managers. By 11 p.m., DBCM had found ten firms each of which would take $100 million (see **Exhibit 8** for a list of colead managers).

TABLE 1   THE LIBYAN SHARE REPURCHASE

Type of shares	Shares sold by Libya	Shares acquired by DBCM/Mediobanca	Shares retained by IFI
Ordinary	205.1 million	115.1 million	90.0 million
Preferred	88.3 million	88.3 million	—
Savings	29.3 million	29.3 million	—

[2]*Rapporto Annuele 1985,* "Comitato Direttiro degli Agenti di Cambio della Borsa Valori di Milano."

The offering price for the equity was fixed in U.S. dollars at $11.28 for the ordinary shares, $7.08 for preference shares, and $6.75 for the savings shares. These prices were discounted 4 percent, 5 percent, and 4 percent, respectively, from the September 23 closing prices in Milan, which represented the highest prices ever realized for Fiat shares. Underwriters were required to take a preset mix of shares including 61 percent ordinary shares, 30 percent preference shares, and 9 percent savings shares. In an unusual move, Fiat also chose to fix the offering price in dollars rather than lire.[3] However, as of September 23, Deutsche Bank had not specified whether the securities to be offered were regular Fiat shares with full trading rights in Milan, or global certificates merely representing ownership in Fiat, which could later be exchanged for Fiat shares.

As business wrapped up on September 23, the principals involved in the deal seemed quite comfortable with the arrangement. Libya was satisfied with its stock sale, and Fiat was relieved to be able to repurchase its shares. For their part, Deutsche Bank and Mediobanca were proud to be leading the largest Euro-equity offering to date.

THE ORDEAL

Despite initial hopes and optimism, problems emerged almost immediately after the Fiat offering began. Major underwriters complained of the way Deutsche Bank appeared to handle the deal. Deutsche Bank was revealed to have sold many of its own shares before the syndicate members had a chance to start selling their allotments. When syndicate members called their regular investors, they found that Deutsche Bank had already contacted them. Some investors were reported to have been called as many as thirty times in one day. The syndicate head of one U.S. investment bank expressed his feelings about Deutsche Bank's syndicate managers: "They were at best vague, at worst misleading." It was at this stage that "the deal got a stink it never got rid of."[4]

Fiat's stock price in Milan started to drop on September 24, and by September 28 some investors tried to cancel their commitments to buy the stock. Collective losses were estimated at $50 million, and 60 percent of the issue was apparently unsold. Deutsche Bank revealed on September 29 that it had spent several hundred million dollars supporting Fiat's share price. Much of investors' concern revolved around the still unclear settlement procedures. Deutsche Bank tried to resolve this issue by announcing that Fiat shares could be traded in Milan. But after experiencing a drop in price to Lit14,980 from Lit16,600 in just 5 days of trading, many syndicate members were themselves ready to cut their losses by selling some of their shares directly into the Milan market. By October 1, Deutsche Bank had spent $300 million to $400 million to support the Fiat price, while it had sold only $450 million of its $600 million allotment. Collective underwriting losses were estimated at $100 million as of October 1.

In mid-October, Fiat's stock traded at about Lit15,000 to Lit15,500, and it remained low through the end of 1986 (see **Exhibit 3** for a stock price history). Some

---

[3]The Libyans reportedly wanted to be paid in dollars.
[4]*Euromoney*, November 1986, p. 25.

underwriters suggested that aggregate underwriting losses on the deal totaled $250 million. One notable exception was the experience of the Arab Banking Corporation, which not only sold its $100 million allocation, but actually requested more shares.

Following the Fiat deal, professionals in the Euromarket tried to understand the causes of the debacle. Fiat's profitability had been increasing, and the maturing Euromarket had appeared ready for its biggest challenge. Yet nothing seemed to work according to plan. Many wondered what implications this deal had for the future of the Euro-equity market.

EXHIBIT 1   FIAT—FIVE-YEAR FINANCIAL REVIEW* (LIRE MILLIONS, EXCEPT NUMBER OF SHARES AND RATIOS)

	1985	1984	1983	1982	1981
Sales	27,101,573	23,812,756	21,985,442	20,618,618	20,312,265
Net income	1,326,143	626,745	253,402	137,346	90,167
Total assets	31,662,822	29,291,291	26,358,374	25,117,923	22,846,862
Net worth	7,304,988	6,318,975	5,105,665	4,902,852	3,589,000
Common shares (millions)[†]	1,350	1,350	900	900	900
Stock price low-high, lire	2,065–6,030	1,675–2,312	818–1,690	740–998	700–1,305
Ratios					
Return on equity, %	18.15	9.92	4.96	2.80	2.51
Price/earnings	17.40	12.10	15.60	13.20	21.40
Price/book value	1.11	0.46	0.30	0.16	0.22
Earnings per share, lire[‡]	655	310	318	203	134
Dividends per share, lire	110	110	60	53	47
Debt/total capital, %	43.44	43.95	44.64	44.59	45.74

*Balance sheet and income statement figures are for the consolidated company.
[†]In addition to common shares, Fiat had 675,000 shares of 10 percent preferred stock with a par value of Lit1000 outstanding in 1984 and 1985. Prior to these years, it had 225 million shares of such preferred stock outstanding (although with a par value of Lit500). This preferred stock had preference as to assets and noncumulative dividends up to 6 percent of par; after common shares received, 6 percent of its par, both classes share alike in further distributions.
[‡]Based on both common and preferred shares adjusted for stock splits and a restructuring of equity capital in 1984.

EXHIBIT 2   FIAT'S OWNERSHIP STRUCTURE,* MAY 31, 1986 (1000-LIRE SHARES)

	Ordinary	Preference[†]
Total shares outstanding	1350 million	675 million
Percentage ownership		
Agnelli family	32.2%	0.0%
Libya	15.2	13.1
Mutual funds		
Italian	6.3	8.7
Luxembourg-based	7.4	5.8
Mediobanca	3.1	0.2
Pirelli S.p.A.	0.5	1.0
Other institutions	1.9	5.5
Foreign	3.2	6.8
Small investors	30.2	58.9

*Excluding 225 million nonvoting savings shares.
[†]Holders of preference shares vote only at extraordinary shareholders' meetings.
Source: The Economist, September 27, 1986, p. 69.

EXHIBIT 3   SHARE PRICE, MARKET INDEX, AND EXCHANGE RATE DATA (LIRE)

	Fiat	Milan Index	Lire/$
December 30, 1985	6,030	460	1666
1986			
January 31	6,460	477	1627
February 28	9,060	567	1515
March 30	10,750	712	1582
April 30	12,440	758	1489
May 31	13,600	782	1591
June 30	11,476	665	1507
July 31	14,550	737	1436
August 29	16,000	817	1400
September 1	16,230	823	1395
September 2	15,900	818	1400
September 3	15,800	813	1398
September 4	15,800	811	1398
September 5	15,480	791	1412
September 8	15,000	773	1426
September 9	14,950	784	1419
September 10	14,550	770	1420
September 11	14,600	770	1441
September 12	14,250	755	1421
September 15	14,100	756	1412
September 16	14,700	768	1412
September 17	15,020	751	1400
September 18	15,800	764	1374
September 19	15,800	744	1376
September 22	15,950	741	1401
September 23	16,500	765	1414
September 24	16,450	764	1413
September 25	15,700	755	1414
September 26	15,480	750	1414
September 29	15,250	746	1400
September 30	14,800	738	1401
October 1	15,000	742	1398
October 2	14,700	739	1388
October 3	14,950	750	1382
October 6	14,800	746	1376
October 7	14,480	739	1382
October 8	14,500	739	1381
October 9	14,900	749	1385
October 10	15,280	756	1370

EXHIBIT 3 SHARE PRICE, MARKET INDEX, AND EXCHANGE RATE DATA (LIRE)
(CONTINUED)

	Fiat	Milan Index	Lire/$
October 13	15,100	754	1369
October 14	15,000	754	1366
October 15	15,000	753	1361
October 16	15,280	765	1366
October 17	15,500	773	1367
October 20	15,460	777	1376
October 21	15,420	777	1376
October 22	15,400	770	1372
October 23	15,600	778	1379
October 24	15,740	769	1401
October 31	15,600	768	1421
November 7	15,750	768	1426
November 14	14,950	743	1387
November 21	13,550	702	1388
November 28	14,330	722	1367
December 5	13,800	694	1385
December 12	13,030	677	1397
December 19	13,430	702	1391
December 30	14,250	716	1355

EXHIBIT 4 HISTORY OF FIAT SHARE PRICE AND INDEX FOR THE MILAN EXCHANGE SEPTEMBER 1, 1986–OCTOBER 31, 1986 (INDEX FROM BANCA COMMERCIALE ITALIANA, BASE 1972 = 100)

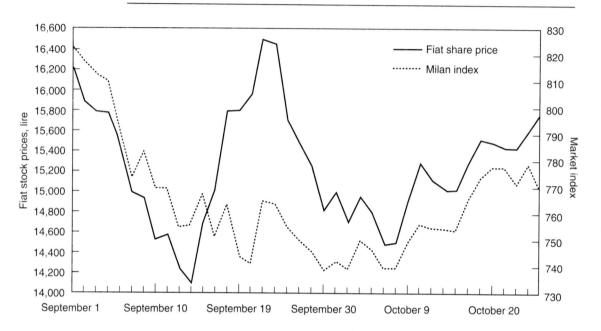

EXHIBIT 5   STRAIGHT EURO-EQUITY—THE LARGEST ISSUES (AS OF SEPTEMBER 1986)

Issuer	Amount,* $ millions	Total number of shares[†]	Issue price, $	Lead manager	Date[‡]
British Telecom	782	3,012,000,000	1.55	Nomura/Morgan Stanley Swiss Bank Corp./McLeod Young Weir	1/84
Nestlé	143	300,000	478.38	Crédit Suisse First Boston	6/85
Nestlé	148	250,000	593.93	Crédit Suisse First Boston	9/85
Nestlé	134	200,000	668.804	Crédit Suisse First Boston	10/85
Rhône-Poulenc	129	3,300,000	38.42	Société Générale	10/85
Singapore Airlines	236	100,000,000	2.359	Development Bank of Singapore	11/85
Daimler-Benz	1,510[§]	3,400,000	455.00	Deutsche Bank	12/85
Cie. Financière de Suez	129	2,163,350	122.00	Banque Indosuez	1/86
KLM	167	15,000,000	20.50	Algemene Bank Nederland	2/86
Electrolux	306	8,000,000	38.76	Enskilda Securities	4/86
Winterthur Swiss Reinsurance	165	50,000	3,309.20	Union Bank of Switzerland	5/86
Swiss Reinsurance	244	150,000	1,628.55	Crédit Suisse First Boston	6/86
Hanson Trust	207	75,000,000	2.76	Crédit Suisse First Boston	7/86

Note: All dollar amounts reflect the exchange rate at the time of issue.
*Raised outside the domestic market.
[†]Including those offered domestically, if any.
[‡]Of announcement.
[§]Estimates.
Source: Special Survey on International Equities, *Euromoney,* November 1986, p. 25.

EXHIBIT 6   PUBLIC INTERNATIONAL STRAIGHT EQUITY OFFERINGS (1983–SEPTEMBER 1986)

Bookrunner ranking*	Amount, $ millions	No. of issues	% of dollar volume
1. Deutsche Bank†	3,657.34	6	32.52
2. Crédit Suisse First Boston	2,268.11	28	20.17
3. Morgan Stanley International	732.76	11	6.52
4. Swiss Bank Corporation	577.24	9	5.13
5. Union Bank of Switzerland	526.29	7	4.68
6. Banque Nationale de Paris	450.13	2	4.00
7. Enskilda Securities	416.32	3	3.70
8. Nomura Securities	388.32	4	3.45
9. S. G. Warburg & Co.	327.04	3	2.91
10. Development Bank of Singapore	235.96	1	2.10
11. Shearson Lehman Bros. International	219.86	6	1.96
12. Merrill Lynch Capital Markets	208.20	6	1.85
13. Algemene Bank Nederland	167.08	1	1.49
14. Crédit Commercial de France	148.89	1	1.32
15. Banque Indosuez	128.95	1	1.15
16. Société Générale	126.81	1	1.13
17. Salomon Brothers	116.49	3	1.04
18. Amsterdam-Rotterdam Bank	87.01	1	0.77
19. McLeod Young Weir	85.23	1	0.76
20. Crédit Industriel et Commercial	81.29	1	0.72
21. Daiwa Securities	72.39	3	0.64
22. Goldman Sachs International	66.38	1	0.59
23. Pierson Heldring & Pierson	66.21	1	0.59
24. Nikko Securities	33.55	1	0.30
25. Prudential Bache Securities Int.	29.79	1	0.26
26. Banque Paribas	18.71	1	0.17
27. Kidder Peabody International	9.53	1	0.08

*The bookrunner receives the full amount of each issue.
†This does not include the Fiat deal.
Source: Special Survey on International Equities, Euromoney, November 1986, p. 26.

Stock Exchange

		Tokyo	New York	Toronto	United Kingdom	Frankfurt	Paris	Zurich
No. of listed companies	(Domestic)	1,476	1,487	912	2,116	212	489	131
	(Foreign)	21	54	54	572	177	189	184
No. of listed issues [Stocks]	(Domestic)	1,487	2,240	1,379	1,804	247	546	205
	(Foreign)	21	58	59	491	186	243	190
[Bonds]	(Domestic)	617	3,602	—	3,040	4,968	2,053	1,406
	(Foreign)	237	254	—	1,551	681	181	776
Total market value ($ millions)	(Stocks)	948,264	1,882,668	157,424	353,629	167,534	79,096	84,085
	(Bonds)	512,529	1,313,873	—	335,578	240,512	200,105	80,588
Trading value ($ millions)	(Stocks)	396,828	970,479	31,626	76,267	39,712	20,184	217,479
	(Bonds)	348,594	9,047	—	205,867	49,217	94,915	
No. of member firms		93	599	74	225	101	45	25

Stock Exchange

		Amsterdam	Milan	Sydney	Taiwan	Korea	Far East	Singapore
No. of listed companies	(Domestic)	232	147	1,117	127	342	219	122
	(Foreign)	242	—	24	—	—	7	194
No. of listed issues [Stocks]	(Domestic)	289	214	1,585	130	414	263	322
	(Foreign)	303	—	39	—	—	7	
[Bonds]	(Domestic)	1,308	1,223	2,245	37	3,728	8	129
	(Foreign)	156	29	—	—	—	1	
Total market value ($ millions)	(Stocks)	59,363	58,502	72,479	10,432	7,381	34,134	11,069
	(Bonds)	70,807	172,833	30,448	1,378	13,481	na	89,133
Trading value ($ millions)	(Stocks)	20,431	15,678	10,895	4,899	4,067	3,975	2,981
	(Bonds)	16,510	2,838	18,036	27	4,019	na	21
No. of member firms		141	115	40	37	25	432	24

Source: (Tokyo: International Affairs Department of the Tokyo Stock Exchange), p. 67.

EXHIBIT 8   CO−LEAD MANAGERS OF FIAT'S INTERNATIONAL EQUITY OFFERING*

Deutsche Bank Capital Markets, Ltd.		Mediobanca	
ABC Investment and Services Co. (E.C.)	Banque Paribas Capital Markets, Ltd.	Commerzbank, A.G.	Crédit Suisse First Boston, Ltd.
Daiwa Europe, Ltd.	Dresdner Bank, A.G.	Salomon Brothers International, Ltd.	Shearson Lehman Brothers International, Inc.
	Swiss Bank Corporation International, Ltd.		Union Bank of Switzerland (Securities), Ltd.

*Co−lead managers are listed as they appeared on the published tombstone for Fiat's international equity offering.

NOVO INDUSTRI
A/S—1981

In January 1981 the management of Novo Industri A/S (Novo) was considering how best to fund the expansion planned for the next several years. Projections in the company's budget revealed a deficit of 220 million Danish kroner (DKr) in 1981 and DKr127 million in 1982. After exploring financing opportunities inside and outside Denmark, three major alternatives had been chosen for further evaluation. These alternatives were (1) convertible debt to be issued in the Eurobond market or the United States, (2) a preemptive rights offering at par to current shareholders, or (3) a general public offering of new shares to overseas investors in London and/or the United States. As the largest external financing executed by the company to date, it was important that Novo's choice be consistent with its overall corporate strategy and financial policies, and that it reflect management's concern for shareholder interests.

COMPANY AND INDUSTRY BACKGROUND

Novo Industri A/S, founded in Denmark in 1925 by Harald and Horvald Pedersen, was a leader in the manufacture and sale of insulin, enzymes, and other pharmaceutical and biochemical products. It was incorporated in 1940, a time during which it exported insulin to over thirty countries. Since then, Novo had developed two major product segments through its strength in research and process technologies: enzymes and pharmaceuticals (primarily insulin).

This case was prepared by Research Associate Glyn Ferguson under the supervision of Professor W. Carl Kester. Copyright © 1986 by the President and Fellows of Harvard College. Harvard Business School case 286-084. A major source of background information for this case was Arthur I. Stonehill and Kåre B. Dullum, *Internationalizing the Cost of Capital* (New York: John Wiley & Sons, 1982).

Enzymes are proteins that act as catalysts in biochemical processes and have a variety of industrial uses. They are produced by extraction from animal or vegetable tissues or by fermentation of microorganisms. Novo, firmly established as the world leader in industrial enzyme production, made an operating profit of DKr135 million on this division in 1980 compared with DKr96 million for pharmaceuticals. The majority of its clients were in the detergent and starch industries. Although many large companies produced their own enzymes, Novo held about 50 percent of the noncaptive market, estimated at DKr1.6 billion in 1980.

Novo's pharmaceutical manufacturing was based on the process of extraction, although fermentation and synthesis processes were also used. Its most important products from this division were insulin preparations. In 1980 Novo ranked as the second largest producer of insulin after Eli Lilly and Company. It was estimated that Eli Lilly captured 85 percent to 90 percent of the U.S. insulin market in 1980 while Novo controlled 60 percent of the European market. Most of Novo's pharmaceutical products were sold under prescription only. Their introduction, pricing, and marketing were subject to control by the public authorities in the various international markets in which they were sold.

Novo's corporate goal was to remain a highly specialized basic manufacturer within a well-defined biological and biochemical area, primarily based on its own research and development. It pursued this objective through a strategy of international expansion. In 1980 it was estimated that 97 percent of Novo's business originated outside Denmark. The company operated production plants in Denmark, France, Switzerland, and South Africa, and established two subsidiaries in the United States. The development of a production plant in Japan was also under way. A summary of Novo's consolidated operations is shown in **Exhibit 1**.

Research, development, and quality control were cornerstones of Novo's strategy. About one-fourth of Novo's employees in Denmark were located in laboratories and approximately 10 percent of annual sales were devoted to research and development. Additional research and technical support were conducted in the United States, Switzerland, and Japan.

By 1981 Novo had become locked in one of the first great battles for a genetically engineered product. Both it and Eli Lilly were spending millions to develop a less expensive human insulin to replace the animal insulin that was then most prevalent in world markets. Each intended to use the product to spearhead a push in the other's home market, hoping to break its competitor's dominant position there. Comparative data for Novo and several of its major competitors are shown in **Exhibit 2**.

FINANCIAL HISTORY

Two classes of common stock were established when Novo was founded. The A shares (par value DKr100), which were nontransferable and granted ten votes per share, were issued to the Novo Foundation, a nonprofit organization comprised of scientists, academicians, and businessmen who distributed income from the stock for humanitarian, scientific, and cultural purposes. The B shares (par value DKr100), which were each granted one vote, were given to the founders and their families. Although the

Novo Foundation initially controlled more than 75 percent of voting rights, it did not involve itself directly in the management of Novo. Nevertheless, it did make clear its intention of preserving at least a two-thirds voting majority.

In 1974 the company was taken public primarily to enable family members to trade their stock and secondarily to provide access to additional equity funding. Initially, only the required minimum of 10 percent of transferable shares was listed on the Danish After-Market (Efterbørsen) and, later, on the Main Copenhagen Stock Exchange (Copenhagen Fondsbørs).[1] The public price per share was DKr150 when offered, although the book value was DKr241 per share.

Prior to 1981, Novo conducted four major financings in the open market (see **Exhibit 3**). The first was a rights offering in December 1974, a time when Novo's stock price was at an all-time high of DKr275. This rights issue increased the number of outstanding shares by 50.6 percent, raised net proceeds of DKr46.8 million, and added DKr6 million to Novo's dividend payments.[2]

A second rights issue was offered in December 1977 and included both A and B shares. Novo's share price at this point was around DKr300. This offering represented a 39.7 percent increase in the shares outstanding and netted Novo DKr56.5 million. Overall, this issue improved the group's capital base, with total liabilities as a percentage of total assets decreasing from 53 percent in 1976 to 47 percent in 1977.

In 1977 Novo's management became concerned about Novo's ability to obtain the funds necessary for continued expansion, especially given its future growth predictions showing a large and continued demand for capital. Denmark was a country where domestic capital was scarce and expensive. In fact, the prior Novo rights issue was regarded as a large issue for the Danish market and represented 25 percent of the total new equity funds raised in Denmark that year. Novo's future needs were expected to exceed that issue.

Furthermore, Novo, with 95 percent of its sales outside Denmark, was planning to invest actively abroad. This was complicated by the fact that the Bank of Denmark was insisting all foreign investment be financed abroad to conserve the Bank's low foreign-currency reserves. To resolve these problems, Novo explored various financing alternatives with its principal overseas bank, Morgan Guaranty. Two foreign sources of capital were identified as potentially viable: a private placement of straight debt in the United States, and a convertible bond issue in either the United States or the Eurobond market.

A private placement was eventually ruled out since Novo was not a well-known company in the U.S. financial community. It would, therefore, have to overcome

---

[1]Although called a stock exchange, relatively little trading in shares takes place on the Main Exchange, which is largely a secondary market for mortgage bonds. Most stock trading takes place in the After-Market, which is subject to the same fundamental rules as the Main Exchange even though it is an unofficial market. Two important exceptions are that securities can be traded in the After-Market by telephone between banks rather than by specialized stockbrokers, and that it is open from 8:00 a.m. to 6:00 p.m. rather than just the few hours to which the Main Exchange is limited.

[2]A preemptive rights offering is a method by which new shares are offered to existing shareholders first. This technique is based on the notion that shareholders are entitled to anything of value that the company may distribute and, therefore, shall have a preemptive right to subscribe to new offerings. Existing shareholders have the option to exercise, sell, or disregard these rights.

significant information asymmetries to achieve a successful offering. Convertible bonds issued in the Eurobond market were believed to be a better alternative, though this too would require Novo to heighten its visibility abroad.

The first step in overcoming information asymmetries occurred when British stockbrokers Grieveson, Grant and Co. decided to add Novo Industri to its research portfolio. Its reports in 1977 were optimistic, and Novo was classified as a "buy." Morgan Grenfell in London was called in as Novo's main advisor, and it was decided that the London firm would manage a convertible bond issue denominated in U.S. dollars. Novo's management also took steps to convert the company's B stock from registered shares to bearer shares and to obtain a listing of the B shares on the London Stock Exchange.

Finally, in October 1978, Novo asked its shareholders to give up their preemptive rights and authorize a $20 million issue of bonds convertible into B shares at a 10 percent premium over the listed price on the Copenhagen Stock Exchange at the time of the offering. Other details of the bond issue are provided in **Exhibit 3**.

Although the convertible bond was well received by both investors and the financial press, it did little to lift Novo's stock price. In fact, Novo's stock price, which had been declining slowly since mid-1977, continued its fall to DKr200 by early 1979. Some analysts viewed this as an undervaluation, while others argued that it was a natural response to the eventual dilutive impact of the convertible issue.

Whatever the cause, European investors' interest in the convertible bond encouraged management to begin promoting Novo's stock abroad. During 1979 presentations to investors were made throughout Europe. Numerous banks, underwriters, and financial publishers were also invited to visit the company. Some promotional literature was published in English, and in the spring of 1980 a special seminar was held in New York City for journalists and financial analysts. The seminar discussed the development of the biotechnology industry in general and Novo's position in that industry in particular. The upshot of this public relations effort appeared to be several encouraging "buy" recommendations and substantial foreign buying of Novo's shares through the London market. The price per share rose to a high of DKr300 by the end of June 1980.

Finally, in the fall of 1980, Novo announced another rights offering that was expected to raise DKr125.2 million. It was structured in two parts (see **Exhibit 3**). The first would raise the number of A and B shares by 20 percent at a price of DKr105 per new share. The second part would increase the B shares by yet another 10 percent at a price of DKr250 per share—a 15 percent discount from market value. Concurrent with the rights offering, the company also announced a dividend increase. The dividend on the A shares was increased from ½ percent of par value to 6 percent, and on B shares, from 12 percent to 13 percent of par value. Copenhagen Handelsbank and Gudme Raaschou & Co. underwrote the rights offering. A rising stock price during the offering period helped ensure that the entire issue was sold. Since much of the subscription took place in London, it was estimated that about 50 percent of Novo's shares were now held abroad, primarily in the United Kingdom and the United States.

THE CURRENT DILEMMAS FACING MANAGMENT

In early January 1981, members of Novo's top management met in Copenhagen with financial advisors from the Copenhagen Handelsbank, Morgan Grenfell (London), and Goldman Sachs (United States). The agenda for the meeting was Novo's 1981 funds needs and a plan to execute the financing that would be necessary. Three alternatives were developed, each involving equity or an equity-linked security, as follows:

1. A second U.S. dollar convertible bond to be issued either in the Eurobond market or in the U.S.

2. A preemptive rights offering to existing shareholders at a subscription price 10 to 15 percent below market

3. A general public offering of Class B common shares to overseas investors in London or the United States.[3]

Novo's stock price had continued climbing during the fall of 1980, lifted in part by a general rise in the Copenhagen and London stock markets (see **Exhibit 4**). It eventually reached DKr700 by January 1981. At this level, many analysts believed a near-term high had been reached, though others remained generally bullish (see **Exhibit 5** for a selection of comments and recommendations).

The convertible bond alternative seemed attractive in light of the success enjoyed by the first issue in 1978. Although that issue had not yet been fully called, investors had already converted roughly a quarter of the issue in 1980. At the current rate of conversion, one could expect less than half the issue would remain outstanding by the end of 1981.

A second convertible could be offered with terms similar to the first, except that under current market conditions the conversion price would likely be set at DKr770 per DKr100 par value B shares at a fixed exchange rate of DKr5.3650 = $1. The coupon on the bond would probably be fixed at 8.00 percent.

A preemptive rights offering would present a means of raising new equity capital without diluting the ownership share of existing Class B shareholders, assuming all such shareholders exercised their subscription privilege. This would allow current shareholders to reap the rewards of future growth entirely for themselves. The risk of a rights offering was that the issue might not be fully subscribed, thus yielding less capital than required by the company. Typically, this risk was covered by an oversubscription privilege allowing subscribing shareholders to purchase all unsubscribed rights on a pro rata basis, or by entering into a purchase and standby agreement with an underwriter. Under such an agreement, an underwriter would stand ready to purchase all the unsubscribed shares at the subscription price less a take-up fee. For this service, underwriters were usually paid a standby fee of approximately ½ percent of the size of the issue, and a take-up fee of another ½ to 1 percent.

---

[3]Arthur I. Stonehill and Kåre B. Dullum, *Internationalizing the Cost of Capital* (New York: John Wiley & Sons, 1982), p. 56.

A general public offering of Class B common shares represented the surest way of raising equity capital immediately at current market prices. At issue was the question of how best to do so. One possible approach was to issue shares directly in London, where the stock was already listed. However, this was complicated by the fact that London Stock Exchange rules restricted general public offerings without preemptive rights for existing shareholders to a size no greater than 5 percent of total shares outstanding. This rule would effectively limit the size of Novo's equity offering to 152,626 Class B shares.

Should Novo choose to offer equity in the United States, it would have to consider setting up an American depository receipt system as a prerequisite to listing on one of the exchanges. This was usually accomplished by having a U.S. bank or trust company hold the newly issued shares against which American depository receipts (ADRs) would then be issued. By using ADRs, Americans wishing to buy shares of foreign companies could execute all transactions, including the receipt of dividends, in U.S. dollars.[4]

Of perhaps greater concern regarding a U.S. general public offering was the fact that a host of initial public offerings by biotechnology companies was hitting the market at the same time. Genentech had gone public in late 1980 with annual revenues of $9 million and operating cash flow of only 6¢ per share. Its stock sold for $35 per share at the time of the issue, a level quickly surpassed in the immediate after-market despite the lack of a commercially viable product or an established operating record. Cetus Corporation, another biotechnology company with virtually no earnings, was also planning a public offering in early 1981. A number of other such companies were rumored to be preparing initial public offerings as well. With this rush of new companies coming to market, there was a threat that U.S. equity investors would become saturated with biotechnology stocks, thus diminishing their incentive to add Novo to their portfolios. Furthermore, from a public relations viewpoint, it was questionable whether or not Novo should allow itself to be linked to such companies in the public's mind by issuing equity at the same time. Misperceptions about Novo's current businesses and future prospects could set the stage for investors' disenchantment later if unrealistically high expectations were not met.

In choosing among these financing alternatives, a number of considerations seemed pertinent. Novo's present and future need for funds, the cost of the capital raised, the likelihood of a successful offering and its effect on Novo's reputation, and current shareholder control of the company were issues meriting careful thought in the decision-making process. This, the biggest financing of Novo's history, would be a milestone in its development and could set a precedent that would influence future financing decisions.

---

[4]In 1981 dividends paid by Danish companies to U.S. residents were subject to a withholding tax of 30 percent. Dividends paid to Danish shareholders would be taxed as ordinary income at marginal rates up to 75 percent. Capital gains were taxed domestically at a rate of 50 percent for shares held more than 2 years and at personal tax rates for shares held less than 2 years.

EXHIBIT 1   CONSOLIDATED FINANCIAL STATEMENTS AND RATIOS (DKr MILLIONS,
EXCEPT WHERE NOTED)

	1977	1978	1979	1980
Sales	864	939	1275	1579
Pretax income	103	97	138	239
Net income	73	75	103	176
Sales abroad (as a % of total sales)	96	96	96	97
Capital expenditure	75	160	126	201
Total assets	1027	1391	1498	1994
Long-term debt	na	na	387	418
Net worth	545	590	667	959
Return on assets, %	7.1	5.4	6.9	8.8
Return on net worth, %	13.4	12.7	15.4	18.4
Debt to net worth ratio, %	na	na	58	44
Earnings per DKr100 nominal amount of A and B shares, primary	22.33	22.28	30.54	50.01
Fully diluted earnings per DKr100 nominal amount of A and B shares	22.33	20.98	28.88	47.02
Stock price, DKr				
High	362.50	266.50	227.50	684.0
Low	241.25	215.50	199.75	207.0
Dividends per share, DKr				
A shares	0.50	0.50	0.50	6.00
B shares	8.00	10.00	12.00	13.00

EXHIBIT 2   COMPARATIVE DATA ON SELECTED COMPETITORS, 1980

	Novo Industri A/S		Gist Brocades		Eli Lilly & Co., $ millions	Miles Labs, $ millions
	DKr millions	$ millions	NFI millions	$ millions		
Revenues	1579.0	280.2	1415.4	711.9	2558.6	686.1
Net income	175.8	31.2	24.2	12.2	342.0	7.4
Total assets	1993.9	331.5	1074.8	504.7	2607.5	635.9
Total debt	655.1	108.9	300.0	140.9	217.6	108.1
Total equity	959.0	159.4	350.3	164.5	1736.7	318.3

	Novo Industri, A/S	Gist Brocades	Eli Lilly & Co.	Miles Labs
Growth rates, %				
Revenues	23.9	12.2	13.7	15.3
Earnings	70.1	5.2	2.5	208.4
Return on sales, %	11.1	1.7	13.4	1.1
Return on equity, %	18.3	6.9	19.7	2.3
Current ratio	1.8	1.4	2.1	1.7
Interest coverage	4.7	2.2	30.7	na
Debt/capital, %	40.6	46.1	11.1	25.4

EXHIBIT 3   MAJOR FINANCINGS, 1974–1981

1. *1974*
Novo goes public on the Copenhagen Stock Exchange with a secondary offering of 90,000 B shares. At the time, a total of 450,000 A shares and 900,000 B shares were outstanding.

2. *December 4, 1975*
Rights issue:
  –One new B share at DKr105 for every three A or three B shares held. B shares increased by 450,000. Net proceeds: DKr46.8 million.
  –Bonus issues: One new B share for every six A or six B shares held.
  –8470 new B shares issued to employees.

3. *December 1, 1977*
Rights issue:
  –One new A share at DKr105 for every four A shares held.
  –One new B share at DKr105 for every four B shares held.
  A shares increased by 112,500.
  B shares increased by 395,860.
  Net proceeds: DKr56.5 million.
  –Bonus issues: One new A share for every eight A shares held and one new B share for every eight B shares held.
  –45,030 new B shares issued to employees.

4. *October 3, 1978*
Convertible Eurodollar bond:
  –7% convertible bonds due 1989; par value, $20,000,000.
  –Convertible from April 15, 1979, through December 30, 1988, into fully paid B shares.
  –Conversion ratio: 20.631 B shares per $1000 face value (effective conversion price of DKr259 per B share at a fixed exchange rate of DKr5.3435/$1).
  –Bonds are callable in whole or in part at the option of the company at premiums declining from 2½% to ½% starting in 1980.

5. *October 1, 1980*
Rights issue:
  –One new A share at DKr105 for every five A shares held.
  –One new B share at DKr105 for every five B shares held.
  –One new B share at DKr250 for every ten A or ten B shares held.
  A shares increased by 123,750.
  B shares increased by 732,150.
  Net proceeds: DKr125.2 million.

6. *During 1980*
Conversion of U.S. dollar convertible bond:
  –Conversion of $580,000 into 11,966 B shares.
  –Conversion of $3,675,000 into 77,819 B shares.

EXHIBIT 4   END-OF-YEAR STOCK MARKET INDICES AND EXCHANGE RATES

	Stock exchange indices			Exchange rates	
	New York*	London†	Copenhagen	DKr/$	DKr/£
1974	68.56	66.89	75.63	6.0550	14.4957
1975	90.19	158.08	100.41	5.7462	12.7669
1976	106.88	151.96	100.18	6.0450	10.9185
1977	95.10	214.53	96.42	6.0032	10.4786
1978	96.11	220.22	88.96	5.5146	10.5853
1979	107.94	229.79	87.37	5.2610	11.1617
1980	135.78	292.22	95.61	5.6359	13.1108

*Standard & Poor's Composite Index.
†*Financial Times*—Actuaries All-Shares Index.
Source: Financial Times, London (various issues).

EXHIBIT 5   **SAMPLE COMMENTS FROM ANALYSTS' REPORTS: AUGUST 1980–**
JANUARY 1981

1. *Danish Børsinformation*

September 5, 1980—Novo's P/E at 10. Novo (stock) passed 400 last week and the increase must be regarded as fantastic. We are inclined to regard the rights offering as negative, but the stock price movements and international stockownership may negate this tendency.

November 5, 1980—An increasing international portfolio interest in Novo's stock is an important determinant when explaining the relatively rapid appreciation of the stock price. Partly, it is due to the fact that Novo has received a valuation as an expansionary research based biochemical firm. Stock price will depend on foreign exchanges. At the present time we do not recommend the stock for short term investment.

2. *Grieveson, Grant and Co., UK*

September 2, 1980—Recommendation: Strong Hold. The share price has risen sharply this week as selling by Danish holders dried up in anticipation of the statement. While we believe the existing holders should maintain their stakes, we suggest that intending buyers should wait to see how the market develops.

January 6, 1981—We rated the shares a hold at 610 at the end of October 1980. We now feel that on the short view they are high enough, and that intending investors in what we still regard as a first class growth company can wait until later in 1981.

3. *Cazenove & Co., UK*

September 8, 1980—The recent rise in Novo's share price recognizes both the strength of the company's current earnings and of its technical and commercial position in the field of biotechnology. These appear to us to merit at least the current rating [price], which is not excessive for an international specialist in a growth phase.

4. *Quilter, Goodison & Co., UK*

September 1, 1980—Recommendation: Buy. We continue to think that the shares are substantially undervalued despite the rise in price from 217 at the beginning of 1979.

Source: Arthur I. Stonehill and Kåre B. Dullum, *Internationalizing the Cost of Capital* (New York: John Wiley & Sons, 1982).

LSI LOGIC CORPORATION

At the beginning of 1987, the managers of LSI Logic Corporation of Milpitas, California, had to decide on the form of the company's next financing. Along with the usual decisions concerning amount, timing, debt ratio, etc., this financing also raised the question of ownership structure. Since its founding in 1980, LSI Logic had pursued an unusual global financing strategy. The company established wholly owned foreign subsidiaries in Europe and Japan, each of which then sold minority equity positions to local investors in each market. Both subsidiaries had received very attractive prices for their shares. While LSI Logic retained majority ownership, each subsidiary operated with considerable independence and raised its own capital.

The parent company's last public issue of securities had taken place in December 1985, when it raised $23 million through a sale of subordinated convertible Swiss franc notes to European investors. Since then LSI had relied primarily on bank borrowings to meet its external funds needs. In 1987 the company anticipated raising between $100 and $150 million. These funds would be used to meet anticipated cash needs through 1988, which would arise from planned expansion in the United States and Canada and possibly from refinancing some or all of the outstanding bank debt. The company had several options to consider: (1) a seasoned equity offering by the parent company in the United States; (2) an offering of subordinated debentures or subordinated convertible debentures by the parent company in either the United States or Europe; (3) an initial public offering of a minority interest in the company's Canadian subsidiary, LSI Logic Corporation of Canada, Inc.; or (4) some combination of (1) through (3).

This case was prepared by Professor Timothy A. Luehrman. Copyright © 1990 by the President and Fellows of Harvard College. Harvard Business School case 290-035.

COMPANY BACKGROUND

LSI Logic was founded by Mr. Wilfred Corrigan in November 1980 to design and produce application-specific integrated circuits (ASICs), which were essentially custom-designed semiconductors. LSI sold ASICs and related design and technology services to customers in the electronic data processing, defense and aerospace, and telecommunications industries. The company promoted ASICs as being able to produce cost and design efficiencies in complex electronic systems by eliminating the need for dozens, perhaps hundreds, of standardized semiconductors and printed circuit boards in a single system. Hence for some applications, ASICs resulted in smaller, faster, cheaper, and more reliable systems, while allowing systems manufacturers to retain control of proprietary systems logic.

Although by 1986 the company had developed some standardized integrated circuit products, most of its sales were derived from the production of custom-designed semiconductors, from technical design services, and from the licensing of proprietary design software. Revenues in 1986 were $194 million compared with $140 million in 1985. Net income was $3.9 million in 1986, down from $10.1 million in 1985. Recent financial statements for LSI Logic are summarized in **Exhibits 1** and **2**.

At the end of 1986, the semiconductor industry had not yet recovered from a softening of demand and erosion of profits that had begun in 1984. LSI had performed better than most semiconductor manufacturers because of continued growth in its ASIC market segment, and because of the profitability of its design services. Sales of such services accounted for about half of LSI's revenues and all of its profits in 1986. As the industry recovered and the market for ASICs grew, competition in the segment was expected to intensify. Large companies such as Fujitsu, Toshiba, NEC, and Intel had already entered the ASIC market segment. There was also the threat that large customers of LSI such as IBM and DEC would integrate backward to design and produce their own ASICs.

LSI Logic's business strategy called for a high degree of customer involvement in the process of designing and developing ASICs for particular end products. To promote such involvement and improve the responsiveness of LSI's design engineers to customer needs, Mr. Corrigan felt it was essential to have locally based design, manufacturing, and marketing capability in each of its three major markets, North America, Japan, and Western Europe. Since its founding, LSI had established subsidiaries in the United States, Canada, Europe, and Japan. Of these, only the U.S. and Canadian subsidiaries were wholly owned. The subsidiaries shared technologies, and certain research and development activities were centralized in the United States. Otherwise, each subsidiary was expected to operate independently. In 1986, non-U.S. affiliates opened twelve new design centers worldwide and accounted for 21 percent of LSI's consolidated revenues.

LSI Logic Europe Limited was incorporated in the United Kingdom and operated nine ASIC design centers located throughout Western Europe. It also had begun construction in 1986 on a $50 million manufacturing facility in West Germany. This subsidiary's sales to European customers represented about two-thirds of LSI's non-U.S. revenues. The parent company owned 82 percent of LSI Logic Europe.

LSI had two Japanese affiliates. LSI Logic K.K., 70 percent owned by the parent, operated two design centers in Tokyo and one in Osaka. In addition, LSI and Kawasaki Steel Corporation had jointly formed Nihon Semiconductor, Inc. in 1985. LSI retained a 64 percent interest in Nihon Semiconductor, which had recently begun construction of a $100 million wafer manufacturing facility in Japan, scheduled to commence operations in 1987. Nihon Semiconductor would not compete to serve LSI Logic K.K.'s Japanese customers.

LSI Logic Corporation of Canada, Inc. began operating in 1986. It had sales offices and design centers in five Canadian cities. In conjunction with the University of Alberta, the subsidiary had begun construction of a facility in Edmonton to perform metalization fabrication, ceramic packaging, and ASIC testing. Although this Canadian subsidiary was 100 percent owned by LSI, the company was considering whether to sell a minority equity interest to Canadian investors.

Previous Financings

Several months after its founding, the company's nearly 5 million shares of common stock were still owned principally by its founders. Most of these shares had been purchased for $0.03 per share. In January 1981 LSI privately issued 6.5 million shares of Series A preferred stock at $0.90 per share to a group composed largely of U.S.-based venture capitalists, and some officers and directors. In February 1982 the company privately placed another 1.4 million shares of Series B preferred stock at $7.00 per share. Most of the Series B shares were sold to European venture capitalists, primarily in the United Kingdom. Series A and B preferred shares had similar rights of conversion with respect to future issues of common stock.

A year later, in May 1983, the company went public in the United States with an initial public offering of 7 million shares at a price of $21.00 per share and net proceeds of $19.78 per share. In the transaction, each share of Series A and B preferred stock was converted into 1.5 shares of common stock. Thus, the implied total value of the company's equity at the time of this offering exceeded $500 million.

In April 1984, LSI sold a 30 percent interest in its newly formed Japanese subsidiary, LSI Logic K.K., to twenty-five Japanese institutional investors for $18.8 million. The implied valuation of $63 million for the Japanese start-up was considered extraordinarily high by U.S. standards, even compared to the very strong U.S. market environment for initial public offerings of technology-driven companies. LSI Logic K.K. subsequently obtained very attractive terms for lines of credit from several Japanese banks.

Two months later, LSI sold 18 percent of its European subsidiary, LSI Logic Europe Limited, to a small group of European investors for $13 million. Once again, the shares were placed with institutions, including British, Swiss, and German venture capitalists. The implied valuation of this new subsidiary was also quite high.

In December 1985, LSI (the parent company) issued 5-year subordinated convertible notes in bearer form and denominated in Swiss francs. The face amount of the issue was 50 million Swiss francs (SF) with an annual coupon of 3.75 percent. The notes were convertible into 1,363,239 common shares of the parent company, implying a conversion price of SF36.67. At the prevailing spot exchange rate of SF1.95/$1, the dollar equivalent conversion price was $18.83 per share, which represented a 24 percent premium over the company's recent closing stock price of $15.125. Net proceeds of this issue were approximately $23 million, which the company used to finance growth in working capital for its U.S. operations. Effective February 21, 1986, the parent company's stock was split 3 for 2, and conversion terms for this issue were adjusted accordingly.

Prospective New Financings

In 1987, LSI faced a need to finance growth in working capital and fixed assets in its U.S. and Canadian operations. The company's consolidated cash balance of about $200 million, consisting primarily of deposits held by overseas affiliates, could not be used in the United States without adverse tax consequences. In any event, using these funds would be inconsistent with the company's decentralized approach to raising capital, and would only create a future need for funds in the non-U.S. subsidiaries. Internal sources of funds were inadequate, due to recent low profitability, so the company was forced to turn to external sources until earnings in the semiconductor industry improved.

Decisions about whether to issue debt or equity, and in what amounts, were linked. At the end of 1986, the parent company's senior indebtedness, including capitalized leases, was nearly $80 million. Of this amount, $65 million was in the form of floating rate notes issued to three U.S. banks. The average interest rate on these loans was about 1 percent below the banks' prime lending rate. Loan agreements provided for repayment in sixteen equal quarterly installments beginning March 31, 1988. These agreements also required a number of restrictive covenants concerning operating ratios and profitability, and they limited such senior notes to a total of $65 million. The company was considering whether to refinance some or all of this $65 million, either with longer-term fixed-rate obligations, or some form of equity.

Meanwhile, LSI's outstanding Swiss franc convertible notes appeared to be "hung": The company's stock price was still well below the notes' conversion and call prices. Moreover, the fall in the value of dollar, to SF1.52/$1 by the end of January 1987, had increased the effective dollar cost of the required Swiss franc debt service. The issuing currency, maturity, and conversion terms of any further issue of Euroconvertibles would have to be carefully evaluated in light of the outstanding Swiss franc issue.

Finally, the company had to decide whether to proceed with an offering of a minority equity stake in its Canadian subsidiary to Canadian investors. On the one hand, this sort of offering, like similar ones in Europe and Japan, had been contemplated at the time the subsidiary was organized. It would put this subsidiary on an equal footing with the others and force it to begin sourcing Canadian financing. On the other hand, the timing for an unseasoned equity issue, even a private one, might be poor. The market for technology-driven IPOs had cooled considerably in the United States since its peak in 1983–1984. The Canadian market was believed to be even thinner, especially for issuers in the depressed semiconductor industry. Further, such an equity issue would add to the complexity of LSI's unusual global capital and ownership structure. Already some analysts were wondering whether LSI should not begin to make plans for an eventual consolidation of its equity ownership. Some elements of LSI's ownership structure are depicted in **Exhibit 3**. Selected data on market interest rates and LSI Logic's stock price performance are shown in **Exhibits 4** and **5**, respectively.

EXHIBIT 1   CONSOLIDATED BALANCE SHEETS

	Years ending December 31 (in $ millions)					
	1981	1982	1983	1984	1985	1986
Assets						
Cash and investments	$3.8	$7.3	$156.9	$161.0	$167.7	$203.0
Accounts receivable	0.1	1.7	10.6	23.1	38.0	44.5
Inventories	0.0	1.8	6.0	21.7	33.8	26.6
Prepaid taxes	0.0	0.0	0.6	1.7	3.2	3.1
Other current assets	0.0	0.2	0.4	1.3	2.1	3.3
Total current assets	3.9	11.0	174.5	208.8	244.8	280.5
Plant and equipment	3.2	9.0	39.1	121.0	160.7	221.6
Less: Depreciation	0.1	(1.0)	(3.8)	(13.7)	(36.3)	(62.5)
Net plant and equipment	3.3	8.0	35.3	107.3	124.4	159.1
Other assets	0.3	0.2	0.8	1.6	3.3	11.8
Total assets	$7.5	$19.2	$210.6	$317.7	$372.5	$451.4
Liabilities and shareholders' equity						
Accounts payable	$0.5	$1.9	$4.2	$17.9	$14.6	$14.8
Income taxes payable	0.0	0.0	0.9	0.0	2.7	3.3
Current portion—LTD	0.4	1.1	4.1	6.1	7.0	1.7
Other current liabilities	0.3	0.9	2.9	6.6	8.5	12.3
Total current liabilities	1.2	3.9	12.1	30.6	32.8	32.1
Long-term debt	2.2	5.4	21.4	67.2	81.9	106.9
Deferred taxes	0.0	0.0	1.1	6.1	9.6	11.7
Minority interest	0.0	0.0	0.0	8.3	16.6	49.7
Total long-term liabilities	2.2	5.4	22.5	81.6	108.1	168.3
Common stock	6.0	15.6	169.1	186.6	191.8	196.4
Retained earnings	(1.9)	(5.7)	6.9	22.3	32.5	36.3
Cumulative translation adjustments	0.0	0.0	0.0	(3.4)	7.3	18.3
Total equity	4.1	9.9	176.0	205.5	231.6	251.0
Total liabilities and shareholders' equity	$7.5	$19.2	$210.6	$317.7	$372.5	$451.4

EXHIBIT 2   CONSOLIDATED INCOME STATEMENTS

	Years ending December 31 (in $ millions)					
Income Statement	1981	1982	1983	1984	1985	1986
Revenues	$ 0.0	$ 5.0	$34.8	$84.5	$140.0	$194.3
Costs and expenses						
Cost of goods	0.7	5.2	19.3	47.5	88.5	129.1
Research and development	0.8	2.3	4.4	11.9	14.4	21.6
Selling, general, and administrative	1.2	1.8	5.9	15.6	26.8	40.2
Total costs	2.7	9.3	29.6	75.0	129.7	190.9
Income from operations	(2.7)	(4.3)	5.2	9.5	10.3	3.4
Interest expense	0.0	(0.6)	(1.2)	(6.1)	(8.1)	(6.9)
Interest income	0.8	1.2	9.8	17.0	13.1	12.0
Net interest income	0.8	0.6	8.6	10.9	5.0	5.1
Income before tax and						
extraordinary items	(1.9)	(3.7)	13.8	20.4	15.3	8.5
Taxes	0.0	0.0	4.0	4.9	4.7	4.1
Income before						
extraordinary items	(1.9)	(3.7)	9.8	15.5	10.6	4.4
Extraordinary items	0.0	0.0	2.6	0.0	0.0	0.0
Minority interests	0.0	0.0	0.0	0.1	0.5	0.5
Net income	(1.9)	(3.7)	$12.4	$15.4	$ 10.1	$ 3.9

EXHIBIT 3   EQUITY OWNERSHIP STRUCTURE, LSI LOGIC AND CONSOLIDATED SUBSIDIARIES

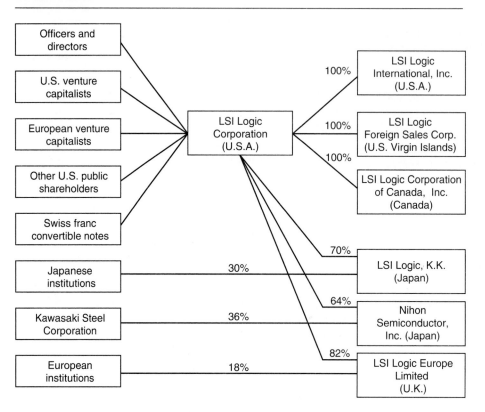

EXHIBIT 4 SELECTED FINANCIAL MARKET DATA

	1986		1987	
	November	December	January	February
Long-term domestic corporate bond yields (AA-rated or equivalent), %				
United States*	8.88	8.88	8.50	8.55
Canada	10.21	10.18	9.67	9.90
Japan	6.05	5.93	5.46	5.35
United Kingdom	11.43	11.71	11.30	10.58
Switzerland	4.71	4.72	4.62	4.56
Long-term domestic government bond yields, %				
United States	7.69	7.79	7.17	7.62
Canada	9.26	9.23	8.94	9.10
Japan	4.73	4.61	4.25	3.96
United Kingdom	10.58	10.17	10.64	9.51
Switzerland	4.07	4.05	3.93	4.01
Domestic Treasury bill rates (3-month bills), %				
United States	5.44	5.73	5.66	5.49
Canada	8.24	8.22	7.24	7.28
Japan	2.89	2.89	2.89	2.89
United Kingdom	10.96	10.75	10.56	10.47
Switzerland	na	na	na	na
Commercial bank prime lending rates, %				
United States	7.50	7.50	7.50	7.50
Canada	9.75	9.75	9.25	9.25
Japan	4.45	4.35	4.28	4.24
United Kingdom	11.00	11.00	11.00	11.00
Switzerland	5.75	5.75	5.25	5.25

*At the end of 1986, Standard and Poor's index of 400 U.S. equities traded at a market value/book value multiple of 2.11 times, the highest multiple since 1968.
Sources: Morgan Guaranty Trust Company of New York; Data Resources, McGraw-Hill, Inc.

EXHIBIT 5   HISTORICAL ADJUSTED SHARE PRICES, PARENT COMPANY

Year-quarter	Share price, $ High	Low
1983-I	na	na
1983-II	20.50	15.33
1983-III	17.50	13.42
1983-IV	16.83	12.17
1984-I	15.50	9.83
1984-II	12.00	8.67
1984-III	13.17	7.83
1984-IV	11.33	7.33
1985-I	11.83	7.83
1985-II	10.33	7.33
1985-III	12.17	9.17
1985-IV	16.17	9.67
1986-I	21.17	13.50
1986-II	20.00	9.00
1986-III	12.00	8.50
1986-IV	11.38	8.00

Note: All figures adjusted for the 3-for-2 stock split effective February 21, 1986. On December 26, 1986, LSI Logic Corporation's closing stock price was $10.125 per share.

THE AN TAI BAO COAL MINING PROJECT

Plans to develop China's An Tai Bao Mine, the world's largest open-pit coal mine, began in 1978. The government of the People's Republic of China invited the Occidental Petroleum Corporation, led by its chairman, Dr. Armand Hammer, to be a foreign partner in the project. As originally conceived, the project would require $400 million from Occidental, all of which would ideally be raised through nonrecourse project financing. Occidental expected to own half the mine and be exposed to essentially no postcompletion risk. With an internal rate of return of 30 percent, the deal was also expected to be quite financially rewarding for Occidental.

In fact, the loan agreement that Occidental, a Bank of China subsidiary, and a syndication of 39 banks were preparing to sign in late 1986 differed in a number of important respects from the original plan that Occidental had envisioned. Despite these differences, a sharp drop in world coal prices, and a provision that Occidental make an equity investment of $20 million in cash, Armand Hammer was still fully committed to the project.

BACKGROUND ON COAL IN CHINA

Coal is the most important of China's generous endowment of natural resources. Total coal reserves were estimated in the early 1970s at 1.5 trillion metric tons, giving China probably the largest concentration in the world. Worldwide reserves totaled 6.2 trillion metric tons in 1986. Worldwide production of coal grew from 3.7 billion metric tons in 1976 to 4.8 billion in 1985.

This case was prepared by Research Associate Richard P. Melnick and Professor W. Carl Kester. Copyright © 1988 by the President and Fellows of Harvard College. Harvard Business School case 288-041.

Almost two-thirds of China's reserves were located in its northern region, with 25 percent in Shanxi province alone (see map in **Exhibit 1**). Production in this northern region was 316 million metric tons in 1985, which was 36 percent of that year's total for China. Though reserves were smaller in other parts of the country, coal existed in 60 percent of the nation's counties. All major coal mines were far from the consumption centers, however. In 1985, three regions accounting for only 15 percent of China's coal reserves produced 45 percent of its total coal output that year simply because development had centered on small reserves near industrial centers.

Since the 1950s, when coal provided 95 percent of China's energy, coal had been the country's most important energy fuel. Falling to 70 percent in the mid-1970s, coal use increased again to 75 percent by 1985. Coal was commonly used because it was abundant and cheap. The transportation sector relied on coal for more than half of its energy in 1980, and coal provided 90 percent of household commercial energy the same year.

The central government tightly controlled energy by regulating the marketing and pricing of coal as well as establishing consumption quotas. For many years, despite the uneven distribution of coal, the government encouraged local areas to be self-sufficient because of the country's poor transportation system. Small, commune-controlled mines appeared all over the country, and by the 1970s there were thousands of pits that provided 30 to 40 percent of total coal output. Pressure was placed upon the Ministry of Coal Industry to produce more coal to help the Chinese economy expand. Finally, in the 1980s there was a change in focus. A number of large-scale mines were started in the northern region. Another important change was the decontrol of "local" or nonstate mines. This new program accomplished its goal of increasing production, though increases in output for the rest of the decade were not expected to match the 1981–1985 growth.

Problems with the Chinese coal industry persisted, however. It was difficult to regulate the large number of new mines that had appeared since 1983. Many of these local mines did not invest in safety equipment and, therefore, had fatality rates fifty times higher than those in the United States. While the quantity of Chinese reserves was substantial, the quality of delivered coal was often poor because there were few incentives to clean it. Unfortunately, the increase in quantity had come at quality's expense, and this was exacerbated by the measurement of state-mine production quotas in terms of raw coal.

Coal also remained a labor-intensive industry employing 4.3 million miners, in part because the average reserves were four times as deep in China as they were in the United States. The problem of moving coal from where it was found to where it was needed was a problem of such magnitude that what improvements had been made in transportation seemed insignificant.

Finally there was the pricing issue. The state price for coal was approximately 25 percent of the international free-market price. The Ministry of Coal Industry wanted to increase the price, but government planners opposed the idea, fearing that it would increase inflation and bring financial ruin. As a compromise, government officials agreed to let coal produced above a mine's quota be sold at prices above the regulated price. Nevertheless, the artificial state price for coal severely impaired the cash-generating ability of the state-owned industry in China.

Chinese investment in coal increased steadily between 1966 and 1980 and production almost doubled in the 1970s. After production setbacks in 1980 and 1981, there was a steady recovery in the 1980s (see **Exhibit 2** for investment in the coal industry from 1953 to 1985). Between 1985 and 1986, China's coal exports increased 30 percent to slightly less than 3 percent of world trade in coal and Chinese industry officials became increasingly concerned about the quality of its coal. Historically the major markets to which China exported coal were Japan, North Korea, and Hong Kong, but China expected new customers as coal exports increased.

Foreign investment in the industry increased in the 1980s through loans and direct investment, primarily from Asia. Joint ventures were dominated by Asian and European countries, with half of the initiatives coming from Hong Kong alone.

ARMAND HAMMER AND THE OCCIDENTAL PETROLEUM CORPORATION

As a young businessman, Armand Hammer conducted various business ventures in Russia during the 1920s and established himself as an American willing to do business with Eastern bloc countries. It was not surprising, therefore, that as relations between the United States and China improved in the 1970s, Dr. Hammer, chairman and chief executive officer (CEO) of Occidental Petroleum Company, was eager to be one of the first American businessmen in Beijing. An opportunity presented itself in 1979. Dr. Hammer learned of a dinner to be held in honor of Deng Xiaoping in Texas. Although not on the official guest list, Dr. Hammer and his wife took the initiative to attend. As they stood in the receiving line, Deng said, "You don't need to introduce Dr. Hammer. We all know you. You're the man who helped Lenin when Russia needed help. Now you must come to China to help us."[1] Dr. Hammer responded that he would love to, but that he would only fly on private aircraft, which the Chinese forbade.

Nonetheless, in May 1979, on his private airplane, Armand Hammer took sixteen executives from various areas of Occidental Petroleum to China. Within a week, he had signed preliminary agreements for oil exploration, coal mining, and several other activities. The following month, Kang Shien, China's vice premier and chairman of the State Economic Commission, visited the United States and invited Occidental to be the first foreign oil company to visit China's inland basin and to participate in seismic studies in the South China Sea.

In 1978 China's Ministry of Mines decided to develop the An Tai Bao Mine to produce steam coal for both domestic use and export. The mine was 450 kilometers southwest of Beijing in the Shanxi province. It was an ambitious project that would cover 17 square kilometers and would produce 15 million metric tons of raw coal annually, which would be converted to 11.5 million metric tons of clean coal. Given the magnitude of the project, the Ministry of Coal quickly came to the conclusion that

---

[1] Armand Hammer with Neil Lyndon, *Hammer* (New York: G. P. Putnam's Sons, 1987), p. 458.

it had to find a joint venture partner with enough coal mining experience to develop the mine. It was hoped that the partner would also help the mine overcome China's reputation for poor-quality coal and erratic delivery.

By 1984, Occidental and Peter Kiewit Sons emerged as two potential foreign partners for the project. Occidental Petroleum Corporation was a California-based company that explored for, produced, and marketed crude oil, natural gas, and bituminous coal. It also manufactured industrial chemicals and processed beef and pork. The company had struggled since its birth in the 1920s, but was rejuvenated by Armand Hammer, who became president and chief executive officer in 1957. Occidental bought Island Creek Coal Company, the third largest coal company in the United States, in the late 1960s. By 1986, Island Creek owned or managed 22 million tons of coal per year, with 95 percent of its output from underground mines and the rest from surface mines. A 5-year financial summary of Occidental appears in **Exhibit 3** and line-of-business information is provided in **Exhibit 4**.

Occidental retained First Boston as its financial advisor in connection with the An Tai Bao project in 1983, and negotiations proceeded between Occidental and the Chinese regarding a feasibility study. This study was completed in May 1984. Peter Kiewit, a construction company based in Nebraska, also entered the deal in April 1984 with the goal of expanding its international operations. Its primary experience prior to 1984 was in the building of federal highways, a source of tremendous growth for the company in the 1950s and 1960s. Kiewit had also developed and operated several major coal mines in the United States. It entered the An Tai Bao project with the understanding that it would be completely project-financed on a nonrecourse basis.

PROJECT FINANCING

In project financing, a project is typically isolated from the parent company with the lenders looking solely to the cash flow and assets of the project itself for loan repayment. Projects financed in this way often have at least two equity holders, with no holder having more than a 50 percent interest to avoid consolidation with parent company accounts, and are generally of very large scale in order to justify the legal and banking fees involved. The loans are usually extended to the project, which is commonly set up as a corporation or a joint venture partnership.

The project owners can structure various contractual obligations to the project. Though many equity sponsors of these projects seek pure nonrecourse financing (i.e., no liability on the part of the sponsors with respect to loan repayment), very few lenders are willing to look only to the project for repayment. Most of these financings are, therefore, "limited recourse" in which the equity holders do have some contingent liability with respect to loan repayment. Most project financings also include a completion guarantee. When there is such a guarantee, the project must produce a certain quantity and quality of its product on or before some predetermined date, failing which it continues as a full-recourse term-loan project.

Project risks are ultimately spread among its various participants. Risk surrounding the participation of a sponsor is generally handled by an agreement among the equity investors to buy out a sponsor if that sponsor needs to be removed from the partnership because of financial weakness. Lenders are sometimes willing to accept some degree of production or market risk (when a project has operating difficulty or general market conditions are less favorable than expected such that the project is unable to service its debt), and are usually willing to accept those insurable risks of *force majeure,* which are events outside the control of the principals (e.g., a flood or earthquake). In an ideal project financing, risks of various types are allocated to those parties that are best able or most willing to absorb them. Debt becomes increasingly expensive to the extent that lenders are forced to take on more and more of a project's risk themselves.

The advantages of project financing are manifold. Because project cash flows can be dedicated to lenders, sponsors can often get more leverage than if the debt were based on their own borrowing capacity. The repayment schedule for the loan is usually flexible since it is tied to cash flows from the project. One advantage cited by financial managers (though increasingly less so) is the favorable impact on financial statements: Project financing can be "off balance sheet" to the extent that a participant has an equity interest of not more than 50 percent. The arrangement fees on these financings range from ⅛ to 2 percent of the principal involved.

Each party in the An Tai Bao deal, namely, Occidental, Peter Kiewit, China, and the banks, had different motives and attitudes toward project financing in this case. Occidental and Peter Kiewit were interested in this deal only if the loans were nonrecourse, or at least limited-recourse, to protect them from large and unusual risks. Occidental's cost of debt had recently increased and it had been downgraded from Baa2 to Baa3 by the rating agencies. Furthermore, the company wanted its contribution limited to a fixed-equity investment and the remaining financing to be off its balance sheet.

For their part, the Chinese were inexperienced with this sort of financing since all of China's previous major loans had been on an unsecured (but fully guaranteed) basis. Nonrecourse funding concerned them. Specifically, one of Occidental's Chinese partners in this venture worried that, if Occidental were not responsible for its share of the debt, it might have a weaker commitment to the project. The banks, meanwhile, had financed similar coal projects in other countries, but were interested in executing new business in China.

OWNERSHIP STRUCTURE OF THE COAL MINE

As the ownership structure for the mine unfolded, Occidental and Peter Kiewit originally planned to own collectively 50 percent of the mine without investing any equity capital. Notwithstanding this attractive proposition, the prospect of protracted negotiations prompted Kiewit to withdraw by September 1984. This left Occidental without a partner.

Fortunately, the Bank of China offered to fill the void left by Kiewit. After a minor restructuring of the financing plan, Occidental invested $20 million of equity through its unguaranteed subsidiary called Occidental China Coal Incorporated.[2] The Bank of

---

[2]Roughly half this amount took the form of credits for previous cash expenditures. Thus, only about half of the $20 million represented new, incremental cash invested.

China created a subsidiary entitled Beijing BOCTC (Bank of China Trust Company) An Tai Bao Coal Development Company, Ltd. (itself a subsidiary of the Bank of China Trust and Consultancy Company, the merchant banking subsidiary of the Bank of China), through which it also invested $20 million. Together these two subsidiaries formed a 50-50 joint venture called Island Creek of China Coal, Ltd. (ICCC), which was a Bermuda-based company that held approximately 50 percent of the mine. The third partner in this project, China National Coal Development Corporation (CNCDC), was an agency of China's Ministry of Coal Industry. CNCDC created an indirect subsidiary called Ping Shuo First Coal Company (PSF), which, along with China International Trust and Investment Corporation, held the remaining 50 percent of the mine (see **Exhibit 5**, which diagrams the organization of the project).

ICCC was to be responsible for managing the mine until 1997. Chinese nationals would receive training during this time period and, eventually, would take control. By 1997 PSF would be in charge of running the mine. Subject to termination clauses, the joint venture would continue for 30 years.

The CNCDC would provide domestic resources for production of the coal. Infrastructure development included building and upgrading railroads, expanding the Qinghuandao port to handle 40 million metric tons of coal a year, building a village that would support 17,000 people, supplying power and water to residential areas, and diverting the Qi Li River. While local labor, materials, and taxes had been a problem in many foreign investment ventures, these dilemmas were minimized in this case since all local expenses were negotiated as a package.

The China National Coal Import and Export Comapny (CNCIEC), a sister company to CNCDC, also agreed to market the mine's coal. Eighty percent of the coal would be exported and 20 percent would be sold domestically. The domestic coal would sell at the Chinese government-regulated price of $6.81 per metric ton, substantially below the anticipated $35 market price per metric ton. While CNCIEC agreed to sell ICCC's portion of the coal, ICCC could market the coal itself if it believed it could obtain better prices.

All borrowings for the Occidental and BOCTC share of the project would be directed through ICCC, which would independently determine its profit and taxes. The tax situation for ICCC in China was as follows: (1) During the first 2 years of profitable operations, ICCC would receive tax forgiveness; (2) the following 3 years, ICCC would be taxed at 25 percent; and (3) thereafter, the tax rate would be 50 percent. Furthermore, equipment investments could be depreciated over 5 years. During the "Investment Recovery Period," which was projected to last until 1995, ICCC would receive 52.49 percent of the project's coal. After 1995 the Chinese would receive 60 percent and leave ICCC with the remainder.

THE LENDING SYNDICATE

The $475 million proposed debt financing was being lead-managed by the Bank of China, Bank of America, Crédit Lyonnais, Industrial Bank of Japan, and the Royal Bank of Canada, all of which had experience with China or coal mining. These banks collectively agreed to loan $130 million while a syndicate of thirty-four other banks would provide the remaining $345 million.

The proposed financing was divided into seven tranches that provided precompletion and postcompletion credits as shown in **Exhibit 6**. Tranches A, B, and C shown in **Exhibit 6** actually would exist both pre- and postcompletion, but would differ according to whether they were project-supported or sponsor-supported. These six tranches plus tranche D totaled seven tranches altogether.

Tranches A and B, which were production loans and production credits totaling $300 million for 9.5 years, were the true project-supported, limited-recourse loans. Included here were letters of credit that could be used to back up issues of commercial paper and export credits. When the $300 million became project-supported (i.e., nonrecourse) postcompletion, the banks would assume certain project risks such as sovereign risks, operating risks (e.g., equipment failure, strikes, etc.), and market risks.

Tranche C was a price-sensitive, 9-year credit line for $100 million. According to a formula, if the price of Chinese coal delivered to a port in China (which generally cost about $10 per metric ton less than the average world price for steam coal) averaged between $38 and $42 per metric ton within any 6-month period after production began, $50 million would become tranche A nonrecourse loans. If the average price reached or exceeded $42 per metric ton, the second $50 million would also become tranche A nonrecourse loans.[3] The D tranche for $75 million was a revolving standby facility for covering debt service obligations and was only available postcompletion. For all of the tranches, the pricing would be ½ percent over LIBOR precompletion and 1 percent postcompletion, increasing to 1⅛ percent and finally to 1⅜ percent if and when the debt became nonrecourse to Occidental and BOCTC.

As important as the pricing, however, was the proposed deal's credit structure. ICCC was to be the borrowing entity, with Occidental and BOCTC jointly and severally fully guaranteeing the loans precompletion. According to the proposed venture agreement, ICCC would be responsible for the operation of the mine while PSF would be responsible for developing the infrastructure to support the mine. The banks and the sponsors agreed to four completion tests that related to the removal of overburden from the mine, the delivery of raw coal to the preparation plant, the processing of raw coal into clean coal, and the loading of clean coal into railroad cars. Since there would be full recourse until these tasks were deemed completed, there was a strong incentive for ICCC to achieve completion of the mine.

While the banks wanted all four tests satisfied concurrently for 91 consecutive days, ICCC and First Boston negotiated so that the tests could run independently for 91 days, with the four tests running concurrently for only 45 days. Further interruptions were allowed during the balance of the 91-day test period. The permitted interruptions, including *force majeure* and infrastructure failure, allowed the sponsors to suspend the completion tests for up to 1 year. Thus, the completion tests could ultimately be satisfied nonconcurrently and on nonconsecutive days.

---

[3]The last-known major sale of steam coal by China was to Japan at $35.30 per ton.

Since ICCC wanted the loans to become nonrecourse, it naturally wanted to reach completion quickly. This could take considerable time if interruptions in the 91-day test period arose. As ICCC's advisor, First Boston persuaded the banks to accept limited recourse in consideration of partial completion. Thus, for every 1 percent the mine was below completion parameters, $5 million would remain sponsor-supported postcompletion. If performance were below 80 percent of the standard completions test, all of tranches A and B would remain sponsor-supported.

Yet another obstacle to the completion of this deal was the availability of mortgage financing. The lending banks wished to have a mortgage on the ICCC assets in China, but the Chinese government would not agree to this. Since a mortgage was not available, the banks then asked for advance approval from the Ministry of Foreign Economic Relations and Trade (MOFERT) to be assigned ICCC's shares in case of default. However, MOFERT refused to approve such an advance assignment. Ultimately, the banks sought a covenant whereby the sponsors would be required to repay all the debt outstanding in the event of a default and no assignment approval from MOFERT. An innovative solution to this impasse suggested by First Boston was to have the sponsors buy back the project from ICCC, and ICCC transfer proceeds to the banks if there were postcompletion default with no cooperation from MOFERT. A net present value calculation using 10 years of cash flows forecasted by an independent consultant approved by the banks and the sponsors and discounted at 15 percent would determine the purchase price. This value was believed to be approximately equivalent to what the banks could obtain if ICCC shares were sold in the open market.

Finally, the banks required that foreign exchange proceeds from the sale of export coal would be received and deposited in the Bank of America's New York branch. As was standard practice in financings involving sovereign governments, it was also agreed that BOCTC would waive the right of sovereign immunity. This would allow banks to undertake legal action in the United States in the event of default or noncompliance on the part of the Chinese government.

CLOSING THE DEAL

By the time this deal was ready for closing in December 1986, it differed substantially from what Occidental had first envisioned. While the company had wanted no postcompletion risk, it was now exposed to some risk under the terms of the current agreement. Meanwhile, as the deal's terms were being negotiated, the average world price of coal fell from $52 in 1983 to $46 by 1986 (see **Exhibit 7** for a price history of coal).

Still, despite these changes, Armand Hammer thought the project's overall importance outweighed other considerations pertaining to the structure and financing of the deal. As the intrepid Dr. Hammer put it, this contract had been "as hard to create as a Stradivarius."[4] It now appeared difficult to persuade him into any course of action other than going forward with the An Tai Bao project under the proposed financing terms.

---

[4]Armand Hammer with Neil Lyndon, *Hammer* (New York: G. P. Putnam's Sons, 1987), p. 460.

EXHIBIT 1   LOCATION OF CHINA'S COAL RESERVES

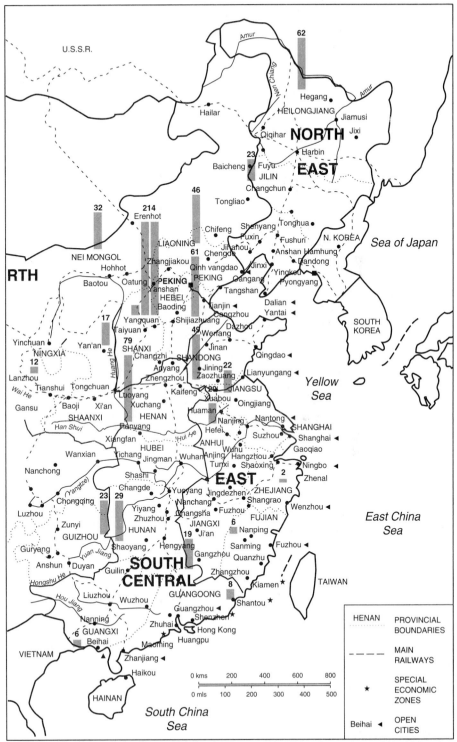

Source: The Economist Intelligence Unit Special Report 1089, "China: Energy Sector Outlook" (London: Economist Publications Ltd.), p. 13.

EXHIBIT 2   **INVESTMENT IN THE CHINESE COAL INDUSTRY, 1953–1985 (IN MILLIONS YUAN, EXCEPT PERCENTAGES)**

Period	Investment in new capacity		Investment in existing mines*		Total investment,
	Yuan	%	Yuan	%	Yuan
1953–1957 plan	2,433	82.0	535	18.0	2,968
1958–1962 plan	6,111	70.3	2,587	29.7	8,698
1963–1965 plan	2,404	95.6	111	4.4	2,515
1966–1970 plan	2,594	55.6	2,071	44.4	4,665
1971–1975 plan	5,217	57.5	3,857	42.5	9,074
1976–1980 plan	8,691	63.8	4,934	36.2	13,625
1978	2,067	65.0	1,113	35.0	3,180
1979	2,072	65.0	1,114	35.0	3,186
1980	2,178	65.1	1,169	34.9	3,347
1980–1985 plan	13,892	68.3	6,440	31.7	20,332
1981	2,127	91.9	188	8.1	2,315
1982	1,709	57.3	1,276	42.7	2,985
1983	2,866	71.5	1,141	28.5	4,007
1984	4,000	72.5	1,514	27.5	5,514
1985	3,190	57.9	2,321	42.1	5,511

Year	(Yuan/$)
1976	1.8803
1977	1.7300
1978	1.5771
1979	1.4962
1980	1.5303
1981	1.7455
1982	1.9227
1983	1.9809
1984	2.7957
1985	3.2015

*The difference between total investment in the coal industry and investment in newly added capacity.
Sources: China Statistical Yearbook, 1986; and International Financial Statistics (Washington, DC: International Monetary Fund), 1986.

EXHIBIT 3   OCCIDENTAL PETROLEUM CORPORATION—5-YEAR SUMMARY OF SELECTED FINANCIAL DATA (MILLIONS, EXCEPT PER SHARE AMOUNTS AND NUMBERS OF SHARES)

	Through September 30, 1986	For the years ended December 31			
		1985	1984	1983	1982
Results of operations					
Net sales	$11,175.2	$14,534.4	$15,586.3	$19,115.7	$17,717.1
Income before discontinued					
operations and extraordinary gain	152.0	455.0	568.7	480.2	136.4
Net income	161.0	696.0	568.7	566.7	155.6
Preferred dividend					
requirements (fully diluted)	61.2	223.7	260.7	367.5	86.9
Primary earnings per share from					
continuing operations	0.63	2.21	3.08	1.15	0.49
Fully diluted earnings per share					
from continuing operations	0.69	2.20	3.05	1.15	na*
Common dividends declared per share	2.50	2.50	2.50	2.50	2.50
Average shares outstanding					
(thousands)	145,343	103,843	99,618	96,569	96,051
Financial position					
Total assets	$17,595.5	$11,585.9	$12,273.1	$11,775.4	$15,772.5
Senior funded debt, net	5,623.8	1,954.9	2,012.0	2,684.3	4,128.5
Subordinated debt, net	1,822.9	1,795.5	1,763.1	—	—
Capital lease liabilities, net	97.8	94.3	106.5	134.9	201.4
Redeemable preferred stocks	171.6	336.7	1,443.5	2,001.2	2,131.4
Stockholders' equity	4,394.7	3,281.0	2,903.6	2,640.9	2,689.7

*Not applicable, as the effect of the calculation is antidilutive.
Source: Occidental Petroleum Corporation, *1986 Annual Report,* p. 25.

EXHIBIT 4 OCCIDENTAL PETROLEUM CORPORATION—INDUSTRY SEGMENTS (MILLIONS)

	Oil and gas		Chemical products		Coal		Agribusiness		Corporate		Total	
	1985	1984	1985	1984	1985	1984	1985	1984	1985	1984	1985	1984
Total revenues	$6805.1	$7208.3	$1621.1	$1645.4	$ 542.9	$540.5	$6612.2	$6166.2	$164.5	$227.2	$15,643.9	$16,237.6
Pre-tax profit (loss)	1942.0	1969.3	100.3	83.3	3.0	(40.4)	103.0	57.6	(330.7)	(425.0)	1,817.6	1,644.8
Net income	829.6	891.6	91.1	76.4	3.2	(40.3)	52.2	34.4	(280.1)	(393.4)	696.0	568.7
Capital expenditures	715.4	625.1	124.4	115.8	35.7	35.1	51.1	48.5	5.5	11.9	932.1	836.4
Depreciation, depletion, and amortization	713.2	703.0	84.1	82.2	29.8	34.7	41.6	39.3	11.5	26.2	880.2	885.4
Total assets	6774.4	7119.7	1721.3	1537.5	1015.9	958.7	1047.2	1062.6	1027.1	1594.6	11,585.9	12,273.1

Source: Occidental Petroleum Corporation, 1986 Annual Report, p. 56.

EXHIBIT 5   THE PROPOSED OWNERSHIP STRUCTURE OF THE AN TAI BAO COAL MINING PROJECT

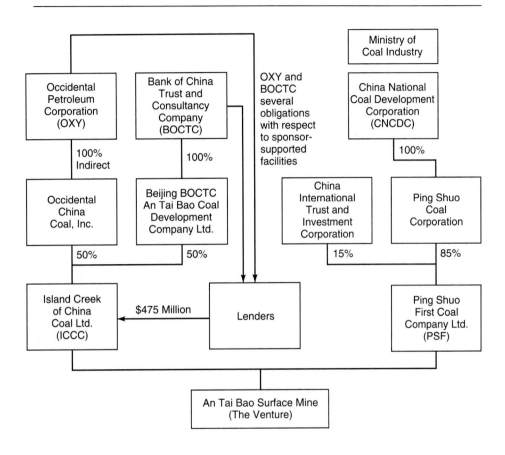

Note: BOCTC is a wholly owned subsidiary of the Bank of China.
Source: The First Boston Corporation.

EXHIBIT 6   FINANCING FOR THE PROJECT

Tranche	Amount, millions	Type
A	$230	Production loans and production credits
B	70	Production credits in the form of letters of credit to support export credits
C	100	Coal price−sensitive production loans and production credits
D	75	Revolving standby facility
	$475	

	Project-supported, millions	Sponsor-supported, millions	Total, millions
Precompletion			
Export credits	—	$ 70 (B)	$ 70
Commercial bank loans and L/Cs	—	330 (A, C)	330
Total	—	$400	$400
Postcompletion			
Export credits	$ 70 (B)	—	$ 70
Commercial bank loans and L/Cs	230 (A)	$100 (C)	330
Total	$300	$100	$400

Note: Repayment schedules were complex and dependent upon coal prices and percentage of loans remaining sponsor-supported postcompletion. Generally, tranche B was expected to be repaid in twenty semiannual installments; repayment of tranche A would be the *greater* of 75 percent of cash available for debt repayment or all available such cash less tranche B requirements; and repayment of tranche D would be the *lesser* of the outstanding balance or 25 percent of the cash available for debt repayment.
Source: The First Boston Corporation.

EXHIBIT 7 AVERAGE WORLD PRICE FOR STEAM COAL*

	Price, metric ton
1978	$46.74
1979	42.52
1980	52.22
1981	62.97
1982	62.45
1983	52.66
1984	46.65
1985	47.37
1986	46.26

*The price of Chinese coal followed world price trends, although its price at a Chinese port averaged about $10 less per ton than the prevailing world price.

Source: Coal Information 1987 (Paris: International Energy Agency, OECD), p. 11.

PART **FIVE**

INTERNATIONAL
MERGERS, ACQUISITIONS,
AND CORPORATE
RESTRUCTURINGS

THE DISTILLERS
COMPANY PLC

On January 20, 1986, Arthur Guinness & Sons PLC announced a record £2.3 billion bid for the Distillers Company, the world's leading producer of Scotch whisky. The proposed merger offer was the largest in British history. If completed, it would transform Guinness overnight into one of Britain's ten largest firms.

This development was watched with great interest in New York by John Monroe, a partner and head of arbitrage in the Wall Street investment banking firm of Thorton, Fraser & Long, Inc., and by Todd Sheridan, a risk arbitrageur reporting to Mr. Monroe. Thorton had taken a position in Distillers's stock when the company was first hit by a bid from the Argyll group in December 1985. Guinness's competing offer made it tempting to raise the stake involved. However, given the rules and regulations governing British mergers, the new bid also complicated the situation and presented additional risks to Thorton, Fraser & Long. Messrs. Monroe and Sheridan had to reevaluate Thorton's position quickly if they wanted to make the most of the new situation.

THE TARGET COMPANY

The Distillers Company PLC (Distillers) had been considered a potential takeover target for many years. Founded in Scotland in 1877, Distillers was the parent company of numerous subsidiaries whose principal activities were the production, marketing, and sales of distilled spirits. Scotch whisky was the largest part of the business with

This case was prepared by Research Associate Richard P. Melnick and Professor W. Carl Kester. Copyright © 1987 by the President and Fellows of Harvard College. Harvard Business School case 287-062.

brand names including Dewar's White Label, Johnnie Walker, White Horse, and Black & White. The company was one of Scotland's best known industrial concerns and Britain's largest liquor company. It also produced Gordon's Gin, made several brands of yeast, and sold carbon dioxide gas. Distillers's overseas interests were important, as the group earned 95 percent of its pretax profits abroad in 1985. Recent financial statements for Distillers appear in **Exhibits 1**, **2**, and **3**. A comparison to other major distillers appears in **Exhibit 4**.

Distillers's problems originated in the 1960s when its biochemicals subsidiary was sued for marketing thalidomide to pregnant women.[1] Distillers never quite recovered from the tragedy that shook this subsidiary: It fell from the rank of twenty-first largest company in the United Kingdom in 1970 to seventy-third by 1985. Between 1973 and 1984, Distillers's share in the world Scotch market also dropped from 48 percent to 35 percent, while its share in the U.K. market fell from 54 percent to 15 percent. Much of this dramatic drop resulted from the removal of its top-selling Johnnie Walker Red Label from Britain in 1977.[2]

Industrywide problems also plagued Distillers during the late 1970s and 1980s. Sales of the major Scotch producers—Distillers, Arthur Bell, Allied Lyons, and Seagrams—plunged at the beginning of the 1980 recession. Between 1977 and 1983, demand for Scotch in the United States (representing 28 percent of worldwide sales in 1983) dropped 18 percent, and total Scotch sales in 1985 remained 15 percent below 1979 levels. Reasons for the decline included the recession of the early 1980s, a health-motivated switch in the United States to wine, better marketing of rival products, and increased interest in local whiskies. After closing or mothballing 20 percent of capacity between 1980 and 1984, which eliminated 7500 out of 25,000 jobs, the industry was operating at 45 percent of capacity in 1985.

During this 4-year period, Distillers's pretax profits stagnated under the £200 million level and it closed twenty-one distilleries. Pretax profits on exports actually increased 9 percent in 1985 due to the strong U.S. dollar and some product price increases. However, Distillers lost overall market share as world exports increased 5 percent while its export volume decreased 1.9 percent. Continued concern over these trends prompted the company to close ten more distilleries.

Industry problems notwithstanding, many institutional shareholders believed that Distillers could be far more profitable than it was. Some analysts believed that Distillers underperformed other spirits companies because it failed to defend its market position aggressively, and never seriously tried to adjust for the decline in Scotch consumption. The strong brand names of Dewar's, Johnnie Walker, and Black & White in the U.S. market appeared to be valuable assets that simply needed better management. Incumbent management seemed protected from replacement via

---

[1]Thalidomide was a drug taken to prevent morning sickness in pregnant women. It was eventually proved to be a cause of severe birth deformities.

[2]The European Economic Community (EEC) had ruled that dual pricing (higher prices charged for export than for domestic consumption) violated the Treaty of Rome. Distillers chose to withdraw Johnnie Walker Red from the British market rather than raise its home price to uncompetitive levels or lower the price of its exports to EEC countries.

takeover, however, because of a large contingent of stable Scottish shareholders who were reluctant to let the company fall into non-Scottish hands.

THE ARGYLL GROUP

The Argyll Group PLC was a £1.7 billion British-based food and drink company employing 36,000 people. It grew extensively in the 1980s, principally through acquisitions arranged by its aggressive chairman, James Gulliver. Argyll Foods, a subsidiary of the group, was one of Britain's largest food retailing concerns. One of its companies, Presto, operated 161 stores, with more than 2.5 million square feet of store area, and accounted for half of Argyll's food sales. The group's drink division produced, marketed, and distributed liquor products principally in the United States through its subsidiary Barton Brands, Ltd., and also in the United Kingdom. Financial data for the Argyll Group are presented in **Exhibits 5** and **6**.

Mr. Gulliver's planning of a bid for Distillers appeared to begin as early as 1984 when he managed to put several Scottish directors on Argyll's board. However, active speculation about such a bid did not develop until late August 1985 when rumors circulated that Argyll was about to tender for Distillers. *The Times* of London reported on August 31 that a major British food company would make "an ambitious and audacious bid for Distillers." Argyll admitted that its long-term strategy was to develop a major food and drink business, and that it did view Distillers and other companies as a possible means to grow through acquisition. It denied, however, that a bid was imminent, and affirmed that it would not presently make a bid. According to the U.K. Takeover Code, once a company made such a denial, it was then forbidden to make a bid for 3 months.

On December 2, the first date allowed under the Code, Argyll did, in fact, begin a £1.8 billion takeover campaign for Distillers. At the time, it was the largest takeover bid in British history. Announcing the bid, Mr. Gulliver said, "For shareholders, Distillers's management failure is all too plain," and he criticized Distillers's executives for surrendering market share, producing low profits, and paying dividends that could not even keep up with inflation.[3] In response, Distillers's chairman, John Connell, accused Argyll of being "upstarts" that would destroy Distillers's strong overseas franchises. Mr. Connell said, "Distillers is a high margin international company, and Argyll lacks experience and information about how to operate in international markets."

Argyll eventually published its formal offer on December 17. The basic offer for every ten Distillers shares was: (1) eight new Argyll ordinary shares, (2) 10 new Argyll convertible preference shares, and (3) £14.50 in cash. The preference shares would have a yield of 6.5 percent on 100 pence par value and would be convertible at the rate of 28 Argyll common shares for every 100 new Argyll preference shares (an implied conversion price of approximately 357 pence per common share). Shareholders could also choose a "cash alternative" to the above offer, which was 485 pence for each Distillers share (see the appendix for discussion of cash alternatives). The first

[3]*The New York Times*, December 3, 1985, p. D1.

closing date for both the basic offer and the cash alternative was January 7, 1986, at 3:00 p.m. The offer was subject to many conditions, including (1) that acceptances were received for not less than 90 percent of Distillers shares for which the offer was made, and from not less than 75 percent of Distillers's shareholders; and (2) that the Office of Fair Trading (OFT) did not refer the acquisition to the Monopolies and Mergers Commission (MMC). Pro forma 1985 financial statements for the Argyll Group after combination with Distillers were published in Argyll's formal offer document, and are shown in **Exhibit 7**.

Using the price of Distillers stock on August 20, 1985 (before bid speculation started), Argyll claimed that its basic offer and the cash alternative represented a premium on Distillers stock of 73 percent and 62 percent, respectively. Stock price data for Argyll, Distillers, and Guinness are presented in **Exhibit 8**, along with other financial market information. At the date of the offer, Distillers had 358,609,544 common shares outstanding, of which 1.26 percent was already owned by Argyll.

By January 7, only 2.72 percent of Distillers's shareholders had actually accepted Argyll's offer, bringing Argyll's total position in Distillers stock to 3.98 percent. Argyll then announced that it would extend its existing offer until January 28. British authorities helped Argyll's cause considerably when, on January 9, they announced that they would not refer this offer to the Monopolies and Mergers Commission. Analysts responded that the clearance greatly increased Argyll's chances of winning control of Distillers, either with this bid or a subsequent higher one. Distillers's executives reasserted their claim that Argyll's bid was "unwelcome and inadequate."

THE MERGER WAVE IN THE UNITED KINGDOM

Argyll's bid for Distillers was only one of many hostile takeover efforts in the United Kingdom in 1985 and 1986. Much of this activity was occurring in the financial services sector, which was anticipating radical changes in stock exchange membership rules following the "Big Bang" scheduled for October 27, 1986.[4] However, many mergers and acquisitions were also occurring in certain industrial sectors such as chemicals and food processing. Combinations were taking place in these industries in an effort to create globally competitive companies. A bull market in London, lots of corporate liquidity, and the free-market orientation of the Thatcher government helped fuel this wave. By the end of 1985, 111 acquisitions totaling £7.0 billion had been completed, with twenty-one more deals worth about £5.0 billion still pending. In 1981, the total volume of completed deals was only £882 million.

British analysts and economists appeared to agree that takeovers were welcome when directed at companies with poor management. However, many feared that some large takeovers in Britain were primarily financial deals that did not increase productivity or create jobs. Most of the largest bids in 1985 were hostile, and one

---

[4]"Big Bang" referred to the cessation of fixed-commission brokerage, and a host of other liberalizations of security market regulations.

analyst claimed that many British takeovers had gone beyond the role of disciplining poor management and were, instead, "corporate cannibalism." Such claims led to pressure on the government to slow the merger wave.

Merger regulations were enumerated in the Fair Trading Act of 1973, and merger and acquisition activities were governed by three different bodies: the Office of Fair Trading, the Monopolies and Mergers Commission, and the Panel on Takeovers and Mergers. In its design, this system of governance was intended to impart a bias against government intervention. The Takeover Panel, for instance, consisted of a group of senior executives from Britain's financial services sector. It was created by the "City" (London's financial community) as a self-regulatory mechanism to function in lieu of formal government control such as that exerted by the Securities and Exchange Commission in the United States. The panel promulgated rules of conduct (the U.K. Takeover Code), heard complaints, and attempted to resolve disputes involving violations of its code. Formally, the panel did not have the force of law and could do little more than publicly censure a company for misconduct in a takeover battle. Nevertheless, it was a widely respected body. Merchant bankers would often complain of inconsistencies in the panel's policies or excessive rigidity, but few preferred to see an extensive legal code replace the self-regulatory code of the panel.

The Office of Fair Trading (OFT) was the body vested with the statutory responsibility of advising the secretary of state for Trade and Industry as to whether or not a proposed combination should be referred to the Monopolies and Mergers Commission (MMC) for a review. A referral would be likely if a combination resulted in a 25 percent market share or more, or if the assets being acquired totaled more than £30 million. These criteria served as a trigger for review and possible reference by the OFT. While the stated policy was to refer bids based on competitive considerations only, other factors such as the degree of debt financing involved in a takeover, or national reciprocity in cases involving foreign bidders, were also used in practice as reasons for referral. A referral could, in principle, be made at any time.

If reference were made, the job of the MMC was to determine whether or not the merger could be expected to operate against the public interest. This process could take 6 months or more, crippling one company's bid while leaving an unchallenged rival free to offer shareholders an immediate deal. If the combination was deemed not to be against the public interest, the matter ended. Ministers had no further statutory power to intervene. The bidding company would be free to proceed with a new offer. If the MMC found the proposed combination to be against the public interest, the secretary of state then had discretion to stop the merger or impose conditions to avert the adverse effects. The director of the OFT would normally be consulted for further advice at this stage.

Technically, Britain's merger guidelines contained no special provisions inhibiting the acquisition of British companies by foreign concerns. While this was the rule, practice sometimes seemed to reflect a different reality. Elders IXL, an Australian brewing company, made a hostile bid worth £1.8 billion for Allied Lyons in 1985. Although Elders had no brewing, food, wine, or spirits businesses in the United Kingdom, the bid was referred to the Monopolies and Mergers Commission, ostensibly because of the heavy leverage that would result from the proposed deal. In contrast to this, the Office of Fair Trading cleared Argyll's £1.9 billion bid for Distillers fairly quickly. Some contended that this evinced a bias against foreign bidders by British antitrust officials and explained the conspicuous lack of foreign "white knights" bidding for large British companies in 1985.

A regulatory bias also appeared to exist for certain types of combinations among U.K. firms. For example, United Biscuits's announced merger with Imperial Group was referred on competitive grounds. The Office of Fair Trading did not, however, refer the subsequent rival hostile bid by Hanson Trust for Imperial, giving Hanson an easier takeover position. This created the impression that the government favored conglomerate mergers over intra-industry deals.

THE MERCHANT BANKS

Actively involved in the British merger wave, and a major guiding force, was a cadre of U.K. merchant banks. These banks not only advised clients on offensive and defensive takeover strategies, they also acted as agents by purchasing stock on the open market, soliciting shares from stockholders, and underwriting cash-alternative offers. As the merger wave accelerated in the United Kingdom, these banks sometimes adopted controversial tactics, eliciting claims from injured parties that even included reports of burglaries at executives' homes and the tailing of directors.

Morgan Grenfell, advisor to Guinness on the Distillers deal, was described as "the bank all others love to beat."[5] It had a reputation for stretching the City's Takeover Code to the limit and taking bold risks in the purchase of target companies' shares on behalf of their clients. For example, it is believed to have spent nearly £500 million purchasing Imperial Group shares for United Biscuits. This prompted the Bank of England and the London Stock Exchange to suggest that merchant banks avoid putting more than 25 percent of their own capital at risk or spending more than 25 percent of their client's net worth without getting client shareholders' approval.

Kleinwort Benson, another large and well-known merchant bank, acted as adviser to Distillers in its defense. Argyll engaged Samuel Montagu, a smaller and less active merchant bank in the merger and acquisition business compared to Morgan Grenfell and Kleinwort Benson, but one noted for its innovativeness. A ranking of U.K. merchant banks according to their involvement in public takeovers is provided in **Exhibit 9**.

THE GUINNESS OFFER

Following its December 2 announcement, Argyll had 28 days to publish its formal offer document (actual publication occurred on December 17). Once the published offer appeared, it then had 16 days under British regulations to take over the target. The forty-sixth day was the last day it could amend its offer, since the shareholders must be given at least 2 weeks in which to make a decision. If it failed to win control within

---

[5]"The City Spins with Merger Mania," *Euromoney* (Supplement), July 1986, pp. 22–24.

this time, it would not be allowed to bid for another year. However, if a new bidder entered the contest, the timetable would start anew at the date of the new offer.

This is what happened when Arthur Guinness & Sons PLC, acting as ''white knight'' for Distillers, made its bid on January 20.[6] Guinness's bid offered Distillers's shareholders the choice of 8 Guinness shares plus 700 pence cash for 5 Distillers shares, or a cash alternative of 584.8 pence per Distillers share. It too was conditional on receiving 90 percent of the shares outstanding and at least 50 percent of the shareholder vote currently exercisable at general meetings.

Guinness, the £1.2 billion brewing and publishing company (see **Exhibits 10** and **11** for financial statements), was headed by Ernest Saunders, an executive well known to British investors for his marketing acumen and aggressive management style. Mr. Saunders took control of Guinness 4 years earlier when profits were sagging. He sold 140 companies in an effort to concentrate the organization. By the mid-1980s, he was rebuilding through acquisition. In 1985 he acquired Arthur Bell and Sons, maker of Britain's best-selling Scotch whisky, in a £356 million hostile takeover effort. If the Distillers bid were successful, Mr. Saunders would double the size of Guinness and, according to him, create a British company that could compete aggressively in international markets. Mr. Saunders and Distillers's executives emphasized that this would be a promising merger because both companies were international in their scope of operations. The new Guinness would have 38 percent of the U.K. Scotch market and 41 percent of the worldwide market after the proposed combination. Pro forma financial statements for the proposed combination were not yet available since Guinness had not yet published its formal offer document.

THE NEXT MOVE

With the new Guinness bid, Mr. Sheridan was charged with the responsibility of reassessing the situation and reporting to Mr. Monroe. Although Mr. Sheridan was an experienced risk arbitrageur, the Distillers deal represented his first foray into the comparatively new world of international risk arbitrage. Certain tasks remained the same, of course. Mr. Monroe was a strong advocate of fundamental research before taking positions. For Mr. Sheridan, this meant studying all available financial statements and other publicly available information (data on recent deals are shown in **Exhibit 12**). He would then have to gauge the intrinsic worth of Distillers and that of the competing offers. He would also have to determine what the potential upside was for Distillers stock, and where it would go if the proposed deals collapsed. However, the idiosyncrasies of British merger and acquisition activity, the fact that transactions were executed in pounds, not dollars, and his sheer distance from the City complicated his job significantly. Thorton, Fraser & Long had already invested heavily in Distillers stock. Mr. Sheridan had to study all angles of this deal quickly but carefully before proposing any changes in that position to Mr. Monroe.

---

[6]In an unusual move, Distillers agreed to pay all of Guinness's fees and other costs incurred in connection with the bid.

EXHIBIT 1   DISTILLERS GROUP PROFIT AND LOSS STATEMENTS (YEARS ENDED MARCH 31) (MILLIONS, EXCEPT PER SHARE ITEMS AND NUMBER OF SHARES)

	1985	1984
Turnover	£1274.3	£1134.1
Excise duty	(342.1)	(327.3)
Turnover excluding excise duty	932.2	806.8
Cost of sales	(619.9)	(551.8)
Gross profit	312.3	255.0
Distribution costs	(28.8)	(27.8)
Administrative expenses	(50.0)	(45.8)
Other operating income (charges)	(0.3)	0.2
Total net operating expenses	(79.1)	(73.4)
Trading profit	233.2	181.6
Share of profit (loss) of related company	4.2	(1.1)
Income from investments	9.0	7.2
Net interest income (expense)	(13.6)	1.9
Surplus on realization of investments	3.4	2.0
Profit on other activities	3.0	10.0
Profit on ordinary activities before taxation	236.2	191.6
Taxation	(102.9)	(63.3)
Profit on ordinary activities after taxation	133.3	128.3
Extraordinary items less attributable taxation	(7.5)	(9.5)
Profits for the year	£ 125.8	£ 118.8
Dividends	£ 54.4	£ 49.5
Earnings per share, pence	36.7p	35.4p
Dividends per share, pence	15.0p	13.6p
Shares outstanding	363,169,545	363,169,545

EXHIBIT 2   DISTILLERS GROUP CONSOLIDATED BALANCE SHEETS (YEARS ENDED MARCH 31) (MILLIONS, EXCEPT PER SHARE ITEMS)

	1985	1984
Fixed assets		
Tangible fixed assets	£ 305.3	£ 299.3
Investments	67.6	60.3
	372.9	359.6
Current assets		
Stocks	874.5	813.1
Debtors	258.1	237.8
Short-term deposits	166.7	57.4
Cash at bank and in hand	32.5	19.8
	1331.8	1128.1
Creditors (due within 1 year)	(294.2)	(204.4)
Net current assets (liabilities)	1037.6	923.7
Total assets less current liabilities	1410.5	1283.3
Creditors (due after 1 year)	(305.9)	(103.0)
Provisions for liabilities and charges	(67.4)	(67.9)
Net assets	£1037.2	£1112.4
Capital and reserves		
Called-up share capital	£ 181.6	£ 181.6
Reserves	62.3	232.0
Profit and loss account	770.3	680.9
	1014.2	1094.5
Attributable reserves of related company	23.0	17.9
Total capital employed	£1037.2	£1112.4
Book value per share, pence	279.3p	301.4p

EXHIBIT 3   DISTILLERS GROUP 5-YEAR FINANCIAL REVIEW (YEARS ENDED MARCH 31) (MILLIONS, EXCEPT PER SHARE ITEMS)

Group profit summary	1985	1984	1983	1982	1981
Turnover	£1274.3	£1134.1	£1127.2	£1083.9	£1041.3
Trading profit	233.2	181.6	201.7	181.6	174.7
Share of profit (loss) of related company	4.2	(1.1)	0.2	(0.5)	(0.4)
Income from investments	9.0	7.2	6.7	5.8	5.5
Interest	(13.6)	1.9	0.7	(6.1)	(5.2)
Surplus on realization of investments	3.4	2.0	—	—	8.7
Profit on ordinary activities before taxation	236.2	191.6	209.3	180.8	183.3
Taxation	(102.9)	(63.3)	(70.1)	(49.0)	(56.0)
Minority interests	—	—	—	0.5	—
Profits on ordinary activities after taxation	133.3	128.3	139.2	132.3	127.3
Extraordinary items	(7.5)	(9.5)	(11.2)	(2.9)	(4.1)
Dividends	(54.4)	(49.5)	(47.2)	(42.7)	(39.0)
Transfer to deferred taxation	—	(60.3)	—	—	—
Profit retained	£ 71.4	£ 9.0	£ 80.8	£ 86.7	£ 84.2
Earnings per share Based on profit on ordinary activities after taxation, pence	36.71p	35.35p	38.29p	36.44p	35.07p
Dividends per share* Excluding associated tax credit, pence	15.00	13.65	13.00	11.75	10.75
Including associated tax credit, pence	21.43	19.50	18.57	16.79	15.36
Balance sheet summary Tangible fixed assets	£ 305.3	£ 299.3	£ 280.1	£ 252.9	£ 234.3
Investments	67.6	60.3	65.4	64.9	53.9
Net current assets	1037.6	923.7	866.6	810.7	753.1
Long-term creditors	(305.9)	(103.0)	(102.5)	(102.8)	(104.1)
Provisions	(67.4)	(67.9)	(7.4)	(5.1)	(4.7)
Minority interests	—	—	(0.1)	(0.3)	(0.8)
Capital and reserves	£1037.2	£1112.4	£1102.1	£1020.3	£ 931.7

*Under U.K. tax law companies paying dividends are obligated to pay an advance corporation tax to the U.K. Inland Revenue at the rate of 3/7ths of the amount of dividend paid. U.K. resident individual shareholders are then entitled to a tax credit of 3/7ths of the dividends received.

EXHIBIT 4 COMPARATIVE DATA ON DISTILLERS (MILLIONS, EXCEPT PERCENTAGES AND RATIOS)

	Company (year ended)					
	Distillers (3/31/85)	Arthur Bell (6/30/84)	Allied Lyons (3/2/85)	Highland Distillers (8/31/84)	Seagrams (1/30/85)	Hiram Walker (9/30/85)
Revenues	£1274.3	£256.7	£3174.0	£92.2	£2505.5	£1956.8
Net income	125.8	21.2	110.3	6.1	340.7	165.8
Total assets	1704.7	254.7	2522.0	65.7	4969.7	2987.4
Total debt	329.7	30.4	708.4	0.2	969.9	1006.2
Total equity	1014.2	164.8	1346.0	50.8	2734.9	1190.2
Growth rates						
Revenues, %	5.2%	3.2%	8.8%	9.4%	0.4%	6.3%
Earnings, %	0.5	12.7	20.9	6.2	6.2	6.3
Return on sales, %	9.9	8.2	3.5	6.6	13.6	8.5
Return on equity, %	12.4	12.9	8.2	12.0	12.5	13.9
Current ratio	4.5	3.1	4.4	3.9	4.9	5.0
Interest coverage	8.6	15.1	5.1	28.7	5.9	3.1
Debt/total capital (book value), %	24.5%	15.6%	34.5%	0.3%	26.2%	45.8%
Price/earnings ratio						
Primary	7.65	8.35	5.47	10.60	9.66	10.72
Fully diluted		9.31			10.06	11.65
Dividend payout ratio	0.43	0.28	0.46	0.35	0.19	0.51

Notes: (1) Growth rates are calculated for the following years: 1981–1985, Distillers, Allied Lyons, and Seagrams; 1981–1984, Arthur Bell; 1980–1984, Highland Distillers. (2) The Seagrams figures are converted to pounds at the January 31, 1985, rate of £1 = $1.26. (3) Allied Lyons produces nonbeverage as well as beverage items. In 1985, wine, spirits, and soft drinks accounted for 31.8 percent of revenues and 31.5 percent of profits before taxes. (4) Hiram Walker is in the gas utility and the distilled spirits industries. In 1985, spirits accounted for 40.3 percent of revenues and 42.4 percent of profits before taxes.

EXHIBIT 5 ARGYLL GROUP PROFIT AND LOSS STATEMENTS (YEARS ENDED MARCH 31) (MILLIONS, EXCEPT PER SHARE ITEMS AND NUMBER OF SHARES)

	1985	1984
Turnover	£1755.6	£1515.6
Less: Value-added tax	(78.6)	(67.3)
	1677.0	1448.3
Cost of sales	(1383.0)	(1200.1)
Gross profit	294.0	248.2
Net operating expense	(236.7)	(203.5)
Operating profit	57.3	44.7
Net interest payable	(3.7)	4.7
Other income (expense)	(0.5)	—
Profit on ordinary activities before taxation	53.1	40.0
Tax on profit on ordinary activities	(13.3)	(6.0)
Profit on ordinary activities after taxation	39.8	34.0
Minority interests	(0.3)	(0.3)
Profit before extraordinary items	39.5	33.7
Extraordinary items	(11.5)	(3.5)
Profit for the financial year	£ 28.0	£ 30.2
Dividends	12.5	9.8
Earnings per average share (before extraordinary items), pence	20.0p	17.6p
Dividends per average share, pence	6.3p	5.1p
Average shares outstanding	197,288,451	192,131,063

EXHIBIT 6   ARGYLL GROUP CONSOLIDATED BALANCE SHEETS (YEARS ENDED MARCH 31) (MILLIONS, EXCEPT PER SHARE ITEMS)

	1985	1984
Fixed assets		
Tangible fixed assets	£229.6	£184.8
Investments	—	0.4
	229.6	185.2
Current assets		
Stocks	184.9	150.9
Debtors	54.3	37.5
Cash at bank and in hand	54.9	47.1
	294.1	235.5
Creditors (due within 1 year)		
Bank overdrafts	(5.8)	(4.9)
Loans	(12.1)	(8.6)
Other creditors	(296.8)	(224.8)
	(314.7)	(238.3)
Net current assets (liabilities)	(20.6)	(2.8)
Total assets less current liabilities	209.0	182.4
Creditors (due after 1 year)	(69.6)	(65.5)
Provisions for liabilities and charges	(17.2)	(5.7)
Net assets	£122.2	£111.2
Capital and reserves		
Called-up share capital	£ 50.0	£ 48.5
Share premium account	12.5	3.1
Reserves	2.4	18.0
Profit and loss account	55.9	40.5
	120.8	110.1
Minority interests	1.4	1.1
Total capital employed	£122.2	£111.2
Book value per share, pence	61.2p	57.3p

EXHIBIT 7　**1985 PRO FORMA FINANCIAL STATEMENTS FOR AN ARGYLL-DISTILLERS COMBINATION (MILLIONS, EXCEPT PER SHARE ITEMS)**

Pro forma profit and loss account	Argyll	Distillers	Enlarged Argyll Group (pro forma)
Turnover (excluding value-added taxes)	£1677.0	£1274.3	£2951.3
Profit before interest	56.8	249.8	306.6
Net interest payable	(3.7)	(13.6)	(17.3)
Pro forma interest on cash consideration*	—	—	(72.0)
Profit before taxation	53.1	236.2	217.3
Taxation	(13.3)	(102.9)	(116.2)
Tax relief on pro forma interest*	—	—	28.8
Profit after taxation	39.8	133.3	129.9
Minority interests	(0.3)	—	(0.3)
Profit before extraordinary items	39.5	133.3	129.6
Extraordinary items	(11.5)	(7.5)	(19.0)
Profit after extraordinary items	28.0	125.8	110.6
Pro forma preference dividends†	—	—	(23.6)
	£ 28.0	£ 125.8	£ 87.0
Earnings per share, pence‡	20.0p	36.7p	21.7p

*Pro forma interest payable at an annual rate of 12 percent has been provided for in respect of the cash element of the consideration and the estimated expenses of the offer. Corporation tax relief at the rate of 40 percent has been assumed in respect of such interest.

†Pro forma annual preference dividends amounting to £23.6 million have been assumed to be paid in respect of the new Argyll convertible preference shares to be issued as part of the consideration to Distillers's shareholders and assuming that the offer was for the whole of the issued share capital of Distillers.

‡Pro forma earnings per share of the enlarged Argyll Group shown above are based on the pro forma profit (after taxation, minority interests, and preference dividends) of £106.0 million and on the aggregate of the weighted average number of Argyll shares in issue during the year ended March 31, 1985, of 197.3 million together with the 290.6 million new Argyll ordinary shares to be issued under the offer assuming that the latter had been in issue throughout the year and assuming that the offer was for the whole of the issued share capital of Distillers.

EXHIBIT 7   1985 PRO FORMA FINANCIAL STATEMENTS FOR AN ARGYLL-DISTILLERS COMBINATION (MILLIONS, EXCEPT PER SHARE ITEMS) (Continued)

Pro forma net tangible assets	Argyll	Distillers	Enlarged Argyll Group (pro forma)
Fixed assets			
Tangible fixed assets	£229.6	£ 305.3	£534.9
Investments	—	67.6	67.6
Revaluation of listed investments§	—	—	86.1
	229.6	372.9	688.6
Current assets			
Stocks	184.9	874.5	1059.4
Debtor	54.3	258.1	312.4
Short-term deposits	—	166.7	166.7
Cash at bank and in hand	54.9	32.5	87.4
	294.1	1331.8	1625.9
Creditors (due within 1 year)	(314.7)	(294.2)	(608.9)
Net current assets (liabilities)	(20.6)	1,037.6	1,017.0
Total assets less current liabilities	209.0	1410.5	1705.6
Creditors (due after one year)	(69.6)	(305.9)	(375.5)
New loan facility§	—	—	(600.0)
Provisions for liabilities and charges	(17.2)	(67.4)	(84.6)
Deferred taxation on revaluation¶	—	—	(24.0)
Net assets	122.2	1,037.2	621.5
Less minority interests	(1.4)	—	(1.4)
Net tangible assets	£120.8	£1037.2	£620.1

§Adjustment has been made in the pro forma to state listed investments of Distillers at their market value at March 31, 1985, less provision for taxation thereon, as disclosed in the Distillers Annual Report for the year to that date.
¶The amount shown in the pro forma for the new loan facility represents the cash consideration under the office amounting to £526.6 million, together with estimated expenses of the offer amounting to £73.4 million.

EXHIBIT 8   SELECTED PRICES AND YIELDS 1985–1986

| Date | | Closing stock prices, pence | | | FT Index | 3-Month yields, % | | Dollar/sterling exchange rates | |
		Distillers	Argyll	Guinness		Euro $	Euro £	Spot	3 Mos. fwd.
Aug.	16	292	317	271	975.3	8.0625	11.2500	1.4005	1.3899
	23	313	328	270	991.2	7.9375	11.5000	1.4025	1.3902
	30	360	313	266	1011.0	8.0000	11.6250	1.3925	1.3801
Sept.	6	392	307	291	1018.2	8.1875	11.7500	1.3250	1.3134
	13	390	320	279	1011.0	8.2500	11.3750	1.3405	1.3307
	20	393	340	275	1002.4	8.1250	11.4375	1.3695	1.3591
	27	395	323	270	987.9	8.0625	11.4375	1.4060	1.3943
Oct.	4	416	343	282	1010.7	8.0000	11.4375	1.4145	1.4026
	11	428	335	306	1025.2	8.1250	11.5000	1.4115	1.4000
	18	432	335	304	1050.5	8.0625	11.5000	1.4270	1.4150
	25	440	333	306	1047.9	8.1250	11.5625	1.4220	1.4101
Nov.	1	465	330	313	1070.6	8.0000	11.6250	1.4400	1.4269
	8	451	335	313	1074.3	8.0000	11.5625	1.4180	1.4055
	15	475	340	315	1084.4	8.1250	11.5000	1.4220	1.4104
	22	495	340	306	1131.9	8.0000	11.5625	1.4535	1.4412
	29	510	337	303	1142.1	8.0625	11.5625	1.4880	1.4757
Dec.	6	495	335	293	1115.6	8.1250	11.5625	1.4770	1.4647
	13	491	330	283	1104.8	7.8750	11.6250	1.4365	1.4240
	20	477	325	294	1105.8	7.8750	11.8125	1.4240	1.4110
	27	500	335	307	1122.5	8.0000	11.8125	1.4375	1.4250
Jan.	2	497	343	316	1138.1	7.8750	11.8125	1.4500	1.4366
	3	495	350	320	1148.8	7.9375	11.8125	1.4385	1.4252
	6	493	350	318	1143.2	8.0000	11.8125	1.4355	1.4222
	7	487	347	307	1134.3	7.9375	12.0000	1.4395	1.4255
	8	497	345	303	1123.7	7.9375	12.5625	1.4430	1.4270
	9	525	340	299	1104.6	8.0625	12.8750	1.4525	1.4357
	10	531	350	313	1116.6	8.0625	12.7500	1.4540	1.4379
	13	535	358	305	1109.1	8.1875	13.0625	1.4425	1.4260
	14	532	358	300	1093.1	8.1875	13.0000	1.4400	1.4233
	15	538	357	310	1100.1	8.0625	12.8750	1.4415	1.4249
	16	552	375	302	1113.6	8.0000	12.9375	1.4380	1.4216
	17	567	370	303	1119.6	8.0000	12.8125	1.4370	1.4207
	20	562	355	290	1108.8	8.1250	13.3125	1.4150	1.3978

EXHIBIT 9 1985 M&A LEAGUE TABLE: FINANCIAL ADVISERS IN U.K. PUBLIC TAKEOVERS (RANKED BY VALUE OF TAKEOVERS)

Financial advisers	No. of bids	No. of defenses	Total	Value, £ millions
1. Morgan Grenfell	23	9	32	3143
2. S. G. Warburg	22	7	29	3129
3. Kleinwort Benson	18	7	25	1714
4. Schroders	15	7	22	1482
5. County Bank	12	4	16	1386
6. N. M. Rothschild	13	1	14	1279
7. Baring Brothers	10	—	10	752
8. Robert Fleming	12	1	13	685
9. Hill Samuel	13	3	16	629
10. Hambros Bank	8	1	9	606
11. Samuel Montagu	9	3	12	472
12. Henry Ansbacher	5	2	7	436
13. Barclays Merchant Bank	7	2	9	303
14. Lazards	5	1	6	265
15. Charterhouse Japhet	4	2	6	245

Note: Table based on completed and failed public takeovers in 1985. Where there are two financial advisers to one company, each adviser is given the full value of the bid.

EXHIBIT 10 **GUINNESS PLC CONSOLIDATED PROFIT AND LOSS STATEMENT (FOR YEAR ENDED SEPTEMBER 30, 1985) (MILLIONS, EXCEPT PER SHARE ITEMS AND NUMBER OF SHARES)**

	1985	1984
Turnover	£1187.7	£923.7
Net operating costs	1102.3	858.8
Trading profit	85.4	64.9
Exceptional items	4.0	4.0
	81.4	60.9
Share of profits of related companies	17.7	16.5
Net finance charges	13.0	7.0
Profit on ordinary activities before taxation	86.1	70.4
Taxation on profit on ordinary activities	26.3	25.1
Profit on ordinary activities after taxation	59.8	45.3
Minority interests	6.1	7.3
	53.7	38.0
Extraordinary items	2.9	9.8
Profit attributable to stockholders	50.8	28.2
Dividends	20.6	12.1
Retained earnings	30.2	16.1
Earnings per share, pence	25.3p	20.9p
Dividends per share	10.26	8.97
Paid, pence	7.20	6.44
Gross equivalent, pence	10.29	9.20
Shares outstanding (millions)	212.5	181.4

EXHIBIT 11 GUINNESS PLC CONSOLIDATED BALANCE SHEET (YEARS ENDED
SEPTEMBER 30, 1985) (MILLIONS, EXCEPT PER SHARE ITEMS)

	1985	1984
Fixed assets		
Tangible assets	£441.9	£280.3
Investments	64.1	65.7
	506.0	346.0
Current assets		
Stocks	251.5	127.7
Debtors	193.5	113.3
Cash at bank and in hand	57.7	61.4
	502.7	302.4
Creditors (due within 1 year)	416.1	254.2
Net current assets (liabilities)	86.6	48.2
Total assets less current liabilities	592.6	394.2
Creditors (due after 1 year)	224.2	89.5
Provisons for liabilities and charges	66.5	25.9
	290.7	115.4
Net assets	£301.9	£278.8
Capital and reserves		
Called up share capital	£ 74.7	£ 48.2
Share premium account	—	0.5
Revaluation reserve	48.9	52.3
Profit and loss account	92.0	82.9
Related companies	49.3	55.7
Stockholders' equity	264.9	239.6
Minority interests	37.0	39.2
	£301.9	£278.8
Book value per share, pence	124.7p	132.1p

EXHIBIT 12 SELECTED STATISTICS ON CONTEMPORARY U.K. ACQUISITIONS (£ THOUSANDS, EXCEPT PERCENTAGES)

	Jan. 5, 1984	Feb. 17, 1984	Nov. 22, 1984	Dec. 19, 1984	Apr. 15, 1985	Oct. 24, 1985	Oct. 28, 1985
Target	Candecca Resources	Alexander's Discount	Western Board Mills	Sir Joseph Causton & Sons	MFI Furniture	Brook Street Bureau	Owen-Owen
Market value	72,607	20,401	11,678	17,935	500,143	16,750	47,142
Bidder	Trafalgar House	Mercantile House Holdings	David S. Smith	Norton Opax	Associated Dairies	Blue Arrow	Ward White Group
Market value	537,006	273,813	5,953	22,936	1,253,692	23,361	223,818
Merchant bank	Kleinwort Benson	S. G. Warburg	Laing & Cruikshank	Samuel Montagu	Morgan Grenfell	Lloyds Merchant Bank	Morgan Grenfell
Bid premium	0.8%	10.0%	22.3%	2.3%	5.6%	9.3%	3.5%
Value of offer at close	60,758	28,812	15,458	17,151	526,362	17,765	48,944
% of shares electing cash alternative	10.0%	10.0%	50.3%	15.9%	1.7%	62.1%	15.3%

APPENDIX: CASH ALTERNATIVES IN U.K. TENDER OFFERS

The most common form of bid financing in the United Kingdom is an exchange of securities, usually accompanied by a ''cash alternative'' offer that target company shareholders could elect in lieu of the paper alternatives. In fact, a cash alternative is required under Rule 11 of the U.K. Takeover Code if the bidder owned or sought to acquire more than 15 percent of a company. Generally, the cash alternative is priced at a discount relative to the paper alternative.

Cash alternatives are usually underwritten by the merchant banks advising the bidding companies. They receive fees as compensation for their exposure, regardless of whether or not they pay out any cash. Underwriting costs are generally 2 percent of total exposure for the first 30 days and 1/8 percent per week thereafter. Guinness, for example, paid underwriting costs of £5.08 million on a total underwriting exposure of £253.9 million when it took over Bell. Samuel Montagu, advisor to Argyll in the Distillers bid, added a new twist to the fee structure by building in a 1.25 percent ''success commission'' to be paid on top of ordinary fees if Argyll's bid was successful. In the event of failure, ordinary commissions would be about 0.5 percent lower than usual.

The election of the cash alternative (or, for that matter, the receipt of any cash in exchange for shares) has tax implications for tendering shareholders under U.K. law. An exchange of shares or debentures for the target company's stock will normally be tax-free to target company shareholders if the bidding company owns more than 25 percent of the ordinary shares of the target company after the exchange, and there are bona fide business reasons for the transaction. The original tax basis of the tendering shareholders in the target company's stock will be transferred to the securities received. A capital gains liability is deferred until the shares or debentures are disposed. If cash is received for shares, however, a capital gains liability is incurred immediately. For purposes of computing any chargeable gain (or allowable loss) when both cash and securities are received for the tendered stock, a target company's shareholder will have his or her tax basis in the tendered stock apportioned among the elements received by reference to the market value of the new securities on the day that dealings in them commence.

MINEBEA COMPANY, LTD.

On October 28, 1985, Trafalgar Holdings Ltd. and Glen International Finance Services Co. offered $1.4 billion to acquire Minebea Company, a Japanese manufacturer of ball bearings and electronic parts. Trafalgar Holdings was a Los Angeles–based corporate finance concern controlled by Charles W. Knapp, the former chairman of Financial Corporation of America. Its partner, Glen International, was a London-based securities and investment firm headed by Terence Ramsden. Trafalgar-Glen claimed that it had acquired control over 23 percent of Minebea's stock in the form of warrants, common stock, and convertible bonds. Minebea promptly rejected the bid and took steps to defend itself by approving the placement of 20 million more shares in the form of convertible bonds with selected friendly investors.

It was unclear how effective this defensive tactic would be in deterring the bidders. Other factors such as shareholder and government reactions were sure to play critical roles in determining the final outcome. Historically, hostile takeovers had been considered taboo within Japan. However, recent trends toward financial liberalization, officially supported and promoted by the government, could result in a changed attitude. Thus, the financial world watched with considerable interest as bidder and target locked in battle in this the first hostile tender for a Japanese company attempted by a foreign concern.

BACKGROUND

Minebea Co., established in 1951 as Nippon Miniature Bearing Company, was the world's largest producer of miniature ball bearings with total 1984 sales of ¥131

This case was prepared by Professor W. Carl Kester. Copyright © 1986 by the President and Fellows of Harvard College. Harvard Business School case 287-022.

billion. By 1984 it had become a highly diversified company, however, with products ranging from kimonos to computer keyboards. Sales by business segments were ball bearings, 33 percent; electronic devices, 43 percent; machinery components, 17 percent; and household and other products, 7 percent. Approximately 40 percent of its sales came from overseas markets. Financial data for Minebea are presented in **Exhibits 1**, **2**, and **3**.

Minebea's president and chief executive officer was the flamboyant and often outspoken Takami Takahashi. Mr. Takahashi had built the company through a series of twenty-four acquisitions over 14 years. He exerted considerable personal control over Minebea, a managerial style unique among Japan's consensus-oriented managers. Mr. Takahashi himself controlled 6 percent of Minebea's stock through a foundation. Other information about Minebea's ownership structure is shown in **Exhibits 4** and **5**.

Mr. Takahashi's aggressive acquisition and diversification strategy, and his willingness to take risks by ignoring conventional wisdom, sharply differentiated him from other Japanese chief executives. He reportedly advocated a company drive to become a one-trillion-yen enterprise through additional corporate acquisitions.[1] Traditionally, most Japanese companies expanded from within, making Minebea's growth by acquisition relatively uncommon in Japan.

Minebea began its acquisition activities in the early 1970s when it acquired several Japanese and overseas companies in related businesses through stock-for-stock exchanges. Strong employee opposition to such a combination in one of its Japanese acquisitions, that of the Tokyo Keiki Company, eventually forced Minebea to sell its interest. Thereafter, Minebea focused on companies in which all major stockholders and a majority of employees were willing to merge the company or have it acquired. For the most part, this meant acquiring poorly performing companies in need of rehabilitation. Inevitably, this took considerable time, effort, and capital. In some cases Minebea eventually decided to divest the acquired company rather than put more money into it.

Eventually, Minebea turned away from poorly performing companies as acquisition targets. Instead, it sought companies meeting three major criteria: (1) a business related to that of Minebea and its affiliates; (2) profitability; and (3) the ability to be acquired at a price and by a means that would not ''undermine Minebea's performance'' (e.g., dramatically lower earnings or dilute earnings per share). By 1985 Minebea had taken over more than twenty firms at home and abroad, including several companies in the United States.

THE BID FOR SANKYO SEIKI MANUFACTURING COMPANY

In August 1985, Mr. Takahashi defied a Japanese commercial taboo by attempting a hostile takeover of a $400 million Japanese manufacturer of robots and music boxes, Sankyo Seiki Manufacturing Company. Starting in early 1984, Minebea had quietly purchased 19 percent of Sankyo's shares on the open market, making it Sankyo's

---

[1]''Acquisitions Weigh Heavily in Minebea's Strategy,'' *The Japan Economic Journal,* June 25, 1985. p. 33.

largest shareholder. Mr. Takahashi wanted to merge the two companies because both produced micromotors and had plants operating in Nagano Prefecture. He also said a merger would help "consolidate the management position." Minebea established a $200 million credit line in the Euromarkets with which to launch a full-scale bid for the maker of robots and music boxes. Sankyo, for its part, vowed to fight back. Its banks and other major holders declared their support for Sankyo.

This hostile bid, the first of its kind in Japan, was monitored closely by Japanese businesses and by foreign executives considering acquisitions as a potential means of gaining a foothold in Japan. There had never before been a contested takeover attempt in Japan because of the close relations that typically existed between companies, banks, and broader industry groups. Mergers and acquisitions were generally arranged privately among these groups. Mr. Takahashi was the first to challenge this "teahouse" approach to mergers with a bolder "American-style" tender.

TRAFALGAR HOLDINGS LTD.

In November 1984 Charles W. Knapp became chairman and chief executive officer of a start-up investment bank, Trafalgar Holdings. This occurred just 2 months after he resigned as chief executive officer of Financial Corporation of America (FCA). By the end of 1985, Mr. Knapp and several former FCA employees had raised $1.5 billion of capital and had ten deals in progress.

Many regarded Mr. Knapp's fund-raising ability as remarkable given his tarnished reputation as FCA's CEO. In that position he transformed a small thrift into the nation's largest through aggressive lending and risky bets on the direction of interest rates. Misjudgments in 1984, however brought about FCA's near collapse. Mr. Knapp was forced to resign in August 1985 after a quarterly profit of $25 million was restated as a $79 million loss.

Outside investors in Trafalgar Ltd. remained anonymous but were claimed by Mr. Knapp to be "successful individual investors and companies" in the United States and abroad. Their funds were used by Trafalgar to finance acquisitions organized by others. For example, Trafalgar backed Carl C. Icahn's bid for Phillips Petroleum Co. with $100 million. In addition, Trafalgar's participation in T. Boone Pickens's run on Unocal Corporation was reported to be $45 million (although insiders suggested it may have been as high as $140 million). With the bid for Minebea, Trafalgar was initiating a hostile tender for the first time together with a London partner, Glen International Financial Service Company.

GLEN INTERNATIONAL FINANCIAL SERVICE COMPANY

Terence Ramsden, a former stockbroker's clerk and the 33-year-old proprietor of Glen International, described himself as the world's foremost expert on Japanese securities. Beginning in 1975, he gradually mastered the details of Japan's financial system and learned to engineer complex transactions in Japanese securities issued in the Euromarkets.

Like Trafalgar Ltd., Glen International's investors also remained anonymous but were said to include a number of very influential Japanese investors, as well as wealthy Swiss, Arab, and German individuals. Mr. Ramsden himself claimed to have a net worth of more than £100 million. "If everything goes my way," he once noted, "I could end up the first self-made English billionaire".[2]

Mr. Ramsden's investment in Minebea began when he acquired a block of equity warrants on Minebea stock. Warrants were frequently issued by Japanese companies as part of foreign-currency bond-warrant units issued in the Euromarkets.[3] They typically traded anonymously in bearer form. Minebea had three such issues outstanding, the terms of which are presented in **Exhibit 6**. Exchange rates between the yen and the various other currencies involved are shown in **Exhibit 7**.

Upon learning of Minebea's bid for Sankyo Seiki, Mr. Ramsden moved quickly to acquire 10 million shares of Minebea on the Tokyo Stock Exchange. He did so through a Swiss private bank and a British securities company, which placed orders through Marusan Securities Co. At the conclusion of these transactions, Glen International owned securities representing roughly 23 percent of Minebea's 218 million outstanding shares.

THE TENDER OFFER

Upon acquiring his stake in Minebea, Mr. Ramsden reportedly offered to let Minebea repurchase Glen's holdings at a price the equivalent of ¥1150 per fully diluted share, nearly double its recent price on the Tokyo Stock Exchange (see **Exhibit 8**). Minebea rejected this offer, after which Mr. Ramsden allegedly presented the same deal to Sankyo Seiki. This proposal was also turned down. At this point, Glen International sold Trafalgar Ltd. an option to purchase the 23 percent stake in Minebea. The two companies also established a partnership known as Trafalgar-Glen to pursue the investment opportunity further. News of the sale and partnership agreement drove Minebea's stock price to ¥845 in less than 2 weeks.

On September 11, Minebea's board approved in principle the issuance of ¥16 billion of subordinated debentures convertible into 20 million shares of common stock. The debentures were to be placed with "stable" shareholders such as Mr. Takahashi, the Long-Term Credit Bank of Japan, and other banks with which Minebea did business. A final decision to issue the bonds would actually be made at a later date. However, the mere announcement of the planned issue caused Minebea stock to fall about 10 percent in price.

Finally, on October 25, Trafalgar-Glen presented a formal offer to Minebea's directors for all of Minebea's outstanding common stock. If accepted, the Trafalgar-Glen partnership would buy all the shares and then merge with Minebea in Japan.

For each fully diluted Minebea share, Trafalgar-Glen offered a unit consisting of $0.70 cash, a 20-year 3½ percent yen-denominated convertible bond valued at ¥550

---

[2]"A Brash Briton Plays Shark in Japanese Waters," *Fortune*, December 9, 1985, pp. 129–130.
[3]Prior to January 1, 1986, Japanese investors were prohibited from purchasing foreign-currency warrants.

(approximately $2.56), and a 30-year zero-coupon bond with a current value of ¥200 ($0.93) per share and a par value of ¥2000 ($9.30) at maturity.[4] The convertible carried an exercise price of ¥1125 ($5.23) per share and would be convertible into shares of the new (postacquisition) Minebea. The zero-coupon bond was to be secured by U.S. Treasury bonds.

The total package was valued at nearly ¥900 per fully diluted common share of Minebea, or approximately $1.4 billion. Mr. Ramsden claimed the offer was supported by several American and European banks, which he would not name. Some special incentives were also offered to those Minebea executives that cooperated with the bidding partnership. A November 4 deadline was placed on the offer. At the time of the offer, Minebea's stock had returned to ¥800 per share. There was no change in price on the day the actual offer itself was announced.

Top management's reaction to the tender offer was swift and sharp. Iwao Ishizuka, Minebea's executive vice president, declared the offer to be an insult to Minebea's Japanese shareholders. Mr. Takahashi vowed that Minebea would use all necessary measures to thwart the takeover attempt. As this war of words escalated, investors watched eagerly to see what the next move would be in this vanguard case of a hostile takeover by a foreign company in Japan.

---

[4]Values reported were estimated by Trafalgar-Glen.

EXHIBIT 1 **CONSOLIDATED INCOME STATEMENT (MILLIONS, EXCEPT PER SHARE ITEMS)**

	Fiscal year ending September 30		
	1984	1983	1982
Sales	¥130,707	¥94,140	¥91,131
Cost of sales	115,892	85,003	79,727
Gross profit	14,815	9,137	11,404
Expenses			
Selling, general, and administrative	7,684	5,577	5,690
Operating income	7,131	3,560	5,714
Net nonoperating income (expense)	2,040	1,492	1,184
Net extraordinary gains (losses)	(518)	(674)	179
Income before taxes	8,653	4,378	7,077
Provision for taxes	3,996	1,882	3,590
Net income	4,657	2,496	3,487
Dividends	2,054	1,733	1,247
Directors' bonuses	10	10	10
Shares outstanding (millions)	217.80	203.90	166.30
Earnings per share, ¥	21.38	12.24	20.97
Dividends per share, ¥	9.43	8.50	7.50

EXHIBIT 2   CONSOLIDATED BALANCE SHEET (MILLIONS)

	Fiscal year ending September 30	
	1984	1983
Cash and marketable securities	¥ 61,503	¥ 32,857
Notes receivables	16,139	7,481
Accounts receivable	37,975	27,948
Inventories	21,253	19,395
Other current assets	7,669	6,673
Total current assets	144,539	94,354
Net plant and equipment	19,028	16,462
Land	3,359	619
Long-term investments	59,191	41,657
Intangible assets	442	559
Deferred assets	818	747
Total assets	¥227,377	¥154,398
Notes payable	¥ 19,667	¥ 10,924
Accounts payable	22,315	14,803
Short-term debt	20,929	15,947
Short-term liability reserves	3,641	1,609
Other current liabilities	4,980	2,237
Total current liabilities	71,532	45,520
Bonds	61,642	23,920
Other long-term debt	4,203	6,039
Long-term liability reserves	463	603
Other long-term liabilities	1,655	—
Paid-in capital	71,377	64,725
Earned surplus	11,268	10,477
Unappropriated earnings	5,237	3,114
Total stockholders' equity	87,882	78,316
Total liabilities plus equity	¥227,377	¥154,398

EXHIBIT 3   FIVE-YEAR FINANCIAL SUMMARY (MILLIONS, EXCEPT RATIOS, PERCENTAGES, PER SHARE DATA, AND TOTAL MARKET VALUE)

	Fiscal 1984	Fiscal 1983	Fiscal 1982	Fiscal 1981	Fiscal 1980
Sales	¥130,707	¥94,140	¥91,131	¥73,533	¥45,116
Net income	4,657	2,496	3,487	1,729	1,286
Dividends	2,054	1,733	1,247	704	506
Liquid assets	77,642	40,338	39,050	28,760	23,840
Current assets	144,539	94,354	88,698	53,307	41,313
Total assets	227,377	154,398	134,898	87,763	74,031
Notes payable and short-term debt	40,596	26,871	30,690	20,480	23,039
Current liabilities	71,532	45,520	48,245	33,967	31,153
Long-term debt	65,845	29,929	29,692	16,754	18,395
Stockholders' equity	87,882	78,316	56,349	37,042	24,483
Return on sales	3.6%	2.7%	3.8%	2.4%	2.9%
Return on equity	5.3%	3.2%	6.2%	4.7%	5.3%
Dividend payout, ¥/share	¥ 44.1	¥ 69.4	¥ 35.8	¥ 40.7	¥ 39.3
Current ratio	2.0	2.1	1.8	1.6	1.3
Debt/total capital, %	54.8%	42.1%	51.7%	50.1%	62.9%
Interest coverage	2.5	2.4	2.6	2.1	1.5
Stock price (yearend), ¥/share	695	898	525	648	675
Total market value (¥ billions)	151,224	182,287	87,308	75,929	68,293
Price-earnings ratio	32.5	73.0	25.0	43.9	53.1

STOCK DISTRIBUTION (SHARE NUMBERS IN MILLIONS)

EXHIBIT 4

	1982		1983		1984	
	Shares	%	Shares	%	Shares	%
Financial institutions	65.73	39.5	73.33	36.0	75.90	34.8
Individuals	44.98	27.1	45.01	22.1	58.74	27.0
Business corporations	36.77	22.1	38.79	19.0	47.65	21.9
Foreigners	12.44	7.5	32.81	11.7	22.26	10.2
Investment trusts	0.00	0.0	11.21	5.5	706.00	3.2
Securities companies	6.37	3.8	20.66	10.1	11.11	5.1
Government	0.01	—	0.01	—	0.01	—
Total*	166.30		203.86		217.80	

*Percentages do not necessarily sum to 100 percent due to rounding and some overlap in categories (e.g., foreigners and individuals).
Source: Daiwa Services Research Institute *Analyst's Guide* (various years).

EXHIBIT 5   MAJOR SHAREHOLDERS OF MINEBEA COMPANY, LTD., IN 1984

	Number of shares owned	
	Millions	%
Takahashi Sangyo Keizai Kenyu Foundation	12.347	5.7
K. K. Keiaisha	11.136	5.2
Long-Term Credit Bank of Japan	6.801	3.2
Sumitomo Trust and Banking	6.801	3.2
Nomura Securities	6.035	2.8
Swiss Credit Bank	4.564	2.1
Total	47.684	22.2

EXHIBIT 6   RECENT BOND ISSUES BY MINEBEA COMPANY, LTD.*

Issue: SF100 million 6½% convertible bonds due 1992

Date:	August 1982
Denomination:	SF5000 in bearer form
Interest:	Paid annually on September 30
Convertible:	Into Minebea common stock from October 1, 1982, at ¥553.7 per share
Callable:	As a whole on coupon dates only with 90-day notice from September 30, 1987 at: 103 September 30, 1988 102 September 30, 1989 101 September 30, 1990 100
	All bonds may be redeemed on or after September 30, 1986, if the closing price for the company's shares was at least 150% of the effective conversion price for 30 consecutive business days. Redemption will be at the same prices as above, except redemption on September 30, 1986, must be at 104.
Listed:	Zurich, Basel, Geneva, Lausanne, Bern
Comanagers:	Bank Hofmann AG, Banque Centrale, Schweizer Deposit und Kredit

Issue: $80 million 5½% convertible bonds due 1998

Date:	April 1983
Denomination:	$1000 in fully registered form
Interest:	Paid annually on September 30
Convertible:	Into Minebea common stock from May 17, 1983, at ¥667 per share
Callable:	As a whole or in part at any time on 30 days' notice from September 30, 1986, at 104 and declining thereafter at 0.5 annually until par in 1994. No call before September 30, 1988, unless common stock is at least 150% of the conversion price for 20 days preceding the 15th day prior to call notice.
Listed:	Luxembourg
Lead manager:	Nomura International, Ltd.

Issue: $100 million 6¼% bonds with warrants due 1989

Date:	February 1984
Denomination:	$5000 in bearer form
Interest:	Paid annually on February 27
Warrants:	Each bond issued with one warrant entitling the holder to 1545 Minebea common shares at a price of ¥761 cash per share. The warrants are exercisable from March 5, 1984, to February 20, 1989.
Callable:	As a whole on 30 days' notice only if tax status changes
Listed:	Luxembourg
Guarantor:	Long-Term Credit Bank of Japan
Comanagers:	Nomura International, Ltd., Baring Bros. & Co., Daiwa Europe, Ltd., Lloyds Bank International, Long-Term Credit Bank, Ltd.

*All the issues described in this exhibit contain an antidilution clause that requires adjustment of the conversion price if new shares are sold at less than the prevailing market price at the time of issue, or if convertible or exchangeable securities are sold with conversion prices less than the prevailing market price for Minebea's stock at the time of issue.

EXHIBIT 6   RECENT BOND ISSUES BY MINEBEA COMPANY, LTD.* *(continued)*

Issue: £50 million 8¼% bonds with warrants due 1990

Date:	February 1985
Denomination:	£5000 in bearer form
Interest:	Paid annually on March 30
Warrants:	Each bond issued with one warrant entitling the holder to 2141 Minebea common shares at a price of ¥683 cash per share. The warrants are exercisable from March 1, 1985, to March 15, 1990.
Callable:	As a whole only if tax status changes
Listed:	Luxembourg
Guarantor:	Long-Term Credit Bank of Japan
Lead manager:	Baring Brothers

Issue: SF120 million 3½% bonds with warrants due 1993

Date:	May 1985
Denomination:	SF5000
Interest:	Paid annually on September 30
Warrants:	Each bond issued with three warrants entitling the holder to 250 Minebea common shares per warrant at a price of ¥632 cash per share. The warrants are exercisable from June 14, 1985, to September 9, 1993.
Callable:	As a whole only if tax status changes
Listed:	Luxembourg
Guarantor:	Sumitomo Trust
Lead manager:	Crédit Suisse

*All the issues described in this exhibit contain an antidilution clause that requires adjustment of the conversion price if new shares are sold at less than the prevailing market price at the time of issue, or if convertible or exchangeable securities are sold with conversion prices less than the prevailing market price for Minebea's stock at the time of issue.

EXHIBIT 7   **BILATERAL EXCHANGE RATES BETWEEN THE YEN AND SELECTED CURRENCIES (YEN/FOREIGN-CURRENCY UNIT)**

1985		¥/$	¥/SF	¥/£
January		254.65	95.11	287.12
February		259.51	91.66	282.86
March		252.50	96.47	313.86
April		252.24	97.56	313.87
May		251.83	96.60	320.73
June		248.94	97.19	322.41
July		236.64	103.79	338.10
August		237.24	103.96	332.15
September	6	241.35	100.67	322.44
	13	243.40	101.14	325.30
	20	241.70	102.03	327.02
	27	222.50	101.62	313.06
October	4	212.10	99.46	303.83
	11	215.80	98.76	304.71
	18	215.35	99.47	306.87
	25	216.00	99.68	307.45

EXHIBIT 8   RECENT STOCK PRICE MOVEMENTS FOR MINEBEA COMPANY (1985)

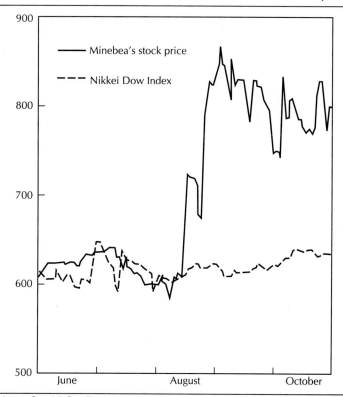

Source: James Capel & Co., *The International Bond Manual, 1986* (London: February 8, 1986), p. 649.

NOTE ON CORPORATE GOVERNANCE SYSTEMS: THE UNITED STATES, JAPAN, AND GERMANY

As business continues to become more global in the 1990s, the incidence of cross-border investment rises. Increasingly, managers are encountering different corporate governance systems—or, broadly, different sets of incentives, safeguards, and dispute resolution processes used to control and coordinate the actions of various stakeholders. There are many such systems. This note distinguishes among three found in the developed industrial world: the American, the Japanese, and the German models.

Awareness of different forms of corporate governance and the economic purposes that these various arrangements of ownership and control are intended to serve will better enable managers to contract abroad, structure joint ventures, and control foreign investments. Managers' ability to maneuver deftly within and across these systems will, in part, determine their success in the international business environment.

AMERICAN CORPORATE GOVERNANCE[1]

Predicated upon the ideal of shareholder democracy and the perceived need to prevent abuse of corporate power, the American corporate governance system is the product of constantly evolving American jurisprudence. It seeks to promote allocative efficiency

---

[1]The primary elements of corporate governance in Australia, Canada, New Zealand, the United States, and the United Kingdom bear many similarities. Thus, one might generally refer to an "Anglo-American" style of corporate governance. Because of numerous specific legal differences, however, this note will describe only the American system as a somewhat representative example of this larger class.

This case was prepared by Professor W. Carl Kester and Research Associate Robert W. Lightfoot. Copyright © 1991 by the President and Fellows of Harvard College. Harvard Business School case 292-012.

through antitrust laws that separate the interests of numerous stakeholders and that keep them in atomistic competition with one another, and seeks to maintain the accountability of corporate managers to corporate owners through the board of directors and the proxy-voting mechanism.

Current American economic performance has cast doubt on the competitiveness of American business and on the effectiveness of the American corporate governance system in promoting that end. Although the system may prevent the abuse of monopoly power and may ensure management accountability to shareholders, it may also be poorly suited to attaining other economic goals. Consequently, Americans find themselves in the middle of a debate over shareholders' rights and the ability of the corporate governance system to foster internationally competitive businesses.

The Board of Directors

The American corporate governance system relies on the board of directors as its main organ. Elected by shareholders, the board safeguards shareholder interests by overseeing management and board selection, reviewing financial performance and allocation of funds, and ensuring that the corporation acts in a legally and socially responsible manner.[2]

Generally, membership on American boards does not mirror a company's close commercial or financial relationships, as it often does in Japan and Germany. Rather, board composition in the United States tends to reflect an American affinity for outside directors, or those with no direct affiliations to management. No doubt the fact that American firms are less likely to enter into tight, long-term supply and banking contracts than their Japanese or German counterparts explains part of the difference in board composition. More significant, however, is the American emphasis on accountability of managers to directors, and of directors to shareholders. Companies have responded to burgeoning liability litigation, which has shifted the onus of legal responsibility to directors, by choosing outside directors who are considered essential for maintaining a neutral board capable of objective oversight.

The reliance on outside directors, however, introduces information asymmetries to the board: Managers, who report to the board, are intimately connected to the workings of the corporation. Directors, however, who usually meet together for 3 to 6 hours only five to nine times per year, must rely on information solely from management. The problems associated with information asymmetry are compounded by the shortage of time most directors can devote to their board positions. One reaction to the time and information constraints on directors has been the use of committees for delegating some board responsibilities: Three-quarters of all boards have three to five committees to ease the work load on the full board.[3]

---

[2]Jay W. Lorsch and Elizabeth MacIver, *Pawns or Potentates* (Boston: Harvard Business School Press, 1989), p. 9.

[3]Ibid., pp. 58, 87.

Several aspects of the board system may promote the selection of directors sympathetic to incumbent managers, thereby diluting management's accountability to the board. The existence of the joint chief executive officer–chairman of the board blurs the separation between management and oversight functions in many companies. In fact, chief executive officers (CEOs) also chair the board in 80 percent of all American corporations, and although CEOs can neither hire nor fire directors, they often choose the nominating committee for the directors, or even indirectly nominate the directors themselves. Voting procedures for the election of directors may also diminish management's strict accountability to the board: Most shareholders who vote for or against a slate of management-nominated directors vote by proxy. Although write-in candidates are allowed, the effort required to coordinate enough shareholders to install an alternative board is infeasible in most situations. The composition of corporate boards reveals a propensity to choose members inclined to support management: 63 percent of all board members are CEOs of their own corporations.[4]

Share Ownership in America

American shareholders are by no means a homogeneous group. Approximately half of all shares in American companies are held by individuals, and the other half by institutions. Institutional share ownership has been rising since 1950, when institutions with assets of $107 billion owned 8 percent of all outstanding equity. By 1980, institutions with assets of $2 trillion owned 33 percent of outstanding equity, and by 1990, with assets of $6 trillion, institutions controlled about 20 percent of all financial assets and 45 percent of all outstanding equities.[5] In 1989, pension funds controlled about two-thirds of stock held by institutions, and investment companies and endowments each controlled about one-sixth. Because individual shareholders tend to be more stable investors than institutions and tend to hold diversified stock portfolios, their incentive and ability to participate actively in corporate governance are attenuated.

Although individuals own about half of all shares, they do only about 20 percent of the trading, whereas institutions do about 80 percent.[6] Heavy institutional trading is not surprising, however, when one considers the types of institutions that hold major equity positions in American companies: pension funds, investment companies (mutual funds), and endowments. Indeed, most equity-owning institutions are financial in nature. Notably absent from this list are commercial banks and other deposit institutions, which American law prohibits from owning stock outside of their trust departments, and nonfinancial corporations, which hold virtually none of one another's stock.

[4]Ibid., pp. 2, 18.
[5]William Taylor, ''Can Big Owners Make a Big Difference?'' *Harvard Business Review* (September/October 1990): 70.
[6]Jay O. Light, *The American System of Corporate Governance* (unpublished draft, November 1990), pp. 2–10.

Legal and Effective Restrictions on "Big Owner" Board Representation

Often preferring to take a passive role in corporate governance, large shareholders—especially mutual funds and pension funds—are conspicuously absent from the rosters of corporate boards. American law explains why big shareholders are not represented in many instances, and why they are loathe to participate actively in governance.[7] **Exhibit 1** lists the major laws that influence share ownership and board representation.

Commercial Banks and Other Deposit Institutions   The Glass-Steagall Act of 1933 prohibits banks from owning stock directly, or indirectly through affiliations with investment banks. The Bank Holding Company Act of 1956 prohibits banks from owning more than 5 percent of the voting stock in any nonbank company or from otherwise controlling an industrial firm. Additionally, the tax code encourages diversification of bank-managed trust holdings so that no more than 10 percent of a bank's trusts are invested in any corporation. Finally, financial institutions that exert actual or effective control over a company could be subject to "equitable subordination" of their loans in the event of a bankruptcy proceeding, and might ever be subject to other liability, including penalties under the Racketeer Influenced and Corrupt Organizations law, or RICO.

Pension Funds   Although pension funds control two-thirds of institutionally owned equities, they have virtually no representation on corporate boards. Individually, no pension fund may hold more than 10 percent of the stock of any company if it wishes to receive favorable tax treatment as a diversified fund. As a result, no individual fund has that much voting power. Pension funds might obtain considerable power if they voted as a block. Any attempt to sway shareholder opinion, however, could founder on legal obstacles: If a participant in a proxy fight tries to influence more than ten stockholders, he or she must obtain prior Securities and Exchange Commission (SEC) approval.

Other laws discourage pension funds from becoming too involved in anything resembling a management issue. The Employee Retirement Income Security Act of 1974 establishes a prudent standard for fiduciaries: Managers of pension funds must be "prudent experts" in the business they undertake. Pension funds are in the business of managing money, not corporations. If pension fund managers were on boards of business corporations, they could be liable to meet higher standards of care in their investments. Even those pension fund managers who do wish to play an active role in governance are constrained by a variety of other factors: Pension funds could be suspect because of their political ties (many pension fund managers are appointed), because they could be seen as unstable investors more interested in short-term stock price swings than in the health of the firm, or because they frequently own stock in competing businesses.

---

[7]The following discussion is based on Franklin R. Edwards and Robert A. Eisenbeis, *Financial Institutions and Corporate Myopia: An International Perspective* (unpublished draft, 1990), pp. 53–71. See also Taylor, op. cit., pp. 70–82.

Mutual Funds   Like pension funds, mutual funds tend to refrain from exercising large shareholder rights in order to receive favorable tax treatment. If a mutual fund is not diversified, its income is taxed first at the corporate rate and then again when it is distributed to its shareholders. To be considered diversified under the tax code and the Investment Company Act of 1940, a fund must have at least half its investments in companies that constitute 5 percent or less of its portfolio, and cannot own more than 10 percent of any company's stock. Even if a fund owned 5 percent of a company's stock, the portfolio company would become a statutory affiliate of the mutual fund and its principal underwriter. If the fund wished to exercise control with another affiliate, it would need prior SEC approval.

Insurance Companies   Insurance companies in America are regulated primarily by state laws. Those that wish to operate nationwide must abide by the strictest of those laws, the strongest of which prohibit an insurance company from putting more than 2 percent of its assets into a single company and from owning more than 5 percent of the voting stock of any corporation.

When Shareholders Take Control

Although most institutional shareholders refrain from interfering with management, the United States has seen considerable experimentation with shareholder activism in the 1980s and early 1990s. The number of shareholder proposals sponsored by institutions rose from 28 in 1988, to 70 in 1989, and to 120 in 1990. The 1991 proxy season saw a decrease in shareholder resolutions: Only 101 of 153 of those submitted by institutions came to a vote.[8] Sometimes, shareholders try to get involved in strategic management issues. Carl Icahn, a well-known corporate raider, tried to persuade USX, the holding corporation that controlled U.S. Steel and Marathon Oil, to spin off its U.S. Steel holdings. In a hot proxy fight, shareholders eventually voted to spin off the subsidiary. In another case, Time Warner withdrew a rights offering after shareholders, including at least three pension funds, sued the company in fourteen separate actions. Shareholder sentiment alone, however, did not stop the deal. Shareholder influence became pivotal, but only after the SEC raised objections to the offering. The senior vice president of INB Financial Co., a fiduciary for one million of Time Warner's shares, commented, "We hope this is the first step of management recognizing that the company has to be run with an eye to shareholder value."[9]

Corporate Governance and the Market for Corporate Control

Theoretically, the threat of hostile takeover should ensure that assets are controlled by those best able to manage them, and in the United States, with its well-developed market for corporate control, hostile takeover is the ultimate check on management.

---

[8]"Cutting Loose from Shareholder Activists," *Business Week,* July 8, 1991, p. 34.
[9]"Time Warner Feels the Force of Shareholder Power," *Business Week,* July 29, 1991, pp. 58–59.

When shareholders fail to take an interest in the governance of a company, or when their governance proves ineffective, low-quality managers are able to remain in power or management's allegiance to the shareholder may falter. In either of these cases, a company's share price should drift lower so as to form a gap between the stock's actual price and its potential value. If the gap between a company's market value and its perceived potential value were to grow large enough, a takeover would ensure that control over the company's assets eventually would go to those who could earn a higher return on those assets. The existence of employee stock ownership plans, poison pill defenses, staggered boards, and supermajority provisions diminishes the threat of takeover in many instances.

To some, the hostile takeover enhances social welfare by ensuring the efficient deployment of resources. There is evidence that hostile takeovers enhance shareholder wealth substantially. Professor Michael Jensen estimated that, from 1977 to 1986, mergers and acquisitions produced gains for selling-firm shareholders aggregating $346 billion (in 1986 dollars).[10] Some researchers have shown that in the American manufacturing sector, takeover targets demonstrated subnormal productivity levels before being taken over, and demonstrated higher productivity growth after takeover.[11] Others, however, argue that the threat of hostile takeover diverts management resources to short-term strategies that harm firms' competitiveness. Tom Barrett, president and CEO of Goodyear Tire & Rubber Company, argues,

> The takeover frenzy is vivisecting our industrial base and our competitive future. The victims are America's competitive position in the global market, its industrial base, and thousands upon thousands of hard-working Americans whose livelihood is being destroyed. . . .
>
> It forces management to ignore or slight such landmarks as the needs of markets for goods and services from which it draws its revenues . . . and to short the planning and investment it should be doing for the years ahead.[12]

JAPANESE CORPORATE GOVERNANCE

A prominent feature of Japanese corporate governance is the tendency for large corporations to engage in tight, long-term commercial relationships. Such corporate networking achieves its highest expression in the *keiretsu*, an affiliation of related companies whose interests are aligned partly through long-lasting and informal supply contracts, intercompany personnel transfer, and reciprocal equity ownership. Some *keiretsu*, such as the Mitsubishi, Sumitomo, Mitsui, and Fuyo groups, are actually descendants of pre–World War II *zaibatsu*, which were tighter groupings of companies centered around a common holding company. Others are newer

[10]Michael C. Jensen, "Takeovers: Their Causes and Consequences," *Journal of Economic Perspectives,* 2, no. 1 (Winter 1988): 21–48.

[11]Frank C. Lictenberg and Donald Siegel, "The Effect of Ownership Changes on the Employment and Wages of Central Office and Other Personnel," *Journal of Law and Economics* (October 1990): 282–408; "The Effects of Leveraged Buyouts on Productivity and Related Aspects of Firm Behavior," *Journal of Financial Economics* 26 (1990): 165–194.

[12]Remarks by Tom H. Barrett to the Subcommittee on Manufacturing and Finance, Manufacturing Studies Board, Washington, DC, May 12, 1988.

groups that sprang up around a major bank such as the Industrial Bank of Japan or the Dai-Ichi Kangyo Bank, or around a major industrial corporation such as Toyota, Hitachi, or Nippon Steel.

Companies belonging to *keiretsu* account for only one-tenth of 1 percent of all incorporated businesses in Japan. But group members are generally much larger than the median Japanese firm. They account for roughly a quarter of total sales and paid-up capital of all Japanese corporations, and just over half of all listed corporations in Japan are members of an industrial group. Most of the Japanese competitors encountered by Western companies are likely to have a group affiliation. Even those that do not are likely to have entered into various reciprocal shareholding and trade agreements with other Japanese firms.[13]

These networks exhibit a number of common (within Japan) business practices that have important governance functions. The most distinctive and important of these are widespread reliance on reciprocal trade and relational contracting; management transfers; extensive information sharing; cross-shareholding arrangements; and the capacity for selective intervention by major stakeholders, particularly banks.

Reciprocal Trade and Relational Contracting

Japanese *keiretsu* tend to be characterized by a great deal of stability in group affiliation and loyalty as far as the favored status group members give each other in their business dealings. If a manufacturer can source parts and equipment within its own group, it is highly likely to do so, though never on an exclusive basis. Furthermore, intragroup trade will tend to be reciprocal to the extent practical. Thus, Mitsubishi Motors is sure to be sourcing some of its steel requirements from Mitsubishi Steel and some of its equipment from Mitsubishi Heavy Industries. They, in turn, will be sure to include Mitsubishi Motors' autos and trucks in their vehicle fleets. Data on intragroup sales and procurement are provided in **Exhibit 2**.

The contracts that typically govern such trading relationships are quite different from their Anglo-American counterparts. In the automobile industry, for example, a business relationship between two companies will formally begin with the signing of a "basic agreement," usually a long-term contract subject to annual renewal. Rather than addressing a specific transaction, basic agreements are expressions of intent to engage in mutually beneficial business transactions, to establish and maintain an atmosphere of mutual trust in business dealings, and to respect each other's autonomy. Although the agreement usually does contain certain legal stipulations (such as confidentiality clauses), executives in Japanese companies do not necessarily view them as legally binding nor are they generally willing to resort to court enforcement of the agreement. Indeed, basic agreements generally also contain articles stipulating that any disagreements concerning the contracts be settled amicably upon deliberation and mutual consultation. Basic agreements

---

[13]W. Carl Kester, *Japanese Takeovers: The Global Contest for Corporate Control* (Boston: Harvard Business School Press, 1991), pp. 54–55.

receive much of senior management's time, for considerable due diligence is done before entering into a close, long-term relationship.

Management Transfers and Board Composition

Ongoing relationships require effective communication between the contracting parties, and management transfers and lifetime employment develop lines of communication. Midcareer managers or engineers may be temporarily transferred to a related company to help solve specific problems or to work on joint projects. Such transfers provide extensive webs of enduring personal relationships between individual managers in related companies, webs that may facilitate future transactions between the companies by enhancing trust between the company's managers.

Reinforcing monitoring and communication at the managerial level are ties at the level of the board of directors. Though outwardly similar in some respects, Japanese boards differ from those of most Western companies in numerous ways. For example, large Japanese companies are controlled by boards consisting of about twenty to twenty-five directors. However, unlike the practice in Anglo-American economies, it is rare to find independent, outside directors on Japanese boards. Instead, virtually all Japanese directors are *inside* managing directors chosen from the ranks of top management itself. Although formally elected by (usually unanimous) shareholder votes at annual meetings, the slate is nominated by management itself.[14]

Nevertheless, major share-owning stakeholders in a Japanese company often obtain indirect representation through former executives that assume positions on the boards of companies with which their former employers do business. Typically, an executive from a share-owning corporation, bank, or other financial institution who is late in his career (most often in his mid-fifties) will be "retired" from his first job and start a "second career" as a director of the associated company in question. In some instances, midcareer executive transfers become permanent when the transferred executive rises relatively quickly to a managing director position.

Information Sharing: Informal and Institutionalized Lines of Communication

In addition to the informal network for communication provided by management transfers, with its reliance on the trust and forbearance of managers, many Japanese industries have institutionalized networks that foster information sharing. A company's main bank, which often holds both a company's debt and equity, closely monitors that

---

[14]Except for managers in companies in which founder-owners continue to play a prominent managerial role, most have no material share ownership in the companies they manage, nor are stock options a component of compensation. Semiannual cash bonuses are paid to all managers and employees alike, but they are only loosely tied to corporate performance in the previous year. Employees generally regard such bonuses as a more or less reliable part of their annual income.

company's business and financial condition—especially in times of distress. Because the main bank is usually the company's largest supplier of capital and has the best information on the company, it is likely to intervene in times of financial difficulty. Such intervention differs in the United States, where equitable subordination of loans keeps banks from getting involved in a client's affairs until those loans have been breached.

Further, groups of related firms often have some sort of organization of senior officers. For example, the presidents of the twenty-eight major Mitsubishi companies are members of the *Kinyo-kai,* a council that meets monthly to "promote friendship" and exchange views on sundry business and economic matters.

Suppliers of some large manufacturers also meet in *kyoryokukai,* or "cooperation clubs." These associations do promote friendship, but they also serve an important function for suppliers, many of which rely on the same company for the majority of their business. Suppliers meet to collect and disseminate information about their experiences with one another and with the manufacturer. Discussions in this forum amplify each party's reputation and diminish the existence of hidden information. Any firm that tries to exploit its market power at the expense of a supplier might find its reputation—and its ability to do business with other firms on favorable terms in the future—injured. The magnification of the manufacturer's reputation may lessen the risk to each supplier of a small customer base.

Reciprocal Equity Ownership

Reciprocal equity ownership generally also links companies with important business relationships. Cross-holdings usually involve only minority equity positions with no more than a few percent of outstanding shares being exchanged on a bilateral basis (see **Exhibit 3**). In the aggregate, however, about 25 percent of the stock of member companies in an industrial group is owned under cross-shareholding arrangements within the group itself (see **Exhibit 4**). Substantial numbers of shares are also typically owned by corporations and financial institutions with important business ties to companies within a group, even if they are not themselves part of that group. Individual ownership of listed Japanese corporations is small and declining (see **Exhibit 5**).

Most institutional holdings are covered by widely understood and rigorously observed agreements not to sell any shares held in connection with an ongoing business relationship. To the contracting businesses, such agreements signal a commitment to one another and serve to cement business relationships. They are also a barrier to takeover and, thus, serve to entrench management.

A more subtle effect of cross-shareholding arrangements between transacting companies is to commingle the types of claims against the company held by various stakeholders. Key suppliers are often also important suppliers of credit and major equity owners. Likewise, banks and insurance companies provide both debt and equity capital to companies, as well as participating in other contractual relationships. In effect, they own something like a "strip" of a company's capital base.

Selective Intervention[15]

Perhaps the most powerful safeguard in the Japanese corporate governance system is the ability of one or more equity-owning stakeholders to intervene from time to time directly and explicitly in the affairs of another company when necessary to correct a problem. This is by no means a routine or highly frequent occurrence, but it is common—indeed, expected—under certain circumstances. Typically, such intervention is undertaken by a company's main bank, usually to remedy nonperformance in the face of impending financial distress. This "responsibility" generally falls to the troubled company's main bank because it usually is the largest single supplier of capital and has quicker access to more information than most other equity-owning stakeholders. It also typically holds both debt and equity claims against companies for which it acts as main bank. Whereas fear of triggering so-called "equitable subordination" of their loans keeps most American lenders on the sidelines until a loan agreement is formally breached, and even then restrains their degree of intervention, Japanese main banks effectively assume such subordination from the outset and take far-reaching, early steps to limit the damage. For example, the Dai-Ichi Kangyo Bank, main bank for the Kojin Corporation, voluntarily repaid all of Kojin's debts to other banks when Kojin failed. DKB then assumed sole responsibility for recovering loans from Kojin.

Main bank intervention may also occur for reasons other than financial distress. Dispute resolution and sheer dealmaking (though seldom on a fee basis) by banks among client companies are also observed. For example, a Tokai Bank executive assumed the presidency of a client company, Okuma Machinery Works, in order to resolve a bitter dispute between labor and management over who was to succeed the company's founder-president. The Sumitomo Bank's financing of companies such as Nissan, Mazda, and Matsushita Electric has allowed it to act as a go-between in arranging sheet-metal supply contracts for Sumitomo Metal Industries, one of its group clients.[16]

Intervention is by no means limited to banks, however. Although less common, major industrial stakeholders will take quick, decisive steps to supplant an important supplier's or customer's autonomy with temporary de facto administrative control when nonperformance becomes imminent. Mitsubishi Electric, for instance, played a leading role in the restructuring of Akai Electric, a major supplier and purchaser of electronic parts and equipment within the Mitsubishi group. Nissan Motor also assumed effective operating control of Fuji Heavy Industries, the maker of Subaru automobiles. Although Nissan owned only 4 percent of Fuji's stock, it consistently sent executives to become directors of Fuji, relied on Fuji to produce Nissan brand passenger cars until 1986, and collaborated with Fuji in the manufacture of aerospace and marine products. The de facto "takeover" occurred without the restructuring of

[15]W. Carl Kester, *Governance, Contracting, and Investment Time Horizons* (Harvard Business School Working Paper 92-003) (Cambridge, MA: Harvard Business School), pp. 29–31.

[16]Michael Gerlach, "Business Alliances and the Strategy of the Japanese Firm," *California Management Review* (Fall 1987): 126–142.

any debt or a single share of stock changing hands among Fuji's major equity-owning stakeholders.

GERMAN CORPORATE GOVERNANCE

Although commonly grouped with Western capitalist organizations, German corporations operate within a system of corporate governance distinct from that of their Anglo-American and French counterparts. Indeed, German corporate governance arguably has more in common with the Japanese system than the Anglo-American. The tremendous global success of German corporations in the postwar period suggests that this system has been extremely successful. It comes as no surprise, therefore, that corporate governance practices in neighboring countries such as Austria, Switzerland, and Sweden have been heavily influenced by the German system. Many Eastern European enterprises are also being privatized with governance systems similar to the German model.

Two-Tiered Board Structure

One of the most unique features of German corporate governance is the structure of its board of directors. Whereas the American board of directors is intended to provide objective, albeit shareholder-oriented, oversight of a company's management, its German counterpart, the *Aufsichtsrat,* or ''supervisory board,'' is not chosen for its impartiality or its strict commitment to shareholder interests. Its membership frequently reflects the company's financial and commercial relationships and provides other stakeholders with a voice in the company. Indeed, the two-tier governance system was created in the 1870s to give *bankers* an organ of control with which to oversee their investments.[17] Today, all public corporations with more than 500 employees must have a two-tiered board structure, with both a supervisory board and a management board that meet together quarterly.

The nine to twenty-one members of the *Aufsichtsrat* appoint an actual management board, rather than just a CEO, who would, in an American corporation, be responsible for selecting his or her own management team. In fact, no overlap in membership is allowed between the two boards (although the chair of the *Aufsichtsrat* is frequently the most recently retired chair of the *Vorstand,* or ''management board''). The five to fifteen members of the management board are responsible for the day-to-day operation of the company. Each member typically has a functional specialty, and the members are supposed to run the company by consensus. In practice, many management board chairmen wield significantly more influence than do the supervisory board members, who appoint the members of the *Vorstand* for 5-year terms and set their compensation.

---

[17]Christel Lane, *Management and Labour in Europe: The Industrial Enterprise in Germany, Britain and France* (Aldershot, England: Edward Elgar), p. 56.

Membership on the Supervisory Board and "Big Shareholder" Representation

In Germany, employees and shareholders nominally enjoy equal representation on the *Aufsichtsrat,* although a law requiring workers to elect at least one manager of the firm usually tips the balance in favor of shareholders. *Aufsichtsrat* chairs are also usually shareholder representatives.

It is difficult to ascertain the identity of most large shareholders in German corporations, and, thus, to determine whether they are represented on boards. The anonymity of shareholders, who hold most stock in "bearer" form, precludes detailed study of cross-shareholdings. The evidence, however, suggests that among business corporations, significant reciprocal holdings do exist. In 1984 there were at least eighty-eight cross-holdings among Germany's largest 100 corporations, up from eighty-five in 1982.[18]

Shareholder representatives on supervisory boards are often chosen for their ties to German industry. Through varied membership of the *Aufsichtsrat,* German companies can gain knowledge of related industries and of business and economic conditions throughout Germany. The largest shareholders—business corporations, insurance companies, and banks—do have considerable representation on supervisory boards. Representation does mimic some commercial and financial business ties, and personal relationships, particularly in family-controlled companies such as Porsche, can be important on the supervisory board.

It is unclear whether supervisory board contacts can help a company win contracts. Although many managers say no, clearly some board members expect preferential treatment. When the chairman of one bank accepted an offer from an unrelated contractor to build a new building, a fellow board member is reported to have exclaimed, "Are you mad? We own about 30% of a [competing] construction company, and I sit on its supervisory board. You've chosen a rival firm. You're throwing good money away."[19] **Exhibit 6** shows share ownership, and **Exhibit 7**, which profiles membership on the supervisory boards of the Germany's major automotive companies and banks, illustrates the interconnections among industrial companies and financial institutions.

Special Position of Banks

Banks enjoy a special position in German industry. A historically deficient capital market and an annual net asset tax on corporations (1 percent per annum) have inclined corporations to finance with bank debt rather than equity. Banks also own a significant fraction of equity in German companies, although the exact percentage of bank-owned shares is not known. For example, the country's largest bank, Deutsche Bank, owns 28.1 percent of Germany's largest industrial concern, Daimler-Benz. As a group,

[18]David Shirreff, "Bankers as Moral Monopolists," *Euromoney,* March 1987, p. 72.
[19]Ibid., p. 71.

banks own nearly 9 percent of all domestically listed shares and more than 25 percent of at least thirty-three major industrial corporations.

In addition to direct share ownership, banks serve as depositories for stock owned by other shareholders. At the end of 1988, they held shares worth DM411.5 billion, or 40 percent of the total market value of outstanding domestic shares. Banks also enjoy *Vollmachtstimmrecht,* or the right to vote shares held on deposit on behalf of the depositor. Effectively, banks control virtually half of German shares. German law has been amended to require that banks solicit voting instructions from shareholders whom they represent and renew the right of proxy for shares held on deposit every 15 months. In the event of a takeover offer, banks must inform shareholders of pending bids only if the offer is published. Still, banks continue to obtain wide latitude in the voting of shares held on deposit. **Exhibit 8** profiles ownership of shares on deposit in banks.

As in Japan, firms tend to have strong relationships with one or a few banks, called *Hausbank*s. A *Hausbank* would be a primary lender to a company and would often enjoy representation on the supervisory board or an equity position in the company. Supervisory board members from such banks are valued for their knowledge of business and economic conditions, as well as for their detailed knowledge of the company. In times of financial crisis, the *Hausbank* would tend to be more willing to aid the company than would other banks. As in Japan, shares owned by *Hausbank*s are seldom traded. (**Exhibit 9** profiles traditional German *Hausbank* relationships in the automotive industry.)

A few episodes in Daimler-Benz's relationship with its *Hausbank,* Deutsche Bank, illustrate how a such bank can aid a German corporation and also the influence that it may have in the company's management. Since the bank brought together the two predecessors of Mercedes-Benz in 1926, it has maintained a special relationship with the automotive giant. With 28.6 percent of the auto company's stock, Deutsche Bank is its major shareholder, and the chair of Daimler-Benz's *Aufsichtsrat* is customarily a Deutsche Bank executive. In the 1970s, Daimler-Benz came under pressure from an unfriendly investor who wished to acquire a 38 percent share in the company and force it to make a major foreign investment. Deutsche Bank bought 28 percent of Daimler-Benz at a large premium to market value, thereby thwarting the unfriendly investor's plan. Deutsche Bank then formed the Mercedes-Benz Holding company, whose stock it placed in the hands of several German financial and automotive supply companies. The ownership in the holding company has been stable since the company was founded. In the 1980s, however, Deutsche Bank exerted a different kind of influence on the board. It helped bring about a major restructuring of Daimler-Benz's *Vorstand,* which resulted in the appointment of a new chairman and tilted the board in favor of a major diversification strategy.[20]

---

[20]"The Banker Behind the Shakeup at Daimler-Benz," *Business Week,* July 27, 1987, pp. 36–37; "We Are Still Saying Hello to Each Other," *Forbes,* May 18, 1987, pp. 94–98.

Merger and Acquisition Activity

The threat of hostile takeover is not a significant element of German corporate governance. Indeed, friendly mergers are uncommon, and hostile takeovers virtually unheard of: from 1982 to 1988, there were only twenty-nine mergers in West Germany.[21]

The special position of banks, government antitrust policy, and the structure of the corporation all discourage unfriendly takeovers. A takeover would be virtually impossible without the support of the major banks because of their extensive stock holdings, their control over shares held on deposit, and the fact that they write the rules on takeovers. In fact, there are no statutory takeover rules in Germany, only guidelines rigorously enforced by banks. (The takeover guidelines require the bidder to inform appropriate stock exchanges of an offer, refrain from insider trading before publication of the offer, publish the terms of the offer, and give those who may have accepted a lower bid for their shares the higher price in the event that a second offer is made.)

The government Cartel Office must clear any bid if the new concern would have more than DM2 billion in sales annually. Also, the Cartel Office has the authority to review the merger and require divestment ex post.

Several other structural aspects of German corporations and corporate law impede takeovers. Major changes to the corporation require 75 percent approval by shareholders, law prohibits golden parachutes, and strict conflict-of-interest rules impede most would-be management buyouts. Because companies with more than 2000 workers have equal employee and shareholder representation on the *Aufsichtsrat*, employee support is virtually a prerequisite for a successful takeover.

SUMMARY AND COMPARISON

Modern corporations are frequently described as a nexus of contracts among stakeholders of many types—shareholders, creditors, managers, workers, customers, suppliers, and so forth. While these diverse groups have a strong incentive to cooperate in order to further their individual economic welfare, they are also frequently tempted to exploit the corporation's resources to further their own individual objectives at the expense of others. Various organizational forms and systems of corporate governance have evolved in different parts of the world to attenuate these universal hazards of self-interested opportunism.

The plethora of different legal organizational forms populating capitalist economies is evidence of the wide breadth of responses to problems of governance of which such economies are capable. The diversity within even a single country's borders can be staggering, making it problematic to define any one system of governance as prototypical of an entire nation. Nevertheless, broad differences do appear to separate the systems most commonly found among large corporations headquartered in different countries such as Germany, Japan, and the United States.

By and large, Anglo-American companies have tended to address the hazards of self-interested opportunism among cooperating stakeholders by delineating the

[21]*International Financial Law Review Special Supplement* (February 1990): 100.

responsibilities of one to another, as much as possible, in formal, explicitly written contracts enforced by courts, and by relying heavily on arm's-length, price-oriented transactions with a large number of competitive lenders, suppliers, customers, subcontractors, managers, and so forth (i.e., relying upon the incentives and discipline of the market to ensure mutually beneficial behavior). Where market incentives are insufficient to control the hazards of opportunism, vertical integration takes place. Indeed, at times, higher degrees of vertical integration *and* a greater reliance on a fragmented, highly competitive market relative to foreign competitors can be found in American industry. General Motors and Ford, for example, tend to be more vertically integrated (only about 30 percent of GM's parts are purchased outside the company, while for Ford the amount is approximately 50 percent) than most of their major Japanese and German counterparts, and yet rely on more than 2000 different primary parts suppliers—five to ten times the number typically used by overseas firms.[22]

Traditionally, stakeholder groups are distinctly separate in the typical Anglo-American corporation, and there are reasonably clear boundaries separating a firm from the factor and product markets in which it transacts. The primary responsibility of the Anglo-American board of directors is to safeguard the interests of one particular stakeholder, the equity investors, and to ensure that management seeks to maximize the value of the shareholders' stake in the corporation. Consistent with the Anglo-American propensity to rely upon competitive markets to induce satisfactory behavior among contracting parties, a relatively free and active market for corporate control is relied upon to correct failures of the board of directors to act as a safeguard of shareholder interests.

German and Japanese companies govern relationships among corporate stakeholders transacting with one another rather differently. They tend to rely more extensively on implicit, relational contracting, and on somewhat different safeguards and dispute resolution processes to enforce adherence to agreements.

By tying themselves to one another in groups through equity participation and various personal and institutionalized information-sharing networks, yet eschewing outright majority ownership and control, Japanese corporations have been able to exploit powerful market incentives that derive from independent asset ownership. Concurrently, the close involvement of major stakeholders in a firm enables them to adapt their relationship with the company to the prevailing environment. In lieu of arm's-length transactions among many strictly autonomous market participants, or extensive integration of asset ownership under large administrative hierarchies, Japanese corporations engage in tight commercial relationships, formed by relational contracts, personal trust among managers, and extensive information sharing. The existence of large minority equity claims among major stakeholders helps mitigate the abuse of such business relationships.

Of course, such a system of governance is not without its faults. Excess work force, excessive product proliferation, *over*investment in declining businesses, unrelated

---

[22]See United States General Accounting Office, National Security and International Affairs Division, *Foreign Investment: Growing Japanese Presence in the U.S. Auto Industry* (GAO/NSIA 0-88-111) (Washington, DC: General Accounting Office, March 1988), pp. 32–33.

diversification beyond organizational capabilities, and mismanagement of corporate excess cash balances are relatively commonly observed inefficiencies of business in Japan.[23] A positive effect, however, has been to foster considerable transactional efficiencies among Japanese companies doing business with one another. These efficiencies may help promote investment and global competitive success.

German contractual governance bears many similarities to the Japanese system, particularly regarding the maintenance of long-term lender-borrower relationships and bank ownership of equity. In at least one important respect—the composition of corporate boards of directors—German governance provides stronger safeguards against the moral hazards associated with information asymmetries than does the Japanese system. Japanese boards tend to be heavily dominated by strictly inside managing directors. Retired executives of important equity-owning stakeholders sometimes join these directors as "alumni" representatives of their former employers. German supervisory boards, in contrast, are at least half-composed of salaried executives of the corporation's major institutional shareholders or other important stakeholders.

In many other respects, however, German contractual governance provides somewhat weaker safeguards for the preservation of long-term relationships. Although supervisory board representation is concentrated among a relatively small number of executives who sit on many boards, the sort of temporary personnel transfers at lower levels of management that are so common in Japan are not so common in Germany. Information sharing is less institutionalized in Germany than in Japan, where inter-company management and supplier organizations are commonplace. Differences between Germany and Japan are more matters of degree than of kind, however, especially in comparison to common practice in the United States.

All three nations have evolved highly effective systems of contracting and corporate governance. None of them, however, are static. As the world's capital and product markets integrate, and as companies domiciled in different nations engage in various cross-border investments and transactions (e.g., joint ventures and cross-border acquisitions), these systems are increasingly coming into direct contact and, sometimes, conflict with one another. As they do so, the advantages and limitations of each become more clearly exposed. From this process is emerging a somewhat Darwinistic "competition" among systems of governance that is likely to engender further evolution in the three models described here.

---

[23]W. Carl Kester, *Japanese Takeovers: The Global Contest for Corporate Control* (Boston: Harvard Business School Press, 1991), pp. 219–235.

EXHIBIT 1   **MAJOR LAWS INFLUENCING CORPORATE OWNERSHIP AND GOVERNANCE BY FINANCIAL INSTITUTIONS IN THE UNITED STATES**

- Glass-Steagall Act of 1933
- Securities and Exchange Act of 1934
- Investment Company Act of 1940
- The Bank Holding Company Act of 1956
- Employee Retirement Income Security Act of 1974 (ERISA)
- Various state insurance regulations

EXHIBIT 2   **INTRAGROUP SALES AND PROCUREMENT IN MAJOR JAPANESE *KEIRETSU*, 1981**

	Six major *keiretsu*	Original *zaibatsu* groups*	Modern groups[†]
Average intragroup sales[‡]			
Presidents council members	10.8%	13.4%	8.6%
All group companies	20.4	29.0	14.9
Average intragroup procurement[‡]			
Presidents council members	11.7%	14.8%	9.1%
All group industrial companies	12.4	18.6	8.2

*The Mitsubishi, Mitsui, and Sumitomo groups.
[†]The Fuyo, DKB, and Sanwa groups.
[‡]Statistics are exclusive of group financial institutions.
Source: Kigyo Shudan no Jittai ni tsuiti, June 21, 1983.

EXHIBIT 3   **SELECTED CROSS-SHAREHOLDINGS IN THE MITSUBISHI GROUP, 1990**

	Mitsubishi Bank	Mitsubishi Corp.	Mitsubishi Heavy Industries
Mitsubishi Bank	—	5.0%	3.6%
Mitsubishi Corp.	1.7%	—	1.6
Mitsubishi Heavy Industries	3.0	3.2	—
Total owned by Mitsubishi group	18.1	25.5	17.2

Source: Industrial Groupings in Japan, 9th ed., 1990–1991 (Tokyo: Dodwell Marketing Consultants, 1990).

EXHIBIT 4   PERCENTAGE OF RECIPROCALLY OWNED SHARES IN JAPANESE INDUSTRIAL GROUPS, 1987

	Percent reciprocally owned
Mitsui group	
Mitsubishi group	25.3%
Sumitomo group	24.5
Fuyo group	18.2
DKB group	14.6
Sanwa	10.9

Source: Industrial Bank of Japan.

EXHIBIT 5   JAPANESE SHARE OWNERSHIP BY TYPE OF INVESTORS, ALL LISTED COMPANIES (%)

	1980		1985		1989	
Government (all levels)	0.2%		0.2%		0.7%	
Financial institutions	38.8		39.6		45.6	
All banks		17.1%		18.3%		22.1%
Investment trusts		1.9		1.1		3.1
Annuity trusts		0.5		0.5		1.0
Life insurance companies		12.3		12.7		13.1
Other insurance companies		4.9		4.8		4.2
Other financial institutions		2.1		2.2		2.1
Business corporations	26.1		25.9		24.9	
Securities companies	2.0		1.9		2.5	
Individuals and others	30.4		26.3		22.4	
Foreigners	2.5		6.1		4.0	
Total	100.0%		100.0%		100.0%	

Source: Tokyo Stock Exchange.

EXHIBIT 6   GERMAN CORPORATE OWNERSHIP STRUCTURE, 1989

		Market value, billions		Percent of market value
Government		DM 61.1		6.8%
Financial institutions		215.2		19.5
Banks	DM 98.5		8.9	
Insurance companies	116.7		10.6	
Business corporations		433.4		39.2
Private households and others		185.4		16.8
Foreigners		160.3		17.1
Total		DM1055.4		100.0%

Source: Deutsche Bundesbank, internal report, May 1990.

EXHIBIT 7 SUPERVISORY BOARD PROFILES OF MAJOR GERMAN AUTO COMPANIES AND BANKS, KNOWN AFFILIATIONS BY INDUSTRY[a]

Company (no. of supervisory board members)	No. of labor reps.	Financial institutions: (Total no.) Company, position, board type	Industrial corporations: (Total no.) Company, position, board type	Other known affiliations: (Total no.) Affiliation
BMW (22)	11	(1) Dresdner Bank[b]	(6) Altana Industrie-Aktien und Anlagen AG (holding co.)[b] Siemens AG[c] NV Philips' Gloeilampenfabrieken[c,d] Linde AG (eng. & constr.)[c,d] Maschinenfabrik Goebel GmbH (eng. & constr.)[c] Gevaert NV (textiles)[c,d]	(4) Federal High Court Lawyer Two other lawyers BMW, former member of management board
Daimler-Benz (21[e])	10	(6) Bayerische Landesbank Girozentrale[c] Commerzbank[c,d] Deutsche Bank AG (3)[d] Dresdner Bank, Speaker[c,d]	(1) Deutsche Shell AG (energy)[c,d]	(1) Mercedes-Automobil-Holding AG[c,d,f]
Porsche (12)	6	(1) Landesgirokasse öffentliche und Landessparkasse (bank)[c,d]	(2) AUDI AG[c,d] Nixdorf Computer AG[c,d]	(0)
Volkswagen (20)	NA	(3) Allianz AG Holding (insurance holding)[c,d] Deutsche Bank AG[c] Dresdner Bank AG[b,d]	(2) Preussag AG (nonresidential construction)[b] Ruhrgas AG (energy)[c,d]	(5) Berlin Senate, former member[g] German Stockholders' Association, president Government of Lower Saxony (2)[f]: Minister of Finance, Minister for Economic Affairs, Technology and Transport Volkswagen AG, senior executive

		(3)	(2)	(3)
Bosch (20) (1987 data)	NA	Allianz Versicherungs-AG[c,d] Bank für Gemeinwirtschaft AG[c] Union Bank of Switzerland (honorary president)	Unilever NV (former dep. chair board of directors) Wieland-Werke AG (nonferrous metals)[c,d]	Max-Planck-Institut für Festkörperforschung, director Robert Bosch, two former members, management board
		(1)	(6)	(0)
Commerzbank (21[e])	NA	Allianz Lebensversicherungs-AG (life insurance)[c,d]	Bayer AG (chemicals, pharmaceuticals, petroleum)[b,d] Hoechst AG (chemicals, pharmaceuticals)[b] MBB Messerschmitt-Bölkow-Blohm GmbH (air/electronics) RWE AG (energy)[c] SMS Schloemann-Siemag AG (eng. & constr.)[c,d] Volkswagen AG[c,d]	
		(0)	(5)	(0)
Deutsche Bank (22[e])	10		Beiersdorf AG (chemicals, pharmaceuticals)[b] Robert Bosch GmbH (2), general counsel[c,d] Otto-Versand GmbH & Co. (retail trade)[c,d] Siemens AG[b,d]	
		(2)	(5)	(1)
Dresdner Bank (22[e])	NA	Banque Nationale de Paris, SA, director general Münchener Rückversicherungs-Gesellschaft AG (insurance)[c,d]	Altana Industrie-Aktien und Anlagen AG[b,d] Hoechst AG[b,d] Maschinenfabrik Goebel GmbH[c,d] NV Philips' Gloeilampenfabrieken, president and chair, board of managing directors Thyssen AG (holding/industrial conglomerate)[c,d]	Professor of Business Economics, University of Bonn

[a]For banks, "Financial institution" affiliations include only external affiliations.
[b]Member of supervisory board.
[c]Member of management board.
[d]Board chair
[e]Number includes honorary chair.
[f]Mercedes-Automobil-Holding AG owns 25.1 percent of Daimler-Benz and is itself owned by major financial institutions and industrial corporations, including Allianz, Robert Bosch, and Siemens.
[g]The government of the Federal Republic of Germany owned approximately 20 percent of Volkswagen until 1988. The state of Lower Saxony still owned, in 1991, approximately 20 percent of Volkswagen.
Sources: Annual reports.

EXHIBIT 8   SECURITIES DEPOSITS IN GERMAN BANKS BY GROUP OF INVESTORS, 1988

		Market value, billions		Percent
Government		DM 23.5		5.7%
Financial institutions		50.2		12.2
Insurance companies	DM 21.9		5.3	
Investment companies	28.3		6.9	
Nonfinancial business companies		125.5		30.5
Private households and others		121.4		29.5
Foreigners		90.9		22.1
Total		DM411.5		100.0%

Source: Deutsche Bundesbank, *Monthly Report,* May 1989.

EXHIBIT 9   TRADITIONAL GERMAN *HAUSBANK* RELATIONSHIPS IN THE AUTOMOTIVE INDUSTRY

Company	*Hausbank*
BMW	Dresdner Bank
Daimler-Benz	Deutsche Bank
Porsche	Landesgirokasse öffentliche Bank und Sparkasse
Robert Bosch	Deutsche Bank
Volkswagen	Deutsche Bank
	Dresdner Bank

Source: Company interviews.

KOITO MANUFACTURING, LTD.

. . . putting a stockholder whom the American courts had labeled a greenmailer on our board would be highly irresponsible. Greenmailers—Japanese or American—are not welcome on Koito's board. (Takao Matsuura, "Boone-San, Either Put Up or Shut Up," *The Wall Street Journal,* April 18, 1990, p. A22)

All I've asked for is representation. . . . Give me a chance. Is that an unusual request for someone who has bought a substantial part of a company? (T. Boone Pickens, Jr., *The Japan Economic Journal,* July 7, 1990, p. 2.)

On the morning of June 29, 1990, T. Boone Pickens, Jr.—Texas oilman, corporate raider, and self-styled champion of shareholder rights—prepared for that day's annual meeting of Koito Manufacturing, Ltd. (Japan). By accumulating 26.4 percent of Koito's stock from Kitaro Watanabe, a reputed Japanese greenmailer, Mr. Pickens had displaced Toyota Motor Corp. as Koito's largest shareholder. Still, his efforts to gain board representation and the access to company records afforded him by Japanese law had been frustrated for more than a year. Despite Mr. Pickens's stated intent—only to participate in Koito's long-term management and growth—Koito's management suspected Mr. Pickens's ultimate motives.

Mr. Pickens blamed his inability to exercise his "shareholder rights" on the Japanese *keiretsu* system—the federation of groups of companies around a major bank, trading company, or large industrial firm. To Mr. Pickens, *keiretsu* "look and act just like old-fashioned cartels," facilitating long-term market-domination strategies,

This case was prepared by Research Associate Robert W. Lightfoot under the supervision of Professor W. Carl Kester. Copyright © 1991 by the President and Fellows of Harvard College. Harvard Business School case 291-027.

raising consumer prices, stymieing foreign competition, prejudicing Japanese producers toward Japanese suppliers, and inflating share prices in an already overvalued stock market.[1] He complained that the Japanese market was essentially closed to American investors wishing "to invest with full rights in Japan," and that the problem was made more difficult "because the most powerful impediments in Japan were not legal restrictions, but silent barriers produced by business customs and practices."[2]

The Japanese view of *keiretsu*, however, differed. To some, the *keiretsu* system was a product of Japanese culture and history. It also happened to be an effective form of business organization well suited to long-term business planning and large joint projects. Its economic success would seem proof enough of its merits. Within it, the corporation was viewed as part of an extended family whose members included all of its stakeholders: employees, suppliers, customers, creditors, and shareholders. "The obligation to shareholders is met by a reasonable return on capital, which is all that institutional investors, who are the most important shareholders, expect. The rest of the wealth generated by the enterprise is retained on behalf of other constituencies, the most important of which are its members—those working in the enterprise."[3]

COMPANY HISTORY

Koito Manufacturing, Ltd. was founded in 1915. It was incorporated in 1936, at which time it began supplying lighting equipment to Toyota and Nissan Loom Works, the two companies chosen by the Japanese government to produce trucks domestically for military purposes. For more than 50 years, Koito had retained its product focus on automotive lighting and its customer affiliations with Toyota and Nissan: 92 percent of its 1990 sales were in automotive lighting equipment, and, in 1986, Toyota and Nissan bought 62 percent of Koito's output. Koito also manufactured aircraft parts (6 percent) and other products, including power window regulators and electronic parts for precision instruments and communications equipment (2 percent).

Koito enjoyed a special relationship with the Toyota Group. Toyota was Koito's largest customer and, behind Pickens, its second-largest shareholder, with 19 percent of its stock. The Toyota Group's purchases accounted for more than half of Koito's revenues.[4] (See **Exhibits 1** and **2**.)

In the year ending March 1990, Koito earned ¥3.7 billion on ¥123.5 billion in sales. (See **Exhibits 3** and **4**.) Shareholders' average annual return (capital gains plus dividends) for the 9 years to March 31, 1990, was an impressive 24 percent. During the same period, net income grew at 5 percent per annum, and sales at nearly 9 percent.

---

[1]T. Boone Pickens, Jr., "Secrets Koito Hoped to Hide by Keeping Me Off Its Board," *The Wall Street Journal*, March 28, 1990, p. A14.

[2]T. Boone Pickens, "T. Boone's Bone to Pick," *The International Economy* (September/October 1989): 90.

[3]Gene Gregory, "A Stake in Japan," *Management Today* (November 1989): 110.

[4]Takao Matsuura, "Boone-San, Either Put Up or Shut Up," *The Wall Street Journal*, April 18, 1990, p. A22.

In the 9 years to March 1986, however, these annual figures were 8 percent, 12 percent, and 11 percent, respectively.

Koito's stock performed extremely well after being listed on the Second Section of the Tokyo Stock Exchange on March 1, 1988 (see **Exhibit 5**). Although it more than doubled in value between 1982 and 1987, when it was traded over the counter, it increased nearly five-fold in the next 3 years. In fact, the rapid rise of Koito's stock after its Second Section listing spurred the Finance Ministry to investigate possible order-padding by Japanese brokerage firms. Takao Matsuura, president of Koito, also held billionaire Kitaro Watanabe responsible for the 18-month run-up in Koito's shares, from about ¥700 in 1988 to more than ¥5,000 in 1989.[5]

JAPANESE AUTO MANUFACTURER-SUPPLIER RELATIONSHIPS

Virtually all Japanese auto manufacturers (OEMs) were associated with industrial groups known as *keiretsu* (see the "Note on Corporate Governance Systems: The United States, Japan, and Germany" for a more thorough discussion of *keiretsu* and Japanese corporate governance in general). Mitsubishi Motors, for example, was a member of the Mitsubishi *keiretsu,* the modern descendant of the pre–World War II Mitsubishi *zaibatsu*. The contemporary groupings of suppliers, dealers, insurers, and other automotive affiliated companies around Toyota and Nissan were newer *keiretsu* that emerged in Japan's postwar economic development.[6] **Exhibit 6** shows Toyota's group affiliations in 1990.

The Structure of the Japanese Automotive Supply Industry

In the immediate postwar period, Japanese automobile makers found it nearly impossible to imitate U.S.-style mass production of automobiles.[7] The difficulty was due to fragmented demand for small numbers of many types of automobiles and trucks, strict labor laws imposed by the Allied Powers, a shortage of capital and foreign exchange, and the persistent threat of foreign entry into the Japanese automobile market. After the war, the Japanese government had intended to build an independent automotive supply industry to take advantage of economies of scale, but the Japanese OEMs chose to cultivate tight supplier relationships of their own.

Toyota divided its suppliers into two tiers. From performance specifications, first-tier suppliers designed and developed components with Toyota engineers and with other suppliers. In turn, first-tier suppliers bought individual parts from second-tier suppliers, which were manufacturing specialists, not engineering specialists. Three

---

[5]Ibid.

[6]Honda is not normally considered a core company of an industrial group (one of its main banks, in fact, is the Mitsubishi Bank). Nevertheless, like the other major Japanese auto assemblers, it too maintains steady, close vertical relationships with a stable network of suppliers, dealers, and providers of capital.

[7]The American automobile industry was then and is still characterized by a high degree of vertical integration. Independent suppliers bid for the few parts that are contracted out (approximately 30 percent of the value of the car), and short-term contracts are usually awarded on the basis of some clearly defined criteria, such as best price or best quality.

difficulties surfaced from this organizational structure. First, suppliers competing with one another for the same business were prone to restrict the flow of information and cost-saving technologies to fellow Toyota suppliers. Such behavior tended to enhance individual suppliers' competitiveness at the expense of others, including Toyota. Second, Toyota had little information about or influence over its suppliers' quality control, leading to greater variances in quality than was thought desirable. Finally, the flow of supplies was not as efficiently controlled as it could have been, leading to a greater investment of scarce capital in inventory than was necessary.

To solve these problems, Toyota created a new ownership structure among its suppliers. First, it spun off its in-house supply operations into quasi-independent suppliers in which it retained some equity and purchased minority equity positions in its other, formerly independent suppliers. Each supplier then purchased equity in some other suppliers of the same tier. Second, Toyota's suppliers created a *kyoryokukai* ("cooperation club"), called *"Kyohokai,"* which meant "a club for coprospering with Toyota." Members collected and disseminated information about Toyota and one another, and met regularly to discuss ways of improving their interaction with Toyota. The resulting pyramidal structure is shown in **Exhibit 7**.

Although other Japanese OEMs did not copy Toyota's supplier structure identically, most evolved broadly similar networks of supplier relationships. Thus, the eleven Japanese OEMs relied on 1400 first-tier suppliers and at least 10,000 second-tier suppliers. Each OEM had between 150 and 300 affiliated and independent suppliers, which typically were members of a *kyoryokukai*. Whereas Toyota's 176 suppliers belonged to one *kyoryokukai,* Nissan's belonged to two: one primarily for affiliates (105) and the other for independents (58), many of which also supplied Toyota.[8] In contrast to their American counterparts, major Japanese OEMs were much less vertically integrated in parts production. Toyota, Nissan, and Mitsubishi Motors, for example, were each about 30 percent vertically integrated, and Honda 22 percent. In contrast, Ford and General Motors were 50 percent and 70 percent vertically integrated, respectively. Despite higher vertical integration, the American OEMs each relied on 2000 to 5000 primary external parts suppliers.

Business Practices within Automotive *Keiretsu*

The conduct of business within *keiretsu,* including the Toyota group, differed sharply from that commonly observed in other economic environments. There was generally a high degree of loyalty among member companies, which translated into substantial reciprocal trade. If an OEM could source parts and equipment within its own group, it was highly likely to do so, although rarely on an exclusive basis. Toyota, for example, relied heavily on Koito for halogen lights but also bought lighting equipment from Ichikoh Industries and Stanley Electric. Likewise, group suppliers also sold to other OEMs, although no other single company would typically account for as much of sales as its own group's OEM.

[8]Dodwell Marketing Consultants, *Structure of the Japanese Automobile Supply Industry* (Tokyo: Dodwell, 1986), pp. 5–6.

Given the long-standing relationships between OEMs and suppliers in Japan, supply contracts were usually quite informal and bore little resemblance to the sort of explicit written contracts more commonly used in Western business environments. Underlying these informal contracts were carefully nurtured trust relationships among managers of the OEM's and their associated suppliers. These were created and supported by frequent temporary personnel transfers between assemblers and suppliers in connection with collaborative projects. OEM's also indirectly monitored assemblers by providing some of their ''retiring'' executives to sit on the board of directors or in other senior management positions of key suppliers. Former Toyota executives, for example, sat on the boards of Nippondenso, Koito, and most other major Toyota group suppliers.

From an outside perspective, management transfers often led to ambiguity about whose interests were really being represented. Mr. Pickens, for example, claimed that three members of Koito's twenty-three-person board were de facto Toyota representatives by virtue of their former employment at Toyota. Koito's president, Mr. Matsuura, contested this claim by observing that the directors in question had left Toyota's employ years ago.

Finally, as commonly observed in other Japanese industries, automotive *keiretsu* typically engaged in extensive reciprocal equity ownership. Member companies in the Toyota group, for example, were estimated to have at least 26 percent of their shares held within the group. In general, corporations and financial institutions with which Toyota had business dealings owned 87.7 percent of its shares; individual shareholders held only 9.3 percent of Toyota's common stock (see **Exhibit 8**).

MERGERS, ACQUISITIONS, AND GREENMAIL IN JAPAN

True hostile takeovers were virtually unheard of in Japan, due, many observers believed, to a widespread Japanese abhorrence of such activity. Japanese managers tended to perceive their companies as extended ''families,'' which lent a sense of ''flesh peddling'' to the sale of corporations. Indeed, the very terms commonly used to express the concept of corporate takeovers, *nottori* (''hijacking'') and *baishu* (''bribery''), connoted opprobrious behavior.

The image of mergers and acquisitions in Japan was tainted also by connections to *yakuza,* organized crime groups that extort companies after having acquired large stock holdings. One such scheme involved two groups. The first, ''The Man With 21 Faces,'' extorted Fujiya, a major confectioner, by threatening to poison the company's candy, while a second group attempted to greenmail the company. *Yakuza* money was also thought to support certain *shite* (or ''corner'') groups, which greenmailed companies whose stock was thinly traded. *Shite* purchased shares on margin and harassed incumbent management by threatening to exercise large shareholder's rights.

Despite these taboos, greenmailing (the buyback of shares from an unfriendly investor) occurred in Japan with surprising frequency and increasingly at the hands of legitimate—even if unpopular—investors. One source documented forty-one successful greenmailings in Japan between 1976 and 1985, and estimated that their value ranged between ¥3.4 billion and ¥76.8 billion. Another estimated that, in 1988, 120 *shite* held stock in 156 listed corporations worth ¥1.5 trillion.[9]

Toyota itself had paid greenmail once before to rescue its affiliate and former parent corporation, Toyoda Automatic Loom Works (TALW). In mid-1986 the *shite,* or "corner group," Nihon Gendai Kigyo, started buying shares in TALW at about ¥1000 per share. By March 1987, Nihon Gendai owned 17.7 million (7.1 percent) of TALW's shares, which it then asked Toyota to buy back. Although Toyota conceded that the price was high, it did not want to be troubled by undesirable major shareholders. Circumventing a Japanese restriction against stock buybacks, Toyota Motor and three other Toyota group companies purchased Nihon Gendai's holdings for approximately ¥2000 per share in April 1987.

Since then, the Toyota group strengthened its cross-holding. Bitter from its last experience, Toyota made it clear that it was not interested in greenmail: "It is a breach of other shareholders' trust to buy the stock at prices far higher than its real worth," Toyota President Shoichiro Toyoda maintained.[10]

Special Shareholder Rights, Proxy Contests, and Tender Offers

As in most other nations, shareholders without direct or close indirect representation on corporate boards had little voice in the control of Japanese corporations. Certain rights, however, did exist for large shareholders. Those with 1 percent ownership or more could add items to the agenda at shareholders' meetings (normally quite perfunctory in Japan, often lasting less than 30 minutes). With 3 percent of the stock, they could call a special shareholders, meeting (at their own expense) and could apply to a court to remove a director. A 10 percent holding for more than 6 months could allow a shareholder to inspect a company's accounting records and to apply to a court to appoint a special auditor for this purpose. Finally, owners of 34 percent or more of the outstanding stock could propose special shareholder resolutions.

Advance review of proxy materials by the Ministry of Finance was abolished, even under circumstances in which a battle for control could be at stake. Provisions requiring designated proxy agents to follow the voting instructions of the shareholders solicited also were deleted; blank proxies, which were quite common in Japan, were routinely cast as votes in support of management's position. Although penalties for the violation of proxy regulations did exist, they were generally considered weak. Indeed, no sanctions were ever imposed, perhaps because proxy regulations extended narrowly to only the *solicitation* of shareholder proxies, *not* to corporate action taken in light of those proxies. Thus, the prevailing view among Japanese legal scholars was that, even if sanctions for proxy law violations ever had

---

[9]W. Carl Kester, *Japanese Takeovers: The Global Contest for Corporate Control* (Boston: Harvard Business School Press, 1991).

[10]"Hostile Investment in Koito Worries Toyota," *The Japan Economic Journal,* April 15, 1989, p. 4; "Tokyo Watch," *Euromoney,* May 1989, p. 22.

been imposed, they would not have affected the validity of any action taken at the shareholders' meeting itself.[11]

Regulations governing tender offers were put into effect in 1971, with an amendment to the Securities and Exchange Law. Between 1971 and 1990, only two tender offers were formally registered and concluded, both of them friendly offers designed to achieve sufficient share ownership to permit consolidated financial reporting.

Regulation of tender offers was required if the offeror and its affiliates acquired more than 10 percent of the shares outstanding or if the interest was nonbeneficial. Although advance review of proxy statements was not required, ministerial approval was. The offeror had to file with the Ministry of Finance a tender offer registration statement, which became valid 10 days after acceptance. The statement had to include the offer's purpose and duration (minimum 20 days, maximum 30 days); the number of shares to be purchased; the existence of withdrawal rights; the offer price (which had to be uniform); the source of funds; and a description of the offeror, its affiliates, and its holdings in the target company. For a cash offer to be validated, a deposit in the amount of the offer had to be made in a Japanese bank (the Japanese subsidiary of a foreign bank would qualify), which was designated as the "commissioned agent" for the bidder. The offer then had to be published in at least two or more daily newspapers, and the target firm notified. If the target's management chose to make recommendations about the tender offer, any agreements between management and the bidder had to be disclosed. If management made no official recommendations, side deals did not have to be disclosed. The bidder was not allowed to repay loans with cash derived from the target's assets because doing so would violate the Japanese law against a corporation repurchasing its own shares.[12]

KOITO BECOMES A TARGET

Kitaro Watanabe was a World War II orphan who amassed great wealth through dealings in used cars and real estate. At some (undisclosed) time in the mid-1980s, he started buying Koito stock from Mitsuhiro Kotani, a speculator known for his "stock-cornering" activities. Mr. Watanabe continued to add to his holdings on the open market and may eventually have acquired as many as 50 million shares. He approached Koito's most important customer and shareholder, Toyota, on two occasions and reportedly threatened to sell his stock to an American bidder if Toyota did not buy his shares.[13] Toyota did not oblige. It was at this juncture that Mr. Watanabe opened discussions with T. Boone Pickens in the United States.

---

[11]See Misao Tatsuta, "Proxy Regulation, Tender Offers, and Insider Trading," in *Japanese Securities Regulations*, eds. Louis Loss, Makoto Yazawa, and Barbara Ann Banoff (Tokyo and Boston: University of Tokyo Press and Little, Brown & Co., 1983), pp. 159–171.

[12]Ibid., pp. 172–191.

[13]"T. Boone Pickens: Greenmail on the Mind?" *Tokyo Business Today* (June 1989): 38–39.

T. Boone Pickens

T. Boone Pickens became widely known among American executives as an aggressive, tenacious, and generally hostile bidder for corporations that he targeted as undervalued investment opportunities. He had been bought out at a substantial profit in at least three of sixteen different bids for control of other companies, and had given up his bid for control in seven. Mr. Pickens's profits from investments in Cities Service, Gulf, and Philips Petroleum alone were reported to be $500 million. Subsequent bids met with less success. Unocal responded to his acquisition of 13.6 percent of its stock with a stock buyback that excluded him, and his bids for Newmont Mining, Homestake Mining, and KN Energy failed.

Pickens Acquires Koito Stock

In 1989, Koito represented one of Mr. Pickens's latest and most remarkable investments. After meeting with Kitaro Watanabe more than ten times, Mr. Pickens announced on April 4, 1989, that his merchant bank, Boone Co., had bought 32.4 million Koito shares (20.2 percent) from an undisclosed seller for an undisclosed amount. Because 60 percent to 65 percent of Koito's stock was in "friendly" hands, analysts considered a takeover unlikely. However, with more than 10 percent of the stock, Mr. Pickens could demand that Koito turn over confidential financial documents and then raise potentially embarrassing questions. "We don't mind at all that the U.S. shareholder investigates our business ties with Koito," Toyota Motor President Shoichiro Toyoda protested, but most analysts disagreed.[14] Some independent Japanese suppliers hoped that Mr. Pickens would be able to upset the close relationship between Toyota and Koito, thereby improving their negotiating position with carmakers. As one complained, "Ford . . . will pay higher prices for better parts from us. Japanese carmakers will not."[15]

The high price Mr. Pickens allegedly paid for his stock, as well as his refusal to disclose the source of his stock and its associated financing, added to the suspicion that he intended to greenmail Koito. Observers estimated that Mr. Pickens's average purchase price was ¥3375 per share,[16] which was well below the ¥5090 March closing price, but a substantial multiple of Koito's 1989 per share earnings of ¥17.90. Some observers also conjectured that Mr. Pickens was not the real owner of the stock, but a front man for Mr. Watanabe or other investors. Unable to greenmail Toyota, Mr. Watanabe might have resorted to giving Mr. Pickens some sort of buyback agreement in order to unload his large position. Later, Mr. Pickens wrote of his meetings with Mr. Watanabe, "Mr. Watanabe figured that if an outsider were ever going to break through the closed corporate culture, it would have to be an American. So we met to discuss the possibility of buying into Japan Inc."[17]

---

[14]Yuko Inoue, "Pickens, Koito Spar before September Showdown," *The Japan Economic Journal,* July 1, 1989, p. 2.

[15]"Pickens Keeps Bucking Odds to Crack Koito," *The Japan Economic Journal,* November 18, 1989, p. 7.

[16]Inoue, op. cit., p. 2.

[17]T. Boone Pickens, "T. Boone's Bone to Pick," *The International Economy* (September/October 1989): 88.

Toyota and Koito presented a united front against paying greenmail. Junsuke Kato, executive vice president of Koito, vowed, "We will never accept any request to take over the acquired stock, or act as a mediator in arranging its transfer to others." And at an April 20 press conference, Toyota president Shoichiro Toyoda confirmed, "Toyota will neither ask Boone Co. for a meeting, nor try to buy back the stock to take over the leadership of Koito management."[18] Still, analysts said that Toyota might have no choice but to act if Mr. Pickens, as the number 1 shareholder, charged the Japanese automotive supply industry with using market power unfairly to force suppliers to cut price.[19]

Mr. Pickens Meets with Mr. Matsuura

After receiving formal approval of his investment from the Japanese Ministry of Finance, Mr. Pickens met with Koito's president, Takao Matsuura, on April 20. The purpose of the meeting was to request board representation and to discuss "management problems," including low dividend payout and the company's close links with Toyota Motor.[20] According to Mr. Matsuura, Mr. Pickens began by explaining that Boone Co.'s philosophy was to put stockholder interests first. Mr. Matsuura replied, "In our case, we have to consider the interests of our employees, our clients and the local communities where we operate, as well as those of the shareholders."[21] Mr. Pickens denied that he had any hostile intentions, but called the purchase a " 'test case' to determine the accessibility of the Tokyo market." He hinted at the possibility that U.S. sentiment toward Japan would become hostile if Japan did not open its markets more widely to American investors.[22]

Regarding Mr. Pickens's request for board representation, Mr. Matsuura told the press, "We gave no specific answer but explained generally that it is not a custom in Japan to just say, 'I've become a major shareholder so I should become a director.' " One of Koito's general managers, Mr. Aoyama, scoffed at the idea of letting Mr. Pickens participate in Koito's management. "Mr. Pickens works in the oil business and does corporate buy-outs. But he has no experience in a manufacturing industry, so we don't recognize him as a manager."[23]

By a voice vote at the 1989 annual meeting, Mr. Pickens was overwhelmingly denied board representation. He cast the only vote in favor of his proposal, later saying that the 60 percent of shareholders who had voted him down were in management's pocket. Mr. Pickens called the meeting the most unusual one of his life and complained that his wife, Bea, had been blocked from entering the meeting by two bankers from Nomura Wasserstein Perella Co. Further, he objected that hiring the investment bankers was unnecessary and wasteful: Mr. Pickens, a "long-term investor" who was

[18]Megumu Kondo and Toru Machida, "Toyota Plays Cards Close in Pickens Gamble," *The Japan Economic Journal,* April 29, 1989, p. 1.

[19]"Hostile Investment in Koito Worries Toyota," *The Japan Economic Journal,* April 15, 1989, p. 4.

[20]Inoue, op. cit., p. 2.

[21]Takao Matsuura, "When a Stranger Comes Knocking," *Business Tokyo* (February 1990): 56.

[22]"Koito Plans to Ask Pickens to Become a Friendly Holder," *The Wall Street Journal,* April 19, 1989, p. A15.

[23]"Pickens Encounters a Waiting Game in Koito Meeting," *The Wall Street Journal,* April 21, 1989, p. A12.

paying one-fifth of the bill, told the shareholders, ''I know how expensive these guys are. You cannot afford to waste money.'' After the meeting, Mr. Matsuura commented, ''We will continue to deal with Mr. Pickens as our major shareholder, with respect and courtesy.''[24]

The Dividend Issue

Once the 6-month waiting period for exercising one's shareholder rights expired, Mr. Pickens was able to wield new weapons against Koito. On September 20, 1989, Mr. Pickens called on Koito to increase its September 30 semiannual dividend to ¥7 from ¥4 per share and, the next day, stepped up his pressure on Koito by arranging to buy another 10 million shares. (This purchase brought his stake to 42.4 million shares, or 26 percent.)

On November 22, Koito announced that it would not raise the dividend. Management was concerned that such a move would benefit Mr. Watanabe, with whom Koito still suspected Mr. Pickens of being in cahoots. If Mr. Pickens's shares had been purchased on margin, the annual interest burden of carrying them would have been between $50 million and $100 million, well above the stock's roughly $2.5 million dividend. Rumors were circulating that Mr. Watanabe's real estate holdings were suffering, and, the next week, *The Wall Street Journal*'s ''Heard on the Street'' column predicted a cut in the dividend on Mr. Pickens's Mesa Limited Partnership. Any increase in Koito's dividend would make it easier for whoever held the Koito stock to cover margin interest. Mr. Pickens criticized the board's move for neglecting individual shareholder interests. A full 7 months after Mr. Pickens challenged Koito to raise its dividend, Koito did so, from ¥8 to ¥10 per share (¥5 semiannually).

Final Maneuvers

On January 15, 1990, Mr. Pickens filed a lawsuit in Japan to gain access to Koito's books and announced plans to file another seven lawsuits against Koito, including one that demanded compensation for dumping practices that benefited Toyota. On March 9, 1990, Koito again rejected Mr. Pickens's demand to review company accounts. On March 30, Mr. Pickens announced that the Bank of Japan had approved his application to acquire an additional five million shares of Koito stock and that he planned to increase his stake to 30 percent. Responding to criticism that he was a greenmailer, Mr. Pickens asked Koito to adopt a proposal prohibiting it from paying greenmail.

Days before Koito's June 26, 1990, annual meeting, Boone Co. and Koito launched publicity campaigns against each other. Mr. Pickens distributed a 38-page press pack describing more than a year's history of his dealings with Koito and pledged to raise his stake in the company. Koito's bankers announced that they had proof that Boone Co. did not actually own the stock, and Koito once again accused Mr. Pickens of attempted greenmail. Boone Co.'s 1989 Delaware Franchise Tax Report showed total

---

[24]''Pickens and Koito Fight to a Draw as He Is Denied Presence on Board,'' *The Wall Street Journal*, June 30, 1989, p. A10.

gross assets of only $1.9 million, although Boone Co.'s Koito stock alone was worth $950 million. Koito claimed that these figures proved Boone Co. was not the legitimate owner of the Koito stock that Mr. Pickens claimed to represent. Retorting that the filing included only domestic assets, Boone Co. then produced an amended filing that included its Koito holdings. Mr. Pickens acknowledged that he purchased his shares from Mr. Watanabe, but refused to give details of how the shares were financed and whether or not he had a buyback agreement with Mr. Watanabe.

A Clash of Cultures

As the rhetoric became more heated, camps on both sides of the Pacific prepared for yet another sharp confrontation during the approaching annual meeting. At one level, the struggle was seen as just another tempest among strong personalities vying for power in a medium-sized company. Others, however, saw it as but the first of many clashes yet to come between two divergent philosophies concerning appropriate methods and objectives of corporate governance.

EXHIBIT 1   KOITO MANUFACTURING, LARGE-OWNER PROFILE

Owner	Holdings, March 1990, %
Boone Co.	26.4%
Toyota Motor	19.0
Nissan Motor	5.9
Matsushita Electric Industrial	5.3
Nippon Life Insurance	4.1
Dai-Ichi Mutual Life Insurance	3.3
Matsushita Real Estate	2.5
Japan Securities Finance	2.3
Mitsubishi Bank	1.5
Sumitomo Bank	1.5
Dai-Ichi Kangyo Bank	1.5

Sources: T. Boone Pickens, "Secrets Koito Hoped to Hide by Keeping Me Off Its Board," *The Wall Street Journal,* March 28, 1990, p. A14; "Pickens Tries Histrionics at Koito," *The New York Times,* June 29, 1990, p. D1.

EXHIBIT 2   KOITO MANUFACTURING, MAJOR CUSTOMERS

Customer revenues	% of Koito's total revenues
Toyota Motor	48
Nissan Motor	14
Mazda Motor	9
Mitsubishi Motors	5
Fuji Heavy Industries	3
Daihatsu Motor	3
Hino Motors	2

Source: Dodwell Marketing Consultants, *The Structure of the Japanese Auto Parts Industry,* 3rd ed. (Tokyo: Dodwell, 1986).

EXHIBIT 3   KOITO MANUFACTURING, INCOME ACCOUNTS, 1982–1990 (FISCAL YEAR ENDING MARCH 31, MILLIONS)

	1982	1983	1984	1985	1986	1987	1988	1989	1990
Sales	¥70,932	¥72,998	¥78,297	¥84,505	¥93,117	¥96,891	¥106,011	¥111,442	¥123,543
Cost of goods sold	60,444	62,266	65,396	70,620	78,287	82,956	88,958	94,920	106,545
Gross profit	10,488	10,732	12,901	13,885	14,830	13,935	17,053	16,522	16,998
SG&A expenses	6,695	7,188	8,547	8,994	9,855	10,328	11,827	12,175	13,091
Operating income	3,793	3,544	4,354	4,891	4,975	3,607	5,226	4,347	3,906
Nonoperating income	1,588	1,717	1,803	2,251	2,499	2,636	2,447	2,746	3,031
(Int. and div. received)	1,199	1,354	1,504	1,871	2,170	2,033	1,973	2,350	2,272
Nonoperating expenses	428	391	397	486	419	675	332	290	583
(Int. and discounts)	301	263	183	172	155	141	180	80	79
Recurring profit	4,953	4,870	5,760	6,656	7,055	5,568	7,341	6,803	6,354
Extraordinary gain				1,406	40		1,457		1,227
Extraordinary loss	162	164	470	247	326	292	653	191	394
Income before taxes and special reserves	4,791	4,706	5,290	7,815	6,769	5,276	8,145	6,612	7,187
Transfer from reserves	58	89							
New appropriations to reserves	10								
Income before taxes	4,839	4,795	5,290	7,815	6,769	5,279	8,145	6,612	7,187
Provision for taxes	2,477	2,471	2,856	3,702	3,801	2,980	4,730	3,741	3,510
Net income	2,362	2,324	2,434	4,113	2,968	2,296	3,415	2,871	3,677
Dividends	942	942	942	1,071	1,153	1,154	1,255	1,282	1,603
Directors' bonuses	45	45	60	65	72	72	77	76	78
Retained earnings	1,375	1,337	1,432	2,977	1,743	1,070	2,083	1,513	1,996

Source: Daiwa Institute of Research.

	1982	1983	1984	1985	1986	1987	1988	1989	1990
Assets									
Current assets	¥29,416	¥30,309	¥34,514	¥41,683	¥42,341	¥51,747	¥60,439	¥54,475	¥61,408
Cash and deposits	3,295	2,969	2,855	4,244	4,906	11,868	23,919	19,146	18,540
Notes receivable	6,026	5,191	6,047	7,158	7,260	7,797	1,527	2,495	2,380
Accounts receivable	6,708	7,499	7,804	7,563	8,146	8,072	16,085	18,635	22,531
Securities	8,247	10,280	12,552	16,830	15,825	16,808	12,896	7,893	10,586
Inventories	4,114	3,641	4,447	4,839	5,259	4,572	4,603	4,870	5,794
Fixed assets	21,160	21,508	21,470	23,620	26,049	27,788	26,223	32,914	35,579
Tangible fixed assets	16,499	16,366	16,240	17,305	20,009	22,065	21,314	22,574	24,410
Depreciables	13,360	13,386	13,109	14,181	16,003	17,974	16,740	18,101	19,649
Land	2,840	2,844	2,893	2,641	3,317	3,675	3,785	4,029	4,016
Construction in progress	299	136	238	483	689	416	789	444	745
Nontangible assets	172	158	145	133	123	113	100	88	77
Investments	4,497	4,984	5,085	6,182	5,917	5,610	4,809	10,252	11,092
Securities	3,058	3,179	3,291	3,655	3,841	3,841	4,255	9,647	9,946
Long-term loans	1,197	1,604	1,614	2,172	1,601	1,273			
Total assets	¥50,584	¥51,817	¥55,984	¥65,303	¥68,390	¥79,535	¥86,662	¥87,389	¥96,987
Liabilities									
Current liabilities	¥20,020	¥19,872	¥21,727	¥22,734	¥24,074	¥23,814	¥28,374	¥26,936	¥33,931
Notes payable	9,891	9,615	10,459	11,140	11,219	11,897	12,518	11,705	14,861
Accounts payable	4,314	4,517	4,630	5,108	5,455	5,436	6,385	7,581	10,113
Short-term debt	655	475	322	263	250				
Liability reserves	3,220	3,146	3,819	3,757	4,347	3,700	5,140	2,716	4,121
Long-term liabilities	3,211	3,345	4,210	4,684	4,369	14,698	5,555	6,019	6,296
Bonds	213	86			20	10,015	456	268	261
Long-term debt			13	330					
Liability reserves	2,824	2,853	3,741	3,870	3,845	4,172	5,097	5,748	6,032
Total liabilities	23,431	23,217	25,937	27,418	28,443	38,512	33,929	32,955	40,227
Equity									
Stockholders' equity	27,153	28,600	30,047	37,885	39,947	41,023	52,733	54,434	56,760
Capital stock	6,730	6,730	6,730	9,106	9,261	9,264	14,043	14,137	14,141
Additional paid-in capital	9,567	9,567	9,567	11,943	12,098	12,101	16,881	16,975	16,978
Legal earned surplus	1,683	1,682	1,682	1,732	2,302	2,316	2,377	3,529	3,535
Voluntary earned surplus	6,500	7,910	9,228	10,581	12,941	14,542	15,520	16,454	17,895
Unappropriated	2,673	2,711	2,840	4,523	3,345	2,800	3,912	3,339	4,211
Total liabilities and equity	¥50,584	¥51,817	¥55,984	¥65,303	¥68,390	¥79,535	¥86,662	¥87,389	¥96,987

Source: Daiwa Institute of Research.

EXHIBIT 5 KOITO MANUFACTURING, SHARE DATA, 1982–1990 (FISCAL YEAR ENDING MARCH 31)

Investment Criteria	1982	1983	1984	1985	1986	1987	1988	1989	1990
Stock price, ¥	302	390	513	625	541	600	1,910	5,090	2,950
Volume, millions of shares	58.77	39.64	165.93	130.46	82.04	38.10	141.25	42.13	4.30
Earnings/share, ¥	17.55	17.27	18.08	28.63	20.58	15.92	21.34	17.90	22.93
Dividends/share, ¥	7.00	7.00	7.00	7.50	8.00	8.00	8.00	8.00	10.00
Net assets/share, ¥	203.22	212.48	233.23	263.71	276.93	284.37	329.58	339.48	353.95
Cash flow/share, ¥	49.55	51.07	53.61	62.33	56.42	67.63	66.88	60.96	66.01
Price/earnings ratio, times	17.21	22.59	28.37	21.83	26.29	37.70	89.49	284.28	128.65
Dividend yield, %	2.32	1.79	1.36	1.20	1.48	1.33	0.42	0.16	0.34
Market value/book value	1.49	1.84	2.30	2.37	1.95	2.11	5.80	14.99	8.33
Total market value, ¥ millions	40,649	52,494	69,050	89,599	78,039	86,556	305,600	816,166	473,062
No. shares outstanding, millions	134.60	134.60	134.60	143.66	144.25	144.26	160.00	160.34	160.36

Source: Daiwa Institute of Research.

EXHIBIT 6 THE TOYOTA MOTOR GROUP

Assemblers
  Toyota Motor
  Daihatsu Motor (passenger cars)
  Hino Motors (diesel trucks and buses)

Automotive parts/subassemblers
  Toyota Auto Body
  Kanto Auto Works
  Daihatsu Diesel Mfg.
  Hino Auto Body
  Sawafuji Electric
  Araco Corp.
  Aisin Seiki
  Toyoda Gosei
  Toyoda Machine Works
  Toyoda Automatic Loom Works
  Aisan Industry
  Futaba Industrial
  Nippondenso Co.
  Aichi Steel Works
  Toyoda Boshoku
  Kyowa Leather Cloth
  Toyota Kako
  Koito Manufacturing
  Jeco Co.
  Tokai Rika
  Chuo Malleable Iron
  Chuo Spring
  Tokyo Sintered Metal
  Koyo Seiko
  Trinity Industrial

Dealers/insurors
  Tokyo Toyota Motor
  Tokyo Toyo-pet Motor Sales
  Osaka Toyopet
  Toyota Tokyo Corolla
  Chiyoda Fire & Marine Insurance

Research and development
  Toyota Central
  Research & Development Laboratories

Nonautomotive industries
  Toyota Tsusho
  Towa Real Estate
  Nakanihon Theatrical

Source: Dodwell Marketing Consultants, *Industrial Groupings in Japan* (Tokyo: Dodwell, 1990), p. 251.

EXHIBIT 7   OEM-SUPPLIER RELATIONSHIP IN THE JAPANESE AUTOMOTIVE INDUSTRY

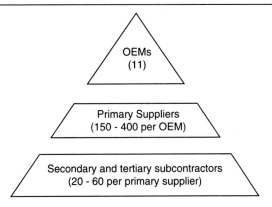

From Dodwell Marketing Consultants, *Structure of the Japanese Auto Parts Industry* (Tokyo: Dodwell, 1986), p. 14.

EXHIBIT 8   OWNERSHIP STRUCTURE OF MAJOR JAPANESE AUTOMOTIVE ASSEMBLERS, 1989 (%)

	Toyota	Nissan	Honda	Mitsubishi Motors
Financial institutions	65.6%	61.9%	57.7%	18.8%
Business corporations	22.5	24.4	17.4	51.7
Securities companies	0.4	1.2	1.7	0.9
Individuals and others	9.5	8.7	14.2	5.7
Foreigners	2.0	3.8	9.0	22.9
Total	100.0%	100.0%	100.0%	100.0%

Source: Daiwa Securities Company, Ltd., *Analysts Guide, 1990* (Tokyo: Daiwa Securities Co., 1990).

FUJIYA CO., LTD.

At the end of November 1986, the directors of Fujiya Co., Ltd. met to determine their best course of action in response to a threatened takeover of the company. An investor group led by a well-known Japanese speculator had accumulated a large block of Fujiya's shares and threatened to offer it to a large foreign food company if Fujiya did not arrange for one of its affiliates to purchase the shares. Fujiya's options were to ignore the threat and try to keep 50 percent of its shares in friendly hands; to arrange the repurchase demanded by the hostile investor group; or to accede to a merger, with either a foreign partner or a Japanese "white knight."

FUJIYA CO., LTD.

Fujiya was one of five major confectioners in Japan. The company manufactured and distributed candies, cakes, ice cream, soft drinks, and other specialty foods throughout Japan. Operations were organized in two divisions. The chain store division consisted of retail candy shops, tea rooms, and restaurants. At the end of March 1986, there were 948 such outlets, of which 792 were operated by franchisees and 156 were managed directly by Fujiya. Ten Fujiya factories supplied products to these outlets. The company had plans to expand its chain store operations despite the fact that, in recent years, sales growth had not kept pace with growth in the number of stores and some of the franchise shops had recently closed.

The wholesale division operated five factories and produced branded chocolates, candies, and soft drinks for sale to independent wholesalers and retailers throughout

This case was prepared by Professor Timothy A. Luehrman. Copyright © 1987 by the President and Fellows of Harvard College. Harvard Business School case 288-027.

Japan. A few products were licensed from foreign companies such as Baskin-Robbins Ice Cream Co., Hershey Foods Corporation, Frito-Lay (PepsiCo, Inc.), and Rowntree Mackintosh, plc. Some of these products were imported directly while others were manufactured in Japan by Fujiya and distributed under the foreign brand name. Hershey products, sold by Fujiya, comprised the leading brand of imported chocolate.

Net income for the year ended March 31, 1986, was ¥950 million on sales of ¥124,287 million. The chain store division accounted for 45 percent of sales and about 50 percent of net income. Fujiya's financial statements and historical financial data are given in **Exhibits 1** through **3**.

THE JAPANESE CONFECTIONERY INDUSTRY

The confectionery industry in Japan was dominated by a small number of large firms that owned or controlled distribution channels and was characterized by slow growth and relatively low profits. Sales had grown at an average annual rate of less than 5 percent for the 5 years ending in March 1986. Income from confectionery operations had been declining; this decline was offset as companies diversified and earned income from passive investments in cash and securities. Even so, industry profits had displayed little growth since the mid-1970s, and in 1986 the industry's return on assets was less than 4 percent. **Exhibit 4** gives comparative data on Japanese confectionery companies.

Although the Japanese confectionery market was the second largest in the world after that of the United States, penetration by foreign manufacturers was quite low. Imports made up about 1 percent of Japanese candy consumption in 1985. Recent increases in imports were mostly accounted for by chocolates. Some industry observers felt that this signaled a shift in Japanese tastes. Historically, Japanese consumers had favored individually wrapped, sugar-coated candies and sweet cakes over chocolate products. By comparison, consumers in the United States and especially in Europe consumed far more chocolate than any other type of candy. As chocolate consumption increased in Japan, foreign producers quickly sought licensing agreements with Japanese companies or announced plans to enter the market independently. **Exhibit 5** presents data on major foreign confectioners.

The Japanese government imposed a 20 percent tariff on imported chocolate in 1986, but was studying proposals to reduce the tariff substantially. Industry observers in Japan and abroad expected the tariff to be lowered, if not eliminated, by the end of 1987. Meanwhile, the recent strengthening of the yen had increased the attractiveness of the Japanese market to foreigners and slowed plans by Japanese confectionery companies to expand their exports.

The Man With 21 Faces

One of the industry's most recent problems was a gang of extortionists calling itself "The Man With 21 Faces." In December 1984, Fujiya received a letter from the group threatening to put poison in some of the company's candy products just before

Valentine's Day unless the company paid the gang ¥ 100 million. Similar threats had been received by two other confectioners earlier in the year. Sales and profits of Morinaga & Co. and Ezaki Glico were suffering as certain of their products were pulled off retail shelves in some parts of the country.

On February 12, 1985, poison-laced chocolate bars were found in Tokyo and Nagoya. The contaminated candies were found in various public locations and carried labels warning of poison danger. Police reported that some of the chocolate bars contained as much as 0.4 grams of cyanide, an amount considered lethal. The contaminated products belonged to five of Japan's largest confectioners: Ezaki Glico, Morinaga, and, for the first time, Fujiya, Lotte, and Meiji Seika. The Man With 21 Faces contacted Japanese newspapers and claimed responsibility for the act.

In May 1985 Ezaki Glico and Morinaga reported sharply lower sales and earnings for the year ended March 31. Net income for both companies fell more than 75 percent from the previous year and both blamed The Man With 21 Faces for the decline. Other major confectioners reported small decreases in earnings.

In December 1985, several companies again received threats from extortionist groups. On February 18, 1986, news media in Japan reported that Fujiya and Meiji Seika had each paid ¥ 500,000 within the past month to groups threatening to poison their candies. Other confectioners were reported to have refused to make any such payments.

TRADING ACTIVITY IN FUJIYA SHARES

Fujiya shares were listed on the First Section of the Tokyo Stock Exchange (TSE). Until 1982, ownership and management of the company was dominated by the Fujii family. Mr. Goro Fujii and Mr. Kazuro Fujii, sons of the company's founder, were chairman and president, respectively. Two grandsons of the founder were directors of the company and were expected to replace the elder family members when the latter retired. The Fujii family was thought to control, directly and indirectly, about 20 percent of the company's stock.

In 1982, Mr. Ginzo Korekawa, an experienced private investor, began to purchase Fujiya shares. By the end of March 1983, Mr. Korekawa had registered 15.457 million shares under the name of Tokiwa K.K., a private company owned by Mr. Korekawa and engaged in securities and precious metals trading. Another 380,000 shares were registered to Mr. Korekawa and his wife. An additional 6.42 million shares were registered to Sanyo Securities Company, a firm through which Mr. Korekawa often conducted trading. Analysts in Tokyo estimated that Mr. Korekawa might control as much as an additional 15–18 million of the total 126.344 million shares outstanding. Thus, estimates of Mr. Korekawa's interest in the firm ran as high as 30 percent. Fujiya's stock price rose steadily during this period, from ¥ 295 on March 31, 1982, to ¥ 590 one year later.

In 1984, Mr. Korekawa approached the management of Fujiya and offered to sell his shares. As a listed public company, Fujiya was not permitted to purchase its own shares, but could arrange for the shares to be purchased by trusted stable investors. Outside observers later estimated that Mr. Korekawa had offered to sell for about

¥500 per share. Opinions within the Fujii family appeared to be divided, however, preventing the company from responding positively or negatively to the offer, which Mr. Korekawa eventually withdrew.

In late 1984, amid growing threats from The Man With 21 Faces, the trading volume of confectionery companies' shares on the Tokyo Stock Exchange increased substantially. At this time, Video Seller, a company ostensibly engaged in selling and leasing videotapes and recording equipment, began to accumulate shares in Morinaga and Fujiya. Video Seller was known in financial circles as the leader of a coalition of investors that assembled substantial stakes in listed companies and then resold them at a profit, usually to an affiliate of the target company. Such coalitions were called *kaishime*.

At the end of 1984, Mr. Korekawa sold his interest in Fujiya to Video Seller in an off-market transfer for a price estimated to be between ¥500 and ¥600. On December 31, 1984, Fujiya's stock closed at ¥855 on the TSE. Video Seller continued to acquire Fujiya shares in 1985, both privately and on the open market. On June 28, Fujiya closed at ¥1620 and Video Seller was thought to control in excess of 50 million shares.

Two months later, with the stock trading at ¥2100, Video Seller approached Fujiya and offered to sell its shares back to the company. Fujiya declined. Although unable to ascertain exactly how many shares were controlled by Video Seller, the management of Fujiya felt confident that it was less than 50 percent and that Video Seller had financed most of its purchases with borrowed money. Nevertheless, in the fall of 1985 Fujiya undertook a program to ensure that 50 percent of its shares were in the hands of well-identified, stable shareholders sympathetic to management. Shortly afterward, Kazuro Fujii announced the success of the program to the Japanese financial press.

On October 19, 1985, the president of Video Seller suffered a heart attack and died. The price of Fujiya's stock fell from ¥2160 to ¥1540. However, leadership of Video Seller was quickly assumed by Mr. Yoshio Kurihara, a former stockbroker, and Fujiya's stock price recovered to ¥2020 by October 28.

In December 1985, a block of 5.4 million shares was registered by Mr. Daisuke Kawai, making Mr. Kawai the third largest single shareholder. Mr. Kawai was not believed to be related to the Video Seller group, nor could he be considered a stable shareholder, having been involved previously in an attempted takeover of Yomiuri Land. Analysts in Tokyo speculated that Mr. Kawai bought his shares off-market from shareholders previously considered by Fujiya to be stable. They reasoned further that Mr. Kawai would cooperate with Video Seller's efforts to force a purchase by Fujiya. Fujiya's stock closed on December 31, 1985 at ¥2470.

Recent Events

In 1986, the price of Fujiya shares continued to rise as rumors circulated that foreign firms had become interested in the company and were investigating its finances and operations. It was also rumored that Video Seller had engaged a Wall Street law firm to find a buyer for its shares in the United States. At the end of April 1986, the stock reached a high of ¥3790. As the stock price became increasingly volatile, the Tokyo Stock Exchange announced steps to curb speculation and assure an orderly market for Fujiya shares. These included restrictions on daily price movements, an increase in margin requirements, and limitations on the number of shares that could be purchased on margin.

On September 25, 1986, six members of the Video Seller coalition registered part of their holdings, a total of 14.489 million shares. Mr. Kurihara, the president of Video Seller, stated that while his firm did not have a majority, it controlled more than 60 million shares (47.5 percent) and intended to continue attempts to secure a majority. Privately, Video Seller again indicated its willingness to sell to Fujiya and confirmed that buyers were being sought elsewhere. The management of Fujiya estimated that Video Seller controlled 61.4 million shares. Fujiya itself controlled nearly 63 million. **Exhibit 6** presents data on changes in stock ownership.

On November 3, Mr. Kawai committed suicide. The news media reported rumors of his involvment with *boryoku-dan* ("gangsters") in connection with trading in Fujiya stock.

After nearly 2 months of fitful, low-volume trading of Fujiya shares, the Tokyo Stock Exchange suspended trading indefinitely on November 26, 1986. The last trade had taken place at ¥2810. Data on Fujiya's stock price and other contemporary market data are given in **Exhibits 7** and **8**. A chronology of events appears in **Exhibit 9**.

EXHIBIT 1 FUJIYA CO., LTD.—BALANCE SHEETS (MARCH 31, MILLIONS)

	1986	1985	1984
Assets			
Current assets			
Cash and securities	¥ 7,516	¥ 5,540	¥ 4,212
Notes receivable	4,100	4,972	4,634
Accounts receivable	8,499	9,035	8,881
Inventories	6,897	7,337	7,473
Other	1,734	2,669	3,058
Total current assets	28,746	29,553	28,258
Fixed assets			
Land	1,267	1,267	1,267
Depreciable assets (net)	18,107	18,002	16,927
Construction in progress	1,166	398	1,374
Total fixed assets	20,540	19,667	19,568
Investments			
Securities	2,347	2,046	2,249
Long-term loans	2,742	2,663	3,137
Total investments	5,089	4,709	5,386
Other assets	5,757	5,592	5,112
Total assets	60,132	59,521	58,324
Liabilities and equity			
Current liabilities			
Notes payable	9,059	9,331	10,283
Accounts payable	3,846	4,026	4,256
Short-term debt	4,305	3,080	2,080
Liability reserves	3,892	3,942	3,533
Other	4,445	7,263	4,069
Total current liabilities	25,547	27,642	24,221
Long-term debt	111	1,517	1,550
Pension liability reserves*	10,023	9,316	8,636
Other liabilities	1,120	1,069	1,006
Shareholders' equity			
Paid-in capital	16,200	16,200	16,200
Retained earnings	7,131	6,962	6,711
Total liabilities and shareholders' equity	¥60,132	¥59,521	¥58,324

*The reserve equals 40 percent of the lump sum severance settlements that would be incurred if all employees left voluntarily on the balance sheet date.

EXHIBIT 2 FUJIYA CO., LTD.—STATEMENTS OF INCOME (MARCH 31: MILLIONS, EXCEPT PER SHARE ITEMS)

	1986	1985	1984
Sales	¥124,287	¥124,086	¥120,960
Cost of goods sold	69,472	70,646	69,984
Gross profit	54,815	53,440	50,976
SG&A expenses	52,632	51,130	48,604
Operating profits	2,183	2,310	2,372
Nonoperating income	1,882	1,266	1,294
Nonoperating expense	760	736	865
Recurring profit	3,305	2,840	2,801
Extraordinary loss	855	282	97
Profit before taxes	2,450	2,558	2,704
Provision for taxes	1,500	1,580	1,701
Net income	950	978	1,003
Supplementary information			
Dividends	¥ 758	¥ 758	¥ 758
Depreciation charges	3,749	3,706	3,552
Earnings per share	7.52	7.74	7.94

EXHIBIT 3 FUJIYA CO. LTD.—HISTORICAL FINANCIAL DATA (MILLIONS, EXCEPT AS NOTED)

Year ended March 31

	1986	1985	1984	1983	1982	1981	1980	1979	1978
Revenues	¥124,287	¥124,086	¥120,960	¥114,014	¥109,235	¥104,173	¥103,720	¥106,491	¥105,493
Operating income	2,183	2,310	2,372	2,404	2,870	2,764	724	1,467	2,534
Net income	950	978	1,003	1,329	1,201	10	399	806	1,204
Total assets	60,132	59,521	58,324	56,922	54,080	53,883	53,355	46,449	46,433
Long-term debt	111	1,517	1,550	1,923	5,336	5,671	8,578	2,493	975
Short-term debt	4,305	3,080	2,080	1,469	335	1,277	1,136	1,826	2,870
Equity	23,331	23,162	22,911	22,346	18,897	18,408	15,360	15,648	14,461
Book value/share, ¥	185	183	181	178	159	147	137	140	132
Stock price, ¥	2,550	900	660	590	295	273	286	470	335
Earnings/share, ¥	7.52	7.74	7.94	10.60	10.11	0.08	3.57	7.22	11.02
Dividend/share, ¥	6.00	6.00	6.00	6.00	6.00	3.00	3.00	6.00	6.00
Price/earnings ratio, times	339.10	116.28	83.12	55.66	29.18	—	80.11	65.10	30.40
Return on sales, %	0.76	0.79	0.83	1.17	1.10	0.01	0.38	0.76	1.14
Return on beginning equity, %	4.10	4.27	4.49	7.03	6.52	0.07	2.55	5.57	11.28
Capital expenditures	4,622	3,805	4,759	5,343	3,222	2,806	3,862	2,281	2,752

EXHIBIT 4   COMPARATIVE DATA ON JAPANESE CONFECTIONERY COMPANIES (MILLIONS, EXCEPT AS NOTED)

	Fujiya, 3/86*	Ezaki Glico, 3/86*	Morinaga, 3/86*	Meiji Seika, 3/86*	Yamazaki Baking, 12/85*	Morozoff, 1/86*	11-Firm average,† 1986
Revenues	¥124,287	¥112,357	¥108,858	¥203,472	¥207,203	¥25,471	¥96,998
Net income	950	3,762	(1,710)	3,721	6,660	1,432	2,529
Operating income	2,183	2,596	(2,917)	4,379	10,848	2,010	3,746
Total assets	60,132	109,070	74,707	170,467	134,694	19,752	69,222
Cash and securities	7,516	61,509	3,755	23,540	25,147	7,125	17,278
Short-term debt	4,305	0	3,898	12,178	13,788	1,950	4,408
Long-term debt	111	0	4,472	3,964	427	1,999	1,402
Equity	23,331	60,058	30,243	97,161	70,549	10,858	36,633
Capital expenditures	4,622	4,133	3,029	6,300	13,902	2,453	—
Stock price, ¥	2,550	820	490	660	812	640	—
Earnings/share, ¥	7.52	31.63	(7.83)	9.71	39.41	49.48	
Price/earnings ratio, times	339.10	25.92	—	67.97	20.60	12.93	64.24
Market/book value	13.81	1.62	3.54	2.60	1.95	1.71	3.58
Dividends/share, ¥	6.00	10.00	0.00	6.00	10.00	8.00	
Payout ratio	0.80	0.32	0.00	0.62	0.25	0.16	0.38
Return on sales, %	0.76	3.35	(1.57)	1.83	3.21	5.62	2.61
Return on equity, %	4.07	6.26	(5.65)	3.83	9.44	13.19	6.90
Current ratio	1.13	2.46	1.10	1.91	0.68	1.75	1.41
Cash flow/net income	4.95	1.83	(0.79)	2.44	2.40	1.58	2.57
Interest coverage	5.69	—	(2.79)	2.62	10.66	10.07	10.81
5-year growth rates							
Revenues, %	3.59	−0.11	1.18	2.73	5.30	na	3.01
Net income, %	148.63	−6.16	—	5.27	3.52	na	0.27

*Dates indicate fiscal yearends.
†Eleven confectionery companies listed on first section of TSE, including Fujiya.

EXHIBIT 5 SELECTED DATA FOR NON-JAPANESE FOOD AND CONFECTIONERY COMPANIES (YEAR ENDED DECEMBER 31, 1985; VALUES IN CURRENCIES INDICATED IN COLUMN HEADINGS, EXCEPT WHERE NOTED OTHERWISE IN TABLE BODY)

	Borden, Inc., $ millions	Hershey Foods Corporation, $ millions	PepsiCo, Inc., $ millions	Nestlé S.A., SF millions	Cadbury Schweppes plc, £ millions	Rowntree Mackintosh plc, £ millions
Revenues	$4,716	$1,996	$7,653	SF 2,225	£1,874	£1,205
Net income	194	112	544	1,750	42	44
Total assets	2,932	1,197	5,893	25,188	1,213	794
Cash and deposits	141	111	939	3,853	30	42
Long-term debt	533	110	1,036	4,707	195	134
Equity	1,408	728	1,838	11,238	471	328
Stock price (Nov. 26, 1986)	$52.00	$24.50	$28.00	SF 9,757	179p	422p
Earnings/share	2.50	1.19	1.89	515	9.31p	36.00p
Price/earnings ratio, times	20.80	20.59	14.81	18.95	19.23	11.72
Dividend/share	0.76	0.48	1.31	145	5.90p	12.20p
Payout ratio	0.30	0.40	0.69	0.28	0.63	0.34
5-year growth rates						
Revenues, %	-0.99	8.38	7.74	11.52	10.86	13.85
Net income, %	5.56	12.56	14.70	20.70	0.48	20.25

Interest and exchange rates	December 1985	November 1986
90-day commercial paper rate, $	8.01%	5.79%
90-day interbank deposit rate, SF	4.50%	4.00%
90-day interbank deposit rate, £	12.75%	11.44%
Yield on 20-year U.S. government bonds, $	9.49%	7.69%
Avg. yield on Swiss Confederation bonds, SF	4.42%	4.16%
Yield on 25-year U.K. government bonds, £	10.35%	10.58%
Spot exchange rates, SF/$	2.0595	1.6415
$/£	1.4450	1.4340

EXHIBIT 6   CHANGES IN STOCK OWNERSHIP OF FUJIYA CO., LTD, 3/82–3/86

	3/82	3/84	3/86
Number of shareholders	18,015	6,819	5,476
Percentage of shares registered to:			
Financial institutions*	26.6%	26.2%	26.6%
Securities companies†	6.5	22.3	19.7
Other institutions‡	6.0	16.8	17.8
Foreigners§	0.0	0.8	1.0
Individuals¶	60.9	33.9	34.9
Total	100.0%	100.0%	100.0%

*Financial institutions are primarily Japanese banks and insurance companies. In 1986 the company listed as bank references: Kyowa Bank, Dai-Ichi Kangyo Bank, Bank of Yokohama, Fuji Bank, and Tokai Bank. Of these, Kyowa and Dai-Ichi Kangyo held 4.3 percent and 2.9 percent of Fujiya's shares, respectively. Other banks had smaller holdings.
†Securities companies consist of members of Japanese stock exchanges.
‡Other institutions represent nonfinancial Japanese corporations, including affiliates of Fujiya.
§Foreigners include non-Japanese stockholders, both individual and institutional.
¶Individuals are private Japanese citizens.

EXHIBIT 7 **FUJIYA CO., LTD., CLOSING STOCK PRICES, 1982–1986**

Date	Closing stock price, ¥/share	Date	Closing stock price, ¥/share
Jan. 1982	¥296	Jan. 1985	¥730
Feb.	309	Feb.	870
Mar.	295	Mar.	900
Apr.	326	Apr.	1070
May	299	May	1210
Jun.	343	Jun.	1620
Jul.	314	Jul.	1620
Aug.	312	Aug.	1980
Sep.	300	Sep.	1990
Oct.	334	Oct.	2050
Nov.	417	Nov.	2080
Dec.	419	Dec.	2130
Jan. 1983	541	Jan. 1986	2650
Feb.	522	Feb.	2400
Mar.	590	Mar.	2550
Apr.	540	Apr.	3790
May	575	May	2750
Jun.	560	Jun.	3600
Jul.	590	Jul.	3060
Aug.	719	Aug.	3000
Sep.	730	Sep.	2950
Oct.	680	Oct.	2800
Nov.	626	Nov. 26	2810
Dec.	642	Trading suspended	
Jan. 1984	659		
Feb.	660		
Mar.	660		
Apr.	667		
May	705		
Jun.	750		
Jul.	720		
Aug.	724		
Sep.	715		
Oct.	815		
Nov.	882		
Dec.	855		

EXHIBIT 8 SELECTED MARKET PRICES AND YIELDS, 1985–1986

Date	TSE new index, ¥/share	Yield on 90-day (¥) gensaki,* annualized %	Avg. yield on long-term gov't. bonds, annualized %	Avg. short-term bank lending rate,† annualized %	Spot exchange rate, ¥/$
Jan. 85	¥931.06	6.26%	6.25%	5.70%	¥254.65
Feb.	977.30	6.32	6.31	5.70	259.50
Mar.	999.30	6.27	6.31	5.70	252.50
Apr.	967.28	6.25	6.31	5.70	252.25
May	997.03	6.25	6.31	5.70	251.85
Jun.	1026.03	6.30	6.31	5.69	248.95
Jul.	992.13	6.29	6.25	5.69	236.65
Aug.	1018.50	6.30	6.31	5.69	237.25
Sep.	1026.10	6.33	6.38	5.70	217.00
Oct.	1026.30	7.11	7.06	5.70	211.50
Nov.	1006.50	7.55	6.94	5.70	202.00
Dec.	1049.40	7.03	6.38	5.71	200.50
Jan. 86	1041.60	6.12	6.00	5.70	191.80
Feb.	1090.70	5.92	6.56	5.64	179.70
Mar.	1265.93	5.16	5.06	5.42	179.60
Apr.	1251.88	4.53	4.69	5.24	168.30
May	1300.11	4.66	4.88	5.04	174.30
Jun.	1359.24	4.64	4.63	4.95	163.03
Jul.	1428.92	4.65	4.69	4.57	153.92
Aug.	1526.73	4.53	4.63	4.52	154.70
Sep.	1517.28	4.75	4.88	4.48	154.33
Oct.	1407.96	4.54	4.56	4.48	163.64
Nov.	1490.90	4.43	4.50	4.45	161.92

*Gensaki are long-term government bonds with repurchase agreements attached.
†Rate quoted is the average of twelve city banks' contracted short-term lending rates to prime corporate borrowers. Compensating balances may be required in addition to the contracted rate.

EXHIBIT 9   CHRONOLOGY OF EVENTS

January	1982	Stock price at ¥296/share. Korekawa begins to accumulate shares.
March	1983	Korekawa thought to control 30%.
	1984	Korekawa proposes buyback by Fujiya. Fujiya fails to respond. Video Seller begins acquiring stock.
December	1984	Fujiya threatened by The Man With 21 Faces. Video Seller acquires Korekawa's stake.
February	1985	Poison found in candy in Tokyo and Nagoya.
May		Confectionery companies report earnings for fiscal 1985.
June		Stock price reaches ¥1620/share. Video Seller continues buying.
August		Video Seller proposes buyback. Fujiya declines.
September		Fujiya attempts to ensure that 50% of its stock is controlled by stable shareholders.
October		President of Video Seller dies from heart attack.
December		Fujiya receives more extortionist threats. Kawai registers 5.4 million shares.
February	1986	Fujiya reported to have paid ¥500,000 to extortionists.
April		Video Seller rumored to have hired U.S. law firm to find buyer for its shares. Stock price reaches ¥3790/share. TSE imposes restrictions on trading in Fujiya's shares.
September		Video Seller registers part of its holdings. Announces control of over 60 million shares; again proposes buyback.
November		Kawai commits suicide. TSE suspends trading of Fujiya shares. Last trade at ¥2810/share.

KYOCERA/AVX

Between April and September 1989 the senior managements of AVX Corporation, an American company, and Kyocera Corp., a Japanese company, had been in discussions regarding the possibility of a joint undertaking or combination of their businesses. Both firms were worldwide manufacturers of ceramic components that were heavily utilized in semiconductors. Kyocera dominated the global market with a 64 percent share of ceramic housings for semiconductor chips. In 4 of the prior 5 years, Kyocera had been selected by Japanese executives as the most admired Japanese firm for entrepreneurship and technological progress. Kyocera was much larger than AVX (see **Exhibits 1**, **2**, and **3**), but AVX had significant operations (with considerable excess capacity) in Europe where Kyocera was relatively weak (see **Table 1**).

During early 1989, senior management at AVX sought to address two issues: (1) the failure of the market to reflect adequately the value of AVX in the price of AVX's common stock; and (ii) the excess capacity available in AVX's European manufacturing facilities. AVX's senior management and financial advisors considered various alternative transactions designed to increase the market value of AVX's common stock, but none of these alternatives was deemed to be financially viable. Management of AVX considered the possibility of a going-private transaction in April 1989 and considered possible joint ventures thereafter. However, no offers were made or received by AVX. In order to address the problem of a need for additional products to utilize available capacity, AVX and its financial advisors considered a number of alternative transactions including acquisitions of, or joint ventures with, various companies that had the technological capabilities to utilize AVX's manufacturing skills

This case was prepared by Professor William E. Fruhan, Jr. Copyright © 1990 by the President and Fellows of Harvard College. Harvard Business School case 291-003.

TABLE 1   SALES BY GEOGRAPHIC AREA (MILLIONS)

	Kyocera	AVX
Japan	$1748	$ 67
United States	520	233
Europe } Other	297	109
Total sales	$2565	$409

and facilities. Kyocera was among the companies AVX considered as a possible joint venture partner.

In early 1989, senior management at Kyocera investigated various means of expanding their business in both Europe and the United States. In February, Kyocera approached AVX with the possibility of a joint undertaking or combination. In April 1989, discussions took place in New York between senior managers of the two firms. Additional discussions took place in Tokyo in June. In July, senior managers of Kyocera toured AVX's major production facilities in the United States and Europe. Detailed discussions were undertaken as to the possible terms of a merger.

Discussion continued over several additional months. Kyocera then indicated to AVX's management that it might be prepared to acquire all of AVX's common shares at a purchase price of $32.00 per share, a premium of 50 percent over AVX's price of $21.00 per share on May 8. (Prior stock price and stock price index data for both firms are presented in **Exhibit 4**. Stock trading volume is presented in **Exhibit 5**.)

Just prior to this indication, Kyocera had announced an agreement to purchase Elco Corp., a wholly-owned subsidiary of Wickes Companies, Inc., for $250 million cash from WCI Holdings. Elco manufactured electronic connectors and interconnecting systems for the electronic equipment industry. Its parent had been purchased by WCI in a leveraged-buyout transaction in December 1988.

THE STRUCTURE OF THE PROPOSED TRANSACTION

The management of both Kyocera and AVX continued to discuss how the proposed transaction might be structured. Kyocera could easily acquire the outstanding AVX shares for cash since the $561 million total purchase price[1] would represent less than one-third of Kyocera's cash equivalents (see **Exhibit 3**). Another alternative, however, was to exchange Kyocera's common stock in the form of American Depository Receipts (ADRs) for AVX's common shares. Such a transaction would represent the

---

[1]Includes the cost of common stock issued in conversion of convertible debentures and from exercises of stock options.

first time a Japanese company had acquired an American corporation entirely for stock. A stock transaction would emphasize, in the words of Kyocera's chairman, that AVX was:

> . . . a partner that would remain intact. When we buy with cash, there is a connotation—certainly in Japan and maybe in the United States as well—that we bought the company, it is ours, and we can do anything with it. This is certainly not the spirit of the arrangement.[2]

Since 1986, numerous acquisitions of large U.S. companies (see **Exhibit 6**) by foreigners had ignited discussions in Congress about limitations on acquisitions in the United States by any country with barriers to American investment. Some U.S. government officials had also hinted at a broader interpretation of "national security" reasons for blocking a merger to include economic as well as military factors. A transaction structured as an exchange of stock rather than a cash purchase might defuse some of the criticism of Japanese takeovers of U.S. companies.

KYOCERA'S ADRs

Kyocera's ADRs had been trading in the United States since 1976 when the company sold 3.24 million ADRs[3] and raised $23 million for investment in its U.S. subsidiary. In 1980, the company announced a second issue of 5.2 million ADRs and raised $54 million. At this point Kyocera's ADRs were listed for trading on the New York Stock Exchange. By 1989, Kyocera's ADRs were the seventh most widely held of the 142 Japanese firms with ADRs outstanding (see **Exhibit 7**).

Historically American investors held rather small amounts of non-U.S. equities. While the market value of publicly held U.S. equities exceeded $3 trillion in 1988, only about $60 billion of non-U.S. equities were held by American investors (see **Exhibit 8**). Only about $5 billion of this total represented Japanese equities held by American investors.

[2]Paul B. Carroll, "Kyocera Corp. of Japan Agrees to Buy AVX," *The Wall Street Journal,* September 29, 1989, p. A4.
[3]Each Kyocera ADR equaled two shares of Kyocera common stock. All numbers noted are after stock splits.

EXHIBIT 1   SELECTED FINANCIAL DATA FOR AVX, 1984–1988 (MILLIONS, EXCEPT PER SHARE DATA AND NUMBER OF SHARES)

	1984	1985	1986	1987	1988
Net sales	$231	$178	$195	$272	$409
Net income	15.5	(12.3)	(3.1)	15.8	27.6
Total assets	243	274	251	420	424
Long-term debt	69	112	51	140	123
Net worth	115	128	154	186	208
Depreciation	8	13	16	19	28
Capital expenditures	25	48	11	30	33
Net income per share*	1.65	(1.20)	(.25)	1.20	2.07
Cash dividends per share	0.32	0.24	—	—	0.18
Shares outstanding	9.4	10.2	12.3	13.2	13.3

*Primary earnings per share. Fully diluted earnings per share in 1988 was $1.88.

EXHIBIT 2 SELECTED FINANCIAL DATA FOR KYOCERA, 1985–1989*

	¥ billions, except per share data, exchange rates, and shares outstanding					$ millions, except per share data, exchange rates, and shares outstanding
	1985	1986	1987	1988	1989	1989
Net sales						
Ceramic and related products			¥195	¥211	¥234	$1777
Electronic equipment			45	52	66	497
Optical and precision instruments			36	37	39	292
Total	¥325	¥279	¥276	¥300	¥339	$2566
Operating profit (loss)						
Ceramic and related products			¥ 43	¥ 53	¥ 60	$ 450
Electronic equipment			(1)	1	4	32
Optical and precision instruments			(3)	(2)	(2)	(13)
Total			¥ 39	¥ 52	¥ 62	$ 469
Identifiable assets						
Ceramic and related products			¥288	¥305	¥348	$2635
Electronic equipment			66	72	91	688
Optical and precision instruments			64	66	63	478
Total			¥418	¥443	¥502	$3801
Net income	¥ 38	¥ 18	¥ 17	¥ 22	¥ 30	$ 225
Total assets	379	355	427	451	521	3950
Long-term debt	—	1	61	43	74	558
Net worth	287	292	300	330	364	2760
Depreciation	15	17	16	14	15	114
Capital expenditures	35	21	14	17	21	159
Net income per share†	254	123	116	141	183	1.45
Cash dividends per share	44	44	44	44	44	0.33
Exchange rate, ¥/$1	223	175	146	121	121	121
Shares outstanding, millions		150.0	150.0	153.9	154.5	154.5

*Fiscal year ended March 31.
†Primary earnings per share. Fully diluted earnings per share in 1989 was $1.39.

EXHIBIT 3 COMPARATIVE BALANCE SHEET DATA FOR KYOCERA AND AVX CORP. ($ MILLIONS, EXCEPT NUMBER OF SHARES)

	Kyocera, 3/31/89	AVX, 12/31/88		Kyocera, 3/31/89	AVX, 12/31/88
Cash and equivalents	$1801	$ 25	Accounts payable	$ 303	$ 15
Other short-term investments	56	—	Accrued liabilities	247	36
Notes receivable	179	—	Current maturities of long-term debt	14	5
Accounts receivable	460	52	Other current liabilities	19	5
Inventories	374	82	Total current liabilities	583	61
Deferred taxes and other current assets	70	16	Long-term debt	558	123
Total current assets	2925	175	Other non-current liabilities	46	32
Property, plant, and equipment	571	204	Minority interest in subsidiaries.	3	—
Investments and advances to affiliates	149	—	Net worth	2760	208
Securities and other investments	141*	—	Total liabilities and net worth	$3950	$424
Other assets	164	45	Number of shares outstanding (millions)	154.5	13.3
Total assets	$3950	$424			

	Shares of bank owned by Kyocera, thousands	%	Shares of Kyocera owned by bank, thousands	%
Bank of Kyoto	5772	2.41%	6874	4.45%
Sanwa Bank	5377	0.19	7444	4.82
Daiwa Bank	1807	0.13	4072	2.64
Sumitomo Bank	885	0.03	5011	3.24

*Valued at cost; market value was higher by $340 million and included cross-holdings of various banks as noted in second part of table.

EXHIBIT 4 AVX AND KYOCERA STOCK PRICES AND STOCK MARKET INDICES, 1980–1989

	Nikkei Index, ¥	Nikkei Index, $	S&P 400 Index	AVX Corp.,* $/share	Kyocera ADRs,* $/ADR	Exchange rate, ¥/$	Index of real yen exchange rate to 15 industrial country currencies[†]
12/31/80	7,116	35.04	154.45	20.33	18.03	203.05	
12/31/81	7,681	34.98	137.12	9.25	19.69	219.63	
12/31/82	8,016	34.12	157.62	14.33	24.12	234.93	
12/31/83	9,893	42.68	186.24	27.17	51.50	231.83	
12/31/84	11,542	45.90	186.36	17.50	53.09	251.49	
12/31/85	13,083	65.33	234.56	14.50	43.81	200.25	97.0
12/31/86	18,701	118.25	269.93	10.62	48.09	158.15	115.4
12/31/87	21,564	178.06	285.96	15.12	80.71	121.10	119.6
12/31/88	30,159	241.56	321.26	17.00	79.52	124.85	125.9
3/31/89	32,838	247.78	339.42	17.25	67.38	132.53	122.3
6/30/89	32,984	228.84	363.48	18.75	77.73	143.98	116.6
9/30/89	35,636	255.26	397.95	21.63[‡]	79.00	139.61	114.8

*Kyocera and AVX share price data are adjusted for stock splits and stock dividends. Each Kyocera ADR equaled two shares of Kyocera common stock.

[†]1980–1982 = 100.

[‡]Price prior to public announcement of acquisition discussions.

EXHIBIT 5 ANNUAL STOCK TRADING VOLUME, 1985–1988 (HUNDREDS OF SHARES OR ADRs)

	Kyocera shares	Kyocera ADRs*	AVX shares
1985	487,750	19,573	89,518
1986	501,000	15,170	96,720
1987	1,275,000	25,389	120,607
1988	614,750	12,347	79,202

*One Kyocera ADR equals two shares of Kyocera common stock.

EXHIBIT 6 MAJOR JAPANESE ACQUISITIONS OF NONFINANCIAL AMERICAN BUSINESSES, 1986–1989

Date	Japanese buyer	U.S. acquisition/investment	Amount, $ millions
12/86	Dainippon Ink and Chemicals, Inc.	Graphic Arts Material Division (Sun Chemicals Corp.)	550.0
8/87	Dainippon Ink and Chemicals, Inc.	Reichhold Chemicals, Inc.	540.0
10/87	Aoki/Bass Corp.	Westin Hotel and Resorts (Allegis Corp.)	1530.0
11/87	Sony Corp.	CBS Records, Inc. (CBS, Inc.)	2000.0
3/88	Bridgestone Corp.	Firestone Tire & Rubber Co.	2600.0
4/88	Paloma Industries, Ltd.	PACE Industries, Inc. (Rheem Manufacturing Co.)	820.0
9/88	Seibu/Saison Group	International Hotel (Grand Metropolitan)	2300.0
9/88	Nippon Mining Co., Ltd.	Gould, Inc.	1100.0
9/88	Settsu Corp.	UARCO Inc. (Printing Holdings, L.P.)	400.0(E)
2/89	Hitachi, Ltd.	National Advanced Systems (National Semiconductors)	398.0
3/89	Yamanouchi Pharmaceutical Co., Ltd.	Shaklee Corp.	395.0
7/89	Kyocera Corp.	Elco Corp. (Wickes Companies, Inc.)	250.0
9/89	Sony Corp.	Columbia Pictures	3400.0
9/89	Sony Corp.	Guber-Peters Entertainment Co.	270.0
9/89	Secom Co., Ltd.	HMSS Inc.	250.0

Source: Ulmer Brothers, Inc.

EXHIBIT 7 **MARKET VALUE OF THE TEN LARGEST OUTSTANDING ADRs OF JAPANESE FIRMS, 1989**

	Market value of ADRs, $ millions	Number of ADRs, thousands
Honda Motor Co., Ltd.	203	7770
Sony Corp.	200	3800
NEC Corp.	200	2986
Hitachi, Ltd.	150	1474
Ito-Yokado Co., Ltd.	112	1067
The Tokio Marine & Fire Insurance Co., Ltd.	88	1372
Kyocera Corp.	55	708
Canon Inc.	42	682
TDK Corp.	40	995
Mitsui & Co., Ltd.	17	121

EXHIBIT 8 TOTAL MARKET VALUE OF U.S. HOLDINGS OF NON-U.S. CORPORATE COMMON STOCKS (MILLIONS)

	Holdings of all non-U.S. corporate equities					Holdings of all Japanese corporate equities				
	Start-of-year position	Purchases less sales	Price changes	Exchange-rate changes	End-of-year position	Start-of-year position	Purchases less sales	Price changes	Exchange-rate changes	End-of-year position
1988	$54,669	$ 909	$8882	$(1729)	$62,731	na				na
1987	51,442	(2358)	(1053)	7701	55,732	5002				na
1986	39,839	741	6430	3894	50,904	3941				$4718
1985	27,926	3959	6303	2534	40,722	2289				3851
1984	26,551	1127	3041	(2817)	27,902	2742				2878
1983	18,568				26,551					
1982	17,360				18,568					
1981	19,166				17,360					
1980	14,834				19,166					
1979	11,236				14,834					

Source: U.S. Department of Commerce, "The International Investment Position of the United States," *Survey of Current Business* (various June issues, 1985–1989).

GRUPO INDUSTRIAL ALFA, S.A., 1982

In October 1982, Sr. Rafael Páez had been the chief executive officer (CEO) of Grupo Industrial Alfa, for a little more than a year, succeeding Sr. Bernardo Garza Sada, who remained chairman. His short tenure as CEO had been consumed by a difficult struggle to guide his company through tumultuous economic conditions in Mexico. In 1981, Alfa was Mexico's largest private company and ranked 193 on *Fortune*'s list of the world's largest non-U.S. industrial companies. Beginning in the late 1970s, the company had borrowed heavily in U.S. dollars to finance its rapid growth in operations. Now, in the midst of a severe worldwide recession, plummeting petroleum prices, rapid devaluation of the peso, and hyperinflation in Mexico, the company's ability to continue servicing its debt was very much in doubt. Already in December 1981, the Mexican government had (i) made various equity contributions (subscribing preferred shares) to fifteen different GIASA subsidiaries, which in the aggregate amounted to 5.4 billion pesos (MP) ($216 million) and (ii) extended a line of credit for factoring transactions in the amount of MP5 billion ($200 million). Four months later, in April 1982, the company had been forced to suspend payments of principal on all its outstanding bank debt. By October it was clear that Sr. Páez had two choices: bankruptcy or an out-of-court restructuring of the company's debt.

EVOLUTION OF GRUPO ALFA

In 1890 two brothers-in-law, Isaac Garza and Francisco Sada, together with José Calderón and others, founded a brewery, Cervecería Cuauhtémoc, in Monterrey. The

This case was prepared by Research Associate Rajiv A. Ghatalia under the direction of Professor Steven R. Fenster. Copyright © 1991 by the President and Fellows of Harvard College. Harvard Business School case 292-008.

business was started with two vats, three wooden kegs, and a supply of grain and hops. From this modest beginning, the company integrated backward by forming companies to supply the brewery's bottling operation: Titán was formed in 1936 to supply labels, Hylsa in 1942 to supply bottle caps, and Vitro in 1936 to supply bottles. Titán eventually grew into a paper and packaging company; Hylsa, into a steel company; and Vitro, into a glass manufacturer. These companies comprised the core of what became known as the Monterrey Group, which was based in Monterrey, and which dominated the Mexican private sector in the 1950s and 1960s.

In 1974 the Group was still controlled by the two founding families. Recognizing the disparate goals and objectives of the two families, the founders' principal heirs agreed to divide the Group into two smaller conglomerates: Visa and Alfa. Visa continued to hold a majority of the Monterrey Group's businesses. Grupo Alfa began with Hylsa, Titán, a 25 percent stake in Televisa, a television broadcasting company, and a 30 percent interest in Cysda, the Monterrey Group's petrochemicals subsidiary. Don Roberto Garza Sada was appointed president of the newly formed Alfa and his son, Sr. Bernardo Garza Sada, was named director general, an office he had held at Hylsa during the preceding decade.

As director general of Hylsa in the 1960s, Sr. Bernardo Garza Sada had significantly expanded and modernized steelmaking operations. Hylsa quickly became Mexico's second largest steel company and its pioneering innovations in the direct reduction process enabled it to export some of its technology abroad. At the time Alfa was formed, Hylsa was by far its largest component, accounting for approximately 80 percent of Alfa's revenues and assets.

Upon becoming director general of Alfa, Sr. Garza Sada immediately launched an aggressive expansion and diversification program to reduce Alfa's dependency on the regulated Mexican steel market. Speed was considered essential in this effort, to take advantage of healthy economic growth in Mexico, relatively easy access to financing, and a fairly benign regulatory attitude toward expansion by large businesses and the consequent concentration of economic power. Historically, none of these factors had been present consistently in Mexico's closed economy; to have them all present at the same time represented a unique opportunity. Hence, expansion and diversification were to be undertaken quickly, primarily through acquisitions and joint ventures with leading multinational corporations.

In the second half of 1975, Alfa made its first acquisition, a 51 percent interest in Nylmex. Nylmex produced synthetic fibers such as nylon, polyester, and lycra under license from E. I. Du Pont de Nemours, which owned a 40 percent interest in the business. As a result of recent financial problems at Nylmex, Alfa was able to purchase a 51 percent stake from Nylmex's creditors for $60 million and negotiate a cession of operating control from Du Pont to Alfa. Nylmex was the first of the collection of businesses that formed the ''New Alfa,'' as compared to businesses like steel and paper and packaging that represented the traditional Alfa.

Many acquisitions and joint ventures followed. In 1975, Alfa acquired Philco, Ford Motor's industrial electronics division in Mexico, and Polioles, a producer of glycols and polyols. In 1977, it acquired Fibras Químicas, a synthetic fibers manufacturer, and created a joint venture with Hitachi to produce electric motors. In 1978 and early 1979, it acquired Petrocel, a supplier of synthetic fibers, and the Mexican operations of Admiral and Magnavox, which together with Philco formed PAM, Alfa's consumer electronics division. In the same year, Alfa contracted with Ford Motor Co. to manufacture automobile cylinder heads. Acquisition activity continued through 1981, by which time Alfa operated hundreds of individual businesses in diverse industries such as steel, petrochemicals, auto parts, carpeting, paper and packaging, consumer products, and food processing. Alfa also engaged in joint ventures with large firms such as Du Pont (nylon fiber), Hitachi (electronics), Hercules (raw material for polyester fiber), BASF (polyurethane), and Dravo (construction), among others. **Exhibit 1** summarizes Alfa's principal businesses and markets at the end of 1981.

As Alfa grew, so did its role as a leader in the Mexican business community, and in Mexican social and cultural affairs. In 1978, it completed construction of the Alfa Cultural Center in Monterrey, which was open to the public and included the most advanced planetarium and children's science museum in Central and Latin America. In Mexico City's Chapultepec Park, Alfa participated in financing a new museum housing the extensive twentieth-century art collection of painter Rufino Tamayo.

By 1980, Grupo Alfa had become a symbol of anticipated growth and prosperity in Mexico, mirroring the rise in the country's exports of manufactured goods and petroleum. In that year Alfa was composed of 143 subsidiaries and had 49,000 employees. Its revenues had quadrupled from 1976 to revenues of MP46.7 billion ($2 billion) and net income of MP3.7 billion ($161 million) in 1980. **Exhibit 2** gives a summary of consolidated financial results for this period.

Grupo Alfa's impressive expansion and diversification program was financed primarily with debt, of which over 87 percent was denominated in U.S. dollars. The company borrowed dollars for two reasons. First, Alfa's huge external financing needs during 1976–1980 exceeded the combined peso lending capacity of Mexico's commercial banks. Second, as Mexico's most powerful conglomerate and the joint venture partner of leading global corporations, Alfa was a favored customer of many banks eager to expand their international lending, and therefore received attractive terms on its foreign debt. **Figure 1** shows the increase in the number of Alfa's businesses and the corresponding increase in debt from 1974 through 1981. At the end of 1981, Alfa's total debt was $2.8 billion. By comparison, this figure was approximately 3.5 percent of the size of Mexico's outstanding sovereign debt.

Some of Grupo Alfa's equity was owned by the public and traded in the public equity market. However, a large majority, over 80 percent of the outstanding shares, was closely held by insiders. Most prominent among these were members of the Garza Sada family, led by Sr. Bernardo Garza Sada. The ten-member board of directors was composed exclusively of family members and long-time family associates, such as Sr. Páez. Family members also played an active role in the management of the Group, having occupied many key executive positions since the company's founding. In general, the top executives at Alfa were well paid, receiving about 20 percent more in salary and benefits than the average for the Mexican corporate sector.

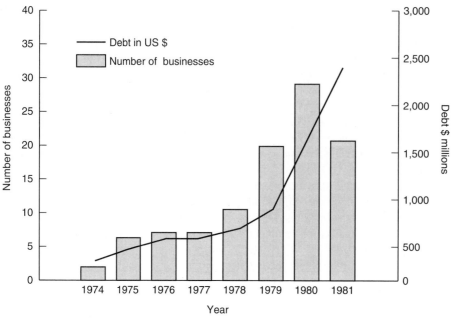

FIGURE 1   Evolution of Alfa's portfolio, 1974–1981.

THE MEXICAN ECONOMY IN 1982

The 1982 economic crisis in Mexico could be traced in part to the country's macroeconomic and industrial policies of the preceding 10 years. In the early 1970s Mexican public policy of subsidizing businesses in targeted industries helped Mexico achieve 7 percent real growth in gross national product (GNP) in 1971 and 1972. The discovery of major oil deposits in 1973 gave Mexico another potential engine for economic growth, but led directly to the imposition of restrictions on foreign investment and ownership of Mexican assets. Hence, the subsequent expansion of Mexico's economy was financed by massive foreign borrowing, and consumer prices rose dramatically during 1973–1975. The Mexican peso, which had been pegged to the U.S. dollar at MP12.50/$1 since 1954, came under tremendous pressure and capital began fleeing the country. President Echeverría was forced to seek a devaluation of the peso to MP20.00/$1 in 1976. Soon afterward he was succeeded as president by Sr. José López Portillo.

President López Portillo strongly encouraged oil exploration, which was handsomely rewarded as proven reserves increased from 6 billion barrels in 1976 to 70 billion in 1981. Mexico, which had been an importer of oil in 1973, was exporting 2 million barrels per day by 1981 and earning foreign exchange at a rate of $80 billion per year. Meanwhile, real gross domestic product (GDP) grew at more than 8 percent per year during 1978–1981, and investment rose 20 percent per year. However, inflation also increased, to over 25 percent per year by 1980. Once again, the combination of high inflation and a fixed exchange rate caused capital flight, as people converted their pesos to dollars in an effort to preserve purchasing power. This contributed to a large current account deficit, despite oil export earnings, that the country financed with more foreign debt.

In 1981, as world oil prices dropped, Mexico held its quoted prices firm in an effort to preserve foreign exchange earnings. Oil contracts were soon canceled or not renewed and oil exports dropped by 400,000 barrels per day, or approximately 27 percent. Holders of pesos continued converting into dollars, fearful of further dramatic declines in the value of the Mexican currency. This activity further drained the country's reserves, and the government turned once more to foreign lenders to supply necessary capital. The new borrowings were primarily short-term, and when they came due in 1982, the overextended economy finally collapsed. On February 18, 1982, the peso was devalued from MP26.20/$1 to MP38.50/$1. At the beginning of August 1982, the Banco de México stopped supporting the peso. On August 12, Mexico's finance minister froze all dollar accounts in Mexican banks and announced that they could only be exchanged for pesos. This move by the government came 4 months after Alfa had suspended principal payments on its outstanding bank debt. **Exhibit 3** presents historical data on peso/dollar exchange rates. **Exhibit 4** presents historical inflation figures.

EFFECTS ON ALFA'S BUSINESSES

The economic crisis of 1982 acutely affected most of Alfa's operations and showed up immediately in the company's financial results (see **Exhibit 2**). Perhaps more ominously, Alfa's access to necessary credit was seriously impaired by the country's precarious economic condition. Alfa's managers responded by implementing consolidation and reorganization plans, some of which had been developed already in 1981. They focused on businesses in which the company had the most experience or in which they felt there was the most potential for growth. Spending was reduced to a bare minimum; some projects near completion were delayed, and many longer-term projects were abandoned. Some decision making was decentralized, and subsidiary managers were made responsible for their use of capital and urged to cut overhead wherever possible. Some unprofitable operations were eliminated entirely.

The Group's activities were reorganized into six principal sectors: basic steel, paper and packaging, petrochemicals, consumer goods, capital goods, and food. Grupo Industrial Alfa, S.A. (GIASA) was a holding company, with thirteen sub–holding companies and more than 130 subsidiaries. In August 1981 Sr. Rafael Páez was named chief executive officer of the Group, succeeding Sr. Bernardo Garza Sada, who retained the office of chairman. Like Sr. Garza Sada before him, Sr. Páez had previously been the top executive at Hylsa. As the new CEO, Sr. Páez was given authority to take all measures necessary to implement the new consolidation plans.

In 1982, Hylsa was still the largest part of Alfa, accounting for 50 percent of Alfa's revenues and assets. Hylsa accounted for 23.6 percent of the country's steel output and was by far the most efficient major steel producer in Mexico. Nevertheless, Hylsa was hit hard by the nearly 50 percent decline in Mexican steel consumption during 1982.

As the recession deepened, Hylsa cut production, changed its output mix, and took steps to reduce inventories. As part of this program, Hylsa found it necessary to lay off a significant fraction of its work force. Employees dismissed in this fashion received a severance payment of 3 months' wages plus an additional 20 days' wages for each year of service as provided by Mexican labor law. Finally, Hylsa announced that it would reconsider planned capital expenditures on Project 1600, a major plant expansion project designed to double productive capacity and improve its cost structure. Unfortunately, nearly 20 percent of Hylsa's assets in mid-1982 were accounted for by new projects that were incomplete and had yet to produce revenue. Internally prepared operating and financial projections for steel operations are presented in **Exhibit 5**.[1]

The petrochemicals sector consisted of an integrated group of companies organized in seven divisions that produced and/or consumed petrochemicals, and that generated significant foreign exchange through exports. Primary products were synthetic fibers such as lycra, nylon, polyester; raw materials for synthetic fibers, produced both for export and for use within the sector; petrochemical derivatives such as ethylene oxide, polystyrene foam, and industrial polyols; and polyurethane foam and mattresses. In some product lines, over half the sector's output was exported. Equally important, some products were manufactured almost wholly from imported raw materials. Because of the high priority the Mexican government gave the petrochemicals industry, such raw materials were expected to be sufficiently available to meet demands of the domestic petrochemical industry. In the recent past, the industry had been supplied in part by the state-owned petrochemical concern, Pemex. In the event of a severe shortage of a particular input, Pemex was authorized to purchase the material abroad and sell it to domestic producers at a domestic market price. Projections for the petrochemical sector are presented in **Exhibit 6**.

The core of the paper and packaging sector was Titán, one of the original companies of Alfa. This sector produced molded cellulose, kraft paper, and corrugated cardboard. Having operated successfully in the paper industry for over 40 years, Titán itself was a mature business with a strong market share. Demand for sector's packaging materials was directly tied to the level of industrial output in Mexico of goods for both domestic and export markets. As in the petrochemicals sector, the high price of imported raw materials raised operating costs. Titán responded to the crisis in 1982 by embarking on cost reduction and productivity improvement programs, aimed particularly at reducing and improving its use of expensive energy and chemicals. It remained unclear whether these programs would sufficiently address the contraction in demand. Projections for the paper and packaging sector are presented in **Exhibit 7**.

The consumer goods sector was a relatively new one for Alfa, away from its traditional focus on heavy industry, and requiring substantial additional infusions of capital to fully develop. It manufactured a wide range of products, from television

---

[1]Sector financial projections presented in **Exhibits 5** through **10** were prepared internally in 1982, using macroeconomic assumptions contained in **Exhibit 4** and additional sector-specific assumptions supplied by Alfa's managers. The projections presented in **Exhibits 5** through **10** *exclude* intracompany commercial and financial transactions. The projections do not reflect any proposed restructuring of Alfa's debt.

sets and shoe soles to fishing nets and carpets. In addition, the sector owned and operated resort facilities, primarily hotels, and developed real estate in resort areas. The devaluation of the peso was expected to boost the tourism industry eventually; in the short run, however, the severity of the recession in the United States was causing American tourists to cut back their travel. Similarly, Mexican consumers were expected to demand fewer of this sector's various products for the duration of the recession and perhaps beyond. Already a Philco plant had been closed, resulting in layoffs of 1200 employees. Projections for this sector are presented in **Exhibit 8**.

Just as Alfa was cutting unnecessary capital spending, so were the customers of its capital goods sector. Companies in this sector produced machine tools, electric motors (Alfa was the only domestic maker of certain electrical motors and equipment), agricultural equipment, and automotive parts. Much of the sector's output would normally be exported, and benefit from a devaluation, but many critical inputs were imported. Many of the companies in this sector were in the midst of capacity additions and were forced to defer completion and start-up of new installations. As a result, assets in the sector were underutilized. Rationalization programs were instituted to improve productivity and cut administrative costs. By October, 30 percent of the sector's work force had been dismissed. Projections for the sector are given in **Exhibit 9**.

Finally, the food sector consisted of Fud Alimentos, S.A., one of Alfa's most recent acquisitions. It was Mexico's largest producer of processed meats and livestock, and it also produced vegetable oils and canned foods. In 1981, Fud Alimentos operated 50 companies in sixteen Mexican states and the Federal District, and it was six times larger than its largest competitor. Demand for its products was fairly robust in recession. Further, the sector represented an attractive opportunity to reap operating efficiencies from rationalization, automation, and economies of scale. Alfa believed that modern techniques in food processing would effectively limit foreign participation in this industry. In the short run, however, returns were hurt by price controls on some products and by rapidly inflating costs. Moreover, the sector brought with it relatively high levels of dollar-denominated debt. To cope with these problems, Fud Alimentos terminated employees, discontinued low-margin and capital-intensive businesses, and disposed of unproductive assets. Detailed projections for this sector are presented in **Exhibit 10**.

Operating and financial projections for the six sectors are added together and summarized in **Exhibit 11**. The figures presented in **Exhibit 11** exclude intercompany transactions and transactions between the holding company, GIASA, and third parties. For example, some of Alfa's debts were obligations of the holding company rather than particular subsidiaries, and so are not reflected in the sector projections of **Exhibits 5** through **10**. The other primary cash flows for the holding company were dividends from the sectors and certain tax credits paid by the operating subsidiaries to the holding company. The credits would be paid in cash and reflected the difference between taxes that would be owed by profitable subsidiaries if they were independent and the (lower) taxes actually paid by the consolidated entity, which was expected to have operating losses during some years. These and other projected funds flows for GIASA are given in **Exhibit 12**.[2] Consolidated projections for the entire Group are presented in **Exhibit 13**, which combines the sector projections of **Exhibit 11** and the holding company projections of **Exhibit 12**.

In summary, the immediate effects of economic turmoil on Grupo Alfa as a whole were outlined clearly in the company's consolidated peso accounts, given in **Exhibit 2**. The income accounts showed healthy increases in revenues and operating income from 1981 to 1982, part of which were due to inflation. However, the peso cost of servicing dollar-denominated debt also rose, more than offsetting the increase in operating income. Total debt, expressed in pesos, increased from MP63 billion in 1981 to over MP200 billion a year later. Part of this increase reflected new borrowing, but the largest fraction reflected the sharp decline in the value of the peso, which resulted in a huge increase in the peso value of dollar-denominated debt.

The anticipated longer-term effects were outlined in the macroeconomic projections of **Exhibit 4** and the operating projections of **Exhibits 5** through **13**. The combination of recession and significant peso depreciation would, if they persisted or worsened, further increase the peso burden of servicing dollar debt. Approximately 87 percent of Alfa's debt in 1982 was denominated in U.S. dollars. **Exhibit 14** presents a schedule of Alfa's debt by term and denomination.

The Group's complex money management practices added two additional layers of complexity to its capital structure. First, funds borrowed externally by one subsidiary would commonly be lent to another through intercompany transactions, known within Alfa as the "current account." In the ensuing financial crisis, creditors had difficulty untangling the complex web of transactions to determine the financial health of specific subsidiaries, and hence the riskiness of certain outstanding loans.

Second, the debt obligations of a given subsidiary would sometimes be guaranteed by another subsidiary or by a sector-level holding company. Such guarantees were known as *"avals"* and were used to enhance the credit of some subsidiaries. *Avals* operated much like ordinary parent guarantees of a subsidiary's debt, except that a creditor demanding payment was not required to seek it first and foremost from the debtor, but could instead present a note directly to the guarantor for payment. The complexity of such arrangements made it more difficult to assess the solvency of individual entities within the Group, especially those that were both debtors and guarantors.

THE ALTERNATIVES: BANKRUPTCY OR RESTRUCTURING

In October 1982 it appeared impossible for Alfa to meet all the demands to which it had committed itself. According to Mr. David Thomas, then a vice president at Lehman Brothers, any further cutting, squeezing, and rationalizing of operations would be exceedingly difficult and, in any event, not enough. There remained, he argued, only two courses of action, bankruptcy or restructuring.

[2] For simplicity, the data in **Exhibit 12** are presented as if GIASA were the only holding company. In reality, Alfa was composed of numerous holding companies at different levels of the organization, in addition to GIASA. **Exhibit 12** consolidates data for sector- and subsidiary-level holding companies with data for GIASA.

Bankruptcy (a process initiated by either the creditor or debtor) or *suspensión de pagos* (a process initiated only by the debtor) would bring the Mexican legal system in between the company and its creditors. Corporate law in Mexico, including that pertaining to suspensión de pagos and bankruptcy, fell under federal jurisdiction. Unlike many Anglo-Saxon legal systems, Mexico's system was based on a Napoleonic code of law. That is, each case was decided more or less in isolation and on its merits, without regard to court precedents. Mexico had a system of both federal and state courts, including appellate and supreme courts in each state. There was one national supreme court which was the highest court of appeals. Any matter, state or federal, and any procedural question in any court could be brought, at the outset, before the supreme court for resolution. In general, Mexican society was not a litigious one; litigation was usually pursued only in the most intractable matters. In practice, even comparatively simple orders, such as an *amparo,* or injunction, could sometimes take many months to process.

The role of the courts made the outcome of a suspensión de pagos difficult to predict. After a company has defaulted on its obligations, an impaired creditor could force the company to file with a court for a suspensión de pagos. The priority of claims would be preserved basically intact. After filing, the company would continue to operate, usually under incumbent management, and the court would order negotiations between shareholders and creditors aimed at restructuring the company's obligations. Any negotiated settlement would have to be approved by the court. Alternatively, the court, in its sole discretion, could reach a finding that the parties were unable to reach an agreement, and therefore order a liquidation. In the event of a liquidation, the court would appoint an ''intervener'' to effect the sale of company assets so as to maximize value for the creditors. The intervener typically would be a disinterested member of either the Mexican chamber of commerce or an industry association. The whole process could be expected to consume a large amount of time and to involve considerable costs and embarrassment for many of the parties involved. Two recent examples of suspensión de pagos by large companies had resulted in the defaulting debtors being liquidated.

An out-of-court restructuring would require the company and its lenders to reach voluntary agreement on a wide range of complex issues. First, and most fundamental, was the size and scope of the restructured Alfa's businesses. Would Alfa continue to be a grand company or would it emerge considerably shrunken? Lenders could be expected to press for the sale of some operations to generate cash. However, Alfa's directors wanted to defend what they felt were basically sound acquisitions that would perform very well once the crisis had passed. Each sector and subsidiary would have to be carefully evaluated.

Second, there was the question of how much of what type of debt each subsidiary and GIASA could support after the restructuring. It seemed clear that the amount, timing, and/or currency denominations of outstanding obligations would have to be substantially altered, regardless of how extensively Alfa's operations were restructured. This would require complex negotiations among a large group of lenders that included some of the largest banks in the world. Chase Manhattan, Citibank, Bank of America, Continental Illinois, and a host of non-U.S. banks had very large exposures to Alfa. Several were believed to be in excess of $100 million. For the most part, these lenders had been completely unprepared for such serious problems with a customer as strong as Alfa. As recently as June 1981, the company's credit had been good enough to float a public issue of $75 million of floating rate notes. In August 1981, Hylsa had been able to borrow $60 million under a new facility arranged with several Texas banks. The dramatic reversal of Alfa's fortunes had likely cost it some credibility with its lenders.

Third, the lenders could be expected to demand substantial equity to compensate them for the concessions they would have to grant and to protect themselves from conceding too much in debt reduction. Alfa's stockholders, united by family ties, patriotism, and economics, would stoutly resist giving up a significant amount of control in the form of equity.

Fourth, a viable recapitalization would have to include mechanisms for avoiding future problems with creditors. The outstanding loans to Alfa had relied on comparatively few covenants, which events had shown to be inadequate. For example, one covenant had provided that total debt could not exceed 1.5 times consolidated net worth, a limit that would be exceeded in 1982. New loans would have to contain more provisions for effective monitoring of whatever arrangements were agreed to by the company and its banks. Alternatively or additionally, Alfa's procedures and practices for corporate governance might have to be modified.

Finally, even if the role of the Mexican courts was minimized, the Mexican government would undoubtedly be deeply involved in any restructuring. For one thing, the government was a large stakeholder, having recently made equity contributions and extended a line of credit to the various Alfa subsidiaries. Furthermore, in pursuit of national economic development objectives, the government strongly influenced or directly controlled many parts of the economy in which Alfa participated. In particular, government ministries wielded substantial influence over the allocation of domestic credit and the setting of certain output prices such as steel and some consumer goods. For these reasons, the government might normally be expected to ally itself with Alfa in any protracted struggle with foreign banks. However, in 1982 the government had its own very difficult problems with the same foreign banks. Moreover, with so many Mexican companies suffering acute financial difficulties, it was impossible for the government to help them all, and it would be politically difficult to appear to favor a large family-dominated conglomerate such as Alfa. In short, Alfa had adversaries as well as friends within the Mexican government. Hence, there was considerable uncertainty about how the Ministry of Finance would behave in the course of lengthy negotiations with foreign creditors.

As Sr. Páez pondered his alternatives, his company was rapidly running out of cash. He and Sr. Bernardo Garza Sada had recently met with Sr. Jesús Silva Herzog, the minister of finance, to discuss Alfa's looming debt crisis. At the end of their meeting, the minister of finance said, "I would like to show the rest of the world, using the example of your group, that in Mexico we are capable of solving in an orderly manner any complex difficulty." Those present at the meeting understood that Alfa represented modern Mexico. Although there were important foreign interests at stake, the process of resolving the current problems had to remain under Mexican control.

EXHIBIT 1 SUMMARY DESCRIPTION OF ALFA'S BUSINESSES IN 1982

Company	Products	Markets
Basic steel		
Hylsa	Flat and structured steel	Construction, commercial, and electrical equipment
Paper and packaging		
Titán	Paper and packaging	Foods, pharmaceuticals, and textiles
Celulósicos Centauro	Cellulose and paper	Paper
Petrochemicals		
Akra	Synthetic fibers	Textiles and tires
Polioles	Petrochemical products	Synthetic fibers, mattresses, pharmaceuticals, detergents
Petrocel	DMT and TPA*	Synthetic fibers
Selther	Mattresses and polyurethane foam	Padding and automotive
Consumer goods		
Casolar	Real estate and tourism	National and international tourism, real estate
Electronics (PAM)	TVs, modular equipment	Consumer electronics
POM	Polyurethane shoe soles	Footwear
Terza	Rugs and carpets	Construction
La Marina	Canvas, fishing nets	Rubber tire, transportation, agricultural, and fishing
Capital goods		
HyL	Steel technology	Direct reduction
Draco	Nonferrous minerals	Electronics, petroleum, aeronautics
Galvak	Galvanized sheet metal	Construction and manufacturing
Megatek	Electric motors, generators	Steel, cement, petrochemicals, industrial equipment
Agromak	Tractors and farm implements	Farming and livestock, construction
Atlax	Specialty steels	Automotive, auto parts, capital goods, mining
Metamex	Specialty steels	Automotive, agriculture, capital goods, consumer goods
Makrotek	Industrial and heavy machinery	Siderurgical-electric, chemical, brewing, mining, and glass
Nemak	Aluminum heads for motors	Automotive and steel
Formacero	Industrial steel parts, structures	Construction, petrochemical, cement, and paper
Food	Meat processing, vegetable oils	Food
TIM	TV broadcasting	Communications

*DMT = dimethyl terephthalate; TPA = terephthallic acid.

EXHIBIT 2 HISTORICAL CONSOLIDATED FINANCIAL DATA (MILLIONS)

Income statement data	1978	1979	1980	1981	1982
Revenues	MP19,061.4	MP30,010.5	MP46,739.5	MP 62,664.0	MP 82,600.0
Gross margin	6,289.5	10,066.2	15,353.0	20,591.0	26,992.0
Operating expenses					
Administrative	(1,997.7)	(3,338.9)	(6,518.0)	(9,087.0)	(10,368.0)
Selling	(664.6)	(1,223.5)	(1,721.6)	(3,394.0)	(3,506.0)
Operating income	3,627.1	5,503.7	7,113.4	8,110.0	13,118.0
Interest income/(expense)	(1,565.9)	(2,030.4)	(3,521.6)	(8,533.0)	(22,575.0)
Other income, net	119.5	228.0	305.5	933.0	2,008.0
Pretax income	2,180.7	3,701.4	3,897.3	510.0	(7,449.0)
Income taxes	(276.6)	(915.0)	(42.9)	(98.0)	(18.0)
Net income before extraordinary items	1,904.1	2,786.4	3,854.4	412.0	(7,467.0)
Monetary exchange-rate fluctuations*	(14.4)	(80.1)	(121.4)	(2,399.0)	(23,974.0)
Extraordinary items	0.0	0.0	0.0	(3,873.0)	(1,428.0)
Net income	MP 1,889.8	MP 2,706.3	MP 3,733.1	MP (5,860.0)	MP (32,869.0)
Net assets					
Cash and equivalents	MP 592.2	MP 699.5	MP 1,044.5	MP 3,797.0	MP 14,894.0
Net working capital	6,389.6	10,853.8	22,056.7	22,316.0	3,068.0
Net property, plant and equipment	22,122.7	33,780.2	52,771.4	74,636.0	166,510.0
Investments and other assets	1,225.1	1,781.9	2,270.5	4,301.0	6,116.0
Deferred charges, net of deferred credits	376.0	489.8	1,603.1	1,755.0	10,643.0
Provision for divestitures	—	—	—	(1,586.0)	—
Excess of cost over book value of subsidiaries	272.5	568.2	2,936.2	3,002.0	1,694.0
Tax benefit due to monetary exchange losses*	—	—	—	—	25,403.0
Other assets, net of liabilities	(95.9)	(167.1)	(285.2)	(779.0)	15,076.0
Net assets	MP30,882.2	MP48,006.3	MP82,397.2	MP107,442.0	MP243,404.0
Capitalization					
Short-term debt	MP 1,352.0	MP 1,909.2	MP 3,240.3	MP 4,129.0	MP 20,924.0
Short-term bank loans	2,475.7	3,957.9	12,770.0	23,388.0	80,428.0
Long-term debt:					
Mortgage bonds	671.5	579.5	890.3	788.0	322.0
Debenture bonds	569.7	600.0	859.4	863.0	1,169.0
Bank loans and notes payable	9,616.2	13,610.4	25,921.0	33,683.0	107,551.0
Total debt	14,685.1	20,656.9	43,681.0	62,851.0	210,394.0
Common equity	16,197.1	27,349.4	38,716.1	44,591.0	33,010.0
Total capitalization	MP30,882.2	MP48,006.3	MP82,397.2	MP107,442.0	MP243,404.0

*Reflects translation adjustments from exchange-rate fluctuations of the peso against foreign currencies and tax deductions arising from exchange rate losses.

EXHIBIT 3 **MONTHLY NOMINAL SPOT EXCHANGE RATES—MP/$, 1978–1982**

Date	MP/$	Date	MP/$	Date	MP/$
January 1978	22.72	August 1979	22.81	March 1981	23.65
February 1978	22.72	September 1979	22.78	April 1981	23.85
March 1978	22.74	October 1979	22.81	May 1981	24.09
April 1978	22.74	November 1979	22.86	June 1981	24.33
May 1978	22.73	December 1979	22.81	July 1981	24.57
June 1978	22.80	January 1980	22.81	August 1981	24.78
July 1978	22.84	February 1980	22.82	September 1981	25.04
August 1978	22.84	March 1980	22.85	October 1981	25.36
September 1978	22.76	April 1980	22.83	November 1981	25.68
October 1978	22.77	May 1980	22.84	December 1981	26.01
November 1978	22.79	June 1980	22.88	January 1982	26.43
December 1978	22.74	July 1980	22.97	February 1982	31.33
January 1979	22.71	August 1980	23.02	March 1982	45.26
February 1979	22.76	September 1980	23.00	April 1982	45.92
March 1979	22.81	October 1980	23.06	May 1982	46.76
April 1979	22.83	November 1980	23.15	June 1982	47.62
May 1979	22.82	December 1980	23.19	July 1982	48.52
June 1979	22.84	January 1981	23.34	August 1982	78.03
July 1979	22.83	February 1981	23.48	September 1982	87.00

MONTHLY MOVEMENT IN MP/$ EXCHANGE RATE, JANUARY 1978–DECEMBER 1982

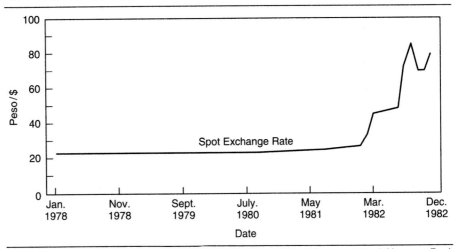

Source: International Financial Statistics Database (Washington, D.C.: International Monetary Fund, 1978–1982).

EXHIBIT 4   PROJECTIONS OF SELECTED MACROECONOMICS INDICATORS*

	Actual							Forecasted									
	1976	1977	1978	1979	1980	1981	1982	1983	1984	1985	1986	1987	1988	1989	1990	1991	1992
Mexico																	
Price index (annual average)																	
Consumer	15.8	29.1	17.5	18.2	26.3	27.9	59.8	82.8	39.6	35.5	27.8	25.7	26.6	—	—	—	—
Wholesale	22.2	41.2	15.8	18.3	24.5	24.5	60.5	91.6	37.7	34.1	26.0	25.8	23.2	—	—	—	—
GNP deflator	19.6	30.5	16.8	20.1	28.7	26.8	60.2	87.5	38.6	34.8	26.9	25.6	23.4	21.0	19.0	17.0	15.0
Interest rate (CPP %)†	—	—	15.2	16.4	20.7	28.6	40.5	49.0	38.3	37.4	30.9	29.0	27.2	25.0	23.0	21.0	19.0
Exchange rate																	
Average	15.4	22.6	22.8	22.8	23.0	24.5	—	97.3	135.1	171.7	209.1	247.4	289.3	335.8	386.0	436.0	484.0
Yearend	19.9	22.7	22.7	22.8	23.2	26.2	76.4	118.2	152.0	191.4	226.7	268.0	310.6	361.0	411.0	461.0	507.0
United States																	
Price index (annual average)																	
Consumer	5.8	6.5	7.7	11.3	13.5	10.4	6.2	5.9	5.7	5.3	5.3	5.0	4.8	—	—	—	—
Wholesale	4.4	6.5	7.8	11.1	13.5	9.2	4.1	6.4	5.5	5.4	5.3	5.3	5.0	—	—	—	—
Interest rates																	
LIBOR	5.6	6.0	8.7	12.0	14.0	16.8	13.5	11.5	10.2	9.9	9.3	9.5	8.7	9.0	8.0	8.0	7.0
Prime	6.9	6.8	9.1	12.7	15.0	18.9	14.9	13.0	11.7	11.4	10.8	11.0	10.2	—	—	—	—
Long-term																	
Government bond	7.6	7.4	8.4	9.4	11.5	13.9	11.0	9.8	8.8	8.5	8.1	8.3	8.0	—	—	—	—

*Projections estimated as of June 1, 1982.

†The CPP rate is a weighted average cost of funds for Mexican banks. Each month, the Bank of Mexico computes this rate from the previous month's data. The CPP rate moves in a similar manner to the Cetes Rate, which is the Mexican short-term Treasury bill rate.

EXHIBIT 5 FINANCIAL PROJECTIONS FOR THE STEEL SECTOR (MILLIONS)

	1983	1984	1985	1986	1987	1988	1989	1990	1991	1992
Selected income data										
Revenues	MP54,734.0	MP79,807.0	MP105,259.0	MP130,436.0	MP161,226.0	MP195,098.0	MP236,027.0	MP285,593.0	MP345,574.0	MP418,159.0
EBIT	15,053.0	23,035.0	31,278.0	38,119.0	43,961.0	46,742.0	50,502.0	56,372.0	62,814.0	69,356.0
Interest expense	(12,883.0)	(16,256.0)	(19,468.0)	(21,501.0)	(25,226.0)	(29,190.0)	(34,082.0)	(37,127.0)	(40,267.0)	(43,888.0)
Net income	(765.0)	6,494.0	8,667.0	13,130.0	14,908.0	17,612.0	17,188.0	19,358.0	22,567.0	26,515.0
Selected funds flow data										
Sources										
Depreciation	2,574.0	5,064.0	6,817.0	9,136.0	11,848.0	15,578.0	19,207.0	23,815.0	29,538.0	36,634.0
Accounting exchange losses*	3,715.0	939.0	—	—	—	—	—	—	—	—
Net borrowing and deferred credits	8,706.0	—	—	—	8,650.0	29,046.0	—	28.0	—	4.0
Uses										
Working capital	8,840.0	3,135.0	416.0	2,455.0	4,626.0	3,275.0	4,802.0	7,841.0	3,456.0	5,917.0
Capital expenditures	2,080.0	1,352.0	1,794.0	5,510.0	17,046.0	18,123.0	6,375.0	5,526.0	6,814.0	8,402.0
Other assets	—	4,728.0	5,869.0	4,505.0	—	—	655.0	2,178.0	18,694.0	15,304.0
Debt repayments	3,310.0	1,806.0	3,685.0	5,445.0	6,806.0	13,384.0	15,765.0	19,062.0	23,949.0	22,246.0
Dividends to holding company	—	—	3,716.0	4,334.0	6,564.0	7,454.0	8,806.0	8,594.0	9,679.0	11,284.0

*Reflects translation adjustments from exchange-rate fluctuations of the peso against foreign currencies and tax deductions arising from exchange-rate losses. Treated as a noncash charge and therefore a source.

EXHIBIT 6   FINANCIAL PROJECTIONS FOR THE PETROCHEMICALS SECTOR (MILLIONS)

	1983	1984	1985	1986	1987	1988	1989	1990	1991	1992
Selected income data										
Revenues	MP37,945.0	MP59,965.0	MP87,217.0	MP116,337.0	MP149,860.0	MP187,215.0	MP231,644.0	MP296,596.0	MP348,258.0	MP424,661.5
EBIT	7,252.0	12,108.0	18,256.0	74,525.0	30,100.0	37,851.0	47,034.0	57,773.0	58,287.0	71,176.9
Interest expense	(3,274.0)	(3,904.0)	(4,810.0)	(5,851.0)	(7,201.0)	(7,690.0)	(7,556.0)	(9,433.0)	(10,401.0)	(11,485.0)
Net income	3,058.0	4,597.0	6,665.0	7,615.0	9,265.0	12,210.0	15,596.0	19,169.0	17,208.0	21,347.0
Selected funds flow data										
Sources										
Depreciation	1,852.0	3,131.0	4,433.0	6,151.0	8,230.0	10,384.0	12,871.0	15,947.0	19,560.0	23,858.6
Other assets	1,288.0	0.0	0.0	0.0	0.0	0.0	0.0	0.0	0.0	0.0
Net borrowing and deferred credits	80.0	1,698.0	2,171.0	2,227.0	(102.0)	(1,162.0)	(1,780.0)	(1,349.0)	(539.0)	378.0
Uses										
Working capital	3,320.0	4,751.0	6,337.0	7,161.0	7,596.0	6,830.0	9,428.0	10,994.0	3,418.6	13,640.6
Other	(101.0)	180.0	368.0	181.0	0.0	0.0	0.0	0.0	0.0	0.0
Capital expenditures	1,379.0	2,514.0	3,473.0	3,305.0	2,139.0	2,622.0	3,189.0	3,871.0	4,691.0	5,642.0
Dividends to holding company	1,083.0	1,560.0	2,363.0	3,450.0	3,978.0	4,903.0	6,452.0	8,230.0	10,137.0	8,118.0

EXHIBIT 7 FINANCIAL PROJECTIONS FOR THE PAPER AND PACKAGING SECTOR (MILLIONS)

	1983	1984	1985	1986	1987	1988	1989	1990	1991	1992
Selected income data										
Revenues	MP8,447.0	MP14,879.0	MP19,884.0	MP24,323.9	MP35,982.3	MP44,365.0	MP54,004.0	MP70,459.8	MP80,705.3	MP97,618.4
EBIT	837.6	1,622.2	2,642.2	3,613.5	5,099.3	6,865.9	8,844.0	11,433.8	14,365.7	21,795.6
Interest expense	(1,318.4)	(1,683.6)	(2,257.2)	(2,832.7)	(3,483.3)	(3,927.2)	(4,538.1)	(5,020.9)	(5,559.7)	(5,887.7)
Net income	(406.1)	(392.3)	884.5	1,871.0	2,267.6	3,555.7	3,087.6	4,262.5	6,104.3	7,943.6
Selected funds flow data										
Sources										
Depreciation	214.3	308.4	358.8	528.2	643.0	830.1	1,055.0	1,316.9	1,702.1	2,145.1
Net borrowing and deferred credits	2,950.8	4,577.4	2,006.7	2,516.7	2,659.7	651.3	0.0	0.0	0.0	0.0
Uses										
Working capital	928.0	1,261.0	1,498.0	1,359.0	1,611.0	1,840.6	1,726.4	1,990.7	2,299.1	2,659.6
Capital expenditures	1,442.2	2,652.0	2,870.4	3,408.2	4,767.4	4,066.5	5,634.0	5,651.1	7,927.1	9,071.8
Debt paydown	1,524.0	4,613.7	530.0	794.5	1,159.2	1,572.6	69.8	1,244.1	485.4	2,009.3
Corporate overhead	161.0	211.0	267.0	334.0	399.5	466.9	540.8	627.4	728.9	848.0
Other assets	3,210.0	460.0	576.0	531.0	400.0	300.0	275.0	275.0	250.0	250.0
Preferred dividends	408.0	408.0	408.0	408.0	408.0	408.0	408.0	408.0	408.0	408.0

EXHIBIT 8   FINANCIAL PROJECTIONS FOR THE CONSUMER GOODS SECTOR (MILLIONS)

	1983	1984	1985	1986	1987	1988	1989	1990	1991	1992
Selected income data										
Revenues	MP10,258.0	MP15,066.0	MP17,878.0	MP22,326.3	MP25,086.5	MP32,275.5	MP37,891.9	MP44,328.2	MP51,286.3	MP61,675.2
EBIT	(557.3)	(119.9)	432.6	1,970.6	3,058.2	4,357.1	5,716.0	7,378.3	9,500.8	12,313.0
Interest expense	(628.5)	(705.6)	(791.7)	(849.7)	(905.2)	(924.6)	(930.5)	(893.4)	(813.0)	(670.9)
Net income	(1,680.2)	(1,604.4)	(881.8)	309.9	949.6	1,356.5	2,078.0	3,086.6	3,928.5	5,090.6
Selected funds flow data										
Sources										
Depreciation	751.5	903.1	1,080.0	1,288.3	1,541.8	1,838.5	2,182.8	2,587.0	3,083.1	3,670.8
Other assets	(362.0)	664.0	42.0	80.0	65.6	70.7	61.2	64.3	67.5	70.9
Net borrowing and deferred credits	1,786.4	919.2	501.3	547.2	219.9	53.2	56.4	105.7	135.0	48.1
Uses										
Working capital	(21.0)	1,295.0	1,476.0	1,377.0	1,589.9	1,651.1	1,887.4	2,128.0	2,406.4	2,799.2
Debt paydown	2,061.1	0.0	0.0	142.4	229.6	241.7	434.5	826.7	1,238.9	0.0
Corporate overhead	163.0	217.0	273.0	341.0	399.0	474.5	532.1	582.0	648.5	735.2
Capital expenditures	944.8	1,106.3	1,355.7	1,592.6	2,028.1	2,424.0	2,834.6	3,623.9	4,426.3	5,360.7
Preferred dividends	460.0	460.0	460.0	460.0	460.0	460.0	460.0	460.0	460.0	460.0

EXHIBIT 9   FINANCIAL PROJECTIONS FOR THE CAPITAL GOODS SECTOR (MILLIONS)

	1983	1984	1985	1986	1987	1988	1989	1990	1991	1992
Selected income data										
Revenues	MP14,003.0	MP20,890.7	MP28,604.1	MP35,166.6	MP43,308.7	MP50,293.6	MP58,482.4	MP67,919.1	MP75,481.9	MP89,804.1
EBIT	(437.9)	368.1	1,028.2	1,975.3	3,866.1	4,524.4	4,768.9	5,194.7	5,072.4	6,020.1
Interest expense	(774.1)	(1,243.7)	(1,587.0)	(1,924.8)	(2,280.6)	(2,647.2)	(3,078.0)	(3,511.0)	(3,943.8)	(4,342.3)
Net income	(2,099.0)	(936.7)	(466.3)	445.2	1,263.1	1,684.3	1,704.6	1,932.4	2,058.7	2,461.1
Selected funds flow data										
Sources										
Depreciation	1,057.2	1,295.1	1,567.5	1,842.4	2,192.0	2,527.8	3,026.3	3,508.1	4,042.0	4,620.3
Net borrowing and deferred credits	1,831.1	2,482.4	208.6	451.6	51.2	40.8	12.9	66.6	57.2	49.7
Uses										
Working capital	2,293.7	2,455.2	2,668.5	2,648.4	3,269.4	3,800.0	4,423.1	5,141.3	5,718.9	6,799.0
Capital expenditures	1,110.0	1,359.8	1,645.8	1,750.3	2,082.4	2,401.4	2,875.0	3,683.5	4,244.1	4,851.3
Corporate overhead	136.0	188.0	243.6	305.8	367.0	422.0	485.3	558.1	613.9	736.7
Other assets	322.0	441.6	578.4	712.9	869.9	1,006.7	1,166.1	1,349.7	1,494.7	1,783.5
Preferred dividends	80.0	80.0	80.0	80.0	80.0	80.0	80.0	80.0	80.0	80.0

521

EXHIBIT 10 FINANCIAL PROJECTIONS FOR THE FOOD SECTOR (MILLIONS)

	1983	1984	1985	1986	1987	1988	1989	1990	1991	1992
Selected income data										
Revenues	MP17,926.0	MP26,005.0	MP36,989.0	MP50,950.0	MP69,962.0	MP93,572.0	MP123,515.0	MP160,569.6	MP205,529.0	MP258,966.6
EBIT	1,822.0	2,529.0	3,618.0	5,156.0	7,151.0	9,553.0	12,610.0	16,392.9	20,983.0	26,438.5
Interest expense	(1,838.0)	(1,825.0)	(2,068.0)	(2,145.0)	(2,409.0)	(2,530.0)	(3,642.1)	(4,146.5)	(4,651.0)	(5,115.0)
Net income	(2,600.0)	(1,380.0)	(983.0)	565.0	1,859.0	3,977.0	5,249.6	6,824.5	8,735.4	11,006.6
Selected funds flow data										
Sources										
Depreciation	257.0	475.0	620.0	881.0	1,174.0	1,582.0	2,088.2	2,714.7	3,474.8	4,378.3
Exchange loss	2,512.0	2,047.0	2,410.0	2,180.0	2,551.0	2,631.0	2,762.6	2,900.7	3,045.7	3,198.0
Other assets	282.0	165.0	—	—	—	—	—	—	—	—
Net borrowing and deferred credits	105.0	—	—	—	—	—	—	—	—	—
Uses										
Working capital	711.0	1,484.0	2,129.0	2,602.0	3,537.0	4,317.0	5,698.4	7,408.0	9,482.2	11,947.6
Capital expenditures	—	—	523.0	673.0	848.0	1,059.0	1,397.9	1,817.2	2,326.1	2,930.9

EXHIBIT 11 SECTOR CONSOLIDATED FINANCIAL PROJECTIONS (MILLIONS)

	1983	1984	1985	1986	1987	1988	1989	1990
Selected income data								
Revenues	MP143,313.0	MP216,612.7	MP295,831.1	MP379,539.9	MP485,425.5	MP602,819.1	MP741,564.4	MP925,465.6
EBIT	23,969.3	39,542.4	57,255.0	125,359.4	93,235.6	109,893.4	129,474.9	154,544.8
Interest expense	(20,716.0)	(25,617.9)	(30,981.9)	(35,104.3)	(41,505.0)	(46,908.9)	(53,826.6)	(60,131.7)
Net income	(4,492.4)	6,776.6	13,885.4	23,936.1	30,512.2	40,395.5	44,903.9	54,633.0
Selected funds flow data								
Sources								
Depreciation	6,705.9	11,176.6	14,876.3	19,826.9	25,628.8	32,740.4	40,430.4	49,888.7
Accounting exchange losses	6,227.0	2,986.0	2,410.0	2,180.0	2,551.0	2,631.0	2,762.6	2,900.7
Net borrowing and deferred credits	15,459.3	9,677.0	4,887.6	5,742.5	11,478.8	28,629.2	(1,710.7)	(1,148.7)
Uses								
Working capital	16,071.7	14,381.2	14,524.5	17,602.4	22,229.3	21,713.8	27,965.4	35,503.0
Capital expenditures	6,956.0	8,984.2	11,661.9	16,239.1	28,910.9	30,695.9	22,305.5	24,172.8
Other assets	2,063.0	6,638.6	7,433.4	6,009.9	1,335.5	1,377.4	2,157.4	3,867.0
Debt repayments	6,895.1	6,419.7	4,215.0	6,381.9	8,194.8	15,198.3	16,260.3	21,132.8
Corporate overhead	460.0	616.0	783.6	980.8	1,165.4	1,363.4	1,558.3	1,767.5
Dividends to holding company	1,083.0	1,560.0	6,079.0	7,784.0	10,542.0	12,357.0	15,258.0	16,824.0
Preferred dividends	948.0	948.0	948.0	948.0	948.0	948.0	948.0	948.0

EXHIBIT 12   ESTIMATED FUNDS FLOW FOR GIASA (HOLDING COMPANY) (MP MILLIONS)

	1983	1984	1985	1986	1987	1988	1989	1990
Projected dividends								
Hylsa	—	—	MP 3,716.0	MP 4,334.0	MP 6,564.0	MP 7,454.0	MP 8,806.0	MP 8,594.0
Petrochemicals	MP 1,083.0	MP 1,560.0	2,363.0	3,450.0	3,978.0	4,903.0	6,452.0	8,230.0
Estimated tax credits	922.0	2,650.0	4,400.0	2,300.0	—	—	—	—
Total income	2,005.0	4,210.0	10,479.0	10,084.0	10,542.0	12,357.0	15,258.0	16,824.0
Interest expense	9,268.0	10,666.0	12,108.0	13,718.0	15,841.0	18,007.0	20,223.0	22,495.0
Preferred dividends	948.0	948.0	948.0	948.0	948.0	948.0	948.0	948.0
Total servicing requirements	10,216.0	11,614.0	13,056.0	14,666.0	16,789.0	18,955.0	21,171.0	23,443.0

EXHIBIT 13 GROUP CONSOLIDATED FINANCIAL PROJECTIONS (MP MILLIONS)

	1983	1984	1985	1986	1987	1988	1989	1990
Selected income data								
Revenues	MP143,313.0	MP216,612.7	MP295,831.1	MP379,539.9	MP485,425.5	MP602,819.1	MP741,564.4	MP925,465.6
EBIT	23,969.3	39,542.4	57,255.0	125,359.4	93,235.6	109,893.4	129,474.9	154,544.8
Interest expense	(29,984.0)	(36,283.9)	(43,089.9)	(48,822.3)	(57,346.0)	(64,915.9)	(74,049.6)	(82,626.7)
Net income	(3,570.4)	9,427.6	18,285.4	26,236.1	30,512.2	40,395.5	44,903.9	54,633.0
Selected funds flow data								
Sources								
Depreciation	6,705.9	11,176.6	14,876.3	19,826.9	25,628.8	32,740.4	40,430.4	49,888.7
Accounting exchange losses	6,227.0	2,986.0	2,410.0	2,180.0	2,551.0	2,631.0	2,762.6	2,900.7
Net borrowing and deferred credits	15,459.3	9,677.0	4,887.6	5,742.5	11,478.8	28,629.2	(1,710.7)	(1,148.7)
Uses								
Working capital	16,071.7	14,381.2	14,524.5	17,602.4	22,229.3	21,713.8	27,965.4	35,503.0
Capital expenditures	6,956.0	8,984.2	11,661.9	16,239.1	28,910.9	30,695.9	22,305.5	24,172.8
Other assets	2,063.0	6,638.6	7,433.4	6,009.9	1,335.5	1,377.4	2,157.4	3,867.0
Debt repayments	6,895.1	6,419.7	4,215.0	6,381.9	8,194.8	15,198.3	16,260.3	21,132.8
Corporate overhead	460.0	616.0	783.6	980.8	1,165.4	1,363.4	1,558.3	1,767.5
Preferred dividends	948.0	948.0	948.0	948.0	948.0	948.0	948.0	948.0

EXHIBIT 14   DEBT OUTSTANDING AT JUNE 30, 1982 (IN MILLIONS)

| | Total third-party debt | | Short-term debt | | | | Long-term debt | | | |
| | | | Peso-denominated | | $-denominated | | Peso-denominated | | $-denominated | |
	In pesos	In $	In pesos	In $	In pesos	In $	In pesos	In $	In pesos	In $
Basic steel	MP 38,128.4	$ 798.5	MP 298.0	$ 6.2	MP14,491.0	$303.5	MP 3,332.0	$ 69.8	MP20,007.0	$ 419.0
Paper and packaging	7,339.2	153.7	234.0	4.9	2,927.0	61.3	560.0	11.7	3,619.0	75.8
Petrochemicals	10,743.8	225.0	210.0	4.4	1,958.0	41.0	1,285.0	26.9	7,291.0	152.7
Consumer goods	9,249.2	193.7	77.0	1.6	3,987.0	83.5	455.0	9.5	4,730.0	99.1
Capital goods	7,811.9	163.6	377.0	7.9	2,827.0	59.2	710.0	14.9	3,896.0	81.6
Food	3,156.3	66.1	158.0	3.3	2,579.0	54.0	189.0	4.0	232.0	4.9
Holding companies	34,890.9	730.7	429.0	9.0	9,846.0	206.2	5,944.0	124.5	18,670.0	391.0
Consolidated total	MP111,319.6	$2,331.3	MP1,783.0	$37.3	MP38,615.0	$808.7	MP12,475.0	$261.3	MP58,445.0	$1,224.0

Note: The contractual denomination of each debt issue is as indicated. Translations are computed, for illustration, at an exchange rate of MP47.75/$1.

COMPAGNIE GÉNÉRALE D'ELECTRICITÉ

In January 1987 the French government announced that Compagnie Générale d'Electricité (CGE), the telecommunications and energy giant, would be privatized in May 1987. CGE would be the sixth of sixty-five companies to be privatized under a program established by the Chirac government when it took office in 1986. The planned privatization was announced 1 month after CGE completed its acquisition of ITT's worldwide telecommunications businesses in a transaction valued at $2.3 billion.

To prepare for the privatization, CGE set up a task force that was given a broad mandate to oversee an abundance of preparations and decisions that had to be made before the sale of shares could take place in May. The task force had just 4 months in which to make recommendations concerning a number of vitally important issues, including the determination of an appropriate capital structure for the company, the establishment of a core shareholding group, and an appropriate price for the shares being offered. Clearly, the recommendations to be made would affect not only the success of the offering in the near future, but the long-term success of the company as well.

BACKGROUND

Compagnie Générale d'Electricité was founded in 1898 to generate and sell electrical power. During the next 50 years, the company expanded in the areas of power

This case was prepared by Research Associate Richard P. Melnick and Professor W. Carl Kester. Copyright © 1988 by the President and Fellows of Harvard College. Harvard Business School case 289-002.

generation, power distribution, and the production of equipment related to those activities. By 1965 CGE's chairman, Ambroise Roux, focused the company's future on three primary activities: energy, telecommunications, and utilities and construction. This focus eventually led to the acquisition of a major company in each area: Alsthom in energy, Alcatel in telecommunications, and Société Générale d'Entreprise in construction. The CGE Group was managed in a decentralized manner, allowing its many subsidiaries broad autonomy within strategic goals set by the parent. By 1968 the parent operated exclusively as a holding company while it assisted subsidiaries in new activities and encouraged efficiencies among its sectors. An organization and ownership chart of the group as of March 1987 is shown in **Exhibit 1**. Financial statements are provided in **Exhibits 2**, and **4**.

By the 1980s, CGE's strategy focused primarily on international expansion in the energy and telecommunications fields with the goal of establishing leading worldwide positions in these basic activities (geographic and sectorial data are provided in **Exhibit 5**). Because of this strategy, the 1980s were a time of tremendous change for CGE. Société Générale d'Entreprise, a source of great growth in the 1970s, was sold to Saint Gobain in 1983. In 1985, CGE's subsidiary, CIT Alcatel, acquired Thomson Telecommunications and formed a new subsidiary named Alcatel. Following this merger and others involving cable companies, CGE ranked fifth worldwide in telecommunications equipment, and second in cables manufacturing. Furthermore, CGE bought a minority interest (40 percent) in, and assumed management responsibility for, Framatome in 1986. By purchasing this manufacturer of nuclear power plant reactors, CGE complemented its energy production activities.

When Socialist President François Mitterrand was elected president in 1982, many French companies were nationalized, including CGE. Despite the nationalization, CGE managed to pursue the major elements of its corporate strategy. This was largely due to the fact that existing management remained in place with only the chairman of the board being replaced, first by J. P. Brunet, a former ambassador with a reputation for sound business judgment, followed by George Pebereau, who was himself from the top ranks of CGE's executives. Also, CGE's decentralized structure, with several partially owned subsidiaries listed on the Paris Bourse, made it difficult for the Socialist government to force changes upon the company as a whole.

But if strategic direction did not change, the execution and financing of CGE's strategy certainly did. As a nationalized company, public authorization was required to undertake certain transactions involving the buying and selling of assets. Dealing with customers and other companies in the buying and selling of assets was further complicated by CGE's unique state-owned status in comparison to that of its major competitors.

Finally, as a nationalized company, CGE found it more difficult to raise sufficient capital to fund its strategy. At the heart of the problem was difficulty in establishing the equity base needed to support growth. With the state as primary shareholder, profits from CGE were frequently diverted to support other publicly owned companies in weaker financial condition (CGE was one of only a few nationalized French companies to show a profit steadily). During its 5 years as a nationalized company, CGE paid out 800 million French francs (FF) in dividends to the government while raising only FF700 million externally.

To replace permanent capital absorbed by the government, CGE pioneered the use of a new type of financing instrument called *titres participatifs* (TPs), which were nonvoting participating securities. They were actually debt instruments paying a return that varied with the issuing company's performance. In October 1983, CGE issued FF1 billion TPs at par (FF1000). The interest, payable annually, contained two parts: (1) a fixed portion equal to 34 percent of the median interest rate on bonds guaranteed by the French Republic; and (2) a variable portion indexed annually to the variation, from its 1982 level, of the CGE Group's share of consolidated cash flow (adjusted for the immediate impact of any acquisitions or divestitures). CGE's TPs had a floor under the interest rate of 8.5 percent but no ceiling. The TPs were nonvoting securities redeemable only at the company's option in 1998 at a price of FF5000 per FF1000 face amount (starting in 1990, they could also be repurchased by CGE in the open market or through a tender offer). A similar issue of 1.1 million TPs was sold in 1985 for FF1.573 billion. The average yield on these securities for 1986 amounted to 9.5 percent of par value.

EXPANSION IN TELECOMMUNICATIONS

One of CGE's last major developments as a nationalized company was its acquisition of ITT's worldwide telecommunications businesses (which were heavily concentrated in Europe) in December 1986. CGE paid ITT $1.5 billion in cash and assumed about $800 million of ITT's liabilities for a 55.6 percent interest in these properties.

Telecommunications technology had undergone rapid change since Alcatel CIT's introduction of its digital central office switch in 1972. Because of their ability to decrease noise and process signals more quickly, digital switches quickly began to replace more conventional analog switches. However, with development costs of a billion dollars or more, competing successfully in the digital switch industry required substantial capital, large-scale manufacturing, and exportation to recoup investment outlays. Long-run profitability was estimated to require at least an 8 percent to 10 percent share of the market worldwide. Because of its size and the opportunities created by the AT&T divestiture in January of 1984, the U.S. market was particularly important to the achievement of this global share. Hence, significant foreign penetration had occurred in the U.S. market, often by means of joint ventures formed between U.S. and foreign companies. Competition was fierce with more than two dozen companies in, or planning to enter, this market. Comparative data on several major competitors are provided in **Exhibit 6**.

The telecommunications businesses of ITT were merged into Alcatel to form one of the largest telecommunications companies in the world, second only in size to AT&T, and placing CGE in the forefront of the European telecommunications industry. In its new form, Alcatel NV was 55.6 percent owned by CGE and 37 percent owned by ITT. Also, Crédit Lyonnais participated in the ownership of the new Alcatel with a 1.7 percent share of the equity, and Société Générale de Belgique, Belgium's largest industrial and financial holding company, owned 5.7 percent. Alcatel was reorganized as a holding company incorporated in the Netherlands and headquartered in Brussels. Reflecting CGE's decentralized management style, Alcatel was to be governed by a management committee to be led by CGE, which would control planning, finance, research and development, and other staff functions. Operating responsibility was left in the hands of six product group managers that reported directly to this committee.

One of the managing committee's major tasks would be to integrate the new Alcatel's many products and companies brought together by the purchases from ITT. CGE had its own digital switch that was being installed in Europe at the rate of 1.7 million lines per year. ITT had developed its own System-12 digital switch that was also being installed at the rate of 2 million lines per year. However, some questions had been raised about the design integrity of the System-12 and its adaptability to the U.S. market. Nevertheless, it was expected that Alcatel would continue to support both product lines for the foreseeable future. Roughly 80 percent of Alcatel NV's revenues were expected to come from products other than digital switches such as cables, private telephone exchanges, screen and videotex terminals, and facsimile machines.

THE TREND TOWARD PRIVATIZATION IN EUROPE

Privatization entails the transfer of whole or partial ownership of companies from governments to the private sector. It emerged as a widespread global phenomenon in the 1980s, first taking root in the United Kingdom and later spreading to Europe and other parts of the world. Free-market economists promoted privatization, arguing that the rigors of risk and reward in the private sector would eliminate waste, increase efficiency, and allow for a more efficient allocation of resources than generally took place among state-owned enterprises. In addition, privatization was heralded as a means of reducing the administrative and financial burdens placed on governments by weakly performing companies. For some economies, it was also seen as a means of broadening and deepening capital markets.

The British Program

Under British Prime Minister Margaret Thatcher's leadership, privatization of state-owned enterprises became an important objective of Britain's Conservative Party in 1979. By 1987, $40 billion dollars of assets and 600,000 jobs were transferred from the state to the private sector, while an estimated 3 million people became shareholders in the United Kingdom for the first time. (The percentage of U.K. citizens who held shares fell from 35 percent to 14 percent between 1961 and 1981. By 1987, this trend had been reversed, with 28 percent of the population owning shares.)

One of the privatizations to take place under the Thatcher government was that of Jaguar, the well-known British producer of automobiles. Jaguar's productivity and quality suffered during its period of nationalization (1975–1984), but starting in 1980, in anticipation of privatization, management improved productivity, technology, and training. Average output per worker increased from 1.3 cars in 1980 to 3.4 cars in 1983. The company provided a return on equity of 37 percent, and it had the second best customer satisfaction ratings in the United States behind Mercedes-Benz. Though not always as noticeable in all privatized firms, this company was clearly more profitable in the private sector. Other major British privatizations included British Telecom in 1984 and British Gas in 1987. British Telecom, with 1984 pretax profit of 990 million pounds sterling (£), had an international floatation of shares worth nearly £4 billion. British Gas had pretax income of almost £2 billion in 1985 and was the largest privatization in British history with a stock offering of £5.6 billion.

The Italian Program

Italy also had an active privatization program, but one considerably newer than that in the United Kingdom. The Ministry of State-owned Companies in the Italian government encompassed three state-owned holding companies: IRI (manufacturing and banking), ENI (petro-chemicals), and EFIM (diversified enterprises). IRI, which had holdings in banking, steel, and telecommunications, was the most deeply involved in privatization. The first large IRI company to be privatized was Alfa Romeo. The car company had been a chronic problem for IRI because of its low market penetration and consequent lack of profitability. It also did not fit the Italian philosophy of owning only those companies in industries deemed strategically important to the nation's future, but with insufficient domestic demand to sustain it. Plans to privatize Alfa Romeo essentially turned into a process of appraising rescue plans put forward by two large private buyers with an international focus in the automobile industry: Ford and Fiat. After extensive negotiations among Fiat, Ford, and IRI representatives, Fiat paid $736 million and assumed $491 million in debt to buy Alfa Romeo. Fiat announced plans to invest an additional $3.9 billion in the company over the next 7 years.

The French Program

France's privatization program began under Jacques Chirac, who was appointed Prime Minister in March 1986. Like Mrs. Thatcher, M. Chirac believed that the rigors of unsubsidized competition in the private sector were essential for companies to be well managed and efficient. M. Chirac also saw privatization as a way of decreasing government spending and reducing the budget deficit. During the election, he promised to implement a privatization program that would return sixty-five recently nationalized banking, insurance, and manufacturing companies to the private sector (the industrial companies nationalized in 1982 and slated for privatization are shown in **Exhibit 7**). Despite efforts by President Mitterrand to cancel the privatization program in July 1986, Prime Minister Chirac successfully pushed through new legislation and had the program on track by September 1986.

The French government's central figure administering the privatization program was the finance minister, Edward Balladur. M. Balladur had worked in the private sector for 10 years before becoming finance minister, most notably as the president of Ceac, an industrial batteries business in the CGE Group, and GSI, a subsidiary specializing in computer services and systems engineering. He, too, saw the privatization program as an attractive source of revenue for other Chirac programs. It had been estimated that FF200 billion to FF250 billion might be realized over the next 5 to 10 years if all the proposed companies were privatized as planned.

Under M. Balladur, a seven-person privatization commission led by Pierre Chatenet, a former minister under Charles de Gaulle and a member of the Council of the State, was formed. This committee presided over the process in which the companies, the financial advisers, and the government implemented privatizations. The steps in the process included: (1) a legislative modification of the company's status, (2) the selection of experts to determine the minimum price and means by which shares would be sold, (3) the preparation of a prospectus by accountants and lawyers, (4) the development of an advertising and information dissemination campaign for investors, and (5) a 2-week subscription period. By law, the offering of shares to foreigners was limited to 20 percent. No individual (domestic or foreign) could obtain more than 5 percent of one of these companies. Commissions were fixed at 0.25 percent for lead underwriters, 1.25 percent for the remaining underwriters collectively, and 0.25 percent for brokers.

The French program was initiated in November of 1986 with the privatization of Saint Gobain, a large glass and engineering company with strong cash flow, consistent earnings, and stable management. Prior to privatization, the French Republic owned 84 percent of the company with the remaining 16 percent being held by nationalized banks and other financial institutions. Following redistribution, ownership was 70 percent in the hands of domestic shareholders, 10 percent in employees' hands, and 20 percent in the hands of international shareholders. When Saint Gobain was offered at FF310 per share, over 1,600,000 French investors rushed to buy the stock. On the first trading day for Saint Gobain, the shares could not be quoted because buy orders completely overwhelmed the number of shares available for sale.

A similar result was obtained in the case of Compagnie Financière de Paribas, France's largest and highly prestigious merchant bank and the second French company to be privatized. The Paribas issue was oversubscribed by a factor of 40 times, resulting in a rationing of four shares per investor rather than ten. Trading in Paribas' stock in the unofficial grey market took place at prices as much as 25 percent higher than the official subscription price of FF405 per share. In commenting on the oversubscriptions of the early offerings, M. Balladur declared that he would rather be "overwhelmed by success than submerged by defeat."[1]

CGE's PRIVATIZATION

When the Chirac government announced the privatization program in 1986, CGE asked immediately to be privatized. But the government was reluctant to make an early commitment on the timing of CGE's privatization (some officials even sought to delay it until after the May 1988 elections). In the meantime, however, they did begin preparations for an eventual privatization by replacing CGE's current chairman with Pierre Suard, who had been chief executive officer of Alcatel. By the end of 1986, M.

---

[1]*Daily Telegraph,* March 6, 1987, p. 70D.

Suard undertook to persuade the government that a rapid privatization of CGE would help smooth the successful completion of ITT acquisitions and would enable the company to finance these acquisitions freely. The government agreed and announced in January 1987 that CGE was scheduled to be privatized in May 1987.

After the government's decision had been made, CGE itself needed to prepare for the process. To do so, the company created an internal task force, led by M. Bilger, executive vice president, that included financial, legal, industrial, communication, and accounting executives from throughout the holding company. Of the numerous policy and implementation issues that the task force had to resolve, the most prominent included (1) establishing an appropriate capital structure, (2) determining how to handle the outstanding TPs, (3) determining an appropriate ownership structure for the equity, and, of course, (4) determining an appropriate offering price for the stock.

Capital Structure   By March 1987, CGE still owed ITT $577 million (FF3.52 billion at the prevailing exchange rates) for its 55.6 percent stake in the new Alcatel company. In light of this debt burden should CGE attempt to raise new equity? If so, how much? Should it be done before (through a rights offering to the government), concurrent with, or after the privatization itself? The privatization would probably be so large that it was not clear when, if ever, would be an appropriate time to raise new equity capital.

Titres Participatifs   Closely associated with the capital structure decision was the question of what to do with the previously issued TPs. The company could leave them outstanding or provide for their conversion into equity at some appropriate rate of exchange. Again, there was also the issue of whether to undertake any conversion before, during, or subsequent to the privatization. In November 1986, TPs were being traded heavily and were increasing in both price and volume (see **Exhibit 8**). On March 7, 1987, trading in TPs was suspended indefinitely.

Ownership Structure   The task force was also expected to make recommendations concerning the ownership structure of CGE's privatized shares. Although the majority of the shares would be sold to the French public at large, special provisions could be made to extend or limit the sale of shares to employees, foreigners, or so-called *noyaux durs*—preselected "hard-core" shareholders.

Employee participation in the ownership of companies had traditionally been low in France. Privatization was viewed by many as an opportunity to develop this potential ownership base further (although the law restricted employee ownership to 10 percent of the company). Employees could be induced to purchase shares by offering them a discount of 5 percent or possibly as much as 20 percent from the subscription price. Restrictions on the transferability of the shares could be established to prevent immediate resale. Another possibility to encourage employee ownership would be to place shares in an employee mutual fund. The latter would entail giving employees some representation on the board of directors.

The French Privatization Law restricted the offering of shares to foreigners to not more than 20 percent, but CGE could elect to restrict that percentage still further at the time of the offering if it wished. The rationale underlying the restriction on foreign ownership was to limit foreign control and reduce the possibility of a foreign takeover.

This concern was further reflected in the *noyaux durs* concept that was employed in the privatization of St. Gobain and Paribas. In both those cases, key institutional shareholders had been asked to purchase shares in the newly privatized companies as a means of providing some stability of share ownership and to diminish the likelihood of a foreign takeover. Paribas's stable shareholders are listed in **Exhibit 9**. In CGE's case, 12.8 percent of its 9.4 million shares outstanding were already owned by a small group of nationalized and private banks. At the time of the privatization, more common stock could be placed in stable hands.

Alternatively, an *Action Specifique* (commonly referred to as a ''golden share'') could be created, which would give the government the right to subject to its authorization the acquisition of more than 10 percent of CGE's shares by one or more persons acting jointly. Generally, however, the government sought to avoid putting such a mechanism in place.

Pricing   Certainly one of the most important technical issues to be addressed was the pricing of CGE's equity. The offering price would have to be attractive enough to entice individual investors to purchase the stock, yet not so low as to provide the state with insufficient value for the shares sold, which would create an opening for criticism from the opposition. At the time, there was considerable public enthusiasm around the world for equity investing. In New York, the stock exchange had doubled in value during the 5 years since 1981. The Tokyo Stock Exchange had risen by nearly 250 percent during the same period, as had the Paris Bourse. This seemed a propitious time to float shares.

A number of factors could be used to value the company. The book value of the common equity, adjusted for the acquisition of the ITT properties, was FF8.4 billion. A revaluation of certain assets to market value would boost this figure by FF5.6 billion. Consolidated sales for 1987 were expected to exceed FF130 billion, with CGE's share of earnings tracking consolidated sales at the same percentage experienced in 1986. Although no price/earnings multiple was directly observable for CGE, management thought the French equity market as a whole seemed to be trading at twelve times earnings. However, based on multiples observed for other French companies in the electrical and telecommunications sector, CGE's stock might be expected to trade at a slightly lower multiple, perhaps equal to 90 percent to 95 percent of that for the market as a whole. Outside forecasts of CGE's performance, such as that shown in **Exhibit 10**, were also made by security analysts around the time of the privatization. Analysts considered an appropriate rate at which to discount future dividends was 12.5 percent.

Complicating the pricing of the issue were the decisions concerning a possible capital increase and the treatment of the TPs. Besides simply increasing the number of shares outstanding, a capital increase at the time of the privatization, if sizable enough, could influence the price at which the equity could be successfully sold. In the case of the TPs, if a holder were given a conversion option at the time of the offering, an appropriate conversion ratio would have to be established to prevent the common stock from being diluted. In the weeks prior to suspension of trading in CGE's TPs, their unit price had risen in heavy volume to FF3010.

Reaching Consensus

The opportunity to return to the private sector and operate on the same terms as its competitors was clearly an important and exciting event for CGE's management. But given the size and complexity of the company, it was equally clear that the job would not be an easy one. CGE's task force had only a few months in which to prepare for this momentous event, a relatively short amount of time in view of the many parties involved and the need to coordinate with the government.

EXHIBIT 1 FINANCIAL ORGANIZATION CHART OF THE CGE GROUP

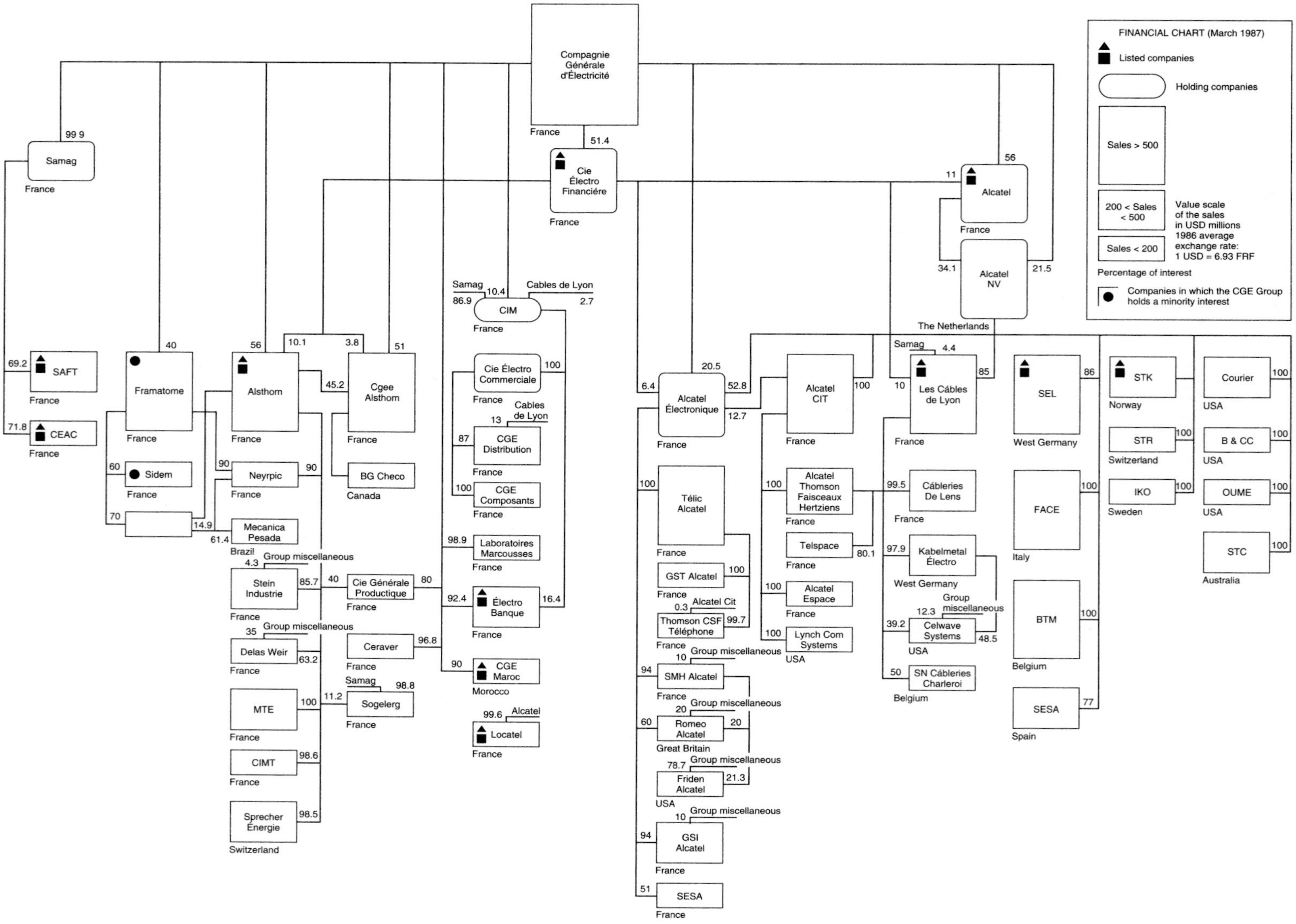

EXHIBIT 2   BALANCE SHEET (MILLIONS)

	1986*	1985
Assets		
Current assets		
Cash and equivalents	FF 8,128.2	FF 8,810.1
Marketable securities	13,800.5	7,776.8
Loans receivable within one year	5,857.6	4,918.0
Accounts receivable, trade	24,874.3	21,331.1
Advances and prepaid expenses	4,861.0	2,302.2
Inventories and work in process	51,699.7	45,212.5
Total current assets	109,221.3	90,350.7
Fixed assets		
Tangible fixed assets	25,729.0	23,686.6
less depreciation	(14,648.2)	(13,638.3)
Intangible fixed assets	447.3	430.7
less amortization	(221.7)	(149.0)
Financial fixed assets, net		
Shareholdings accounted for by the equity method	5,259.9	922.9
Goodwill of consolidated companies	5,029.9	838.7
Shareholdings in nonconsolidated companies	1,791.7	1,374.3
Others	1,636.0	1,220.2
Total fixed assets	25,023.9	14,686.1
Deferred taxes	1,185.1	933.0
Total assets	FF135,430.3	FF105,969.8

*ITT's former subsidiaries were accounted for by the equity method through Alcatel NV. At December 31, 1986, the rate of exchange with the U.S. dollar was FF6.45.

EXHIBIT 2   **BALANCE SHEET (MILLIONS) (CONTINUED)**

	1986*	1985
Liabilities		
Accounts payable, trade	FF 14,193.9	FF 11,299.7
Prepayments from customers	59,257.9	46,860.8
Other nonfinancial debts	10,970.2	10,381.1
Subtotal	84,422.0	68,541.6
Borrowings from financial institutions		
Subordinated loans	575.0	861.0
Convertible bonds[†]	701.9	455.2
Other bonds	2,979.1	1,272.6
Bank and other borrowings	12,339.7	9,781.9
Subtotal	16,595.7	12,370.3
Provisions		
Provisions for risks and expenses	12,498.0	10,027.7
Deferred taxes	822.4	964.5
Subtotal	13,320.4	10,992.2
Capital and surplus (before distribution)		
Capital (9.414 million shares outstanding)	941.4	884.3
Reserves	4,897.1	4,634.6
Premiums	1,429.3	1,086.7
Net income	1,159.5	761.5
Net worth, group share	8,427.3	7,367.1
Minority interests in net worth	10,091.9	4,125.6
Total capital and surplus	18,519.2	11,492.7
Titres participatifs		
(2.1 million TPs outstanding)	2,573.0	2,573.0
Total equity	21,092.2	14,065.7
Of which: Group share	11,000.3	9,940.1
Total liabilities and equity	FF135,430.3	FF105,969.8

*ITT's former subsidiaries were accounted for by the equity method through Alcatel NV. At December 31, 1986, the rate of exchange with the U.S. dollar was FF6.45.
†Convertible into approximately 1.2 million shares of CGE.

EXHIBIT 3   INCOME STATEMENT (MILLIONS)

	1986*	1985
Sales	FF80,902.8	FF71,942.2
Other operating revenues	6,836.9	6,277.1
Total operating revenues	87,739.7	78,219.3
Operating expenses		
Cost of goods sold	(46,320.5)	(41,930.0)
Personnel expenses	(27,271.5)	(24,622.6)
Taxes	(1,799.5)	(1,579.6)
Allocations to operating provisions	(6,885.4)	(5,992.3)
Depreciation and amortization	(2,833.3)	(2,351.9)
Total operating expenses	(85,110.2)	(76,476.4)
Operating Income	2,629.5	1,742.9
Income from joint ventures	58.0	110.6
Income from investment portfolio	1,109.5	698.5
Interest income	1,215.5	1,425.4
Total financial income	2,325.0	2,123.9
Interest expense	(1,857.5)	(1,755.4)
Allocations to financial provisions	(341.9)	(201.0)
Total financial expense	(2,199.4)	(1,956.4)
Net financial income	125.6	167.5
Nonrecurring expenses, net	(346.2)	(389.6)
Employee profit sharing	(93.3)	(66.4)
Income taxes[†]	(754.9)	(407.9)
Currency gains (losses)	4.6	(50.0)
Net income of consolidated companies	1,623.3	1,107.1
Income from companies accounted for by the equity method	98.1	78.4
Net income	FF1,721.4	FF1,185.5
Of which: Group share	1,159.5	761.5
Minority interests	561.9	424.0

*Excluding companies acquired from ITT Corp. on December 30, 1986. The average exchange rate against the dollar for 1986 was FF6.93.
[†]The French marginal corporate tax rate was lowered in 1986 from 50 percent to 45 percent.

EXHIBIT 4 STATEMENT OF CHANGES IN FINANCIAL POSITION (MILLIONS)

	1986*	1985
Sources of funds		
Consolidated net income	FF1,721.4	FF1,185.5
Noncash expenses:		
Depreciation and amortization	2,742.2	2,329.3
Provisions	1,701.3	1,665.5
Less		
Earnings from companies accounted for		
by the equity method	(98.0)	(78.4)
Other changes	(798.1)	(230.5)
Funds provided by operations	5,273.8	4,871.4
Of which:		
Cash flow from operations (net		
income plus depreciation)	4,463.6	3,514.8
Proceeds from disposals of fixed assets	4,504.8	1,698.3
Other reductions in financial		
fixed assets	549.7	256.5
Capital increases	1,729.5	243.7
Increase in nonvoting participating		
securities	—	1,573.0
Increase in borrowings	6,569.7	1,905.8
Other sources	56.7	42.2
Total sources	FF18,684.2	FF10,590.9
Uses of funds		
Dividends and distributions	FF497.8	FF372.1
Purchase of fixed assets:		
Tangible and intangible assets	3,321.4	2,814.3
Financial assets	10,030.6	1,409.7
Increase in expenses attributable to		
other years	47.7	15.8
Reduction of capital	35.5	19.1
Reduction in borrowings	2,710.3	1,783.7
Total uses	FF16,643.3	FF6,414.7

*The average exchange rate against the dollar for 1986 was FF6.93.

EXHIBIT 5 BREAKDOWN OF ACTIVITIES (1986)

Sector	Sales		Net income		Cash flow		Capital spending	
	FF millions	% Total	FF millions	% Total	FF millions	% Total	FF millions	% Total
I. Sector								
Energy and transportation	22,402.4	27.7	357	20.8	1,181	26.4	693	17.8
Nuclear	5,201.2	6.4	231	13.4	326	7.3	177	4.5
Batteries	2,945.5	3.6	120	7.0	282	6.3	237	6.1
Telecommunications and business systems	25,715.6	31.8	392	22.7	1,418	31.7	1,765	45.3
Cables	10,591.0	13.1	265	15.4	742	16.6	576	14.8
Electrical contracting and industrial process control	10,348.0	12.8	103	6.0	230	5.1	229	5.9
Services and other	3,699.1	4.6	253	14.7	290	6.6	220	5.6
Total	80,902.8	100.0	1,721	100.0	4,469	100.0	3,897	100.0

EXHIBIT 5   SALES BREAKDOWN (1986) (CONTINUED)

	FF millions	% Total
II. Location		
France	51,842.8	64.1
West Germany	3,856.7	4.8
United Kingdom	1,050.8	1.3
Other EEC countries	2,479.6	3.1
Rest of Europe	3,590.0	4.4
Africa	3,392.9	4.2
United States of America	2,696.7	3.3
Canada	819.9	1.0
Latin America	2,233.8	2.8
Middle East	2,388.0	3.0
Far East	1,184.4	1.5
China	401.2	0.5
Rest of Asia	2,349.8	2.9
Rest of the world	2,636.2	3.3
Total	80,902.8	100.0

EXHIBIT 6   COMPARATIVE DATA ON KEY COMPETITORS, 1986 ($ MILLIONS, RATIOS AND GROWTH RATES)

	AT&T	Northern Telecom	Siemens A.G.	NEC	Philips	L. M. Ericsson
Financial statements						
Revenue	34,087.0	4,383.6	23,270.6	13,381.0	25,108.1	4,640.6
Net income	1,843.0	313.2	729.6	151.4	463.0	82.6
Assets	38,883.0	3,961.1	28,866.9*	14,399.5	23,097.6	5,020.1
Debt	24,421.0	1,694.1	8,906.3	11,626.5	11,643.2	2,682.7
Equity	14,462.0	2,267.0	19,960.7	2,773.1	11,454.4	2,337.4
Selected financial ratios						
Net profit margin, %	5.41	7.14	3.14	1.13	1.84	1.78
Return on equity, %	12.74	13.82	3.66	5.46	4.04	3.53
Asset turnover	0.88	1.11	0.81	0.93	1.09	0.92
Current ratio	1.39	2.20	1.60	1.20	1.70	1.90
Debt/total capital, %	62.81	42.77	30.85	80.74	50.41	53.44
Price/earnings ratio	15.24	17.90	22.30	135.40	10.00	17.30
Annual growth rate 1981–1986						
Revenue, %	−10.10	18.70	6.40	17.50	5.40	14.30
Net income, %	−23.10	27.40	26.50	4.20	23.20	5.60

*Siemens' total assets included $10.8 billion of cash and marketable securities.

EXHIBIT 7   INDIVIDUAL COMPANIES SELECTED FOR PRIVATIZATION

Compagnie Générale d'Electricité
Pechiney, S.A.
Saint-Gobain
Rhône-Poulenc, S.A.
Thomson, S.A.
Compagnie des Machines Bull
Compagnie Générale de Construction Téléphonique
Matra, S.A.
Société Nationale Elf-Aquitaine

EXHIBIT 8   TRADING DATA FOR TPs (FF/SHARE, EXCEPT TRADING VOLUME)

	High	Low	Median	Average daily trading volume, number of shares
1983	1059.5	1008.0	1032.37	5643
1984	1595.0	1055.1	1375.54	4054
1985	1640.0	1375.0	1476.96	2624
1986	2940.0	1622.0	2516.93	5286
1987 (through March 10)	3010.0	2450.0	2752.14	6563

EXHIBIT 9   STABLE SHAREHOLDERS FOR COMPAGNIE FINANCIÈRE DE PARIBAS*

Shareholder	% Ownership
Total—Compagnie Française des Pétroles	4.00
Union des Assurances de Paris	4.00
Assurances Générales de France	2.67
Mutuelles Unies Assurances	2.67
Paror (L'Oréal)	1.33
Caisse Nationale de Prévoyance	0.80
Compagnie Financière S.G.T.E. (Schneider, S.A.)	0.80
Compagnie Générale des Eaux	0.80
Compagnie de Navigation Mixte et Vie	0.80
France—Developpement (Frandev)	0.80
Groupe des Assurances Nationales (GAN)	0.80
Groupe Bruxelles—Lambert France, S.A.	0.80
Genet Comit Gestione, S.A.	0.80
G.M.F. Vie	0.80
Groupe des Populaires d'Assurance	0.80
Kuwait Investment Authority	0.80
Sumitomo Life Insurance Company	0.80
Total stable shareholding	24.27

*By agreement, stable shareholders must keep 80 percent of the shares allocated to them in the public offering for at least 2 years. After 2 years, Paribas had a pre-emptive right for 3 years with respect to 80 percent of any stable shares offered for resale.

EXHIBIT 10   INDEPENDENT FORECASTS OF CGE'S PROFIT AND DIVIDEND GROWTH (FF MILLIONS, EXCEPT PERCENTAGES)

	1987	1988	1989	1990	1991
Net profit (group share)	1745	1990	2190	2440	2690
Growth,	—	14.0	10.0	11.4	10.2
Payout ratio, %	28.7	30.2	31.8	33.4	35.0
Dividends	500	601	696	815	941

Source: Fauchier-Magnan, Durant des Aulnois, S.A.

COMPREHENSIVE REVIEW
AND SYNTHESIS

DAINIPPON INK AND CHEMICALS, INCORPORATED

On June 25, 1987, Mr. Shigekuni Kawamura, president of Dainippon Ink and Chemicals (DIC), sent the following letter to members of the Board of Directors of Reichhold Chemicals, Inc.:

Members of the Board:

As I am certain you are aware, in a letter delivered to your chairman, Mr. Powell, on June 9, 1987, Dainippon Ink and Chemicals sought to press forward the discussions we have been engaged in with Reichhold since the early Spring looking toward an acquisition of Reichhold by DIC. . . . I had hoped that the transaction outlined in my letter would provide the basis for continued negotiations. However, since our discussions with your financial advisors have not been fruitful, we believe we have no choice at this time but to take our offer to Reichhold's stockholders for their consideration.

Accordingly, an indirect wholly-owned subsidiary of DIC has today commenced a tender offer to purchase all of the outstanding shares of Reichhold's common stock (together with the associated Preferred Stock Purchase Rights) for $52.50 in cash per share. . . .

By the end of July, neither Reichhold nor DIC had won the battle that followed the announcement of DIC's unsolicited tender offer. Reichhold had not located a buyer willing to outbid DIC and many analysts asserted that the low value of the U.S. dollar would prevent the rescue of Reichhold by a U.S. white knight. Nevertheless, Reichhold's stock price stubbornly remained above the $52.50 per share offered by DIC. DIC had twice extended the open period of its offer, most recently to August 28,

This case was prepared by Professors Timothy A. Luehrman and Kevin Rock. Copyright © 1989 by the President and Fellows of Harvard College. Harvard Business School case 289-067.

1987, but had refused to increase its bid. During the first week of August, Mr. Kawamura and DIC's directors considered what might be done in the face of a continuing stalemate.

COMPANY BACKGROUND

DIC was one of Japan's leading diversified chemical companies, specializing in printing inks, organic pigments, and synthetic resins. It was the world's largest producer of printing inks, having acquired leading ink manufacturers in the United States and the Federal Republic of Germany during 1986. It was also the world's third largest producer of organic pigments. In the fiscal year ending March 31, 1987, DIC had sales of 448,951 million yen (¥) and net income of ¥6472 million. A summary of recent operating and financial results is presented in **Exhibits 1** and **2**.

DIC's objective was to become a global market leader by using its strengths in research and development to develop competitive advantages in otherwise mature markets. DIC's managers felt that this could not be accomplished with an export strategy. To be responsive to customers' needs, DIC's research and development (R&D) capability had to be located near its customers. Moreover, the specialized inks and resins developed for use in high-speed offset printing equipment could not be shipped long distances. As a result, DIC's operations were carried out by a globally dispersed group of 135 companies in twenty-nine countries and DIC had been an acquirer of North American and European companies for more than a decade.

THE PRINTING AND GRAPHIC ARTS BUSINESS

DIC's major strategic thrust of the 1980s had been in the printing and graphics arts business that grew from its traditional strengths in organic pigments and printing inks. Although demand in the industry had long been considered mature, by 1980 technological advances had begun to affect competition among printers and among their suppliers and customers. The changes were especially visible in two areas.

First, high-quality four-color printing had become faster and less costly. Color originals could be digitized and the digital information stored on optical disks or other high-capacity electronic storage media. This digital information could then be fed into computerized automatic drawing, mask-cutting, image-processing, proofing, and film-composing systems. Such systems were capable of further processing the digital image, merging it with other images, and performing layout tasks, such as combining images with text on a page. The systems also were capable of outputting fully laid-out text and illustrations onto photographic negatives. The negatives could then be used with photosensitive plates to produce offset plates for high-speed color offset printing presses. The digitization of inputs and the extensive computerization of printing and preprinting processes had eliminated the need for many skilled, experienced operators and thus lowered printing costs.

Advances in color printing resulted in increased use of color by advertisers in newspapers and magazines, and hence more four-color periodicals. Color printing also became more economical for the growing business of mail- and telephone-order catalog retailing. Since the various technologies had come from diverse sectors of the economy, equipment and materials suppliers included both small specialized firms producing a few system components, and large multinationals such as Eastman Kodak, Polaroid, Xerox, and Du Pont.

The second major area of technological advancement was in high-speed transmission of digital data over long distances via satellite, telephone cable, and fiber optic networks. This permitted many preprinting functions to be centralized and their output transmitted in digital form to presses located near distribution channels. Transmitting data rather than shipping printed periodicals resulted in significant transportation cost savings and spurred the growth of national and international readership for daily newspapers such as *The Wall Street Journal, The New York Times,* the *Financial Times,* and *USA Today.* In addition, the development of service bureaus offering a full range of graphic arts, preprinting, and printing services made the technical advances in color printing and image transmission available to smaller customers.

An early move by DIC into the broader printing and graphic arts business came with its acquisition in 1979 of Polychrome Corporation, a U.S. manufacturer of printing plates and supplies. Polychrome's platemaking technologies and DIC's development of light-reacting polymers had since resulted in advances in photosensitive platemaking processes. In July 1981, DIC organized a Printing Supplies Division to coordinate the company's graphic arts and printing related businesses. By 1987, DIC's product offerings spanned nearly the entire range of equipment and supplies related to modern commercial and industrial printing. They included inks, pigments, adhesives, preprinting systems, printing presses, and printing supplies. A summary of the printing and graphic arts product line is presented in **Exhibit 3**. In industry parlance, DIC was a "mega-vendor," able to design, manufacture, and/or provision the necessary satellite downlinks, workstations, electronic prepresses, and specialized inks, papers, presses, computer, data transmission, and process technologies for an efficient color printing operation.

Some of DIC's products were manufactured in Japan, partly from imported raw materials, both for sale domestically and for export. Others were not manufactured by DIC, but purchased from original equipment manufacturers (OEMS) integrated into DIC-designed and -supplied systems for resale to DIC's customers. For example, DIC imported and sold multicolor offset printing presses produced by an OEM in Germany. Still other products were produced and sold outside Japan by DIC affiliates and subsidiaries. For particular products, DIC had active, often strong competition, both from Japanese and non-Japanese manufacturers. Summary data on selected Japanese ink and chemical producers are presented in **Exhibit 4**. However, none of the Japanese competitors had yet emerged as a dominant mega-vendor.

ACQUISITION OF SUN CHEMICAL'S GRAPHIC ARTS DIVISION

DIC's most recent acquisitions reflected a long-held strategic objective. The Hartmann Group, a leading European ink manufacturer, was acquired in 1986 for $55 million. The purchase of Sun Chemical's Graphic Arts Division for $550 million in November

1986 gave DIC a strong position in the United States, the world's largest printing market.

Sun Chemical was the leading U.S. producer of pigments and printing inks. DIC's attempts to acquire the company dated back to negotiations initiated in 1980, not long after the purchase of Polychrome. At that time, DIC and Sun could not agree on a price, and negotiations stalled, then deadlocked, and eventually were broken off. In early 1986, DIC publicly announced its willingness to purchase either Sun's graphic arts business for $425 million, or the entire company for $600 million ($77 per share). DIC commenced a tender offer at this price in April 1986. Sun Chemical's chairman resisted the offer and increased his personal holdings of Sun Chemical stock to 44.6 percent of the outstanding shares. Sun then also hastened efforts to complete an acquisition of Chromalloy American Corporation, in an effort to thwart DIC's takeover attempt.

DIC's attempt to acquire Sun was another in which analysts felt exchange-rate levels played a significant role. At the time DIC first approached Sun, the yen/dollar exchange rate had been falling and had recently dropped below ¥250/$1. The dollar then rose and remained strong through 1984. In early 1985, however, the yen began to rise, and during 1985 and 1986, it was the strongest major currency in the world. By the end of April 1986, the time of DIC's bid for Sun, the yen/dollar spot rate stood at ¥175/$1 (see **Exhibit 5**).

In May 1986, DIC increased its bid for Sun Chemical to $665 million. With the share purchases by Sun's chairman under investigation by the U.S. Securities and Exchange Commission, with Sun's credit rating under review by bond rating agencies, and with numerous shareholder lawsuits seeking to block Sun's acquisition of Chromalloy American, Sun Chemical agreed in June to reopen negotiations with DIC for the sale of its graphic arts division. Sun and DIC signed a definitive agreement for the sale of the business for $550 million on November 20. The exchange rate was ¥155/$1. The purchase was financed in part by DIC's sale in August 1986 of $250 million of U.S. dollar 3.5 percent 7-year notes with detachable warrants.

DIC's 1987 report to shareholders reviewed the company's recent advances in the global graphic arts business. It stated that DIC planned to continue its efforts in graphic arts and to realize future growth in its other businesses by similarly pursuing global leadership through R&D. Other main businesses included synthetic resins, new recording media, plastics, petrochemicals, biochemicals, and building materials.

REICHHOLD CHEMICALS, INC.

Reichhold Chemicals was a manufacturer of specialty chemicals, including adhesives, resins, and other polymers and serving primarily industrial customers. The company was based in White Plains, New York, and organized in six divisions. The Swift Adhesives Division produced industrial adhesives. It had been acquired in 1985 and had sales of $106 million in 1986. The Chemical Coatings Division was organized in 1986 and contained Reichhold's architectural and industrial coatings businesses, which had sales in 1986 of $98 million. The Newport Division also was created in 1986 and focused on resins for adhesives, printing inks, and papermaking. It had 1986 sales of $69 million. The Emulsions Polymers Division produced a broad line of latexes for paper coatings, paints, adhesives, carpet backing, and plastics. This division had been especially active in product development—80 percent of its products had been introduced within the last 5 years. Sales in 1986 were $129 million. The Reactive Polymers Division, with 1986 sales of $86 million, produced saturated polyester resins and catalysts for the transportation, construction, and recreation industries. Finally, Reichhold had major foreign subsidiaries in Canada, Switzerland, and Mexico, producing a broad line of adhesives, resins, and polymers, and accounting for $224 million in sales in 1986. Divisional sales and operating profits are presented in **Exhibit 6**.

In 1987 Reichhold Chemicals was nearing the completion of a two-stage restructuring program. The program was undertaken in 1982 following the retirement of Henry H. Reichhold, the company's founder and chairman. Mr. Reichhold founded the company in 1928 and, as chairman, he had placed a heavy emphasis recently on sales growth, adopting a goal of $1 billion in sales. In 1981, the year before Mr. Reichhold retired, sales reached $950 million. However, return on sales and return on equity had been disappointing at 1.5 percent and 8.5 percent, respectively, and the company's stock price languished well below book value. Historical financial data for Reichhold are presented in **Exhibit 7**.

Mr. Reichhold's replacement, C. Robert Powell, was recruited from outside the company. He immediately embarked on a program to raise return on equity to 20 percent. This was to be accomplished in stages. The first stage involved foregoing unprofitable sales and exiting marginal businesses, thus shrinking sales and improving margins. The second stage involved acquisitions, divestitures, and plant upgrades, and increased R&D expenditures to extend product lines and lower costs. The first stage was completed by the end of 1983. In 1984, Reichhold's managers published a set of financial goals for 1987. These included: return on average equity of 20 percent; return on sales of 5 percent; return on average capital of 13 to 14 percent; a payout ratio of 20 to 25 percent; and a single-A credit rating.

Two problems in 1985 and 1986 interrupted the progress of the second stage of the restructuring. First, a number of acquisitions during this period were made for cash and preceded planned divestitures. As a result, the company's debt and associated interest expenses increased substantially. Second, many of Reichhold's U.S. customers, primarily manufacturers of finished goods, had suffered erosion of their market positions during the period of the dollar's strength, from 1981 through 1984. Although Reichhold itself had not suffered greatly from direct foreign competition, the company reported that damage to its customers resulted in lower than anticipated volume and margins in 1985 and 1986. Recent financial statements for Reichhold appear in **Exhibits 8** and **9**.

At the end of 1986, many analysts forecasted a strong recovery from these problems as divestitures were completed, as the company further realigned production facilities to lower costs, and as the dollar weakened. Wall Street analysts expected 1987 earnings per share of about $3.50; with the stock trading at $31 per share in December 1986, many recommended purchasing the shares.

DIC's Attempts to Acquire Reichhold

DIC operated in nearly all of Reichhold's product lines and felt that substantial synergies could be realized by combining the companies' development efforts in synthetic resins and polymers. These would complement both DIC's synthetic resins and its printing and graphic arts businesses, including the newly acquired Sun Group. Moreover, Reichhold's location in the Northeast near established satellite downlinks and large print media markets was attractive. DIC's alternative to an acquisition of a company such as Reichhold was to build the desired manufacturing and distributing capacity from scratch.

DIC began to purchase Reichhold shares on the open market in December 1986. By mid-March 1987 DIC owned 338,900 (4.54 percent) of the outstanding shares. Beginning in March, a number of meetings took place between top management at DIC and Reichhold to discuss possible business combinations, including the acquisition of Reichhold by DIC. On June 9 Mr. Kawamura proposed to Mr. Powell that DIC purchase Reichhold for $50 per share, a 37 percent premium over the closing price of $36.38 on June 8. Reichhold responded that it was unwilling to enter into discussions with DIC unless DIC was prepared to consider a substantially higher price. DIC declined to pursue discussions on this basis and launched its tender offer on June 25 at a price of $52.50 per share. Reichhold's stock price reacted swiftly, opening at $56.00 and closing at $60.50 on June 25. See **Exhibit 10** for daily stock price and exchange-rate movements.

On July 1 Reichhold's board of directors formally rejected DIC's offer as inadequate and urged shareholders not to tender their shares while the company pursued alternatives. These included a management buyout or other recapitalization, breaking up the company and selling its pieces, and merger with a white knight. Reichhold had adopted numerous antitakeover defenses, such as a supermajority provision and a poison pill. Moreover, 15 percent of Reichhold's shares was owned by Teledyne, Inc., and another 10 percent was owned or controlled by management and directors.

On July 8, Reichhold agreed to give DIC access to certain nonpublic information being provided to other potential bidders. In return, DIC extended the expiration date of its offer to August 6 and said it would consider whether to revise its bid based on the new information. On July 21 DIC again extended the expiration date of its tender offer, this time to August 28. The following day, July 22, DIC notified Reichhold and the financial community that it had decided not to increase its offer of $52.50 per share. Reichhold's stock price fell from $62.25 on July 21 to $59.88 on July 22. On July 31 it closed at $59.38.

The continuing stalemate puzzled many observers. On the one hand, Mr. Powell expressed his belief that Reichhold was worth $70 per share. The firm's investment bankers were known to be aggressively seeking buyers for the company and/or its pieces. However, by the end of July, many major chemical companies in the United States and Europe were thought to have examined the company and decided not to bid. A leveraged buyout was thought to be feasible only at a rather small premium to DIC's cash offer.

The lack of competing bids was often explained in the financial press by the strength of the yen and/or the high level of the Japanese equity market. These factors supposedly gave DIC an advantage over U.S. and European bidders and many observers felt the company would inevitably be acquired by DIC. Nevertheless, Reichhold's stock price remained well above DIC's $52.50 offer. In early August, Mr. Kawamura and DIC's directors had to decide whether to change tactics or simply to leave their offer outstanding and wait. Contemporary macroeconomic and capital market data appear in **Exhibit 11**.

EXHIBIT 1   DAINIPPON INK AND CHEMICALS, INCORPORATED—CONSOLIDATED FINANCIAL STATEMENTS; YEAR ENDED MARCH 31 (BILLIONS)

	1987	1986	1985
Net sales*	¥448.0	¥472.8	¥459.4
Income before taxes and equity in unconsolidated gains or losses	15.8	11.4	12.6
Equity in unconsolidated gains (losses)	(0.8)	0.2	(0.5)
Net income	6.5	4.2	6.3
Assets†			
Cash, deposits, and securities	59.5	54.7	54.2
Notes and accounts receivable	127.1	112.6	121.3
Inventories	73.1	64.3	68.0
Other	14.8	7.6	7.1
Total current assets	274.5	239.3	250.6
Fixed assets	150.4	108.0	102.3
Investments and long-term loans	46.7	34.5	33.4
Other assets	37.1	2.7	6.6
Total assets	508.7	384.5	392.9
Liabilities and equity†			
Notes and accounts payable	121.8	116.1	126.8
Short-term bank debt	125.3	73.7	62.6
Current portion of long-term debt	17.0	17.0	17.5
Other current liabilities	30.1	22.2	19.3
Total current liabilities	294.2	229.0	226.2
Long-term debt	109.4	58.1	73.4
Pension liability reserves‡	7.6	7.0	6.4
Other liabilities	1.8	0.2	—
Shareholders' equity	95.7	90.2	87.0
Total liabilities and equity	¥508.7	¥384.5	¥392.9

*Net sales for 1987 are consolidated, but exclude the Sun Group and Hartmann Group, which were acquired near the end of their respective fiscal yearends.
†Balance sheet data for March 31, 1987, include both Sun and Hartmann Groups.
‡The reserve equals 40 percent of the lump sum severance settlements that would be incurred if all employees left voluntarily on the balance sheet date.

EXHIBIT 2   DAINIPPON INK AND CHEMICALS, INCORPORATED—UNCONSOLIDATED HISTORICAL FINANCIAL DATA; YEAR ENDED MARCH 31 (BILLIONS, EXCEPT AS NOTED)

	1987	1986	1985	1984	1983	1982	1981	1980	1979	1978
Revenues	¥390.0	¥415.3	¥401.5	¥398.0	¥379.4	¥368.6	¥351.8	¥325.3	¥261.2	¥240.9
Operating income	15.1	12.9	14.7	14.4	14.9	14.0	16.5	16.0	10.2	10.7
Net income	5.5	5.0	4.9	4.5	4.2	4.2	4.7	4.6	4.1	3.7
Cash and securities	47.0	44.9	30.1	42.8	41.3	37.4	34.2	42.0	30.6	33.8
Total assets	382.9	342.1	348.4	347.5	341.8	337.3	321.2	297.1	234.7	225.7
Long-term debt	86.4	50.5	57.9	72.9	78.1	83.8	78.5	76.6	59.7	61.8
Short-term debt	54.6	49.0	43.4	50.4	55.8	52.3	52.2	38.3	28.5	31.2
Equity	101.4	97.8	94.6	76.8	70.9	68.1	60.0	48.9	44.6	38.1
No. shares, millions	606.0	599.7	593.3	534.5	493.5	487.0	463.0	428.3	380.5	358.4
Book value/share, ¥	167	163	159	144	144	140	130	114	117	106
Stock price, ¥/share	621	387	274	267	242	198	255	265	239	184
Earnings/share, ¥	9.08	8.34	8.26	8.42	8.51	8.62	10.15	10.74	10.78	10.32
Dividend/share, ¥	6.00	6.00	6.00	6.00	6.00	6.00	6.00	6.00	6.00	6.50
Price/earnings ratio, times	68.4	46.4	33.2	31.7	28.4	23.0	25.1	24.7	22.2	17.8
Return on sales, %	1.4	1.2	1.2	1.1	1.1	1.1	1.3	1.4	1.6	1.5
Return on beginning equity, %	5.6	5.3	6.4	6.3	6.2	7.0	9.6	10.3	10.8	10.5
Capital expenditures	12.1	10.8	9.5	8.3	5.9	14.4	20.6	9.6	9.7	7.6
Depreciation	9.6	9.1	8.3	8.5	8.8	8.3	7.6	7.2	6.8	6.3

Note: These figures are not consolidated and therefore are not directly comparable to those in Exhibit 1.

EXHIBIT 3 **DAINIPPON INK AND CHEMICALS' PRINTING AND GRAPHIC ARTS PRODUCT OFFERINGS**

Printing inks: offset, web offset, gravure, flexo, news, letterpress, screen, jet

Pigments: organic and synthetic, specialized coloring agents

Resins: alkyds, acrylics, polyurethanes, polyamides, water-bornes, hard resins, synthetic latexes, perfluorochemicals, flame-retardants, epoxies

Adhesives: dry-laminating, heat-sealable, solventless, hot melts

Varnishes

Can coatings: interior and exterior, metal-decorating inks

Printing and process work supplies: graphic arts films, presensitized plates, platemaking chemicals

Preprinting equipment: layout scanners, color film classifying machines, automatic drawing and mask cutting systems, automated page makeup systems, film processors, platemaking machinery, ultraviolet and infrared curing systems

Pressure-sensitive adhesive materials: paper and film, marking film, labels and seals

Imaging and reprographic products: magnetic tapes and coatings, specialty coatings for optical fiber and compact disks

Printing presses: sheet-fed offset, web offset, rotary gravure, and flexographic printing presses; metal-decorating machines and coaters

Prepress equipment: rotogravure cylinder processing equipment

Postpress and bookbinding equipment: paper-folding, -cutting, -punching, and -gluing machines

EXHIBIT 4 COMPARATIVE UNCONSOLIDATED FINANCIAL DATA FOR SELECTED JAPANESE CHEMICAL MANUFACTURERS (YEAR ENDED MARCH 31, 1987; IN BILLIONS, EXCEPT AS NOTED)

	Toyo Ink Mfg.	Dainichiseika Colour & Chemicals	Kanegafuchi Chemical Ind.	Shin-Etsu Chemical	Kyowa Hakko Kogyo	Kureha Chemical Ind.
Industry classification	Inks and pigments	Inks and pigments	Synthetic resins	Synthetic resins	Fine chemicals	Fine chemicals
Revenues	¥166.8	¥106.2	¥175.3	¥216.4	¥224.3	¥114.9
Operating income	8.1	4.2	12.7	16.8	17.2	20.9
Net income	4.0	1.8	5.7	7.7	5.5	9.5
Cash and securities	21.9	9.4	39.8	14.2	14.9	19.7
Total assets	127.0	76.7	167.7	195.6	230.4	135.0
Long-term debt	0.5	3.4	21.2	26.7	17.8	15.2
Short-term debt	3.4	15.3	31.3	28.0	19.0	11.8
Equity	76.4	20.6	70.0	65.7	97.7	59.5
No. shares, millions	266.9	82.9	314.2	294.5	386.1	218.8
Book value/share, ¥	286	248	223	223	253	272
Stock price, ¥/share	560	671	730	1280	1833	1240
Earnings/share, ¥	14.92	21.94	18.04	26.15	14.21	43.24
Dividend/share, ¥	7.00	10.00	6.00	6.00	6.00	7.50
Price/earnings ratio, times	37.5	30.6	40.5	48.9	129.0	28.7
Return on sales, %	2.4	1.7	3.3	3.6	2.5	8.3
Return on equity, %	5.3	10.0	8.4	12.9	6.0	13.2
Capital expenditures	5.9	2.7	14.1	11.8	8.9	11.6
Depreciation	5.0	1.7	10.7	9.8	8.4	7.0

Note: These figures are not consolidated.

EXHIBIT 5 END-OF-PERIOD QUARTERLY YEN/DOLLAR AND DEUTSCHE MARK/DOLLAR EXCHANGE RATES, I-1978 THROUGH II-1987

Quarter	¥/$	DM/$	Quarter	¥/$	DM/$
1978-I	¥223.4	DM1.9976	1983-I	¥239.3	DM2.4287
II	204.5	2.0717	II	239.8	2.5439
III	189.2	1.9404	III	236.1	2.6309
IV	195.1	1.8205	IV	232.0	2.7278
1979-I	209.3	1.8683	1984-I	224.8	2.6603
II	217.0	1.8366	II	237.5	2.7825
III	223.5	1.7413	III	245.4	3.0238
IV	239.5	1.7274	IV	250.3	3.1365
1980-I	249.8	1.9309	1985-I	250.7	3.0863
II	217.6	1.7581	II	249.0	3.0599
III	212.9	1.8067	III	222.8	2.6568
IV	209.3	1.9677	IV	202.9	2.4870
1981-I	211.4	2.1227	1986-I	180.0	2.3175
II	225.8	2.3824	II	165.9	2.2125
III	227.8	2.3354	III	154.4	2.0420
IV	220.3	2.2366	IV	163.2	2.0065
1982-I	246.6	2.3955	1987-I	149.0	1.8222
II	257.2	2.4829	II	147.1	1.8257
III	265.8	2.5085			
IV	235.3	2.3742			

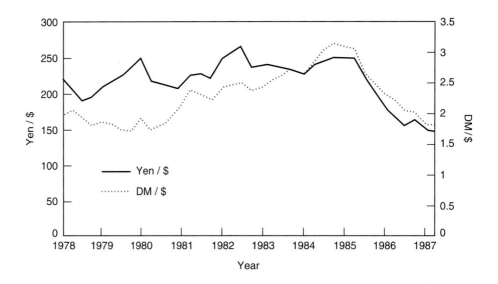

EXHIBIT 6   REICHHOLD CHEMICALS, INC., SEGMENT DATA (MILLIONS)

Division*	1986	1985
Swift Adhesives†		
Sales	$106.1	$ 65.0
Operating profit	6.0	2.1
Chemical Coatings		
Sales	98.0	107.3
Operating profit	2.3	(4.8)
Newport		
Sales	69.0	72.5
Operating profit	1.2	(6.0)
Emulsion Polymers		
Sales	129.2	132.3
Operating profit	14.0	4.4
Reactive Polymers		
Sales	86.0	91.6
Operating profit	1.3	(2.2)
Foreign Subsidiaries		
Sales	223.8	186.5
Operating profit	14.0	9.4

*Figures for operating profits in all divisions reflect some charges related to Reichhold's restructuring program.
†The Swift Adhesives Division was acquired in 1985; figures for that year do not represent a whole year's operations.

EXHIBIT 7 REICHHOLD CHEMICALS, INC.—CONSOLIDATED HISTORICAL FINANCIAL DATA; YEAR ENDED DECEMBER 31 (MILLIONS, EXCEPT AS NOTED)

	1986	1985	1984	1983	1982	1981	1980	1979	1978
Net sales	$765.6	$822.5	$801.4	$747.3	$814.9	$950.1	$885.1	$874.9	$753.9
Interest expense	12.0	10.2	4.4	2.6	5.4	6.6	6.7	7.7	7.4
Net income	15.9	(28.4)	25.7	21.7	4.7	14.7	16.1	12.2	12.0
Working capital	70.1	55.4	95.0	98.5	117.5	129.8	124.3	120.4	106.3
Total assets	458.4	496.1	373.8	384.8	366.9	408.6	428.2	429.3	397.6
Long-term debt	92.9	104.6	48.1	50.7	58.6	73.9	81.2	91.7	76.7
Preferred stock	—	—	—	30.0	35.0	35.0	35.0	35.0	35.0
Common equity	196.1	178.9	208.4	183.6	168.3	174.8	172.4	163.5	159.7
Earnings/share, $	2.13	(3.85)	3.63	2.74	0.25	2.04	1.90	1.34	1.32
Dividends/share, $	0.80	0.80	0.65	0.51	0.48	0.48	0.61	0.74	0.74
Book value/share, $	26.31	24.14	28.37	26.33	24.28	25.23	24.88	23.58	23.04
Stock price, high, $/share	38.25	43.13	35.63	38.88	19.63	16.00	15.00	16.00	16.63
Stock price, low, $/share	28.38	29.75	23.00	18.25	10.00	11.13	9.63	11.25	10.75
Beta	0.90								
Return on sales, %	2.1	(3.5)	3.2	2.9	0.6	1.5	1.8	1.4	1.6
Return on average equity, %	8.5	(15.1)	12.2	10.3	2.3	7.1	7.7	6.0	6.1
Capital expenditures	40.9	35.0	24.2	19.3	20.5	15.9	22.7	26.1	24.3
Depreciation	21.5	23.4	20.2	19.0	20.1	20.9	20.3	19.6	20.3

EXHIBIT 8   REICHHOLD CHEMICALS, INC.—CONSOLIDATED BALANCE SHEETS, YEAR
ENDED DECEMBER 31 ($ MILLIONS)

	1986	1985	1984	1983
Assets				
Cash and securities	$ 15.74	$ 9.15	$ 8.71	$ 7.34
Accounts receivable	93.22	108.02	99.03	106.34
Inventories	64.22	75.85	56.40	59.15
Other current assets	22.67	26.41	11.69	11.47
Total current assets	195.85	219.43	175.83	184.30
Net fixed assets	202.99	203.97	172.22	175.72
Investments in affiliates	14.77	12.07	13.33	14.01
Goodwill (net)	32.15	44.18	2.01	2.48
Other assets	12.70	16.43	10.44	8.24
Total assets	$458.45	$496.08	$373.83	$384.76
Liabilities and equity				
Bank notes	$ 11.17	$ 28.83	$ 3.13	$ 7.56
Current portion of long-term debt	5.19	6.49	5.57	5.61
Accounts payable	53.88	58.54	53.22	49.08
Accruals	55.55	70.21	18.96	23.54
Total current liabilities	125.79	164.07	80.88	85.79
Long-term debt	92.94	104.59	48.13	50.71
Deferred taxes	23.81	20.98	33.11	30.68
Other liabilities	15.51	9.41	1.04	1.10
Minority interests	4.32	18.14	2.25	2.92
Preferred stock	—	—	—	30.00
Common equity	196.09	178.89	208.43	183.57
Total liabilities and equity	$458.45	$496.08	$373.83	$384.76

EXHIBIT 9   REICHHOLD CHEMICALS, INC.—CONSOLIDATED STATEMENTS OF INCOME; YEAR ENDED DECEMBER 31 ($ MILLIONS, EXCEPT AS NOTED)

	1986	1985	1984	1983
Net sales	$765.59	$822.53	$801.36	$747.26
Cost of goods sold	591.97	669.62	644.81	605.87
Selling, general, and administrative expense	148.78	144.72	112.99	106.86
Operating income	24.84	8.19	43.56	34.53
Restructuring program	14.60	(39.58)	1.00	2.19
Equity in income (loss) of affiliates	2.93	(0.41)	2.13	2.22
Minority interest	(0.43)	(1.17)	0.19	(0.16)
Interest expense	(14.31)	(12.66)	(6.53)	(5.02)
Interest income	2.30	2.43	2.09	2.47
Other, net	(1.10)	(4.34)	(0.23)	2.47
Income before taxes	28.83	(47.53)	42.20	38.69
Provision for taxes	12.97	(19.10)	16.49	16.99
Net income (loss)	$ 15.86	$(28.43)	$ 25.71	$ 21.70
Earnings/share, $	2.13	(3.85)	3.63	2.74
Average common shares outstanding, thousands	7430	7381	7193	6943

EXHIBIT 10 SELECTED EQUITY AND CURRENCY MARKET DATA, 1987

Date	DIC stock price, ¥/share	TSE index	Reichhold stock price, $/share	S&P 500 index	¥/$ exchange rate
June 1, 1987	¥760	2156.68	$36.625	289.83	¥145.75
2	750	2136.68	36.375	288.46	144.35
3	753	2158.92	36.250	293.47	142.70
4	747	2190.35	36.500	295.09	144.14
5	738	2180.01	36.375	293.45	143.36
8	766	2195.28	36.375	296.72	142.91
9	770	2196.01	36.625	297.28	142.81
10	761	2243.07	37.125	297.47	141.89
11	770	2258.56	38.625	298.73	142.85
12	765	2255.67	39.625	301.62	143.26
15	763	2241.08	40.625	303.14	144.64
16	757	2231.13	40.500	304.76	144.10
17	745	2241.59	42.250	304.81	144.75
18	755	2221.82	44.500	305.69	144.39
19	754	2174.81	43.500	306.97	144.60
22	735	2109.07	43.750	309.65	145.55
23	748	2117.29	43.500	308.43	146.75
24	750	2117.09	42.250	306.86	144.75
25	760	2134.25	60.500	308.96	146.05
26	795	2130.64	61.000	307.16	146.20
29	795	2076.91	60.875	307.90	146.70
30	780	2039.08	60.750	304.00	147.05
July 1, 1987	795	2042.53	63.125	304.93	146.65
2	790	2072.39	64.000	305.63	147.12
3	775	2050.52	holiday	holiday	148.53
6	769	1991.49	64.000	304.92	149.35
7	772	1993.27	63.125	307.40	149.25
8	759	1961.03	64.000	308.29	150.75
9	760	1983.34	63.375	307.52	149.35
10	755	2017.74	62.750	308.37	150.90
13	764	2020.50	62.125	307.63	151.10
14	760	1998.76	62.625	310.68	150.85
15	751	1995.54	62.750	310.42	151.10
16	750	2004.23	62.625	312.70	149.85
17	759	1996.69	61.750	314.59	152.00
20	748	1939.21	61.750	311.39	153.00
21	728	1915.64	62.125	308.55	152.23
22	730	1888.27	62.250	308.47	152.30
23	730	1918.19	59.875	307.81	151.19
24	748	1999.35	59.875	309.27	150.05
27	735	2007.33	60.250	310.65	149.40
28	753	2028.28	60.375	312.33	150.70
29	779	2022.81	60.375	315.65	150.35
30	770	2018.06	59.875	318.05	150.56
31	775	2015.11	59.375	318.66	149.40

EXHIBIT 11   SELECTED INFLATION RATES AND INTEREST RATES

| Year | Annual rates of consumer price inflation, % | | |
	United States	Japan	Germany
1978	7.64%	4.27%	2.59%
1979	11.39	3.71	4.12
1980	13.48	7.65	5.48
1981	10.31	5.05	6.29
1982	6.15	2.73	5.23
1983	3.23	1.81	3.35
1984	4.32	2.30	2.41
1985	3.52	2.04	2.15
1986	2.00	0.60	−0.20
1987*	4.93	0.70	1.00

| Investment | Selected market interest rates at July 31, 1987, % | | |
	U.S. $	Japanese ¥	German DM
90-day T-bills	6.11%	2.38%	na
Long-term government bond yield	8.88	4.44	6.39
Commercial paper	6.98	3.74	3.85
High-grade corporate bond yield[†]	9.90	5.35	6.75

*Figures for 1987 are annualized, for the period January–June 1987.
†Bond ratings are not directly comparable across currencies. The U.S. dollar rate is for A-rated issues.

ELDERS IXL LIMITED—1986

In September 1986, the Australian conglomerate Elders IXL Limited (Elders) purchased Courage/John Smiths, the sixth largest U.K. brewer, from Hanson Trust PLC for 1.4 billion pounds (£) [about 3.2 billion Australian dollars (A$)]. Six months earlier, Elders had bought an 18.2 percent stake in the Broken Hill Proprietary Company, Limited (BHP), Australia's largest company, for A$1.7 billion. Totaling nearly A$5 billion, these two investments tripled Elders's assets and had significant repercussions on the liability side of its balance sheet. In particular, Elders had assumed a considerable amount of sterling-denominated debt in connection with the Courage acquisition and the need to execute yet another major external financing. An intriguing possibility for this financing was a multicurrency convertible bond suggested by Crédit Suisse First Boston. This novel proposal had some appeal for a company with an increasingly global scope of operations, but not everyone was convinced such an offering was right for Elders at this stage of its evolution.

COMPANY BACKGROUND

Elders was founded in Australia in 1839 and originally concentrated in pastoral (farming and livestock) and woolbroking activities until 1981. Much of the company's early growth emanated from Elders's pastoral roots. Farmers, for example, required financing to operate their farms. This led Elders into financing activities. An International Group was also established as a trading operation to sell primarily grain, meat, and wool.

This case was prepared by Research Associate Richard P. Melnick and Professor W. Carl Kester. Copyright © 1988 by the President and Fellows of Harvard College. Harvard Business School case 288-042.

In 1982 Elders merged with Henry Jones IXL, a Tasmanian jam producer that had achieved considerable growth since being acquired and managed by John Elliott. Mr. Elliott became the new chairman of the combined company, Elders IXL. The new company grew both internally and through acquisitions into one of Australia's largest corporations (financial statements and a 5-year financial review are provided in **Exhibits 1**, **2**, and **3**). By 1980, Elders was divided into four core businesses: brewing, pastoral, finance, and international. Each area is described briefly below (segment data are provided in **Exhibit 4**).

Brewing

Brewery operations were conducted by Carlton and United Breweries (CUB), which contributed A$80.5 million, or 46 percent of the company's pretax profits, in 1986. CUB produced 48 percent of the beer consumed in Australia in 1986. The Australian beer market was considered mature with two major players, CUB and Bond Brewing. CUB's strategy was simply to maintain market share. In New South Wales (where 35 percent of Australians live) CUB's share actually increased from 42.4 percent to 46 percent in 1986 while Bond's dropped from 56.7 percent to 51.8 percent. The other major market in Australia was Victoria (with 26 percent of Australian beer consumption), in which CUB had almost a 96 percent market share. Carlton's leading brand, Fosters Lager, was the largest-selling packaged beer in Australia and held a 20 percent market share. One of Elders IXL's goals was to make Fosters the best-recognized brand name in the world.

Pastoral

Elders's pastoral activities included woolbroking, farming, and livestock activities. In contrast to the success of brewing, the Pastoral Group reported a 45 percent decrease in pretax profits in 1986 because of a downturn in the industry as well as a loss of market share in some of its woolbroking business. The group was still the largest woolbroker and livestock agent in Australia, with a 45 percent market share and a 450-branch network in Australia and New Zealand. Pastoral's primary competitive challenge came from small operators who competed on the basis of price. The company expected to defend its market position with its larger scale (it was the largest rural agent of real estate and insurance), its lower cost structure, and its dominant branch network.

International

The International division traded commodities around the world and provided shipping and chartering services to the company. The division had a difficult but improved trading year in 1986. It was the second largest exporter of Australian wool and the largest exporter of New Zealand wool. The International Group was reorganized in 1986 into a two-tier structure divided by region (Europe, Asia, America, and Australia) and product (wool, meat, brewing materials, and grain). Elders expected this reorganization to improve profitability by better focusing management's attention on local client needs and facilitating the transfer of information about local markets within the division.

Finance

Elders's Finance Group sustained its 30 percent annual growth from 1984 to 1986 by recording a 41 percent increase in profit after taxes in 1986. The division, which concentrated in merchant banking, financial services activities, and property finance, was the largest Australian-owned nonbank financial institution. Mr. Ken Jarrett, the group's managing director, said his strategy was basically to extend the international commodity dealing and financing that the Pastoral Group had been doing for years. His group was expanding into the New York, London, and Asian markets. It presently operated in fourteen countries and worked closely with most of Elders's other major groups.

Overall, Elders IXL's performance for the year ending June 1986 had been outstanding, with sales of A$7.7 billion and net income applicable to shareholders of A$205 million, an increase of 91 percent over the previous year. To celebrate the profitable year, Elders announced a one-for-three bonus stock issue for shareholders. The cash dividend, for which the new shares would also be eligible, was being paid at an annual rate of 21¢ (Australian) per share.

CORPORATE CULTURE AND STRATEGY

Elders IXL's success was in large part a result of the corporate culture established by its forceful leader, John Elliott. His biographer, Peter Denton, said of Mr. Elliott, "[Elliott] thrives on challenges, [and he] has achieved the utopian ideal that does not differentiate between work and leisure. He lives for now and sees no point in dwelling on the past, except if there is something to be learned from mistakes once made."[1]

The company's business strategy was oriented around balancing a portfolio of safe and aggressive positions. As a base, Elders maintained a solid set of core businesses that provided a stable and healthy cash flow to which newly restructured acquisitions could be added. Simultaneously, the company constantly searched for new growth opportunities in markets with potentially attractive returns. To find such opportunities, the company focused most of its attention on overseas markets.

Management was highly decentralized and, with the exception of accounting and finance (which was controlled by a small corporate headquarters), much authority was delegated to the operating groups. This minimized layers of corporate bureaucracy and fostered effective, hands-on decision making. So long as a division maintained the company goal of 15 percent annual earnings-per-share growth, corporate headquarters allowed it considerable autonomy. Repeated failure to meet the target would generally result in divestiture. (In 10 of the last 14 years, Elders

---

[1]Peter Denton, *Elliott, A Biography* (Bedford, U. K.: Little Hills Press, 1986).

achieved its 15 percent growth objective on a consolidated basis.) Other consolidated corporate targets included a 1:1 debt/equity ratio and a 25 percent pretax return on capital. Analysts forecasted a decline in Elders's dividend payout ratio to 25 percent by the late 1980s.

The treasury function was the primary exception within this decentralized company. Local treasurers did not finance projects themselves and could only receive funds earned from local production and sales. Whenever a local company needed additional capital, it would apply to headquarters for funds. Foreign exchange dealings were also managed centrally. A foreign exchange exposure manager at headquarters bought and sold currencies at market rates and controlled the exchange rates available internally to Elders's managers. Since local managers were evaluated in Australian dollars, there was an incentive to cover exposures completely at the local level. Occasionally, corporate treasury would take an unhedged foreign exchange position itself, but it did not speculate on a large scale. It also had its own target return on capital of 15 percent after tax.

ELDERS IXL'S MERGERS AND ACQUISITIONS

Between 1983 and 1986, Elders IXL's major financings and their impact on its ownership and capital structure were driven by a series of major acquisitions. The details of the deals are described below.

Carlton United Breweries

In December 1983, Elders acquired Carlton United Breweries (CUB) for A$988 million. Conservatively managed, CUB could be described as a mature "cash cow" with high, steady margins and virtually no debt. Retention of earnings, however, had contributed to a bloating of the capital base and a consequent decline on its return on capital. Under Elders's management, CUB's capital base was reduced from A$980 in 1984 to A$700 in 1986. Much of this use of funds was offset by a buildup in ordinary trade credit, which increased from A$94 million in 1983 to A$200 million in 1986. Accompanying these changes was a sharp turnaround in return on capital (see **Exhibit 5**).

Immediately following the CUB acquisition, Elders's debt ratio approached 85 percent of total capital. By June 1985, this ratio had been cut to 50 percent. This reduction was achieved through the issuance of new equity and the sale of some "nonstrategic" assets owned by CUB. Specifically, Elders sold whole or partial interests in 300 of CUB's 350 hotels. Approximately A$270 million was realized through these sales. Another A$320 million was raised through the sale of new equity in Australia, and $160 million was provided by the sale of Elders's first U.S.-dollar-denominated convertible bond in June 1984. Despite a 25 percent depreciation in the Australian dollar since the date of the convertible bond issue, the bonds consistently traded above the original issue price of $93 per $100 par value. Although not yet called by the company, all but $35 million of the bonds had been converted by late 1986. The remainder were expected to be converted before maturity.

Broken Hill Proprietary Company Limited

Acting as a white knight, Elders bought 18.2 percent of Broken Hill Proprietary Company Limited (BHP) for A$1.7 billion in April 1986. BHP, the giant Australian steel and natural resources concern, was Australia's largest company. Elders was helping defend BHP from Robert Holmes à Court of Bell Resources, which already held 18.8 percent of BHP. In his fourth hostile bid for BHP since 1983, Mr. Holmes à Court offered A$2 billion for an additional 20 percent of the company, which would have given him effective control.[2] Mr. Elliott described Elders's investment in BHP as "long term" and "a sound strategic share purchase at a good time."[3]

Simultaneously with Elders's purchase, BHP acquired A$216 million of Elders's convertible bonds in the Euromarkets which, if converted, would give BHP 12.6 percent of Elders's outstanding shares. BHP then invested an additional A$1 billion cash in Elders in exchange for new 6.75 percent preference shares with detachable common equity warrants redeemable by Elders in 1993. These nonvoting shares could be used to exercise the warrants at a price of A$4.35 per share. However, only A$140 million of the preference shares could be used immediately to receive common shares in April 1986. The remaining A$860 million could be exchanged for common shares after 1988. Since Australian law prohibited a company from acquiring more than 20 percent of another company's shares without making a formal bid for that company, neither Elders nor BHP was expected to increase its holding in the other in the immediate future.[4]

These arrangements between Elders and BHP made it more difficult for Mr. Holmes à Court to win direct control of BHP because, in order to do so, Bell would have to execute the daunting task of securing another 30 percent of BHP. Some analysts speculated that Mr. Holmes à Court might eventually target Elders, or instead, that Elders and BHP would eventually merge. The future of this cross-holding deal was far from clear.[5] In September 1986, Elders's top twenty shareholders controlled 60 percent of the company. Two of these, BHP Nominees Pty. Ltd. and Charmes Limited, controlled 30.2 percent.

---

[2]The previous year BHP had acted as a white knight for Elders when it bought some Elders shares held by Mr. Holmes à Court.

[3]*Financial Times*, April 11, 1986, p. 44.

[4]But even at its present level, the cross-holding arrangement was controversial. Australia's National Companies and Securities Commission announced a public hearing to determine if BHP and Elders had violated the takeover law. The commission concluded that the acquisitions were not unacceptable.

[5]In September 1986, Elders, BHP, and Bell established the following guidelines regarding their cross-holdings: (1) The companies agreed not to increase their respective shareholdings in any one company unless they consulted with the others and were ready to launch a full bid for that company; (2) if a company wanted to sell shares in another, it had to be acceptable to both other companies; (3) all legal disputes between BHP and Bell over the takeover bid were to be terminated and new action was not to be taken; (4) Mr. Elliott and Mr. Holmes à Court were to join the BHP board, and BHP's managing director, Brian Loton, was to be appointed to Elders's board. Finally, AFP Investment Corporation (an investment concern nominated by Elders) acquired an option over the A$860 million worth of Elders 6.75 percent convertible preference shares that BHP had purchased in April. AFP paid Elders A$40 million in cash to change the documentation so as to improve the rights of the equity warrants associated with the preference shares.

Allied Lyons

The geographic scope of Elders's acquisitions was not confined to Australia. In October 1985, Elders made a hostile takeover bid of £1.8 billion for Allied Lyons, the second largest brewer in the United Kingdom and a company with a market capitalization four times larger than that of Elders.

This bid startled the City and found many opponents in the United Kingdom. Concerned about the takeover attempt, Allied purchased a Canadian brewery, Hiram Walker Spirits, for £400 million. This allowed Allied to take on an additional £466 million of debt, largely in an attempt to make itself a less attractive takeover target. Allied also launched a war of words designed to attract the attention of the Monopolies and Mergers Commission (MMC), by claiming that the acquisition would disastrously raise Elders's leverage. S. G. Warburg, Allied Lyons's merchant bankers, claimed that Elders's debt would exceed 80 percent after the takeover. The Bank of England was also concerned about the postacquisition leverage and said as much to the MMC.[6] Ultimately, the bid was referred to the MMC for its consideration.

Courage

Following a 9-month study, the MMC cleared Elders's bid for Allied Lyons on September 3, 1986. Despite the allegations of opponents to the acquisition, the MMC was impressed with the quality of Elders's management and the company's success in reducing leverage following the CUB acquisition in Australia.

Nevertheless, Elders abandoned its bid for Allied and turned its attention to Courage/John Smiths breweries. On September 18, 1986, Elders bought Courage from Hanson Trust PLC for £1.4 billion, or A\$3.3 billion. Mr. Elliott said about the move that ''It has become clear that the purchase of Courage represents a far more attractive way of fulfilling our aims.'' In another interview he explained, ''We're not in the takeover business for the sake of it. We are in the business of building a worldwide brewing company. Courage gave us a cheaper entry into the U.K. market.''[7]

Courage was the sixth largest brewer in the United Kingdom, with a 9 percent market share that was concentrated in the south of England and Yorkshire. Its purchase represented the largest overseas takeover in Australian history and the largest in British brewing history. It also made Elders one of the ten largest brewing companies in the world. The acquisition had three major components: (1) Courage, with three breweries and 5005 pubs (3671 tenanted public houses and 1334 public houses under management); (2) Saccone and Speed, a wine and spirits wholesaler; and (3) Roberts and Cooper, Ltd., a chain of 386 off-license liquor stores. Collectively, these properties represented the drinks businesses of Imperial Brewing and Leisure, Limited, a part of the Imperial Group that had recently been purchased by Hanson Trust.

---

[6]Reportedly, the Bank of England gave evidence of Elders's borrowing needs, representing the first time it ever took such an action during a takeover attempt.

[7]*Financial Times,* September 19, 1986, p. 1.

FINANCING THE COURAGE ACQUISITION

To pay for the £1.4 billion Courage acquisition, Elders utilized Courage's own £100 million net cash position, relied on a syndicated bank facility for £1 billion, and hoped to raise £300 million by issuing securities. The bank syndicate included twenty-two banks, most of which had been originally assembled during the earlier bid for Allied. The loans required interest payments of 10.5 percent and represented bridge financing until Elders could refinance them with long-term debt or equity. When Elders announced the Courage takeover, Mr. Elliott said he wanted to raise 700 million of the £1.4 billion by selling equity interests in Courage's 5005 pubs to landlords. Besides raising cash, it was hoped that changing the ownership structure of the pubs would induce pub owners to utilize their assets better, thus improving returns on capital.

The Alternatives

Three major financing alternatives were available for raising the remaining £300 million: straight debt, subordinated convertible debt, and new equity. Straight debt would most likely be issued at fixed rates with a 10- to 12-year maturity in either the Eurobond market or the domestic sterling market. Prevailing yields in these markets are provided in **Exhibit 6**. Exchange rates are provided in **Exhibit 7**. Volume data by currency and type of issue are provided in **Exhibit 8**.

Elders had favorable prior experience with convertible bonds when it issued its convertible note in June 1984. The original issue size of $130 million was increased to $160 million due to the strength of demand. But at £300 million (approximately $450 million), a new convertible bond issue would be one of the largest in history. (Texaco executed $1 billion and $500 million convertible bond issues in the Eurobond market in 1984.) Launching such an issue would require considerable ingenuity and planning.

A proposal made by Crédit Suisse First Boston was to denominate the convertible bonds in several currencies and issue them simultaneously in multiple markets. Specifically, it was proposed that the bonds be issued in four separate tranches representing deutsche marks, pounds sterling, Swiss francs, and U.S. dollars. Alternative currencies under consideration were Dutch guilders, French francs, and European Currency Units (ECUs). The Swiss franc and deutsche mark tranches would be issued in the Swiss and German domestic markets, respectively, while the dollar and sterling issues would be issued in the Euromarkets. Crédit Suisse First Boston also recommended the inclusion of a put option on the bonds, which would permit investors to put the bonds back to Elders at a price sufficient to guarantee some minimum yield to redemption. Other proposed terms for the convertibles are presented in **Exhibit 9**.

The raising of new equity would be executed by means of a rights issue that would be governed by Australian securities law. Such a deal would probably take the form of an underwritten one-for-two rights (i.e., one new share of stock for every two rights) issue at A$4.25 per share (a discount from market price of approximately 15 percent). Again, at £300 million (A$690 million), such a rights offering would be one of the largest in Australian history.

THE TREASURY'S CHALLENGE

Elders IXL clearly had entered a dynamic, fast-paced period in its corporate evolution. Its asset base and competitive position in world markets changed dramatically as it acquired one new company after another. With each new acquisition came equally dramatic changes on the liability side of its balance sheet and in its ownership structure. The challenge presented to the treasurer's office as it faced this next major financing decision was to prepare Elders for the future while exploiting the best available capital market opportunities in the present.

EXHIBIT 1   **ELDERS IXL's CONSOLIDATED INCOME STATEMENT (FOR THE YEARS ENDED JUNE 30; THOUSANDS)**

	1986	1985	1984
Revenue	A$7,658,665	A$6,994,822	A$5,581,600
Total net operating profit before income tax*	236,849	133,449	86,748
Income taxes	(27,577)	(24,880)	(14,572)
Net operating profit after income tax	209,272	108,569	72,176
Extraordinary items	(2,436)	4,781	(3,290)
Net income from all sources	206,836	113,350	68,886
Outside preference and minority shareholders' interests therein	(4,622)	(1,665)	(730)
Net income applicable to Elders IXL Limited shareholders	A$ 202,214	A$ 111,685	A$ 68,156

*Depreciation and amortization expenses (in A$ thousands) were A$51,009 in 1986; A$51,227 in 1985; and A$37,739 in 1984. Interest expenses were A$522,615 in 1986; A$360,487 in 1985; and A$220,412 in 1984 (also in A$ thousands).

Source: Elders IXL Annual Reports.

EXHIBIT 2 **ELDERS IXL'S CONSOLIDATED BALANCE SHEET (FOR THE YEARS ENDED JUNE 30; A$ THOUSANDS)**

	1986	1985	1984
Assets			
Current assets			
Cash and deposits	A$753,609	A$29,880	A$49,392
Debtors	416,901	473,043	430,840
Stocks	187,400	282,895	456,841
Total	1,357,910	785,818	937,073
Noncurrent assets			
Fixed assets	969,276	986,184	1,135,067
Investments	2,157,774	146,898	197,903
Other noncurrent assets	112,748	90,102	76,079
Total	3,239,798	1,223,184	1,409,049
Finance subsidiaries	197,680	138,216	92,125
Total assets	A$4,795,388	A$2,147,218	A$2,438,247
Liabilities and shareholders' equity			
Current liabilities			
Creditors	A$567,122	A$499,798	A$458,848
Borrowings	140,485	119,384	241,189
Provisions	61,869	63,894	58,719
Total	769,476	683,076	758,756
Noncurrent liabilities			
Secured debt	1,793,790	27,271	285,726
Unsecured debt	96,710	488,479	646,009
Other	91,984	78,827	76,128
Total	1,982,484	594,577	1,007,863
Convertible bonds	168,427	168,427	168,427
Minority interests	13,681	13,320	11,755
Shareholders' equity*	1,861,320	687,818	491,446
Total liabilities and shareholders' equity	A$4,795,388	A$2,147,218	A$2,438,247

*Shares outstanding: 333,877,166 in 1986; 254,112,844 in 1985; and 157,498,000 in 1984.
Source: Elders IXL Annual Reports.

EXHIBIT 3 ELDERS IXL—5-YEAR FINANCIAL REVIEW (MILLIONS, EXCEPT RATIOS AND PER SHARE AMOUNTS)

	1986	1985	1984	1983	1982
Revenue	A$7659	A$6995	A$5582	A$3694	A$2767
Profit and loss					
Net operating profit	209	109	72	64	61
Extraordinary items	(2)	5	(3)	—	(3)
Minority interest	(5)	(2)	(1)	(1)	(1)
Net income	202	112	68	63	57
Dividend received by shareholders	64	50	32	33	28
Results per ordinary share					
Net income, A$	0.54	0.44	0.29	0.26	0.24
Dividends, A$	0.21	0.22	0.16	0.14	0.11
Market price, A$	4.06	0.82	2.36	1.88	1.91
Balance sheet					
Total assets	4795	2147	2438	1198	1258
Total debt	2199	804	1417	458	524
Total equity	1861	688	491	415	387
Return on equity, %	16	19	15	16	20
Payout ratio, %	32	45	47	52	49

Source: Elders IXL Annual Reports.

EXHIBIT 4   ELDERS IXL, SEGMENT DATA (THOUSANDS, EXCEPT FOR RETURN ON CAPITAL)

	Carlton, 1985	Pastoral, 1985	Finance, 1985	International, 1985	Other, 1985
Revenue	A$1,630,688	A$3,331,056	A$337,363	A$1,385,249	A$310,466
Earnings before interest and taxes	142,963	55,031	25,955	35,989	38,772
Profit before taxes	64,963	30,031	25,955	11,989	511
Capital employed	738,000	221,000	118,000	221,000	173,000
Return on capital employed, %	19.37	24.90	21.99	16.28	22.41

Source: Bache Cortis & Carr Limited.

EXHIBIT 5 **RETURN ON CAPITAL FOR CARLTON AND UNITED BREWERIES PRE- AND POSTACQUISITION (1984) BY ELDERS IXL***

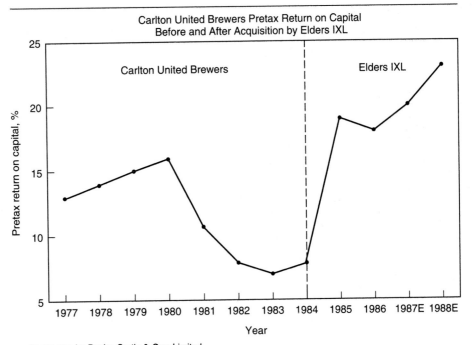

Carlton United Brewers Pretax Return on Capital
Before and After Acquisition by Elders IXL

*Estimates by Bache Cortis & Carr Limited

EXHIBIT 6 SELECTED BOND YIELDS

	1983, Dec.	1984, Dec.	1985, Dec.	1986							
				Jan.	Feb.	Mar.	Apr.	May	June	July	Aug.
Domestic government bond yields (long-term issues, at or near end of month), %											
United States	12.00	11.61	9.49	9.45	8.31	7.50	7.70	8.37	7.79	7.88	7.51
France	13.96	12.70	11.33	10.79	10.00	9.19	8.53	8.58	8.65	8.55	8.05
Germany	8.38	7.17	6.57	6.64	6.32	6.21	5.78	6.31	6.17	6.07	5.95
Japan	7.45	6.47	5.92	5.57	5.33	4.67	4.79	5.57	4.90	4.83	4.57
Netherlands	8.58	7.72	6.96	6.81	6.84	6.44	6.15	6.39	6.38	6.22	6.03
Switzerland	4.53	4.60	4.42	4.42	4.27	4.16	4.24	4.39	4.49	4.39	4.26
United Kingdom	9.94	10.25	10.35	10.56	9.83	8.75	8.73	9.11	9.32	9.45	9.32
Domestic corporate bond yields (long-term issues, at or near end of term), %											
United States	12.63	12.25	10.15	10.38	9.00	8.63	9.00	9.20	9.00	9.25	8.63
France	14.35	12.94	11.76	11.38	10.81	10.13	9.82	9.44	9.85	9.12	8.37
Germany	8.30	7.20	6.90	6.80	6.80	6.70	6.60	6.40	6.50	6.60	6.40
Japan	7.09	6.21	6.90	6.70	5.96	5.40	5.14	5.20	5.14	4.74	5.14
Netherlands	8.51	7.51	na	na	6.86	6.53	na	na	na	na	na
Switzerland	4.92	5.09	4.93	4.78	4.71	4.64	4.96	4.77	4.83	4.84	4.77
United Kingdom	11.57	11.64	11.47	11.59	10.88	9.96	9.80	10.05	10.32	10.49	10.32
International corporate bond yields (U.S. companies operating in the following markets), %											
Eurodollar	11.59	11.25	9.68	9.60	9.27	8.78	8.93	9.27	9.09	8.97	8.60
Euromark	7.34	6.95	6.73	6.73	6.61	6.67	6.62	6.74	6.65	6.55	6.55
Swiss franc	5.83	5.73	5.49	5.47	5.52	5.63	5.65	5.62	5.63	5.56	5.63

Source: Morgan Guaranty Trust Company, World Financial Markets, various issues 1983–1986.

EXHIBIT 7   DOLLAR EXCHANGE RATES*

	U.K. pounds	Australian dollars	German marks	Swiss francs	Japanese yen	Dutch guilders	French francs
1981	1.9090	0.8865	2.2460	1.7890	219.60	2.4610	5.6960
1982	1.6170	1.0205	2.3770	2.0070	234.75	2.6265	6.7325
1983	1.4510	1.1117	2.7220	2.1800	231.50	3.0575	8.3150
1984	1.1585	1.2110	3.1535	2.6015	251.50	3.5570	9.6425
1985	1.4450	1.4645	2.4450	2.0595	199.00	2.7475	7.4825
1986:1	1.4125	1.3990	2.3885	2.0265	192.70	2.6975	7.3100
1986:2	1.4465	1.4285	2.2300	1.8870	180.40	2.5155	6.8600
1986:3	1.4835	1.4025	2.3250	1.9475	179.40	2.6205	7.1525
1986:4	1.5505	1.3495	2.1635	1.8105	167.50	2.4405	6.8900
1986:5	1.4720	1.3950	2.3245	1.9315	174.45	2.6135	7.4050
1986:6	1.5320	1.4805	2.2010	1.7950	163.65	2.4745	7.0175
1986:7	1.4920	1.6770	2.0925	1.6750	153.70	2.3585	6.8000
1986:8	1.4880	1.6375	2.0345	1.6415	154.45	2.2935	6.6650
1986:9	1.4465	1.5915	2.0265	1.6455	154.30	2.2915	6.6400

Pound exchange rates†

	Australian dollars	German marks	Swiss francs	Japanese yen	Dutch guilders	French francs
1981	1.6930	4.2850	3.4300	419.00	4.6900	10.8700
1982	1.6450	3.8400	3.2400	379.50	4.2450	10.8800
1983	1.6093	3.9500	3.1600	336.00	4.4400	12.0659
1984	1.4020	3.6450	3.0100	291.00	4.1100	11.1650
1985	2.1180	3.5300	2.9725	288.25	3.9800	10.8525
1986:1	1.9755	3.3700	2.8600	272.00	3.8075	10.3275
1986:2	2.0835	3.2225	2.7275	260.50	3.6350	9.9250
1986:3	2.0770	3.4450	2.8850	265.75	3.8850	10.6125
1986:4	2.0920	3.3525	2.8050	259.25	3.7800	10.6850
1986:5	2.0660	3.4200	2.8400	256.50	3.8425	10.9025
1986:6	2.2780	3.3700	2.7475	250.25	3.7875	10.7525
1986:7	2.5045	3.1175	2.4975	229.00	3.5150	10.1475
1986:8	2.4450	3.0250	2.4400	229.50	3.4100	9.9200
1986:9	2.3010	2.9275	2.3775	222.85	3.3100	9.6075

*Units of foreign currency per dollar, except pounds.
†Units of foreign currency per pound.

EXHIBIT 8   EUROBONDS AND INTERNATIONAL ISSUES: CURRENCY VERSUS TYPE OF INSTRUMENT (FIRST 9 MONTHS OF 1986)

	All issues		Straights		FRNs		Convertibles		Equity warrants	
	No. of issues	Amount, $ millions	No. of issues	Amount, $ millions	No. of issues	Amount, $ millions	No. of issues	Amount, $ millions	No. of issues	Amount, $ millions
U.S. dollars[a]	683	92,581.04	379	49,010.77	137	29,924.66	47	4,021.45	120	9,624.17
Yen[b]	163	17,948.68	155	17,345.07	6	374.29	0	0.00	2	229.32
Swiss francs	296	16,250.56	208	11,991.01	2	101.03	30	1,650.06	56	2,508.46
Deutsche marks	154	13,708.22	119	10,288.25	9	1,498.42	1	101.05	25	1,820.50
Pounds[c]	79	10,406.05	55	4,723.40	20	5,484.03	1	70.50	3	128.12
Canadian dollars[d]	68	4,107.58	68	4,107.58	0	0.00	0	0.00	0	0.00
ECUs[e]	64	5,665.79	54	4,426.17	6	987.23	2	59.99	2	192.40
Australian dollars[f]	83	3,654.35	78	3,215.11	5	439.24	0	0.00	0	0.00
French francs	40	3,196.53	33	2,594.33	5	452.85	1	49.12	1	100.23
Dutch guilders	31	2,161.05	26	2,010.52	4	117.92	1	32.61	0	0.00
Danish kroner	25	1,023.76	23	945.88	2	77.88	0	0.00	0	0.00
Luxembourg francs	77	719.86	76	652.74	0	0.00	0	0.00	1	67.12
New Zealand dollars[g]	18	627.63	17	574.71	1	52.92	0	0.00	0	0.00
Italian lire	7	531.41	7	531.41	0	0.00	0	0.00	0	0.00
Hong Kong dollars	8	480.72	2	64.11	6	416.61	0	0.00	0	0.00
Belgian francs	5	305.04	4	257.99	1	47.05	0	0.00	0	0.00
Finnish markkae	1	48.37	1	48.37	0	0.00	0	0.00	0	0.00
Spanish pesetas	2	29.74	2	29.74	0	0.00	0	0.00	0	0.00
Austrian schillings	1	27.74	1	27.74	0	0.00	0	0.00	0	0.00
Swedish kronor	1	20.63	0	0.00	1	20.63	0	0.00	0	0.00
Total	1806	173,494.75	1308	112,844.90	205	39,994.76	83	5984.78	210	14,670.32

[a] Including Yankee issues.
[b] Including Samurai and Shibosai issues.
[c] Including Bulldogs.
[d] Including Shogun bonds.
[e] Including U.S. debt issues in ECUs.
[f] Including U.S. debt issues in Australian dollars.
[g] Including U.S. debt issues in New Zealand dollars.
Source: *International Financing Review* (London: IFR Publishing, 1986).

EXHIBIT 9   TERMS OF THE MULTICURRENCY ISSUE

Guarantor: Elders IXL Ltd., on a subordinated basis

Amount: Four-tranche unsecured subordinated convertible issue comprising $175 million (A), DM200 million (B), £40 million (C), SF200 million (D)

Maturity: 12 years (due November 5, 1998)

Conversion premium: 20.72% over the October 10 Melbourne Stock Exchange closing price of A$4.97

Tranche A

Amount:	$175 million
Coupon:	5¼% payable annually on November 5, starting in 1987
Issue price:	100
Conversion period:	November 6, 1986, to October 27, 1998
Conversion price:	A$6, representing a 20.72% premium; each bond is convertible into 261.23 shares
Exchange rate:	A$1 = US$0.6380
Denominations:	$1000 bearer and registered
Amortization:	Bullet
Put option:	At 125 on November 5, 1993, giving a yield to redemption of 8.05% per annum
Call option:	At 106 on or after 30 days after the exchange date, declining by 1% per annum to 100 on November 5, 1992, but not before 1993 unless the closing price for ordinary shares on the Melbourne Stock Exchange equals or exceeds 130% of the conversion price for a specified period
Listing:	Luxembourg
Governing law:	English
Commissions:	1½% (management, underwriting 1%, selling 1½%)

Tranche B

Amount:	DM200 million
Coupon:	3%
Issue price:	100
Conversion period:	November 6, 1986, to October 23, 1998
Conversion price:	A$6, representing a 20.72% premium; each bond is convertible into 130.39 shares
Exchange rate:	A$1 = DM1.2782
Denominations:	DM1,000 and DM10,000
Amortization:	Bullet
Put option:	At 123 on November 5, 1993, representing a yield to redemption of 5.76%
Call option:	At 101% in 1991; at 100 in 1992; there is also a trigger clause (130%, 30 trading days)
Listing:	Frankfurt Stock Exchange
Governing law:	Federal Republic of Germany
Commissions:	2½% (management, underwriting 1%; selling 1½%; in addition, there is a listing fee of ½%).

EXHIBIT 9 TERMS OF THE MULTICURRENCY ISSUE *(Continued)*

Guarantor: Elders IXL Ltd., on a subordinated basis

Amount: Four-tranche unsecured subordinated convertible issue comprising $175 million (A), DM200 million (B), £40 million (C), SF200 million (D)

Maturity: 12 years (due November 5, 1998)

Conversion premium: 20.72% over the October 10 Melbourne Stock Exchange closing price of A$4.97

Tranche C

Amount:	£40 million
Coupon:	8% payable annually on November 5, starting in 1987
Issue price:	100
Conversion period:	November 6, 1986, to October 27, 1998
Conversion price:	A$6, representing a 20.72% premium; each bond is convertible into 373.11 shares
Exchange rate:	A$1 = £0.4467
Denominations:	£1000 bearer and registered
Amortization:	Bullet
Put option:	At 124 on November 5, 1993, giving a yield to redemption of 10.49% per annum
Call option:	At 106 on or after 30 days after the exchange date, declining by 1% per annum to 100 on November 5, 1992, but not before 1993 unless the closing price for ordinary shares on the Melbourne Stock Exchange equals or exceeds 130% of the conversion price for a specified period
Listing:	Luxembourg
Governing law:	English
Commissions:	2½% (management, underwriting 1%; selling 1½%)

Tranche D

Amount:	SF200 million of subordinated bonds convertible into shares of Elders IXL
Maturity:	12 years (due November 5, 1998) with a put option for investors after 7 years
Coupon:	2½% payable annually on November 5
Issue price:	100 (+0.3% Swiss federal stamp duty)
Terms fixed:	October 15
Conversion period:	November 6, 1986, to October 27, 1998
Conversion price:	A$6, representing a 20.72% premium; each bond is convertible into 800 shares
Exchange rate:	A$1 = SF1.0417
Denominations:	SF5000
Amortization:	Bullet
Put option:	At 120% in 1993 to yield 4.96%
Call option:	Forced conversion: at any time at 106%, decreasing thereafter by 1% annually if the price of the shares during 20 consecutive days represents at least 130% of the conversion price
Listing:	Zurich, Basel, Geneva, Lausanne, and Berne Stock Exchanges
Governing law:	Switzerland
Commissions:	2⅞% (management ½%, underwriting 2⅜%)

Source: International Financing Review (London: IFR Publishing, 1986).

MONTEDISON
S.p.A.—1983

In the spring of 1983, the board of directors of Montedison S.p.A., a diversified multinational chemical company headquartered in Italy, met to consider a proposal made by Wertheim & Co., Inc., a New York investment banking house. Wertheim had proposed that Montedison consolidate its pharmaceutical and diagnostic equipment subsidiaries, incorporate the unit offshore, and offer equity on the New York Stock Exchange. The objective in doing so was to spotlight some value believed to have been buried in Montedison's complex array of business. If executed as proposed, the health care subsidiary would be the first Italian company ever to do an initial public offering on the New York Stock Exchange.

The proposal was not without its risks, however. The benefits of a cross-border equity issue were not entirely clear cut, and any of several potential problems could arise to undermine the deal. If this happened, it would represent an embarrassment to Montedison and a setback in its hard-fought campaign to regain profitability and respectability as a leading multinational business.

BACKGROUND

Montedison was created in the 1966 merger of two Italian companies: Edison, founded as an electrical utility concern in 1884, and Montecatini, founded in 1888 for the mining of copper and pyrites. At the time of their merger, Montecatini was a diversified company with businesses in such areas as fertilizers, dyestuffs, fibers,

This case was prepared by Professor W. Carl Kester. Copyright © 1985 by the President and Fellows of Harvard College. Harvard Business School case 286-032.

pharmaceuticals, and aluminum. Edison had been Italy's largest electric utility, supplying one-quarter of the nation's electric power in 1962, the year in which Italy nationalized its electricity generating industry. In anticipation of that event, Edison had also diversified into petrochemicals during the 1950s, becoming Italy's second largest chemical company by the 1960s.

The early 1970s marked the beginning of a new thrust for Montedison. The company's commitments to businesses such as food, insurance, electromechanics, and financing were reduced to make way for its new emphasis on chemicals and related processes, especially pharmaceuticals. But they also marked the beginning of a decade of political interference, labor unrest, and poor economic conditions. The economic boom of the 1960s led to a tight labor market and rising wages. Montedison's labor costs increased from 29 percent of sales in 1969 to 34 percent by 1972. Its meager profits changed to large losses. Leverage also rose, with debt constituting 64 percent of total capital by 1972. In response to the deteriorating situation, the government took strong action by acquiring a 17 percent interest in Montedison through Ente Nazionale Idrocarburi (ENI), a state-owned energy company.

More than 10 years of poor market conditions and overmanned, inefficiently operated plants ensued. The oil shock in 1973–1974 and the devaluation of the lira (Lit) contributed further to Montedison's poor performance. By 1978 Montedison's losses were Lit267 billion on sales of Lit5839 billion. To reduce losses, the company divested its share in some chemical joint ventures and sold its U.S. polypropylene business to U.S. Steel. These divestitures resulted in a small profit for 1979 (0.3 percent of sales), but losses continued thereafter, reaching 6 percent of sales in 1980 and 7 percent of sales in 1981, or over Lit600 billion. Recent financial data for Montedison are provided in **Exhibit 1**.

ASSET RESTRUCTURING

In 1980 Mario Schimberni, former vice president for finance within Montedison, was appointed president of the company. He took office with the objective of returning Montedison to profitability by 1984, the company's centenary year. With this in mind, he immediately began negotiating the return of Montedison to the private sector upon assuming office. He succeeded in June 1981 when a group of prominent Italian industrialists bought ENI's 17 percent interest for approximately Lit49 billion.

His next step to rationalize the company's operations was to reorganize it as a holding company and strengthen its equity base. Ten major business areas were defined, and the principal divisions within each were set up as autonomous operating companies. Lit640 billion in new equity was also raised in early 1982. The deal was sweetened by inclusion of warrants for equity in two of Montedison's prominent operating companies, Farmitalia Carlo Erba (pharmaceuticals) and SELM (electric power).

A top priority of the managers of the new business units was to control fixed costs and capital expenditures so that more cash could be directed toward reducing

Montedison's immense debt burden. Interest on this debt amounted to 12 percent of Montedison's annual consolidated sales. This was extremely high in comparison to comparable averages of 4 percent of sales for European competitors and 2.5 percent of sales for U.S. chemical companies.

A classic ''business portfolio'' analysis was also made of all Montedison's business units to determine which were to be fostered, which were to provide funds for other units, and which were to be divested or deemphasized. With the exception of pharmaceuticals, parts of all Montedison's operating subsidiaries were deemed candidates for divestiture or restructuring as joint ventures.

In plastics, the company chose to concentrate on polystyrene and polypropylene. Five other commodity plastic operations that were losing Lit200 billion annually were sold to ENI for Lit435 billion. Polyesters and acrylics were selected for emphasis in the fibers areas. Its nylon assets in France and Italy were liquidated, and Montedison's share of a British nylon venture was swapped for some acrylic assets owned by the Monsanto Company in West Germany and Ireland.

Fertilizers, detergents, and pesticides were also considered candidates for sale, although their poor performances hampered efforts to divest them. Possible joint ventures in these areas with ENI for the purpose of rationalizing these industries in Italy were discussed. The continued involvement of ENI in the restructuring of Montedison prompted some critics to argue that perhaps Montedison should be nationalized outright rather than bailed out at the government's expense.

THE CROWN JEWELS

Despite its reorganization and sale of low returning assets, Montedison was still heavily concentrated in mature commodity markets. It did, however, have two lines of businesses in which it saw great future promise: plastics and health care.

Plastics

Montedison had fostered the development of polypropylene during the early stages of this product's development shortly after World War II. Over the following several decades, its polypropylene technology fell behind that of the other major competitors. In the early 1980s, Montedison joined Mitsui Petrochemical to work on a third-generation process in an attempt to regain its technological dominance. The two companies eventually developed a new high-yield catalyst and polymerization technology that promised energy and other production-cost savings. A test of the process for the production of polypropylene on a large scale yielded production-cost savings of 10 to 20 percent at a very low level of investment, while the quality of the output was superior to that of conventional processes.

Montedison enjoyed a leading position in the European market for polypropylene. It expected the demand for polypropylene to increase substantially during the coming decade.

Health Care

Montedison's health care businesses had been growing at a 20 percent rate over the past several years. The company was involved in three sectors of health care: pharmaceuticals, diagnostics and reagents, and instruments and equipment. Its principal health care subsidiary was Farmitalia Carlo Erba, Italy's largest pharmaceutical company. In 1982 Farmitalia contributed 56 percent of Montedison's total health care sales, earning about Lit52 billion on sales of Lit450 billion. This represented the largest contribution margin of any unit in the Montedison group. Between 1983 and 1985, Montedison planned to spend Lit150 billion on new research and production facilities for Farmitalia, as well as continuing to spend approximately 8 percent of sales annually for research and development.

Farmitalia's primary product was Adriamycin, an anticancer drug used in chemotherapy. By the end of 1982, Adriamycin had become the world's leading chemotherapy drug, accounting for 33 percent of Montedison's ethical pharmaceutical sales that year. Farmitalia considered itself the world leader in anticancer drugs and concentrated much of its research efforts in that area (approximately one-quarter of its research and development budget). Three new anticancer drugs were in the clinical testing phase in 1982. However, Farmitalia also had a wide range of drug products coming to the market in the mid-1980s in various other therapeutic groups such as antibiotics, analgesics, and anti-inflammatory and neurological products. In general, these new products and Farmitalia's ongoing research were directed at common diseases heavily affecting industrialized countries.

Besides Farmitalia, the health care group consisted of Adria Laboratories, Inc.; Lark, S.p.A.; Alpharm, S.A.; and Kallestad Laboratories. Lark (an Italian corporation) and Alpharm (a Swiss corporation) engaged in the manufacture and sale of bulk pharmaceuticals. With the acquisition of Kallestad Labs (a U.S. corporation) in 1982 for $87 million, Montedison diversified into immunodiagnostics equipment. Steady income from less risky areas such as medical equipment was important for supporting a pharmaceutical company's research efforts, particularly since the typical product development period was so long and new products had a high failure rate. Many of them never reached the consumer market.

Adria Labs had been created in 1974 as a joint venture between Hercules, a major U.S. chemical company, and Montedison. The joint venture was arranged to market Farmitalia's drug products, primarily Adriamycin, in the United States and Canada. In fact, the joint venture was given an exclusive right to market any of Farmitalia's products that were brought to North America. The majority of the drugs Adria marketed were obtained from Farmitalia as fully developed and proven products. Thus, Adria Labs avoided the long, expensive research projects that typically characterized proprietary ethical drug development.

Like many other multinational drug companies, Montedison sought entry to the U.S. market because of the market's large relative size (the largest single national market in the world) and the fact that no single national market for drugs in a particular therapeutic group was big enough to allow recovery of development costs. Hercules was chosen as a U.S. partner because Montedison had done business with it before and was familiar with its management. Under the terms of the joint venture agreement, each company contributed one-half of the partnership's initial capital (approximately $2 million) and elected one-half of the board of directors.

Adria Labs's management was newly hired, as was its sales force, which specialized in oncology (the study of tumors). This provided Adria Labs with a competitive advantage since it could service the entire country with only eighty-five to ninety sales representatives, roughly one-quarter the number that would have been necessary if nonspecialists were used. The initial joint venture agreement was due to expire in 1984, at which time it could be renewed with the consent of both parties, renegotiated, or allowed to expire.

WERTHEIM'S PROPOSAL

In connection with Montedison's restructuring, the New York investment banking firm Wertheim & Co., Inc., had approached the company with a proposal to reorganize its health care operations. The essence of the proposal was quite simple. A new company, to be called "Erbamont," would be created to consolidate Montedison's worldwide pharmaceutical and health care operations. It would be listed on a major stock exchange, and some of its equity would be sold to the public. Specifically, Wertheim recommended that Erbamont be incorporated in the Netherlands Antilles, that it be listed on the New York Stock Exchange, and that approximately 15 percent of a total of 45 million shares be sold in a public offering at a price of $18 per share. The composition and ultimate ownership structure of Erbamont as described in this proposal would be as shown in **Exhibit 2**. Consolidated financial statements for the proposed health care group are provided in **Exhibits 3**, **4**, and **5**. Some contemporary cross-border equity deals executed in New York are listed in **Exhibit 6**.

Wertheim's proposal was not without its risks and drawbacks, however. The New York Stock Exchange was uncharted territory for Italian companies. No other Italian company was listed on the Exchange, and the proposed deal would represent a first for Italian business. If the offering went poorly, it would be an embarrassment to Montedison and the prominent business families now controlling it.

Under Italian securities law, the Ministry of Commerce would have to approve the deal before it could be executed. At the time, the Italian government was strongly encouraging companies to list on the Milan Borsa as part of an effort to reduce the dominance of a small number of powerful Italian industrial families.

The Italian banks had to be dealt with as well. Virtually all of the assets to be placed in Erbamont were pledged to banks, as was Montedison's stock in these subsidiaries. To complete the deal, the banks would have to approve it, release the shares on which they had liens, and accept new Erbamont shares instead. This was no mean task in light of the fact that Montedison borrowed from a consortium of more than 100 banks.

There was also a potential "flow back" problem to consider. Common stock sold outside of the domestic market often could become concentrated in the hands of home country investors, particularly during declining markets. The Dutch electronics company, Philips Gloelampenfabrieken NK, for example, once had over a third of its equity held by American investors. When the market's opinion of the company soured, large blocks of the stock flowed back to Amsterdam, severely disrupting local trading.

This would also happen when waves of interest in foreign stock buying proved to be short-term fads. There was some concern that recent American and British interest in the Italian "big five," which included Montedison, was of this "faddish" nature.[1]

Negotiations with Hercules, Inc.

Finally, there was Montedison's U.S. partner, Hercules, Inc., with which to contend. Given its 50 percent ownership of Adria Labs, its cooperation would be critical to the success of a U.S. public offering. This might have been taken for granted but for the fact that the two partners were not seeing eye to eye on the joint venture's management. Hercules preferred to see Adria Labs evolve into a stand-alone pharmaceutical company conducting its own research and product development in the United States as well as marketing Farmitalia's active products. Furthermore, Hercules had some concern that Adria was not being given access to all of Farmitalia's new products.

Montedison, in contrast, preferred to control research and development in Italy and to use Adria Labs primarily as a marketing arm in North America. These different visions of the joint venture had created a desire by Montedison to buy out its U.S. partner. This issue undoubtedly would come to a head as the joint venture agreement approached expiration. However, the proposed equity deal effectively shortened the time frame within which a resolution could be achieved.

Further complicating Montedison's relationship with Hercules at this time were negotiations concerning a possible polypropylene joint venture in North America and Europe. If created, the joint venture would have total assets of $600 million at inception and would be expected to generate first-year sales of $750 million.

At stake in the negotiations was the relative ownership shares of the two partners. Montedison sought a 50 percent ownership position in consideration for 380,000 tons per year of polypropylene resin capacity in Europe and its new cost-saving technology that would be contributed to the venture. Hercules wanted two-thirds ownership in consideration for its contribution of 750,000 tons per year of highly profitable capacity in North America.

The polypropylene joint venture would be a completely separate entity from Adria Labs. However, as a practical matter, it would be difficult for Montedison to raise the Erbamont proposal with Hercules concurrent with the polypropylene negotiations without inviting some linkage between the two deals in the process.

Given the many complications, some members of Montedison's board wondered if alternatives to Wertheim's proposal should be developed and studied more closely. A decision would have to be made soon, however, if Montedison wished to exploit the favorable market conditions that were developing in the United States in early 1983 (see **Exhibit 7**).

---

[1]The other four major Italian companies were Fiat, Olivetti, Generali, and Rinascente.

EXHIBIT 1 CONSOLIDATED FINANCIAL STATEMENTS AND RATIOS, 1978–1982 (LIT BILLIONS, EXCEPT PER SHARE AMOUNTS, NUMBER OF SHARES, PERCENTAGES, AND RATIOS)

	1982	1981	1980	1979	1978
Sales	9019	8927	7793	6843	5839
Net income	(859)	(619)	(449)	19	(267)
Operating cash flow	(268)	(342)	(44)	223	(89)
Earnings per share, Lit	(150.83)	(304.48)	(220.86)	9.35	(133.55)
Total assets	10,283	9179	8624	7904	7553
Long-term debt	1911	2008	1784	1493	1622
Net worth*	1338	364	918	647	302
Book value per share, Lit	235.05	179.05	451.55	318.25	151.05
Market value per share (yearend), Lit	102.50	160.25	180.25	172.50	165.75
Number of shares outstanding, millions	5692.4	2033.0	2033.0	2033.0	1999.3
Return on sales, %	(9.5)	(6.9)	(5.8)	0.3	(4.6)
Return on net worth, %	(64.2)	(170.1)	(48.9)	2.9	(88.4)
Current ratio	0.7	0.7	0.7	0.7	0.7
Debt/total capital, %	58.8	84.7	66.0	69.8	84.3
Interest coverage	0.2	0.2	0.3	0.6	0.0
Market value/book value	0.44	0.90	0.40	0.54	1.10
Exchange rate (Lit/$)†					
Average	1361	1145	863	829	845
Yearend	1371	1193	930	804	831

*Annual changes in net worth do not reconcile with net income due to a series of capital restatements during this period.
†By June 1983, the spot exchange rate for the dollar was Lit1512.

EXHIBIT 2   THE PROPOSED ERBAMONT GROUP OF HEALTH CARE COMPANIES (PERCENTAGES SHOWN REPRESENT OWNERSHIP INTEREST)

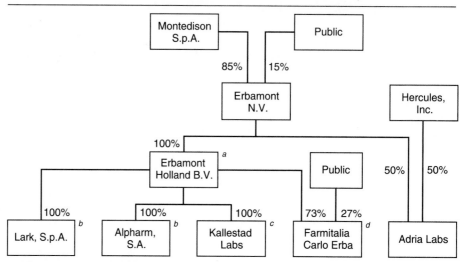

[a]To be incorporated in the Netherlands.

[b]The bulk pharmaceuticals operations were collectively valued by health care consultants at Lit70 billion approximately ($50 million) at the end of 1982.

[c]Kallestad Labs were acquired in 1982 for $87 million (approximately Lit118 billion). General appreciation in the level of equity prices since the time of purchase would result in a value of $100 by the end of 1982.

[d]The publicly traded portion of Farmitalia Carlo Erba trades on the Milan, Brussels, and Antwerp Stock Exchanges. Its stock was recently quoted in Milan at Lit11,000. Total shares outstanding were 78.9 million.

EXHIBIT 3   CONSOLIDATED STATEMENT OF INCOME FOR THE PROPOSED ERBAMONT GROUP* (YEARS ENDED DECEMBER 31)

	Millions of Italian lire		
	1982	1981	1980
Net sales	Lit797,012	Lit695,307	Lit560,250
Operating costs and expenses			
Cost of products sold[†]	379,200	334,498	284,592
Marketing and administrative	228,716	180,266	150,607
Research and development	79,336	67,404	53,947
	687,252	582,168	489,146
Operating earnings	109,760	113,139	71,104
Interest income	77,599	48,909	25,941
Interest expense	80,332	77,325	46,898
Other expense (income) net[‡]	(2,416)	(7,481)	1,853
Income before taxes and minority interests	109,443	92,204	48,294
Income taxes[§]	39,507	35,807	18,538
Income before minority interests	69,936	56,397	29,756
Minority interests	19,590	10,535	3,718
Net income	Lit 50,346	Lit 45,862	Lit 26,038

*Statements were prepared in accordance with the provisions of FASB No. 52.

[†]Noncash expenses for 1980, 1981, and 1982 (all in Lit millions) included depreciation and amortization of 17,531, 18,601, and 21,411, respectively, and provision for employee termination benefits of 11,882, 14,653, and 14,782, respectively.

[‡]Includes foreign exchange gains (losses) (all in Lit millions) of (211), 2296, and 4272 in 1980, 1981, and 1982, respectively. Also includes equity earnings on Adria Laboratories, Inc. of (2393), 2649, and (2199) for 1980, 1981, and 1982, respectively.

[§]Includes deferred taxes (in Lit millions) of 2851, (1115), and (5169) in 1980, 1981, and 1982, respectively.

EXHIBIT 4 CONSOLIDATED BALANCE SHEETS FOR THE PROPOSED ERBAMONT
GROUP* (YEARS ENDED DECEMBER 31)

	Millions of Italian lire	
	1982	1981
Current assets		
Cash	Lit 9,550	Lit 2,844
Marketable securities	31,884	299
Trade receivables	215,049	175,643
Due from related parties†	276,978	242,957
Inventories	199,228	181,163
Prepaid expenses and other current assets	32,855	33,131
Total current assets	765,544	636,037
Due from related parties†	9,904	10,220
Property, plant, and equipment, at cost	363,603	270,520
Less accumulated depreciation	136,996	125,789
Net property, plant, and equipment	226,607	144,731
Goodwill, at cost less amortization	115,244	28,300
Other assets‡	31,871	26,641
Total assets	Lit1,149,170	Lit845,929
Current liabilities		
Bank loans and overdrafts	Lit 197,935	Lit156,180
Current maturities of long-term debt	62,101	25,664
Trade payables	102,769	89,270
Income taxes payable	16,462	27,887
Due to related parties†	29,855	25,024
Other current liabilities	73,854	64,798
Total current liabilities	482,976	388,823
Long-term debt, less current maturities	170,751	146,051
Due to related parties†	47,542	9,600
Deferred income taxes	15,302	17,988
Employee termination benefits§	86,190	78,648
Minority interests	80,489	35,637
Total liabilities	883,250	676,747
Shareholders' equity	265,920	169,182
Total liabilities plus shareholders' equity	Lit1,149,170	Lit845,929

*Statements are prepared in accordance with FASB No. 52.

†Current amounts due from related parties represent advances to Montedison by various health care subsidiaries. They include accrued interest, are unsecured, and payable on demand. The long-term amount due from related parties is an 8 percent note receivable denominated in U.S. dollars and payable in annual installments of $1,000,000. Amounts due to related parties are also denominated in U.S. dollars. Montedison has guaranteed Lit81,074 million of bank loans, overdrafts, and long-term debt of the health care subsidiaries at December 31, 1982.

‡Erbamont's 50 percent interest in Adria Laboratories, Inc., has been accounted for by the equity method and is included in other assets.

§The Italian Civil Code entitles all employees to severance pay, regardless of the reason for termination of employment. Such pay is considered normal remuneration that has been deferred, and approximates 1 month's pay, including bonuses, for each year of service, revalued each year on a basis linked to cost-of-living indices.

EXHIBIT 5 **GEOGRAPHIC AREA INFORMATION FOR THE PROPOSED ERBAMONT GROUP (PERCENTAGES)**

	Italy	Western Europe	United States	Latin America	Asia and Africa
Net sales from operations within each area	61.3%	17.8%	1.5%	16.6%	2.8%
Italian sales to customers by geographic area	57.3	12.1	15.5	1.1	14.0
Operating earnings	77.2	5.6	(0.7)	14.5	3.4
Identifiable assets	74.8	4.5	12.2	6.9	1.6

EXHIBIT 6 FOREIGN EQUITY ISSUES IN THE UNITED STATES, EARLY 1983*

Date	Company	Amount, $ millions	No. of shares offered† (millions)	Offer price per share, $	Price/earnings ratio	Recent price, $	Managers
January 18	Elscint	28.2	1.2 OS	23.50	34.1	24.00	Prudential-Bache Securities/Robertson/Shearson-Amex
March 22	Biogen N.V.	57.5	2.5 OS	23.00	‡	16.50	Warburg Paribas Becker/Salomon Bros.
March 29	Rodime	23.75	1.25ADR	19.00	70.4	24.00	Goldman Sachs/Warburg Paribas Becker
April 14	Novo Industri	103.75	2.0 ADR	51.875	24.1	60.125	Goldman Sachs
May 10	L. M. Ericsson	228.125	3.65ADR	62.50	28.4	61.50	Dillon Read/Morgan Stanley
May 11	Elron Electronic Industries	26.75	1.5 OS	17.50	31.25	17.50	L. F. Rothschild, Unterberg/Prudential-Bache Securities
May 26	Scitex	39.6	1.8 OS	22.00	26.8	22.75	L. F. Rothschild, Unterberg
May 27	Norsk Data	56.625	1.5 ADR	37.75	41.5	39.50	Morgan Stanley

*All offerings were listed on the NASDAQ Over-the-Counter Market, except Novo Industri's, which was listed on the New York Stock Exchange.
†OS = ordinary shares; ADR = American Depository Receipts.
‡Biogen had not shown a profit since its founding in 1978.

EXHIBIT 7   RECENT PERFORMANCE OF SELECTED STOCK MARKETS*

| | Europe | | | | | | | United States | | |
	Belgium	France	Germany	Italy	Netherlands	Switzerland	United Kingdom	NYSE	AMEX	OTC
1982										
January	100.0	100.0	100.0	100.0	100.0	100.0	100.0	100.0	100.0	100.0
February	104.0	107.8	101.7	106.5	94.0	99.5	95.6	97.4	90.0	95.2
March	106.0	102.9	103.7	106.0	102.2	100.7	98.9	94.0	88.0	93.2
April	100.9	108.9	103.5	100.2	106.9	101.2	99.9	98.6	91.5	98.0
May	95.8	108.1	101.7	92.1	105.7	99.9	103.3	98.8	91.7	94.8
June	95.0	98.6	98.8	84.0	99.1	95.6	99.0	92.9	84.8	90.9
July	95.9	96.1	98.9	89.0	99.6	95.4	102.1	92.5	84.2	88.8
August	101.8	101.0	97.8	92.4	101.8	97.8	104.8	92.6	94.7	94.3
September	105.6	98.6	102.8	88.8	102.9	98.6	110.7	103.4	95.8	99.6
October	102.4	100.3	101.7	89.3	111.0	104.9	113.6	112.1	108.2	112.9
November	100.7	100.8	103.7	92.8	108.4	108.7	114.1	117.4	113.7	123.3
December	105.5	99.2	110.8	91.1	114.4	113.4	115.3	118.2	115.2	123.4
1983										
January	107.0	105.6	109.8	104.7	118.4	115.6	119.8	122.6	122.6	131.8
February	110.1	108.7	117.8	113.6	121.5	119.8	120.5	124.8	126.2	138.4
March	119.6	118.1	132.3	122.2	142.2	120.3	124.7	128.8	131.6	143.7
April	127.7	124.1	140.4	113.8	148.1	125.0	134.8	133.4	144.2	155.6
May	124.9	128.9	132.6	109.7	146.8	121.5	134.4	139.3	155.8	163.9

*European indexes are based upon data reported by Capital International Perspective of Geneva. U.S. figures are based upon composite indexes reported by each exchange. All indexes are based upon changes in local currencies. NYSE = New York Stock Exchange; AMEX = American Stock Exchange; OTC = NASDAQ Over-the-Counter Market.

JAGUAR plc—1989

October 16, 1989—Sir John Egan, chairman and chief executive of Jaguar plc, looked over the letter that he had just received from Mr. Lindsey Halstead, vice president of Ford Motor Co. and chairman of Ford of Europe. The letter reiterated the intentions that Mr. Halstead had made clear earlier that day in a meeting with Sir John: Ford wished to make a friendly bid for all of Jaguar, and, although it could not specify an offer price immediately, it would do so within 2 weeks.

Sir John was personally identified with Jaguar's independence. In the mid-1980s he was credited with returning Jaguar to profitability, restoring its tarnished reputation for quality, and revamping employee pride in the company. Had he not taken over Jaguar's management in 1980, claimed many Britons, Jaguar would have been liquidated. For his efforts, Mr. Egan won a popular reputation as "England's Lee Iacocca," and was knighted in 1986.

After 3 years of declining profitability, however, Jaguar badly needed resources for plant modernization and for product design and development. Jaguar had to link up with a larger company to survive, and two American manufacturers, General Motors (GM) and Ford, proved the most ardent suitors. Respecting Jaguar's desire to remain independent, GM was willing to enter manufacturing, marketing, and other commercial joint ventures while holding only a minority stake in Jaguar. Just 4 weeks earlier, GM's executives had expressed their willingness to purchase 30 percent of Jaguar's shares. In contrast, Ford sought 100 percent of Jaguar's shares. Jaguar had previously

This case was prepared by Research Associate Robert W. Lightfoot under the direction of Professor Timothy A. Luehrman. Copyright © 1991 by the President and Fellows of Harvard College. Harvard Business School case 291-034.

broken off talks with Ford during the summer of 1988 because of Ford's insistence on total ownership.

Preferring an arrangement that would leave Jaguar with some independence, Sir John had so far resisted Ford's bid. He realized, however, that Ford's recent aggressiveness might signal its willingness to pay a handsome premium for total control of the company. Before negotiating further with either company, Sir John needed to decide how much Jaguar was worth to each, and how he might obtain the best price for his shareholders.

PRIVATIZATION OF JAGUAR, 1984

In 1984, Jaguar had been a unit of state-owned British Leyland (BL) for a decade. Prime Minister Thatcher's Conservative government had decided to sell Jaguar to the public as part of its broader political program to end state ownership of British industry.[1] Eager to complete its political agenda of privatizations and mindful of the upcoming offering of British Telecom, a much larger state-owned enterprise, the Thatcher government priced the Jaguar offering attractively. The offering was eight times oversubscribed. Jaguar issued 177,880,000 shares to the public at 165 pence each, for a total of £294 million. On August 10, 1984, Jaguar shares initially traded at 176 pence per share, and were widely held by small investors. As of March 1985, more than 85 percent of Jaguar's shareholders owned 1 to 500 shares. These shareholders controlled 7.6 percent of Jaguar's stock.

At that time, Britons regarded Jaguar as the jewel of their domestic auto industry and valued its independence highly. To quell fears that Jaguar would become the target of a hostile tender offer, the Secretary of State for Trade and Industry retained a "special share" in the company. This provision, popularly known as the "golden share," effectively prevented a hostile takeover by giving the Department of Trade and Industry (DTI) the right to veto any change in the company's articles of association. Jaguar's bylaws restricted any individual from owning more than 15 percent of the company, and any change in the company's bylaws required approval from 75 percent of Jaguar's shareholders and from the DTI. The golden share was scheduled to expire on December 31, 1990, unless relinquished earlier by the government.

JAGUAR'S PERFORMANCE, 1984–1988

Jaguar was extremely successful in the years following its sale to the public. Reflecting strong demand for Jaguar cars, a strong dollar, and efficiency gains, Jaguar extended its financial recovery of the early 1980s throughout 1984 and 1985. In 1983, Jaguar earned 51.1 million pounds sterling (£) on sales of £472.6 million. Jaguar's pre-tax profit surged to £91.5 million on sales of £634.1 million in 1984 and £121.3 million on sales of £746.5 million in 1985. By the end of 1985,

---

[1]Jaguar's 1984 privatization is described in *Jaguar plc, 1984*, Harvard Business School case 290-005 (Cambridge, MA: Harvard Business School), which appears in Part 3 of this book.

Jaguar's share price had risen to over 330 pence. **Exhibits 1** and **2** summarize key financial and operating data. **Exhibit 3** presents data on Jaguar's stock price performance.

Jaguar set new sales records in 1984 and 1985. Accounting for 54 percent of unit sales in 1985, the U.S. market was particularly strong and appeared to offer the greatest opportunity for growth: Jaguar estimated that 75 percent of its potential customers resided in the United States. In 1985, Jaguar sold 20,528 cars in the United States, up from 15,815 in 1983 and 18,044 in 1984. Worldwide unit sales reached 37,952, up from 28,467 in 1983 and 32,956 in 1984. Jaguar relied on just two basic models for nearly all of those sales, the Series III XJ-6 saloon and the XJ-S sport coupe. This narrow product range made Jaguar particularly vulnerable to an unsuccessful new model launch, and considerably less flexible than its primary competitors: The Japanese producers enjoyed a much shorter product development time, and the German luxury carmakers enjoyed the security of broad product lines. Jaguar had introduced the XJ-6 in 1968, and the XJ-S in 1975.

To reduce its exposure to currency fluctuations while expanding in its foreign markets, Jaguar started a forward-exchange hedging program toward the end of 1984. Sir John claimed that the company preferred stable profits to wild swings in profits caused by exchange-rate fluctuations. Immediately after privatization, Jaguar adopted a policy of selling forward 50 percent to 75 percent of the next 12 months' anticipated dollar receipts in the interbank forward market. Jaguar intended this rolling 12-month hedge to give its managers some time to respond to dramatic currency swings, not to hedge all of Jaguar's foreign-currency exposure. In 1984, Jaguar sold forward a large fraction of its anticipated 1984 and 1985 dollar receipts, and in 1985, Jaguar expanded its dollar hedging program. By the end of 1988, Sir John said Jaguar's policy was to hedge at least 75 percent of its dollar revenues on a rolling 12-month basis. Jaguar had hedged its dollar revenues at $1.28/£1 in 1986, $1.44/£1 in 1987, and $1.55/£1 in 1988.[2] Such hedging helped soften the blow of falling dollar exchange rates during 1985–1988. **Exhibit 4** presents data for the exchange rates of major currencies against sterling.

From 1986 to 1988, Jaguar continued to boost production, but financial performance suffered, largely due to a falling dollar and the impact of the October 1987 stock market crash, which directly affected many consumers' willingness to purchase luxury cars, and which caused Jaguar's stock price to drop nearly 50 percent. After peaking in 1986, unit sales in the United States drifted 6 percent lower in 1987 to 22,919, and 10 percent lower in 1988 to 20,727. Pre-tax sterling profits were flat in 1986. Turnover topped a billion pounds in 1987 and 1988, but profits fell dramatically—18 percent in 1987 and 53 percent in 1988. Furthermore, the immediate prospects for the U.S. market remained poor. Sir John predicted, ". . . although 1989 will not be an easy year for our Company, we will continue to trade profitably and be able to fund our ambitious capital investment and new model programmes from our own resources."[3]

---

[2]"Jaguar Profits Dip 19.7% on Continued Weakness," *Financial Times*, March 12, 1988, p. 1.
[3]Jaguar, *1988 Annual Report*, p. 9.

After investing £200 million over 7 years, Jaguar successfully introduced a new saloon model in the United Kingdom in October 1986, and in the United States in April 1987. It was Jaguar's first completely new saloon since the XJ-6 was launched in 1968, and even this was delayed for 2 years because of concerns over quality and styling. The new car was marketed under the same XJ-6 name, and sold in the United States for $40,500. The car let Jaguar surpass minimum corporate average fuel economy standards in the United States, thus avoiding fines of about $8 million per year. It also reduced Jaguar's production costs and increased quality enough that Jaguar could offer a roadside assistance program. Jaguar designed the new XJ-6 to have a production life span of about 9 years, half that of its older models.

Jaguar remained committed to investing in new plant, equipment, and design facilities during the mid-1980s. In July 1985, Jaguar announced that it would automate its plants at a cost of £500 million from 1985 to 1990. At the end of 1985, Jaguar committed £37 million over 2 years for a new engineering center at Whitley, Coventry. The engineering center eventually cost £55 million, and was completed in 1988. By 1988, however, Jaguar needed to pare down its ambitious capital spending plans to conserve cash. It announced that capital expenditures in 1989 and 1990 would be less than £100 million per year. In March 1989, Jaguar initiated a cost control program aimed at slashing operating expenditures by £50 million over 2 years.

JAGUAR'S SITUATION IN 1989

In 1989, Jaguar faced tough, new competition. Honda, Nissan, and Toyota all wished to claim a share of the upscale American market through their own luxury divisions. Although Honda's Acura division did not compete directly with Jaguar, Acura's 1986 debut proved how quickly the Japanese producers could enter the upscale American market. Acura entered the market in 1986 with only 60 dealers and two basic models, the $11,000 Integra and the $20,000 Legend. In 1988, Acura's 290 American dealers sold 128,000 cars, more than Mercedes-Benz, Porsche, and Jaguar combined. While critics sniped that Acura cars were not true luxury cars, the impending introduction of Toyota's Lexus cars and Nissan's Infiniti cars promised stiffer competition in the luxury segment of the market.

Infiniti and Lexus both challenged Jaguar's definition of luxury, its technology, and its price. Infiniti models were launched with an innovative advertising campaign designed to redefine luxury. In contrast, Lexus portrayed its cars as sensibly priced, technologically superior alternatives to BMW and Mercedes models that cost twice as much. The 1990 Infinitis arrived on the market in September 1989, and industry observers expected Lexus's 1990 models in November. One analyst predicted that the European automakers' sales might be down 20 percent in 1990 due to Nissan's and Toyota's entry.[4] Priced at $36,000 and $38,000, respectively, the Infiniti and Lexus enjoyed a $6000 to $8000 price advantage over the cheapest Jaguar. **Exhibit 5** presents data on price points in the U.S. market.

---

[4]*The Wall Street Journal*, September 12, 1989, p. A21.

Jaguar responded to discounting by competitors and to the new Japanese entrants by offering rebates. In June 1989, Jaguar offered 11,000 Jaguar owners a $5000 rebate if they purchased an XJ-6 before July 10. This temporary price cut put the XJ-6 in the same price range predicted for the top-line Lexus and Infiniti. The rebate failed, however, until Jaguar offered it to an additional 14,000 Jaguar owners and extended it until August. In September, Jaguar introduced a stripped-down version of the XJ-6. The new model had a simpler suspension system, less interior walnut trim, and no sun roof. Analysts called the move bold, because Jaguar was the first European luxury-car producer to respond to the Japanese threat by *removing* options. Jaguar announced that it would charge $39,700 for the stripped-down XJ-6, and cut the XJ-6's price to $43,000. It continued to offer the $48,000 Vanden Plas XJ-6, and added a special trim version of the XJ-6 for $53,000. What Jaguar really needed, one analyst said, was a completely new car.[5] Faced with high production costs and an earnings slump, Jaguar did not have the resources to build one without some sort of product development link with another manufacturer.

Jaguar's U.S. unit sales continued to slide during 1989, and so did its profits. Jaguar's sales declined 6 percent in the first half of 1989, although it fared better than most of its European competitors. During the first 7 months of 1989, Jaguar's sales fell 5.2 percent, while Mercedes-Benz's sales dropped 16.2 percent, Porsche's 43.6 percent, and BMW's 2 percent. In the first half of 1989, Jaguar earned a paltry £1.4 million before taxes, versus a profit of £22.5 million for the same period in 1988. **Exhibit 6** presents selected data on Jaguar's European and Japanese competitors.

The Suitors

A long-time Jaguar supplier and the world's largest auto company, GM had several reasons to acquire all or part of Jaguar. Jaguar would add diversity to GM's interests in luxury cars, and strengthen its presence in the United Kingdom, where GM trailed Ford. In 1988, Ford U.K. sold more than twice as many cars as GM's U.K. Vauxhall unit. Vauxhall's Opel brand had a solid image, and its newest products were well received in the European market. Still, Opel lacked the allure of the Jaguar marque, and building a new luxury brand from scratch would be expensive. An alliance with GM would help Jaguar finance development of a wider range of cars, including an executive model in the under £25,000 ($39,400) price range. Jaguar had already produced designs for executive model cars, but lacked resources to develop them. Such a product line extension would reduce Jaguar's dependence on the XJ-6 and might greatly increase unit volume, thus lowering development, production, marketing, and distribution costs.

Like GM, Ford hoped to gain entry to the top segment of the luxury car market through an acquisition of Jaguar. Jaguar could fill a gap in Ford's luxury market presence. While Ford's Lincoln division held a large share of the U.S. market, Lincoln's top-price cars sold for $30,000, almost $10,000 less than the stripped-down XJ-6. Ford's efforts to expand into the higher end of the luxury segment through new

[5]Ibid., p. A21.

product introductions and acquisitions had been largely unsuccessful. Ford had failed three times before to sell a European car line through its Lincoln-Mercury dealers, with the German Capri coupe, the Italian Pantera, and the German Merkur. Ford had introduced the Merkur XR4Ti sports coupe in 1985 and Scorpio sedan in 1987, but both cars flopped in the American marketplace. Ford eventually dropped the Merkur brand name from its advertising for the two cars, and tried instead to promote the products themselves. These attempts also failed, because, according to some dealers, the car was overpriced by $8000 to $10,000.[6] In October 1989, Ford canceled the 1990 Merkur line in the American market.

Ford also had attempted acquisitions previously, without notable success. The year 1986 was particularly rough. Backbench British politicians blocked a Ford takeover of Austin Rover, the BL unit, because they feared a nationalist outcry when the public learned of GM's concurrent deal to buy Land Rover and Leyland Trucks from BL. Ford also lost a bid for Alfa Romeo, the Italian sports car maker, to Fiat. The next year, Ford revived talks with Austin Rover, which would have increased Ford's U.K. market share by 50 percent. The talks fell through, however. Ford did manage to acquire 75 percent of Aston-Martin (U.K.), the specialty sports car company, but Aston-Martin did not have the same presence in the marketplace as Jaguar. Ford's Mr. Halstead acknowledged, "There are not an excessive number, actually I would say there are damn few prestige or noble brands with tradition, history, recognition and presence in the marketplace, that might offer us an opportunity to participate in that [luxury] segment. We don't participate effectively at the moment. It is an opportunity for growth."[7] In October 1989, Ford broke off talks with Saab-Scania when it decided that Saab had little appealing technology or image to offer.

Either GM or Ford could provide Jaguar with the financial and technological resources necessary to develop new models and increase its annual production. Ford was believed to have more aggressive plans, assuming it could gain control of Jaguar. These included tripling Jaguar's production to 150,000 cars per year before the end of the 1990s, and using its market power to obtain better prices from Jaguar's suppliers. Such an increase in volume would most likely entail developing a broader product range as quickly as possible, and necessitated large research and development expenditures. **Exhibit 7** gives projections for certain operating and financial variables for a hypothetical scenario in which Jaguar's volume is increased to 150,000 cars per year by 1995. Given stiff new competition in Jaguar's market segment, such an aggressive expansion would likely have to be accompanied by competitive wholesale pricing. Accordingly, the projections in **Exhibit 7** include only modest price increases in each market. At the same time, Jaguar's unit production costs are assumed to be improved, in real terms, by the increase in volume, by new purchasing economies, and by Jaguar's most recent capital expenditures. Capital expenditures and depreciation for 1990–1995 are not projected in **Exhibit 7**, but tripling production would surely entail heavy spending, at least in the short term. Analysts estimated that such a program could cost £300 million to £600 million over 3 to 4 years.

---

[6]*Automotive News,* October 23, 1989, p. 1.
[7]*Financial Times,* September 21, 1989, p. 25.

At the end of 1988, Ford's automotive unit had approximately $5.5 billion of cash and equivalents, $3.8 billion of marketable securities, and long-term debt of $1.3 billion. GM had $5.8 billion of cash, $4.3 billion of marketable securities, and long-term debt of $4.5 billion. Selected consolidated operating and financial data for GM and Ford are summarized in **Exhibit 8**.

Jaguar's Defenses

With less than 3 percent of Jaguar's stock owned by employees and management, Jaguar was not in the strongest position to defend itself against a takeover. However, it had several other defenses that enhanced its bargaining position. Foremost among these was the golden share, which was scheduled to expire at the end of 1990. Until then, Ford and GM could each buy up to 15 percent of Jaguar on the open market, but could launch no takeover bid without government support.

Once the golden share expired, Jaguar's bylaws still restricted anyone from holding more than 15 percent of the company. The 75 percent vote needed to change the bylaws, however, would probably not prove difficult to obtain if Jaguar's financial performance did not improve sharply. Furthermore, recent takeover speculation had increased the share of Jaguar's stock owned by risk arbitrageurs to an estimated 30 percent.

Jaguar management was uncertain how the government and the unions would act. The unions were not strong supporters of Sir John, but would oppose any offer that did not guarantee security for British jobs. This could work for or against the company. A rich acquirer might be able to persuade the unions that Jaguar was not viable as an independent company. The government had voiced strong support for Jaguar's independence in the past, but Ford had recently been courting the support of British politicians and touting its commitment to investing in Britain. Ford was in the midst of a 5-year, £1.8 billion U.K. investment program. Already it employed 47,900 workers in U.K. plants.

Public relations concerns limited Ford's and Jaguar's range of options. As the market-share leader in the United Kingdom, Ford did not want to damage its image by upsetting British consumers. Conversely, Jaguar might suffer in *its* largest market if it appeared too anti-American. Such risks did not appear to be as great for GM, which was less exposed to the British market.

Negotiations with GM and Ford

GM had first expressed interest in acquiring Jaguar during 1984, when the British government sold off the prestigious automaker. Mr. Egan was incensed by the suggestion that Jaguar be sold to an American firm, however, and Mrs. Thatcher also wanted Jaguar to remain in British hands. Although she thought she could get a good price from GM and that Jaguar would prosper under its ownership, she ruled out any GM purchase.

Ford approached Jaguar during the summer of 1988. Mr. Alex J. Trotman, then vice president of Ford and chairman of Ford of Europe, contacted Sir John to discuss possible business combinations. All of those business combinations would have resulted in Ford's majority ownership of Jaguar. From October to December, executives from the two companies continued to discuss different options, but negotiations were discontinued after Mr. Petersen, Ford's CEO, spoke with Sir John on December 9, 1988. During that conversation, Sir John emphasized the company's resolve to remain independent, and Mr. Petersen emphasized Ford's desire to own a majority holding.

GM renewed its quest for a stake in Jaguar in September 1989, the weekend after Jaguar announced its disappointing interim 1989 financial results. In secret internal meetings on September 16 and 17, GM executives decided to pursue a 30 percent stake in Jaguar. Immediately afterward, GM and Jaguar executives met to discuss possible manufacturing, marketing, and other commercial joint ventures. GM also began studying ways of injecting capital into Jaguar, a task that was complicated by the government's golden share. Jaguar had permission to issue 9 million new shares, or about 5 percent of equity, without the approval of shareholders and the DTI.

On September 19, just 2 days after GM's decision to seek a tie-up with Jaguar, Ford notified Sir John that Ford would file a Premerger Notification and Report Form with the U.S. Federal Trade Commission (FTC) and the Antitrust Division of the Justice Department, and announced to the public that it sought a 15 percent stake in Jaguar. This notification was required under the Hart-Scott-Rodino Act, which requires American companies that intend to take a major stake in a foreign company to file their intentions with the FTC and the Antitrust Division, and to wait 30 days before purchasing significant quantities of the target company's stock. On October 5, 1989, U.S. authorities waived the 30-day waiting period.

GM and Jaguar countered by publicly announcing on October 9 that they were engaged in high-level, advanced discussions of marketing, manufacturing, and other commercial joint ventures between the two companies. On the same day, GM notified U.S. authorities of its intention to begin acquiring a stake, with the aim of eventually owning 25 percent to 29.9 percent of the company.

One week later, on October 16, Ford's Mr. Halstead met with Sir John and gave him the following letter:

Dear Sir John:

In order to make Ford's position clear with respect to its intentions, we offer the following:

1. With Jaguar's support, Ford is prepared to make a full bid for 100% of the outstanding shares of Jaguar and jointly seek removal of the "Golden Share". In addition, Ford will positively consider the development of a plan that would provide Jaguar's stock to Jaguar's management employees.
2. Ford believes Jaguar is best served for future growth and development by maintaining a single self-contained activity. Ford, however, would be required to exercise normal financial and operational control responsibilities toward its investment.
3. Ford's intention would be to maintain Jaguar's premium product image and would expect manufacturing to continue to be centered in Coventry. Ford would plan to jointly develop a business plan with Jaguar that would address in more detail the product and manufacturing plan that could lead to significant volume growth.

4. It is expected that Jaguar's dealer network would remain intact. Cross franchising with Ford dealers is not planned.

This proposal is not legally binding and is subject to the approval of the Ford Board of Directors. It is intended that this approval, including a specific purchase price per share, will be obtained within two weeks. During this period Ford will develop a better understanding of Jaguar's financial and operating position.

/s/ L. Lindsey Halstead

Sir John's Decision

Sir John weighed the merits of the two courses Jaguar might take. GM would help Jaguar remain independent, but Ford might well offer a substantially higher price. Sir John also considered what the government and the unions might do. Nominally, they supported Jaguar's independence. However, the right bidder might be able to convince them that financial security would be a better safeguard for British industry and British jobs than Jaguar's independence.

As takeover rumors intensified, Jaguar's stock price once again rose sharply, and had recently closed at over 700 pence per share. At this price, Jaguar's 190 million shares outstanding were worth over £1.3 billion. Some observers thought this placed a rather high value on the company's equity. Nevertheless, many market participants appeared to be wagering that Ford, or someone else, could be induced to pay at least this much, perhaps more. If this were true, Sir John faced a tactical dilemma. Any actions he took to ensure that Ford could succeed *only* by paying a very high price might effectively put the company in play. This would virtually guarantee that Jaguar would not remain independent. Additional, supplementary financial market data are given in **Exhibit 9**.

EXHIBIT 1 JAGUAR FINANCIAL INFORMATION, 1984–1988 (MILLIONS)

	1984	1985	1986	1987	1988
Consolidated profit and loss account					
Turnover	£634.1	£746.5	£830.4	£1,002.1	£1,075.5
Cost of sales	(495.1)	(577.8)	(646.2)	(832.9)	(945.4)
Gross profit	139.0	168.7	184.2	169.2	130.1
Distribution costs	(18.0)	(19.7)	(20.6)	(23.9)	(28.0)
Administrative expenses	(34.3)	(41.2)	(56.8)	(60.7)	(62.7)
Operating profit	86.7	107.8	106.8	84.6	39.4
Share of profits of related companies	0.2	0.4	0.1	1.0	2.9
Interest receivable	5.8	14.0	18.3	21.8	17.7
Interest payable	(1.2)	(0.9)	(4.4)	(10.4)	(11.9)
Pre-tax profit on ordinary activities	91.5	121.3	120.8	97.0	47.5
Taxation on ordinary profit	(34.4)	(33.7)	(37.4)	(35.7)	(19.1)
Profit on ordinary activities after tax	57.1	87.6	83.4	61.3	28.4
Extraordinary items	(14.5)	0.0	0.0	0.0	0.0
Profit for the financial year	42.6	87.6	83.4	61.3	28.4
Dividends*	0.0	(24.1)	(17.2)	(19.0)	(20.1)
Transfer to reserves	42.6	63.5	66.2	42.3	8.3
Consolidated balance sheet					
Fixed assets	£137.3	£176.6	£238.4	£ 323.6	£ 373.6
Stocks	77.2	87.0	104.7	111.7	126.7
Debtors	31.8	48.4	43.2	60.6	35.4
Investments		53.3	120.8	109.1	45.8
Cash at bank and in hand	100.3	102.9	150.8	146.1	135.4
Current assets	209.3	291.6	419.5	427.5	343.3
Creditors					
Amounts falling due within 1 year†	(174.2)	(234.2)	(346.2)	(420.6)	(381.4)
Portion of above that is funded debt†	(13.9)	(30.7)	(120.5)	(145.9)	(111.7)
Long-term liabilities					
Finance leasing liabilities, 2–5 yrs.	21.4	15.8	10.0	4.1	—
Other accruals incl. warranty	23.2	30.6	48.0	41.9	35.2
Net current (liabilities)/assets	35.1	57.4	73.3	6.9	(38.1)
Total assets less current liabilities	172.4	234.0	311.7	330.5	335.5
Provision for liabilities and charges	(19.5)	(19.5)	(19.5)	(19.5)	(19.5)
Called-up share capital	45.0	45.2	45.2	45.3	45.7
Share premium account		2.8	2.8	5.3	8.9
Other reserves	7.8	1.1	1.0		3.5
Profit and loss account	55.5	119.0	185.2	214.4	222.7
Capital and reserves	£108.3	£168.1	£234.2	£ 265.0	£ 280.8

Note: The figures above reflect U.K. GAAP; they differ from U.S. GAAP principally with regard to: forward currency exchange contracts (need only be included in financial statements to settle foreign currency accounts); deferred taxation (U.K. GAAP requires provision for deferred taxation on timing differences only where it is reasonable to assume that a liability will crystallize); and dividends (under U.K. GAAP, dividends are provided in the financial year in respect of which they are declared or proposed by the directors, whereas under U.S. GAAP, dividends are not included in the financial statements until the calendar year in which they are formally declared).

*1984 dividend was appropriated in 1985 as a first interim dividend paid in lieu of a final dividend for 1984.

†Bank loans and overdrafts, and commercial paper.

Source: Jaguar Annual Reports.

EXHIBIT 2   JAGUAR OPERATING FIGURES, 1984–1988

	1984	1985	1986	1987	1988
Vehicle wholesales, no. of units					
New XJ-6 saloon	—	—	2,610	31,414	38,857
Series III saloon	26,730	29,976	29,449	7,241	2,083
XJ-S sports car	6,070	7,760	9,008	10,367	9,493
Limousine	156	216	189	178	170
Total	32,956	37,952	41,256	49,200	50,603
Production, no. of units	33,437	38,500	41,437	48,020	51,939
U.S. retail sales, no. of units	18,044	20,528	24,464	22,919	20,727
Worldwide retail sales, no. of units	33,424	37,952	40,971	46,612	49,498
U.S. sales/worldwide sales, %	55	54	59	47	41
Geographic analysis of turnover, £ millions					
United Kingdom	108.8	130.7	131.5	217.4	309.4
United States	451.6*	469.4	544.1	555.1	467.6
Canada		44.7	59.3	60.1	59.0
Europe	40.8	61.5	63.2	107.1	150.8
Rest of the world	32.9	40.2	32.3	62.4	88.7
Turnover, £ millions	634.1	746.5	830.4	1,002.1	1,075.5
Turnover, $ millions	734.9	1,079.4	1,231.5	1,889.0	1,945.6
Pre-tax earnings, £ millions	91.5	121.3	120.8	97.0	47.5
Pre-tax earnings, $ millions	106.0	175.4	179.1	182.8	85.9
Capital expenditure, £ millions	38.1	57.2	93.9	132.0	103.8
Research and development, £ millions	19.6	22.9	35.6	50.4	55.7
Depreciation, £ millions	10.4	14.9	28.9	44.2	58.9
Earnings per share, pence	31.7	48.5	46.1	33.8	15.6
Dividends per share, pence	4.75	8.60	9.50	10.50	11.00

*1984 U.S. turnover includes Canada.
Source: Jaguar Annual Reports.

EXHIBIT 3 JAGUAR STOCK PRICE, QUARTERLY THROUGH 1988, AND MONTHLY FOR 1989 (£/SHARE)

Quarter	Stock price	Quarter	Stock price	Month end	Stock price
August 17, 1984	£1.72	I-1987	£5.95	January 1989	£3.07
III-1984	1.95	II	5.47	February 1989	3.11
IV	2.54	III	5.64	March 1989	3.22
		IV	3.13	April 1989	3.02
I-1985	2.96			May 1989	3.58
II	2.66	I-1988	2.76	June 1989	3.49
III	2.71	II	2.84	July 1989	3.87
IV	3.32	III	2.48	August 1989	4.15
		IV	2.69	September 1989	5.70
I-1986	4.51			October 13, 1989	6.77
II	5.40				
III	5.10				
IV	5.17				

Note: Jaguar's 1989 beta, measured with respect to the London Stock Exchange, was 1.10.
Source: Interactive Data Corp.

Jaguar weekly stock price August 17, 1984, to October 13, 1989

EXHIBIT 4   SELECTED EXCHANGE RATES, 1984–1989

Quarter	$/£	DM/£	¥/£
1984-I	1.443	3.738	324.0
II	1.357	3.773	322.0
III	1.235	3.778	303.5
IV	1.159	3.650	291.5
1985-I	1.238	3.801	310.0
II	1.310	3.968	325.5
III	1.407	3.762	304.3
IV	1.446	3.540	289.6
1986-I	1.473	3.424	256.8
II	1.534	3.368	250.0
III	1.447	2.935	223.3
IV	1.483	2.849	234.5
1987-I	1.607	2.900	234.4
II	1.613	2.944	236.8
III	1.627	2.996	238.0
IV	1.885	2.960	228.3
1988-I	1.886	3.125	234.2
II	1.707	3.107	228.2
III	1.692	3.168	226.7
IV	1.809	3.208	225.8
1989-I	1.688	3.198	223.7
II	1.574	3.109	223.9
III	1.615	3.022	225.5

Source: Interactive Data Corp.

Monthly sterling exchange-rate indices

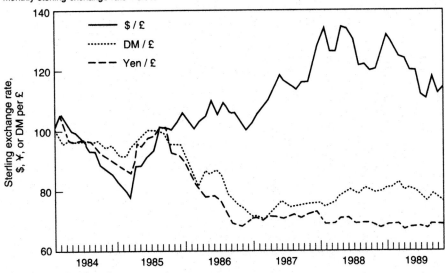

Source: Interactive Data Corp.

EXHIBIT 5   JAGUAR AND COMPETITORS: MODEL RANGES AND U.S. PRICES, 1989

Model	Price		
	Four-door, $	Two-door, $	Convertible, $
Jaguar			
XJ6	$44,000		
Vanden Plas	48,000		
XJ-S V-12		$48,000	$57,000
BMW			
525i	37,000		
535i	43,600		
635CSi		47,000	
735i	54,000		
735iL	58,000		
750iL V-12	70,000		
Mercedes-Benz			
190E	31,590		
260E	39,200		
300CE		53,880	
300TE wagon	48,210		
300SE	51,400		
300SEL	55,100		
420SEL V-8	61,210		
560SEL V-8	72,280		
560SL		64,230	
560SEC		79,840	
Porsche			
944		33,245	
944-S2		41,900	
911		51,205	59,200
911 Targa		52,435	
911 Speedster		65,480	
911 Turbo		70,975	85,060
911 Targa Turbo		77,065	
928-S4 V-8		74,545	
Acura			
Integra RS	12,060	11,260	
Integra LS	13,900	13,070	
Legend V-6	22,600	24,760	
Legend L V-6	25,900	27,325	
Legend LS V-6	29,160	30,040	
Infiniti			
Q45 (1990 model, introduced 11/89)	38,000		
M30 (1990 model, introduced 11/89)		23,500	
Lexus			
LS400 (1990 model, introduced 9/89)	36,000		
ES250 5-speed manual (1990 model)	21,050		
ES250 4-speed automatic (1990 model)	21,800		

Source: Automotive News, *Annual Market Data Book.*

EXHIBIT 6 SUMMARY OF OPERATING AND FINANCIAL DATA FOR SELECTED AUTOMAKERS (ALL CURRENCIES IN MILLIONS OR BILLIONS, EXCEPT STOCK PRICES AND PER SHARE ITEMS)

	Jaguar, £ millions	BMW, DM millions	Daimler-Benz, DM millions	Porsche, DM millions	Honda, ¥ billions	Toyota, ¥ billions	Nissan, ¥ billions
Year ended	12/31/88	12/31/88	12/31/88	7/31/89	3/31/89	6/30/89	3/31/89
Revenues	£1,075.5	DM20,673	DM73,495	DM2,526.3	¥3,489.3	¥8,021.0	¥4,811.7
Operating profit	39.4	421	968	53.4	117.1	467.9	186.0
Profit after taxes	28.4	379	1,675	54.2	97.3	346.2	114.6
Depreciation	58.9	1,288	3,207	181.8	130.9	295.0	188.8
Interest expense	11.9	129	637	0	47.5	84.1	99.2
Cash and marketable securities	135.4	1,958	8,292	459.4	247.3	2,204.6	898.9
Total assets	716.9	11,562	56,303	1,596.5	2,284.4	7,152.9	4,742.7
Common equity	280.8	3,483	10,529	591.5	901.4	3,709.6	1,649.3
Debt	111.7	160	5,748	0	356.7	1,573.8	1,797.3
Long-term	0.0	138	3,121	0	301.6	1,219.5	642.6
Short-term	111.7	22	2,627	0	55.1	354.3	1,154.7
Stock price (10/14/89)	677p	DM 587	DM 761	DM 860	¥ 1,900	¥ 2,790	¥ 1,540
Shares outstanding, thousands	182,926	15,000	43,000	700	948,000	2,993,690	2,477,317
Earnings per share	15.6p	DM 25.28	DM 38.84	DM 77.43	¥ 98.48	¥ 102.17	¥ 47.62
Dividends per share	11.00p	DM 12.50	DM 11.65	DM 11.00	¥ 12.00	¥ 19.00	¥ 14.00
Units sold	50,603	495,787	801,171	29,017	1,903,000	3,968,673	2,789,341
Employees	12,611	65,812	223,219*	8,218†	71,200	67,814	117,330

*Mercedes-Benz division employees only.
†1988 employees.
Source: Worldscope; various annual reports; Daiwa Institute of Research, Ltd.; Value Line.

EXHIBIT 7   SELECTED OPERATING AND FINANCIAL PROJECTIONS ASSOCIATED WITH TRIPLING UNIT VOLUME BY 1995 (ALL CURRENCIES IN MILLIONS)

	1990	1991	1992	1993	1994	1995
Unit sales, thousands						
United States	25.0	30.8	37.8	46.5	57.2	70.4
United Kingdom	15.0	17.9	21.2	25.3	30.1	35.8
Europe	7.0	9.1	11.8	15.4	20.0	26.0
Rest of world	8.0	10.6	14.2	18.8	25.0	33.3
Total units, thousands	55.0	68.3	85.0	106.0	132.3	165.5
Turnover						
United States, $	850.0	1076.9	1364.3	1728.4	2189.7	2774.2
United Kingdom, £	324.0	404.8	505.8	632.1	789.8	986.8
Europe, DM	434.0	572.7	755.6	997.1	1315.6	1735.9
Rest of world, £	172.8	241.3	337.0	470.6	657.2	917.8
Cost of sales, £	1045.0	1350.4	1730.9	2222.1	2829.5	3608.8
Distribution, administrative, and R&D costs, £	122.0	147.3	177.9	214.8	259.4	313.2
Increase in net working capital, £	113.2	34.5	45.1	59.0	77.3	101.5

Note: The costs projected above do not include depreciation, interest expense, or interest income. Nor do they provide for taxes or reflect capital expenditures. Turnover projections are expressed in *local* currencies.
Source: Public information and casewriter estimates.

EXHIBIT 8 SELECTED OPERATING AND FINANCIAL DATA: GM, FORD AND U.K. SUBSIDIARIES (ALL UNITS OF MEASURE IN CURRENCIES INDICATED, EXCEPT WHERE NOTED OTHERWISE)

	1984	1985	1986	1987	1988*
General Motors, $ millions					
Net sales and revenues	$83,889.9	$96,371.6	$102,813.0	$101,781.0	$121,816.0
Operating income	4,700.0	4,214.4	2,717.8	2,568.5	12,210.0
Net income	4,516.5	3,999.0	2,944.7	3,550.9	4,856.3
Cash and equivalents	8,567.4	5,114.4	4,018.8	4,706.4	5,800.3
Total receivables	7,357.9	8,735.8	12,894.8	23,950.1	92,017.5
Fixed assets	19,401.5	24,653.0	30,376.3	32,040.4	36,935.8
Total assets	52,144.8	63,832.7	72,593.0	87,421.9	164,063.0
Short-term debt	2,350.5	2,208.3	2,328.7	2,557.6	47,376.5
Long-term debt	3,508.4	3,314.1	9,926.7	18,615.5	41,048.4
Other liabilities	6,461.2	7,813.5	8,036.3	8,974.4	10,941.7
Stockholders' equity	24,214.3	29,524.5	30,677.9	33,225.1	35,671.7
Car and truck sales, units worldwide	8,256,352	9,304,600	8,575,866	7,764,869	8,107,528
Vauxhall, £ millions					
Turnover	£1,302.8	£1,565.1	£1,499.2	£1,688.0	£2,048.5
Net income (loss)	(9.4)	(47.4)	(61.7)	31.0	151.9
Vehicle sales, units	299,901	336,826	305,329	304,006	353,546
Ford Motor Co., $ millions					
Net sales and revenues	$52,366.3	$52,774.3	$62,715.7	$71,643.4	$92,445.6
Operating income	3,422.2	2,729.7	4,056.5	6,201.2	13,447.5
Net income	2,906.8	2,515.4	3,285.1	4,625.2	5,300.2
Cash and marketable securities	5,943.2	5,903.8	8,553.1	10,097.0	14,770.0
Receivables	2,526.1	2,851.9	3,487.8	4,401.6	95,686.6
Fixed assets	10,549.0	12,421.3	13,200.6	14,033.5	15,992.2
Total assets	27,485.5	31,603.5	37,933.0	44,955.7	143,366.0
Short-term debt	696.7	956.6	1,230.1	1,803.3	32,098.8
Long-term debt	2,762.2	2,475.2	2,211.0	1,831.3	37,849.5
Other liabilities	2,430.5	3,071.9	3,877.0	4,426.5	8,593.2
Equity	9,837.7	12,268.5	14,859.4	18,492.7	21,529.0
Car and truck sales, units worldwide	5,667,162	5,634,348	5,984,081	6,115,288	6,517,186
Ford (U.K.), £ millions					
Turnover	£3,752	£4,045	£4,374	£5,211	£5,936
Operating profit (loss)	(14)	88	45	295	608
Profit on ordinary activities after tax	50	115	79	217	437
Vehicle sales, units	653,000	660,000	656,000	745,000	779,000

*Effective 1988, Statement of Financial Accounting Standards (FAS) Number 94 required the full, line-by-line consolidation of all majority-owned subsidiaries. For GM and Ford, adoption of FAS #94 resulted in line-by-line consolidation of GMAC and Ford Motor Credit for the first time. For both companies, reported 1988 figures are not comparable to those of 1987, and the change does not reflect operating changes.

Source: Standard & Poor's Compustat; GM's, Ford's, Vauxhall's, and Ford (U.K.)'s Annual Reports.

EXHIBIT 9   SELECTED CAPITAL MARKET DATA BY COUNTRY, END OF SEPTEMBER 1989

	U.K.	Germany	U.S.	Japan
Selected interest rates, %				
Domestic government bonds (long-term)	9.81%	7.18%	8.31%	5.06%
Domestic corporate bonds (long-term)	11.58	7.30	9.14	5.31
Treasury bill rates	14.41	—	8.21	3.14
Money market rates	14.88	7.85	9.15	4.96
Commercial prime lending rates	14.00	8.50	10.50	4.88
Forward rates against sterling, end of September 1989				
Spot		DM2.9575	$1.5640	¥224.00
1 month		2.9400	1.5555	222.31
3 month		2.9083	1.5397	219.20
6 month		2.8652	1.5172	215.03
12 month		2.7878	1.4790	207.62
Inflation rates: yearly, 1984–1988; quarterly, 1989; %				
1984	6.2%	2.4%	5.1%	1.9%
1985	5.6	1.5	3.8	1.4
1986	3.7	−1.0	1.1	−0.3
1987	3.8	1.0	4.4	0.8
1988	6.8	1.8	4.4	1.0
1989-I	1.8	1.4	1.5	0.0
1989-II	2.8	0.8	1.5	2.3
1989-III	1.0	0.0	0.7	0.6

Note: Inflation calculated from Consumer Price Indices. 1989 quarterly rates are *not* annualized.

Sources: Morgan Guaranty Trust Company, *World Financial Markets,* October 12, 1989; *The Economist,* October 7, 1989; *Financial Times;* Citicorp Database.

GLOSSARY OF ABBREVIATIONS AND ACRONYMS

Corporate and Governmental Terms and Organizations

AG	Aktiengesellschaft (German public limited corporation)
AMEX	American Stock Exchange
A/S	Aktieselskab (Danish public limited corporation)
BHP	Broken Hill Proprietary Company (Australia)
BID	Bank for International Development
BL	British Leyland
BMH	British Motor Holdings
BOCTC	Bank of China Trust Company
Cetes	Mexican short-term treasury certificates
CFC	Controlled Foreign Corporation (United States)
CGE	Compagnie Générale d'Electricité
CNCDC	China National Coal Development Corporation
CNCIEC	China National Coal Import and Export Company
CSFB	Credit Suisse First Boston
CUB	Carlton and United Breweries (Australia)
DBCM	Deutsche Bank Capital Markets
DEC	Digital Equipment Corporation
DIC	Dainippon Ink and Chemicals (Japan)
DKB	Dai-Ichi Kangyo Bank (Japan)
DTI	Department of Trade and Industry (United Kingdom)
EC	European Community or European Commission
EEC	European Economic Community
EDF	Electricité de France
EMS	European Monetary System
ENI	Ente Nazionale Idrocarbum (Italy)
ERISA	Employee Retirement Income Security Act of 1974 (United States)
ETC	Export Trading Companies Act (United States)
FAS	Financial Accounting Standards (United States)
FASB	Financial Accounting Standards Board (United States)
FCA	Financial Corporation of America
FDA	Food and Drug Administration (United States)
FICORCA	Fideicomiso para la Cobertura de Riesgos Cambiarios (Mexican Trust for Coverage of Foreign Exchange Risks)
Fracdev	France—Development
FTC	Federal Trade Commission (United States)
FT Index	Financial Times index of ordinary U.K. shares
G-5	Group of Five (major Western industrial countries; France, Germany, Japan, United Kingdom, United States)
G-7	G-5 plus Canada and Italy
GAO/NSIA	General Accounting Office, National Security and International Affairs Division (United States)
GAN	Groupe des Assurances Nationales (France)
GDF	Gaz de France

GIASA	Grupo Industrial Alfa, S.A. (Mexico)
GM	General Motors
GMAC	General Motors Acceptance Corporation
GmbH	Gesellschaft mit beschränkten Haftung (German private limited corporation)
G&W	Gulf & Western Industries, Inc.
HKK	Hintz-Kessels-Kohl (Austrian auto manufacturer)
IBJ	Industrial Bank of Japan
IBM	International Business Machines
ICCC	Island Creek of China Coal, Ltd.
IFI	Istituto Finanziario Industriale (Italy)
IMF	International Monetary Fund
IMM	International Money Market
IPI	International Pharmaceuticals Incorporated
IRS	Internal Revenue Service (United States)
K.K.	Kabushiki Kaisha (Japanese public limited corporation)
LDCs	Less developed countries
Ltd.	Limited (British equivalent of Incorporated)
MGL	Morgan Guaranty, Ltd.
MMC	Monopolies and Mergers Commission (United Kingdom)
MOF	Ministry of Finance (Japan)
MOFERT	Ministry of Foreign Economic Relations and Trade (China)
MSD	Merck Sharpe & Dohme
MSDI	Merck Sharpe & Dohme International
NHI	National Health Scheme (Japan)
NMB	Nippon Merck-Banyu (Japan)
NTT	Nippon Telephone and Telegraph (Japan)
N.V.	Naamloze vennootschap' (Dutch public limited corporation)
NYSE	New York Stock Exchange
OECD	Organization for Economic Cooperation and Development
OFT	Office of Fair Trading (United Kingdom)
OKB	Oesterreichische Kontrollbank Aktiengesellschaft (Austrian Export-Import Bank)
OPEC	Oil Producing and Exporting Countries (international cartel)
OPIC	Overseas Private Investment Corporation (United States)
OTC	NASDAQ Over-the-Counter Market (United States)
Pagafes	Mexican federation treasury bills
plc	Public limited corporation
PruAsia	Prudential Asia Investments Limited
PSF	Ping Shuo First Coal Company (China)
RJR	R. J. Reynolds Industries, Inc.

RTZ	Rio Tinto-Zinc
S.A.	Societe Anonyme; Sociedad Anonima; and Sociedade Anonima (public limited corporation in France, Spain, Mexico, and other Spanish-speaking nations; and Brazil, Portugal, and other Portugese-speaking nations; respectively)
SDI	Strategic Defense Initiative (United States)
SEC	Securities and Exchange Commission (United States)
SGTE	Societe Generale de Techniques et d'Etudes
SJL	Simmons Japan Limited
SNEA	Société Nationale Elf Aquitaine (France)
S&P	Standard & Poors
SpA	Societá per Azioni (Italian public limited corporation)
TALW	Toyoda Automatic Loom Works (Japan)
T-bills	Treasury bills (United States)
T-bonds	Treasury bonds (United States)
TSE	Tokyo Stock Exchange
U.K.	United Kingdom
U.S.	United States
U.S.S.R.	Union of Soviet Socialist Republics
WB	World Bank
WCI	Wickes Companies, Inc.
WTI	Wafer Tools, Inc.

Currencies

A$	Australian dollar
As	Austrian schilling
C	Costa Rican colon
DKr	Danish kroner
DM	Deutsche mark
ECU	European Currency Unit
FF	French franc
Fl	Dutch guilders
Lit	Italian lire
MP	Mexican peso
p	British pence
Pts	Spanish pesetas
SF	Swiss franc
¢	U.S. cent
$	U.S. dollar (also appears sometimes as US$)
£	British pound sterling
¥	Japanese yen

Financial and Business Terms

ACT	Advance corporation tax
ADRs	American depository receipts

B/As	Banker's acceptances
CAPM	Capital asset pricing model
CEO	Chief executive officer
CIA	Covered interest arbitrage
C.O.D.	Cash on delivery
CPI	Consumer price index
CPP	Weighted average cost of funds for Mexican banks
CTA	Cumulative translation adjustment
DFE	Domestic Fisher effect
EBIT	Earnings before interest and taxes
EPS	Earnings per share
FCF	Free cash flow
FP	Forward parity
FRN	Floating rate note
FX	Foreign exchange
GAAP	Generally accepted accounting principals
GDP	Gross domestic product
GNP	Gross national product
IFE	International Fisher effect
IPO	Initial public offering
IRP	Interest rate parity
L/C	Letter of credit
LIBOR	London Interbank Offered Rate
LOOP	Law of one price
LTD	Long-term debt
NDA	New drug application
NPV	Net present value
OEM	Original equipment manufacturer
OS	Ordinary share
P/E	Price/earnings (ratio)
PPP	Purchasing power parity
R&D	Research and Development
SDR	Special drawing right
SG&A	Selling, general, and administrative
TMO	Taux moyen mensuel du marché obligataire
TPs	Titres participatifs (French financial instrument)
WACC	Weighted average cost of capital
WPI	Wholesale price index
% p.a.	Percent per annum

Scientific, Technical, and Medical Terms

ASIC	Application-specific integrated circuit
CAT	Computerized axial tomography
CVD	Chemical vapor deposition
DMT	Dimethyl terephthalate
kWh	Kilowatthour
LNG	Liquid natural gas
LSI	Large scale integration
NCEs	New chemical entities
TPA	Terephthalic acid
VLSI	Very large scale integration

Index